Topsy-Turvy 1585

THE SHORT VERSION

a translation and popular introduction of the famous treatise by Luis Frois S.J. listing 611 ways Europeans & Japanese are contrary

by
robin d. gill

"with a little help from my friends"

道 可 道
非 常 道

paraverse press

This is the fifth book published by paraverse press,
home of truly creative nonfiction, which is to say,
nonfiction that is neither journalism, nor history,
nor how-I-overcame-this-or-that. We are afraid
our books will not help you get rich, healthy
or up-to-date. Whatever their subject,
they offer one thing, always the same
yet different; and that is ideas,
*"food for thought,
all you can eat!"*

©
2005
paraverse press
all rights reserved

but, please do not let that trouble you
for you may quote whatever you want, so long as
you cite this book and take care to check the *Errata* at
our web site: www.paraverse.org

We hope the Library of Congress will help us catalog
someday, for as you can see below, we need help! Meanwhile
our Publisher's Cataloging-in-Publication:

Topsy-Turvy 1585
THE SHORT VERSION
a translation and popular introduction
of the famous treatise by Luis Frois S.J.
listing 611 ways Europeans &
Japanese are contrary.
by robin d. gill

ISBN# 0-9742618-3-1 (pbk)

1. Comparative Culture – Europe vs. Japan
2. Japan – Culture – 1500-1600 (Momoyama+Muromachi)
3. Europe – Culture – 1500-1600 (Renaissance+Reformation)
4. Identity – Collective – Europe/Japan(+China)
5. History – Jesuit – Accommodation Policy in Japan
6. Orientalism – Occidentalism (comparative culture)
7. Nonfiction – Literature – Translation+Essay
8. Men, Women, Children, Religion, Food & Drink, Weapons, Horses, Medicine, Writing, Architecture, Gardens, Boats, Entertainment
9. Luis Frois's *"Tratado em que se contem..."* (1585)
10. Luis Frois (Luís Fróis) S.J. (1532-1597)

1st edition (May Day 2005) of the short version
[created from the long version (740 pgs)1st edition (7/30/04)]
printed by Lightning Source
in the United States and United Kingdom.
Distributed by Ingram, Amazon , B&N, etc.

To learn more, please visit our website, or send a stamped envelope to:
Paraverse Press / pmb #399 / 260 Crandon blvd, suite 32 / Key Biscayne, FL 33149-1540

TOPSY-TURVY 1585

THE SHORT VERSION

611 Ways Europeans and Japanese are Contrary

*a translation and popular introduction of Luis Frois S.J.'s famous treatise (**Tratado**)* – by robin d. gill

> "The Jesuits had aimed for El Dorado but landed in the Antipodes," writes Professor George Elison in *Deus Destroyed* (E:DD). "There was no foothold to be had without an inversion of past attitudes. How difficult it was to perform to perform that headstand is apparent from a look at Padre Luis Frois's attempt at cultural analysis, a treatise he composed in 1585 on *Contradictions and Differences of Custom between the Peoples of Europe and this Province of Japan*."

Luis Frois S.J. (1532-1597) left his native Portugal in his teens and sailed for the East as a boy-scribe. He arrived in Goa (East India) just after proselytizing began in Japan, which he reached in his mid-twenties. A prolific letter writer, he sent more information about Japan to Europe than anyone before or since. *Unique* is an overused word that will soon mean little more than "remarkable," just as "incredible" is now all too easy to believe; but this treatise (*Tratado em que se contem* . . .), written in his fifties, probably at the behest of the Visitador A. Valignano, in connection with the revolutionary new policy of Accommodation (the practice of cultural relativism), is truly unique. Herodotus made *dozens* of black and white contrasts between Egypt and the Greco-Roman civilization he called "the rest of the world;" Alberuni (Il Bîrûnî) did the same for India and the West (mostly what Occidentals now call the Middle East); but no one found *hundreds* as did Frois for Europe and Japan.

Since Father Josef F. Schütte discovered the worm-eaten original (Portuguese with some Japanese words mixed in) of the *Tratado* in a Library in Madrid and published a German translation with notes and the original transcribed into print, popular and semi-scholarly Japanese translations have gone through countless pocket-book printings. Frois's 611 skeletal distiches – two lines we might call *heroic contrast!* – are highly regarded because, excluding those dealing with religion, they are not judgmental but, rather, objective, i.e. descriptive in the manner of naive cultural anthropology. As such, they are often quoted as first-hand evidence by historians. Laymen, on the other hand, enjoy the *Tratado* because it is also (Elison again), "a booklet of amazing banality." Who but Frois would have noticed we pick our noses with different fingers, sniff melons from opposite ends, fear or fear not snakes, pay or get paid for the removal of our bowel movements, etc. *and* bothered to write it down!

Best known for a series of books deconstructing stereotypes of difference and demonstrating the hidden *similarities* between Japanese and Occidentals written and published in Japanese in the 1980's, with this book, the translator-critic Robin D. Gill finds *himself* in a topsy-turvy world; for, in order to do justice to Frois, he now dons another cloak, that of the contrast-monger. Not only has he done this, but for the sake of argument (something he loves) and amusement (an independent scholar needs not keep a stiff upper lip), he has gone out on a limb, adding enough new contrasts, which he dubs *Faux Frois,* to bring the total distiches in the book to a thousand or so. *Guinness*, are you reading?

注！ Readers who want *more* notes and quotations, *longer* digressions and the uncut Annotated Bibliography, and (until the 2nd *edition*) can tolerate many *typos, stylos* (stylistic problems) and *mistakos,* are advised to give this little book to a friend and buy the 740-page Long Version.

paraverse press may be found at www.paraverse.org

Or, keep this book, which is, after all, far better edited and look up the additional material on-line. The long version (called *TT-long* in the course of this book) is now up at Google Print, which is searchable. It may be up at Amazon, too, for it was sent the same day (but, as of this writing, is tardy).

Robin D. Gill. A native Floridian (Key Biscayne). Working as an acquisitions editor and translation-checker in Japan of top nonfiction literature for Kousakusha and editions Papyrus, he introduced scores of books including Eiseley: *The Star Thrower*, Levi: *Periodic Table*, Lovelock: *Gaia*, Lopez: *Winter Count*, Prishvin: *Nature's Diary*, Thoreau: *Cape Cod*, etc., while writing seven non-fiction books in Japanese (publishers include the major publisher Chikuma-bunko, academic Hakusuisha and the avant-garde Kousakusha) in the 1980's. Most of these books deconstructed stereotypes of difference. One concentrates on the reduction of culture to climate, one on antithetical stereotypes of the mutually exotic tongues of English and Japanese, one on the relationship of mistranslation to prejudice. More information on the content of the books and reviews may be found at the www.paraverse.org website. Note that Gill wrote as "Robin Gill" (ロビン・ギル) in Japan/ese, but now uses his middle initial "D." religiously, because there is a theologian connected with Oxford University Press also named Robin Gill, who is a prolific writer.

Robin D. Gill's *first* book in English, **Rise, Ye Sea Slugs!** (Paraverse Press: 2003), a translation and essay of 1,000 holothurian haiku, was highly acclaimed (Blurbs and Reviews in the appendix), "a classic" from the start according to some reviewers. The sea cucumber poems, many of which are hundreds of years old, are arranged by metaphor and dressed with natural and unnatural history. Because haiku are not overly precious and the book is full of ideas (and what one reviewer calls "quirky facts"), even readers who *hate* most poetry may be surprised to find they enjoy it. According to a review in the Spring 2005 issue of *Metamorphoses: the journal of the five college faculty seminar on literary translation*, "For all the eccentricities one might expect (and does find) in a [480 pg] book devoted entirely to haiku on the sea slug, the author is an accomplished haiku writer, a very talented and engaging critic capable of reading with an astute understanding of culture and cultural differences. Haiku enthusiasts, scholars of Japanese literature and marine biology, and professional and amateur translators alike will certainly welcome this interesting book." (Thomas H. Rohlich, Professor of Japanese at Smith College – the full review is at paraverse.org)

His *second* in English, **Orientalism & Occidentalism** – *is the mistranslation of culture inevitable?* should appeal to serious students of Japan, comparative culture and language, nationalism and translation, or any literate polyglot. It reworks some of the ground covered in his Japanese work with the non-Japanese reader in mind. *O & O* is especially recommended to readers as balance (penance?) for the differences played up and enjoyed in *Topsy-turvy 1585*.

The *third*, **Fly-ku!** breaks new ground concerning anthropomorphism and thematic development in poetry. According to Jane Reichhold in her on-line journal LYNX: "The way Gill translates is not only marvelous, it is absolutely revolutionary. Instead of giving the reader the idea that there is only one way to translate a haiku, he offers a word-for-word translation and then goes into great detail explaining the ambiguities of the Japanese language along with the secrets of Japanese behavior . . . The book is full of humor and information given in Gill's distinctive way. His mind makes huge leaps so all the information about flies or Japanese and everything else in between feels as if it has been stirred in a great cosmic blender and poured out, in a decorative manner, suggesting a teahouse snack." (First issue of 2005)

His fourth, the **LONG** version of **TOPSY-TURVY 1585**, and this, the **SHORT** version, will be followed by **Cherry Blossom Epiphany** on the poetry and philosophy of flower viewing, and **The Fifth Season**, on that neglected season of traditional haiku, the New Year, which is vol. I of *In Praise of Olde Haiku*, (IPOOH) a poetic almanac of five seasons.

At this moment, books are his entire life, so he has nothing more to say about it.
..

 robin d. gill
(*aka* keigu)

This book is a work in progress – if you have anything to contribute, please write us!

> "I wonder
> if I shall fall
> right through the earth!
> How funny it will seem
> to come out among
> the people that walk
> with their heads
> downwards!
>
> The antipathies, I think –"

(Alice, as she tumbles down the rabbit hole)

..

The cover is the most famous of the 36 Views of Fuji by the world's most prolific artist Hokusai (1760-1849)

TABLE OF
CONTENTS

Preface to the original *Tratado* (treatise)____9

*Fore*word: *The Appeal of Topsy-Turvydom* _____11

I = Men in Europe and Japan_____29
II = Women in Europe and Japan_____81
III = Children in Europe and Japan_____129
IV = Monks in Europe and Japan_____153
V = Temples and Images in Europe and Japan_____187

*Mid*word: *China vs Japan*____209

VI = Food and Drink in Europe and Japan____219
VII = War and Weapons in Europe and Japan_____257
VIII = Horses and Riding in Europe and Japan_____279
IX = Diseases and Medicine in Europe and Japan_____297
X = Writing and Books in Europe and Japan_____309
XI = Home and Garden in Europe and Japan_____327
XII = Boats in Europe and Japan_____363
XIII = Drama and Music in Europe and Japan_____377
XIV = Sundry Things in Europe and Japan_____401

*Post*word: *"The JappyKnee Oppositioner"* _____441
Shortened Annotated Bibliography   English = 444; Japanese - 451
Acknowledgements_____453
Reviews of Previous Work (Later to be exchanged for reviews of *this* book, the funnier the better, in the Norton Critical Anthology style!) _____454

Complete chapter by chapter, *item by item* contents_____455

桃山・室町時代に詳しい方のご協力を乞う。　本書に未解決の問題、まだある。
英語を読むのが苦手の場合、＜フロイス問答場＞　を訪ねてみて下さい。

Look at that! Sometimes, it would seem, only the silverfish knew exactly what Frois wrote!

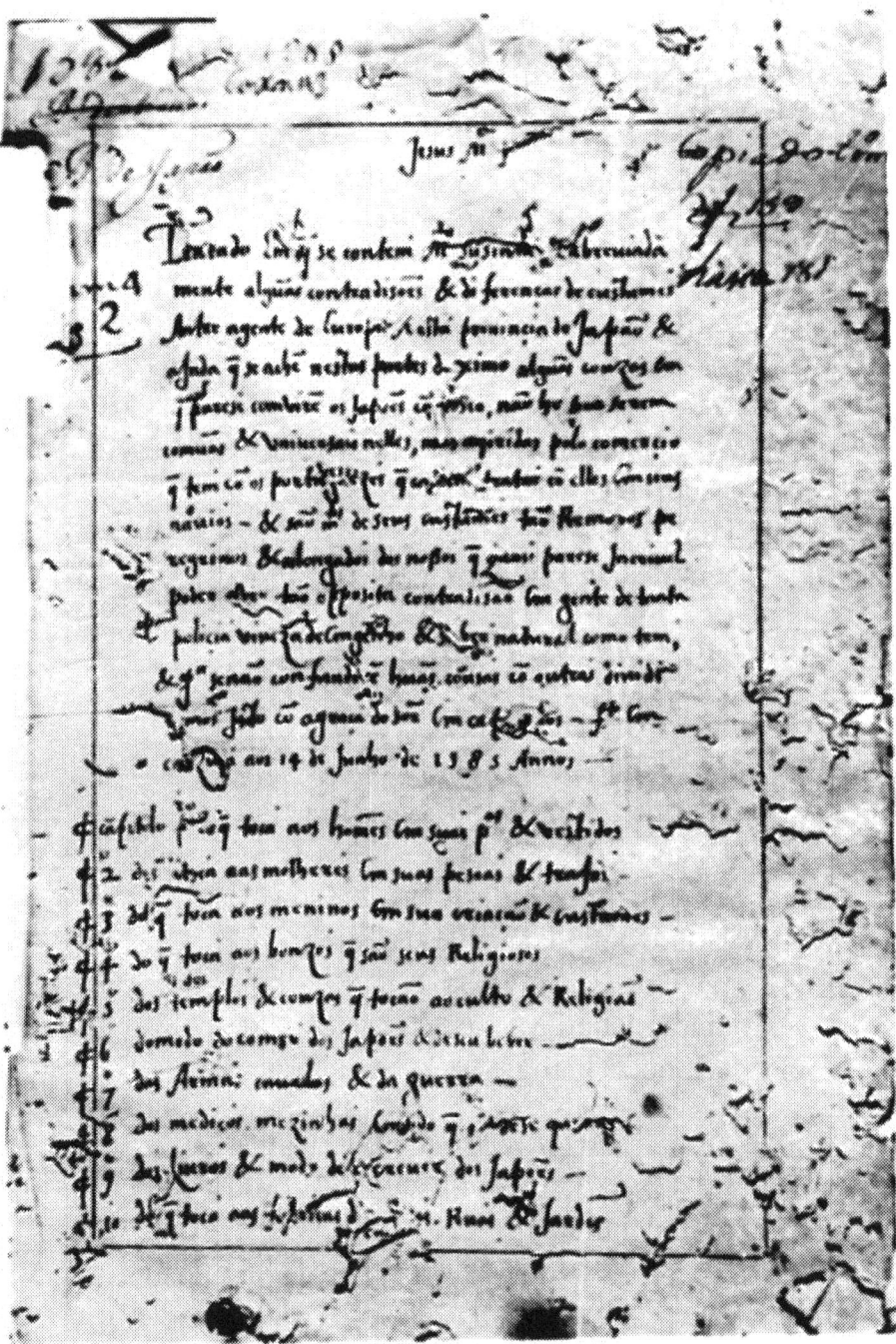

This is a copy of a copy of a photo of the first page of Frois's *Tratado* from mss Jes. 11-10-3/21 at the Biblioteca de la Académia de la História in Madrid borrowed (with apologies for not asking permission) from *Kulturgegensätze Europa-Japan* (1585) by Josef Franz Schütte, S.J. (Sophia University, Tokyo 1955 (F(S):T)). I hope to pay for a good copy from the Académia for a future edition, but am now lack time = money. I nevertheless include it, partly to prove it is real (for much will amaze the reader!) and partly to show its condition. The holes on the next page, reproduced in the pocketbook-sized translation by Matsuda & Jorissen (J/F(M&J):T), show much larger holes! It is amazing how few words Father Schütte failed to read or guess.

Preface

to the original untitled manuscript of Luis Frois S.J.

Jesus - Maria

This short treatise briefly outlines some contradictions and differences in customs encountered among the people of Europe and the people of this province of Japan. Although there are a number of [cultural] items where Japanese appear similar to us in Shimo [today, West Kyushu], these were adopted to facilitate trade with the Portuguese who come here, and are not widespread. Many of their customs are so far removed, so alien from ours it is hard to believe; as it is that so opposite a contrariety can exist in people so civilized, lively with ingenuity and natural understanding as these [of Japan]. In order that the diverse matters concerning us and them are not further confused, with the help of our Lord God, I have divided them into chapters. – written in Canzusa [Katsusa] on 14 June, 1585.

a
Jesus-M

Tratado em que se contem muito [susinta e] abreviadamente algumas contradisões & diferenças de custumes Antre a gente de Europa & esta provincia de Japão & ainda que se achem nestas partes do ximo algumas couzas em que parese comverem os Japões connosco, não he por serem commuas & universais nelles, mas aqiridas polo comercio que tem com os portuguezes que ca vem tratar com elles em seus navios – & são muitos de seus custumes tão Remotos, peregrinos & alongados dos nossos que quasi parese Incrivel. Poder aver tão opposita contradisão em gente de tanta policia viveza de emgenho & saber natural como tem, & pera se não confundirem humas cousas com outras, dividimos isto com a graça do senhor em capitolos – feito em Canzusa Aos 14 de Junho de 1585 Annos –

This ↑ was borrowed from the transcription of Schütte S.J. with a few changes based on the photo of the original. The ampersands are restored and I tried to capitalize as Frois did (Schütte put it in all caps). I left the expansions of Frois's shorthand of "m" and "q" with lines over them for *muito* and *que*, respectively, but restored *Maria* to her abbrev. state.) I think Frois meant to remove *"susinta e"* as redundant, and bracketed it. The photo is from Schütte:1955 work (F(S):T). A pg. from the body in J/F(M&J):T is far more worm-eaten. I couldn't have read it!

Well Said

When they wish to do us great honor, they say that we resemble them.

                        Balthasar Gago *Cartas* (Sept 23, 1555)

To see how everything is the reverse of Europe, despite the fact that their ceremonies and customs are so discerning and rational for those who really understand them, is a thing of no little surprise.

                    Alessandro Valignano, S.J. *Summario* . . (1583)
..

When the Dutch laughed at their customs, they [the Japanese] laughed at the Dutch; but with submission to the learned commentator, that was rather an agreement than a difference.

                Editor's note *Golownin's Captivity in Japan* (1824)

The discovery of the highly-developed Japanese culture and civilization, which had grown up quite independently of Europe came as a salutary shock.

               Michael Cooper, S.J. *They Came to Japan* (1965)

"Yes, Japan may well be, as you write, a country in a looking glass. There are indeed many ideas and customs opposite to those of Europe. But, Brother Frois, take out a mirror and look at it closely. For sure, everything in the mirror is reversed left and right, but are Heaven and earth upside-down?"

          Inoue Hisashi *Waga Tomo Furoisu* [my friend frois] (1999)

 One of the few places the short version of the book is longer than the long.   The first and last quotes are new.

THE APPEAL OF TOPSY-TURVYDOM

foreword

i
the origin of topsy-turvy

There has always been a *Land of Topsy-Turvy*. The literature of cultural anthropology tells us of an *other* world, underground, inverted, a place where men walk upside-down and backwards, eat feces and spit up food. Knowing this, who can doubt the literal Antipodes, the crudely depicted foot-over-head folk we identify with the Medieval imagination, was born long before Pliny? Indeed, self-identity of any sort requires others and the ultimate other, the antipodes, whether part of a belief system or invented by the sub-conscious of an individual has a permanent presence among us.

But, the *practice* of Froising (dare I name it after its master?) i.e., listing numerous opposite features of another living and real culture – not the more easily invented monster – is not so commonly encountered. Of course, people in one tribe have always said *We do this, while they do that*. Doubtless, someone in a purely oral tradition listed contraries sometime, somewhere, but the first *example* I know of comes from Herodotus, (BC 484-425), our entertaining "father of history," who contrasted the "rest of the world" with Egypt, where women went out to do business while men stayed home and wove, men carried burdens on their heads and women on their shoulders and women rather than men made water standing.

Al-Bîrûnî, in AD 1030 (AH 420) carried on the tradition contrasting "our country" to the Hindus in India where – they sip the stale of cows, but do not eat their meat, besmear their bodies with dung instead of perfumes on festive days, and in all emergencies take the advice of the women. Al-Bîrûnî, whose reading of Hindu math, science and religion was far deeper than Herodotus's reportage or any study of exotic culture previous to that of the Jesuits in the 16c, noted: "the reader must always bear in mind that the Hindus entirely differ from us in every respect, many a subject appearing intricate and obscure which would be perfectly clear if there were more connection between us." (Edward C. Sachau trans. *Alberuni's India*). I believe that the well-argued cultural relativism of Frois's superior Valignano – one of his points was that Europeans and Japanese had to become familiar with, that is *experience*, one another's customs to appreciate them – may owe something to Al-Bîrûnî, though the style of making our side as well as theirs explicit in the contrast would seem to owe more to Herodotus. Be that as it may, these great scholars only listed dozens of differences, not hundreds like our humble brother Frois.

We can only guess what Frois's unprecedented and still unbeaten six hundred and eleven item list was for. His preface says only that there are these incredibly contrary customs he was trying to record and arrange, with God's help, in chapters. Valignano included so many of the *Tratado* contrasts in his Summary of Japan written in 1582-3 (which developed from his Summary of India written in 1579), that he must have relied upon Frois, who served as his interpreter and scribe when he visited Japan, for much if not most of that information. Frois's list probably started because Valignano requested it – Frois had made a number of observations found in the Tratado as early as 1565 – but the simple *We this; They that* form is not seen and appears to have originated with his logically-minded Superior. Once begun, however, I believe the list may have continued because Frois got carried away in the manner of any collector of oddities. Since collecting quickly becomes its own reason, it is possible that the *Tratado* may not have been intended for anything other than sharing with intimates.

If the *Tratado* was intended for more, the readership would have been Europeans in the Far East who knew some Japanese, or wished to, as there is more than a smattering of (un-translated) Japanese words in the text, and the message between most of the lines would support the position toward Japanese culture adopted by the Jesuits at the 1580 Consultation of Bungo (also called the Usuki Deliberations), and the policy of Accommodation that was officially adopted as a result of the consensus. That is to say, like Valignano's 1582-3 writing, his *Summary of Japanese Things* that was translated by Maffei into Latin and became the fount of topsy-turvy Japanology, the Tratado is an *apologia* (or, ammunition for an *apologia*) for the first modern declaration of cultural equality (I do not say racial equality for, as we shall see, the Japanese and Chinese were considered *white*). What Valignano wrote, in a word, is that: 1) Matters of religion aside, our cultures and the people who make them up were of equal worth, each more or less advanced, more or less good/bad in different respects; 2) Yet, the two cultures were incredibly "contrary in all" and the Japanese so wedded to their customs that they would not change "though the world should flood over." 3) So, if Japan could not be conquered (which was clearly the case), Europeans in Japan had to accommodate themselves, i.e., adopt Japanese culture if they hoped to win the respect of the natives and thrive; 4) And, because of 1), above, i.e., *this was a matter between equals*, doing things their way – *when in Japan do as the Japanese do* – was also only natural, which is to say morally correct. This was no academic problem, for as St. Xavier pointed out decades earlier, when "the heathen" saw that non-European converts were looked down on by the Portuguese, they avoided conversion and, this was particularly true for Japanese whose strong pride in their own culture and race was noted by all. Even the *appearance* of prejudice had to be avoided.

In the "Relations of the Japanese to the Society" (part of the *modus viviendi/ operendi* worked out at Bungo), the part regarding the "close union" of the European and Japanese missionaries where the "greatest hindrance" was said to lie in the immense difference between their respective customs has these blunt words: "Many things which for us denote politeness and good breeding wound the feelings of the Japanese." Living in Japan, the Europeans had to "learn and observe Japanese etiquette." Such words were meant to be acted upon:

> They should not speak disparagingly of the native customs, as newcomers from India usually do. As soon as they arrive in Japan, their attention must be drawn to the matter; the Superior is to see that from the start they impress on their memories Japanese usages in keeping with the "Rules for the ceremonial and customs which Ours are to observe in one another's company and with strangers." Someone well acquainted with Japanese etiquette should introduce them to these customs and drill them thoroughly in them for some days, so that they may not be taken for uncouth and unmannerly people. (S(C):VMP)

Reading this, one can imagine the *Tratado's* 611 contrasts used to induce culture-shock and break down Eurocentric prejudice, thereby speeding the accommodation to Japanese manners on the part of newcomers to the Jesuit Order.

ii
the nature of topsy-turvy

In 1565, Frois wrote that "the Japanese are superior to the Spanish in more ways than I can say." These words reflect not only his experience, but the views of the Saint Xavier which he would have read and those of the self-described scoundrel Mendez Pinto which he would not have known. Frois was not besotted with the Japanese as was Organtino who, in 1577, wrote that "apart from the faith we hold, no matter how wise we fancy ourselves to be, when compared with them it is we who are most uncivilized (*comparati a loro siamo barbarissimi*) and in 1589, even after the persecution of Christians began, that "any Jesuit who comes to Japan and does not foster a love for this bride of wondrous beauty, not caring to learn her language immediately nor conforming to her ways, [deserves] to be packed back to Europe as an inept and unprofitable worker in God's vineyard." (S:VMP) Frois the observer and scribe had a cooler personality. He had what I would call a healthy admiration of the Japanese.

This is important for, the selection of items to contrast, like the selection of what news to broadcast, is itself an editorial decision, one that inevitably reflects our bias. Had Frois been too biased either way we would not have the contrasts that put the respective parties into a good or bad light. His character is also important because if, as the old English proverb goes, *comparison is odious*, then, *contrast* by its very nature is downright dangerous. Whether or not value-judgments are explicit, every cultural contrast has the potential to harm, because readers who do not respect the other from deep in the heart (in which case, good faith prevents harsh interpretation) can not help but judge difference. "We do *this* while they do *that* " is, after all, what supports the largely uncomplimentary stereotyping called Orientalism (Western stereotypes about the East) and Occidentalism (Eastern stereotypes about the West). Once overall equality is granted, however, difference, *provided it is properly explained,* can be turned around and used to break the single scale backbone of prejudice.

I emphasize *properly explained*, because years of following pop-Japanology (*nihonjinron* – books that boost Japanese self-esteem by selective contrast with a stereotypical Occident) in Japan taught me that relativism all too often backfires because it serves as a cover for making outlandish contrasts without taking the time to appraise their validity and significance. I came to know that whenever an author made a big deal of disavowing any value judgment with respect to claims of difference he introduced, *look out!* He was likely to be highly prejudiced. My reading in this pop-sociology was almost entirely confined to Japanese, so I cannot say whether the same holds true for books written in English, but, in Japan, I would submit that the fiction of insignificant difference actually spreads prejudice. Mark my words, difference is *never* insignificant. Even as we enjoy reading about it (after all, exotic, a word meaning no more than "foreign" or "outside", *is* fascinating) we must hold it suspect.

Frois wrote so much and analyzed so little that the scholarly consensus (at least most of what I have seen written in English) has is that he was not much of a thinker. True, he had neither the scholarly background nor genius of a Valignano or a Ricci. But, Frois was far from naïve. Lacking the advantages of these men – Frois was always the servant of the elite and had little time left over for himself – he was still the first person I know of to take the problem of *the incommensurability of terms* by the horns. Valignano does not do this until 1601, years after Frois did at far greater length in his Prologue to the otherwise lost first book of his *History of Japan*, explaining that one of the purposes of this Summary volume was to rid Europeans of mistaken ideas about Japanese resulting from the use of terms liable to being misunderstood when left without qualification. About half of the dozen or so terms are items found in *Tratado*. Since much of The Table of Contents of the lost book was also identical to the chapters of the *Tratado*, it is safe to say that Frois intended for contrasts to be *properly explained* either *viva voce* or in print. Here is the most entertaining of the qualifications:

> Told that Japanese blow their nose but once per *handkerchief*, the European reader will find it odd if not ludicrous. It is like being told that the kings of Malabar eat just once from the same plate. They eat on banana leaves, so when the meal is over, they throw them away. Thus, when it is said that once a handkerchief has been spit in or blown upon, the Japanese throw it away without washing it, the following must be explained: that the Japanese, go about with many handkerchief-like thin, folded papers in their pocket[bosom], instead of handkerchiefs. As this paper is very cheap, for a very small outlay, they can use as much as they please. The gentry keep one white or blue linen cloth with the paper which is only used to wipe sweat. But merchants and ordinary folk, besides the paper, keep a cheap hemp rag tucked in their sashes for both wiping off sweat and for using when they wash their face or hands. (J/F:HISTORIA)

With no word for what we now call "tissue paper," as such did not exist in the West, the generic "handkerchief" was used to translate what Japanese call *chirigami*, literally "scatter-paper" or *fukurogami*, "pocket-paper." The former now means "toilet paper," while it is called teishyu (tissue) and still more popular than *hankachi* (handkerchiefs). Before the picky reader snorts at what Frois chooses to explain, let me take responsibility. Frois did not neglect more important items such as incommensurable number units and the problematic title of "king."

iii
some types of topsy-turvy

Difference is real. We cannot long pretend not to see or minimize difference to support our catechism that "we are all alike." When push comes to shove (such as in a trade-war), empathy built on a fiction does not hold up. We must stare right at the difference and figure out how, correctly understood it proves we are, *at some deeper level*, similar. To do this, the clearer initial picture we can get the better. That is why we need black & white contrast, crude though it may seem, in a world that is ultimately grey.

But not all contrasts interest or effect us in the same way.

There are items in the *Tratado* which beautifully betray our expectations by demonstrating that not only is the past a foreign country but, at times, the very antipode of the present. When time stands a contrast on its head – the illusion of timelessness being one of the marks of all cultural stereotyping – we immediately realize that our ideas of "us" and "them" are too shallow. Considering modern Occidental stereotypes about Japanese women as virtual slaves, how pleasant to read numerous items suggesting they once enjoyed far more personal freedom than European women. Contrasts 2-1, -20, -24, -30, -32, -34, -35, -38, -45, -54 show, respectively, that *they* were *not forced to be chaste, could walk barefoot, show their legs, own property (and lend it to their husbands), divorce their husbands, go out when they please, have abortions, knew how to write, and could drink and even get drunk!*

On the other hand, even the confirmation of hoary differences can be instructive. Is it not worthwhile to learn that even back then (before the Tokugawa Era (1603-1867) with its long, in some ways, authoritarian rule) *most Japanese were more disciplined than most Occidentals* (14-2), *did not whip their children as we did* (3-7) and *were paid rather than paying for the hauling away of human waste* (11-21)? These things, if I may editorialize, all speak well for Japanese, and suggest we in the Occident still have something to reflect upon, or, better yet, learn. Humans will need all the self-discipline we can muster to keep from turning the earth into hell; all too many children continue to be mistreated; and, the waste of good waste is still a serious problem.

If some contrasts such as *our showing much emotion when we lose our fortune or our house burns down, whereas Japanese grin and bear it* (14-2), or *we only execute big-time robbers while Japanese kill all thieves* (14-7) have been observed by many visitors before and after Frois, others, such as *"With us, killing flies with the hand is [considered] filthy; In Japan, lords and gentlemen do so, pulling off their wings and throwing them away."* (4-23) or *"When we warm our hands, the palm faces the fire; When the Japanese warm them, the back of the hand faces the fire."* (14-43), could only have been recorded by someone actively seeking examples of difference.

The arrangement of the 611 contrasts in thematic chapters ranging from 19 to 74 items each would benefit from additional tiers of organization. For example, *horses* and *boats* might be put into a larger section on *transportation* in which case another chapter on foot-travel (several items concern walking) might have been added, etc., but to do this thoroughly, Frois would have had to invent modern social science. As is, the arrangement of the individual items tends toward the haphazard, which I enjoy for the same reason I prefer listening to the radio not knowing what will come next to a record where I do.

But imagine other possibilities. How about listing them from the most serious ones (*Europeans killing animals easily* vs. *Japanese killing men easily* (14-6)) to the most trivial (the above-mentioned *hand-warming style* or, even less telling, *the hand used to strike a flint* (14- 1)). In that case, one might give explanations of varying length, the longest for the most important contrasts that stand to create prejudice if left unchallenged, and to next to nothing for the minor ones. Or conversely, one could pay little attention to the important contrasts because others may be depended upon to comment on them and confine ourselves to minor observations ignored by others. In this book, Frois's contrasts are left in the original order. And, if there is a method to my commentary, I leave it to the reviewer to find it.

I do not know if I would, after Elison, call Frois's contrasts *banal* in the strict sense of the word, for few are pointed out by others. They are only trite in the sense that life itself is so. But, even with explanation and put into context, it is true that many do not seem individually significant. The word *trivial* rather than *banal,* comes to mind. We cannot help but think of, say, Joao Rodrigues S.J.'s outstanding description of *The Way of Tea* written only a decade or two after *Tratado*. His comprehension of the finer part of Japanese culture, the "art of *suki*" or "good taste" that comes with the *chanoyu*, or tea ceremony, is, to my mind, nothing short of miraculous. Over a century before Chinese-style landscape would be the vogue in England, he wrote:

> "Everything artificial, refined and pretty must be avoided, for anything not made according to nature causes tedium and boredom in the long run. For if you plant two trees of the same size and shape, one in front of the other, and deliberately make them correspond to one another, they will end by causing tedium and boredom; the same applies to other things as well. But lack of artificiality and a note of naturalness (for example, in a complete tree made up of various disordered branches pointing this way and that, just as nature directed them) is never boring, because experience shows there is always something new to be found therein." (Cooper trans. R(C):TIJ)

Compared to this, many of Frois's contrasts seem shallow indeed. But, Rodrigues gives us little if anything new to us *today*. A Japanese reader, or knowledgeable Western reader will not find much he did not know already, for other cultured souls *eventually* wrote about the same exceptionally worthy subjects. Frois, on the other hand, by being less discriminating – something for which he criticized by his superiors – offers us much that is fresh. History itself is topsy-turvy: *with the passage of time, it is the commonplace that becomes rare, the banal that becomes fresh.* I think this is understood today. Is that not why we put common things into time capsules? But it was not always so. Could we call Frois the man who discovered culture with a small c?

iv
tokugawa topsy-turvy

Valignano's listing of dozens of contrasts, rather than Frois's hundreds, made their anonymous way into the drawing rooms of Europe. One finds them in almost every work on Japan published for centuries, sometimes with no mention of Maffei (whose name, rather than Valignano's was on the work). Von Linschoten's 1598 book, which influenced generations of Dutch visitors to Japan, is an exception, for he *also* stole from Valignano's 1579 *Summario* (He was in Goa in 1583) which contrasted "cleane contrary" Chinese and Japanese (See the Mid-word).

Only one work evidently borrows directly from Frois's *Tratado*. This is the oft-published work *My Voyage Around the World* (*Ragionamenti . .*) of Carletti. Valignano is his favorite source. After describing a Japanese peasant who shook his feet "so much his shoes came off" and pardoned himself "instead of removing a hat – which they never wear," as he passed the Florentine merchant on a bridge, he writes:

And as their customs are no less strange than varied, and as they are opposite to us in location of their land, I have made notes about them and contrasted them with ours in every way. But all that was lost with everything else of mine. But to report something that comes back to my memory, what greater strangeness could there be than their way of caring for the sick, whom they feed on fresh and salted fish . . . . and on various raw, sour, unripe fruits, and without ever letting blood, thus in everything doing the opposite of what we do? (transl. Herbert Weinstock C(W):MVAW)

The fine details of shaking off shoes and the humorous way he says they do not take off the hats "which they never wear" is pure Carletti – a fine observer and witty raconteur. But how strange that "their way of caring for the sick" should happen to be the thing to come back to him, for it just happens to be something stressed in Valignano's 1583 *Sumario* (*Mas cousa de espanto es ver la manera del curar*) and is identical down to the details about the food! Yet, as Matsuda and Jorissen point out, part of his "notes" were almost certainly made from Frois's manuscript, which Carletti could have seen while staying in Nagasaki for ten months on the year of Frois's death, 1597; for some observations contrast maritime matters not in Valignano's work, giving them *in the same order they appear* in the *Tratado*. Could Carletti have "requisitioned" that missing first volume of Frois's *Historia*, in which case, it may be lost forever in a shipwreck on the bottom of the sea? *Only the mermaids know.*

In the early 17c, Japan was sealed off to all but a tiny trade with the Dutch, conducted with as much care as we would with aliens from outer space, perhaps carrying germs that could infect and destroy us. A 1670 work ostensibly on the Dutch *Embassy to the Emperor of Japan*, but actually a hodge-podge of history, second-hand reportage and imaginative explanation by Montanus and an early 18c anonymous English translation of a late-17c *History of the Church of Japan*, by "Monsieur L' Abbe de T." (F. Solier's History of same rewritten by F. Crasset SJ) are full of topsy-turvyisms borrowed from Valignano=Maffei. Montanus admits the good characteristics of the Japanese as well as the bad, but sensationalizes the latter to such an extent that, for the first time, we encounter the modern Orientalized East (this aided by fulsome illustrations of monumental realistic idols surrounded by abject worshippers), while Monseiur L' Abbe despite penning an entire volume on gruesome martyrdoms presents everything favorable Valignano wrote about the Japanese character and a few he did not, while touching upon only a couple of their shortcomings!

The German Kaempfer, who spent a few years in the tiny Dutch trading post observed much with the mind of a doctor and amateur botanist instead of a theologian. His thorough 1690-2 book, containing travelogue type observation and locally researched natural history, mythology, etc. with ample drawings, many copied from Japanese books, was the first to contribute substantial information not already found in the Jesuits' writing. While Kaempfer loved oddity as much as anyone in his baroque era – he introduces "the Shogun who loved dogs" twice and spends pages on blowfish – he does not Orientalize and stands out for *not* remarking upon any tendency toward *contrariness* on the part of the Japanese.

But the theme of *contrariety* was pretty much fixed in the literature. Only the credit got lost somewhere. There are two footnotes regarding "some of the extraordinary differences between the Japanese customs and those of Europe" by the anonymous early 19c English editor of the Russian Golownin's reasoned yet touching account of Japan and his captivity there (G:MCJ) While most of the differences ultimately derive from Valignano/Maffei, the editor credits "Dutch writers" and the Jesuits are not even mentioned! Even the otherwise fair Golownin mentions Jesuits only to attack them for making Europeans believe Japanese had a "detestable character" by painting them in "odious colours." Not encountering such "monastic rage" in anything I read, I found the charge dubious until reading of an article by Engelbert Jorissen in the *Bulletin of Portuguese/Japanese Studies* ("Exotic and 'strange' images of Japan in European texts in the early 17th century") which credits (?) S. Gonçalves, S.J. with "creating a strange malevolent image of Japan" in his History (ca.1615), which was picked up by others with the result being that the hitherto *exotic* became *barbaric*. So, the Jesuits may indeed deserve some blame for *bad Japan*.

To his credit, Golownin's editor also adds the first note of caution towards difference-mongering. With respect to a remark of the Swede Thunberg (like Kaempfer, a physician who served the Dutch to see Japan and equally a big Japanophile), claiming Japan was "totally different from Europe," he remonstrated:

> but, not withstanding this is generally true, it is not the less remarkable, that many of their institutions, and much of their manners . . . are absolutely fac-similes of our own feudal times, and demonstrate the existence of that system to a much greater extent than our ablest writers have hitherto imagined; at the same time, corroborating the similarity frequently noticed between Japan and Great Britain, and opening a wide field of speculation for the spirit of political prophecy . . . (G:MCJ)

I did not find that Thunberg stressed difference enough to earn such a riposte in a footnote to a third party's book, but Golownin's editor makes a good point: *differences reviewed from a developmental perspective can be understood as similarity.* Because this implies a ladder of progress, however, one might say that a neutral difference has been reinterpreted as one with a value: for, if Japan is indeed like us, then, by the yardstick of progress, it is backwards, if not inferior.

v
modern topsy-turvydom: alcock

The Age of Nonsense may well have been born in newly "opened" Japan, for the letters of the first English Ambassador to Japan, Sir Rutherford Alcock, were "printed and laid before Parliament" and published in leading journal/s during the decade before Lewis Carroll's *Alice* discovered the "Antipathies." They were published in book form in 1863. *Alice* in 1865. In a page of Alcock's *Capital of the Tycoon* captioned *"Paradoxes and Anomalies,"* a splendid reverie on the bath-houses of Yeddo (Edo/Tokyo), which includes mention of a young Caucasian who "emerged as red as a lobster, and much as that martyr to gastronomy may be supposed to feel before all feeling is boiled out of him" – ends with the dreamy sentence: "Here, if they have any cares, they seem to forget them all in the steamy atmosphere, and forming the very oddest assemblage that can well be conceived." And, as if that steam (rather than a *looking glass*) created a mirage on the brain – in the very next sentence and paragraph Alcock is *there*.

> Japan is essentially a country of paradoxes and anomalies, where all, even familiar things, put on new faces, and are curiously reversed. Except that they do not walk on their heads instead of their feet, there are few things in which they do not by some occult law, to have been impelled in a perfectly opposite manner and a reversed order. They write from top to bottom, from right to left, in perpendicular instead of horizontal lines, and their books begin where ours end, thus furnishing good examples of the curious perfection this rule of contraries has obtained. Their locks, though imitated from Europe, are all made to lock by turning their key from left to right. The course of all sublunary things appears reversed. Their day is for the most part our night, and this principle of antagonism crops out in the most unexpected and bizarre way in all their moral being, customs and habits. I leave to philosophers the explanation – I only speak the facts. There, old men fly kites while children look on; the carpenter uses his plane by drawing it to him, and their tailors stitch from them . . . and, finally, the utter confusion of the sexes in the public bath-houses, making that correct which we in the West deem so shocking and improper, I leave as I find it – a problem to solve. (A:COT)

A word on that kite-flying. Grown men *did* engage in kite battles with strings "covered with pounded glass" (Scidmore) and still do today. Kites can be huge, heavy and very dangerous (some wear helmets and ambulances wait on the side of the field). The teams who fly them run madly about, and children had best stay out of the way lest they be run over! Either the kiting Alcock observed was exceptionally mild stuff or the old men were prepared to meet their maker!

I skipped Alcock's comments on Japanese horses and lady's teeth (the " . . ."), which will be noticed by all subsequent Victorian era visitors, as they are in *Tratado*. While Alcock found more than a few things to praise in Japan (he had a soft spot for simple but effective mechanical devices, the abundance of which mystified him in view of the low cost of labor), he was an opinionated Englishman, writing from a post-industrial revolution perspective of progress-as-the-measure-of-man – which made him far less relative about culture (religion aside) than the Jesuits in Bungo. Yet, sometime over the course of the Victorian era, whether due to the spreading American ideology of equality, Alfred Russell Wallace's testimony of equality based on years of living with alleged primitives, romantic tolerance for the exotic – *the antipodes as cute* – or, whatever, *the modern relativistic outlook began to take root*, plumb in the middle of the heyday of Orientalism, long before the flourishing of the Boas school of anthropology with which it is usually identified. Kipling, a man all too often identified with Imperialism – who, by happy coincidence, was born the very year *Alice* was published – penned a charming page-long children's verse called *"We and They,"* which is as relative as relative can be. The last stanza is especially charming and deserves to be better known:

> All good people agree,
>   And all good people say,
> All nice people, like Us, are We
>   And every one else is They:
> But if you cross over the sea,
>   Instead of over the way,
> You may end by (think of it!) looking on We
>   As only a sort of They!

vi
modern topsy-turvydom: chamberlain

It would seem that Alcock's patent on the "principle of antagonism" was a short one, for by the end of the century, Professor Basil Hall Chamberlain, who, according to Charles E. Tuttle Co.'s book-jacket blurb, "taught Japanese and Japan to the Japanese," is the man most widely identified with the term "topsy-turvydom" today (Next to the ridiculous opera, but let us not go there!). This is not surprising, for there is even a two page *"Topsy-turvydom"* heading in his classic *Things Japanese* (1890) that includes dozens of examples. The heading begins –

> It has often been remarked that the Japanese do many things in a way that runs directly counter to European ideas of what is natural and proper. To the Japanese themselves our ways appear equally unaccountable. It was only the other day that a Tokyo lady asked the present writer why foreigners did so many things topsy-turvy, instead of doing them naturally, after the manner of her country people. (C:TJ)

If Chamberlain read earlier topsy-turvy listings he does not mention any. It is ironic, for he claims his title "which cost us much cogitation" comes from *cosas de Espana,* a phrase meaning "there is no accounting for customs," used by Alcock who also uses the words *things Japanese,* which he probably did not know was once used as a title by Valignano: *las cosas de Japon.* It is hard to excuse Chamberlain's failure to credit Alcock, (whose book he read and liked) for developing the idea of topsy-turvydom; but, Alcock, himself, failed to credit *his* predecessors in topsy-turvydom, and they, theirs and so forth. Time, the ultimate plagiarist, obscured the fathers of *contrary* Japan, Valignano and Frois. *Or, do I protest too much?* As Gulliver noted about his account of the Struldbruggs, as he headed for Japan:

> And if I am deceived [as to the uniqueness of my account], my Excuse must be, that it is necessary for Travellers, who describe the same Country, very often to agree on dwelling on the same Particulars, without deserving the Censure of having borrowed or transcribed from those who wrote before them." (S:GT)

Unlike Herodotus and Frois's contrasts, Chamberlain's instances of "contrariety" follow the style of Al-bîrûnî whose *India* was Englished from German but two years before *Things Japanese*. That is to say, he usually mentions only *their* side. We know *ours*. Here are items mentioned by Chamberlain that Frois missed, which I have not introduced elsewhere. I have trimmed the edges from some:

> *Footnotes are printed at the top of the page.*
> *The reader inserts his marker at the bottom.* [1]
> *The Japanese do not say "north-east," "south-west," but "east-north," "west-south."* [2]
> *Japanese women needle their thread rather than threading their needle.*
> *Instead of running the needle through the cloth, they hold it still and run the cloth upon it.* [3]
> *There are no actresses to speak of; it is the women who fall in love with fashionable actors.*

1. Book Marks. Today, books generally rest on their butts in Japan too, so marks must stick up. Books in Japan were more plentiful than in the West and seldom had hard-covers. Naturally, they laid on their side. If you lay a book on its side in front of you, the bottom of the book is what you would see, hence that is where the markers should stick out. Book-marks of all types far more plentiful in Japan than in the USA because 1) the word *shiori* is so beautiful (it comes from a poetic term for "branch-bending" to mark a trail in the woods) the thing itself appeals more; and 2), because writing and art fit the vertically long format better than ours does and this results in many attractive *shiori*.

2. East-north, West-south. This order comes from the Chinese convention, and is almost invariably used to designate places, but Japanese today often use the Western way for navigation purposes. I think a bolder contrast could have been made:

We think of North as up.
They think of East as up.

Kyoto retains traces of this idea even today. The East of Kyoto is "uptown" for, as they say, it is the side where the sun rises, and the West is "downtown" for the opposite reason. Pre-Renaissance European maps likewise often had the East on top. The Chinese convention may itself have come from the primary importance of the East-West axis for people who look up at the sky rather than down at a compass.

3. Running Clothes On a Needle. When one sews a thin broadly woven fabric using wide stitches proceeding in a simple porpoise-like manner – how I would describe most of the hemming work on traditional Japanese dress – that is the best way to sew. I have folded clothing into a needle without ever seeing anyone do it nor having read about it.

The *Topsy-turvy* heading was not the only place for the topsy-turvy in *Things Japanese*. After writing under "Time," that Japanese have six night-hours and six day-hours, twice as long as ours, beginning with 9 and ending with 4, with sunrise and sunset always at 6, Chamberlain gives us a prime example:

> Why, it will be asked, did they count the hours backwards? *A case of Japanese topsy-turvydom,* we suppose. But then why, as there were six hours, not count from six to one, instead of beginning at so arbitrary a number as nine? The reason is this: -- three preliminary strokes were always struck, in order to warn people that the hour was about to be sounded. Hence if the numbers one, two, three had been used . . . (C:TJ)

His explanation of why Japanese time was counted down to *four* rather than *one* is fine. But how about the broader idea of counting *down*? If you think of time as something you use up – as, we do when contemplating a deadline, or marking off days on a calendar – the idea of counting *down* is not backwards but every bit as logical as counting up. On the whole, Chamberlain is fair, amusing and still may be the best and most thorough guide to traditional Japan, but deep explanations are sometimes neglected for breathless "topsy-turvy" exclamations such as we saw above. Why such laziness in this prolific and generally conscientious writer? See what he wrote about "Logic" –

> Sometimes, after a recurrence of astounding instances [problematic business transactions], one is apt to exclaim that Japanese logic is the very antipodes of European logic, that it is like London and New Zealand, – when the sun shines on one, 'tis night-time in the other, and *vice-versa*. Were it really so, action would be easy enough: – one would simply have to go by the "rule of contraries." But no; the contradiction is only occasional, it only manifests itself sporadically and along certain, – or uncertain – lines . . . .
>
> *Race*, yes, that is it. The word slipped accidentally from our pen; but racial difference is doubtless the explanation of the phenomenon under discussion, – an explanation which, it is true, explains nothing . . . . (C:TJ)

By this, Chamberlain is only saying the Japanese are like that because they are Japanese. That his "race" is not the same color-based concept we are familiar with is shown by statements like the following: "Almost all are agreed that the Japanese are the pleasanter *race* to live with, clean, kindly, artistic. On the other hand, the Chinese are universally allowed to be far more trustworthy. . . Japan the globe-trotter's paradise is also the grave of the merchant's hopes." (Ibid. *italics* mine)

vii
modern topsy-turvydom: lowell

> The boyish belief that on the other side of the globe all things are of necessity upside down is startingly brought back to the man when he sets foot in Yokohama. If his initial glance does not, to be sure, disclose the natives in the every-day feet of standing calmly on their heads, . . . it does at least reveal them looking at the world as if from the standpoint of that eccentric posture. For they seem to him to see everything topsy-turvy. (Percival Lowell: *The Soul of the Far East*)

The earliest use of the word "topsy-turvy" to describe the Japanese – as opposed to the idea, which dates back to the 16c Jesuits – to describe Japan that I have found so far belongs to "an intellect" Chamberlain calls "truly meteor-like in its brilliancy," Percival Lowell. The date, 1888. Chances are that Chamberlain, having been on the scene longer, had himself already used "topsy-turvy" in another less famous book or article. Moreover, *Things Japanese* was clearly a work long in the making, so I spotted a few years to Chamberlain, and put Lowell after him in my chronology. But, Lowell should have been squeezed into Chamberlain's *"Topsy-turvy"* heading because the essay appearing at the very start of his "dazzling display of metaphysical epigrams" attacking "the inner nature of the Japanese soul," as Chamberlain himself describes his book, is the longest and most entertaining ever written on the subject. It is with great difficulty that I refrain from quoting *all* of the first eight pages!

> Whether it be that their antipodal situation has affected their brains, or whether it is in the mind of the observer himself that has hitherto been wrong in undertaking to rectify the inverted pictures presented by his retina, the result, at all events, is undeniable. The world stands reversed, and, taking for granted his own uprightness, the stranger unhesitantly imputes to them an obliquity of vision, a state of mind outwardly typified by the cat-like obliqueness of their eyes. (L:SOFE)

Lowell's thinking lies between Thoreau and Barthes – the metaphysical retina of the former and the semiotic oblique eyes of the latter – although neither of them would be such a slave to formal style to use the insipid third-person.

... If personal experience has definitely convinced him that the inhabitants of that under side of our planet do not adhere to it head downwards like flies on a ceiling, – his early *a priori* deduction, – they still appear quite as antipodal, mentally considered. Intellectually, at least, their attitude sets gravity at defiance. ... To speak backwards, write backwards, read backwards, is but the *a b c* of their contrariety. The inversion extends deeper than mere modes of expression, down into the very matter of thought. Ideas of ours which we deemed innate find in them no home, while methods which strike us as preposterously unnatural appear to be their birthright. From the standing of a wet umbrella on its handle instead of its head to dry, to the striking of a match away in place of toward one, there seems to be no action of our daily lives, however trivial, but finds with them its appropriate reaction – equal but opposite. Indeed, to one anxious of conforming to the manners and customs of this country, the only road lies in following unswervingly that course which his inherited instincts assure him to be wrong. // ... Like us, indeed, and yet so unlike are they that we seem as we gaze at them, to be viewing our own humanity in some mirth-provoking mirror of the mind, – a mirror that shows us all our familiar thoughts, but all turned wrong side out.

If Lowell's philosophy/example ratio is exorbitant, it is because he, like Barthes, describes not real Japanese, but idealizations fitting his meta-psychological theory: *"If with us the I seems to be of the very essence of the soul, then the soul of the Far East may be said to be Impersonality."* Lowell does a fine job with a small number of contrasts which support his master contrast such as the way Japanese share the New Year's for a communal birthday whereas we have individual birthdays,[1] and Japanese arranged marriage *vs.* Western love,[2] etc., but quickly poops out. That is to say, he does not notice (or write down) trivial differences unless they matter, in which case they are no longer trivial.

1. *Individual vs Communal Birthdays.* This contrast is Percival Lowell's main proof of his thesis of individual Occidentals and communal Orientals:

> ... the poor little Japanese baby is ushered into this world in a sadly impersonal manner, for he is not even accorded the distinction of a birthday. He is permitted instead only the much less special honor of a birth-year. ... *New Year's day is a common birthday for the community, a sort of impersonal anniversary for his whole world.* ... A communistic age is, however, but an unavoidable detail of the general scheme whose most suggestive feature consists in the subordination of the actual birthday of the individual to the fictitious birthday of the community. ... Then [New Year's day] everybody congratulates everybody else upon everything in general, and incidentally upon being alive. Such substitution of an abstract for a concrete birthday, although exceedingly convenient for others, must at least conduce to self-forgetfulness on the part of its proper possessor, and tend inevitably to merge the identity of the individual in that of the community. (*my italics* L:SOFE)

The part I italicized is *splendid*. Thoreau, with his broader metaphysics would have embraced the New Year idea and celebrated it, rather than call it fictitious, abstract and dangerous for individual identity. Lowell himself seems to have been of two minds about it; he used it for proof of the backwardness of the Asian psyche on the one hand and in another chapter on "Nature" and "Art" praised it. As a matter of fact, the contrast is too sweeping. Pereira observed in the mid-16c that the Chinese not only observed birthdays but had parties!

> They are wont also to solemnize each one his birthday, where-unto their kindred and friends do resort of custom, with presents of jewels and money, receiving again for their reward good cheer. (B:SCSC)

Cruz would repeat this with added detail in the first book on China published in Europe (1569) and a Portuguese editor adds that the great attention given to the Chinese birthday parties implied birthdays were *not* celebrated in Iberia. So, go back a bit and Lowell's flippant East-West contrast can itself be flipped right over! Ball, in *Chinese Things* was more precise :

> As a general rule it may be said that the principle of topsy-turvydom comes into play in the differences in observing birthdays in China and England: here in China the 'grown-ups" birthdays are kept and the child's almost entirely ignored, while with us, in our own lands, the contrary is more commonly the case.

This can also be said for Japan, and it is only logical when you consider that we grow, or should grow more useful, more precious and worth celebrating with each passing year.

2. *Arranged Marriage vs. Love*. According to Lowell, marriage in Japan is "entirely a business transaction." Actually Japanese usually had *some* choice – at least an informal veto – exercised after a preliminary meeting called an *omiai*, literally "look-meeting." True, marriages usually did not *begin* with romance (as was true in parts of Europe, too). But Lowell goes much further, claiming that *youth in Japan do not fall in love!*

> He does nothing of the kind. Sad to say, he is a stranger to the feeling. Love, as we understand it, is a thing unknown to the Far East... The community could never permit the practice, for it strikes at the very root of their whole social system. (L:SOFE)

Nonsense! If Lowell wrote Japanese "neither make love nor woo" as Caron (C:MKJS) wrote, it would have only been a small error (for peasants still had their night-creeping – something like our bundling – and there was *some* other courtship as well (see note 2-16); but customs and the hearts of men are a different matter. Not long before Lowell wrote, the Japanese government passed a new law about double-suicides, a practice where lovers died together rather than live separately. If Japanese were only strangers to "the feeling," such a practice and laws to deal with it would not exist. Lowell concludes that

> with a communal, not to say cosmic birthday, and a conventional wife, he [the Japanese/ Oriental] might well deem his separate existence the shadow of a shade and embrace Buddhism from mere force of circumstances. (Ibid)

This, when, unknown to Lowell, Japanese were and still are *more*, not less, self-conscious than Westerners (This is proven by their suffering from high rates of hyper-consciousness-related phobias and other such *Underground Man type* mental disorders) and, according to Keene, among the world's greatest diarists (K:CJL).

THIS IS AN EXAMPLE (SOMEWHAT SHORTENED) OF THE COPIOUS NOTES IN *THE LONG VERSION* OF THIS BOOK. SO, IF YOU LIKE DETAIL...

> The light of truth has reached each hemisphere through the medium of its own mental crystallization, and this has polarized it in opposite ways, so that now the rays that are normal to the eyes of the one only produce darkness to the eyes of the other. (L:SOFE)

Lowell admitted the equality of the East and the West. And he even suggested that together they provide stereo-vision; but his overriding hypothesis holds that the Eastern personality, or rather lack thereof, to be in a form of arrested development. That is to say, high level of culture or not, Japanese/Orientals are backwards, in the idiomatic sense of the word. No fancy metaphysics excuses this prejudice. We should note that the post-Bungo Jesuits, despite their belief that Japanese needed Christianity and their pride in their own wealthy global civilization and its power, did not exhibit such monumental cultural conceit.

viii
modern topsy-turvydom: knapp

Six years after Chamberlain's classic, Arthur Knapp introduced his "Principle of Inversion" in his little known *Feudal and Modern Japan* (1896-7). Knapp, too, faithfully follows the self-discovery tradition in topsy-turvy, for despite mentioning the opinions of "Professor Chamberlain" many times on *other* issues, he does not mention him (nor anyone else) in this respect. Why introduce yet another statement, when it merely echoes the others? Because, finding the Antipodes alive so far from Medieval times – so close to our times – is thrilling enough to bear repetition. Who says we have to go back a thousand years to find such enchanting naiveté! We cannot fairly judge the Japanese=Oriental (Knapp, like Lowell, conflates the two), he writes, "unless we can succeed in psychologically standing on our heads" because:

> Inversion is the confirmed habit of the far Oriental. It characterizes, not only the general mode as well as every detail of his outward life but also his intellectual and moral being. It is not simply that his ways and thoughts differ from ours. They are the total reversal of

ours. In our childhood we were accustomed to picture the inhabitants of the antipodes as standing upon their heads. We were so far right in our imaginings that that is really the only thing the Oriental does *not* do in the inversion of our ways. (K:FMJ)

These men are writing about the wonder of wonders: to the West, Japan (and the Japanese) was *the biggest wonder in the world*. After regretting he had not kept a memorandum of the "numberless and minute details of art, and thought and life" in Japan that illustrated his principle, his memory provided enough to show "something more than a mere bent of the Japanese mind; that bent is carried so far as to become a somersault." A number of his "details" do not appear in Frois, Alcock, Lowell, Chamberlain or my notes. Some reflect Knapp's warm yet comical bent.

> After-dinner speeches made before dinner, thus assuring brevity, and furnishing the topic for conversation.
> The absorbing desire of the young ladies to grow old that they may share the reverence given to age.

Despite Knapp's crude hyperbole of *inversion* as a "confirmed habit", he was not only "bright," but extraordinarily "sympathetic" (Chamberlain's appraisal) in his approach. Instead of Alcock's backward keys locking "left to right," and Chamberlain's puzzling keys that "turn in instead of out," Knapp writes of "keyholes made upside down, [*so you find*] the keys turning backwards," [1] and teaches you that footnotes turning into headnotes makes more sense because "the larger margin of the page . . . [is] at the top instead of at the bottom." That is to say, the man would make sense of everything. And he went a step further than the general relativism of Valignano, to whom familiarity made all difference (but religious ones) reasonable, and found something missed by the humorous relativism of Alcock, abstract relativism of Lowell, and nihilistic relativism of Chamberlain, who thought he was writing the epitaph for a moribund culture.

> Of course, our first conclusion is that theirs is the wrong way, because it is the opposite of that which we have been taught is the only right way. But an analysis of almost any one of their methods . . . . will show that it possesses manifest advantage over ours. . . . For example, by carefully experimenting with the use of the Japanese saw in comparison with the workings of our own, I am convinced that the former has superior merit in the ease and firmness with which it can be guided in the hand of the workman. So too . . .

Sometimes, *our* way also may have an advantage or two. But anyone who has used a saw that bites on the *pull* rather than the *push* can confirm the general *superiority* of the Oriental saw. Knapp is right. There is no room for relativity in that. A blade that will not buckle when it sticks (and sticks less for being thinner) has a clear advantage over one that will. Here, Knapp teaches us something very important: difference, *even caricatured as "inversion" or "somersault,"* need not imply negative value-judgment. We saw with the accommodating Jesuits that it could be value-neutral; but, if efficient use, ecological benefit, aesthetics and other standards for judgment are taken into account, items of the contrary other can be judged superior as well, and, if we are open to improvement, adopted. All of us, as individuals and as cultures have good and bad points. That is life. With the proper attitude – unbiased *judgment*, rather than a dumb moratorium on all judgment – and a modicum of intelligent explanation, the same apparent differences that naturally put us on guard against others can draw us to them and, in the final event, prove that culture as well as nature, makes all men kin.

---

1. *Keys and Key-holes.* If our key-holes were uniform then, they are not now! One of my keyholes takes the key teeth *up* and one teeth *down* and one of my mother's locks turns one way and one the other! Judging from key-holes, we might say that nowadays, our culture may be too sloppy to reveal patterns capable of generalization. That would make topsy-turvy observation difficult to say the least.

ix
twentieth century topsy-turvydom

Douglas Sladen's *Queer Things About Japan* (1903) and *More Queer Things About Japan* (1905) got 20c antipodalism off to a pleasant start. A humorist, he did not list contrasts but played with them in good, pedagogical humor. In 1932, Ripley (*Believe It or Not*), borrowing without credit from Ball's *Things Chinese*, vulgarized what had been a generally polite game, contrasting us, not to Japan, but to the *"Heathen Chinee"*, using obviously insulting contrasts and vocabulary (see *Midword*). There were similar lists of deprecatory contrasts made against the Japanese in Usanian magazines during World War II, but we shall skip them for the high road of the German economist, Kurt Singer, who, anticipating the essay style of the post-war French academics, glorified difference in 1939, after an eight-year stay. Here is what he had to say about the culture shock facing "a stranger landing on the islands of Japan."

> . . . the sense of orientation and the scales of preference are subtly disturbed by a general "topsy-turvydom" expressing itself in almost systematic exchanges of right and left, before and after, speech and silence. Every gesture, the shape of the vessels, the cadence of a sentence, the etiquette of a household or of a school-class, an arrangement of flowers in a vase – each bears an unmistakable mark peculiar to this country. (*Mirror, Sword and Jewel* — the Geometry of Japanese Life, first publ. 1973.)

So we see Chamberlain's favorite term, *topsy-turvydom* – as always with no credit – used in a book the good critic Donald Richie recently (reviewing the 1997 reprint in *The Japan Times*) called "the best ever written on the Japanese!" Personally, I prefer the timeless magic of Chamberlain's contemporary and close friend Lafcadio Hearn. The misty fairyland quality of his writing on Japan comes in part from an affection for things quaint, old and mysterious – his *Creole* (New Orleans) *Sketches* are a particular treat – and partly from the fact that *his* Japan builds upon a single controlling contrast: *the Brobdingnagian West versus Lilliputian Japan.* It is a good choice. The idea is found only indirectly, if at all, in Frois. Europeans tend to be taller (1-1), Japanese value simple black and white artwork (11-29), give less presents to show love than Europeans (14-26), single blossoms rather than bouquets (14-55), etc.. A generation later, Rodrigues comes closer when he repeatedly comments on the more minimalistic Japanese taste, for the metaphors of *quantity/quality* and *luxury/austerity* are cognate with those of *big/small*. But, it would seem that the clear-cut "big vs. small" contrast is post-Perry, an invention (in the old sense of the word, including "discovery") that had to await an overgrown modern Europe and the *Aren't we a big baby!* America of Walt Whitman. Chamberlain must have shared the still young idea with Hearn, for here is how he began his introduction of sumo:

> The wrestlers must be numbered among Japan's most characteristic sights, though they are neither small nor dainty, like the majority of things Japanese." (C:TJ)

Who does not love miniatures? Through Hearn, even the Japanese learned to love themselves in an age where the Western culture was – at least for a couple decades, it seems – worshipped. But we ought not swallow Hearn like a cormorant (I use a favorite Japanese expression). Like Lowell, we have cultural comparison/contrast *serving* a larger *a priori* topsy-turvy concept. As John Steadman pointed out in his groundbreaking deconstruction of Orientalism *The Myth of Asia* (1969), Hearn blithely matched Gothic cathedrals with Shinto shrines (rather than the large Buddhist temples), sumptuous opera with geisha playing banjo-like *shamisen* (rather than the fancier *kabuki*); that is to say, he compared *incommensurables* to maximize contrast. But, that is one reason Hearn reads well. All good writers exaggerate. I do not fault Hearn for it. I only to wish to point out with respect to him – and Singer and Barthes etc., – that a heavy dose of the topsy-turvy can be found in our most sophisticated work, and our most beautiful. We may talk about the philosophical pitfalls of *dualism* and nitpick all we like, but *black and white*, *upside-down*, *inside-out* high-contrast still makes our day.

In a sense, Frois's *Tratado* is part of *modern* topsy-turvydom, for it only became known after Josef Franz Schütte S.J. discovered the forgotten manuscript in the library of the Royal Academy of History in Madrid, transcribed the badly worm-eaten 16c Portuguese handwriting – which includes many Japanese terms only a bilingual scholar could decipher – and published it in Japan, together with a German translation and notes in 1955. As I write, Frois is not totally unknown in the English language world. Michael Cooper's superbly selected and annotated anthology of "European Reports on Japan, 1543-1640," *They Came to Japan* (1965) includes a score of his contrasts and Endymion Wilkinson's more journalistic *Japan versus Europe* (1980) about an equal number. Citations pop up here and there. But, the fact is that Frois has been neglected. In Japan, two annotated translations of *Tratado* published by major publishers became near best-sellers, pocket-books going through dozens of printings, while no full English translations were published until I published the long version of this book in July of 2004 as *Topsy-turvy 1585*, from my own one-man press. But, *Why this extreme difference in treatment when the subject of topsy-turvy is of interest to all?*

I think it is because modern Japanese identity is almost entirely based upon bi-polar contrast with the West. "They" define themselves as what "we" are not, and see "us" as what "they" are not. Frois's *style* is, thus, not only familiar to them, it is *their* style, and yet (unlike a fifty or hundred year-old book) much of the content is old enough to be fresh. *Nihonjinron*, books of pop-Japanology defining Japaneseness against stereotypes of the Occidental, sold exceptionally well in the 1970s and 80s and Frois, or rather his translators and publishers profited from it. On the other hand, let us be honest: "we" are less interested and aware of the Far East than the vice versa. Some may point out that "without east there is no west, without natives there are no sahibs, without 'them' there is no 'us';" (Littlewood 1996), but our identity, such as it is (we tend not to dwell upon it), is not so dependent on *a single* 'them,' as is the case for Japanese. It is constructed against a host of others (Oriental, African, Puritan, Despotic, Primitive, Communist, Islamic, etc.). Since the psychological importance of the Far East is to us but a fraction of ours to them, Eastern things are relegated to a small number of specialist publishers rather than a general publisher. Marginalized by definition, even a book with content of interest to the general reader, such as *Tratado*, is not given a chance to prove itself.

With the rise of the *Nihonjinron* in Japan and the fall of bold speculation about culture in the stifling "politically correct" atmosphere in the West (most notably the USA), the locus of creation of Topsy-turvy, or what I call antithetical stereotypes of Occident and Orient, shifted from the West to the East. Readers interested in knowing more about it might start with my *Orientalism & Occidentalism* (2004).

~~~~~~

X
"topsy-turvy" in broader perspective

Take those opposite saws. The pop-Japanologists (*nihonjinron-ka*) tie it in to opposite *lifestyles* or psychologies of *boxing* versus *judo*. They trace these back to different primal environments that gave rise to literally *pushy* Western (the Occident including what "we" call the Middle-East) herders fighting off beasts in pastures undergoing harsh desertification *versus* pacific Eastern (the Orient beginning, perhaps, in Burma, according to some Japanese) farming folk peacefully *pulling* on their hoes in little plots tucked into the benevolent moist forest. The only problem is that, as we shall later see, Japanese were more likely to whittle away from themselves (7-13) and pull-saws were, and probably still are, common as far West as Turkey. Okay, for now, let's pass on the environmental reductionism, forget the whittling and re-start the East from Turkey. In that case, the general *push-pull* contrast still holds, but it is put into an entirely different perspective. If *most of* the civilized world used pull-saws, *it is not the Japanese who are the odd-guys out, but us!* This sort of thing is not only true for some of Frois's Japanese items but for much that is treated as uniquely Japanese by modern books about Japan. What tends to be forgotten is the fact that the exotic, by itself, does not exist. Japan is not *exotic* and we (I write as what I am, an Occidental) are not exotic *except in relation to one another*, for our languages are extraordinarily distant and we share less cultural memes than we do with cognate cultures.

My logic-loving side finds radical contrariety interesting in itself. Perhaps that is why I was able to read book after book of pop-Japanology and chuckle even as I dissected and cooked them for my anti-stereotype books. *Push* versus *pull* culture is food for thought. Vector-wise, you can not get more contrary. But is *direction* all of it? An Indian philosopher might laugh aloud at the *push-pull* dichotomy:

> *Away,* you say? *Towards* you say? What of it? In India, we do *neither*. No, I do not mean we do nothing, though some of us are adept at doing that, too. The question is this: *Who says the blade must be moved to cut?* No, this is not what the Japanese call a *koan*. The answer is no paradox: *We cut with the knife in place.* Vegetables and fruit are opened or sliced by passing them through a knife imbedded blade-up in a stationary stone or wooden base. Let me ask you: Is not this lack of movement, as opposed to the direction of movement of the cutting device – and, perhaps, its being blade *up* rather than *down,* too – a much deeper difference?

A heavy handle – and no handle can be as massive as a large stone, concrete or wooden base! – reduces power loss by steadying the blade, so it makes good sense to fix a blade to it, especially if the blade is not very sharp. While such a device fits the metaphysically active=female / still=male image of Kali the Destroyer squatting upon an inert male, I think we have to be careful before using it for proof of the superior position of women, for it also may have kept knives out of women's hands (before the gun, the knife was a great domestic equalizer, for men had to sleep). But let us not get distracted by details, our point is that of the imaginary philosopher: here, the Far East and Far West with their *pull/push* would appear to be mirror-images of each other, while only India, the original Middle East (until the British military command of that name moved) with its *still* blade truly turns the world upside down. If something as simple as a saw or knife offers multiple dichotomies, we might wonder about the validity of even trying to Frois more complex, multifaceted things.

Take the ultimate cultural artifact, without which culture itself dies – what about *language?* Which is farther from English, Chinese or Japanese? Is the all-character writing of Chinese, or the mixed Chinese character and phonetic syllabets of Japanese more alien to us? 100% *character* is the more perfect antithesis of 100% *alphabet*. Seen that way, *Chinese is more exotic*; but a *mixed* system is more perfect an antithesis to a *pure* one, and seen that way *Japanese is more exotic to both English and Chinese.* Or, what about the telegraphic nature of Chinese and the SOV (subject-object-verb) syntax of Japanese? Which is closer/further from us? Classical Chinese – at least, as written – is *unbelievably* spare (not Tarzan and Jane-like, but *utterly alien*), while the syntax is more-or-less the same SVO we use; while Japanese despite its alien SOV (mutually exotic word order) seems stylistically similar to English, i.e., equally redundant, or wasteful, and enjoying a similar degree of freedom with their syntax.   Then there is the poetry. Is the terse rhyming Chinese, or the slacker unrhymed meter of the Japanese closer to ours? The Chinese are part of "our" rhyming world, while the Japanese are not; but the perfectly identical lines of a few characters (4 lines of 8 characters each may be the most common) comprising traditional Chinese verse that comes out looking like rectangles or even perfect squares seems alien to us, whereas Japanese poems, even without rhyme, seem of a more natural (*i.e., familiar*) design. With multi-cultural contrast, opposites quickly produce paradox.

There are dozens of ways both languages are more different from English than the other and more similar. One reason is that Chinese and Japanese belong to language groups that, to use David Pollack's words, "are not only entirely unrelated but appear almost entirely antithetical in their phonological, morphological, and syntactic systems." *The Fracture of Meaning*). That is to say, "Chinese operates in a dominantly synchronic mode, relying almost entirely upon parallelism and rhyme, its logic governed by the association of like categories; Japanese, to the contrary, is a diachronic language governed by hypotactic subordination, its logic predominantly that of the combination of dissimilar categories." (Ibid) Please do not ask me what Pollack's fancy words mean. Enjoy his prose as opera, the aria of which is a florid paragraph equating Chinese to a "black hole" and Japanese to a "supernova." This is surely the most dynamic metaphor of contrast ever invented and suggests that the two Eastern languages might, in important ways be more at odds with each other than with English.

The same can be said about practically *anything*. It might not always be so obvious, or convincing, but it can be said. That is why, every single one of Frois's contrasts (*contradisões e diferenças*) not only is a true contradiction in the sense Valignano made clear – i.e. they do not represent different levels on a developmental ladder of humanity, but describe equally developed cultures that contradict the very idea of a single ladder – but, in one way or another, at one level or another, can themselves be contradicted.

envoi

The thoughtful reader will wonder whether Japanese participated in the history of Topsy-turvy prior to their coming to own it in recent decades. They did, *of course they did*, but I am afraid there are few first-hand opinions in print and most of these are not easy for the poor (lacking money to pay library loan fees) independent (lacking access to academic sources requiring registration) and environment-ally conscious (preferring not to travel across the ocean) scholar to obtain. There are some interesting prints of Europeans and their African umbrella boys (men, actually), and I do not doubt that one is out there – hanging on the wall of some wealthy Occidental who cannot even read Japanese – with a list of topsy-turvy observations accompanying it, i.e. written on the print as Japanese were wont to do. Or, it might be that nothing remains – except for some venomous anti-Christian tracts – for once the persecution started, the possession of anything related to Europeans would have endangered the life of its owner and his or her family. So much for excuses, let me just tell you what I *have* managed to find so far.

Most important and the main excuse for this "Envoi" is a book allegedly by the 4 young Japanese ambassadors, or envoys, Valignano sent on a tour of Europe at the very same time Frois sat back in Japan writing his (huge) *History of the Church* and compiling the (tiny) *Tratado*. Why "allegedly?" Because, the entire book is a dialog between these youths and their Japanese relatives written by Valignano but partly based on what I believe to be the observations of the youths who had been instructed to take ample notes and correspond (If anyone can find and send me copies of their letters from Europe to Goa or to anyone in Japan, I would be grateful!). That is why, when I quote them in this book, I use their Christian names with an equal sign to link them with Valignano, eg.: "Miguel = Valignano," Mancio = Valignano, etc. While topsy-turvydom was not the subject of the book, it was a *reason* for the Embassy. Pater Valignano observed that the Japanese found *us* as contrary as we *them*, and that this made it hard for them to take the idea of Europe seriously, as it was just too different, too wondrous to believe and that this, to quote Miguel =Valignano, resulted in "both countless inconveniences and psychological wounds [to the Jesuits], and less of the thing most desired, [good] results in proselytizing." So, the idea was to obtain first-hand testimony of Europe's grandeur by Japanese eye-witnesses, who, armed with this weapon of their own making, said book DE MISSIONE LEGATORVM IAPONEN (we shall call it *De Missione* (1589) from now on), translated into Japanese, of course, would tell Japan what was what, or rather, who was who in the world. (Note: Valignano wrote in Spanish which was translated into Latin by de Sande, who claims he was not in good form because his mind was deep into his studies of written Chinese, and this I, then, English from a stilted modern Japanese translation from the Latin.)

It was never translated into Japanese. Despite a tenuously maintained friendship with the Shogun Hideyoshi and his successors, the Jesuits had to swallow their pride in Europe as the child of Christianity (and Portugal as its prodigy) and eat humble pie to keep their toehold in Japan. The newly consolidated nation started tightening the screws on potential political competition at the same time the youths were being feted in Europe where their embassy fulfilled its second purpose, that of advertising the importance of the Jesuit enterprise in Japan and gaining support for it in Europe. Like Nobunaga, Hideyoshi massacred entire sects of Buddhists because they would not acknowledge his absolute authority and was preparing a war to conquer China and weaken possible rivals (especially Christians in the South) by conscripting them and their resources toward that effort. Hideyoshi was in a no-nonsense mood and not amused by the quarrelsome Europeans who competed to prove to him just how dangerous to Japan other Europeans were. Suspicious of their motives – especially of the Pope and his emissaries who, like he, himself, wanted to rule the world – unforgiving of the arrogance of some missionaries who did not share the Jesuits willingness to accommodate, and enraged by reports of forced conversion and vandalism of Buddhist sculptures by Christians (including Frois), he had just crucified a number of Christians. To introduce *De Missione*, with its exaltation of Europe and demonstration of its power, to Japan at this time would have been like throwing oil on a fire.

De Missione interests us for two reasons. First, because Valignano, in the person of his dialoging envoys, offers us a fuller contemporary take on the early modernization of Europe than anything else I know of. And second, for its Japanese views of Europe and European ways that touch upon the topsy-turvy. Some of those views must be authentic. I can not imagine Valignano dreaming up things like feeling insecure with toes dangling in the air when seated on a chair or the traumatic experience of dancing *with* someone, to give but a couple of many examples that will be introduced in the course of this book.

p.s. *note to Readers!*

Thanks to Frois, and the assistance of everyone mentioned in the *Acknowledgement*, all of us can now enjoy in these pages a world every bit as wonderful as that visited by Alice. That world, like Alice's, is, as you will discover, not only *theirs*, but *ours*. I hope you will find me a satisfactory guide and heartily welcome your suggestions for addition and revision. – r.d.g.

About the translation

Frois's original *Tratado* is in Portuguese. I first did a draft-translation from the Japanese translations in 1998. Then I rewrote, after seeing the modern Portuguese edition and a sketchy English translation of most chapters by a native speaker that was of minimal help because the difficulty was less in the grammar or vocabulary then in *knowing what Frois was driving at* because the extremely short sentences of the original leave much unsaid, and a revision by DR for about half the chapters based on my earlier translation (before I saw the Portuguese), the native speaker's translation and his good sense as a fine writer and incisive scholar. Later, I rewrote again making a much closer reading of the Portuguese original (with additional dictionaries at hand) Japanese translations, French translation and German translation (see *Acknowledgment*) and my increased understanding based on further research. The biggest dilemma was not how to assure accuracy, but how closely to adhere to the original where it was awkward and the writer in me said "Pretty it up!" while *something* else said "No, just give them the closest thing to what Frois wrote!" I fear my choice has not been uniform. I sometimes let the syntax slip a bit for a smoother translation, other times I went for an ugly direct translation to better make a point in the explanation. I simply cannot pull it off in the smooth manner of the French (or, as I think DR might have done). Part of it may be failings on the part of my English, but mostly it is because of *my attitude toward translation*. I cannot help wanting to show people what does *not* get translated as well as what does.
..
Readers who want to know more about what translation involves will find much more information (mostly notes on the vocabulary) scattered throughout the Long Version of this book.

I

OF MEN, *THEIR PERSONS AND DRESS*
do que toca aos homens em suas pessoas, e vestidos

1-1   Europeans are for the most part tall and well built;
Pola maior parte os homens de Europa são altos de corpo e boa es[ta]tura;

Japanese are for the most part shorter and slighter of build than us.
Os Japões pola maior parte mais baxos de corpo e estatura que nós.

While most of Frois's contrasts are black and white, he deserves credit for qualifying this first one with *pola maior parte,* "for the most part." The height difference that generally held true in 1585, still holds true, though the average height of a Japanese *today* probably exceeds that of the average European in 1585. Since tall Japanese tended to have shorter servants – as the English aristocracy had their "little men" – it is not surprising that one of the Japanese translations of *Tratado* (J/F(M&J)) brings out the possibly belittling connotation of short/low/slight (*baxo*) by making the Japanese "*inferior* (*otoroeteiru*) in build and height." Our psychology of height is evidently similar.

Estatura (physique) is ambiguous for including elements of proportion and bearing but Frois probably means muscularity, for Rodrigues would soon write the mostly "medium build" Japanese "admire well-built men." (C:TCJ) But a *good build* is a matter of opinion and while the first European observer, captain Jorge Alvarez, wrote in 1547 "the natives are for the most part . . . *well made*" (italics mine, in Coleridge C:LLFX), and most 19c visitors found the bodies they spied in the public baths fit enough to be reminded of Eden (LR), Isabella Bird wrote "their physique is wretched, leanness without muscle being the general rule." Perhaps it depends on *where* the brawn is desired. Those who appreciated Japanese men often noted the "well-turned leg" – *the* mark of male beauty in the West prior to the ascendancy of what was women's clothing in much of the world: *trousers* – as Japanese, for their part, found "our" legs lacking. The notorious 18c nationalist Hirata Atsune, pointed out that "the slenderness of their [the Dutch traders'] legs also makes them resemble animals." (K:JDE) I think he means *the calves*, for they, together with our broad toenails are unique to humans.

One problem is there never was *a* Japanese build. In 1690, Kaempfer found "common people . . . of a very ugly appearance, short-siz'd, strong, thick-legged, tawny, with flattish noses," nobles, "somewhat more majestick in their shape and countenance, being more like Europeans," and people in some provinces "short, slender, but well shap'd, of a good handsome appearance." But stocky or slender, handsome or ugly, most Japanese were probably far from ideal Greco-Roman dimensions. As Chamberlain put it, "Compared with people of European race, the average Japanese has a long body and short legs;"(1890). This still holds true today. The head-to-body-length ratio far exceeds the classical 1:8 proportion (a proportion many Japanese, but few Americans, are aware of). Moreover, the less recognized but more important shoulder-to-waist width ratio is noticeably different and relates to different ideals of beauty, or perhaps we should say *power*. Late-20c *Nihonjinron* contrast the broad-shouldered heaven-oriented Occidental Atlas (a triangle standing on its tip) with the earth-bound stability of the sumo-wrestler with his low center of balance (a triangle on its base), and point out the more ecological (?) nature of *their* side.

If height and build are considered *as a unit,* Frois's contrast strengthens, for robust tall Japanese are *very* rare.   And, when we include *posture*, the illusion of absolute difference grows yet stronger, for, if I may be permitted a *Faux Frois,*

> *Europeans go proudly about chin-up and chest-out, looking straight out at the world God made. Japanese are* nekozei *[cat-backed=hunched-over] and think it immodest to appear so full of pride.*

It is possible, however, that Japanese only became this way during the feudalistic Tokugawa era (1603-1867) and still stood straight as Koreans in 1585, but I doubt it.

1-2 Europeans hold large eyes to be beautiful;
Os de Europa tem por fermozura os olhos grandes;

> Japanese think they are horrid, and find eyes beautiful that are pinched shut on the tear[duct]-side. *Os Japões os tem por horrendos, e os fermozos são fechados da parte dos lagrimais.*

The fact that the upper-class for a thousand years or so was a relatively tall *slit-eyed* Mongolian type, as opposed to the relatively *round-eyed* working-class "pudding-faced" (1890 C:TJ) type, obviously enhanced the appeal of the former. But, note, *shape* not *size* was the telling factor. It was *round* eyes that were considered ugly and beastly – "like dogs." Large eyes were admired in Japan too, so long as they were vertically narrow like the Chinese character "one" (一), in which case, the lachrymal part is hidden because eyes narrow most around the edges.   Still, the wide open eyes of the Europeans do show more of themselves than most Japanese eyes and would, indeed, *look* large. A Japanese folk-history of the *Barbarian Temple* (*nambanji-kyôkaiki* c.1700) describes the eyes of Furukomu, a composite character, mostly Frois, as "round, as if they were eye-glasses"(J/E:NBJ). And Thunberg (1775), who thought the "oblong, small," and deep-sunk "organs" of the Japanese and Chinese gave them "almost the appearance of being pink-eyed [conjunctivitis]," recorded that the Japanese called out *"Oranda O-me!* (Dutch Big-eyes!)" whenever they saw Europeans (T:TEAA).

I am surprised that Frois does *not* contrast eyelids, the *différence* that so excited a certain 20c French philosopher. With a nod to Barthes (and Alice Mabel Bacon, who said it first),

> Our eyelids usually are grooved near the edge to delineate the eye from the face;
> Their eyelids usually lack this trimming and closed run right into the rest of the face.

Having spent all his adulthood in Japan, was Frois no longer conscious of this difference, heightened by our eyes tending to be deep-set and theirs flush, as pointed out by Bacon and Barthes? Or, were Europeans themselves less wide-eyed and more familiar with unfringed eyelids at Frois's time than in later centuries? After all, we can see many Madonnas and Saints with eyes which might be considered "Mongolian" in 12-16c European art. With the Westernization of the world in the 20c, Japanese ideals have changed and operations to double eyelids, the better to frame eyes Western style and make them *look* larger have become all too common. Since most Japanese now tend to see *their* single-fold, or rather, unfolded eyelid in terms of *lack,* I was delighted to read Okada's notes to this contrast explaining Occidental show-everything eyes in terms of a *lack:*

> Because European eyes *normally have little adipose tissue* on the upper lid, most lids are double, . . . and the upper eyelid can look sunken and shadowed. When wide open, the red tear-duct can be seen on the inner canthus. (my *italics,* J/F(O):T)

The relationship or lack of relationship between double eyelids and insufficient padding is beyond my ken, but how could one disagree with the aesthetic complaint of the Japanese in Frois's day? The inner quarter inch or so of the eye opening *is* ugly. We see precisely the type of yucky red/pink membrane humans have managed to hide over the course of their evolution from the grosser apes. (The ape's ugliness is not only due to our similarity, but because of that unseemly exposure. Eyelids should conceal the inner canthus as lips conceal gum, the rump conceals the anus and both flesh and hair replace the disgusting genital welt of the non-human female primate.) Membrane takes getting used to. The 16c Japanese were not used to it and, I believe, must have pointed it out to Frois. Today, they *are*, and this difference is no longer significant.

1-3   Among us, having white/bright/translucent eyes is not strange or repulsive;
Antre nós ter os olhos brancos não se estranha;

> Japanese find them monstrous, and it is a rarity among them.
> *Os Japões o têm por mon[stru]oso, e hé couza rara antre elles.*

It is hard to say what Frois means by *olhos brancos.*

If we take *brancos* ("white") literally, as one of the Japanese translations and Schütte's German translation do, we might assume it refers to eye disease (such as pterigiums) that cover the iris and would have been common in South Europe but not in Japan, for it is rare among dark-eyed people, or blindness caused by syphilis, which enjoyed a 50 year head-start in Europe? But aren't we always repulsed by this, even if we ourselves have it (I had pterigiums removed)?

If, with Okada, we take it to mean the *sclera,* or white of the eye, we must assume that Frois, having come to Japan early in life, forgot that the Japanese idea of *shirome,* or, exposing the sclera (*shirome o dasu,* etc.) had no Portuguese equivalent and unwittingly created a confusing neologism. It does make sense though, for *in Japanese*, "to look [at someone] with white eyes" is to look at them with disdain or with cold, merciless eyes, as a demon might. I think of the association with the upturned eyes of the dead, but Okada (shades of Melville!) finds an intrinsic spookiness in the color: "wet, the white takes on the cold gleam of porcelain, which is one reason the eyes appear malevolent." It is also a fact that when eyes bulge with anger, draw a bead on someone, or open wide in "walleyed" fear, the sclera *does* stand out, so Japanese who were not used to open displays of emotion (14-2) would be relatively unused to it. There is also a strange disconnect in body, or rather face-language here. *Faux Frois*, again

> Europeans *find slit-eyes uncanny and associate narrowed eyes with anger;*
> Japanese *admire slit-eyes as discreet and associate narrowed eyes with contentment.*

To "narrow ones eyes" in Japanese means *to be delighted.* This narrowing implies a vertical rather than horizontal closure and holds true for cats as well as humans. Japanese draw happy specimens of either with closed eyes in the shape of gentle arch. Our lack of awareness of this is evident in depictions of people smiling with unrealistically wide open eyes and captions accompanying cats with closed eyes in photographs claiming they are asleep when the rest of their body language says otherwise. People *do* "narrow their eyes in anger," as per English idiom, but this is mostly narrowing *across* (scrunching together), rather than *up and down.* This difference suggests a culture's reading of narrowed/closed eyes can go either of two ways. My feeling is that the main difference is one of *perception*; but Morse suggests it lies in our respective expressions of displeasure.

With us, we usually frown and compress the eyes, but the Japanese when "mad" open their eyes wide; and a boy who has done something wrong will get a scolding, or *Omedama chodai;* literally, "a gift of eyeballs." (M:JDD)

Close-eyed anger and open-eyed anger are associated with different sub-emotions of anger. I would expect a growl or bite more likely from the former and a yell or a pounce from the latter. But, it is generally accepted that wide-open eyes are a primary indicator of anger among primates, so Occidental body-language may be less natural in this respect than the Japanese. Perhaps our ocular ideology (the idea that sustained, unblinking eye contact is a mark of honesty and something good) has reduced the natural scare value of the open-eyed stare.
..

Once I considered Okada's interpretation, one thing led to the next and I almost missed another equally or more likely reading of *olhos brancos,* what the French translation calls *yeux clairs,* or "bright/clear/translucent eyes." Since it is likely Frois would have known enough to write *branco do olho*, or "white of the eye" if that was what he meant, common sense favors this slightly less common reading of *branco,* the 4th in *Aurelio* (a fine large dictionary), *"claro, transparente, translúcido."* I think this means a pupil that is blue, grey or hazel was spooky to people not used to such bright and seemingly translucent irises (I can recall that my father's grey-blue eyes seemed somewhat frightening even to me, but it might have been because of an association: he had a voice like thunder.). Back to that description of Frois by *name* (but Valignano by *time*) in the Japanese folk history of the Southern Barbarian Temple, for it includes a relevant close-up of the Western eye:

> His eyes were round like eyeglasses and within them the eyes [pupils?] were gold colored, . . . he rode standing tall in the stirrups, smoking tobacco (a pipe?) lit from sparks that flew from his own nails, . . . spotting a crow in a tree he would ride closer while the bird would remain transfixed and break off the branch it sat on . . . (J/E:NBJ)

Did those *round gold eyes* paralyze the bird? So long as we are on eyes, another *Faux Frois:*

Europeans think strongly slanted eyes outlandish;
Japanese find them either gallant or coquettish.

But, note: slit-consciousness is not *entirely* different East and West, for exceptionally straight slits are called "fox-eyes" in Japan, and considered hard, untrustworthy and merciless. Moreover, most Japanese do not have oblique eyes, so they are almost as conscious of them as Occidentals are. The difference is that they are common enough not to seem outlandish. I find it intriguing that almost all samurai, geisha and ninja in old prints or today's animation are depicted with eyes drawn up so high as to resemble cat eyes. The humorist Douglas Sladen observed the following in 1905:

..
> The Japanese girl of the lower classes . . . is a most fascinating little creature. Her complexion is not yellow, but of a sunny brown, with rich blood showing through like the best Italian complexions. Her eyes are not obliquely placed or set in slits – she would only be too thankful if they were, for it is vulgar to have the eyes we admire. The paintings of Giotto would seem perfectly beautiful to a Japanese. The merry little maiden like Greuze's *Girl at the Fountain,* with her bright healthy cheeks, and lips like cherries, and innocent round eyes, which Europeans admire so much in Japan, only strikes the Japanese themselves as plebeian: they prefer tragic queens, with lantern jaws and long hooked noses, and pasty white faces, and eyes like cats. (S:MQTJ)

Sladen refers to the women found in Edo era *ukiyoe*. I doubt Japanese taste is really so uniform. As Arthur Marwick (*Beauty in History*) argues, we cannot assume that stylized art reflects what men, or women, *really* find attractive. Art-ificial *haute culture* ideals of beauty may misrepresent our real ideals of beauty, the beauty we *would* if we could.

1-4   Our noses are high, some aquiline;
Os nossos narizes são altos e alguns aquilinos;

Theirs are low with small nostrils.
Os seus baxos e as ventas peqenas.

Frois's "ours" clearly does not hold for the round-headed peasants of parts of North Europe, but to South Europe where even the poor boasted beaks. And most of the 16c Jesuits were of that ilk. An 18c folk history 南蛮寺興廃記 description of Organtino includes this:

> He was about 9 feet tall (kyu-shaku), with a head proportionately small for his body, a red face, round eyes, and a long, long (*takadaka to shite* high, high) nose so that when he looked sideways it would brush on his shoulder. His mouth was so large it reached to his ears . . . (J/E:NBJ)

In Japanese, big/long noses are called "high," with all the favorable metaphorical connotations (and one, unfavorable one, that of conceit) that accompany, while small noses, of course, are called "low" and bear the opposite connotation. A glance at *ukiyoe* prints shows the same association of high-bridged and finely shaped "aristocratic noses" with the nobility and administrative/warrior class and pug-noses with commoners found in parts of Europe, developed to a higher degree in Japan, where farmers were often depicted utterly noseless. Naoko, a farm girl who worked as what is now called an *au pair*, whom I befriended on my first trip to Japan in 1971 (aboard the last voyage of the S.S. Wilson), told me how, as a girl, she had stroked her bridgeless button nose and sang a ditty to try to "heighten" it. To her, it was not *an* indicator but *the* indicator of personal beauty. She thought another woman no better looking than her – not good looking at all, I thought – a real beauty, solely for that reason! A translator friend writes, *no*, it is not so much about class association or aesthetics, as *fortune*: nose size and success go hand in hand. She sent me a book which included this:

> The nose (*hana*) is a flower (*hana*) that is the bloom of your life. The nose reveals the extent of your intellectual and financial fortune. No matter how capable you are, without a grand nose the *hana* of life will not bloom. Strange but true. There are hardly any people with small or somehow lacking noses who actually make it in society. (*Heisei-juninen unmei-hôkan*)

My friend's mother was a professional fortune-teller, so she admits to being more conscious of traditional physiognomy than her contemporaries, but whatever aspect is looked at, the size of the nose has more bearing on one's face-value in Japan than is the case in Europe. This may be because too many Europeans have bridged noses to make its presence or absence a matter for general concern, whereas in Japan and parts of China (where the physiognomy books derive) *variety is the rule*. Again, *Faux Frois*:

> We press our hand against our chest to indicate ourself;
> They point to or touch the tip of their nose with their index finger.

In 1860, the Marquis de Moge noted the same with a twist, on our side:

> When the Japanese wish to designate the I, that is to say their personality, they touch their nose; the tip of the organ being, according to them, the seat of individuality. There is nothing wonderful in all this. When a Frenchman wishes to be very impressive, and to indicate his ego, does he not press his hand upon his stomach?   (M:BGE, *my bracket*)

There was also a subtle difference between male and female ideals of nasal beauty. In Heian Japan (c.800-1200), beautiful women, but not handsome men, were sometimes depicted with neither nose nor nostril. John Bulwer, in 1653, suggested that noselessness as an ideal had a Chinese origin:

The *Chinoyse* doe hold them for the finest women who have small Noses, wherefore from their Child-hood, they use all the art they can possible, to prohibit the encrease of the Noses of their female Children. And indeed, their Noses are very little, and scarece standing forth. The People being in the composition of their Body short nosed, when they make the portraiture of a deformed Man, they paint him with a Long nose. (B:A)

Bulwer felt "the natural Sagacitie" of the Chinese would be somewhat hurt, for short noses do not smell as well as long ones; but beauty-wise, he admits their noses are "not unsuitable unto their broad Faces." A beak of a nose on a wide face would be literally "deformed" for even birds do not boast that combination. And, he adds something about Europe that suggests Frois's contrast may indirectly favor European men:

With us, and with most of Europe, a long Nose is held more Beautiful, especially in Men; for the Midwives as soon as children are born, use with their fingers to extend the Nose, that it may be fairer and longer . . . (B:A)

These precious Occidental noses were extended yet further and turned into outlandish goblin beaks by Japanese *namban-e* (Southern Barbarian Paintings) and illustrations in anti-*kirisutan* literature (where said beak gives away the padre hiding in Japanese dress).

~~~~~~

1-5   European people for the most part have thick beards;
Pola maior parte a gente de Europa tem boa cópia de barba;

> Japanese usually have sparse, poorly shaped beards.
> *Os Japões pola mayor parte pouca e naõ bem composta.*

While Japanese often have so little beard Rodrigues once claimed one might say more appropriately they do not have them (V(A):S&A n99), he also noted that the owner of said [no]beard exercised more freedom over it than Europeans of that time:

They also cultivate their beards in various fashions. Some wear only mustaches . . . and shave all the rest. Others follow the fashion which pleases them best and in this they are imitated out here in the East by the Portuguese, Spaniards and Moors, ... (C:TCJ).

If thick beards were rare, one would *have to* allow a great variety of style, for otherwise they could not be kept trim. But the Jesuits arrived in an exceptionally wild era. Beards followed them out. The samurai in the Era of Seclusion ended up as clean-shaven as the 1950's corporation man of the United States. *Faux Frois* again:

Men in Europe only plucked hair from their noses or ears;
In Japan, men often pluck their beards and chest and even scalps..

The fact that many natives of North America were also hair-pluckers and some, like the Japanese, did not stop with the beard, suggests that even in the absence of a counter-example like the Ainu (the natives of Japan who are so hirsute they have been called "the hairy Ainu"), the poorly bearded groups of men may tend to go for an ideal of smooth skin. Bulwer, writing *circa* 1650 on the way "the people of the whole world" treated their bodies observed that the sparsely bearded Chinese ("not of above twenty or thirty haires"), "when they would describe a deformed man, they paint him with a thick beard." (B:A)

1-6 The dignity and honor of a European is placed upon his beard;
A honrra e primor que a jente de Europa tem boa copia de barba;

> The Japanese put it on a tuft of hair bound at the back of their heads.
> *Os Japões a poem no cabelinho que trazem atado detrás do toutiço.*

The word "honor" was no exaggeration. European men swore by their beards. According to Phillip Camerarius, writing in the 17c, "Among the Anglo-Saxons the penalty for damage to a beard was twenty shillings, while breaking a thigh bone was only twelve" and in many places in Europe "serious criminals, such as fornicators, were punished by having their beards "chopped off publicly with a keen axe." (Londa Schiebinger: *Nature's Body*) Sir Thomas More's last witticism was "Let me lay my beard over the block lest you cut it, for it has never committed treason."

The tuft of hair by which Japanese expressed *their* honor was not bound low at the back of the head like the Chinese queue, but near the top, with 4 to 6 inches of the hair jutting up proudly 6 to 8 inches from the crown, bound into an erect trunk with chord spiraling up and down to create criss-cross intersections or diamonds (as found on sword handles). The extra 1 to 3 inches sometimes bristled up and out freely like a brush. (J/O:KGB) I think of it as the most manly hairstyle in the world. The thickness varied, depending on how much, if any, of the head was shaven. If the head was shaven it was usually relatively thin, waxed and bound with no brush to speak of. Magistrates and samurai in Frois's time already kept it in this *chonmage,* or "bent" style (where the tuft curls forward like a pistol set on the head) that would be used by most classes in the Tokugawa era (1603-1867).

On TV Easterns – which remain more popular than our Westerns! – the losing sword-fighter's *chonmage* is often cut off by the victor as the camera pans the loser, whose remaining hair falls abjectly down. With this psychological baggage, it is amazing that less than a generation after Perry opened Japan, the Japanese cut off their own topknots as part of their effort to take on the West by becoming the West – what Lafcadio Hearn called "the most admirable system of intellectual self-defense ever heard of – by a marvelous national *jiujitsu* [judo]."(in N:MAR)

1-7 With us, men keep their hair trimmed, but consider it an affront to be depilated;
Os homens antre nós andão trosquiados e tem por afronta pelarem;

> Japanese make themselves bald, using a tweezers to be sure not a hair remains. **Pain and tears accompany this.** *Os Japões se pelão com tenazes pera não terem cabelos, e isto com dor e lagrimas.*

"We" were hair moderates, if insisting on a medium-length can be so called. Long hair on men was not allowed and the heads of adults of both sexes was shaved for punishment. This authoritarian barbering must have been unpleasant for free-thinkers, but keeping one's hair cropped was still easier than what custom demanded of most (?) Japanese men. An earlier letter of Frois's, as Englished by Willis, is a good read:

> "bare-headed commonly they go, procuring baldness with sorrow and tears, rooting up with pincers all the hairs of their heads as it groweth, except it be a little behind, the which they knot and keep with all diligence." (The "tears" are in the original 1565 letter, but the connotation of what must be *dor* (i.e. *dolor*) in this case should be *pain* rather than "sorrow!").

Valignano's short-lived *China*-Japan topsy-turvy list of 1579 contrasted Chinese who wore their hair "long like women," with Japanese who "not only cut theirs short but actually pull it out so they remain bald-headed" and Okada backs up Frois with a passage from the *Keichô Kenbunshû* written about 30 years after *Tratado* by the Japanese author (Miura 浄心) where the "old fool [a self-denigrating term]" in his youth observed hair on boy's foreheads removed "not with razors but with large wooden tweezers" in the Kanto (greater Tôkyô) area. He observed "a horrendous amount of black blood flowing down their foreheads."

When Frois wrote, the Japanese were in the process of changing from the excruciating process of plucking the hair out – this "fashionable but painful style" (Rodrigues:C:TCJ) being a perfect masculine rite for the Warring Period – to shaving the head "in a very handsome way." (ibid. It is hard to know if this "handsome" refers to Rodrigues's admiration of the hair-style or the skill of the shaving.) In the early 19c, observing the toilet of ship-wrecked Japanese sailors seated on mats on the deck of the Dutch boat, someone, Seibold, perhaps, writes "above all, we admired their dexterity in shaving their own heads." (in B:MCJ:1841) The topknot, which stuck up from the crown and pointed forward on the shaven pate, was cut off "as a sacrifice to his patron divinity, in acknowledgement of his deliverance from imminent danger." Though I mention "Japanese" doing this or that, there really was more diversity of hair-style than one might imagine from the above. A particularly notable one called *otsugami,* worn by masterless samurai, some sick people, playboys wanting to look cool/bad/tough, might even be called an *anti-style.* It was created by allowing the "moon forehead" clearing to grow into an ugly porcupine (shades of punk!), while the rest of the hair was unbound to hang down. (J/O:KGB)

The origin of the partial head shaving is said to be the need to keep cool wearing helmets in the Warring Years. The shaved part (the crown) was called the *tsukishiro* = "a place to lodge the moon", *tsukibitai* = "moon forehead" (the clearing resembling the moon), or *sakayaki*, a word of debatable etymology. It so happens that many of the most Japanese-looking natives of North Brazil and South Venezuela, the Yanamamo, Cayapo and Tchikrin shave the exact same portion of their heads and all of them consider the tonsure "a graphic representation of the moon's disc." (Robert Brain: *The Decorated Body* 1979) I cannot help but wonder if there is a connection somewhere!

~~~~~~

1-8 We have many freckled men and women;
Antre nós há muitos homens e molheres sardas;

Japanese, though white, rarely have freckles.
Os Japões, com serem alvos, há muy pouqos que o sejão.

The Japanese, collectively, were considered "white," *gente blanca,* to use Valignano's words. This was not only an honorable white status reflecting the respect the Jesuits had for them but how Japanese came to be perceived. The fact that Latins were themselves relatively dark may have something to do with this. Vilela, who proceeded Frois to Japan, wrote that when it came to whiteness (*blanca*), the Portuguese had nothing over the Japanese; and in the same year (1565) Frois himself described "a Japanese youth much paler (*albo*) than the Spaniards" and another who "in his whiteness (*blancura*) of face resembles a German." There were, however, notable exceptions. One complaint Valignano made against Cabral, the head of the church in Japan he had to depose, was that he failed to respect Japanese and justified his mistreatment of them for racist reasons: "*al fin de cuentas eran negros*" = "in the final account, they are only niggers." (from notes to V(A):S&A)

While lightly pigmented, Japanese can sun splotch with age, they do indeed have *few* freckles. Frois's syntax [*with* being white] is not quite so clear as my "though," but his antithetical point must be that Japanese do not freckle *despite* being fair. But seeing the 19c photographs of well-tanned

Japanese, one can't help wondering how much of their whiteness was in the mind's eye. Alvarez-Taladriz cites an observation about the Embassy of Japanese youth sent to Europe in 1582 to the effect that "Although it is said that in Japan skin is white [*suele ser blanco*] and fits the great cold there, these gentlemen for the travail of the road have darkened to the point of appearing to be moors;" and L' Abbe de T., in the late-17c or early 18c, noted that white or not, "they rather incline to an olive colour." Yet, as late as 1860, The Marquis de Moges, denied the "pretty legend" of Japanese originating in China as a select group of young pioneers seeking "the herb of immortality" who never returned, because:

> The Japanese, with skins as white as our own, cannot be descendents of the yellow sons of Han; and indeed they repudiate all idea of common descent with the Chinese ... (M:BGE)

With Moges as pleased with the honorable Japanese ("cleanly to a miracle," "noble and proud") as he was disgusted with the cowardly Chinese ("dreadfully dirty" "sneaking, submissive and cunning"), it would appear that *white is as white does* influenced his perception. But, when did the ridiculous idea of "yellowness" first appear? Was it born in the mid-19c scientific studies of race? Whatever, it soon spread from China to Japan and we find even the scholar Chamberlain writing "the Japanese are Mongols, that is, they are distinguished by a yellowish skin . . ." (C:TJ) The earliest *yellow Japanese* I know date back to the 1880 novel *Yellow Peril* and explorer Isabella Bird's book of the same year where she finds [Caucasian] Ainu features a welcome relief

> "after the yellow skins, the stiff horse hair, the feeble eyelids, the elongated eyes, the sloping eyebrows . . . and the general impression of degeneracy conveyed by the appearance of the Japanese." (B:UTJ)

While not a few Japanese good-naturedly lamented their lack of beauty as a race, they did not readily agree with their new *yellow* label. If they knew some English, they also knew the word had a bad connotation. Despite the auspicious connotations of yellow in the Sino-sphere, as far as I know there were no celebrations of yellowness. Any recognition of a yellow identity was a grudging one. On 4 January 1901, the sickly novelist who now adorns the 1000-yen bill, Natsume Soseki, notes that phlegm in London is black, imagines how dark the lungs of Londoners must be, and admits to shuddering every time he blows his nose. The next day he writes:

> It is hard to understand how people living in this smoke can be so beautiful. It can not be the climate or the weak sunlight. I saw a short, strangely dirty man coming toward me, and then I realized it was my reflection in a mirror. Coming here, for the first time, this matter of our being yellow made sense to me. (LR: Maybe my translation from his diary which I have lost somewhere.)

Yellowism on "our" side peaked during World War II, when Japanese were depicted as literally yellow, denigrated as LYB's (little yellow-bellies) and country stars sang the likes of *"We're gonna find a Fellow Who is Yellow and Beat Him Red White and Blue."* (D:WWM). It revived in a visual format during the Trade Wars of the 1970's, when the European press bannered bright yellow samurai and sumo-wrestlers. In this context, the yellowness was not cowardly, but outlandish and terrifying. (In America, Japanese, Korean and Chinese ethnicities would sue such racist press, so what yellow journalism there is, is minor by comparison!) As trade deficits with China grows at the dawn of the 21c, we shall soon see whether this *yellowism* blooms yet again!

Living 20 years in Japan, I met only one person with yellow skin. Perhaps it was the combination of the chemicals he worked with (he was a lithographer), his consumption of tangerines (up to a half-box a day) and his chain-smoking. On the other hand, I know several Japanese, who thought they, *as Mongoloids*, didn't need to fear the sun like whites, and got badly burned for it! Japanese never identify *themselves* as "yellow" except indirectly, when the press complains about a foreign politician allegedly crusading against "yellow peril," or reports on a Hawaiian metaphor, *banana,* the yellow equivalent of the black-inside white-outside *oreo*. Yet the terms "white" (*hakujin*) and "black" (*kokujin*) are in common use in Japan, as they are everywhere. In the late 1960's, a brilliant Mexican cartoonist suggested his countrymen needed a color to *compete* in the brave new world of color "power" and color "beauty" so as not to be forced out of the running by their overbearing black and white neighbors to the North. Unfortunately, "beige power" and "beige beauty" did not catch on. In matters of color, there would seem to be *a law of the excluded middle.*

1-9   With us, pockmarked men and women are rare;
      Antre nós hé raro serem os homens ou m[olhe]res bixigozas;

            In Japan, they are common and many lose their sight from the pox.
            Antre os Japões hé couza muito commua e cegão muitos d[e] bexigas.

    At the time Frois wrote, descriptions of missing persons suggest that about one in six Englishmen (and women, such as Queen Elizabeth who caught smallpox the year Frois arrived in Japan, 1562) were pock-marked and such young servants were favored because of their immunity. So pockmarks were not *that* rare in some of Europe. Had the globe-trotting Luso-Iberians already gained so much immunity (been sufficiently thinned out) not to show many effects? Were the Japanese hit hard by new strains introduced by the Europeans? There is curious reversal involving small-pox not mentioned by Frois:

    We fear measles, but we fear small pox most of all.
    They say "smallpox takes your looks, measles takes your life." and fear measles more.

    A well-known Japanese proverb reads: "small pox will settle your looks but measles will settle your life." By Frois's time or soon thereafter Japanese evidently found *measles* the more lethal disease. The deadly measles was not something to joke about, but 18c *senryu* (17-syllabet poems of black humor) are full of small pox in the person of pitted brides, called simply "bring-dowries" (for the wealth that b[r]ought them husbands). The high number of pockmarked Japanese still observed when it was reopened in the mid-19c dropped precipitously within a generation of Perry's arrival thanks to appropriate government measures encouraging vaccination for smallpox "which has always been epidemic" in Japan, according to Morse, who also noted in 1877 that "in this matter, as in many others, the Japanese are far ahead of occidental nations"(M:JDD) because of the negative influence of Christian fundamentalism on the spread of scientific knowledge.
..

1-10 We consider it filthy and uncouth to have long finger-nails;
      Antre nós trazer as unhas compridas se tem por sujidade e pouqa criaṣão;

            In Japan, men as well as well-bred women sport some nails like talons.
            Os Japões, asi homens como molheres fidalgas, trazem algumas como de gaviões.

    Okada, annotating Frois, protests: "It is an exaggeration to write that our country has the custom of growing long nails. There were just days when nail-cutting was taboo; it was considered inauspicious to cut them at night or [for punning reasons] before departing on a journey." Indeed, most Japanese depicted in *ukiyoe* prints show nails cut so short the meat of the finger-tip bulges up. But, what Okada and others translate as "sometimes have nails" or ". . . some men and ladies have nails . . . ," Frois probably intended to mean "some nails," referring to the practice of keeping a long fingernail on at least *one* pinkie on the part of some priests, literatae, wealthy merchants and nobles. While Âl-bîrûnî noted that "India/ns let the nails grow long, glorying in their idleness, since they do not use them for any business or work, but only, while living a *dolce far niente* life, they scratch their heads with them and examine the hair for lice." (A(S):AI), the practice apparently came to Japan from China. Rada described 16c Chinese men who "let the fingernails of one of their hands grow very long, . . . as long as their fingers" (trans. Boxer:B:SCSC), and Cruz further claimed that "they keep very clean; and these finger-nails do serve them instead of the chop-sticks for to eat withal." (ibid) The Portuguese editor for the Cruz reprint writes that the nails were coated with silver (*bainhas de prata*). He also notes that no other documentation on *eating* with nails has been found. No documentation, perhaps, but the idea got around, for Bulwer a century later wrote that "these Nailes do serve them instead of Forkes to eate withall; the use of silver Forkes which our Gallants so much used of late was no doubt an imitation of this." (B:A) Bulwer writes tongue-in-cheeke, but chopsticks – called just "sticks" by the Portuguese and Spaniards – were often Englished as *forks*. Dyer Ball, in the late 19c mercifully drops the chopstick/fork idea:

> Long finger-nails are not considered a sign of dirtiness, but of respectability, and of being above manual labour, which, if necessary, would of course prevent them from attaining such length as an inch and a half, two inches, or even three, though it is seldom one sees them all of equal length on all the fingers. It is well that such is the case, as two or three on one or both hands give such a claw-like appearance to the fingers as to make them sufficiently repulsive; fortunately hand-shaking is not in vogue in China, as it would be extremely unpleasant to feel the long talons gripping one's hand. (THINGS CHINESE)

Viewed in retrospect, there is no little irony in the contrast, for in Japan, where the same word was used for "fingernail," "claw" and "talon," having long nails had a strong beastly significance and, as it turns out, *identified with Europeans*! The retrospective folk-description of the kind and gentle Japanophile Organtino S.J., the nose of which we have already seen includes some animal metaphor:

> His teeth are like a horse's, whiter than snow. His finger-nails the claws of a bear. (J/E:NBJ)

Since the same word is used for *nails* and *claws* in Japanese, it might be overdoing it to say that Furukomu (Frois or Valignano) lit his tobacco by striking fire from his own *claws*" (As it is usually translated), but the practice of depicting the other side with spooky fingernails is undeniable. These "claws" disappeared with the opening of Japan, but were returned to the hands – or, rather, paws – of Churchill, Roosevelt and other Anglo-American enemy in WWII Japanese propaganda art! (D:WWM) This art reminds us that we should be careful about equating nails and elegant femininity. (For examples of nails used as weapons by men – not in Japan – see LL-long.)
..

1-11 We think sword scars on the face a deformity;
Antre nós se tem por d[is]formidade ter huma cutil[a]da no rosto;

> Japanese are proud of their wounds and, not taking care with their treatment, make them so much the more deformed. *Os Japões, se prezão delas e como são mal quradas são ainda mais disformes.*

Dueling scars were valued in some parts and eras in Europe, but it would be hard to find a culture as utterly macho as 16c Japan. Every visitor to Japan was favorably impressed with their bravery. This was on the tail-end of the long Warring States Period (Sengoku-jidai: 1338-1568). Continual wars turn people into either chickens or roosters. In Japan's case, it was the latter:

They will not put up with a single insult or even a word spoken in anger. Thus you speak (and, indeed, must speak) courteously even to the most menial laborers and peasants because they will not have it otherwise, for either they will drop their work without giving a second thought to what they stand to lose, or else they will do something even worse. (Alessandro Valignano in C:TCJ).

Jesuits, themselves *warriors for Jesus* and honor-conscious Latins (i.e. Arabized Europeans), found the Japanese recklessness praiseworthy as compared to the Chinese who, many noted, ran "like women." The Japanese served as mercenaries throughout Asia at this time, were proud of their bravery as a people, and did not hesitate to boast about it. This "we are the toughest dudes around" attitude continued throughout the Tokugawa isolation and is one of the main reasons Japan was not colonized by the West.

One still finds scars *at work* in the popular culture, but they serve a different role in a no longer brave society. Sitcoms and comic books frequently show a scarred *yakuza* (or, rather *chinpira,* a *yakuza* underling) intimidating people with his presence alone – for some reason, nine out of ten times in the subway. Beauty is not the only "face value," a scar's scare-effect can gain a man (who may be a coward at heart) a seat and the room to stretch out on it . . . Perhaps, scars, then, functioned as a mark of identity. If sartorial and weapons-related restrictions did not permit many types of gallantry (in the Olde English sense of *showing off*), scars, at least, could not be outlawed!

Concerning male dress
quanto aos vestidos dos homens

(This is the first and last chapter with a double count. It shows Frois's treatise was unfinished.)

1-1+ Our dress is the same for almost all of the four seasons of the year;
Os nossos vestidos quasi em todos os 4 tempos do anno são, os mesmos;

Japanese change their dress three times a year: *i.e., natsu katabira, aki awase, fuyu kimono.* *Os Japões os varião 3 vezes no ano: nac̱cu catabira, aqui avaxe, fuyu qimão.*

Non-Japanese tend to use one word, *kimono,* to describe *all* robe-like clothing worn by Japanese. Japanese would no more do this than we would call a jacket or trousers "a dress" because they are dress. Hence, Frois uses the specific Japanese terms. The *natsu,* or "summer" *katabira* is an unlined, gauze-thin robe, or gown, after nature's the second best suit for sultry weather. It was also held above the head as a parasol of sorts. Today, the closest thing is the *yukata,* worn at home, for some festivals, in hotels and even outside in hot-spring resorts (but never over the head). Until Japanese adopted Western dress, it also served for underwear. The *aki awase* or "autumn combo" is a more substantial two-layered robe which can properly be called a kimono. It was *officially* only worn for a short time, from the first day of the Ninth Month (now, mid-October) until the ninth day of the same, perhaps, partly to air it out before it was stuffed with cotton or flock-silk (for nobles) and turned into a *fuyu kimono,* or, "winter kimono," and this was pulled out to turn it back into an *awase* on the first day of summer (the Fourth Month by the old calendar). This latter is called *hatsu-awase,* or "first *awase*" and the day, "Clothes-Change" Day, or *koromogae*.

Even if he did grow up in Portugal, Frois must have known that much of Europe is freezing cold in the winter, so what does he mean when he says "our dress" remains the same? First, "we" could keep our tights and pompously plump pants on year-round because Western Europe summers are relatively dry. Second, we put a coat *over* our usual suit, while the Japanese replaced or stuffed the suit itself and were more formally attentive to seasonal colors. So our changes were less radical.

While there were formal dates for changing dress and, as Rodrigues noted, "They are most punctilious in the observance of those ceremonies," (R(C):TIJ) (Ibid.) the Japanese were not absolute = irrational about it, for he also writes the *katabira* was worn in the summer "and when it is hot," and, more interesting yet, hints at the practice of frequent, if not day-by-day stuffing and unstuffing: "this costume will be more or less padded in keeping with the natural temperature of the season." *That* is smart. I have long wondered why we don't use inflatable coats in the winter.

1-2+   With us, colorful clothing is considered frivolous and ludicrous;
Antre nós trazer o vestido pintado se teria por liviandade e zombaria;

With Japanese, excepting bonzes and old men of shaven pate, wearing colorful clothing is universal. *Nos Japões hé universal trazerem-nos todos pintados, excepto bonzos e velhos rapados.*

Japanese *never* wore clothing as ludicrous as that of the Renaissance dandy, who boasted tights of different color on each leg! But Fashion is short-sighted. In Frois's day, the West had just begun the historical anomaly someone called the Great Sartorial Renunciation, i.e., the graying of male fashion, when Frois wrote. Until the mid-16c when they warred ferociously with one another over who was the holiest and cut back on their proclivity to play the peacock, European men were second to none in their decoration. They still wore quite a bit of colored (as in, not white or black) clothing with fine adornment when Frois wrote. This makes me believe that his *pintado* may not so much mean colorful in the sense of bright colors as covered with bold *designs,* or *pictures* like those described by Rodrigues: "The outer surface of the material of the robe, whether it be silk, hemp or linen, is generally printed handsomely with flowers in various colours, although some of the silk robes have a striped pattern, others are dyed with one colour, others with two . . ."

Later, Japan would enact strict sartorial laws, but they were never as restrictive as the black & white *mindset* of our puritan forefathers and the modern corporation man in his gray flannel suit! In the 1960's and 70's, conservative Japanese, appalled at the revival of color in menswear in the West, forgot about their own past and the America of a decade earlier and argued such freedom was the result of Occidental individualism, far from drab but productive and safe Japanese conformity. Only the young Japanese construction worker and truck driver remained true to their wild pre-Modern roots. They are the ones you'll find wearing purple and orange trousers and whatever hairstyle they please.

1-3+   We have new clothing and new designs almost every year;
Antre nós quasi cad'ano se inventa hum novo traje e invensão de vestidos;

In Japan, the fashions are the same and never change.
*Em Japão, sempre a fei*s*ão hé a mesma sem nunqa se variar.*

Early modern fashion vs. traditional culture? Hardly so simple. One way or another, humans *will* seek novelty. Men *will* show off. Could restrictive color and graphic design rules in Europe have been offset by more structural changes in the costume from year to year and the vice versa with respect to Japan? Almost a hundred years earlier, Sebastian Brant had snorted *"Shameless and fickle I do brand / Style-slaves who live in every land"* (JH:CER), but there is no question that Europeans – or, at least, the Jesuits who traveled to and from it – were very conscious of the rapid change of fashion in their part of the world. Montaigne, writing at the same time as Frois, discovered what might be called "the fashion cycle," where the acceptable clothing circles back to the styles of earlier generations, and marveled about it using vocabulary that demands quoting:

> The present fashion in dress makes them promptly condemn the old, with such great conviction and such universal agreement that you would think it was a kind of mania that thus turns their understanding upside down. ("Of Ancient Customs" M(DF):CEM)

At any rate, the "us" side of Frois's contrast about Europeans following fashion, was itself old hat. In the report of the contemporary Japanese Embassy to Europe, the Japanese, "Miguel," with a little help from Valignano,★ first describes the sumptuous wall-hangings in Europe, then adds, "you can imagine how much Europeans adorn their bodies." Indeed,

> . . . the first surprising thing is that since Europeans wouldn't think of wearing the same type of clothing all the time and dislike using one item over and over, every year, they think up new modes of dress. Whatever the dress is, the fabric tends to be very expensive thin wool weave, silk . . . and is adorned with gold brocade, so that an enormous sum of money must be spent to keep one's body properly attired. . . . The women, too, like the men, ordinarily invent things that are new and not yet worn by others . . . Moreover, this type of luxury is not confined to the masters, but found among domestic servants and squires as well. The higher the place [his master's social position] of the servant, the more elegant his clothing . . . In the end, the excessive competition with respect to beautiful clothing without regard for money sometimes makes it necessary to restrict this excess prolificacy by law, but whatever the punishment, whatever the threat, at least with respect to tailoring, has no effect on Europeans. (De Missione: 1590 ch 9)
>
> ..

I do not know what, if anything, Valignano or Frois really felt about European innovation. Perhaps they hated it, for the Jesuits usually criticized luxury *in the East* (eg. 4-8) as deriving from a culture with completely worldly interests. But, in *De Missione* – even granting the last line quoted above – Miguel=Valignano *uses* the prodigious expenditure of wealth on architecture and clothing and jewelry, where even servants are fitted out luxuriously, as proof of the overflowing – or rather, overwhelming – wealth of Europe, particularly with respect to their closest rival for global prestige, the Chinese. (J/S:DM, ch.33) Evidently, Christian modesty was overruled by the need to show what bounty the religion has brought to those who believed in it! Still, one wonders what Valignano would have thought of mid-17c (Philip IV) Spain, when fashion extremes reached all-time peaks of absurdity – e.g., all the ladies wearing eyeglasses of different weird shapes (D:DLS)!

The Japanese had, in fact, not made *major* structural changes. Frois's observation was to be repeated by other Western visitors for centuries. But I cannot help entertaining some doubt, for, when Hideyoshi paraded from Nagoya back to the capital in 1593, the members of his retinue were dressed in Portuguese style and, "largely as a result of Valignano's embassy in 1591, every Japanese at court made efforts to obtain at least one article of European dress . . ." (C:RTI) *Does that sound like a fashion-dead culture!* In 1776, Thunberg claimed that almost nothing had changed since Kaempfer visited a hundred years earlier, but the truth is that even if the basic structure of Japanese dress remained pretty constant, fashion was far from dead. Tokugawa intellectuals were self-conscious of their rapidly changing fashions (*ryûkô*), and even "fashion" is too slow a word to describe Edo, where even a street vender could start a *fad* (*hayari*) by a clever advertising gimmick! By the late 20c, Japanese considered themselves, for better or worse, the *most* prone to fads or "booms" as they call them, of all the world's people. In the heyday of *Japan-as-Number-One*, the intellectuals of the Bubble went so far as to call the West (a traditionally-minded "stock culture" incapable of coping with the new) *a museum* for Japanese tourists, incapable of competing with the post-modern, ever-changing "flow culture" of Japan. In a word, modern Japanese managed to reverse the hoary stereotype of the sleepy, changeless East and active protean West.

Yet, for all these contradictions and qualifications, Frois has a point. Japanese traditional clothing (*wafuku*) and footwear even today (though confined to certain places and times) remains basically what it was a thousand years ago, or thrice that if the Chinese roots are included! If Japanese seldom wear it, at least they *do*, whereas Occidental ancient clothing only exists in books of costume. (And the exceptions, the Irish kilt, Greek skirt and Swiss shorts are not worn so often as traditional Japanese clothing.) In this sense, one could argue that the Europe has no *living* traditional clothing in the sense that Japan has. Without a continuous thread of culture, the past is as good as dead and our only alternatives to present fashion are outside (ethnic) or future.

★ 注   *If you missed the explanation of why* Miguel=Valignano, *please read the Envoi of the Foreword.*

1-4+   We are used to wearing a cape/coat over our doublet and shirts;
Antre nós sobre os jibões e palotes se usa de trazer capa;

> The Japanese wear a colored, very thin, front-opening *sambenito*, over their *katabira* [see 1-1+] or *kimono*. *Os Japões sobre o qimão ou catabira trazem hum sambenito pintado muito ralo, aberto por diante.*

Our *jibao*, or *gibao* is a "doublet." But what *is* a "doublet?" Pictures show me a fancy leather jacket with or without sleeves, and a belted waist. Lacking a generic term for a thin garment worn on the outside, Frois calls what is probably a *haori*, or "wing-weave," a *sambenito*, a sleeveless smock, often covered with colorful symbolic designs worn by penitents during the Inquisition trials that to us, today, look like clothing for a fool. *Tratado* translators split as to whether the *muito ralo* applies to the subtlety of the colors or the thinness of the cloth. I go with the latter, as the Iberian Cape was a substantial coat and this strengthens the contrast. Frois would seem to be contrasting an outside garment that is longer, heavier and closed in the West to one smaller, thinner and open in Japan. Clothing terms do not translate well across the ocean of space or time! I wish Frois used *more adjectives,* for nouns mean nothing unless we already know what they mean.

1-5+   Our sleeves are narrow and extend to the butt of the hand;
As nossas [man]gas são estreitas e chegão até o colo da mão;

> Those of Japan are wide; and male, female or bonze stop halfway down the arm.
> *As dos Japões largas, asi homens como molheres e bonzos, chegão-lhe até meo braço.*

Wide sleeves were traditional with Japanese clothing; *short* ones were not. They were a century-long "tradition", perhaps a functional development of the long Warring Period. For most of Japanese history, the sleeves extended to, near or even past the wrist. Okada notes they were also rounded off at the ends at this time, but that they were still loose compared to Europe, where even loose sleeves and voluminous trousers had tight collars and cuffs, and clothing had to be unlooped or unlaced to remove (The exception would be Venetian robes with bell-bottom sleeves. Tight at the armpits, they offered more to the eye than to comfort.). In the more relaxed, pre-warring times in Japan, the sleeves were often wider than they were long, and *"long* sleeves" actually meant *wide* ones, for in Japanese, as in English, the longest side is generally called "the length".

1-6+   Our breeches or drawers open in the front;
Os nossos calsões ou seroulas são abertas por diante;

Those of Japan open on both sides, and a loin-wrap [?] pommel of [. .?]
Os dos Japões tem duas aberturas nas ylhargas e hum tanga[nho] ou arsão de sela de [?]

Boy, did "ours" open in front! The Iberians tended to cover the top of their breeches with skirts (and were in the process of switching to very baggy pants), but even these tended to retain a trace of something Frois's contemporary Montaigne called "that empty and useless model of a member that we cannot even decently mention by name, which however we show off and parade in public." Montaigne's "empty" is telling. Unlike the Dani of New Guinea, who actually stick their penis into the long gourd tube, the codpiece at this time was a total fake.

We parade colorful abstract models of our manhood attached to our breeches every day.
They parade huge realistic members about town on their shoulders once a year.

The Japanese side is harder because of lacuna in the manuscript. "Those" of the Japanese would seem to be *momohiki* (literally: thigh-pullers). Rodrigues describes them as "wide at the bottom and open on both sides from the top down to the knees" and notes that one part is in front without any opening but with ribbons attached by which it is tied, and another is behind also with ribbons . . ." (Ibid. = I forget *what* Ibid! Probably R(C):TIJ) Frois's "loin-wrap" (according to Okada, *tanganho* = a diminutive of *tanga,* an African wrap-around) if it is a loin-wrap, may allude to the manner that a large portion of the cloth itself wraps around to the other hip or further. Be that as it may, the truth be said, Japanese were never big on bifurcated male clothing.   As Rodrigues notes, breeches "are not the ordinary attire of the nation" but purely formal wear, probably invented in "that part of China facing Japan . . . from which . . . Japan was populated."(Ibid)

Okada thinks the puzzling "pommel" may refer to a frontal flap on some formal trousers called *hakama.* A type of these *hakama* worn by high-level administrators in Japan developed beyond, or rather, mutated from their Chinese prototype, until the legs extended down far beyond the man's feet! Rodrigues mentions magistrates who "wear these trousers with their feet hidden within, the trouser legs trail along two or three spans after the feet, and they must exercise diligence lest they fall over."

We wear pantaloons to separate our legs in order to ride easily and move about faster;
They wear hakama *which extend past their feet to slow themselves down and look dignified.*

These long *hakama* intrigued Europeans. Alcock, thought that the effect was such that –

their feet, as they advanced, seemed pushed into what should have been the knees of the garment. The consequence was, that they were compelled to shuffle along like so many people shorn by some general calamity of both legs, and walking upon their stumps, much as a man cut down to his knees might be expected to progress, an effect farther heightened by said prolongations trailing behind on the floor, collapsed and evidently empty. (A:COT)

And Oliphant, in a more perfectly topsy-turvy vein wrote that

they seem to be cut upon *a principle precisely the opposite* to that which regulates our Court-dress. We consider that when we have brought our nether garments down to the knee, we have not only satisfied decency, but have reached the highest pitch of refinement and elegance. The great object of the Japanese is to create an entire misconception in the mind of the spectator as to the situation of that important joint; he wishes it to be supposed that he shuffles into the royal presence on his knees; but finding that process attended with much practical inconvenience, he compromises the matter by having his trousers made about eighteen inches longer than his legs; by these means his feet are made to represent his knees, and he is enabled to walk upon them comfortably with his sham legs dragging after him.(O:LEM *italics,* mine)

Rudofsky, more recently, jokes that they are the *result* of Japanese having short legs, for "true costume emphasizes rather than hides body characteristics." (R:KM) Could Frois have skipped this obvious contrast because he thought they were worn so rarely and by so few, that such a contrast was not worth mentioning? But, let us leave these dragging trousers and proceed to something else Frois missed:

We wrap long pieces of cloth around our necks to keep warm in the winter;
They wrap long pieces of cloth around their privates for cool summer dress.

We think of a loincloth as something primitive and made from crude material;
They make them from silk so even a nobleman can wear one without shame.

We would not think of wearing our underwear outside;
They not only wear their loincloths outside but some even work wearing them.

TT-Long has *much more* on loin cloths, which I like for transporting me to my boyhood dreams about life as an AmerIndian; but let me leave one more Loinclothism that shows how far we have changed with respect to the definition of a certain word in the past century or so:

"the men when naked always wear a loincloth." Isabella Bird (M:JDD1)

~~~~~~

1-7+   Our skirt-pantaloons and imperial tights are made of silk with gold brocade;
As nossas calsas e muslos imperiais são de seda atroceladas d'ouro;

Even when the clothing of Japan is silken, the trousers are *canga*, or *nuno*.
Os vestidos dos Japões, ainda que sejão de seda, os calsões sempre hão de ser de canga [1] *ou* nono.

Canga (*ganga, canque*, etc.) is cotton fabric from China, *nuno* a rougher Japanese weave. Japan, being humid in the summer, like the East coast of North America, rather than dry like Europe, the gentry wore cotton or hemp trousers in Japan because they were cooler. But could Frois be illustrating the fact "we" spend a lot even for the lower part of our body, whereas the Japanese shortchange their extremities? But no additional signification for this contrast changes the fact it is small stuff compared to Âl-bîrûnî's felicitous single-line contrast of the Muslim and Hindu:

They [the Indians] *use turbans for trousers.* (A/S:AI)

Functionally, this is disingenuous for Indians do not really wrap their turbans around their crotches; but there is a resemblance, as both look like swaddling. Even as I marveled at this creative topsy-turvy, I came across the following passage in Michael Cooper's *Rodrigues the Interpreter* describing what actually happened in Japan (as described by our Frois) when the Shôgun Hideyoshi presented white *katabira* robes to the retinue of black guards (the Portuguese always had their slaves with them) after watching their dance performance in 1593:

Rodrigues indicated to the recipients that they should follow Japanese etiquette and raise the presents over their heads as a sign of reverence towards the donor. Obviously misunderstanding his directions, the men proceeded to wind the robes around their heads as if they were turbans, thus unwittingly causing further entertainment for the onlookers. (C:RTI)

1-8+   With us, male clothing can not be worn by women;
Os vestidos dos homens antre nós não hé couza que possa servir aas molheres;

> The Japanese *kimono* and *katabira* are worn by both men and women.
> *Os quimões e catabiras de Japão ygualmente servem às molheres e homens.*

Medieval illustrations show Europeans in what looks like unisex dresses and robes. By the Reformation (16c), only children did this. As Japanese dress is not tailored to the peculiarities of the human body, gender differences would naturally be less pronounced even if the Japanese physique did not exhibit less sexual dimorphism than the European physique to begin with. As a result, Occidentals have always had great trouble telling the sexes apart. The mid-19c visit of the first Japanese Embassy to America provided ample proof that Frois's contrast still held true. Two contemporary correspondents, one of whom was laughing at the Japanese and one of whom was recording the barbarism of his countrymen:

> Don't I wish yeou'd a bin their, Uncle Jack; and if yeou had, yeou'd jave larfed fit tew split. Their wos we, awl in unerform, grate big men; and their wos they, little, peaked, slim chaps, dressed e'enermost like wimmen folks, but as bright and chippur as a school-marm on examanashun mornin.'

> Then at every halt each carriage was surrounded by a mob, who thrust their heads into the carriages, and passed all sorts of comments among themselves upon the appearance of the strangers. One burly fellow swore that all they wanted was to have a little more crinoline and be right out decent looking nigger wenches. (J-A:FJE)

Be that as it may, Japanese men and women do not *wear* clothing in quite the same way. Belts are tied differently, some colors taboo, etc. . *Japanese* had no trouble telling the difference.

1-9+   Our clothing fits the body and is tight and restrictive;
Os nossos vestidos são justos, estreitos e apertados no corpo;

> Japanese clothing is so loose people can easily bare themselves above the waist and think nothing of it. *Os de Japão tão largos que com facilidade e sem pejo se desp[em logo] da sinta pera riba.*

In his outlandish *Kimono Mind*, Rudofsky lets his designer eye portray "our" tight clothing "constructed with an eye to anatomy . . . they represent a sort of hollow casting of their owner. Between airings they hang like human effigies from the gallows of our clothes closets. (R:KM) If Frois had a contemporary European reader, he or she might have read loose morals into the loose clothing of the Japanese, but his wording suggests functional difference. Golownin (in 1811-12) gives an amusing account of how such looseness was used to adjust the warmth of multi-layered *kimonos*:

When a Japanese finds a room too warm, he pulls off the upper coat, and lets it hang upon a girdle [i.e. from the back of his *obi* belt]; if this is not enough, the second, third, &c. are pulled off, and he keeps on only one coat: when he feels too cold, one coat is by degrees put on again over the other. (G:MCJ3)

Frois describes the removal of that last layer – in the summer, nobles wore these fine white robes as underwear, but most people wore only one garment. Slipping out of the top part left their upper torso completely bare. And this was not only true for men. Bird describes "women unclothed to their waists . . . busy stripping mulberry branches." (B:UTJ) Loose clothing was *de rigueur* in Japan for ventilation, wiping off sweat and frequent washing (38+, below).

But not all Japanese fashion is loose and comfortable. When I appeared on Japanese late-night television to discuss men and non-bifurcated clothing, they cinched me up in a kimono as stiff as a straight-jacket (No wonder, thought I, that "binding" – rather than whipping or spanking – is the traditional form of sadomasochism in Japan). Luckily, I puffed out my belly like a sly horse when the fitter put his knee on my back, so I could breathe! Formality, East or West, can be excruciating. Rudofsky calls the enjoyment of such discomfort *sartoriasis,* and claims "the kimono fills that need to perfection." (R:KM)

1-10+ We, because of our buttons and lacing, cannot easily reach our bodies with our hands;
Nós por causa dos botões e atacas não podemos meter a mão no corpo fa[cilmente];

> Japanese men and women, not restricted by such devices, can thrust their hands into their bosom at any time, especially in the winter when the sleeves are left dangling. *Os Japões asi homens como molheres, como não tem nada disto, sempre, specialmente no Inverno, trazem as mangas por f[ora] caídas e as mãos dentro no corpo.*

With little heating and no sweaters, the ability to withdraw *into* one's clothing and fuse the body into one unit is vital to conserving heat. Call it *the mitten effect.* This ability, it turns out, is also useful for hot weather. Rodrigues:

> As the robes are very ample and have wide sleeves, people can insert their hands inside with the greatest of ease and wipe away body sweat [One place wiped was "under the arm-pits!" (Thunberg)] with a handkerchief. (R(C): TIJ)

"But," he observes, to do so "is a grave discourtesy and impertinence in the presence of the gentry, only a master will do it in front of his servants; but on no account whatsoever may a servant do it in the presence of his master." Nor, he continues, could anyone do so at a formal function. This is understandable. Loosely hanging sleeves marked the debonair gambler and other "cool" men-about-town. Dyer Ball notes that Chinese fanned *inside* their "jackets" front and back. To Japanese or Chinese, "our" tubular clothing must have seemed like a straight-jacket. What heroism, what suffering (*what ringworm!*) must have accompanied their adoption of our unsuitable clothing!

1-11+ We wear our best dress on top and the inferior underneath;
Antre nós se veste o milhor vestido em cima e o somenos debaxo;

> Japanese wear the best underneath and the inferior on top.
> *Os Japães o milhor debaxo e o somenos em riba.*

The metaphorical equations *top=outside* and *below=inside* are found in Japanese, Portuguese and English, alike. They speak from the perspective of the body. The Japanese seem to contradict the metaphorical equation, by putting the superior garment "below" the inferior one, and even go against nature, for animals wear *their* decorations on the outside. So, for this contrast, the Japanese side is clearly the one calling for an explanation. Did this reversal begin because of sartorial regulations (sumptuary law)? Because the best dress was preserved for ones intimates and not wasted on the rabble? To preserve good clothing from weathering? To avoid highwaymen or taxes? Or, to avoid envy? Who knows? I do know it is usually explained *today* in terms of subtle Japanese aesthetic preference. It is *shibui* (discriminating, in a subdued way) to keep the best art under cover.

1-12+ With us, a garment must always be better than its lining;
Antre nós sempre o vestido á-de ser milhor que o forro;

> With *dobuku* [vest] of the Japanese gentry, the lining must, as far as possible, be better than the [outside of the] garment. *Em Japão os dubuqus dos senhores hão-de ter o forro milhor que [o] vestido, se poderem.*

The Japanese *dobuku* transliterates as "torso-wear;" it was usually sleeveless and, like Japanese trousers, originated in China Here, Frois probably refers to silk *dobuku*. I cannot say more about the *dobuku* of 1585, but the OJD says it evolved into the silk *haori,* literally "wing-weave," of the Tokugawa era (1603-1867), which usually had sleeves and always had a lining. Wealthy merchants and townsmen vied with one another over who could boast the most ornate lining for their plain black *haori* coats. To me, it is magical. I am reminded of oolite.

..

1-13+ We wear our hide *dobuqus* with the fur on the inside;
Nós trazemos os dobuqus de peliças com a pelle pera dentro;

> Japanese wear it on the outside.
> *Os Japões os trazem com as peliças pera fora.*

Since fur holds heat better facing in, and Japanese, as Buddhists who should not kill animals, might be expected to hide the evidence, it is doubly surprising they wore it on the outside. Was this for the love of natural texture? Fear of fleas? Or some historical accident? Who knows. Fur is now pretty much the prerogative of women in Japan, as in the West. The weasel/ermine/ferret/mink comforters with their little feet and beady black eyeballs never fail to amaze Usanian visitors.

1-14+ We cut or shave the hair on our heads for relief from suffering;
Antre nós trosquia ou rapa hum homem a cabeça pera se aliviar de dores;

> Japanese shave it off out of sadness, for sorrow, or falling out of grace with a master. *Os Japões a rapão por tristeza ou dó, ou por estarem fora da graça de seus senhores.*

As a clear-cut contrast, this fails. The reasons Frois gives for Europeans shaving their pate are unclear. What relief is gained? He doesn't mean *head-lice,* does he? If he means an escape from secular suffering by joining a religious order or going on a pilgrimage, then isn't that the same as the Japanese? The only clear difference to me is the falling out of grace part, for Japanese have long been quick *to take responsibility for things.* And, it is better to shave off one's hair – literally "round one's head" (*atama-o marumeru*) – to show one is contrite and determined to make a fresh start than cut off a finger in the style of the courtesan or yakuza to express the same! But Frois misses something here. More than anything else, shaving the head signified *do-or-die determination* (必死), burning the boats behind you. But that still brings us no closer to a clear-cut contrast. Herodotus, the father of contrast as well as history, does much better:

> Among other people it is the custom in grief, for those to whom the grief comes close to shave their heads; but the Egyptians under the shadow of death let their hair and beards grow long, though at other times they shave. (H(G):HH)

Paradoxically, what Herodotus says about the Egyptians *growing hair* is *also* true for the Japanese, for when someone dies one purpose of shaving is to allow the mourning party to completely ignore grooming for months – as they also do not clean house. (Even today, men with the means to do so, let themselves go for a year after their father dies (I observed this twice but need more information).

Perhaps Frois meant "we only shave our heads for penance and the relief that brings; they do it for many reasons." Anyone?

1-15+ We shave our beards when entering a religious order;
Antre nós rapa hum a barba quando se qer meter em alguma religião;

> Japanese cut off the clump of hair on the back of their head as a sign of leaving the secular world. *Os Japões cortão o cabelinho do toutiço em sinal que deixão as couzas do mundo.*

European monks of some orders shaved part of their heads, too; but with full beards more universal than a full head of hair in the West, sacrificing this precious symbol of manhood to serve God made more sense than it would in the Far East, where many men had less beard and more hair.

If beards are – or, *were* – more significant to Occidentals, hair in Japanese has a more powerful presence then in English or, as far as I know, any Indo-European language. The Yamato (native Japanese) word, *kami,* is homophonic with "god/s" and "upper," while the Chinese-derived pronunciation, *ke,* is homophonic with "filth/pollution." Hair on the head, now generally called *kami-no-ke,* was and is treasured by the native Shinto tradition, whereas hair below may have been thought dirty/impure. Ample body hair was first associated with the less civilized native people of Japan, the Ainu, and, later, the "barbarian" West – Furukomu (Valignano/Frois) is depicted by the Barbarian Temple tales as completely covered with grey hair, with the exception of a tonsure (E:NBJ) – and all hair was loosely associated with *desire.* This idea of hair-as-worldly combined with the significance of the *chonmage* (clump of hair) as a mark of manhood made it the prime candidate for cutting off.

I have seen the last remnant of the practice on TV, many times. I refer to the always tearful hair-cut ceremony of retiring sumo wrestlers! But, like head-shaving, cutting off one's hair in Japan does not so much signify a change of status as having made up ones mind to do so. There is a determining quality, a *once-and-for-all* quality to it commonly expressed by the double-verb *omoi-kitte,* or "think-cut."

Here, again, the Father of History had the more perfect contrast, for if Frois finds different *parts* of the hair cut, Herodotus (H(G):HH) pegged the whole thing:

"In the rest of the world priests of the gods wear their hair long; but in Egypt they shave close."

Âl-bîrûnî captures an even broader hair contrast for it covers the entire man. It is accompanied by an explanation of the contrary Hindhu custom:

They do not cut any of the hair of the body. Originally they went naked in consequence of the heat, and by not cutting the hair of the head, they intended to prevent sunstroke. (A(S):AI)

Here, we must fill in the "we" part: Muslims (like Greeks?) shaved off most of their body hair. The explanation is a bit confusing. There is one good unstated contrast there: "we" (the Muslims) used clothing to protect ourselves from the sun; but the leap from any hair of the body to head-hair is hard to follow. Perhaps, if the more hair the better the protection, then the rest of the body just follows the lead of the head if it were. Maybe Âl-bîrûnî means: "Originally, naked because of the heat, they needed all their hair for protection from the sun, as head-hair protects us from sunstroke." Another Âl-bîrûnî hair contrast looked down. Unlike the Muslim West, the Hindus did not shave their pubic hair. The reason is wonderfully topsy-turvy, considering the identification of hair with lust in the Occident: "They try to make people believe that the cutting of it incites to lust and increases carnal desire."

1-16+ We wrap our clothing right over left;
Antre nós se dobrão os roupões da mão direita pera a esquerda;

Japanese do it left over right.
Os Japões dobrão os quimões da esquerda pera a dereita

..

In Japanese, wrapping ("folding" in old English) the right hem of one's garment over the left is called something that might be Englished as "left flap" (*sajin*) and was used by the Chinese as a derogatory term for "barbarians," i.e., the Japanese, who evidently wore their clothes that way (when not just sticking their heads through a hole in a piece of cloth, Mayan style). In 719, the Japanese officially switched to the left-over-right style called "right-flap" (*ujin*), and about eight hundred years later called Western visitors like Frois and Rodrigues "left-flaps!" As is the case with Western languages, the word "left" has sinister connotations in Japanese, mostly deriving from Chinese. Were a right-over-left wrap called a "right-over," the result might have been the opposite! I found no metaphysical reasons given for European clothing wrapping right-over-left. A search of 15 and 16c artwork made it clear that such was *not* always the case, although it usually was for cloaks – but I did find a discussion of Jewish dress where the *right-over-left* wrap was considered to represent favoring justice and good over its opposite and men advised not to wear suits with the left side *over* the right. I italicize *over* because that is what made it superior. (See TT-LONG for more).

Reading Morse's JAPAN DAY BY DAY, in a section on folk superstition, including *If one's head itches, it is a sign of being happy; if dandruff falls it's a sign of intelligence,* I discovered that "fold" – the same as Frois's *dobrão* – may have been the proper term in English only a century ago:

When a person is getting poor and unfortunate, the expression is used, "*Anoshito no uchi wa hidari mai [mae] ni naru*"; that is, "The man of the house folds his kimono to the left," which is considered unlucky. A corpse is dressed with the kimono folded to the left. (M:JDD2)

Today, "we" wear our clothing in the Sino-Japanese manner. Why did men change? Was it the fact that Turks with whom we were warring in Frois's day wore right-over-left, and we wanted to contradict them? Was it the spread of buttons, which are easiest to undo with the right-hand alone (the left hand left for the reins) if the left side with the holes is on the outside? The commonplace explanation for women's clothing in the West adopting right-over-left is that it was kinder to the servants who did the buttoning. *Perhaps*. But if Frois is correct, it was also traditional.

~~~~~~

1-17+ Our shirts have a mantle and are closed in the front;
As nossas camizas tem manteos e são serradas por diante;

> The Japanese *catabiras* [thin-robes] open in front and have no mantles.
> *As catabiras dos Japões são abertas por diante e não tem manteos.*

This is yet another *closed* vs. *open* contrast deriving from the different climate of Europe and Japan. The *katabira*, a light robe with one side wrapped over the other loosely tied with a thin t sash around (rather than the thick *obi* on the formal *kimono*), was indeed the nearest equivalent of a shirt. But is Frois's *camisa* a shirt in the modern sense of the word? "Dresses" might be more accurate, because they were usually belted and stuck out at the bottom. ("Shirt" and "skirt" are etymologically and historically one.) The *mantle* is a small built-in bib, generally decorative rather than Puritan plain. We see the vestige on our formal dress-shirts. A *Faux Frois*:

> *We use ornate collars to present our still living heads as if they were gifts to the world;*
> *They have no collars wrapping around the neck and only present heads that have been cut-off.*

If the mantle resembles a pretty placemat, the collar resembles a dish, incredibly fancy China serving up the faces of the wealthy. Or should we think of the collars as sepals and faces as flowers? Or, considering the square ones, should we be talking, instead, about picture-frames?

~~~~~~

1-18+ We store our clothing by folding it up with the outside in and the inside out;
Antre nós se dobrão os vestidos pera se guardarem com o direito pera dentro e o aveso pera fora;

> Japanese fold it up with the outside out and the inside in.
> *Os Japões os dobrão com o dereito pera fora e o aveso pera dentro.*

Could this be because (as per 1-11+ and 1-12+) "our" clothing had the best part *outside*, so folding it inside would be safer, whereas Japanese clothing with their precious linings would keep that side in? Or were Japanese storage conditions cleaner so there was less risk of soiling the outside? Or were mantles of shirts and buttons on our coats so costly they were folded inside in order not to tempt the servants?

..

~~~~~~

1-19+ Our handkerchiefs are of extremely thin fabric, embroidered and edged, etc.;
Antre nós os lenços são de pano muito fino, lavrados ou de desfiado, etc.,

> The Japanese use ones of rags or paper.
> *Os dos Japões huns são como de liteiro groso e outros de papel.*

With respect to our method of disposing of snot, a gentleman who only blew his nose by hand asked Montaigne, "what privilege this dirty excrement had that we should prepare a fine delicate piece of linen to receive it, and then, what is more, wrap it up and carry it carefully on us; for that should be much more horrifying and nauseating than to see it dropped in any old place, as we do all other excrements." As a declared relativist, Montaigne admitted that we would find this practice "hideous were it told about another country." I wish I knew if Valignano read the 1572-4 essay (*Of Custome*), for it was a treasure of topsy-turvy that included not only some un-attributed Herodotus but women who show off their loves by wearing tassels for each man they bed, people who drink the dissolved remains of the dead with wine or feed them to dogs, and a people who, when "eating, wipe their fingers on their thighs, on the pouch of their genitals, and on the soles of their feet." (trans. Donald M. Frame) And more important, "The "rags" – *tenugui* (a cotton hand-towel) in one translation and "hempen refuse" in another – and paper" used for wiping brows, drying hands and such were probably as beautiful in their way as the ornate Western handkerchief mentioned. I, at least, prefer naturally colored hand-made paper and the simple prints on Japanese *tenugui* (a handkerchief used either to wipe sweat, rolled up as a sweat-band or tied as a wrapped cap) today to the fancy but usually less tasteful Western handkerchief. For blowing noses, Japanese used only disposable tissues, which is generally still the case. Rodrigues (c1600) noted they were also used for spitting into "when they are in matted rooms."

> This paper is used throughout the kingdom and is very necessary for the sake of cleanliness, and nobody, the gentry or the common folk, women or children, fails to carry this in their bosom. . . . Nobles and gentry observe great cleanliness by immediately throwing away the sheet of paper after they have blown their nose; for this reason there is a great abundance of this paper throughout the whole kingdom. (trans. Cooper – me: *Did Rodrigues and not Carletti get Fros's missing book?*)

Don't get the wrong idea. The paper was not reused. It was collected and recycled. (Paper vats, according to Issa, were a very dangerous place . . . for butterflies). Hygiene, ecology and literacy aligned! In old Japan, there was no telling who once blew his or her nose on the paper you wrote on. If you believe the *ukiyoe* artist, however, the main use of tissue paper in Japan was not for blowing noses or spitting into. It was for love-making. You can estimate the amount of sex engaged in by counting the tissues, and the intensity of it by noticing how crumpled and far-flung they are. Popular brands of tissue paper were used as currency in the Yoshiwara Pleasure Quarters!

~~~~~~

1-20+ We show our courtesy by removing our hats;
Nós fazemos a cortezia com tirar o barrete;

> The Japanese show it by removing their footgear.
> *Os Japões a fazem com descalsar os sapatos.*

As we, when we all *had* hats, once removed them to greet a superior on the street, Japanese removed their footgear. The pariah class, the *eta*, were not permitted to wear foot-wear in *anyone's* presence, ostensibly because it would be inappropriate for their animal (called four-footed, or simply indicated by four fingers) identity, but logically, because they were the inferiors of all others and had to remain physically lower. Incidentally, the removal of one's shoes and the removal of one's hat both make someone lower. *There is a difference, however*, the removal of shoes was something more than a mere *courtesy*, it was a sign of respect shown to one's *superior*, where *courtesy toward equals* was shown by a slight bow, in the manner that we might tip our hat for an equal, and removing the shoes when coming into a house would better be described as a custom and a *necessity* than as a courtesy.

The eclectic (and occasionally wrong) English editor of Golowin's MEMOIRS has it right when he uses the hat *vs.* footgear contrast as one of four examples of why Japanese "have been called our moral Antipodes."

> They salute the foot, instead of the head or the hands, &c (G:MCJv3):

The verb "salute" in mid-19c English meant *"to show respect using."* Today, no one in Japan removes footgear to show respect; neither do the young on both sides of the Pacific (who wear baseball caps backwards because their poor posture makes their necks more likely to burn than their noses) remove or even tip their caps – how could they, with the brim facing back? (I kid, for fashion is mindless, but thanks to Frois, I now realize there is another reason for a brim being in the *front*.)

~~~~~~

1-21+ We use swords that cut on both sides of the blade..
Antre nós se uza d'espadas que cortão d'ambos os gumes;

> The Japanese use a cutlass that cuts on only one edge of the blade.
> *Os Japões de traçados que não cortão mais que de hum gume somente.*

The Occidental *espada* was first a stabbing and second a hacking instrument. Although it presumably cut better than its Gaelic prototype, it was crude stuff compared to the razor-sharp sword that was Japan's top export item to China. In the West, too, if you return to Rome, swords were single-edged, though classic Hollywood gives Romans the double-edged *spatha* they had yet to adopt from the Gauls! Our topsy-turvy scheme is beautifully preserved in this historical flip, when we consider one more fact: the ancient Japanese sword, the *tsurugi,* was double-edged and as long as our medieval "long-sword." So we went from one edge to two, while they went from two to one!

~~~~~~

1-22+ Our scabbards are leather or felt;
As nossas bainhas são de couro ou de veludo.

> Those of the Japanese are of lacquered wood, and the lords' covered with gold or silver. *As dos Japões de pao* vruxadas, *e as dos senhores cubertas d'ouro ou prata.*

The *urushi*, which Frois turns into a Portuguese adjective (*vruxadas*) is lacquer and the wood probably *magnolia hypoleuca.* Lacquer-ware to eat from was generally vermilion, scabbards black. In Frois's list of ten misinterpretations of *things Japanese* in the prologue to his lost introduction to Japan, we find a reference to the lords' scabbards:

> When it is stated that Japanese scabbards are made of gold, this must be understood to mean that the scabbard is wooden and lightly gilded over. The thickness of the gilt depends upon the [financial] capacity of the person the scabbard is made for. (J/F:Historia)

So much for Marco Polo and Columbus's *Zipangu* as El Dorado! The Japanese, like the Balinese, were big on gilt, not *fool's gold,* perhaps, but close to it from the Western viewpoint. Considering the fact that we cannot see inside of objects, the logical view would be that *we* are fools to use solid gold where it is not functional. Unlike leather and felt, lacquer-ware or gilt wood does not get damp and would have helped keep the blade from rusting, so, here, the Japanese item is superior.

1-23+ Our swords have chapes, hilts and pommels;
As nossas espadas tem conteiras, cabos e maçãns;

> Those of Japan have none of these things.
> *As dos Japões nenhuma destas couzas tem.*

The chape is a protective metal fitting for the tip of a "leather or felt" scabbard. The pommel is a big fancy butt for the handle. While the inlaid jewels and other trinkets are functionally worthless, the extra weight improves both the balance (and, thus, control) and the cut (more momentum and reduction of vibration). This was not needed by Japanese swords which had proportionately longer handles gripped with both hands (*viz* 7-2). The *cabo* is problematic for it can refer to either "hilt" (where blade meets guard) or "handle," and Japanese swords had both. The Japanese sword-guard (*tsuba*) was so small in comparison to the huge cross-pieces that literally turned "our" swords into crosses and, the fender-like knuckle-guards sometimes included, that it must have seemed little more than a washer. The grip also seems spare, a mere continuation of the blade in comparison to the more heavily crafted horn handles on Occidental swords. Could Frois have meant the Japanese sword had nothing *we* would consider a proper handle?
..

1-24+ Our swords are tested on lumber or animals;
As nossas espadas se provão em paos ou em animaes;

> Japanese insist upon testing theirs on the bodies of dead men.
> *Os Japões fincão-se pera provar as suas em corpos de homens mortos.*

Orientalism? *No.* Like Damascus steel, the best Japanese swords were sometimes tested if not tempered on flesh. Cooper has a wealth of information on this gory subject including: "a first-class blade sometimes cut through three corpses with one blow, although seven is on record." (see "Sword testing" in the index of C:TCJ) Rodrigues marveled: "the delight and pleasure which they feel in cutting up human bodies is astonishing as is also the way that young boys sometimes indulge in this." (C/R:TIJ). The demand for flesh was such that executed criminals did not suffice even though the bodies were occasionally sewn together to be used a second time! And this continued long after the Warring Period ended. A century after TRATADO, Kaempfer mentions an execution place "where, 'tis said, young people try'd their strength, and the sharpness of their Scymiters, upon the dead bodies, by hacking them into small pieces, scarce an inch long and broad, which they afterwards permitted to be buried." A widely published illustration from this period shows the potential cuts on a headless torso in the same manner as "we" might show the "cuts" of beef or pork, marked on the body of the respective animals, with the difference only that the Japanese illustration names the cuts themselves, whereas the lines on the European illustration divide the meat into named sections.

Lest this makes the Japanese seem inhumane, note that the remains were properly interred. This implies gratefulness toward the flesh/donor, because executed people were usually left to rot, be eaten by beasts, or burned in Japan or the West, where people convicted of especially heinous crimes were *quartered* – pulled apart by horses – not only for painful punishment but because it was popularly believed that broken up people would have a harder time getting it together in the After-life (Since they would seem destined for Hell anyway, I don't see the logic of this, but so be it). In that case, the only thing the victims served was Christian superstition and sadistic spectacle, whereas in the Japanese case, the corpses were not cut up in vain but to improve an instrument that might well be used to save lives.

The closest Western equivalent to sword-testing was dissection. Psychologically it was the

more onerous practice because of the supernatural associations and the accompanying grave-robbing and *Burking* – murdering people to sell their bodies. But this is not to say the Japanese practice was benign. Occasionally, criminal elements and bad people in authority (including one Shogun!) took to testing swords on any poor-looking passerby. This *Sujikire*, "crossroads-cutting," is a favorite theme of Japanese television Easterns but it is hard to say how much actually took place (See 14-6).
..

1-25+ Our cutlasses and scimitar are worn with the convex side downward;
Antre nós os traçados ou alfanjes se trazem com o arcado pera baxo;

The Japanese wear them with the concave side below and the bow on top.
Os Japões os trazem com o concavo pera baxo e o arcado pera sima.

When children play with swords today they tend to wear them hanging straight down. But East or West, they were once hung or stuck into a belt so as to point diagonally or even horizontally. Hence, the top and bottom sides in the contrast. The longer classic Japanese sword, the *tachi,* dangled horizontally from the belt with the convex side downward as did the European weapons mentioned by Frois, but it was out of fashion in 1585 and the *uchigatana* ("striking-sword") was indeed thrust through the belt (see 7-3) diagonally with the curve, barely pronounced enough to notice in artwork, convex-side (that is cutting edge) up. As ER points out, I could also say the cutting edge points *back*. Note that these swords are *always* in the scabbard. The idea was a draw that instantly go to work. This the Japanese got with their new arrangement, which puts the drawn sword out front, whereas ours comes out raised high (better for leading charges than for immediate defense).

1-26+ In rainy weather, we wear felt caps, *beden* [Moroccan capes], rain capes and hats;
Nós uzamos de feltros, bedens *e capas d'agoa e sonbreiros pola chuva;*

Japanese, rich or poor, wear the same very long straw capes and hats.
Os Japões altos e baxos de capas de palha muito compridas e sombreiros de palha.

The Japanese did not need a rain hat for their traveling or working "hat" and "umbrella" were not only homophonic (both *kasa*), but *homomorphic,* which is to say the classic Japanese hat, worn by both sexes, too, was a good deal more effective for rain and, for that matter, UV protection than ours. Not clinging to the head, but supported by a harness, it is better ventilated and more suitable for a muggy climate, too. Their old capes were effective, for the straw is layered like thatch (I do not know if this is true for the *capude palha* (straw cloaks) worn by peasants in North Portugal described by Ball, which Frois may not have known about.)   Japanese kept their *kappa* until modern times but *also* adopted the Portuguese *capa* described by Kaempfer as a "large cloak made of double varnish'd oil'd paper, and withal so very large and wide, that it covers and shelters at once man, horse and baggage." (K:HOJ 1690-2)   It is pleasant to imagine a man wearing one of these crosses between a thatched bungalow roof and a haystack getting out of the rain and shaking himself off like a wet dog.

Rain cloaks made of one form of vegetation or another are found throughout the world (according to Ball, the Chinese, among other things used bamboo-leaves!) but, if I am not mistaken, this natural-wear (for it seems less artificial than paper or cloth) was identified with peasants and what made Japan unique, or rather contrary, was the sight of well-off classes wearing them.

1-27+ We hold walking to be great fun, healthy and refreshing;
Nós temos por grande recreasão, saude e alivio o pasear;

> Japanese have no use for it whatsoever, are puzzled by our doing so, and think we do it for some business or penance. *Os Japões totalmente ho não uzão, antes se espantão e o tem en nós por trabalho e penitencia.*

This contrast held up for centuries. Wondering why Japan couldn't do with less executions and more jail sentences, America's first Ambassador to Japan, Townsend Harris, was told that prisons were not punishment for Japanese because they did not feel a need to walk about in the first place (14-11). The first Japanese Embassy to the West (excluding the 16c mission) contrasted Occidentals who went *out* with Orientals who stay *in* (14-34). Alcock, the first British Ambassador, who arrived in Japan several years ahead of Harris, included *walking* among his "causes of mutual repulsion." Although his book *Capitol of the Tycoon* is about Japan, he makes it clear that this puzzlement belongs to the broader Sinosphere.

> The Chinese and the Japanese, like other people, are very apt to condemn what they dislike or do not rightly understand; and we may rest assured that the foreigner who finds the necessity for 'walking his thousand steps every day,' * or pulling like a bargeman for exercise, or shouting hurrahs with stentorian lungs after dinner for enjoyment, will be regarded as a 'barbarian' by the Chinese, and despised and disliked accordingly . . . (A:COT)

Japanese and Chinese found the idea of "a constitutional" (or a "physique" as Pepys put it closer to Frois's day) ludicrous. Alcock found it explained as a method by which foreign traders computed their accounts! To relax and think, they sat still. Considering the way habitual motion (shaving, washing in the shower and walking) strangely improves creative thought in a way meditation does not, I think the Far East missed out on something good. Who knows but this difference may explain the rise of the West! Exceptions, *for there are always exceptions*, are noted at length in TT-Long. Here, I will only supply a *Faux Frois*.

> *Europeans marching in parades walk as fast or faster than they do normally.*
> *Japanese on parade move one leg at a time so slowly they resemble stickbugs.*
> ..
> This refers to but one of the stylized walks of Japanese pageantry referred to as *neri-aruki,* or "polished walking." There were as many varieties of this walk as those invented by the Ministry of Silly Walks of the *Monty Python Show*, ranging from the rapid and tiny up and down toe-movements used by Shinto float (*dashi*) carriers, which can be seen today, to slow-motion deliberate wobbling and rotating of each foot in turn by courtesans on parade wearing high *geta* clogs and this fish-walk (?) seen by Kaempfer in the train of a great prince in 1692: "Every step they make, they draw up one foot quite to their back, in the meantime stretching out the arm on the opposite side as far as they can, and putting themselves in such a posture, as if they had a mind to swim through the air." (K(S):HOJ)

1-28+ Our swords and valuable goods are highly adorned;
As nossos espadas e cousas de muito preço estão bem guarnecidas;

> Their valuables have no artifice or adornment.
> *As suas preciosas nenhum aparato nem guarnisão tem.*

"In our country there were golden and silver swords made for ritual purposes, but swords for use were not ornate like those of Europe" writes Okada. He overcompensates a bit, for Japanese working swords in Frois's time usually had hilts well adorned with fine metal work. But, even so, it was subtly done, not obvious from a distance. There were none of those globs of jewels that so vulgarize the Occident. The most treasured swords, which were not necessarily used anymore, might not even have a hilt. In Chamberlain's words, "to the Japanese connoisseur the great treasure is always the blade itself, which has been called "the living soul of the Samurai." (C:TJ) Japanese blades are legendary. Rodrigues noted that an ordinary Japanese sword could could "cut a man through the middle in two parts with the greatest of ease"(R(C):TIJ); Montanus claims they could "cut our *European* blades asunder, like Flags or Rushes;" (P:GUG) and Perrine mentions a modern arms collector who "took part in a test in which a sixteenth century Japanese sword was used to cut a modern European sword in two;" and, further, that "there exists in Japan right now a film showing a machine-gun barrel being sliced in half by a sword from the forge of the great fifteenth century maker, Kanemoto II." There is debate on some of these details, but all agree that the Japanese sword was good. What I would like to know is, rather, did the fixation on the blade start because of its excellence or did it become excellent because of the interest in it?

It is said that *millions* of layers of steel of various degrees of hardness had to be hammered out to temper the blade of a sword like this. Even disregarding the above-described "transcendent excellence," (B:MCJ) – a phrase used in 1845, for how else does one describe something as sharp as a razor that can cut nails without notching or bending? (P:GUG)! – the elemental layered and etched beautyof the layers of steel (for which there is a rich aesthetic vocabulary) on the blades of the best Japanese swords impress a person with a modicum of taste far more than glittery jewels. Western aesthetics was, and I fear, still largely is, the aesthetics of the child, or the magpie, rationalized as adult by the value – i.e. high price – of trinkets. Valignano in 1583, does not go so far as to call jewels trinkets; but when he describes old sword blades – in particular, one that "had no adornment of any type, nor gold, but is only a blade of pure iron" for which the King of Bungo paid 4,500 ducats – together with tea utensils and *sumie* (black ink paintings), as the Japanese equivalent of our jewels, he pens a fine paragraph on the Japanese point of view including this line: ". . . at least the things they buy and value so highly serve for something; and, for that reason, the imagination that leads them to pay so much for them is less faulty than that of Europeans who buy little stones that have no use." (in V(A):S&A). Almost a decade later, Miguel=Valignano turns about and makes a spirited defense of jewels, pointing out that, unlike the "tea kettles made of earth, clay or iron," or "piece of paper with a single tree, bird or something painted with black ink black ink" that were terribly expensive *in Japan alone,* pearls were valuable because their worth was recognized not only in Europe but equally throughout Asia and Africa. This proto-free-market rationalization makes sense because Europe had no fine art, in the modern sense of the word, to speak of. Perhaps M=V subconsciously realized there was a weak point in the argument for the value of the pearls was further bolstered by this: "it seems even nature demands this price, for there is a wonderful shine and luster in these gems, some of which can be seen to shine even from afar, and many have the astonishing power to ward off disease or serve as medicine to save human life." (J/S:DM) Leo=Valignano gamely replies that, the best thing would be to find those "tiny rock-like things," sell them to the Portuguese and buy something of aesthetic worth, i.e. the tea kettles. (See TT-Long for the full quotes).

..
The question of whether this or that part of their own culture is or is not internationally viable is *still* discussed in Japan. Such a multi-cultural perspective is part of daily life. In the Occident or, at least in the USA, where we tend to assume our culture is globally applicable, the question generally only comes up with respect to political matters: *i.e.* the suitability of democratic rule and individual rights for non-Western cultures. To my mind, *they* have been ahead of us since 1585.

1-29+   We think it a discourtesy for a servant not to remain standing when his master is sitting;
Nós temos por descortezia não estar o servo im pé quando o senhor estaa asentado;

They think it poor breeding for a servant not to sit, too.
E elles por mao insino não se asentar tambem o criado.

"Our" requirement is cruel for the tired servant, and, even today, we find employers (the new masters) forcing employees to stand out of respect to themselves or customers. But the second half of the contrast is not the result of Japanese being kind enough to allow their servants to rest. It is because Japan shared the extreme *up-down consciousness* of much of South East Asia and the Pacific island cultures where the superior had to be *literally* exalted. K'tut Tantri writes of a Raja in 1930's Bali who would not go under an overpass for fear of losing his dignity should anyone chance to look down on him. They had to stop the car so he could get out and walk over it. (REVOLT IN PARADISE). Heusken, translator for the first United States Ambassador to Japan, described an outing of "His Magnificent Majesty" of Siam: "All the bridges on the route of the Royal Gondola are removed because Royalty cannot bear to pass underneath a path where others place their feet." Also, for this reason one seldom sees two-story houses in Siam." Japanese too could be ridiculously literal. To fold a wife's clothing on top of a husband's would disrespect him, to use a book as a pillow would disrespect the author. It is surprising that Japanese ever allowed the woman superior position in sex! Bowing levels varied minutely to reflect the relative social position of the parties. It still does. Since status is gained with age, the angle of the upper part of the body bowing becomes closer and closer to the vertical. This is, of course, the precise opposite of the case with a certain male part; and I have seen any number of cartoons demonstrating this as an inverse rule of thumb (the *open hand* is shown in front of the body with the thumb demonstrating a youth's erection and an elder's bow, the index finger as a young man's erection or late-middle-aged bow, the baby finger as a youth's bow and an old man's erection, and so forth.)

In 1582/3, Valignano put the contrast more broadly, "To pay honor, *others* stand up, the Japanese sit down." (my italics – S:VMP)   Here, Valignano may be too quick to put Europe in the majority. Since it is convenient to have servants up and running about doing things, I would bet the world is split half-and-half on this one. Even Europeans understood what *lowering* oneself meant. Take this passage from the *Voyage of Van Linschoten.* When elephants and their keepers pay their respect to the authorities,

> the elephants come to the dore and bowe when any thing is given, they kneele on their knees *with great lowliness* [and thankefulnesse] for the good deedes so done unto their keepers (which they think bee done unto themselves)."(my *italics*).

A footnote says the English translator has written "lowliness" for the Dutch word meaning "reverence!"

1-30+   We use black for mourning;
Nós uzamos do preto por dó;

The Japanese white.
E os Japões do branco.

Today, *white* is far less prevalent than *black* at Japanese funerals. This is partly due to Western influence, but the fact is that the use of white in Japan was never as absolute as in neighboring Korea, where it is still *the* color of bereavement (and worn all the time by the elderly as if to say *"I'm ready to go!"*) or China, from where, Rodrigues wrote, the custom came. Even in Frois's time, Japanese men of the *bushi* (samurai) class, at least, only wore white to their *own* funeral, i.e., when committing *seppuku* (formal *harakiri*). Otherwise, they tended to wear dull-black hemp and, as Frois himself noted in a letter Englished by Willis, bonzes wore fine black upper garments to funerals. This makes sense, for the *dark=sad* metaphor is as much part of the Japanese language, as it is of ours. *White*, on the other hand, as befits a color made of the entire spectrum of light, boasts a more complex semiology. It is both the color of the *purity* at the heart of Shinto and the metaphorical "unknowing" of Zen Buddhism. Together with *red*, it comprises the male half of the traditional pair of festive colors. Sometimes the pure, festive and the mourning aspects of white could and were fused, and I have read that "The Japanese bride goes to be married in a pure white mourning robe, which is intended to signify that henceforth she is dead to her old home and her parents, and that she must henceforth look upon her husband's people as her own" (Lorimer in S:MQTJ), but this marriage-as-death idea was developed *much* farther in parts of China and South East Asia. Today, Japanese have little or no consciousness of it and the white veil or cap over the head, which once was "her destined shroud" (B:MCJ), is now known only as a "horn-hider," (*tsuno-kakushi*), a visible reminder that the bride is studying to be good despite her devilish female nature. In other words, the black and white contrast is not so black and white.

But fact never stopped topsy-turvyism. Montanus, in 1670, took the idea all the way to absurdity: "To be clad in Black or Scarlet, amonst them signifies Triumph or Joy, but their Mourning for loss of Friends and other Disastors, is White." (M:EEJ) I have *never*, I repeat, *never!* found black so described by Japanese.

On the other hand, I *have* found white mourning in the West. *Plenty of it.* According to Montaigne, Argive and Roman ladies wore white mourning as ours used to and should have continued to do, if they had taken my advice." He claimed that "there are entire books written about this question." (M(F):CEM). And, more significantly, A. H. Oliveira Marques, writing about Frois's Portugal – Portugal no less! – claimed that whitish or yellowish homespun or sackcloth was the standard "badge of mourning" during the Middle Ages, when only the King and Queen were permitted the luxury of black cloth. Even nobles were not allowed it and it wasn't until the early 16c that it became the official color of mourning. This was unfortunate for many. When Philip (Felipe) II (King of Spain, Portugal (and *mucho* more)) died in 1590, black fabric "began to fetch black market prices" and so many "poor people who could not afford the appropriate black mourning garb were thrown in prison" that "Philip III had to modify the requirements, allowing the poor simply to wear unadorned hats."(E:MP) We tend to think of dark as natural and light as artificial, but the fact most fabrics are naturally closer to white than black probably ensures that the crude clothing favored by most cultures for mourning will be whitish. (The relationship of this natural white and shiny white, which became proof of spiritual purity, gets a page more in *TT-Long* if you are interested).

1-31+ When we walk, we lift up our clothing in front so it is not soiled;
  Nós quando caminhamos alevantamos os vestidos por diante pera os não sujar;

  The Japanese lift it up so high from behind that the entire north is bared.
  Os Japões os alevantão tanto por detrás, que lhe fica todo o norte desquberto.

Today, with our high-heels, it makes sense to lift up in front, but I am not sure why that would have been the case in Frois's time unless it was because keeping a clean front was more important than a clean rear. The Japanese side is easier for Japanese sandals would have flicked up mud, even if the amount would have been lessened by the shortness of the heels (1-59+) and, for a man, the rear is less revealing than the front. Tucking up was standard practice and there is even a name for it (*shiri-karage*) that includes the word buttocks (*shiri*), though only the foreign visitors made a big deal of it. I did not know Latins used "north" that way until reading this contrast. Japanese women, not surprisingly, kept their "norths" covered, and only tucked up – less radically, to be sure – in the front.

1-32+ With us neither commoner nor noble dare reveal so much as a little toe when accompanying his master; *Antre nós os pajens e fidalgos acompanhando seus senhores não lhe á-de aparecer hum dedo do pee;*

Japanese on the road with their master may roll their breeches up clear to their groin. *Os Japões quando os acompanhão polas ruas arregasão os calsões [até às] verilhas.*

If Europeans found their inferiors' nudity insulting, and professed to be disgusted by it, Japanese rather enjoyed it. This attitude lasted well into the Edo era, when Issa wrote haiku of freezing cold winter moon-shine congealing on the rumps of butt-proud footmen. In Japan, a lord would be proud of, rather than embarrassed by the magnificent *gluteus-maximae(?)* on his charges, though he himself remained covered. They were not prurient. The dignity of office forced them to wear too much for the summer and too little for the winter. Other haiku by Issa show his enjoyment of the discomfort of the *daimyo* (feudal lords) in their regular parades back and forth from Edo from the point of view of a poor man, who could lounge naked in the shade or sit at his *kotatsu* heater and watch the big-shots on parade suffer.

Today, the way many Muslims require women to wear veils seems oppressive to "us." But, we (especially in the USA) forget that we too force women to cover their breasts and both sexes to cover their genitals and these laws are at heart based on religion, "our" Adam and Eve *just-so story*. And "we" have not only done this to ourselves but, less forgivably, to others. Read what European ideas of Christian "modesty and propriety" did to the lives of the once nude men in North Mexico in the early 17c.

. . . In order for an indian to return to his lands with clothing for himself and his wife, he will spend half a year or more working in some mining camp or at one of the Spaniard's settlements, especially if the clothing is at all elegant, which they like. This is the degree to which nudity has been uprooted . . . (R(R&A&D):HOT7-7)

To Jesuit Andrés Péres de Ribas, walking "forty or fifty leagues" to work for months or even years at no small risk of death was considered a good bargain, for clothing, considered the *sine qua non* for Christian=civilized living. In the face of such sartorial imperialism, we who do not think the desert religions should dictate their rules of clothing to the rest of the world, are thankful to the Japanese for proving that bare skin and civil society are not intrinsically at odds.

1-33+ We spit at any time;
Nós em todo tempo deitamos o cuspinho fora;

Japanese normally swallow their sputum.
Os Japões commumente emgolem pera dentro os escarros.

"We" who? In England, Frois could have pissed in the corner of a room without an eyebrow being raised, but if he dared the tiniest spit in a Dutch home he would have been brained by a frying pan (LR). There is some irony here, for in the 20c, it was Japanese men who spit too freely for the taste of most of us, who forgot that not long ago we were world-class spitters (This goes particularly for my countrymen – Dickens and Trollop entertain us with pages of outlandish depictions of tobacco-chewing Americans who never let up whether it was in a gale at sea or the floor of the Senate). But 20c Japanese men only did it outdoors. Indoors, the existence of *tatami* (straw mat) ruled out all expectoration. It is curious that the Japanese of Frois's time also refrained *outside*. Okada wonders if it might have been considered impolite. Because most body noises have not bothered Japanese (see 6-60), my guess is that sputum was either considered particularly impure or, like hair and nail clippings, something to be guarded from black magic. But there is another type of expectoration we do but Japanese do that was probably true in Frois's day as it was when I lived in Japan:

We readily blow our noses and can not abide continued sniffling;
Japanese find nose-blowing gross, while sniffling aloud all day long!

In 1-19, an English translation of Rodrigues mentions "nose-blowing," but I suspect it may be misleading, for in many languages (including Japanese with *fuku* and Portuguese with *assoar*) the same verb is used for *blowing* and *wiping*. Frois and others also miss the bodily function considered by some "a privilege of the male sex," that has aroused by far the most international controversy – judging from countless *letters to the editor* in English language papers in Japan – in the latter half of the 20c: namely, *tachi-shoben* or "standing-urination." Japanese men are infamous for doing it practically anywhere at any time. *Senryu* about wise guys pissing on signs forbidding it go back hundreds of years but I will not Faux Frois it because "we" might have been equally, or more flagrant at that time. I recall that Kipling was furious at the new-fangled automobile because it endangered the lives of men relieving themselves by the road-side.

..

~~~~~~

1-34+   The swords we wear are welded with one hand;
A espada que se singe antre nós se joga com huma mão;

        Those of Japan are very heavy and all are welded with both hands.
        As dos Japões, como são muito pezadas, todas se jogão com anbas.

European swords are thought to have lightened up to complement firearms. The rapier took this development to its spinal conclusion in the following century, while the Japanese sword did not change, thanks to firearms being banned (except for some hunting and parades) and a more reverent attitude. By this, I do not so much mean love for the precise form of the traditional sword so much *as the manner in which it was held.* Polite drinking – a mark, not just of formality, but *sincerity* – was done with two hands. As a custom, this apparently comes from China, where Ball writes –

Both hands are used to pass anything, therefore a Chinese is not to be considered clumsy who hands any small articles, such as a cup of tea, in this manner: it would be thought the height of rudeness to do otherwise, for it would evince an unwillingness to take the little trouble necessary.

I feel there is more to this. Cupping an object with two hands seems to sanctify it and affect the cupper. *Something flows between person and thing.* I do not know what it is, but I have felt it. A one-handed grip generally does not satisfy the man who puts his whole heart into his swordsmanship, or the country that understands and admires that type of true dedication. There is no verb for *centering* and being *centered* in Japanese, but it is that English word that comes to mind here.

1-35+ We wear leather shoes and nobles felt ones;
Nós uzamos de sapatos de couro, e os fildalgos de veludo;

>Japanese, high and low, wear sandals made of rice straw.
Os japões altos e baxos de al[pa]rcas feitas de palha d'arroz.

As mentioned twice earlier, Europe is humid in the winter, Japan in the summer. The latter guarantees ringworm (the bane of GI's in Vietnam, who lost more hours of active duty through this fungus – of the foot, calf and crotch – than to combat injuries!) if one wears hot clothing or shoes. It pains me to think of what suffering the spread of Western footwear has caused to people who happen to live in places with sultry summers. Yet, the Japanese have not always been so kind to themselves. Illustrations of Classic times (Heian Era (794-1185)) show the Japanese nobility wore boat-like closed shoes reflecting the influence of the equestrian culture of the less humid continent. That Japanese, in the long run, did not go that way proves common sense can sometimes beat high fashion.

Frois's "high and low" in the Japanese side of the equation is right, and the rhetoric (all classes using cheap material) understandable, but explanation is called for. Rice *straw* or not, the finely woven *zori* of the wealthy and the crudely macramé *waraji* of the poor (and retirees, bonzes, pilgrims, etc.) were, stylistically, and price-wise, a world apart. I think this would have been better:

>*In Europe, poor people usually can not afford to wear shoes.*
In Japan, even the poor always have footwear.

Many European poor went barefoot. Otherwise Cruz (1569-70) would not have noted that *shoes were so cheap many of the poor could walk about shod in China*. The only exception in Japan was the Eta (next to the Imperial family, the only blood lineage, or *caste,* once treated seriously in Japan) who slaughtered animals, cured hide, worked leather and might have made leather footwear were *not allowed* to wear anything on their feet.

The victory over Chinese fashion was brief. Today, sandals are seldom worn by Japanese. The men, like men everywhere, are slaves of corporations who demand they follow Western fashion, and men in small companies who have the freedom to choose would rather fight athlete's foot than risk their toes on the crowded subway – they evidently aren't as brave as women who do not hesitate to wear toeless shoes. And what sandals *are* found in Japan today are mostly hideous plastic slippers.

1-36+ In Europe, a noble would have to be mad to go barefoot before a prince;
Antre nós em Europa seria doudice yr hum fidalgo descalso diante de hum príncipe;

>In Japan, it is improper to wear shoes in the presence of any lord.
[Os Japões] tem por mao insino yr calsados diante de quaisquer senhores que sejão.

This is pretty much the same as 20+ above. I changed "[a mark of] bad learning" (my attempt to approximate the original) to the simple "improper." Content-wise, it bears noting that thanks to their cooler footwear, Japanese feet/socks would not have stunk as ours certainly would have. Still, considering the facts that feet get dirty when shoes are removed outdoors, I feel that the Occidental practice is the more practical one. And, since taking off a hat is relatively easy, I cannot help wondering if it encouraged us to treat our equals like superiors. Who knows but that hat-removing cultures might not have a greater tendency toward equality than shoe-removing cultures.

1-37+ We enter our houses wearing our shoes;
Nós emtramos nas cazas calçados;

> In Japan, that is impolite and shoes must be left by the door.
> *Em Japão hé descortezia e hão-se de deixar os sapatos hà porta.*

There seems to be a larger pattern here: the Pacific island cultures with the custom of removing footwear before one's superior also happen to have finely woven matting – usually made by women for their dowries – which required bare feet inside a dwelling. For cleanliness's sake this had to be. Japanese matting, *tatami,* may be resilient enough to serve as a judo mat, but the sharp edges on soles and nail-heads would damage it, and dirt quickly works its way into the weave.

Removing shoes, the Jesuits were quick to discover, could be inconvenient. As Valignano noted, it meant they could never go anywhere without *komono* (literally "little-people") child-servants "to keep count of the shoes, for to do otherwise was to risk walking home untrod on the street" (n.77 in A:VS). This was not so much because shoes were stolen as they got lost amid hundreds of other shoes – even today, it can be like trying to find a car in a parking lot – or inadvertently worn away by the wrong party. The shoe-carriers were still around when the West came back. Heusken, translator for the first American Ambassador called the shoe-bearer (and the umbrella bearer) his shadow.

Japanese sometimes had trouble themselves. Legend has it that many people took off their shoes to board the first trains and were disappointed not to find them waiting for them when they arrived at their destination. The train ride of modernity is safely over, but the custom of removing shoes remains. What *tatami* started now applies to carpet and clean wooden floors as well. Japanese today generally trade in their Western-style shoes for slippers at the office, and there is often a special rack or container with slippers for guests at homes as well. But all is not well, for unlike the open-heeled traditional *geta* or *zori*, the Western shoe, which modern Japanese seem stuck with, does not easily shake off, so salesmen, messengers and others who for whatever reason do a lot of coming and going are either wizards with the shoe-horn, which usually hangs by the door, or have permanently scrunched down heels!

Morse has found the sole exception to the shoes-off-at-the-entrance rule. Like the clothes "folding" (1-16+), it is an instance of the topsy-turvy dead.

> When the body is carried out of the house, the men performing this function do not remove their clogs as they enter or leave; hence, if one is seen trying on his first clogs on the mat, his friend will say, "Please do not do it; it is a bad sign." (M:JDD)

1-38+ We roll up only our sleeves to wash our hands and face;
Nós pera lavar as mãos e o rosto arregasamos os pulsos somente;

> Japanese bare themselves down to the waist to do the same.
> *Os Japões pera o mesmo effeito se despem nus da cinta pera sima.*

If it is easy to do, and 1-9+ shows it was indeed, stripping to the waist is much more hygienic, for it allows the neck to be included in the face-wash, preventing ring-around-the-collar and, for men, infection of hair follicles. To restate and enlarge upon a weak contrast, ease of dressing and undressing encouraged cleanliness. Here is Kaempfer, one hundred years after Frois:

Besides, as they can undress themselves in an instant, so they are ready at a minute's warning to go into the bagnio. For they need but untie their sash, and all their cloaths fall down at once, leaving them quite naked, excepting a small band [loincloth], which they wear close to the body about their waste. (K:HOJ)

1-39+ The obeisance we show by placing a knee on the ground;
As cortezias que nós fazemos com pôr hum jiolho no chão;

The Japanese show by prostrating themselves, legs, arms and head close to flat on the ground. *Essas fazem os Japões com se pôrem debruços com os pés e mãos e a cabeça quasi no chão.*

Europeans reserved the more extreme forms of two-legged prostration for God or, once in a lifetime, for their goddess: asking a woman's hand. In the West, it seems that only the Pope lies down on the ground – not quite in the style of the Japanese, who always folded their bodies up as they went down (and unlike Muslims, too, for they reach their arms *out*) – or, rather, asphalt, when he kisses it immediately after getting off the airplane.

As far as I know, the Japanese do not prostrate themselves before their gods. Shinto or Buddhist, they may hold their hands together and lightly nod their head or bow, but that is generally it. There is nothing like our kneeling on both legs. Obeisance toward superiors, especially the most powerful is a different matter. Jesuits in Japan had to learn how to show obeisance in the Japanese manner to survive. See Rodrigues (R(C):TIJ) for more details on bowing. I shall only add one thing neither Frois and Rodrigues mentioned: the wordless, but auditory element of Japanese obeisance.

We bow or kneel silently or while saying appropriate courteous words;.
They do so while making sounds like someone about to expectorate or hissing snakes.

The first mention of these weird noises which seem to say *"I am tense and awed! I am tense and awed!"* may be by the English Captain Saris: "... and then clapping their left hand within their left, they put them downe towards their knees, and so wagging or mouing of their hands a little to and fro, they stooping, steppe with small steps sideling from the partie saluted, and crie *Augh, Augh..*" (LR) (Readers wishing to know more about this "strange but impressive way of bespeaking reverence" (Alcock) which is still common in Japan though prostration is not may find a whole page in *TT-Long*.)

In the mid-19c, when Japanese still prostrated themselves, Westerners, who no longer dropped to one knee in the manner described by Frois, experienced mixed feelings not felt in Frois's time, when we took inequality for granted. Some may have been delighted to find old-fashioned obeisance – as W.H. Hudson was thrilled to meet a country maid in England who could still do a proper courtesy – and some Westerners in Japan were delighted to find a maid who went down on their "her little knees" and even "her little nose," as Littlewood notes, but Usanian visitors also criticized what they considered to be excessive servility and humiliation. Young Heusken, shortly after arriving in Japan to assist the American Consul was impressed with the way he was bowed down to but,

The sight of all these human beings, as good as I am or even better, on their knees began to disgust me. Here a white-haired old man bent his trembling knees and lowered his venerable brow; there a young girl turned her lovely face towards the ground and remained in a humiliating posture. It is certainly an excessive honor to see all the beauties of Japan on their knees before oneself; but this honor did not please me; if I had been allowed at least to kneel with her, this thing would have had a different complexion. (H(V&W):JJ)

1-40+ We wear hats of thick cloth that are square or round;
Nós uzamos de barretes de cantos ou redondos de pano;

> Japanese ones are silk, some pointed and others shaped like bags.
> *Os Japões de barretes de seda, huns agudos e outros feitos hà feisão de sacos.*

I do not see much of a contrast between the hats as Frois describes them, unless he means that ours with corners and roundness are real geometric forms, while theirs are ugly points and bags. Moreover, the great poet Bashô, who was born about the time Frois wrote, is usually shown wearing a hat the shape of a cake about two layers high that is neither pointed, nor bag-like. Before and after Frois wrote there was a never-ending gallery of hats in Europe and Japan that defy easy contrast. This is a subject best discussed in pictures.

1-41+ With us, a patch is a lowly thing;
Antre nós hum remendo é couza mui baxa;

> In Japan, even princes put a high value on kimonos and *dobuku* made of nothing but patches. *Em Japão estima hum principe em muite hum* quimão *ou* dobuqu *todo feito de remendos.*

..

The tea masters and poet-aesthetes were patchwork enthusiasts and nobles liked to be "in." This patchwork (*hagi*), mostly of old brocade and other fine material (including not a little gold), was a far cry from that of the poor. The rage became an aesthetic tradition, for two hundred years later, Issa writes of a similar patchwork of paper kimonos – the poor old man's winter dress – which was glued rather than sewn together from a collage of *hanko*, reusable paper scraps from old books, calendars, paintings, manuscript, etc.. *Dobuku*, if you recall, are outside-wear vests.

kiritsuki no bi o tsukushitaru kamiko kana – issa (d.1823)

> milking the beauty
> of collage for all it's worth
> this paper robe

1-42+ In Europe, all our cloth is cut with scissors;
Em Europa todo vestido se corta com tizoura;

> In Japan, all is cut by blades.
> *Em Japão todo se corta com faca.*

I have had tiny *shears*, which is to say, cutting blades where the fulcrum is the end of the handle – or, tong-blades – introduced to me as "Japanese scissors." They are beautiful for their simplicity but hard to keep in correct trim, so it is easy to see why knives were preferred. A specific knife (*monotachigatana* ("thing-cut-off-sword") or, simply, *monotachi*) was indeed used for tailoring in Japan. So why didn't the Japanese use *real* scissors – i.e., two blades on a common fulcrum between the handles and blades, that opening make a cross? Logically speaking, if one blade is sharp enough – and Japanese were the best blade-makers in the world – two are not needed. Still, it is puzzling that a culture where something as complex as guns were copied=learned=adopted in a jiffy did not adopt scissors from the Chinese. Some scissors may have made it to Northern Kyushu centuries earlier and others definitely arrived at the same island the first guns arrived at, Tanegashima in the mid-16c. This latter variety is said to have sharpened itself with each use.

1-43+   In Europe, it would be considered effeminate for a man to carry and use a fan;
Em Europa se teria por cousa afiminada trazer hum homem abano e abanar-se com elle;

In Japan, a man always has a fan in his belt and would be considered vulgar and wretched otherwise. *Em Japão hé baixeza e miseria não o trazer sempre na sinta e uzar delle.*

The original says a man would not "fan" (*abanar-se*) a fan (*abano*). Because "fan a fan" doesn't work in English, I changed the verb to "use." But using *fan* as a verb would bring out "our" prejudicial attitude better, for *fanning* suggests "fluttering," a fine and, therefore, feminine movement. If you have ever faced a large barracuda fanning its fins, you can imagine a samurai with a fan would look tough, even if the fan was rarely if ever used as a lethal weapon (as in the Japanese TV Easterns). No, seriously, in the days before air-conditioning, only a masochist could have summered in Japan without a fan. The same thing could be said of most of South East Asia.

That might seem the end of it. But fans, like so much "simple" technology, are no one-trick wonder like air conditioning; they were good for many things, three pages-worth in *TT-Long*. Summing up long 17c and 19c passages, the fan served the receive dainties or alms, "in lieu of a whalebone switch," "instead of a ferule for the offending schoolboy's knuckles, as a sign for the moment one's head was to be struck off" (B:MCJ:1841), as armor, Buddhist priest's, Noh dancers and umpires props, a winnow, to fan open flowers that are slightly open, as declarations of love, a sign of dismissal (S:JDJ:1891), cooling soup, cooling people fast by dipping an oil-paper fan into water before fanning (M:JDD), as Baeddeckers with road maps, miles, inn recommendations, prices, etc. which the Dutch were not permitted to buy (K:HOJ: 1692), as notepads for spies (M:BGE: 1858), as dildos for women on a legendary all-woman island where the wind was their only lover (this in senryû). Distributed free for the dog-day *bon* dances – folk dances, where they serve for sitting on, cooling off and enhancing dance movements, they now serve as advertisements. The only two I clearly remember were graced with the face of an actor and florescent fireflies on one side, and an advertisement for a local store and a warning on safe driving, respectively on the other.

When it comes to fans, Ball, in *Things Chinese* waxes at far greater length than Chamberlain in his *Things Japanese*. The variety of fans is stupendous. It covers all those found in Japan *and* "octagonal, sexagonal, or polygonal" shaped screen fans; materials ranging from the usual bamboo and paper to silk actually spun on the frame by the silk-worm(!), palm leaf, and goose-feathers arranged in bone or ivory handles in a lyre shape, huge imitation wooden fans used to prevent officials from seeing one another and having to stop when meeting on the highway and, most incredible, fans of pure air, which is to say "open-work spaces are left in walls of the shape." Only one item, the *folding fan* would seem to come from Japan.

1-44+   With us, nobles and princes are preceded by torches of wax;
Antre nós se uza de tochas de sera que vão diante dos fidalgos e principes;

In Japan, they are made from long bundles of old, dry cane or bundles of straw.
Em Japão de molhos de canas velhas, seqas, compridas, ou molhos de palhas.

While Japanese commonly used portable lanterns by this time, the torch, as the ancient method, was probably considered more proper for nobility engaged in ceremony. The common Japanese term for torch is *taimatsu*, literally, "pine-light," because pine resin was generally the fuel, though it was not always rubbed on to pine. The straw might have been crudely bound by peasants, but a proper torch had it bound up within a bamboo (the variety of bamboo in question is the arrow-bamboo *yadake* that I consider a cane) framework.

This is one of the ten items Frois gives as an example of misinterpretation of terms in the Prologue to his missing summary of Japan. He writes that if it were reported that Nobunaga [the Shogun] met the Visitador [Valignano] on such and such a mountain in the light of "two thousand torches" a person would "have to know that they were not of wax, . . . because there is no beeswax in Japan and Japanese torches are made from straw;" and "likewise for India" when a "torch" is mentioned they are talking about a lamp of oil and not beeswax, "so from the European point of view, they are not torches." (J/F:*Historia* v.1) Linguistically, Frois has made an interesting point, but I may be missing something, for this still seems a piddling contrast to me unless the bee's wax has some lofty significance whereas cane and straw seem humble and even wretched materials to "us."

1-45+ In Europe, one would be strangely regarded for baring so much as one leg to warm himself before a fire; *Em Europa descobrir hum pé ao fogo pera se hum aqentar estranha-se;*

> Japanese warming themselves, stand and openly bare their entire posteriors to the fire, without feeling any shame. *Em Japão quem estaa im pé ao fogo pera se aquentar descobre em claro sem pejo toda a trazeira.*

Had Frois been writing in England fifty years earlier, the contrast might have been a bit more difficult. According to a Law passed by King Edward VI in 1548, "Any knight under the rank of a lord, or any other person [is forbidden to wear] any gowne, jaket or cloke unless it be of sufficient length on a man standing upright to cover his privy member and buttokkes." (from A. Parsons: FACTS AND PHALLUSES, 1990) But Europe turned prudish while lack of shame with respect to revealing ones private parts in a non-sexual connection survived Japan's feudal era to shock the 19c West. It was one thing for fishermen to toss books with dirty pictures up to Perry's Black Ships to the joy of the sailors and the anger of the ship chaplain – ports are known for such behavior – and quite another to have a "respectable Japanese" gentleman at home open up his robe and, "taking his privities in his hand," ask "the names of the various parts in English" in plain sight of his mother, wife and daughter, as reported to Townsend Harris, the first American ambassador to Japan by his highly reputed Dutch-American translator-secretary Heusken! (Journal entry: Jan. 21, 1857 H:CJTH).

On the other hand, 19c Japanese found the décolletage of Western women – not to mention emphasizing the figure by various devices – shameful in the extreme and, at first, even took umbrage at the showing of nudes in painting exhibitions, because they had no similar tradition of figure worship. If the Japanese were as rude to *us* as we were to them, they would surely have called us a *figure-idolizing culture*. And, I think, it is because of our infatuation that we periodically over-react by making all nakedness taboo. Call it cultural schizophrenia if you wish.

The eccentric Zen abbot Sengai, who lived in Issa's time, painted himself doing just what Frois describes, with his testicles in plain view; and, punning on their euphemistic name, "golden gems," wrote an accompanying poem about breaking out the gold for all to share! (*kintama-o uchi-akete* . . .) (LR My book is with my library in Japan; the painting is clear in my mind.).

1-46+ We consider it effeminate for a noble to look in the mirror;
Antre nós ver-se hum fidalgo a hum espelho se tem por obra afeminada;

Japanese nobles all have their mirrors to dress in front of.
Os fidalgos japões pera se vestirem tem commumente todos espelho diante de si.

Okada notes that even *Hagakure,* the classic manual for the samurai, recommends that warriors use a mirror to make certain they are properly dressed and groomed. He adds that looking at the mirror at least once before going out was thought to ward off potential disaster. More generally, the mirror in Japan was considered an instrument of self-knowledge, purity and cleansing. A gift from the gods in Shinto tradition and identified with the redeeming light of the Law, i.e. the moon, in Buddhism, its use by either sex was not thought to be narcissistic but, *reflective* in the moral sense of the word. But, religion aside, the use of a mirror was hardly surprising for men who spent as much time grooming as they did. According to Carletti, whole mornings were spent "combing and tying up their hair, smoothing it with great pains and anointing it with scented oils, to make it glisten." (inC:TCJ)

Basically, Japanese men resembled "our" ancient Celts, warriors who bleached their hair in lime-water and painted their eyelids black, the major difference being that the Celts paid more attention to muscular development and were reported to punish young men who exceeded "the standard measure of the girdle." (Peter Beresford Ellis: *Celtic Women* Constable 1995) By Frois's time, European men were evidently not supposed to care about their own appearance, though the paintings of the time suggest that not a few men did sneak looks into mirrors.

1-47+ With us, one would have to be joking or mad to clothe oneself in paper;
Antre nós vestir-se hum de papel seria escarnio ou doudice;

In Japan, bonzes and many nobles wear paper [dress] with a silk front and sleeves.
Em Japão bonzos e muitos senhores se vestem de papel com a dianteira e mangas de seda.

On the one hand, paper was a high fashion material (1-41+). Robes made of fancy paper (glued together with devil's tongue paste) with a fine lacquered finish (persimmon sap), they were evidently a luxury item in Frois's time. On the other hand, paper robes called *kamiko* soon came to be associated with elderly poets and prostitutes. Believe it or not, the haiku association (i.e. seasonality) of the *kamiko* is with *winter.* (In the 1960's, I once went out with a girl wearing a paper dress. It was summertime. New Orleans. Sultry) Recall that winter is the driest part of the year in Japan, so the paper would not dampen. And, as the homeless know, many layers of paper make remarkably good insulation. There is another angle Frois may have missed, given by Thunberg in 1776, only the elderly were allowed to use paper kimonos. I like that for old age can always use a perk.

1-48+ What we would take for house-wear,
Ho que antre nós hé trazer roupão por caza, –

This the Japanese use [to dress up?], wearing sleeveless *dobuqu* [vest/s] over *katabira* [robe/s]. *Disto uzão os Japões vestindo sobre as* catabiras dobuqus *sem mangas.*

I may well be wrong. All other translations (Japanese, German and French) are: "When we would wear house-wear; The Japanese wear sleeveless *dobuku* [vests] over *katabira*". That is closer to the Portuguese but makes the contrast a mere indoor repetition of 1-4+, i.e. Japanese wear vests over their robes while we do not. But is it not possible that by *vestindo* here Frois may not only mean wear/dressed but *dressed up,* i.e. for going out? Then we would have an *indoor-outdoor* contrast. L' Abbe de T. in the late-17c wrote that "when we go abroad, we commonly put on Cloaks and Hats; they on the contrary wear Cloaks in the House, and lay them aside when they go to Town, . . . (A:HCJ) And a note by Golownin's editor suggests something even more perfectly contrary: *"They [the Japanese] wear habits of ceremony or their Sunday clothes in the house: but lay them aside in going out."* (G:MCJ)   Could Frois have been driving at something like this –

Where we put on informal clothing at home and our best clothing to go out;
They get dressed up to stay home but not to go out.

– but got lost in particulars? This makes sense considering Japanese weather and because, as Frois notes elsewhere (14-34), "we" tend to do our entertaining in public while the Japanese do it at home.   Okada writes the *dobuku* was *de rigor* for what would be called professionals today: magistrates, doctors and tea-masters. But, the question here is whether they wore them inside – i.e. dressing up at home – while practicing their profession, outside, or both.

~~~~~~

1-49+   We wash our clothing scrubbing it with our hands;
Antre nós se lava a roupa esfregando-a com as mãos;

> The Japanese wash, kicking the laundry with their feet.
> *Em Japão a lavão pizando-a aos couces com os pees.*

Years without a washing machine taught me that it is *remarkably* easy to stamp laundry clean in a bathtub.   Not only are leg muscles bigger, but the weight of the body can be put to work. Unfortunately, better clothing requires hand-eye coordination, so all cannot be washed that way. As it happens, some people in the West also used their feet. The washer women in Edinburgh. In Dec. 1815, Thomas Hood (H: WTH), the elder described "great bare-legged women" striding around water clothing on the ground while *"you the lasses might spy / In tubs, with their petticoats up to the thigh, / And instead of their hands, washing thus with their feet, / Which they often will do in the midst of the street..."* Frois must have lived in the Edinburgh in Japan, for in most of Japan I think it was done by hand. In Korea, a real contrast with Europe would have been easier to find, for laundry was *pounded* clean or swung into smooth rocks in rivers, whereas in Japan, such pounding was reserved for new silken-cloth. Be that as it may, the *hand* versus *foot* Topsy-Turvy Sweepstake goes to Herodotus, who pointed out that contrary to the rest of the world (the Greeks?)

> They [the Egyptians] knead dough with their feet, but mud with their hands, and they lift dung with their hands. [The dung seems a gratuitous dig, did others use shovels?]

~~~~~~

1-50+   We carry our handkerchiefs and tissue in our pockets or sleeves;
Nós trazemos lenços e papeis na aljibeira ou manga;

> The Japanese stuff it into their bosom; the more there, the more gallant.
> *Os Japões tudo trazem metido no seio, e quanto mais alevantado é mais primor.*

If the same *aljibeira/algibeira* did not appear in 51+, "purse" would be the more likely translation for "our" *pockets* for the transition from an external purse to an internal pocket was not yet finished so the one word applied to both. But since the first pockets were often purses worn within one's clothing and reached through an unmarked slit (side-seam, etc.) or what Chaucer's Wife of Bath) "his nether purs," i.e., the codpiece, no word can substitute for explanation. As might be expected, the bisexual Shakespeare could not resist playing with these baubles: "Enter AUTOLYCUS. // 'twas nothing to geld a codpiece of a purse; . . . (*Winter's Tale* 4-3)

Frois has cheated a bit here so as not to spoil the contrast. Japanese are famous for carrying things in *their* capacious sleeves as well as open bosoms. I confess I thought *our* practice was confined to magicians, but googling found that Rabelais, who, as might be expected, was also big on codpieces (Gargantua's "purse" was made from the cod of an elephant, and others he drew were so large as to require wheels, etc.), wrote of a sleeve-as-pocket and *Webster's* defined it incidental to explaining an idiom:

> After dinner Panurge went to see her, carrying in his sleeve a great purse full of palace-crowns, called counters, and began to say unto her, "Which of us two loveth other best, you me, or I you?"
>
> *To have in one's sleeve* is to offer a person's name for a vacant situation. Dean Swift, when he waited on Harley, had always some name in his sleeve. The phrase arose from the custom of placing pockets in sleeves. These sleeve-pockets were chiefly used for memoranda, and other small articles. (www.websters-dictionary-online.org)

Frois was not exaggerating about the Japanese, the sash about the lower belly turns the entire garment above the waist into an enormous pocket and the contents were by no means limited to tissue. Reading the testimony of kimonos turned into "warehouses" – men even squeezing in their children and up to seven books and a map according to Isabella Bird, in the 19c (B:UTJ) – one cannot help wondering whether the Japanese were not the model for Jonathon Swift's philosophical linguists at the Grand Academy of Lagado. Bird also notes a gruesome use for sleeves. Women filled them with rocks and jumped in wells or rivers to commit suicide.

There may have been a closer equivalent to this Japanese bosom-stuffing in the West than the sleeves mentioned by Frois. In 1653, Bulwer wrote of the capacious breeches comprising the best part of "the garbe of old English Gallantry," about whom a "Chronologer" wrote "that they bestowed more cost of their Arses than they did on the rest of their whole body. The stuffing that originated in the common practice of bolstering one's manhood expanded to encompass the entire garment and thighs of these breeches aped from the continent got so fat men had to walk bow-legged. A man who fell astray of sartorial law against "wearing Bayes [*baize* = a fine cloth introduced by Dutch and French fugitives and subject to sumptuary restrictions] stuffed in their Breeches" stands in court before a judge and –

> began to excuse himselfe of the offense, and endeavouring by little and little to discharge himselfe of that which he did weare within them, he drew out of his breeches a paire of Sheets, two Table Cloths, ten Napkings, foure Shirts, a Brush, a Glasse, and a Combe, Night-caps, and other things of use, saying, (all the Hall being strewed with this furniture) your Highnesse may understand, that because I have no safer store-house, these pockets do serve me for a roome to lay up my goods in, and though it be a straight prison, yet it is a store-house big enough for them, for I have many things more of value yet within it. And so his discharge was accepted and well laughed at . . (B:A)

1-51+ We use pockets;
   Antre nós se uza de aljibeiras;

   The Japanese, small purses suspended from the belt.
   Os Japões de bolsinhas pinduradas da sinta.

The strings by which the Japanese pouches dangled were the purse strings, so they kept closed naturally. These strings wrapped around the *obi* sash or simply passed under it. To prevent the purses from slipping off, a counter-weight large enough not to slip or be easily tugged through the space between belt and belly (it would catch on the edge of the belt) was tied to the other end of the string. This is the *netsuke,* collected throughout the world today for the fine miniature carving. The pouches were made of leather, cotton or wood (with the last, the two strings pass through the lid). The advantage of a pouch as opposed to a pocket is that they rarely spill things when you sit or lie down. Perhaps for this reason Japanese did not adopt the pocket from the Portuguese or, later, the Dutch. When the West returned 250 years after Frois, pockets were still eye-opening. Morse noted that turning his pockets inside-out searching for something excited the Japanese so much he felt guilty of performing an act to catch their attention whenever it happened. (M:JDD)

1-52+ A purse in Europe is used to carry money;
As bolsas servem em Europa de trazer dinheiro;

In Japan, that of a noble or soldier serve for scent, medicine and flint.
Em Japão as dos fildalgos e soldados servem de cheiros, mezinhas e pederneira.

Japanese men, especially nobles, were *very* big on scent. If *The Tale of Genji* is any indication, they used to roam about all night making love to their women, leaving personal scent trails that could be identified by others a whole day later. Unlike tom cats, the scent was pleasant to most, though rivals no doubt thought it stank to high heaven! A generation after Frois wrote, I am afraid tobacco was the main scent left by all men, gentry or peasant. Bird noted – after her translator tripped and cut his head on the brazier while trying to get a light! – that Japanese men even woke up for a puff at night! Medicine might be carried in a wooden or enameled purses, if such is the right word for them. Frois forgot to mention "purses" for writing equipment (I think pipes came later). We shall return to *flint* in chapter 14. Not everyone was allowed to carry one.

1-53+ We bathe at home to completely avoid the eyes of others;
Antre nós a jente lava o corpo em suas cazas muito escondido;

In Japan, man, woman or bonze, they bathe in a public bath or, by night, in front of their homes. *Em Japão homens, molheres e bonzos em banhos publicos ou à noite aas suas portas.*

As Rodrigues observed, in Japan "neither nobles or common folk felt shame in stripping to their loin-cloths or birthday suits for wrestling" or "other activities which require the body to be naked or nude." (R(C):TIJ) We, apparently, did. Some modesty may be natural to our species, but I think it safe to say that for this contrast "we" are in the cultural minority, the odd man out. The Christian mythology of shame and sin made Europe, once a land of naked Pics and barely robed Greeks, pathologically averse to nudity, even as we continued to worship the ideal human body! Still, we were not always the filthy hydrophobic barbarians shown in the movie *Shogun*, either. Europe once enjoyed public baths and we even read of a 14c England, surely Christian, where "men and women could go naked, or nearly naked, through the street to the baths in a way which today would be impossible, except perhaps at a bathing resort, or for undergraduates living out of college at one of the major British universities. (LR: but know date because of this: "The daughters of the nobility thought it an honour to parade naked in front of Charles V.") Unfortunately, baths were put out of business by the Plague and the Reformation, and syphilis (brought back from Africa or America), probably, drove the final nail in the coffin. But even in the heyday of the European public bath, "we" never bathed as often as the Japanese. Had Frois been in Japan *a hundred years later*, he might have written this:

> *Our gentry bathes occasionally and many of us almost never bathe.*
> *Japanese rich or poor bathe every day.*

The Jesuits, like the English depicted in SHOGUN had to learn to bathe more often as part of their efforts to accommodate the Japanese. But they did not have to bathe every day, for that practice developed later after public baths became popular, then taken-for-granted in the Tokugawa Era (1603-1868). This occurred in Edo (the water-city, now called Tokyo which was nothing in Frois's day), where the first commercial bath-house (*sentô*, literally: penny-hotwater) was opened in 1591. Frois would, however, have seen pay bathhouses in Kyoto, where some (called simply *furuya* =bath-rooms) date back to the Muromachi Era (1338-1573). People had to duck under a low door for the room to maintain its heat. Dark and steamy, they would not have offered the eyeful of mixed genitalia modern readers might imagine and it is debatable how much full nudity existed in mixed baths at this time, for there are reports of wrap-around skirts on women and small loincloths on men.

In ancient times, Japanese used a sweat-house + cold river combination like that found in native American culture. It probably had ritual (shamanistic/shintô purification) significance. In Frois's time most of the public baths were run by Buddhist Temples. Some claim the practice of collective bathing started to clean Buddhist sculptures and the laity who got wet doing so caught the habit. Be that as it may, bathing eventually brought Buddhist brownie points and the faithful were encouraged to bath on certain days where the benefit was thought the greatest. Eventually, in Edo, the daily bath was born. By the time the seclusion ended the bathhouse in Japan was, according to Alcock, "what the baths were to the Romans, and what the cafe is to the Frenchman – the grand lounge," and "passing along the streets of Yeddo on a summer's evening, at every hundred steps a bath-house is visible."

Neither Frois nor Rodrigues directly contrast single-sex bathing in Europe *versus* mixed bathing in Japan (Though, as detailed in *TT-Long*, not all bathing in Japan was mixed sex). Perhaps this is because when Europe *did* have baths, they, too, were mixed. In the 19c, however, it scandalized most Western observers with the exception of Alcock who, opined that mixed bathing served to protect the state; "for, though one woman may plot a deed of vengeance, the history of the world does not record an instance of a conspiracy of women, or of any mixed assembly of men and women, for the enactment of scenes of violence and political convulsions." The Japanese government, eager to please the Western powers, did their best to prevent "promiscuous bathing" (as we called it) but two decades after Alcock, Bird observed that "As I rode through on my temporary biped [she preferred quadruped transportation], the people rushed out from the baths to see me, men and women alike without a particle of clothing." (UTJ) – No wonder they bathed "in front of their homes" – *the better to watch the passerby!*

Mixed bathing was quickly chased out of the cities and only remained in a number of medicinal spas that mostly cater to the elderly. But Japanese public baths – with men on one side, women on the other – only began to close down in the last half of the 20c, as more and more people came to have baths at home. I have fond memories of public baths in Tokyo, a pleasant pandemonium, with little boys pulling around choo-choo trains of linked stools and wash-tubs (gallon-sized pails used for washing prior to getting into the baths), the owner's daughter coming in to clean up with me still washing, etc.. Soon, I fear, few Japanese will have such memories. Another *Faux* Frois:

> *Europeans wash themselves with soap inside of the bath;*
> *The Japanese wash themselves first to keep the bath water clean.*

Japanese are warned not to do this in Western hotels where the bathroom floor lacks a drain.

But to return to Frois's contrast, *a different standard of modesty*: I wish someone would do a book on modesty around the world, for every culture defines the private=shameful and public=showable) in its own way. In Bali, not long ago, women gave birth in public view – with younger children shouting "come on, mommy, I see its head!" – yet people ate individually facing the corner behind closed doors, and there was even a fine for disturbing families while they were eating. Birth, including a ringside view of the vulva, was public, while dining was private. (LR) Japanese may not have minded nudity, but they enjoyed eating together while childbirth was taboo for men (and they would not dream of exposing a child to it). In this sense, they were like us, opposite to the Balinese. Since it is unlikely that one culture should be more immodest than another in every way, it behooves us to think of how Japanese may have been more modest than Europeans in 1585. Frois, elsewhere mentions *feelings*. Japanese hid *them*. Isn't that a type of modesty? We will examine *kissing, embracing* and *eye contact,* all avoided by Japanese (at least in public), later.

1-54+ We wear boots or regular footwear when it rains;
Antre nós pola chuva se trazem botas ou o calsado comum;

> Japanese go barefoot or elevated on wooden chapin with staff in hand.
> *Em Japão ou vão descalsos ou levão chapis de pao e bordões nas mãos.*

Boots would be too hot in the Japanese rainy season.

The two Japanese translations differ on the Japanese footwear and walking aid. Okada writes "wooden shoes with pole in hand," while Matsuda and Jorissen write "raised-sole-shoes (*geta* + a gloss for chapin) with an iron cane." I was tempted to turn the *chapin* into a *clog*, but considering the fact that clogs have solid soles of cork or another light wood, whereas the chapin/chopine/choppines actually had the same stilt-like extensions as found on the Japanese wooden footwear, I decided to use the obsolete word and explain it instead. Basically we are talking about two boards attached at vertical angles to the solid sole – the best resemblance is Π (Thank God for the Japanese in my computer, by which I could easily call up the *pi* symbol!), with a bit more overhang fore and aft. Most Japanese chapin, or *geta,* are not very high, but the type called *ashida* has 4-8 inch high stilts. In Frois's time, they were pretty much used for wading mud puddles. They were later worn by prostitutes in parades and some men in the water-trades (entertainment industry). Though a mountain magician on a single stilt chapin (*tengu-geta*) might use a metal staff, wood was normal.

Within 50 years, some English Dandies stood on high stilts in the sunshine. Bulwer chuckled that these gig-like heeles put them into "so tottering a condition, that when they have spun a while in the streets, [they] usually come hobling down, and in this fashion are emblematically presented to be unstable in all their waies." (*Anthropometamorphosis* 1643). There might be a Japanese origin for this.

1-55+ We make our footwear from stiff, thick leather;
Entre nós fazem o calsado de couro forte e grosso;

> The Japanese make *tabi* [*foot-bags*] of glove leather.
> *Em Japão os* tabis *são de couro como luvas.*

The "leather as with gloves" makes it seem like the *tabi* are contrary, for they become a sort of glove for the feet. They were generally "goatskin" but soon would be cotton.) As they were generally worn with sandals or *geta* providing the soles and, if clean, could be worn indoors, they are not really commensurable with shoes and might better be called socks. Frois might better have written:

We change from our slippers to our shoes when we go out.
They wear their slippers upon their shoes when they go out.

Our socks usually cover the entire foot and do not divide the toes;
Japanese ones looks like horse hooves, for theirs separate the large toe from the others.
..

I cannot help but wonder why Frois did not catch at least the second of the above unless Europeans of his day themselves wore split socks. I once read of an American maid, who, seeing *tabi*, jumped to the conclusion that Japanese had only two toes, which amused her employer's Japanese husband who told her that Japanese, for their part, thought Occidentals lacked heels because their shoes were only raised in the back, rather than being flat or raised on two stilts like Japanese shoes.

Our shoes have heels to prevent them from slipping through the stirrup and to elevate us.
Their shoes, raised on stilts or flat on the ground, are perfectly level and have no heels.

In 18c Edo, the term "heel-less ones" become slang for Westerners. A *senryu* quips "in Maruyama / once in a while they bear / heel-less ones" (OJD) (In this Period of Isolation, the authorities tried to discourage sex with foreigners, and, failing that, the birth of mixed-blood babies. But, occasionally there still were accidents.) Frois did not overlook the *heeled/heel-less* contrast: Occidental male shoes generally did not have heels to speak of in the 16c. But he could have written this:

Our shoes are like boats and usually cover the entire foot;
Their shoes are only raft-like soles held to the foot by a strap between the first and second toes.

Today most Japanese only wear *tabi* when they wear Japanese traditional clothing. Carpenters prove the exception to the rule. Young or old, they wear special *tabi* with rough corrugated rubber soles, thin enough to let one get a feel for whatever lies beneath. (Everyone I have shown my pair ro thinks they are *ninja* shoes!) They are the opposite approach to safety of our heavy steel-plated boots. Japanese want to be able to climb and walk across beams with little danger of falling; we are afraid of things falling on us (or stepping on nails)!

~~~~~~

1-56+ Our gloves fold back at the wrist;
As nossas luvas dobrão-se no colo da mão;

Japanese ones sometimes extend to the elbow.
As dos Japões chegão-lhe às vezes até os cotovelos.

Old paintings show the European of Frois's time with a few inches of the glove turned back like a cuff (the "cuff" itself, originally meaning glove or mitten). While such a cuff might, once in a while, serve to prevent blood or some other liquid from flowing up the wearer's arm, I suspect it is 99% a matter of fashion. The long Japanese "gloves" were open palmed, and would appear to derive from archery arm-guards if it were not for the back of the arm being covered as well as the front. The fingers were usually not covered, so we might better call them arm-sleeves! But the main difference between gloves in Europe and Japan has nothing to do with the above details. To *Faux Frois* it:

> *In Europe, gloves are thought elegant, symbolize power, signal duels and serve romantic ends;*
> *In Japan, they are purely practical tools and nothing else whatsoever.*

As the fan was far more than a fan in the Sinosphere, the glove was, to Europeans, far more than gloves. Kings gave them out as tokens of this or that favor granted to a subject, land-grant recipients could show them to illiterates as proof of their domain, used as a proxy for a man who could not be at his own wedding (*Het handschoentje*), as import duties, to convey bribes, for assassination (poisoned and given to the unsuspecting victim), as gauntlets, i.e., thrown down in front of opponents as a challenge, dropped on purpose by women to pick up a man by having him pick up said glove, etc..

Today, gloves in Japan and in the West are considered to be a female accessory – males only wearing them for work – but in Frois's time gloves were still a predominantly male fashion and were just beginning to catch on with women (thanks largely to the example of Catherine de Médicis, queen consort of Henry II of France, and one person rumored to have used gloves as a weapon for assassination).

~~~~~~

1-57+ With us, it would be madness to wear unfinished clothing;
Antre nós seria doudice trazer o vestido por agorentar;

> Pelt *dobuku* [vests] worn by the Japanese seem just as they were torn off the buck.
> *Os dobuqus de peles dos Japões así os trazem como se tirarão dos veados.*

Japanese tend to preserve natural textures and shapes in their architecture, utensils, food and clothing. The natural grain of the wood was preferred to paint (11-7), unglazed pottery was used for formal occasions (6-30), and clothing was worn as it was woven, in the best form (rectangular) to show off the fabric, rather than the human body beneath. Animal pelts, unlike woven cloth, come in different shapes. We have already seen that the fur side is on the outside (1-13+). By leaving the pelt in its apparently natural shape as well, the material is revealed rather than hidden. If you would wear animal fur, then give the animal its due! (14-37) Another way of putting this is that Japanese value the material (fur or fabric), where Europeans value the tailor. Of course, someone must prepare the clothing in Japan, but the main thing is not *how* clothing is cut, but *what* is cut, if it is cut at all.

~~~~~~

1-58+ Our shoes, boots and slippers have leather soles or removable foot-pads;
Antre nós os sapatos, botas e calsas tem solas ou palmilhas postiças;

> Japanese *tabi* have no separate sole, [and are] just one continuous piece of leather.
> *Os tabis de Japão não tem solas sobre si mas todo o couro hé contínuo.*

Note 55+ explains part of why *tabi* had no soles: they were not worn on hard surfaces, but as socks. A better contrast would be to forget about the *tabi* and say that Japanese shoes, being sandals, were *all* sole. Lacking any cushion (foot pad), a wooden *geta* can be literally jarring. Though stone or brick roads were uncommon, there were some hard stretches even in Frois's time. The greater health of Japanese feet (thanks to open footwear) and joints (thanks to sitting on heels and squatting) may have been one factor allowing this. It is also one reason why everyone wore cheap *waraji* (sandals made of thick twisted straw) for travel: they provided some shock absorption.

1-59+ In Europe, wearing shoes with the foot but halfway in would be ridiculous.
Em Europa seria couza rediqulosa trazer o calsado até meio pé somente;

> In Japan, it is stylish.[1] Only bonzes, women and the elderly fit fully into their shoes. *Em Japão hé primor, e o inteiro hé de bonzos, molheres e velhos.*

Because a Japanese shoe is open and can accept feet of various widths, an entire population can use a single medium size. Frois's contemporary Avila noted the opposite side of the coin: that 'it does not matter if the shoe be an inch or two longer than the foot, because even a child of four summers can wear the shoes of his father or mother.'"(C:TCJ Avila was a merchant contemporary of Frois.)

The idea that it is cool to hang a heel remains until the present day. I can recall being taught by Japanese friends that I did not even need the (too small) largest size, for an even smaller one allowing *more* hang-over was more manly. Since I walk and once ran long-distance on the balls of my feet, I could accept *that*, but I could *never* accept the plastic indoor and bathroom slippers all too common today. They are just too hot – I can remember fearing I'd develop athlete's foot while wearing a close-toed plastic slipper at a dermatologist's office (Or was *that* the idea?). Lacking a toe-grip or thong, these plastic atrocities also slip off little feet.

1. *Primor* Translation. The same *primor*, a word dear to Frois's heart, Englished as "dignity" (dignified) in 1-6, "gallant" in 1-50+, and here, "stylish." It is also "dandy," "elegant," "cool," etc. . . You will see more in other chapters.

1-60+ We walk with all of our foot touching the ground;
Antre nós se anda com todo o pé asentado no chão;

> The Japanese, only on the ball of the foot on shoes covering but half of their feet.
> *Em Japão somente com as pontinhas sobre o calsado de meyo pee.*

Because of the reason given in the last contrast, people had to exercise their arches or soil their heels. No wonder, they didn't walk for relaxation! (1-27+)

1-61+ We do not wear clothing thin enough to reveal the body either in the winter or the summer;
Antre nós nem por Verão nem por Inverno se usa de vestidos ralos polos quais se veja o corpo;

> In Japan, summer clothing is so thin that almost everything is visible. *Em Japão são polo Verão tão ralos que quasi tudo se enxerga.*

About 600 years before Frois, the great complainer – or witty connoisseur of life, if you prefer – Sei Shônagon, had something to say about thin clothing in her listing of *"Things that are unpleasant to see"* in her Pillow Book:

> A dark-skinned person looks very ugly in an unlined robe of stiff silk. If the robe is scarlet, however, it looks better, even though it is just as transparent. I suppose that one of the reasons I do not like ugly women to wear unlined robes is that one can see their navels. (trans. Ivan Morris: S(M):PBSS)

When Frois wrote, summer linen was so thin and weak that *haikai* (proto-*haiku*) joke about poor women unable to ford waist-high rivers. Be that as it may, the West still has *a lot* to learn from Japan when it comes to fabric for hot weather. Traditional Japanese sheets soak up and evaporate sweat extremely quickly and, considering the waste of energy on air-conditioning, it is criminal that they are losing out to Western style sheets today.

~~~~~~

1-62+ The hems of our skirts and long robes do not reveal the foot at all;
   As bordas dos nossos sayos ou roupões compridas não são desfalcados em nada;

> In Japan, the front hem of the *katabira* and *kimono* of men and women wants a span. *Em Japão as* catabiras *y* quimões *de homens e molheres falta-lhe hum palmo nas bordas dianteiras.*

Frois's contemporary Rodrigues suggests that the difference was not so clear-cut for women whose "robes were *very long and reach right down*, and they wear underneath a white petticoat from the waist downwards." (R/C:TIJ *italics* mine) Either there was a change in the fashion in the two decades spanning Frois's and Rodrigues's writing, or they are describing different classes of woman or robes. That wonderful metaphysical (or was it *cavalier?*) poem about a woman's feet as mice hidden below the hems but occasionally peaking out at the world shows Frois was not exaggerating about the length of "our" clothing. And, I think, it does *look* better to take a hem all the way down to the ground without a break, as Europeans did, though it must have been hell to keep this clothing clean and I only wonder what percent of the population could afford the time=money to wear it! No one who had to wash their own clothing I would bet!

~~~~~~

1-63+ We never stitch black clothing with white thread.[1]
   Antre nós ho vestido preto não se coze com linhas nem r[etrós=mod Portuguese trans.] branqo;

> Japanese are not troubled when black (clothing) is sewn with white (thread).
> *Os Japões não têm por inconviniente com branqo cozer o preto.*

"This is presumably about the thread used for fitting kimonos. Sometimes part of this is left as 'decorative fitting,'" writes Okada. The neat stitches can be seen as mere adornment, but the fact they are not extraneous makes them a revelation as well. There is a beauty in *not* concealing human work, somewhat akin to the attraction of the grain of the wood or the fur mentioned in 1-57+. If I may wax poetic for a moment, in these stitches we can see the prototype of the pipes on that art museum in Paris, of a functional modern aesthetics. Unlike the pipes, however, we can appreciate the skill of the sewer, who is seen rather than forgotten. Isn't this idea reflected in the open movement of props on stage and the presence of the puppeteer, albeit wearing the invisibility of black, moving about on stage with the puppet in Japanese traditional drama? That, too, is part of the show.

1. **Com linhas nem retros. Translation.** If the modern Portuguese editors' guess is correct, we may be talking about two types of stitching and/or thread. That is beyond me. Like the other translators, I kept it simple.

~~~~~~

(Several blank pages, probably intended for additional contrasts, follow. The same is true for other chapters.)

endnote 1
M*en* 男

The clothes may be the *man*, but so many items in the chapter rightly pertain to *both* sexes, that Frois ought to have made a chapter for *Costume* alone. One wonders if he did not do so because he had far more contrasts specifically about *Women* in the next chapter – and sought to equalize the length. The second, women's chapter is also more interesting, for many contrasts do not only treat appearances but concern lifestyle and, incidentally, overturn current stereotypes. Reading this chapter, I couldn't help wondering if men had lives! The very title of the chapter specifies *"vestidos,"* as if males are but clothes-horses, whereas the next chapter gives Women *"custumes,"* or *customs* as well as *costumes* (only 1 of 4 other translations chose the latter meaning). And how about all those *swords*? Arms are thoroughly contrasted in chapter 7 (on *War and Weapons*). That there could, nonetheless, be that many (seven!) entries about *swords* in this first chapter indicates just how much a part of the male *pessoa,* or person, they were considered.

..
The most important part of the European's *persona*, skin color, was not touched upon because there was no contrast. As we have already noted, most of the Jesuits thought of the Japanese as fellow whites. The Long version of this book has pages on black and white matters including a complex discussion of the origins of color difference in *de Missione,* which, if I am not mistaken, goes beyond Aristotle in the mix of genetics and climate while also trying to come to terms with the Christian mythology (eg. it is pointed out that the Ham story is not in the Bible, though such a Christian story would not be known by Japanese). Jesuit thought is often identified with sophistry. "Jesuit" as an adjective in the dictionary tells us that much (and not only in anti-Catholic England, but in Portuguese as well!). I do not know how much validity is in the charge. But, one thing is certain. The academic question of the worth of the *noble primitive* position (expounded in imaginary debates between Indian ascetics and Alexander the Great, etc.) which engaged Medieval scholars is child's play compared to the task of understanding then explaining a different but equal people to an intellectual tradition that had already placed itself on the top of the pyramid. And this, precisely, was one of the first tasks that the newly formed Company had to do. The Jesuit tradition teethed in a suddenly complex world, where simple black and white explanation was impossible. Skin color provides a good example of this.

Today, skin-color no longer matters for Japanese-Western relations, except in so far that the relative uniformity – few blacks or whites – in Japan makes it difficult for Japanese to comprehend the problems inherent to more obviously poli-ethnic and poli-racial societies (I write *"more obviously"* because Japan *does* have some variety and problems I will not go into in this book). But physical differences *other than skin color* still matter and these differences, I believe, create a gender gap. In a word, Far Eastern women are appreciated more than Far Eastern men. This is because *size* matters. While fashion and the accidents of history may throw a few curve-balls, as a rule, large men and petite women are favored throughout the world and they know it. Western men visiting Japan sometimes feel themselves *too* large, but it is generally a purely practical complaint occasioned upon bumping ones head on the top of the door or spending the night with ones feet outside the futon. The only exception I know is a fine passage in Kipling's *First Letter from Japan* (1889) when he admits to feeling uncomfortably large in the "doll houses" of Japan. "I tried to console myself with the thought that I could kick the place to pieces; but this only made me feel large and coarse and dirty." (C&W:KJ)

But, this is a *bull-in-the-china* situation-induced lament, the "we-as-barbarian" amusement of a humorist that doesn't go nearly so deep as true apprehension over one's appearance. The first lengthy exposition of such a true lament I know of is by Alice Mabel Bacon and is part of a 2½ page footnote on Japanese standards of personal beauty in her 1890 classic, *Japanese Girls and Women* where she gives us the first clear exposition of what we might call *the beauty advantage* of petite Japanese women over large Western women. After contrasting "the mildness of expression" gained by the flatness of the face where the eye-socket was not outlined by brow cheek or nose, the delicacy of colorless cheeks, slender figures and wee, scuffing steps of the Japanese women with "the blue eyes set in deep sockets . . with the bridge of the nose rising as a barrier between them" that imparted "a fierce grotesqueness to the face" that, at first sight, even made the "babies scream with horror" and the "long, clean-stepping walk, and the air of almost masculine strength and independence" of these "slim-waisted, large-hipped" white women, Bacon writes

> *Foreigners who have lived a great deal among the Japanese find their standards unconsciously changing, and see, to their own surprise, that their countrywomen look ungainly, fierce, aggressive, and awkward among the small, mild, shrinking, and graceful Japanese ladies.* (B:JGW, my *italics*)

Note. At this time in the West, broad hips and large busts were not only considered attractive but, as sexual bimorphism meant *specialization* and a high degree of specialization was credited with bringing about Higher Civilization, commonly cited as *proof* the Caucasian race was more highly evolved than Asian races. That this science-backed superiority complex could not only disappear but flip over while one lived in Japan – and I would guess that the first of her "countrywomen" who felt less than happy with herself was Bacon herself – is remarkable! Some of the early Jesuits went over to the Japanese side with respect to *character* (Organtino being the clearest case), but they never admit to feeling *ugly* or seeing their countrymen or women with such Japanese eyes. As men of religion, from a culture where men were not supposed to look in the mirror (1-46+) we wouldn't expect them to, either. But the fact that European males were on the winning side of the male=large=superior equation, makes it unlikely that even secular Occidentals would have found grounds to feel inadequate on the basis of physical characteristics. (Mentally, as we shall see later, it is a different story). Living in Japan in the last quarter of the 20c, I never came across white or black men miserable for being big oafs, but I cannot count the times I ran across remarks similar to Bacon's on the part of Caucasian *women* visiting or living in Japan who suffered from low self-esteem and seemed disappointed or even *angry* that Caucasian males in Japan tended to favor Japanese women. Such jealousy is understandable. So much has been written by Western men on the wondrously wonderful Japanese women that one could make a whole library of their adulation. I must have read the geisha's wit praised at least a dozen times, with each writer pointing out that she is not just a "giggling girl," but, in Menpe's words "a little genius." (M:JRC) Hearn, who was married to a kind and intelligent Japanese woman, has every right to *his* adulation (which, coming from a man who also penned the best homage to blond beauty I have read means something); but I would guess most Occidental males simply liked the fuss Japanese women made of them and were happy to jump on the bandwagon for sanctifying Japanese women in masse. This made a certain Mr. Crosland, writing in 1904, very cross:

> In brief, if we are to believe the books, there is not a shrew in all Japan, and consequently not an uncomfortable husband. On the face of it this is ridiculous. Where you have women you are bound to have shrews; where you have marriage, you are bound to have a considerable number of husbands who are sorry for themselves. (C:TAJ)

..
He was right, of course, but it is of no help for the opposite problem – that of the Oriental males. As Golownin's editor put it in 1824, "all the early writers [mostly 17c Dutch] describe the women as extremely handsome; and yet they represent the men as very ill made." 19c writers were blunter and

not adverse to describing their "ugliness" in excruciating detail (See *TT-Long*). The only exception I know is Morse, who found Japanese men "better-looking than the women" among peasants, who were "on the whole rather plain-looking." Still, he doesn't go so far as to call them handsome. And this was not only true for Japan but for Mongolians in general. Take Cruz on China in 1569. Here is how he began his chapter "Of the apparel and customs of the *men*" (Yes, Frois might have referenced this!):

> Although the Chinas commonly are ill-favoured, having small eyes, and their faces and noses flat, and are beardless, with some few hairs on the point of the chin, notwithstanding there are some who have very good faces, and well proportioned, with great eyes, their beards well set, and their noses well shapen. But these are very few and it may well be that they are descended from other nations . . . (in B:SCSC)

This is Boxer's translation. The original is not "ill-favoured" but simply *feios,* "ugly"! (C:TCC) Compare that to the lead of the curiously named chapter "Of the apparel and customs of the *women*, and whether there are slaves in China."

> The women commonly, excepting those of the sea coast and the mountains, are very white and gentlewomen, some having their noses and eyes well proportioned. From their childhood they squeeze their feet in cloths, so that they may remain small, and they do it because the Chinas do hold them for finer gentlewomen that have small noses and feet. (B:SCSC)

~~~~~~

Today, in an Americanized world where maleness is identified with tallness, powerful chins, broad shoulders and, ridiculously large muscles which Westerners and blacks, with their larger and less neotonous physiques more frequently embody, the Far Eastern male is at an greater disadvantage than ever. Lest you doubt me, look at the sex ratio of clearly East Asian faces in contemporary advertisements. Look at the models in the fashion world. There are always exceptions. But they only go to prove the rule. Until Asian males break free of Western fashion and create an entirely different ideal, they are pretty much doomed to play a losing game. Little can be done about the mean difference in the dimensions of the part nobody mentions (though, the less-endowed can take consolation in the fact they are less likely to suffer prostate cancer and may enjoy a longer active sex life), which to men counts for a good portion of their self image – but I believe the right fashions could pretty well offset the rest of the gap. Japanese (and other largely Mongolian people, starting with the Chinese) should dump the Occidental clothing and hair-styles they adopted to make it in the world, and now that they have made it (and have us literally in their debt) no longer need, and the sooner the better, if they would be happier and more confident in the greater global society, that all of us, thanks to mass media, share today.   Unless, that is, the idea is *to stay ugly* as an incentive to work harder and gain the appeal wealth assures its owner, the Far East should exchange the narrow-waist, broad-shoulder dress of the Occident in favor of the robe and show off their thick, shiny hair by tying it up on top of the head, *etcetera.*

II

OF WOMEN, THEIR PERSONS AND MORES
do que toca as molheres, e de suas pesoas e custumes

~~~~~~

2-1 In Europe, the supreme honor and treasure of young women is their chastity and the preservation of their purity; *Em Europa a suprema honrra e riqueza das molheres moças hée a pudicicia e o claustro inviolado de sua pureza;*

> In Japan, women never worry about their virginity. Without it, they lose neither their honor nor the opportunity to wed. *As molheres de Japão nenhum cazo fazem da linpeza virginal nem perdem, pola não ter, honrra nem casamento.*

Christianity made premarital sex taboo and turned chastity into a fetish. The "preservation of their purity" in more direct translation would be "the inviolate cloister of their purity," and the simple "virginity" the Japanese failed to value would be "virginal cleanliness". The outlandishness of such vocabulary owes something to the fact that English is not Portuguese, but it is also due to our distance from a culture where virginity was esteemed above life and it was believed, to quote the 1912 *Catholic Encyclopedia*, that "the respect for woman rises and falls with the veneration of the Virgin Mother of God." Prior to the Reformation, North Europe was equally enthralled by Virgin Mary – actually, it boasted more Churches under her name – but, by the time Frois wrote, the sanctity of marriage was valued higher than that of virginity in the Protestant countries where the attention given to Mary at the expense of Jesus had come to be considered misguided. Nevertheless, premarital sex and adultery were thought to damage the sanctity of marriage and because the general level of anxiety with respect to sex itself was higher in the Calvinist parts, Frois's generalization probably held equally true for most of Europe. Still, we are talking *ideals*. The very year Frois wrote his first draft of the *Tratado*, 1583, Stubbes, in his *Anatomy of Abuses* ranted about the way (English) people in "every parishe, towne and village . . . run gadding to the woods . . . where they spende all the night in pleasant pastymes" bringing back a "Mai pool (this stinckyng Idoll rather)," with the result that "of fourtic, three score or a hundred maides goying to the woode over night, there have scarcely the third part returned home again undefiled." Clearly, not everyone in Europe was a prude.

In 1585, the Japanese no longer considered virginity a spiritual liability as some claim was true in ancient times, when a virgin might be buried under a road to gain some vicarious experience, but the fertility-worship element of culture survived occasional repression by Buddhist and Confucian authorities and men and women still exchanged bawdy songs as they planted rice and laughed with their children on their shoulders when gigantic phalluses paraded through town. "They" were still as "we" were, once upon a time, when natural generation rather than the fiat of Creation was venerated. A courtship practice called "night-crawling" (*yobai*) sex was preliminary to marriage – if the girl got pregnant or the guy slept-in, the knot was tied – survived right up to the mid-20c in rural areas.

While Christian missionaries like Frois struggled to implant their chaste ideals in their Japan congregations (*cultural rape for virginity?*), other Portuguese, according to the Florentine merchant Carletti, found "this Land of Cockaigne much to their liking." One of the sexual opportunities worldly visitors enjoyed was the open practice of leasing girls for live-in maid+mistresses. These young women (probably in their teens) prostituted themselves for the sake of their poor families. Carletti explained the benefit in it for the girls themselves, observing that not only do they not "lose the occasion of marrying" for "having thus been used," but "many of them never would be able to marry if they did not acquire a dowry in this way." (C(W):MVAW) More importantly, since these girls had not acted from desire – what Buddhism found sinful about sex – but *to help others*, they actually furthered their salvation. And they behaved admirably by obeying and assisting their parents, cardinal virtues in the Confucian ethics common to the Sinosphere. For the same reason, an upper-class girl slated for an arranged marriage who engaged in premarital sex would be in serious trouble, not for losing her virginity but for losing her heart and disobeying the wishes of her parents.

KT remonstrates, *"But didn't Shintô demand virgin priestesses [miko]?"* Many Japanese folklorists and students of religion wonder about that, too. Today, the women who who work at shrines, dancing, handing out predictions, anti-misfortune arrows, etc., are mostly high school girls but originally they were probably of any age. The theory I find most convincing is that Buddhist ideas of "purity" considering women the less enlightened, or, to be blunt, the dirtier sex (Buddhist priests are never female and there are temples out-of-bounds to women (see 2-58)) supplanted Shinto ideas of im/purity which originally may have required abstinence because a *miko* was supposed to be occupied by the *kami* (spirit/god), but would not have required virginity because sex was not thought of as permanent pollution. Did Buddhist-inspired misogyny give men an excuse to run women off the mountain and set apart Japanese religion from the largely woman-run shamanism of Korea and Okinawa, where it survives until today? Most professional *mikô* (i.e. shamanness or mediums who wear white and identify with Shinto) today are not virgin and do not live within shrine precincts.

2-2   European women[1] prize golden hair and do many things to obtain it;
As d'Europa se prezão e fazem muito por ter os cabelos louros;

Japanese loathe it, and do all within their power to make it black.
As japoas os aborrecem e trabalhão quanto podem polos fazerem pretos.

Apparently, blond was big in 16c Luso-Iberia. In that classic best-seller, "The Perfect Wife" (*La Casada Perfecta*), Frois's contemporary, Fray Luis de León wrote: "It often happens that a man of letters does not spend as much on his books as a lady on having her hair dyed blond. May God save us from such ruination!" (L(J&L):LPC) DR hypothesizes that this urge to lighten up might have something to do with Spain's long struggle against the darker haired Islamic and Moorish people to the South. De Leon was less understanding. Those "who alter the color of their hair," he wrote, "are offended by their own nationality; they regret not having been born German or English, and so they try to denaturalize themselves at least in their hair." Up in England, anti-fashion criticism directed equally at men and women likewise played up the shame of aping foreigners, but with Spain self-consciously the world's leading power at this time, it was not just the ignominy of copying at issue but of copying ones inferiors. Moreover, because *rubio* denotes blond *and* red in Spanish, de León could even claim that *with this fiery hair,* women "become omens of their own evil" (burning desire and sooty dirtiness)! If that wasn't enough, he claimed it harmed their health because too much hair-washing dampens the head and this hurts the brain and, worst of all, the practice was sacrilegious, for didn't the Lord say "Which one of you can change a single hair from black to white or from white to black?"

Black hair as an ideal may be hard for us (people raised in the Occidental tradition) to appreciate even though we may feel drawn to it. In my case, though my boyhood awe for blonds changed to love for brunettes as a man, I did not really appreciate dark hair *as an ideal* until reading about the Mende of West Africa, who connected their ideal skin color with black water. What we might call "dark," they found radiant – for still black water was shinier and reflected better than any other. (This concept is developed in the only truly *reflective* look at black beauty I know of: Sylvia Arden Boone: *Radiance From the Waters* Yale 1986). Years later, once my infatuation for tan (growing up on the beach in Florida, we called tan "skin color") ended, I found white skin appealing, and came to appreciate black hair in another way, as a foil. So it makes sense to me that in Japan, where pure white skin was the age-old ideal, raven black hair would also have been the ideal. Psychologically considered, however, the two extremes of golden/light blond and jet-black represent the same ideal: *juvenitude*. Fine, fair hair is more common in infants, and thick black hair the farthest from the thin white crown of age. So it makes sense for either to be pursued to the limit.

But the position of the Southern European women wanting to be blond despite it not being their natural color and the Japanese to whom black hair was not only an ideal but the reality and the only accepted color is itself contrary and raises a question: If black is the natural color in Japan, why should the women be doing all they can to *make* it black? *First*, there are degrees of black and Japanese hair eventually turns white. *Second*, if truth be told, the originally black hair of some Japanese takes on a noticeably reddish-brown tinge with exposure to the sun. This made it the mark of a *marginal* lifestyle; as Valignano noted, *cabellos rubios* (blond=red hair) was "left to the meaner class and the fallen." (V(A):S&A). Not surprisingly, good women did not want to look poor. As Rodrigues wrote: "Their hair *must be* black; *on no account* may it be fair, and for this purpose they dye it after their manner." (*my italics* C:TIJ). I am reminded of the way that for much of the 20c, any hair not jet-black and smooth was considered *ipso facto* proof of juvenile delinquency – both because of the suspicion of dyeing/permanents and the association of immorality with Western women – and girls with natural reddish hair had to dye their hair in order not to be criticized or even sent home from school!

See *TT-long* for a full paragraph of Hearn on blond *vs.* brunette beauty, 19c racism's take on Oriental hair and more. For this book, it is enough to add one more *Faux Frois*, borrowed, with small changes, from the observation of Alice Mabel Bacon:

American ladies take pains to simulate a natural curl when Nature denies them that charm;
Japanese ladies misfortunate enough to have even a ripple in their hair take pains to straighten it.

---

1. Translation: European women in this chapter are almost *always* called "as d'Europa" or "as de Europa," i.e. "those of Europe" or "European ones," where Japanese women are "as japoas" or "the Japanese (of feminine gender)". To refer to the *first* side of the contrast as "those" was too awkward even for this occasionally lenient translator to permit. Note also that the *japoas* are never capitalized while the *Japões*, i.e., the men in the last were! The modern Portuguese translation (1993) quietly fixes this so the women are equally capitalized. I do not know what the story is here. Could a feminist with time on her hands find it and tell me what is what?

2-3   European women make their part on their forehead;
As de Europa fazem sus espertaduras na t[esta];

   Japanese women shave their foreheads and conceal their part.
   As japoas rapão as testas e emcobrem a espertadura.

European women also had a brief fling with shaving to reclaim some scalp as forehead in the 15c. This was to prevent their hairline from protruding from their tall hats (hennin) and emphasize the size of their brows. But most paintings from all ages show European women with parts, which were particularly common and well-defined in Frois's time With Japanese, on the other hand, one finds only a few remnant center parts (common in the Heian Era (794-1185) and none of the parts "we" think natural on the right and left of the head. Generally, hair was tied in the middle of the head, high enough that parts had no call to form and these part-less Japanese engineered their hairlines, instead. Unlike Europeans, they did not think large brows particularly noble or beautiful, but they did have preferred shapes for the boundary of skin and hair. Young woman in Frois's time probably tended to round their brows, while middle-aged women went for "the ideal of the beloved Fuji," or Widow's peak. I feel there was a bit more variety, but historians tend to pay more attention to the hairdo itself than the boundary, so it is hard to be specific. All women may have cleaned up around the edges of the hairline to banish irregularity – this unnatural perfection is one reason why the women look like they are wearing wigs in old prints (and must wear wigs on the TV Easterns to mimic that).

The language of the Japanese side of the contrast is puzzling. Could it mean "shave their foreheads *to* conceal their part?" But, doing away with something altogether is not usually considered concealment. And did Japanese really *conceal* parts? Okada, who shows a picture of a woman (Oinu, who died at age 32 in 1582) whose hair has a clear center part, must have had his doubts, for he translated *testas,* generally thought of as forehead, as head and wonders if the *espertadura,* or "part," might not include a clearing (?) shaved into the scalp called a *nakazori,* or "middle-shave," where a *komakura* (pillowette) was set as the base for a chignon.

2-4   European women perfume their hair with aromatic essences;
            As de Europa perfumão os cabelos com cheiros odoriferos;

            Japanese women go about reeking of the oil with which it is anointed.
            As japoas andão sempre fedendo ao azeite com que os untão.

There is no small irony in this contrast. European women who rarely bathed smelled good thanks to perfume, while Japanese who bathed regularly stunk of oil. Evidently Frois did not care for the cheap and pungent sesame oil, the cloying camelia oil or even the lighter walnut. I would guess that noblewomen who could also afford some clove scent in theirs, would not reek. But scent is a matter of taste. Japanese, for their part probably would have taken issue with that perfume. Even today, many express great displeasure with the perfume many Occidental women drench themselves in. I cannot resist introducing a certain method of toiletry used by some Spanish women a generation after Frois as reported by one Madam d' Aulnoy.

            if the lady had no scent-spray, her maid sucked in the water and projected it in little drops through her teeth all over the face and body of her mistress. (D:DLS)

2-5   European women rarely add any other hair to their own;
            As de Europa raramente uzão de cabelos estranhos ajuntados aos seus;

            Japanese women buy a large quantity of wigs imported from China.
            As japoas comprão muitas cabeleiras que vem de viniaga da China.

In Roman times, the "fashionable ladies of Rome" were said to favor golden hair imported from Germany; but, in the 16c, it would seem that men were "our" big-wigs. The practice was mainly English, upper-class and professional, but, by the next century, most men with any pretensions to being fashionable had to wear their powdered wigs that were so important marks of manhood that even the statues in the Louvre were crowned and re-crowned with the newest fashions. Our strange habit was not known to the first Japanese Embassy to the USA. For, according to the diary of the vice-Ambassador Muragaki-Awaji-no-Kami – here is what they *thought* they saw in the Smithsonian:

On the wall were also hung specimens of the hair of the successive Presidents. What a disgusting custom to exhibit the hair of dead men in a public place! (A:FJE)

Rodrigues suggests one reason why so many wigs were needed: "The longer the hair is, the more dignified it is, and so some find it necessary to insert wigs into their hair."(R(C):TIJ) Noble women wore several lengths of hair *in serial*. Okada notes that most women desiring hair-pieces would have used Japanese hair, for there was a profession of *ochyanai* who went around buying hair that normally comes out when brushing for recycling as inexpensive wigs, and that the imported hair was almost certainly yak, red, black or white, that was not used for wigs proper, but to stuff *mage* (buns). This is backed up by Ôhara Reiko, who notes, as Okada does, that Frois is wrong to call them *kazura* ("wigs" = *cabeleiras*) when they are properly speaking *kamoji* ("tresses/rats"). (J/O:KGB)

2-6   European women use many coiffures to adorn their heads;
As de Europa uzão de muitos toucados pera ornamento da cabeça;

       The Japanese go about with uncovered and unadorned hair, and the noblewomen with their hair loose. *As japoas andão sempre em cabelo, e as fidalgas com elle solto.*

    Yes, we had coronet, tiara and other headwear, or rather hair-wear in Europe, combined with fancy hairdos I lack the vocabulary to describe. The prize contrast here is between the noblewomen, because, in Europe, only the poor would let it hang down loose. Be that as it may, this is a fleeting contrast. Within a hundred years, Japanese women boasted a great variety of sculptured hairdo with enough large hairpins to scare a porcupine, and the hairpin man with his straw-wrapped pole stuck full of his diverse chopstick-sized ware plied the streets of Edo. After Japan reopened, Alcock wrote of women with "forests" of hairpins in their hair and a fad for those "with glass beads, filled with bright-colored liquids;" Sladen calls hairpins "the hatpins of Japan" and notes one exceptional design with "Japanese soldiers dragging Chinese soldiers by the pigtails . . . not in good style"; and Edward Morse found many representing a story or an act, "a child painting a kakemono, a bird-cage, …"

    When Frois wrote, at the tail end of centuries of war, men had most of the decoration. This would change in the peaceful centuries to follow, when women came to enjoy the lion's share of the decoration. For poor women, that apparently meant hairpins.

2-7   European women tie it [their hair] with ribbons at the end of their braids;
As de Europa os atão com nastros até baxo emtrançados.

       Japanese women tie it with a scrap of paper in just one place in back or with paper string in the middle of their head. *As japoas os atão com hum pequeno de papel em hum só lugar detrás, ou os emrolão com hum fio de papel no meyo da cabeça.*

Japanese women, or rather, *ladies*, for Frois has the nobility in mind, who let their hair hang down unbound in his last contrast, now *tie* it. This apparent contradiction resolves when you know that for all practical purposes the hair *was* loose. The tie – obvious half bow-ties with the loop on the left being standard – were so low-down (at mid-back or lower) that viewed above the tie, the hair appears to be unbound. For practical purposes, nothing could be worse than this style, because such hair would catch on things very easily, whereas things would pull through loose hair without such a tie. The second Japanese style mentioned will make far better sense to the reader in a figurative translation: *pony-tail*. This was the style a noblewoman would use if she went riding, but it was not restricted to noble women. The paper cord wrapped around the base sometimes continued upward – or *outward,* for the position of the ponytail varied – for several inches, creating a very perky effect.

So, Frois's contrast is between hair kept tightly bound from scalp to tip, on the one hand, and hair that is bound in only one place, i.e., *free* for the rest of its considerable length. Presumably, the latter – I can't help thinking of the old C & W hit *Behind Closed Doors* (*"but when she lets her hair fall down . . ."*) – would have been found "loose" in both senses of the word in Europe at this date.

2-8   European women wear fine bonnets or silk scarves on their heads;
As de Europa poem beatilhas ou volantes na cabeça;

Japanese women *wataboshi* of silk refuse or a length of white cloth under a mantle. *As japoas hum* vataboxi *de borra ou hum pedaço de pano branqo debaxo do manto.*

The Portuguese for this common European headwear is charming: *beatilhas* and *volantes*. The former has a beatific ring to it, reminding one of our "Sunday best." The latter, literally a "flyer," served to increase a woman's attractiveness even as it veiled her. Both items are fine, while the Japanese items are plain if not crude. *Wataboshi* is cloth beaten out of substandard silkworm cocoons, the remnants, dredges or, in slang *merda* (guess!) of the silk. *Wataboshi* is soft and warm, while the white cloth was absorbent and cool, so the Japanese headwear, if not much to look at, was practical.

In Philip Stubbes *Anatomie of Abuses*, published in 1583, we learn that the above-mentioned hats are but a start, for among the "hats that defy virtue" we find some "sharp on the crowne, peaking up like a sphere, or shafte of a steeple, standing a quarter of a yard above the crowne of their heads . . . Othersome be flat and broad on the crowne, like the battlements of a house . . ." and so forth, for a page. But, with all the variety of headwear, I find it interesting that the head-wear of both sides mentioned by Frois share something. Both developed into wedding dress. I will skip describing "our" side. In the century after Frois, the *watabôshi* lifted up off the head so it seems to float like a huge upside-down soup bowl and now you may find it at the Shinto part of the wedding ceremony hiding the "horns" of the bride.

2-9   European women wash their hair and head in their houses;
As de Europa lavão em suas cazas os cabelos e cabeça;

Japanese women do it in public baths where there are special lavatories for the hair. *As japoas em banhos publicos onde ha partiqulares lavatórios pera os cabelos.*

Here, Frois is probably *not* referring to Japanese noblewomen, who would not be caught dead in a public bath (see 1-53). But it is hard to find solid information about these things. Okada found proof that there were special parts of baths to wash hair 25 years after *Tratado*. I cannot say more. But why does Frois write "hair and head" and not just "hair"?

2-10   The noblewomen of Europe wear long trains;
As nobres de Europa trazem grandes rabos nas fraldas;

> Japanese women in the house of the *Kubo* [shôgun] wear four or five wigs attached one to another that drag three *couvades* [about 6 feet] behind them when they walk. *Os japoas em casa do* Qubo *trazem 4 ou sinco cabeleiras apegadas humas nas outras, que lhe andão arrojando tres covados por detras polo chão.*

Frois usually used *kubo* to refer to the *Shogun* Hideyoshi, whom he had met and who ruled Japan in 1585. Hideyoshi's women – he had at least thirteen, far more than his predecessor Nobunaga, who only had one wife and two mistresses. – would have worn what *looked like* a train of wigs on formal occasions. Actually, *they were not "wigs"* (*katsura*) serially linked, but a single long "tress" (*kamoji*) linked to the real hair a bit below the shoulders with a cord (generally tubular cloth decorated with auspicious motif tied so both ends stick out a few inches each way) and red and white *mizuhiki* paper decoratively tied with half-bows at intervals. I can understand Frois's confusion, for it is hard to see how any unbroken hair (be it from a 4 or a 2-legged animal) can be so long. All of this presumed extremely clean surroundings. The hair generally rested on the long train of the kimono which in turn rested on spotlessly clean tatami mat or floorboards. Japanese noblewomen only wore their hair like this on formal occasions. I suspect the same was true for their European counterparts with their trains.

Ambrose Bierce – who was convinced that all of us unconsciously crave the tail our ancestors actually had (see *The Devil's Dictionary*) – would have been delighted to know that "our" *trains* were called "tails" (*rabos*) by the Portuguese, and that there were women who dragged their hair (not to mention the male equivalent in trousers = *hakama*) mentioned earlier (1-6+notes)) in Japan.

2-11   European women value beautifully fashioned, symmetrical eyebrows;
As de Europa prezão-se das sobrancelhas bem feitas e concertadas;

> Japanese women pluck them all out with a tweezers, leaving not one hair.
> *As japoas as tirão todas com tena sem lhe fiqar hum só cabelo.*

Citing Castiglione's *Il Libro del Cortegiano* (*Venezia, 1528*), M & J note that in parts of Europe, too, women plucked out all their eyebrows, "as seen in some fifteenth century paintings." Yes, I have seen *Mona Lisa*, among others. "In this case," they conclude, Frois's contrast "loses its significance." *I disagree.* In Europe, this was only a fashion, albeit a long-lasting one. In Japan, it was age-old custom; it was *the* style for their civilization. The oldest poetry writes of eyebrows like the new-moon or the crescent moon, etc. in the Chinese style, but they began to disappear as early as the Heian Era (c.800-1200). Although we find a protest in the 12c from *"The young woman who loved caterpillars"* ["hair-bug" in Japanese!], the practice outlived Frois.

The Japanese may have loved nature, but they were not as constrained by a philosophy or rather, theology of the natural, that confused *what is* with what *ought to be* as Europeans, who justified or condemned everything as "natural" or "unnatural." If men in Europe had natural beards, their women had natural eyebrows. When Rodrigues, for all his long years in Japan, fumed "This [eyebrow plucking] is considered very fashionable, but in reality, it is an abuse and is against the decoration which nature herself places on the human face"(R(C):TIJ), he was a typical man of his age. In one sense, he may be *wrong.* This eyebrow-plucking, like male hair plucking, may well be a cultural extension of an unconscious strategy for maximizing natural beauty in a relatively hairless race. In a "Scene" of ANTHROPOMETAMORPHOSIS (1654), titled *Eye-brow Rites, or the Eye-brows abus'd contrary to Nature,* John Bulwer notes that "in the Indies, the Cumanans pluck off all the Haire of their Eye-brows, taking great pride, and using much superstition . . . ," "In Nombre de Dios, the Women with a certaine Hearb, make the Haire of their Eye-brows fall off," "In Peru they use offerings in pulling off the Haire of their Eye-brows, to offer unto the Sun," and "The Brazilians (also) eradicate the Haire of their Eyebrows." Bulwer considered people around the world, so it is notable that these are all, more or less Mongoloid peoples with relatively little facial hair to begin with. And, if I am not mistaken, the women in the 15c European paintings M & J mention are mostly blonds, who tend to share this neotoneous trait with Mongoloids. (Moreover, these thin-haired women were generally put in a *damned if you do and ugly if you don't* situation in Europe, because eye-liner was considered not only artificial but, as painted enticement, *sinful* as well!).

Natural or not, there may be something more to this. Some argue that this eyebrowlessness, combined with make-up minimizing the size of the mouth, helped make women *less expressive*, for it left them bereft of the physical signs of an outgoing personality. Bulwer made such an association with expressiveness in the first paragraph of his *Eyebrow Rites* Scene, memorable because it also reveals that one can both *have* yet *not have* eyebrows.

> The *Russian* Ladies tie up their Foreheads so strict with fillets, which they are used to from their Infancy, that they cannot move their Eye-brows, or use any motion; the meaner sort also affect it . . . . *what a plot have these Women upon Nature, thus to bind their Eye-brows to the observation of so strict and unnatural a silence, to hinder her in one of her most significant operations, and to exclude that part of her mind which useth to be exhibited by the Eye-brows.* (B:A)

About the only retort possible for this concept is that made by Ishida Kaori, in her *Keshô sezu ni wa ikirarenai ningen no rekishi* (The history of humans who cannot live without being made up). After giving the standard take on eyebrowlessness as anti-expression, she notes that people with shaved eyebrows seem spooky" because "you do not know what a person who has shaved eyebrows might be thinking." Put that way, I suppose you could even call the fashion empowering, in a way!

KT asks: *But weren't they drawn back in?* For most of Japan's long eyebrow-plucking history, the eyebrows were indeed redrawn, but not upon their original location; it was far higher, near the hairline, or, considering the fact that the hairline was usually shaved (i.e. *shaped*), more or less *upon* the hairline. Such is the case for Oinu, used as an illustration by Okada. Her thick painted eyebrows are so high up that they bear some resemblance to sunglasses resting on the top of the head. In that respect, the fashion should not be conflated with the Chinese practice of drawing a thin line to replace the eyebrows in more or less the correct place. These Japanese eyebrows, if they can be called eyebrows, were short and thick, and in the most radical version, completely round! Sitting way up there, they served a purely decorative function, for the upper brow is virtually stationary. However, they were not drawn all the time – women relaxing are often shown without them. Noble children of both sexes also had their eyebrows shaved and redrawn.

2-12 European women put cosmetics on their brows to make them white;
As de Europa põem posturas na testa pera a fazer alva;

Japanese noblewomen put some pictures on their foreheads with black paint on festive occasions. *As japoas nobres lhe poem per festa humas pinturas de tinta preta.*

Both Japanese translations have Japanese noblewomen painting their brows with *a little black paint/dye* on *formal* occasions. I follow Frois's *festive* and *pictures* with some trepidation. As noted above, Japanese women painted the edges of their hairline and painted in stubby false eyebrows on the upper part of the forehead. The Japanese translators retain the possibility these eyebrows, or a false hairline is what Frois refers to here. Since these varied in thickness and shape depending on the shape of the woman's face, her preferences and, perhaps, the occasion, were they hyperbolized into "pictures"? If we take Frois at his word on those *pinturas,* as the French edition does, one might think there was a brief-lived fashion of decorating brows with pictures, but the only facial pictures I have come across so far were decorative patches glued on the faces of European women in the 17c. Or did Frois see New Year's games where black circles and other designs are painted on the face when the shuttlecock is dropped, etc.. The contrast seems *black* and *white,* but the meaning is not.

2-13   European women all too soon find their hair turns white;
As de Europa, em breves annos, se lhe fazem os cabelos branqos;

Japanese women's hair does not turn white though they turn sixty, because they oil it. *As japoas são de sesenta e não tem cabelo branco polos untarem com azeite.*

If European men were more fortunate in their full beards, Japanese women were blessed with lasting beauty in their hair, even if their fountain of youth made them smelly (2-4)! Walnut oil, in particular, was reputed to keep hair black, according to a period publication *Onna-kagami,* or "Woman's Mirror (with the punning meaning, "Paragon of womanhood") cited by Okada. I suspect genetics and diet have more to do with it; but wonder if the oil might not protect from sun damage and include something beneficial to the hair that may be absorbed by the scalp.

2-14   European women open holes in their ears and fill them with earrings;
As de Europa furão as orelhas e emchen-nas de arrecadas;

Japanese women neither open holes in their ears nor wear earrings.
As japoas nem furão orelhas nem trazem arrecadas.
..
It is surprising the Japanese did not do this when the Chinese, whose habits they usually adopted were so accustomed to earrings that, according to Ball, "it looks almost as queer to see a Chinese woman without these indispensables, as it would to see an English lady going barefoot; and a Chinese woman would feel ashamed to appear in the one condition, as an English lady would in the other." (B:TC) This puts the West somewhere between Japan and China on this matter! Thunberg, at the end of the 18c, explained the lack of this adornment in Japan in moral terms: "Vanity has not yet taken root among them to that degree, as to induce them to wear rings or other ornaments in their ears." (T:TEAA) But, considering the fact they *did* go in for fancy combs and pins in their hair, I think there must be another explanation. One museum exhibit text states matter-of-factly that decorative clothing absorbed all of the decorativeness leaving no need for any *akusesari* (Japanese call jewelry *accessories*) (http://www.sengoku-expo.net/text/tf/J/kaisetsu_keppatsu.html). But that is too simple. Not a few Japanese women *even today* think of ear-piercing as *unnatural* – as most of us view any other body-piercing (or viewed it until recently) – and damaging the body their parents gave them at birth. They refrain from getting pierced even though they must wear clumsy clamp-style earrings and have

accepted without protest tight Western-style shoes which deform their toes, as they do "ours." With large earlobes (*fukumimi*) synonymous with good fortune, is it not also possible Japanese once felt puncturing the site of one's fortune was not a good idea? Could Chinese, who also had the fortune-ear idea, have concluded the opposite: that puncturing it and hanging valuable metal from it would stretch it and serve as a sort of pump-primer? Maybe the two people have a different assessment of *holes* . . .

Or, could this be a case of *historical trauma* dating back to a time when Japanese were not yet Japanese? According to the historical reconstruction of Tanikawa Kenichi, Japanese did wear ear ornaments from the Jomon period (10,000-300 BC) to the Kofun period (300–c.600). These ancestral Japanese hailing from the sea-people tribes of the Hainan (South China) area were called the *mimi*, or "ear" people. Over the millennia, the ornaments included large rings, strings of heavy *magatama* (comma-shaped beads) and, most notably, ear-lobe plugs, or rather discs up to about 4 inches in circumference. In the Yayoi (300BC-300AD) period, ear ornaments stopped being worn by live people but continued being used as funerary dress. Meanwhile the Ear people and the Eye people intermarried and created Japan. Why the ear-plugs and ear-rings had to go, though, I do not know.

2-15 European women think heavy make-up and embellishment of the face unattractive [a vice]; *Nas de Europa hé defeito parecerem-lhe muyto as posturas e afeites do rosto;*

Japanese women think the more layers of [white] powder applied, the more elegant. *As japoas, quanto mais alvayade poem, tanto o tem por maior gentileza.*

In 1583, Fray de Leon warned that "with the excessive use of these corrosives" women "wither their own flower and thus turn yellow and render themselves easy prey to illnesses through having their skin wasted by the make up they put on it" (L(L&P):LCP). The powder was the same "white lead" about which Swift later wrote *"When Mercury her Tresses mows / To think of Black-head Combs is vain, / No Painting can restore a Nose, / Nor will her Teeth return again"*. But health was not the real reason the Occident was, generally, down on cosmetics. To be heavily "painted" was to be a harlot. An English Puritan between Frois and Swift put it like this: "a painted woman's face is a liver smeared with carrion." (LR) De Leon, more diplomatically, did not insult the body nor "want to talk about the sin which some people find and link to make-up." He acknowledged that most women did use *some* make-up, yet were not by any stretch of the imagination harlots. So, he tried to expose Make-up *himself* as a problem, "a deceitful trickster, who gives them [the women] the opposite of what he promises them, and that as in the game children play, so he saying that he paints them, blackens them . . ." De Leon's logic is often as silly as it is impeccable: since women wash off their make-up before they sleep, they *know* it is dirty, *ergo* "how can they persuade themselves that it beautifies them?" (Ibid)

I have come across *nothing* in Japanese literature treating make-up as a moral issue, unless it is about the social sin of not getting properly made up to fit whatever role one might have in society. This requires no explanation. With most cultures different or excessive decorations might be thought odd or unattractive, but immoral? *We* are the ones needing explanation. Of course, the freedom to plaster oneself can be overdone. The prolific playwright and novelist Saikaku (1641-93) has a protagonist whose face is already white, rubbing in 200 layers of *hachya* (mercury-based white make-up) with freezing cold water in *Honchô Machinin-Kagami* – those were bountiful times, indeed, for Saikaku, on his part, polished off 10,000 haiku in a night and that is no hyperbole! This "two hundred," however, was. It was probably Chinese convention, for "The Bride" in I.T. Headland's CHINESE MOTHER GOOSE happens to use "two hundred rouge-sticks," and, unlike 800, 1000 or 10,000, this 200 is not a common idiom for plentitude in Japanese.

When faced with Japanese make-up, all European visitors I have read become instant Puritans. "We" *insist* upon the natural look. Alcock *detested* the way they "powdered all the face and neck with rice powder until they look like painted Twelfth-night Queens done in pastry and white lead." (A:COT) And Isabella Bird wrote "the habit of painting the lips with a reddish-yellow pigment, and of heavily powdering the face and the neck with pearl powder is a repulsive one." (B:UTJ) Thank goodness, I say, for the likes of Baudelaire, Huysmans and Wilde, who challenged this unnaturally narrow naturalism with their unabashed defense of the artificial, or rather, the natural artificiality of life. None of these famous characters visited Japan. The painter Menpes, who did, gives us the type of argument only a more enlightened thinker and true aesthete is capable of:

> There is nothing of the British scheme – no powder puff hidden in a pocket-handkerchief, no little ivory box with a looking glass in the lid, no rouge-tablet concealed in a muff to be supplied surreptitiously at some propitious moment. The Japanese woman has the courage to look upon her face purely as so much surface for decoration, a canvas upon which to paint a picture; and she decorates it as one might decorate a bit of bare wall . . . the white makes no effort to blend with the natural tone of her neck: it announces itself in a clear-cut, knife edge pattern above the folds of the kimono. (M:JRC)

In other words, pure materialism – i.e. *allowing the make-up materials to speak for themselves* – of the Japanese approach is the more honest one. It beats our naturalism, which is fake by nature. Moreover, the Japanese approach is *kinder*. Heavy white make-up is the equalizer par excellence. It lets everyone have an equally attractive second skin. In the dark, every cat is grey. In the light, every Japanese woman was white. *Bright white*. And, this equality of second nature was not only kind to the dark-skinned woman, but to the light-skinned as well. I owe this idea to Edward Morse. When, for the sake of balance, he mentioned a few absurd Japanese customs after a long talk extolling Japanese good manners as an example of higher civilization Vassar girls might well emulate, he brought up that white powder. "Young ladies going to a party" he wrote, "paint or powder their faces conspicuously white, and presenting a rather objectionable sight to those who associate this habit with the class who usually heavily paint at home." Here is the momentous discovery:

> Yet on inquiry about this practice I found it was extreme modesty that prompted it. Did a girl not paint on these occasions, it would assume she possessed so fair a complexion . . . (M:IGM 1894)

2-16   European women do all they can, use all means to whiten their teeth;
As de Europa trabalhão com arteficio e confeisões por fazer os dentes alvos;

> Japanese use iron and vinegar to make their mouth and teeth as black as [. . .]
> *As japoas com ferro e vinagre trabalhão por fazerem a boca e os dentes pretos como [. . .]*

Only two decades later Rodrigues wrote that noble women and boys did it, but that "the practice has now been given up completely by men and largely by women who now leave their teeth in their natural condition." (C:TCJ) As it turned out, the custom – black teeth being the mark of a betrothed or married woman – was soon to revive, continue strong to the second Opening of Japan and then some. Cooper notes that the (boy) Emperor Meiji still had his teeth dyed in 1868! (Ibid)

Iron and vinegar were probably not the only ingredients. Good dye was hard to make and often included secret ones. *Senryu* mention men dangling their genitalia over tubs of dye to magically increase its blackening power for women who couldn't afford to buy the good stuff! "A noseless maid's tooth-black is always badly made" goes one from YANAGITARU (*hanakuta-na gejo ohyakuro-ga denu toiu* – Y 1-3), with the implication being her pox was so bad that she couldn't find a man to cooperate. Thunberg suggests the source of this superstition, for he describes the *ohaguro* as "prepared from urine, filings of iron and sakki [*sake*]." He also writes it was "so corrosive, that the gums and lips must be well covered while it is laid on, or it will turn them quite blue." (T:TEAA) Apparently, women began their day with this vile substance. Everyday was said to assure top quality black teeth. Every other day, decent black teeth. And, every third day, not so good black teeth.

This habit was perhaps the most widely reported example of Japanese contrariness that was not also Chinese. And it was nowhere made to appear so odd as in the English edition of Van Linschoten's Dutch translation, or rather, *exaggeration* of some topsy-turvy from Valignano's *Sumario* (judging from the proximity of the hair and teeth with the *black* vs. *white* mourning colors):

> . . . and as among other nations it is a good sight to see men with white and yealow hayre and white teeth, with them it is esteemed the filthiest thing in the world, and seeke by all meanes they may to make their hayre and teeth blacke, for that the white causeth their grief, and the blacke maketh them glad. (1598 L:VJHVL)

Ridiculous or not, the idea of black as a happy color is a game attempt to make sense of those teeth. Alcock considered whether the eyebrow plucking and "the mouths thus disfigured . . . like open sepulchres" to give Japanese matrons "unrivaled pre-eminence in artificial ugliness" might not be a clever way to preserve conjugal fidelity by not attracting admirers . . . (A:COT:1853)! But I have never seen anything indicating that Japanese thought blackened teeth ugly. So, we might have to consider other explanations. Could the black stand for the *Yin*, or female part of the Yin-yang universe? I find slightly inward pointing teeth make a woman look more cultured, refined, gentle, whereas buck-teeth make her look tomboyish and less unattractive. Are the black teeth, perhaps, an extension of this psychology, making women less bone-hard looking and thereby more feminine? Or, going even further for the sake of argument, could the black teeth under the red lips rather advertise a woman's sexual readiness by increasing the affinity of the upper and the nether mouth? It was, after all, originally part of Coming of Age and only later became the mark of a married woman.

2-17 European women wear bracelets of gold and silver on their arms;
As de Europa trazem manilhas d'ouro e prata nos braços;

> The noblewomen of Ximo [Shimo] wear thin strings wrapped around [their wrists] five or six times. *As japoas nobres de Ximo humas linhas delgadas em cinco ou seis voltas.*

Precious metals versus paltry threads. While the extent to which "we" delighted in these materials was abnormal, the relative lack of interest in jewelry on the part of the Japanese may have been even more unusual, possibly unique in Southeast and Far East Asia. Unlike earrings, bracelets require no mutilation of the body. All they need is to be put on. Did I, then, pay too much attention to the hole issue with earrings? Is it possible Japanese just did not like the *feel* of these things? I, who do not even wear a wristwatch could appreciate that, but I realize it is no explanation. *Or, is it?* If less than half the cultures in the world wear metal bracelets, then "we" would beg for explanation, rather than "them," right?

In respect to those strings, Okada wonders if Frois might be referring to a charm worn when the arm or fingers were sore, but he does not guess why they would be sore. Young noblewomen wove clothing for their boyfriends. Could it have come from long hours on the loom? Or could it be from too much *koto*, a zither that sounds feminine and was, indeed, generally played by women, but is actually one of the most muscularly taxing instruments in the world? (the thick strings are pressed on the outside of the bridge to bend notes, with the amount of bending dependent on muscle power) Be that as it may, my first guess, based on no evidence, is that the strings were indeed charms, but for romance.

2-18 European women wear jewels and golden chains around their necks;
As de Europa trazem joyas e cadeas d'ouro ao pescoço;

> Gentile women in Japan wear nothing, and Christians relics or rosary beads.
> *As jentias de Japão nada, e as christãs relicairos ou rozairos de contas.*

No need to explain us. As far as I know, we did that back to the Stone Age.

In ancient times, Japanese women wore necklaces. If we had heart-strings, they had *tama-no-o,* or "*gem=soul*-strings." A *tama* is a *gem, jewel, ball, bead* (even if not round), rain or dew-*drop,* as an adjective anything precious, and, most important, the *soul* (different Chinese character but same pronunciation). This pun alone assured necklaces abounded, at least in the ancient poetry where the loss of a lover = a broken string and the gem/s (with no singular/plural, the multiple gems could pun as the singular soul) flying off, and widows might receive an offer to have her soul-string restrung (and reply: *You wish!, I've already found a better guy to restring me!*) Later, as longer poems were polished down to the more impersonal haiku, even a dewy spider's web might become a *tama-no-o* for the now Buddhist world. *Poof! Poof! Poof!* little souls return to the *Atman.* Come to think about it, in Japanese, "head," a round thing, is *atama,* a *tama!* And before Chinese characters turned the two *tama* into heteroscript the ancient *tama* was not a pair of homophones, but a singularity. Yet, the Japanese abandoned their necklaces! *Why?* You wouldn't think they would give up their soul-strings!

I cannot help but think that Frois, as a man of religion, and a poor man (unlike Valignano, who, judging from *De Missione,* clearly appreciated gems), valued Japanese more highly for not adorning themselves. If we were to score the contrasts, this one would go to the Japanese.

2-19 European women have sleeves reaching to the wrist;
As de Europa chegão-lhe as mangas [até] o colo da mão;

> Japanese women have them reaching to mid-arm, and do not think it wanton to disclose their arms and breast. *As japoas, chegão-lhe até meio braço e não têm por dezonestidade descobrir os braços e peytos.*

The Portuguese I translated as "wanton" is *desonestidade;* in Olde English, "dishonest." *Talk about contradiction!* – "we" claimed it dishonest to hide the face with make-up, yet honest to hide the body. Frois's "disclose" (*descobrir*) seems to imply a willful act but such was not the case, for the body parts in question were not considered particularly sexy. A *Faux Frois:*

We sometimes double the cloth under our arms to stop the sweat from running;
The Japanese leave a space open under the arm to let heat out and cool air in.

With wide sleeves and loose collars, the breasts might be spied through the sleeve-hole, the underarm hole of a raised arm, or from in front of a bowing body. But a dirty-minded Japanese man would presumably peek elsewhere, at, say, the nape of the neck . . . Note: *Don't mistake any of this to mean Japan was literally an open society.* In Frois's description of the construction of Nijô Castle, we learn that one day when Nobunaga, the Shogun who unified Japan "happened to see a soldier lifting up a woman's cloak slightly in order to get a glimpse of her face, and there and then . . . struck off his head with his own hand." (*Historia*: this trans. in C:TCJ) And, more generally, if Japan was as liberal (?) as some would have it, *senryû* would not mention men sneaking peeks at blind women micturating, using spy-glasses on women bathing, etc..

2-20 Among us, a woman who walked about barefoot would be thought mad or shameless;
Antre nós, andar huma molher descalsa ter-se'ia por douda ou dezavergonhada;

Japanese women, rich or poor, walk about barefoot for most of the year.
As japoas altas e baxas a mayor parte do ano andão sempre descalsas.

One might say the culture of Europe was literally out of touch with the earth. Everyone who could, wore shoes, inside and out. But did Japanese really walk about barefoot? *Inside*, yes. On the beach, sometimes. Otherwise, they took take care to keep their feet clean as not to soil their immaculate *tatami*. For this reason, even small children were generally not allowed to walk barefoot *outside*. Hence, this contrast provides a perfect example of the kind of misleading term Frois mentioned in the Prologue to his missing Summary. "We" assume "barefoot" – *descalcas,* or "unsocked" in Portuguese – is tantamount to being *shoeless*, because *we* wear socks with shoes. But Japanese rarely wore *tabi* (see 1-55+) during the hot half of the year. Their feet are bare to be sure, but not as we might imagine, because they are *in their sandals* or *on their clogs*. Frois probably put this contrast into the Woman's Chapter because he was not so much thinking of what we think of when discussing bare feet, i.e., *soles against the earth*, as of the *top of the foot*, i.e., the scandalous revelation of skin on the lower half of a woman's body.

As a literal antipode for Japan, China would have been far better than Europe. Chinese women not only kept their feet hidden when they were dressed, but when they were not. In China, feet were a surrogate private part. If Japanese women were loose with their feet, Chinese women were tight, and Europeans somewhere in-between. This is not only true for the degree of exposure, but for the degree to which the feet were tortured. The Japanese were kind to them, the Europeans, with their pointed and symmetrical toes, hard on them, and the Chinese with their foot-binding, very, very cruel to them.

2-21 European women wear their belts very tight.
As de Europa trazem seu sinjidouro muito apertado;

Japanese noble women [wear them] so loose, they are always dropping down.
As japoas nobres tão largo que lhe anda sempre caindo.

Okada writes matter-of-factly that the reason *obi* sashes – bands of cloth "as wide as a horse's girth strap" (de Avila Giron in C:TCJ) and just as stiff – were tied loosely was because of their greater width and the fact they are wrapped around the body several times (In TV Easterns, bad guys strip women by grapping hold of the end of the *obi* and spinning them like tops!). But, from what Rodrigues writes decades after Frois, *fashion* was probably at the heart of the matter, and Frois was catching the tail end of it:

> In olden days and up to the time when we went to Japan, and even long afterwards . . . It was thought fitting to wear them very loose and they always placed both their hands inside the sashes as they walked about the house in order to stop them slipping down to their feet. Nowadays, all the women tie their sashes in the same way as the men do . . . (R(C):TIJ)

During the Seclusion, the *obi* evolved into something notoriously restrictive. The rude French traveler Paul Theroux described the result as "an armor compressing and flattening the breasts" and the Austrian-born Usanian Rudofsky more lyrically depicts "breasts flattened out like flowers in a herbarium." This is definitely a strange development from the socio-biological perspective. If the Japanese were rubbing shoulders with a large-bosomed, wide-hipped people, one might argue this was an unconscious ploy to create an identity by *alternity*. This not being the case, we might hypothesize that the relatively small difference between the male and female body was compensated for by raising and thickening the belt for women to further contrast it to low male belt. At any rate, the Japanese did not compress the breast for anti-erotic or misogynic reasons as did the Puritans with their tight bodices and 17c Spain where, according to Desmond Morris, young women had "lead plates [!] pressed in to their swelling bosoms in an attempt to prevent their development." (INTIMATE BEHAVIOR)

2-22   European women wear rings with gems and other jewelry;
   As de Europa trazem aneis com pedraria e outras joyas;

> Japanese women wear no jewelry made of gold or silver.
> *As japoas nenhuma peça nem joya feita de ouro nem prata uzão.*

As Thunberg seconded, two centuries later, Japanese neither adorned themselves with "shells, beads, and glittering pieces of metal," as did most Asiatic and Africa people, nor wore "the unnecessary European trappings of gold and silver lace, jewels and the like, which serve merely to catch the eye." (T:TEAA) When we recall how the West laughed at the other's childish willingness to accept trinkets in exchange for things of real worth, like, say, Manhattan, the existence of a people mature enough to put *us* on the other side is a wonderful object lesson. True, precious gems and metals are precious, as Valignano pointed out. So, when it comes to international trade, they are not identical with trinkets. *But, that does not mean we had to wear them.* Thanks to Japan, European culture is seen for what it is, a culture of primitive magpie-like taste focusing on things that shine. *Look* at the sword handles and crowns now kept in Museums. *As art, they are almost all atrocious.* If they did not *happen to have millions of dollars worth of precious gems in them,* anyone with any sense would say they are junk of zero value. Amazingly, this is even true for many by famous artisans. In a word "we" as a culture were (and still are, I think) permanently *nouveau riche*. Our art would have been far better if it had to *create* what was precious rather than merely *take* it. If a king had only outlawed the use of anything precious for art, we might have had real art.

Since most cultures possessing precious metal have always worn it, the Japanese side is the one most in need of explanation. I don't have it. That is the kind of thing someone should earn a doctorate on.

Today, Japanese women have largely caught up with their *akusesari* (accessories), as they call jewelry, and almost everyone uses engagement rings, mostly platinum with diamonds. Most, like Germans, favor the right hand with its right=straight=correct connotation over the left hand with its left=heart=spirit-finger affiliation (classic culture says it links to the heart).

2-23   European women wear purses or keys on their girdles and belts;
   As de Europa trazem bolsas ou chaves em seus cordões e singidouros;

> The Japanese gird themselves [above the broader *obi* bands] with some thin strips of silk decorated with gold leaf, but hang nothing from them. *As japoas sinjem humas tiras de seda delgada pintadas com folhas d'ouro, mas não lhe pindurão nada.*

With the loose sleeve corners and bosoms serving as large pockets, Japanese had no need for purses. And if 2-21 was right, and the belts were always dropping down . . . But this is, more strictly, a contrast of the use of chord or chain-like devices to hang things from. Japanese men did not wear baldrics for swords, either. Frois missed a better contrast involving those keys:

> *We present the house-keys to a bride to use and wear with pride.*
> *They are presented with a wooden spoon, for they have no locks.*

The image of a housewife with keys dangling from her waist is a very Western one. Japanese houses could only be locked from the inside, and there were no locked rooms or cabinets, so the women would have had no use for keys from the start. "In Japan, the key to privacy is in the human heart, not in hardware, like in the West" as a pop-Japanologist (*nihonjinronka*) might put it. Actually, this could be inconvenient for, in houses with something worth stealing, it meant someone always had to stay home. He also missed another cord contrast:

> *We wear our clothes loose or tight and clothing cannot be both.*
> *They wear their robes loose but tighten them for work by crisscrossing cords over the chest.*

This thin but tough band of cloth or cord called a *tasuke* trusses up the loose robe (and, less obviously the sleeves) in order to keep it from getting dirty by touching the pail one is carrying, the pot one is throwing, or whatever. It looks cool and should be imitated by the fashion world.
..

2-24   European women's dress is closed in the front so the feet are concealed all the way down to the ground; *Os vestidos das de Europa são serrados por diante e cobren-lhe os pés até o chão;*

> That of the Japanese is completely open in the front so that the feet are visible all the way up the instep. *Os das japoas são todos por diante abertos e chegão até o peito do pee.*

The total concealment of female skin is not a Muslim thing. It was "our" thing.

"Open" with respect to the Japanese dress does not mean cut-away or slit *in order to show the leg*, but only that the overlap of the flaps in front is but a foot or two, so that a large step might show the foot up to the lower calf. But, Japanese women generally took mincing steps, for the narrow cloth of the kimono kept them "leg-tied," if I may borrow a 19c coinage of Consul Townsend Harris.

2-25   European women wear valuable scented gloves;
As de Europa trazem luvas preciosas e odoriferas;

> Japanese women wear mittons/sleeves of silk reaching to mid-arm, with all the fingers showing. *As japoas huns manguitos de seda até meyo braço com todos os dedos fora.*

We pretty much covered gloves in the last chapter (1-56). If European men wore gloves first as armor, then as signs of authority, women apparently wore them to hide their hands, supply something good-smelling for people to kiss, or to accidentally drop in order to attract a man's attention. The Japanese equivalent of this last use was a harder accident to concoct: *a broken clog strap*. Evidently, the first sex of gloves, i.e. gauntlets, were themselves tempted to use perfume, for I googled across a 16c Portuguese document, ORDENAÇÃO DA DEFESA DOS VELUDOS E SEDAS ([royal] order [by Dom João III] for defense of velour and silk) which includes a clause forbidding men of whatever status, quality or condition to wear or carry perfumed gloves of any scent whatsoever while permitting women to wear them as they wish. (Biblioteca Nacional de Lisboa, reservados, códice 3395.)

English has problems translating the *manguitos* (mitton/sleeve). See *TT-long*, if you wish.

2-26 European [noble]women generally wear very long black mantles.
As de Europa trazem mantos muito compridos e pretos

>Japanese noblewomen wear short ones of white silk.
>*As nobres japoas curtos e de seda branca.*

An Iberian mantle was a cross between a hat, veil and cloak. *Long* and *black* vs. *short* and *white* seems as different as different can be; but, considering the fact that both women kept their hair shielded and both colors are manifestly pure and somber, even funereal – though they could be worn on festive occasions – they are at some deeper level, similar. While most Japanese headgear was not colorful (sometimes it was figured satin, but not usually), it is my impression that *many* European women wore colorful mantles, which is why the first part of the distich probably deserves the same "noble" qualification as the Japanese one.

2-27 European mantles have neither sleeves nor colorful designs;
Os mantos de Europa não tem mangas nem pintura alguma;

>In Japan, the same figured *katabira* [light robes] they wear also serve for mantles.
>*Em Japão as mesmas* catabiras *pintadas que vestem servem tambem de mantos.*

The image of a light robe serving as a mantle, or veil – imagine someone warding off a rain shower with a coat – would seem so absurd to the reader that Frois has redundantly put "the same" (*as mesmas*) before the *katabira*, where "also" (*tambem*) was grammatically sufficient. Okada adds that the color (aside from white) of this summer-wear was usually "pale-scallion" or "water-pale-scallion" – light greens and blues – and other light shades. Japanese still feel such colors are *cooling* and even today utilize them, not for mantles but for window and door-screens (which I find very ugly).

2-28 European soldiers wear uniforms on festive occasions;
Os soldados em Europa por festa se vestem de libré;

>Japanese women ordinarily wear *kimono* uniforms in full decor.
>*As japoas vestem ordinariamente qimões de libré e quarteados.*

The translation of *quarteados* is a problem. I think we can extrapolate the idiomatic meaning of being well-proportioned, broad across the shoulders, etc. to mean what we now call "dressed to the T," which in military idiom suggests "full décor." This gives the clothing a correct but still formidable air and fortifies Frois's intended contrast of the informal, far-from-uniform, women's wear in Europe (indirectly alluded to by the soldiers) with their formal well-starched counterparts in Japan. This reading is indirectly backed Rodrigues who writes that Japanese garments "are all cut in only one plain style, and this is true of the dress of men and women, laymen and religious"(R(C)TIJ) and Thunberg who adds, two hundred years later, that "the Japanese always have their coat of arms put on their clokes . . . with a view to prevent their being stolen, which in a country where people's clothes are so much alike in point of materials, form, and size, might easily happen. (T:TEEA)" (I suspect Thunberg's translator failed to imagine how clothing folded into little boxes at public baths would be easily confused and Englished "taken" as "stolen.") These "coat of arms" (if the clan mark can be so called) found on formal outdoor wear also suggest martial dress. A *Faux Frois:*

European women go to dances hoping each to boast her special dress unlike any other;
Japanese women at bon dances come in regiments, outfitted with identical uniforms.

Since the Jesuits in Japan were so down on festivities that they even criticized Japanese for their efforts to create Christian fun, we have no detailed reports of bon dances, but I have been impressed by groups of identically dressed women (including neighborhood groups and the employees of medium-sized companies) participating in bon dances. These uniforms, far from drab are a joy to behold. But, in Frois's time, Japanese men, too, probably wore their livery. Frois missed the most obvious purely female difference; it is time for another *Faux:*

European women wear and show only one or at most two layers of clothing;
Japanese ones wear up to twelve layers of clothing and often show them all.

With Japanese clothing generally fastened in only one place – at the waist – the rest of the vertical hem, from the collar to the waist (and, sometimes from the waist to the feet) was loose enough that each layer of color would show like the layers of tissue opened up by a large surgical incision.

~~~~~~

2-29 In Europe, the men walk in front and the women behind;
Em Europa vão os homens diante e as molheres detrás;

In Japan, the men behind and the women in front.
Em Japão os homens detrás e as molheres diante.

Both Japanese translations turn the subjects into *husband* and *wife* (*otto, tsuma*) rather than "men" and "women." This contrast – before I *knew* it was mistaken – astounded and delighted me (to my embarrassment, I even quoted it in two books), for Europeans visiting Japan after the Seclusion observed Japanese men walking in front of their wives, who were supposed to lag back a bit to avoid stepping on their husband's shadow, or guard against back-stabbing (S:MQTJ), etcetera., while the Japanese, for their part, were shocked to see *our* convention of *"ladies first!"* Chamberlain, describing "Woman (Status of)" in THINGS JAPANESE, makes some interesting associations in this respect:

Two grotesquely different influences are now at work to undermine this state of slavery [i.e. "the three obediences" to father, husband and son] – one, European theories concerning the relation of the sexes, the other, European clothes! The same fellow who struts into a room before his wife when she is dressed *a la japonaise,* will let her go in first when she is dressed *a l'europeenne.*

What a disappointment to find out later that Frois was only contrasting an accompaniment of servants! This cannot be ascertained from the Portuguese original (*homens* = men and *molheres* = women) alone, for Frois elsewhere uses them to mean *husbands* and *wives*. I only discovered what was what from reading Valignano, Van Linschoten and Montanus, respectively:

The women ride horses like the men, and when they bring with them maids (*senoras mocas*), maidens and other women, all of them go in front of them, and the men-servants (*criados*) behind, the opposite of the women in Europe. (V(A):V&S)

The like [contrarie] custome is among the women, for as they goe abroad they have their daughters and maydes before them, and their men servants come behind, which in Spaigne is cleane contrarie, . . . (L:VJHVL)

. . . and so [contrarily] amongst their Women, who when they walk abroad, order their maids and Daughters to go before them, whereas ours follow their Mistresses. (M:EEJ)

Had Frois visited in the 20c, he might have observed, as I did, the following (now changing):

In Usania (I cannot speak for Europe), husbands and wives often go out together.
In Japan, husbands and wives rarely if ever go out together, unless it is to a foreign country.

~~~~~~

2-30   In Europe, property is shared between spouses;
Em Europa a fazenda hé commua antre os cazados;

In Japan, each owns his or her own. A woman sometimes lends hers to her husband. *Em Japão cada hum tem a sua separada e às vezes a molher onzena com o marido.*

DR puts it well: "common property would seem to accompany the Western concept of 'becoming one'." That is doubtless the main contrast and parallels that of 4-5, where Frois contrasts the individual economy of Japanese Buddhist monks with the common property of the Christian Brothers. But the European concept of commonality was belied by the fact that, practically speaking, the fortune generally belonged to the man. M & J cite a mid-17c text which advises that while many responsibilities might be shared, the purse should be in the firm control of the husband and "a lady should fear the touch of money as one would fear fire." Money was thought to become a "despicable weapon" in the hands of a woman and, in Portugal, at least, the marriage contract usually specified an allowance to be paid by a husband to his wife. (J/F(M&J):) That is to say, Frois's idealistic contrast might be restated in terms of which sex held the purse strings.

Samurai-class brides were expected to bring a trousseau, supposedly for make-up and clothing, but really to ensure her proper support. It was to be returned to her (parents') family after an unspecified period or upon her death. Relatively wealthy women often brought their own farming plots and money with them into a marriage and lend them to their husbands at their pleasure, and as Frois's *onzena* suggests, it could be at usurious rates (Though 11% is hardly so onerous as the 13% the criminal credit card company now demands from me so I can write: poor men always pay through the teeth). The relationship of the finances to the respectively high position of Japanese women vis-à-vis European women is brought out by Caron's observation that the bridegroom and his parents often return the gift "being unwilling that the bride should have any colourable excuse to raise her into an opinion of having obliged her Husband," while "the poorer sort do but seldom return these offers as needing them." (C:DOJ) In other words, poor men had no choice but to enjoy equality, but not all Japanese men (or their families) wanted to be indebted to their wives. Neither, however, did all Japanese women want to be indebted to their husbands. Sladen, in 1905, noted that "a girl whose parents were only moderately well off, who was marrying a man no better off than herself, might have a trousseau worth five hundred pounds, in which she was provided with everything she could want during the first few years of married life, except the food which perishes. The theory was, that it might make her husband dissatisfied with her if she had to go on asking for things . . ." (S:MQTJ). However, whatever case the case might be, there was one more contrast here. Faux Frois:

In Europe, men handle the family finances;
In Japan, all accounting is left to wives.

Women, as the 19c visitors would learn to their regret after hiring men who couldn't count to do their accounting, kept all the books for the family bank they guarded (or rather *hid*), made payments and doled out allowances (why Japan did not need Prohibition, according to one letter writer to *The Japan Times*). Generations of Japanese men have joked about being cormorants made to regurgitate their pay for their wives. See TT-long for a page more.

2-31 In Europe, repudiating a woman is a serious sin and the greatest dishonor;
Em Europa, além do pecado, hé suma infâmia repudiar a molher;

In Japan, one may repudiate as many as one pleases. The women do not lose their honor for this, nor their marriageability. *Em Japão dá hum repudio a quantas quer, e ellas não perdem por isso honra nem casamento.*

In reality, separation and divorce may have been more acceptable if not common in Europe, including Iberia, than Frois might have known. In parts of Spain, "couples separated and lived freely with other partners. Many believed that one could separate legally from his or her spouse simply by going to the town notary and obtaining a so-called letter of separation. Others, who sought to annul their marriages, found witnesses willing to lie for them." (Sara T. Nalle (97) (*God in La Mancha: Religious Reform and the People of Cuenca*, 1500-1650: IBERIAN RESOURCES ONLINE) Still, if we are thinking about the professed attitude of responsible parties, the European side of the contrast is beyond dispute. Even Kings were not free to "repudiate" their wives. One English King who wanted to do so found it simpler to behead them and divorce his nation from the Catholic church. Even so, Henry VIII's new Anglican church did not permit others to divorce. It is interesting that Frois frames his contrast in terms of moral approbation or acceptance and not on what was legal or illegal. If people were that afraid of sin, why were laws needed?

Frois noted the Japanese side of the contrast in 1565: They commonly have no more than one woman [wife], but for very slight reasons, they may divorce her . . . and take others [for a wife], and they also leave their husbands, although it is less common, still divorce is so frequent among them, from kings to laborers, that they are not at all upset about it (20-11?2?-65 Cartas or V(A): S&A). Valignano, expanded: "And it is surprising how peacefully they do this, because no ill-feeling remains among the relatives, indeed, they visit, speak and treat one another as they did before." (V(A):S&A)

The reality was complex. Frois's "no more than one woman" suggests he describes commoners who comprised 90% of the country. Most of their divorces were early in the marriage. In many cases, the man may not yet have brought his bride home but was himself commuting to her house until his mother saw fit to turn over the house to her. If either spouse was thought to be a poor worker, they might be deemed unsuitable and the marriage, that might better be called a trial marriage, annulled by their families. With samurai, where marriage tended to be political, divorce required the permission of the lord of the domain. It is often noted that in the Tokugawa era (there is almost no information on Frois's time) women could not remarry without an official letter of divorce which only the husband was free to *grant* or *not to grant*. This gives us the impression that the freedom of repudiation was of greater service to men than to women. The husband-wife relationship has even been described as one of master and vassal in a feudal relationship and the threat of simple divorce only a way to keep women in line. About a hundred years after Frois, moralist Kaibara Eiken in his classic *Onna Daigaku,* "Woman-Great-Study" (or, to use a free rendition suggested by Chamberlain "The Whole Duty of Woman") gave seven reasons for divorce allegedly based on Confucius: disobedience to the father or mother-in-law, barrenness, lewdness, jealousy, leprosy or any like foul disease, disturbing the household harmony by talking too much and too disrespectfully, or being a kleptomaniac. Divorce could even be seen as a moral good. In order to promote frugality, the Tokugawa government (authorities in some fiefdoms, at any rate) decreed additional *Reasons for Divorce,* including things like "too much sightseeing" or "too much tea-drinking!"

The reality was *more* complex. At the time Kaibara wrote the infamous list, the husband *also* needed proper proof of divorce (which meant he needed his wife to write a receipt for his writ of divorce.) If she could be shaved bald and returned to her parent's home for the crime of remarrying without being clearly divorced, he could be banished from his county (see 2-22) if his fault was evident.

Women whose husbands philandered away their fortune might even lend them money against such a signed permission of divorce. Japanese families sometimes included pre-signed divorce writs among their prenuptial agreements. The property of the wife was also detailed so that most men could not divorce their wives even if they wanted to because they did not have the wherewithal to properly return them, as was required. The wording of the writ of divorce includes the phrase "*katte*," which implies fiat, but it also has the connotation (still common today) of selfish individual behavior and came at a price, namely, the responsibility to compensate the other party.

The West was still surprised at Japan's high divorce rate when Japan reopened to the world in the mid-19c. Alice Mabel Bacon wrote there were men and women who had divorced two or three times over and were none the worse for it (B:JGW). The Meiji Civil Code of 1898-9 sought to improve Japan's international reputation by making divorce difficult. In a single year the official rate (which vastly understated the reality) dropped from approximately 3 divorces for every 1000 people/year to 1.5, and by the mid-20c, Japan boasted its Confucian family values explained its extraordinarily low rates vs. the high and rising rates in the USA (the rest of Europe, included many nations with lower rates, conveniently overlooked). The main reason given by Japanese – especially the men in power – for fighting hand and tooth against liberalizing divorce law in the last quarter of the century was concern lest easy divorce would permit men to throw away their wives for someone younger, but when the law did change, as it turned out, it was not so much women as men who had something to worry about, for the number of divorces sought by women was several times more than those sought by men. A large and rapidly growing portion of these were elderly women freeing themselves of dead-weight husbands disparagingly called *sôdai-gomi,* or large crude trash (things too big to fit in the garbage, put out on a special day for collection)!

Jesuits in Japan had mixed feelings about the abundant divorces. On the one hand, it was proof of sinfulness, but when they forced nobles who wished to become Christian to ditch all but one wife, the fact that the others would not be ruined by the divorce was doubtless a relief. In 1592, Valignano had the matter (together with 11 other questions on marriage alone) of divorce in Japan submitted to a famous casuist in Spain and the conclusion was that the original marriage, not being contracted with the presupposition of perpetuity, was not a *bona fide* marriage but *a test*, so the divorce was not a real divorce, and there was no problem with it. (See Proust: *Europe Through the Prism of Japan* (P(B):ETPJ))

2-32 In accord with fallen nature, men are the ones who repudiate women [in Europe];
Segundo a natureza corrupta, os homens são os que repudião as molheres;

In Japan, the women are often the ones to repudiate the men.
Em Japão, muitas vezes, as molheres são as que repudião os homens.

Their fallen nature? *Our* fallen nature? *This* fallen world? English needs a pronoun. If Frois means that men in Europe followed "their natural depravity"(what one translation says), this represents a Virgin/Mother Mary-loving Catholic understanding of what modern day sociobiology claims (the male had the stronger tendency to live dissolutely and seek other sex partners). But, in England, at least, it was women who were generally accused of having an especially sinful nature at this time. As crooked as the rib they came from, they gave in to the snake and corrupted Adam. Late-16c and 17c feminists countered that God made woman of man's flesh that" she might bee purer then he" that is to say, she was not second-hand but double-refined! (Jane Anger, 1589, in Travisky ed. THE PARADISE OF WOMEN, but A. Goreau's THE WHOLE DUTY OF WOMEN is the best book on the subject). But, note, if it is indeed the repudiator and not the repudiated that is corrupted here, the implication of the contrast would be that Japanese women are more "corrupt" than their European counterparts.

While women in Japan did not did gain a formal right to sue for divorce until 1873, there were circumstances when they could do *what amounted to the same* in the Edo period. As Okada notes, a husband who spent a wife's savings and sold her property could be divorced by her family and she could gain a divorce *by his failing to send her an official Summons to Return* (after she went home because he abandoned or maltreated her. It is hard to be precise about what Frois saw. One hint comes from the Japanese Middle Ages. In Tale 10 of book of Buddhist tales called *Shasekishû* (vol.5) written in 1283 describes a husband who goes to the constable (*jitô*) for his assistance in capturing his wife who left him, but the constable found she was a kind person, so she got to stay in the house and he was banished from the county. In the Middle Ages of Japan, it seems, a man could divorce his wife and both could remain in the same county, while a man who was divorced by his wife had to leave. This was good, obviously, for protecting the woman from revenge. (J/M:KZJ)

The samurai class was a different story. The men did not need to divorce to enjoy new love (they could take another wife or a formal mistress); so women would certainly have had a better reason to *want* a divorce than a man would, but in their case, politics and economics made it hard. So, you might say that in Japan, poor women had the advantage. 19c Europeans observed that, among low-class wage earners, women not only divorced drink and gambling-addicted husbands but sometimes escaped marriage for lesser reasons. Bacon mentions one who married on the promise that the bossy Mother in Law would remain with the older son, and when this turned out not to be the case, "sued for divorce and obtained it, and was back in her old place, all in a month's time from the date of her marriage." (B:JGW) In *Queer Things About Japan,* Douglas Sladen *lauded* the high divorce rate in Japan, noting that it was far more reasonable to allow a working woman to divorce her no-good husband than to chain them to utterly irresponsible and violent men by unfair laws of property, as English Law did at the time.

Some or even most of the divorces of men by women that Frois learned of may have been by the women *and* their parents; i.e., where a groom who married into the bride's family either because it had no sons (or only young ones) proved a bad deal. This matrilineal practice, "found only in the Pyrenees region of France, parts of Scandinavia, and parts of India" was common (20% of marriages in Edo (article in *Japan Echo* Oct 2003)) but I cannot give percentages for Frois's time.

2-33 In Europe, the abduction of a female relation threatens the survival of all her family;
Em Europa polo rapto de huma parenta se põe toda a gerasão a perigo de morte;

In Japan, her father, mother and brothers conceal it and just let it pass over.
Em Japão os pais e as mãis e irmãos desimulão e pasão levemente por isso.

"*Rapto*" is hell to translate. I think Frois means eloping without the permission of the family, but it might include marriage-abductions. Apparently, European, or, at least Iberian males were under cultural if not legal obligation to risk death trying to wrest back (or *kill,* as we see in some Islamic countries even today) a stolen or, perhaps, wayward woman and those responsible for taking her, in order to defend the family honor.

In most respects, Japanese were sticklers for honor, but apparently this was one area where they were not so touchy as Europeans, or at least Luso-Iberians (See 2-35, below). But Japanese were not tolerant of all illegal behavior. Adultery sometimes led to horrific and grotesque punishment (if you have the stomach for it, see what Carletti and Caron describe in *TT-long*)! Unlike Caron, Carletti put the cruelty in perspective, writing that the Portuguese were even stricter than the Japanese in this regard!

Not only adultery, but *mere suspicion* justified homicide. Portuguese law (in Goa [2nd account E. Indies p214]) permitted husbands to kill their wives at whim, so that women "frequently die unjustly." He sadly mentions hearing of a "young wife of only a few months, killed by her husband because of a jealousy that he felt of a man who had fallen in love with her when she had been a girl, but who continued to pass through the street in which she lived with her husband." (The legacy of this Portuguese law is still found in Brazil, where news of and, thank goodness, controversy over, perfunctory killings of wives by jealous husbands continues today.) If Frois writes nothing about *adultery,* it is doubtless because there was no contrast. Europe and Japan *both* punished it with death.

2-34 In Europe, the seclusion of daughters and maidens is important and rigorous;
Em Europa, o emcerramento das filhas e donzelas hé muito grande e riguroso;

> In Japan, daughters go out for the whole day, or many, wherever they want to, without telling their parents. *Em Japão as filhas vão sós por onde qerem por hum dia e muitos, sem ter conta com os pais.*

Ah, to breathe the free air of Japan! According to Boxer, the freedom of Japanese women was noted by the first European to write about Japan (at Xavier's request in 1543), Captain Alvarez:

> That Alvarez [see 2-35n] was no uncommon observer, is seen from his remark that, despite the nominally inferior position of women, the gray mare was frequently the better horse. He alludes wonderingly to the relative freedom of movement enjoyed by women who could go out unaccompanied by their menfolk or chaperones – something very daring to an Iberian, for as a result of centuries of Mohammedan rule, Moslem ideas on the seclusion of women were much stronger in the Peninsula than elsewhere in Europe. (B:CCJ)

About forty years later, Valignano contrasted the Chinese women, who "are very retiring and modest and are seen in public rarely or never," with the Japanese "who enjoy more freedom and are looser in their conduct than women anywhere else." (first redaction (1580?), in S:VMP). I am not sure what Frois thought of girls and women having license to roam, but it should have been convenient for the Jesuit mission because it meant that they could proselytize women as well as men.

Despite centuries of generally accurate reporting from China and Japan, writers back home continued to confuse the two cultures. In 1873, Cockburn's literary creation, the "Japanese Scout," is amazed that in London *"you'll see the most lovely young 'lassies' / Taking a walk without any young 'laddies'"* to protect their perfectly figured classical bodies from harm. So London (a violent place in Frois's time) was finally civilized! But, an amazed *Japanese* scout? As if young lassies *ever* needed laddies to escort them in Tokyo!

2-35 In Europe, a wife cannot go out without her husband's permission;
As molheres em Europa não vão fora de caza sem licença de seus maridos;

> Japanese wives are free to go where they please without informing their husbands. *As japoas tem liberdade de yrem por onde qizerem, sem os maridos o saberem.*

This difference may owe something to a lack of public order in Europe, but for the most part it probably reflects a moral philosophy of total control over women on "our" side. The normality of this oppressive state is reflected by an observer of the Carnival preceding Lent in late 16c Barcelona:

The women, too, take their part . . . throughout the year they are so severely restricted that they are not allowed to talk to strangers. But at carnival there are no such shackles and hindrance. They put on masks and run through the streets in complete freedom . . . So, for more than one husband, the cuckoo sings before the Spring [summer?] comes." (Felix Platter in H:CER)

Japanese women, not so tightly shackled in their daily life, did not *need* carnivals to walk in freedom. An abridged Englishing of the 1543 testimony of Alvarez contains this line: Good wives are held in much esteem by their husbands; indeed they altogether rule them, and go hither and thither as they list, without ever thinking of asking leave of their lords." (in C:LLFX) Bernandino de Avila Giron, a Spanish merchant contemporary with Frois, also thought highly of Japanese married women who "may be trusted completely for they are the most upright and faithful women in the whole world." But continuing tongue in cheek, adds, "And, she who errs in this matter pays for it with her head." (C:TCJ) Fifty years later, trader Caron gave a more astute, but possibly jaundiced explanation for the goodness and freedom of wives in Japan. Since men who were not happy with their wives could freely divert themselves with concubines and prostitutes, "this liberty that the Men have, obliges the Women to observe their Husbands and endeavor to endear them to them, by an humble compliance and submission to their humors, being sure else to lose them, and see their Rivals preferred before them."(Ibid.)

Be that as it may, Japanese women in the warrior class and among town-folk emulating them, were not only more likely to read and write than their European counterparts (2-45, below), but to have studied enough martial arts to make them no push-over. You don't hear of *them* fainting away like the European lady. Even if overpowered, they were liable to kill themselves; and just in case there were men so utterly cruel as to want their victim dead, the authorities made sure that "terrifying a person into the commission of suicide" was a capital crime. (See TT-long for a famous case – or urban legend – involving America and a suicide poem: *Tsuyu-wo dani itoo Yamato-no Ominaeshi / Furu America-ni Sode-wa nurasaji*) Still, lest *all* Japanese women appear braver, or more heroic than they probably were, I must qualify. While the women mentioned by Frois could go out *without their husband's permission*, if they were anything more than a servant, they generally did not go out *all* alone but with other women, their servants. By alone, Frois probably means that they did not have male guards.

Centuries later, Chamberlain wrote that while Japanese women neither wore veils nor were beaten in Japan, they were "treated more or less like babies, neither trusted with the independence which our modern manners allow; nor commanding the romantic homage that was a woman's dower in medieval Europe." (C:TJ) This is a very different image, indeed. But, if I am not mistaken, the status of Japanese women changed little between Frois and Chamberlain. That of Europeans did, and with it "our" perspective reversed.

~~~~~~

2-36   In Europe, the love between relations of both sexes for one another is very great;
Ho amor dos parentes e parentas entre si hé em Europa muito grande;

In Japan, it is very little; they act like they hardly know one another.
Em Japão muito pouco, e se hão huns pera com os outros como estranhos.

"Relations" is vague, but "family" to many readers would not include extended relations, while "relatives" would not include "family." The Portuguese *parentes* and *parentas* include both family members and relatives. While all pre-modern Europe may have had families far more extended than what we now call family, Latins were probably especially close (and, Northern Europeans with their clans and Russians, if their complex vocabulary for relations is taken at face value) because they still are.

Many Japanese might find it surprising to be put on the nuclear or individualistic side of the contrast, but the fact is they did not relate as much with their relatives as Latins did. True, the reserve Japanese of the upper classes maintained even between family members (see 3-16) exaggerated that distance somewhat, but, as the proverb confirms, Japanese have traditionally favored *"the stranger close by, over the relative far off."* (*tôi shinseki yori chikaku no tanin*). Japanese families were more liable to adopt children (or husbands) to carry on the family line, despite their pride in lineage, than Europeans. Perhaps, the idea of lineage and rights of heredity had less to do with blood and more to do with the ability to learn skills and trustworthiness to keep secrets transmitted down the generations in Japan, i.e., the survival of the memes rather than the genes. After all, in a culture where skill was highly valued, it would do no good to keep the name and lose the art.

East Asians in the 19th and 20th c have continually talked up the family-like nature of their corporations and politic. But a corporation functioning *like* a family (whether hierarchical or egalitarian) is not at all the same as a society where everything depends upon blood relations. I think Frois called it right and that this attitude of the Japanese was conducive to modernization in general and the building of a powerful skill-based economy that vaulted Japan over the Latin cultures to become an economic super-power.

2-37 In India, barefoot boys hold up parasols/umbrellas to keep the rain and sun off the women; *Na Índia levão os moços sonbreiros de pé aas molheres pola chuva ou sol;*

In Japan, the women hold up parasols/umbrellas for each other.
Em Japão as molheres os levam umas às outras.

This is the only time Frois refers to India instead of Europe! Is it because Europeans didn't yet use umbrellas? Presumably, most Jesuit recruits in Japan or bound for Japan or leaving Japan for Europe would spend some time in Goa and become familiar with Indian life, so India is a good proxy for "our" side. The French translators turn the boys into what they were, "young blacks" (*jeunes Noirs* – why the capital letter?), who, judging from the prints of Europeans in Japan, were generally not boys but men. M & J make them "barefoot," not quite the original "on foot," but I like it and borrowed it for there are ambiguities in the Portuguese (See *TT-long*).

Frois is not talking about women in general, but the women in Japan who have a similar social position to those served by others in India or in Europe (though not yet for umbrellas). *Japanese ladies could do things for themselves.* While some nobility did have help in Japan for almost every aspect of their lives, including "fart-cut-nuns" (*hehiri-bikuni*) who took the blame for their social indiscretions – i.e., the responsibility for their literal and figurative farts! (maybe I am fooled by fanciful literature on this, but it is too good not to mention!) – even such pampered courtesans – women living in court = would usually *fan themselves*, something not true in much of the world. In Japan, only the Emperor's dog had someone to fan his flies away and put bits of ice in his mouth, according to *A Diplomatist's Wife in Japan*, Mrs. Frazer, who sighed "I wish some kind fairy would fan *me* all day and put bits of ice into my mouth!"

Reading of women who held up parasols/umbrellas for one another, we conjure up a vision of women walking side-by-side each extending their parasol out and over the other. That would be exotic, very artsy and a poignant illustration of how equality and dependence can go together if it could be done which in reality it cannot, unless a line of women each held umbrellas over the one in front of them. So my first guess at what Frois really meant was that women often *shared* their parasols/umbrellas. Sharing them was so common there are even terms for it in the dictionary (*aiaigasa, aiyaigasa, aigasa*) and in the Edo era it came to signify a romantic relationship. Even today, where "we" would draw a *heart* within which to insert the names of lovers, Japanese will draw a simple *umbrella* and put the names under it, one on each side of the handle. But, the most common depiction of women with umbrellas has them each carrying their own. So Frois must be referring to noblewomen whose heads were indeed shielded by parasols held by *other* women, who are not lowly servants but (judging from pictures) lower level ladies of the court. *Relatively well-off women doing the menial work of holding up umbrellas* would be contrast enough with women using lowly servants.

2-38 In Europe, granted there are abortions, but they are very infrequent;
Em Europa, posto que o aja, não hé frequente o aborsio das crianças;

In Japan, it is so common there are women who have aborted twenty times.
Em Japão hé tão comum, que há molher que aborta vinte vezes.

Andrés Pérez de Ribas wrote that women in what is now North México aborted on purpose if they were already nursing and, on being "reproached for this abuse and cruelty" replied "'Can't you see that i am looking out for the life of this child that i'm holding in my arms?' thus making it clear that she was killing one child to raise another."(R(R&A&D):HOT) That was generally the reason for abortion throughout the world, including Japan, where nursing was long and each infant treated with great care. Note that these Amerindians mentioned by Pérez de Ribas, the Mayo, are described as "not as fierce as these other nations . . . rather, they are tractable and gentle . . ." (R(R&A&D): HOT) Is it not the case that cultures that permit abortion and infanticide are generally gentle and do so in preference to making war on others or allowing starvation to do the dirty work, whereas cultures that force women to breed generally kill others in order to expand, or exist in a state of mutual war with others of their ilk (people have always known that unrestricted "right to life" is really "a license to kill")? Be that as it may, if Frois is right about those numbers, Japanese medical care for women was far in advance of that in Europe, where a woman wouldn't have a million-to-one chance of surviving that many abortions! But, exaggeration or not, abortion was common enough a century or two later that there are many *senryu* (risqué poems) roasting lady-doctors who specialized in abortion – called colloquially "droppings" (*oroshi*) – salaciously(!?) imagining their work "below the hair-line," and how bold their sons must be with their maids, etc.. That is to say, Japanese were indeed familiar enough with the practice to joke about it.

After the Opening of Japan, militarists eager to push up the population and compete with the West in colonizing the world came down hard on abortion, but once Japan was forced out of the war game and back to peace in the last half of the 20c, women were once again free to choose. This does not mean all was well. Doctors who profited from abortion, blocked the pill. The medical lobby is despicable, but Japanese women who abort their fetus rather than raise it under unfavorable conditions show a far greater love for children than women who would give birth regardless of their capability to mother it. Most women have long been wise enough to realize that a fetus is *not* human, but only a *potential* human. Nevertheless, the guilt felt by some is sometimes taken advantage of by Buddhist temples that take high fees to pray for the so called "water-baby's" soul. At these temples, one can see thousands of small stone statues, many with bibs and candy or toys placed before them.

4-39 In Europe, it is very rare if ever that an infant is killed after birth;
Em Europa, depois da criança nacer, raras vezes ou quasi nunca se mata;

Japanese women put a foot on their throat and kill all that they don't think they can raise. *As japoas lhe põem o pé no pescoço e matão todos os que lhe parese que não podem sostentar.*

As a farming people, Japanese called infanticide *mabiki*, or "thinning." This was no euphemism. Neither was it a callous metaphor. It was reality. This "thinning" was short-term taking of life for the long-term gain of life. When crops failed or didn't keep up with taxes, parents had to make hard choices on how to maximize the chances of survival for their offspring, or, to put it in human terms, do everything possible to keep their children fat and happy. Since a bad year could not be predicted, abortion was not always an option. St. Xavier wrote matter-of-factly "Poor women who have many children kill the youngest that they may not grow up to suffer poverty, and this is not punished." (Coleridge trans.) In 1557, Vilela wrote with even more obvious sympathy, "We fear the lean cows of Pharaoh and pray the Lord will not let them come here, because it is heart-breaking to see how many children are killed in such times." (Cooper trans) He also wrote: "It [Japan] has many people; and if they don't kill the children they bear, they will eat up one another, because the number of children killed at birth is infinite. There are women with 15 or 20 dead [children], and with this, they still have infinite people." Reading between the lines, I cannot help wondering if Vilela realized that killing the youngest child (the newly born) was actually the *kindest* way to cope with famine, and a more benign way to regulate the population than allowing starvation, war and disease to kill older children and adults, whose lives were and still are much more valuable, in so far that they already *have* the humanity an infant only promises. (See Nancy Schieper-Hughes: DEATH WITHOUT WEEPING, on infanticide by neglect in Brazil, today, for an honest witness of reality.)

I think the reason the Jesuits usually mention the reason for infanticide instead of simply decrying it, is that in the West, for over a millennium, the practice was identified with prostitution and because, owing to higher death-rates, there was less need to control the population. Individuals who could not raise a baby in Europe generally *abandoned* it; but this was also done in Japan, so there was no contrast, and the *Tratado* does not mention the practice. (For two pages more, see *TT-long*.)

Note that, as was the case for abortion, the most outspoken critics of infanticide were *those who wanted Japan to "move on and spread all over the world,"* as exemplified by Satô Nobuhiro, who devised programs for the reconstruction and expansion of Japan in the early-19c (T:SJT).

2-40 Pregnant women in Europe loosen their belts in order not to hurt the baby; As molheres prenhes em Europa largão os singidouros por não fazer mal à criansa;

> The Japanese tie on a belt so tightly before giving birth that even a hand cannot be squeezed between the belt and their flesh. As japoas até que pairão se apertão com huma precinta tão rijamente que antre a precinta e a carne lhe não possa caber a mão.

Valignano introduced the Japanese side of this contrast, together with that of contrast 2-21:

Nor is it less surprising to see what women do when they are with child and give birth; because, when they conceive, all the wives and maidens who, before conceiving, went about wearing a belt of silk so loose and wide that it was always liable to fall off, and took pride in walking about so disheveled, bind themselves up so tightly with a *faxa* [?] that it seems they would burst, in such a manner that they seem to have thinner bellies on the point of giving birth than they had before conceiving. And I don't understand how, in doing this, they do not kill themselves with their babies – with all this, they say they know from experience that if they do not go about so restricted, the parturition is bad. (1583. For more creative Englishings of this, see Van Linschoten (1598), Montanus (1670) and L' Abbe (1705) in *TT-long*)

Valignano's principle point was that not only are their customs contrary, but they are so because, they attest, *experience has taught them it is best.* He is amazed experience can teach us such contrary things. Perhaps there are advantages and disadvantages to *both* ways. In a later SUMARIO, Valignano further specifies that the tight *obi* (ceremoniously put on in the fifth month) was thought to prevent miscarriage *and premature birth*. Could looseness improve circulation for us, while support would prevent strain for Japanese?   Inactive European women would benefit most from the former and more active Japanese would require the second. *Opinions, Doctors?*

2-41 European women remain lying down and rest after giving birth;
As molheres em Europa acabando de parir deitão-se e descansão;

Japanese women must remain seated day and night for twenty days after birth.
As japoas hão-de estar depois de parir asentadas 20 dias de dia e de noite.

    Childbirth in Japan was done sitting (as it is in most cultures) rather than on flat beds. The wealthy sat on special legless chairs covered with cushions – if we can call something legless a chair, why not call it a sofa and say "they" invented the sofa or soft arm-chair? – and poor farmers improvised the same with straw. An early 19-c document quoted by Okada mentions no less than twelve bundles of straw covered with a futon. Between day 17 and 21 some straw is removed each night until the woman is flat on her back on the 21st day. Still, considering what was written about the poverty of much of the country, I cannot help doubting that commoners stayed seated all day.

    The idea of this contrast would seem to be that "we" think new mothers should take it easy, but "they" think not. Valignano has them not only being forced to remain seated (because lying down would allow the blood to rise to their head, but bathed with cold water (with the baby) and only given "things of little substance" to eat. "And, with all of this," he marvels, it "takes place among people who live with as much discernment and dignity as we do in Europe." There might be some truth to this *easy* vs. *hard* idea, but sitting, at least, would not be as bad as most Western readers might imagine. First, to Japanese, who usually used no chairs, *back support would be a vacation of sorts*. Second, a slightly curved body is better for the circulation of the belly – something that must mend after the rapid-growth tumor called a baby comes out – than a straight one. Third, since Japanese never walked for exercise to begin with, sitting would not be felt as confining and the woman would, after all, get sufficient exercise every time she went to the outhouse (for the benefits of *squatting*, 11-20).

    A word on Valignano's "things of little substance." Red beans on white rice (*azuki-han*) – celebratory colors – and shellfish may not be hearty food by European standards, but nutritionists would approve of them. But it is possible that pigging out was avoided for commoners, who desired to space-out births would not have wanted a quick return to unwanted fertility, and nobles, who turned over nursing to maids, benefited by keeping the slim figure their husband's desired.

2-42 In Europe, we are strongly on guard against air and wind after birth;
Em Europa se guardão muito do ar e do vento depois do parto;

The Japanese, as soon as they give birth, wash themselves and leave the doors and windows open. *As Japoas em acabando de parir se lavão e estão com portas e janelas abertas.*

    Europeans were afraid of the mother and child catching something from outside. Fear of such "wind" is not restricted to the ancient past or to childbirth. My grandmother, who' lived to be 106 avoided *drafts* like the plague. I, who slept with an open window and fan on in Florida, recall my surprise at her solemn warnings. The right amount of circulation was and is problematic. If *influenza* (in-flow) came from drafts, *malaria* (bad-air) came from stagnant air. It is good to go out and *"get some air,"* yet bad to *"be exposed to a draft."* Confusing, isn't it? The Japanese were also wary of the wind, for the very word for "cold" (the disease) in Japanese *is* "wind," and the 1604 Japanese-Portuguese Dictionary includes *ubukaze,* or "birth-wind," meaning *a cold caught by a newly born.*

Yet, the Japanese, presumably, wanted to vent the pollution of birth, which is, after all, a bloody experience. For most of Japanese history, birth took place in a special separate birth hut, so the main house would not be polluted. It puzzles me that Frois did not note it:

Women in Europe give birth in the same bed they always sleep in;
Women in Japan only give birth in a special hut constructed at a distance from the house.

For the washing part of the contrast, Frois might have gone further. L' Abbe de T, after Valignano, claimed Japanese washed the newly born "in Cold Water to harden and fortify it against the injuries of the Weather," and Montanus, as usual, gave a most outlandish elaboration. I know I should cut it from this abbreviated book, but, for your reading pleasure:

They much exercise their patience in all manners of sufferings and are so inur'd by Custom, that Hunger, Cold, Heat, & Thirst, Watching [?] & Travel are their Play-Fellows; for as soon as they are born, though the weather happen to be extream cold & pinching, they carry out the Infants, & wash them in the Running Streams, where whilst they are cleaning, they let them paddle in the Water to save themselves from sinking. (M:EED)

I doubt this was done often (and if it was done, was only done by some weird samurai family) for it was common after birth to have an *ubuyu,* "birth-warm-water," which is only rarely called *ubumizu,* "birth-[cold]water," as it was in Shikajima prefecture, which happens to be the area where the Jesuits began their work. But, even then, it was generally only a little cold water *after* the warm water.

2-43 In Europe, the cloister and seclusion of nuns is strict and rigorous;
Em Europa a clauzura e emserramento das freiras hé estreito e riguroso;

In Japan, convents for the *bikuni* (nuns) are as good as pleasure quarters.
Em Japão os moesteiros das biqunis quasi que serve de rua de meretrices.

This is a *bad* contrast. Frois, Christian partisan, is not being fair to the real thing. True, most Buddhist nuns were not necessarily religious (for men or women in Japan joining an order was convenient for reasons we will examine in ch. 3), but they were hardly harlots! Yet, whores dressed like nuns were indeed a very visible part of Japan for hundreds of years and apparently did have some Buddhist connections. A hundred years after Frois's *Tratado*, Englebert Kaempfer, explains:

They live under the protection of the Nunneries at Kamakura and Miaco [Miyako: Kyoto, the capitol], to whom they pay a certain sum a year, of what they get by begging, as an acknowledgement of their authority. Some pay besides a sort of tribute, or contribution, to the Khumano Temples at Isje .... They are, in my opinion, by much the handsomest girls we saw in Japan. The daughters of poor parents, if they be handsome and agreeable, apply for and easily obtain this privilege of begging in the habit of Nuns, knowing that beauty is one of the most persuasive inducements to travelers to let them feel the effects of their generosity. The Jammabos, or begging Mountain Priests ... frequently incorporate their daughters into this religious order, and take their wives from among the Bikuni's. (K(S):HOJ)

So, the religious authorities (some, at least) could indeed be charged with complicity in creating these roadside angels (Buddhist papers made travel easier) sometimes identified with Kannon, Buddhist Goddess of Mercy! Frois is only wrong for what he neglects to write – not a word on *real* Buddhist convents (even in his chapter on religion) and nothing to indicate that whores in habit were but one kind of whore in Japan. It was almost as if *he wanted the Buddhists to get the whole blame*. The "wenches" described by the Englishman Cocks, who was in Japan shortly after Frois, were not *bikuni* and the *bikuni* were only one of many types of prostitutes described at length by Kaempfer. But Kaempfer was particularly impressed with *bikuni*, namely, the way they accosted "people of fashion" splitting up with "every one accosting a gentleman by herself, singing a rural song" and keeping him diverted for hours by singing and acting in a manner "neither too bold and daring nor too much dejected and affected, but free, comely, and seemingly modest." Yet, "not to extol their modesty beyond what it deserves . . . they make nothing of laying their bosoms quite bare to the view of charitable travelers all the while they keep him company, under the pretence of its being customary in the country . . ." (K(S):HOJ 1692). I know not whether I should say it *was* customary or that the Bikuni quickly discovered Occidentals were drawn to breasts!

We cannot know if the desire to blame Buddhism was the only reason for Frois singling out *bikuni*. It might just be that he ran into them more than others, for he was often on the road. We might note that prostitution was by no means foreign to religion in Europe. Historian Defourneaux's composite visitor to Phillip II's Spain, observes that "the public *puteria* [whorehouse] is so common in Spain that on entering a town, many people go there before going to church. (D(B):DLS) Considering the power of the Church, it *had* to be involved, even if the women in the *puteria* were not allowed to assume the habits of nuns as did prostitutes in 11c Constantinople and the various convents of the Order of Saint Mary Magdalene whose nuns, with the blessing of Pope Gregory IX in 1227. The latter's habits were white and they were known as the "White ladies." (Gies, Frances and Joseph. *Women in the Middle Ages* 1978). If we take a longer and broader perspective, our differences shrink, but that does not invalidate Frois's contrast even if his description of "our" nuns is, as we shall see, idealistic. A better contrast, though it would not fit this chapter, might be:

In Europe men are ashamed to use prostitutes for we think it a sinful thing to buy or sell sex;
In Japan, men are not at all ashamed and even the authorities think it a fine thing.

When the Seclusion ended in the 19 c, our hypocrisy was at a peak. "We" – particularly American (Puritan) Victorians – even pretended to be repulsed by a man-to-man *discussion* of sex. Here is the American Ambassador about a year after he arrived in Japan, having tea with the "Prince" of Shinano (the exceptionally earthy part of Japan Issa came from):

..
The conversation now took the usual Japanese turn. The lubricity of these people surpasses belief. The moment business is over, the one and only subject on which they dare converse comes up. I was asked a hundred different questions about American females, . . . Bingo-no-Kami informed me that one of the Vice-Governors was specially charged with the duty of supplying me with female society, and if I fancied any woman the Vice-Governor would procure her for me, etc., etc . I was asked if their people could receive some instructions in beating the drum when the next man-of-war came . . . Then – oh, shame! They asked me if *we* had a beat of the drum as a signal to our soldiers to go to the houses of *ill fame,* and I emphatically replied *no*. They evidently did not believe me; for, said they, "We know the Dutch do so at Nagasaki, and all your armies are much the same." I gladly took my leave at three P.M. and reached home quite jaded out. (2/22?/1857)

Poor Mr. Harris! He just couldn't take the Japanese honesty with respect to sex. It is too bad he did not see fit to share his *etceteras* with us. And how ironic, when we consider the countless problems caused by horny GI's stationed around the world, including Japan, over the last decades!

2-44   Our nuns ordinarily do not go outside of the convent;
As freiras antre nós ordinariamente não andão fora de seus moesteiros;

The *bikuni* of Japan are always going out, sometimes visiting military camps.
As biqunis de Japão andão sempre em folguedos e às vezes vão de jindachi.

"Our nuns" include women in over a dozen orders. As I write in English, let me add that England had none; the Crown had dissolved both monasteries and nunneries in the 1530's (*compelling monks to marry nuns, to boot!*), ostensibly for the sake of Reformation and for the punishment of abuse, but actually to gain the resources they accumulated over the centuries. And, as Frois belonged to the Society of Jesus, we might also note that of all the Catholic orders, the Jesuits alone had no parallel order for women. This does not mean they were particularly misogynistic. If anything, they were progressive. They had "a special ministry for prostitutes and their children."(LR) They supported the education of women and thought they could be as valiant as men. But they were very strong believers in chain of command and, hence, very clear about woman's place. Be that as it may, "our" convents were a mixed blessing. They provided a refuge for widows and others with nowhere to go, but they *also* served as prisons for the innocent. "One scholar believes that convents were designed primarily to be a means of controlling the surplus female population of the wealthy or noble classes," writes Mary Springfels (Newberry Consort Repertoire Behind Cloiser Walls: Nun's Music (Googled:LR)). That helps explain why we have so many stories of nuns with lovers. She provides an "eloquent and angry condemnation" of forced claustration by Archangela Tarabotti, herself a victim of this practice.

> It is well known that the majority of nuns cannot attain perfection because they are forced to the religious life . . . by their fathers and kin . . . these unhappy girls, born under an unfortunate star . . . singing pretty love-songs and with their tender limbs forming graceful movements, please the ear and delight the soul of the base fathers who, deceitful, weaving nets of deception, think of nothing but to remove them from sight as soon as possible and so bury them alive in cloisters for the whole of their lives, bound with indissoluble knots. *Paternal Tyranny, or Simplicity Betrayed*, 1654.

There must have been many fine cloisters full of genuine religious volunteers and my only apology for dwelling on the bad is that when it comes to Japanese "nuns," so did Frois. Besides, the *bad* is more interesting. About a hundred years after Tarabotti's *Paternal Tyranny,* the paternalistic (in the good sense) seducer Giacomo Casanova describes one "sort of convent" which amounted to a life sentence, for of hundreds of girls who were there, only 4 succeeded in marrying out in 20 years, mostly because men were not allowed to see them. If he is to be believed, the girls were put in "this prison" by their own families from fear she would otherwise succumb to sin. Only the prettiest girls, as judged by "relatives, some ecclesiastic, a monk, the priest of the girl's parish, and in the last instance the Cardinal, who, if he does not think the child pretty, sends her away, for an ugly girl is believed to run no risk by remaining in the world. So you can be sure that, unhappy as we are here, we curse all those who declared us pretty." (Vol 12 ch 1 of *History of My Life*, transl. Trask)

On the Japanese side, Okada wryly observes with respect to the camp visits mentioned by Frois, "it appears that *bikuni* sell-color [prostitution] was really flourishing."

2-45   Among us, it is not very common for women to know how to write;
Antre nós não hé muito corrente saberem as molheres escrever;

The honorable women of Japan think not knowing how to do so lowers their worth. *Nas honrradas de Japão se tem por abatimento as que o não sabem fazer.*

At the time Frois wrote, literacy was on the rise and education was bullish throughout Europe. But not for women, who were not permitted to go beyond the basics. According to the Banbury Grammar School statutes (1594), "none were permitted to attend 'above the age of nine or longer than they may learn to read English'" (G:WDW). "Thus," an anonymous feminist wrote, "if we are weak by nature; they strive to make us more weak by our nurture. And if in degree of place low, they strive by their policy to keep us more under." (Ibid)   The logic of man's oppression of woman in Europe is puzzling. If women were inferior, as claimed, why would their literacy be a threat? But, that is how all true discrimination operates: *it seeks to create by artificial means the difference it claims is natural.* Perhaps this repression is best understood as men jealously guarding their *property* rights, their two-legged treasures. As Lady Carey put it only a decade or so after TRATADO, for a woman to be published is wrong, for her wedding vow made her husband the sole proprietor of her body *and mind.*

> Then she usurps upon another's right,
> That seeks to be by public language graced;
> And tho' her thoughts reflect with purist light
> Her mind, if not peculiar, is not chaste.
> For in a wife it is no worse to find
> A common body, than a common mind.

That is to say, writing involves *sharing* and women in Europe – or, much of Europe, much of the time, for there were pockets of literacy and times/places when troubadours, paramours and such were not only accepted but *de rigor* – were monopolized. In other words, "our" side has changed the most with respect to this contrast. We, not Japan, are the foreign country. This does not mean Japan in Frois's time was a modern country with 100% literacy. It means that the men and women were more or less equally literate. As Frois wrote in his 1565 Meaco (Miyako=Kyoto) letter, "in the more cultured parts of the land, and wherever there are nobility, both men and women know how to read and write." And, I would add that the accomplishment was far more incredible than his words suggest, for it was not enough to write. One had to write *beautifully*, content and calligraphy-wise. To do so required a tremendous investment. And this went back over a half-millennium. In Murasaki Shikibu's *Tale of Genji* (debatably the first full-length novel ever written: c. 1100-1110) letters rather than looks were the key to a lover's heart as poems written out of sight were passed back and forth in the night.

Lest we get the mistaken impression that all Japanese men were gentlemen about female literacy, let me add that an item included with *"Hateful Things"* (things so enviable they are hated) in the "exhaustive listing" (*mono-wa-tsukushi*) titled *Inu-makura* (the dog-pillow: just about Frois's time) includes "a woman's writing well" (Edward Putzar trans.), and a senryû from the *Mutamagawa* (17c) reads "a man boasting / an illiterate wife / lives in paradise" (*muppitsu no nyôbo motte, gokuraku*). No doubt the idea is: She cannot receive love letters, nor read his.

~~~~~~

2-46 The letters we write to women are signed by the men who write them;
Nas cartas que se escrevem antre nós a molheres, se asina o homem que a escreve;

> In Japan, letters written to women need not bear a signature; nor do women sign their letters nor record the month or year. *Em Japão as que se escrevem a molheres não hão-de levar sinal, nem ellas em suas cartas se asinão, nem poem mes nem era.*

I thought Frois might have been conflating *informality* with gender difference here, for letters between friends need not be signed when each recognizes the other's hand-writing. But reading the short section "On the Letters of Women" in Rodriguez's *Treatise on Epistolary Style*, we find that "letters from women to men have no courtesies [formal phrases to end the letter] at the end of the letter, are not signed and do not give the day of the month." (R(L):TOES) while letters from men to women are signed and bear the day of the month (but not the month or year). This does not necessarily contradict Frois, for Frois does not say they *never* are signed, but we can see how he improved the contrast. It is possible that *formality* vs. *informality* is not the whole story. Sei Shonagon in her *Pillowbook* (c.1000) writes about a man extremely aggravated by her cryptic messages (she sent him a piece of *seaweed* that stood for something) and it might be that women who prided themselves on their fine discrimination found signatures boring whereas men did not want to guess and that this difference became recognized if not formalized by Frois's time. （どうでしょう？）

2-47 With us, women receive the name of a saint;
Antre nós os nomes das molheres são tomados das Sanctas;

Japanese women's names are as follows, namely: kettle, crane, turtle, sandal, tea, bamboo. *Os nomes das japoas são: tacho, grou, cagado, alparqa, chá, cana.*

A sampling of female names in Lisbon in 1565 did show one saint after another (Maria 74, Isabel 71, Caterina 56, etc.). With few exceptions, even the less common names (9 Branca [white/bright/clear] 13, Graçla 6, Luzla 6, Crara 2, Cosma 1, Esperança [hope] 1) were spiritually uplifting. *Portuguese Feminine Names from Lisbon, 1565* by Aryanhwy merch Catmael (Sara L. Friedemann) If I am not mistaken, men, too, often received the name of Saints in Catholic countries. During a home-stay in Mexico (1968), I was asked where I got my name since there was no St. Robin in the calendar (I replied, *he stole from the rich and . . .* wasn't that saintly?).

Of the Japanese names (*Nabe, Tsuru, Kame, ___?, Ocha, Take*) only the fourth would be unfamiliar to Japanese today. Okada, looking up the Portuguese word in the NIPO Dictionary found *gege*, a horribly cacophonic woman's word for straw sandals and guesses it *might* be what Frois intended. It is a homophone for the lowest of the low and was used for low-level male servants, so it may have been used for women, too. But I'd guess *Tabi* (slippers) might be the name intended. Regardless, as Michael Cooper notes, "Frois has certainly chosen some unflattering examples to emphasize the differences between Japanese and European usages; he might have also included more pleasing names such as Spring, Plum, Bounty and Purity." (C:TCJ) *Indeed.* Isabella Bird gave the following examples "among the children's names" in a large family she visited: "*Haru*, Spring; *Yuki*, Snow; *Hana*, Blossom; *Kiku*, Chrysanthemum; *Gin*, Silver;" (B:UTJ) and Lafcadio Hearn left us 48 charming pages, with *hundreds* of fine examples of "Japanese Female Names" broken down by type (*Shadowings*: 1900). The variety is tremendous. *Faux Frois:*

Europeans have a large number of family names and a small number of given names;
Japanese have a small number of family names and a large number of given names.

I do not know about Frois's time, but today there are *over a million* different personal names in use in Japan, though many of these are homophonic, so the number of different sounding names would be an order or two of magnitude less. People combine Chinese characters like copywriters creating a new name for a product. "We", on the other hand, have a large number of *family* names primarily because of the diversity of our roots. Were this the other way around, the pop-Japanologists would use it as "proof" of how individualistic Westerners are. But even with millions of choices, popular names in Japan, like those in the US, show large variation from decade to decade. Women's names in particular, show systematic changes in Japan of a greater magnitude than anything the Anglo-American world has seen. The *~ko* endings of the mid-20c are now almost completely replaced by *mi*'s, *ri*'s, *ka*'s, *na*'s etc..

2-48   In Europe, women wear *chapin* made of leather or Valencia gilt;
Em Europa trazem as molheres chapins de couro ou dourados de Valença;

The Japanese wear ones made of *vruxado* [lacquered] wood, with the big toe separated from the others.   *As japoas os trazem de pao* vruxado *com o dedo polegar dividido dos outros.*

The *chapin* can mean either sandal or clog-like shoes that are open to one degree or another or, simply, fancy shoes. Since some of these European chapin had stilts somewhat like those of the typical Japanese *geta,* or because Japanese were not yet as uniformly up on stilts as they soon would be, Frois concentrates on the material and tops rather than the stilts, which *today* mark the *geta* as unique. Today, we are familiar enough with wooden shoes not to gasp, but to Iberians of his time, they might have been considered odd, and certainly would not have been identified with fine footwear. The beautifully laquered female footwear in Japan usually had a triangular front stilt tapering out to the tip and is called *bokuri* rather than *geta.* Shiny black was probably most common.   All varieties of Japanese footwear came to have the toe separation.   The thongs that separate the toes are generally the most decorative part of the shoe for they are all to be seen above the tabi-wearing foot. But the contrast would have to be with shoe-laces. Did "we" have them yet?

2-49   European women ride side-saddle or on a seat [sedan-chair];
As de Europa andão en silhões ou andilhas;

Japanese women ride in the same manner as men.
As de Japão cavalgão da mesma maneira que os homens.

It would probably be easier for the reader to find a side-saddle in an encyclopedia than for me to describe one. If I am not mistaken, the traveling-seat, or *andilhas,* was somewhat like the platform we see people riding on elephants or camels. I was tempted to translate it as "perch."

Frois's "Japanese" are family of nobles and high-ranking samurai. Others had no horses to ride. Noble and warrior-class women generally had riding experience since childhood, and rode in the same style as their brothers. We are told this is true because Japan was coming off several hundred years of warfare and people of both sexes had to move fast or die. But why not instead ask why European women did *not* ride in a natural way like men. "Our" weird idea that it was obscene for a woman's legs to part is what needs explaining! Other Japanese transported on horseback, such as the middle-class townsmen, wealthy farmers, and brides, often depicted in prints taking the only ride they would have in their life, generally "rode" in the manner (on a perch) ascribed to European women.

2-50   For our women, some pads are placed on the back of the mule under the seat;
Pera as molheres se põe em cima das mulas nas andilhas humas almofadas;

In Japan, a white sheet is draped over the saddle of the horse of noblewomen.
Em Japão pera as molheres honrradas se põe em riba da sela do cavalo hum lençol branqo.

The Portuguese original is ambiguous. All the published translations put cushions on *top* of the seat rather than pads *under* it. But a draft translation by H, a librarian at the National Library of Portugal (BNP) and the long saddle-cloths mentioned in 8-26 affirm the above reading, which improves the contrast by becoming an *over* vs *under* thing. I wonder if the sheet *over* the saddle would have seemed odd for all Europeans of Frois's time. Paintings of the caparisons of knights show them *under* the saddle, but the OED has them *over* it. Either way, a sheet on a horse was considered a male (knight) thing. Is this the prime *Aren't "they" odd!* element of the contrast?

If I am wrong and the *almofada* are *pillows* on the seat, not *pads* below it, the contrast would be one of pampered European behinds *vs.* knightly Japanese women, also not bad. In this case, however, it would need to be pointed out that Japanese had cushions, called *futon* (like the bedding that has recently entered the English language), because their saddles were wooden and they needed them!

2-51 In Europe, women generally prepare meals.
Em Europa ordinariamente as molheres fazem de comer;

> In Japan, men prepare them, and noblemen are proud to go into the kitchen to do so.
> *Em Japão o fazem os homens, e os fidalgos tem por primor y-llo fazer hà cozinha.*

M & J claim Frois exaggerates the contrast, citing Ruperto de Nola (*Libro de Guisados* (1529)) as an example of a male cook in court, but this hardly destroys Frois's contention that there were *more* men in the kitchen in Japan (Frois's *"ordinariamente"* is not absolute). And it is also of little account that cooking became the fashion for noblemen in 17c Europe: Frois never claimed his contrasts were timeless. One thing is certain. The Jesuits were impressed. Rodrigues gives a detailed description of the "public kitchens in the palaces of the lords and other noble people." Perhaps the fact cooking was deemed "a dignified and honorable occupation," and the preparation area was so spacious, beautiful and clean, may help explain the greater role of men, but most important, carving was a major activity in the kitchens of nobility, where there was plentiful game (including fish). As one of the ten principal "liberal arts," it was "a very common and noble office among them" (R(C):TIJ). In the West, too, men dressed game outside and carved meat on the table. In Japan, where, because of chopsticks, everything is carried to the table bite-size, there was a high demand for knife-work and this presumably drew men into the kitchen.

It is easy to imagine a number of competing schools of knife-masters boasting the "shi" (master) suffix on their title (*hôchôshi*) and, judging from illustrations, fine dress, both of which indicate theirs was, indeed, one of the most honorable professions, but this description of a dinner given to Baron Gros's Embassy by the governor of Shimoda in 1858 is nevertheless incredible:

> ..
> First, there were dwarf trees, cut into the shape of flowers and animals; then there was a large fish in a dish of water, imitating a pool of salt water with seaweed floating on it; and lastly there came superb flowers, constructed out of lobster-flesh and sliced turnips. The governor told us with evident satisfaction, that these flowers were the work of his officers; which certainly gave us a high idea of the neat handiness of these gentlemen, although it somewhat lowered our opinion of the character of their occupations. That the principal functionaries of state are free to spend their time in making artificial flowers out of carrots and turnips and lobster-flesh, proves the social machine is well ordered and works smoothly without watchful supervision. (M:BGE)

Who can sort the edible and non-edible part of the Marquis's description! The topiary art, if that is what it is, was, may have been done with the aim of pleasing the foreigners, whose [bad] taste was already known by the Japanese hosts.

Times changed. The 70-80 hour work-weeks that launched the 20c economic miracle did not leave men any time for diddling in the kitchen. By the time the work-week dropped to 50-60 hours (or they retired) most of these corporate warriors (or, company slaves) were totally at sea in a kitchen.

2-52   In Europe, men are tailors;
Em Europa [os]homens são alfayates;

And in Japan, the women.
E em Japão as molheres.

Tinker, Tailor, Soldier, Sailor . . . – the OED dates the word "tailor" back to 1297. That was about the time when the loose robes of the Medieval period were being supplanted with clothing cut to fit the body. Whether that followed the neo-classical reverence for the human form or helped create it I know not; but, with the Renaissance, the primary importance of the *cloth* gave way to that of the *cut,* and so the draper (cloth merchant) to the tailor, who was in some cases actually two people: a cutter-pattern-expert and a sewer-assembler. The title of a book printed in Madrid, then (1589) the fashion capital of Europe, *"Libro de Geometria, Pratica y Traca"* (Book of Geometry [measurement], Practice [construction] and Tracing) by master tailor Juan de Alcega, reveals something of the nature of the trade: highly skilled *and male* (What little I saw reminded me of ballistics and other male sciences). There are a dozen different trades involved in making clothing, many of which (eg. *broger, capper, carder, lister*) most of us would not even recognize. While few women were engaged in any of these as recognized professionals (guild members), they worked behind the scenes and sometimes managed to succeed a deceased husband. As the tailor reached the top of the pinnacle and, by the 16c ranked with the merchant class, women were shut out, though in North Europe, at least, they are reported to have done work for master tailors on commission. *Officially speaking,* then, Frois is right.

On the Japanese side, the dyers (the merchant-manufacturer, not the listers who got their hands wet,) and drapers were still on the top and the cutters and assemblers, or, *tailors* were considered menial labor. In that sense, women in Japan did not really enjoy the prestige of being tailors in the Western sense of the word. They were not an independent calling but *seamstresses* working for drapers. In that sense, Japanese men *always* had a hand in the sewing business in Japan. They ran it. From a customer point of view, leaving out gender difference, it might be *Faux Frois'ed* like this:

When we buy cloth, we hire someone to sew it or do so ourselves.
The Japanese buy the cloth only, and the tailoring comes for free.

Japanese did not buy their kimonos; they bought rolls of cloth so expensive that the creation of the actual product by the in-house labor was free. Upper-class clothing in the West resembles this to a degree, but the proportion of expense and labor that go into the cloth production and tailoring are very different, if not the reverse. When Japan reopened in the 19c, Japanese-style clothing (*wafuku*) continued to be assembled by women, while most cutter-sewers of Western style clothing (*yofuku*) were men who were called *shitateya* (lit. outfitter) now translated as "tailor" or "dress-maker." The *ya* on the tail of the word makes it clear that this is someone with his own shop. While more women may have possessed the requisite skills, men created or took over the business of making Western clothing because in the 19c it was prestigious (as the newest fashion, a nationally endorsed effort), risky (being new and, at first, the clients were foreigners) and predominantly *for* men, because more males visited Japan and Japanese women, following an abortive early attempt to introduce Western dress, largely reverted to their native wear and only Westernized in mass after World War II. Considering the wholesale import of European social institutions at the time, men-as-tailors was also tried simply because it was a male job in the West. Logically speaking, this makes perfect sense, but one still wonders if Japanese men might not have better left the entire business of making clothing to the women, for Westerners in Japan throughout the 19c unanimously put down their product and recommended Chinese tailors. But, this may be unfair to Japanese men. The Chinese, unlike the Japanese had a tradition of tubular clothing. It is possible even Japanese women would have failed.

2-53   In Europe, men eat at high tables and women at a low ones.
Em Europa os homens comem em mezas altas e as molheres em baxas;

> In Japan, women eat at high tables and men at a low ones.
> *Em Japão as molheres em mezas altas e os homens em baxas.*

Women and men tended to eat separately in Europe and Japan and the logic of psychology would suggest a *higher* place for men in *both* cultures. Indeed, the Japanese observation seems contrary to practices suggesting that Japanese had a clear cut sense of up=high=exalted and down=low=base. *So what is happening here?* First, I think it bears noting that there are tables and there are tables. Ours are large raised surfaces where people eat together; theirs, tiny portable writing-desk-like devices with tiny folding legs. Okada shows a picture with a nobleman eating with his table directly in front of him resting on the *tatami* (legs folded up) while the woman diagonally across the room has a table by her side about eight inches high. Since both sit on the floor (see 6-5), no one is looking down on anyone. I can imagine the early male visitors to Japan wishing they had the women's tables so they would have a sporting chance of getting the food to their mouths!

2-54   In Europe, it is thought offensive for women to drink wine;
Em Europa se tem por afronta beberem as molheres vinho;

> In Japan, it is very common, and on festive occasions, they sometimes get drunk.
> *Em Japão é muito freqente, e em festas bebem às vezes até acavesarem [or, avinhaçarem?].*

Perhaps this was true in South Europe, but there is abundant literature indicating that women joined men in drinking in much of Europe as they did in Japan, though the fact that women were generally the sex that served and took care of things meant that they rarely imbibed as freely as men. The Spanish merchant de Avila Giron summed up the situation in Japan very well: "the women drink very little, although their menfolk are like Frenchmen."

2-55   European women, for the most part, eat meat and fish;
As molheres de Europa pola mayor parte comem carne e pexe;

> Japanese noblewomen generally don't eat meat, and many don't eat fish, too.
> *As japoas fidalgas ordinariamente não comem carne, e muitas nem comem pexe.*

Europe is on the rare side of the contrast here, for in most cultures, meat is a male thing. I believe this is less because males hunted or herded (though it may have begun that way) than because men tend to have less efficient intestines – they tend to absorb less – than women. This is why famine kills men at a much higher rate than it kills women, even in cultures such as Japan, Korea and China, where no rules of chivalry said to help "women first." Many if not most women thrive on flour, water, and a bit of greens (I exaggerate a little, here), while men usually end up emaciated from such a diet. They need meat, something easily digested in the stomach, more than women do. I think that is why women in Japan could earn Buddhist brownie points on their karma by forsaking meat and most animal protein, whereas most men, although they may have wanted to, could not do so and remain healthy. Men in this Buddhist culture called their four-legged animal meat "medicine," (see 6-24) and that, was not merely a euphemism. They *needed it*.

Note the "noblewomen" (*hidalgas*) on the Japanese side. Frois specified them because if any woman should be able to afford meat it would be them and, thus, abstaining is doubly contrary for it means they eat like poor women in Europe. But more is involved. Noblewomen were freer to worry about their spiritual betterment than commoners who had other things to worry about, and they had a diet diverse enough (plenty of tofu, sea-weeds and whatnot) not to *need* animal protein. Commoners needed to eat fish or *anything* nutritious whenever they could, which was probably seldom. (Note that Frois's exceptionally nuanced contrast includes 3 qualifications: *most*, *generally* and *many*!)

2-56 European women wearing mantles cover their faces all the more when speaking with someone. *As molheres de Europa, se estão com manto, cobrem-se ainda mais pera falarem com jente;*

Japanese women must remove their head from their mantle, for it would be discourteous to speak with it in place. *As japoas hão-de tirar o manto da cabeça, porque falar com elle hé descortezia.*

Though the Muslims had been driven out almost a hundred years before, European clothing still reflected the influence of what had been, and perhaps still was, the most powerful civilization in the world. Remembering the fervor with which I have heard Muslim women defend their veils, I am unsure as to whether we should speak of women *suffering* "centuries of Islamic as well as Christian enclosure of the body." But, when I consider how *hot* veils would be in the summer, I feel "enclosure" too mild a word for the torture. (It is a easy to be pro-veil today, with air-conditioning.) There is also an ironic twist in the assertion that hiding the face serves modesty. In Frois's time, some argued that veils – especially the half-veil, had become "an instrument of the seductive art," for, by only giving "a hint of the face beneath," it could "add piquancy" to pretty features or "lend imaginative charms to those women who were lacking real ones and knew how to use it to excite the attention of men who without this disguise would not give a second glance." (D:DLS) So, we find the veil in essence equated with heavy makeup! If that isn't confusing enough, as the Council of Castille complained to Philip II, family members can't recognize each other, men mistakenly accost others wives or innocent girls, prostitutes pass off for good women. The King forbade its use in 1590.

Okada points out that Japanese dramas of the time show women carrying on a discussion, mantle in place. But, the dramas were *Kyogen*, meaning "crazy-talk," so Frois's contrast has hardly been compromised. I think this contrast may show that while Japanese women tended to cover their faces, the reasons for it probably were not quite the same as they were in the West. With noblewomen, it might stem more from the principle of social importance being indicated by degree of separation (the Emperor the most hidden); with samurai and merchant class it might have been mainly about protection from the sun and dust or simply being coy. Over the course of the Tokugawa era, commoners, especially townswomen (nobles held out to the late-19c) began showing off their faces more and more. While Western feminist scholars might identify attention to the personal beauty of women with female oppression, some Japanese feminist writers see the cult of public beauties in the Tokugawa era, represented by the *bijin-e* (lit. *"beautiful-women-paintings,"* mostly of *yûjo* (lit.: *play-woman:* usually translated as harlot or courtesan or geisha)), as a mark of a new freedom of women to exist as *persona*, rather than the faceless belongings of men. But, for all this progress (?), I must add one *Faux Frois* about something that may go back a long way:

European women laugh with their hands wherever they might be.
Japanese women always cover their mouths with their hands when they laugh.

Even without the veil of the West or the *byôbu* screen of the noblewoman described in the next contrast, there was a tendency for *all* Japanese women to hide their faces, which we can still see today, though less and less young women now cover their faces when they laugh. When "we" think of modesty, we imagine Adam and Eve clutching their crotches (or crotch and breast). I think if Adam and Eve were Japanese "they" might, rather, cover their faces. Could the absence of this Faux Frois in the real Frois mean that European women *also* covered their mouths when they laughed? Once we have as many contrasts as in the *Tratado*, what is *not* written becomes almost as important as what is!

2-57 European noblewomen speak openly with people who call on them;
As fidalgas d'Europa falão descubertamente com quem vem falar com ellas;

Japanese noblewomen speak to someone they don't know from behind *byôbu* [paper partitions] or bamboo blind. *As senhoras de Japão, se as pessoas não são conhecidas, falão-lhe por detrás de biobus ou esteyras.*

So European noblewoman were not as free as Japanese outside, but freer to reveal themselves inside of their architectural enclosures even when facing people who might be strangers? I am not sure exactly what this implies. Is it deemed useless to pretend to modesty when the wolf is already inside? Is revelation outside thought as advertising whereas this was not so within the house?

This does not contradict what Frois wrote about the freedom of Japanese women (2-34, 2-35) or the previous item, 2-56, because here we are only speaking of noblewomen, who were a special case. The Wizard of Oz-like custom of talking from behind screens goes back at least a half millennium and is why the beautiful "shining" prince Hikaru Genji got stuck with a bony, incredibly ugly mistress with a long pointed red-tipped nose, Suetsumuhana, who, as it turned out was not too smart to boot: he was fooled, or rather misled himself, by not realizing the letters they exchanged at night were actually produced by her retainers! (at least, she was kind, as was Genji to keep her!)

2-58 In Europe, women may enter any church they want to;
Em Europa podem entrar as molheres em qualquer igreja que qerem;

The gentile women in Japan cannot enter some temples that are prohibited to them. *As jentias em Japão não podem emtrar em alguns templos que lhe são prohibidos.*

On the balance, Japan offered *more* freedom of worship – or, more important by far, the freedom *not* to worship – than Europe; but women were and occasionally still are taboo in some (Buddhist) temples. Some mountains – usually an entire mountain rather than one temple – opened up to women only one day a year (In Japan, the mountains and the seashore have official "openings," i.e. times of the year when certain activities are acceptable). Issa fondly haikus old women, who visit such a temple, noting that they *".. first of all, look at the sea."* If they were hard-working farm-wives, chances are it was their only look at the sea for the entire year, so one can forgive them for paying attention to nature before the gods!

Buddhism was not sexist at the outset. Roughly a century after Shakyamuni's death, a doctrine arose that denied women the opportunity for Buddhahood unless they transform themselves into males, either literally, before a public gathering . . . , or symbolically, by becoming a nun and in

Japan, it came to pass that even nuns had to pray to overcome their sex at the moment of death to have a shot at paradise, as there were no women in the Pure Land (J/M:KZJ ch7). Buddhism in Japan was relatively egalitarian. In the Nara period (710–794), nuns were equal with monks and presumably not kept out of temples, but with the Heian Period (794–1185), monks took the lion's share of the public functions reducing the role of nuns while the harsh ascetic regimes of ascetic Buddhism – marked by male comradery and misogyny – literally gained ground that became off-bounds to women, so "by the Kamakura period (1185–1333), formally ordained nuns were a rarity, while their lay counterparts grew in numbers. For the most part, women were treated merely as religious subjects needing to be saved." (K:HWJ) I would add that, reading Kenkô's *Tsurezuregusa* (1330-31), I get the impression that *fear* of women as forces attracting men to stay in this world – rather than denigration or hatred of them, as our term misogyny implies – may have been the salient problem. If you think of the temple as a sort of monastery, it does not seem so outlandish to have female visitors forbidden to the men who want them.

2-59 With us, it would be very strange for women to carry things by *pingah* [shoulder-poles];
Antre nós seria muito estranho levarem as molheres couza à pinga;

In Japan, it is normal for maid-servants to carry water in buckets.
Em Japão hé ordinário acarretarem as servas agoa em baldes.

Pingah, according to the French translators, is a Malay word used in Macao (a Portuguese colony on the edge of China that served as a sort of Jesuit headquarters in the Far East) for poles of bamboo or wood shouldered to carry things suspended from the ends. There is no good Portuguese term, as there is no English term. There is a Japanese one: *tenbinbô,* literally, "scale-pole." There are few fresh-water-carrying maids in print, but many illustrations of "brine-maidens" (*shiokumi*), who used such poles to carry brine to the vats at salt-works, because they were associated with romantic poems and drama (mostly concerning exile on islands such as some the Jesuits knew). Japanese men also used poles, but Frois chose to confine his contrast to women, for the greater psychological contrariety.

I never fail to be amazed at how poor the West is at carrying things on foot and wonder whether it is the result of "our" using more pack animals and better wheels or the cause of it! I recall reading scientific studies proving skinny women put marines to shame in their carrying ability, thanks to the weight being centered on the top of their heads. Head-carrying, more common in Korea than Japan, is difficult to adapt to, and would probably not be good for the neck in the long run; but the use of carrying sticks is just as efficient and easy to adapt to. I find myself wondering further whether the problem with the West might not be in our mindset, which makes the assumption that carrying things is supposed to be uncomfortable and a good way to show off what we so highly value: *muscles*. Or, forgive the excess of theories, could it be that masters and mistresses in the West were less attentive to the needs of their servants and too stingy to provide a pole?

2-60 In Europe, women stand up to greet guests;
Em Europa recebem as molheres os ospedes alevantando-se em pee;

Those of Japan remain seated as they greet them.
As de Japão os recebem deixando-se ficar asentadas.

Frois already mentioned this in 1-29+ and did not need to make it a woman-thing, when both sexes behave the same in both cultures. Let me now add that this did not only apply to *greetings*. Since *Accommodation* had been adopted a few years earlier, Japanese celebrating the Eucharist were allowed to remain seated for the Gospel rather than rising, as it was how *they* showed *their* respect.

On a superficial level the behaviors are opposite: *getting up* vs. *staying down*. On a deeper level they are similar. Both represent the most formal – should we say *stiff?* – postures of the respective cultures. We are all familiar with standing up and, in the case of men, snapping to attention, as the more formal posture in Europe (as opposed to and combined with the actual gestures of greeting: bows, hat-tips, curtsies, kisses, handshakes, etc.). We find it harder to understand how remaining seated could be formal, much less *stiff?* While Western women in finishing schools (What a word! *Finishing schools!*) may learn how to keep their knees together and bend their legs slightly to the side, this is not a proper posture for attentively facing a guest. The Japanese posture of proper seating puts the entire body into a tight rectangle and has a formal name, *seiza,* "correct-seating." It is tiring to maintain for long because the weight of the body rests entirely on the folded legs (see 63, below).

Frois's contrast is not quite perfect: it should be "sit down *or remain seated*," for the Japanese sat down if they were standing, or – this, too, should be noted – changed from a less formal way of sitting to the proper way to show respect for their guests. In short, the Japanese, to use a horrid Usanianism, were as *pro-active* as Westerners when greeting their guests.

~~~

2-61 European women wear *rebuço* [a high collar] in order to walk about unrecognized;
As molheres de Europa, pera caminhar desconhecidas, levão rebuço;

> Those of Japan fasten a towel on their head that hangs from both sides of the face when they walk about. *As de Japão quando caminhão atão huma toalha na cabeça, que lhe cay ambas as pontas diante do rosto.*

Since we have already seen contrasts involving mantles, it is evident that women East and West once had many ways of going *incognito*. The *rebuço* sounds very interesting. The dictionary says it was a high collar or lapel of a cloak or coat which turns up to conceal or protect the face. English had their "French collars" which did the same.

Japanese women generally draped their light robes (*katabira*) over their heads, but some dangled *zukin,* literally head-clothes from them. Today, these light, usually colorful, two-foot-long pieces of cloth are used for headbands for work, neckerchiefs+sweat-wiper at bon-dances, washcloths/towels and cleaning, while white hand-towels (the same weave called towel in the West) are hung about the head for sun protection and wiping sweat off while working in fields or the garden. I would not be surprised if such a practical use rather than concealment was behind the Japanese practice mentioned in the contrast. Regardless, Frois apparently opposes the up-raised collar to dangling cloth.

~~~

2-62 European women keep their hair [long] until they die.
As molheres em Europa conservão seus cab[elos] até morte;

> In Japan, old women and widows cut their hair in place of mourning and sadness.
> *Em Japão as velhas e as que viuvão em lugar de dó e tristeza se rapão.*

To fully understand what hair once meant to European woman, read Pope's *Rape of the Locke*. Mock Epic or not, the conceit depended on the view of a woman's hair as an inviolable treasure.

Frois's "in place of" in the second half of the distich is not quite right, for it suggests that by renouncing this floating world and all its attachments together with the hair, the Japanese magically get over the loss of loved ones and their own beauty (or whatever else they would escape). This, of course, would be impossible. It reminds me of the Japanese psychiatrist who wrote that by saying "Thank you" a Western person had no lingering feelings, unlike Japanese, who continue to feel *much obliged*. (Doi: *Anatomy of Dependence*). I suspect Frois really means only that Japanese women cut their hair off and retire to a convent to age and die gracefully, rather than hanging on to their hair and suffering a grim end at home. In the West, too, widows sometimes withdrew from the world and became nuns, but apparently did not cut their hair to do so.

Entering a convent in Japan could mean a total break with the family, as if the person died. This was generally the case for women who divorced or committed a crime or simply wanted to die alone in peace. On the other hand, it could be done to *maintain* family relationships; i.e., widows often went to pray for the soul of their husbands. In the case of the former motive, all the hair was cut off, for it symbolized cutting off all ties to house/family as well as the world. In the case of the latter, sometimes the hair was only cut half way off (a bit longer than shoulder length) and the woman, after a few years might return to the world and even remarry.

2-63 In Europe, women sit on divans, chairs and stools;
As molheres de Europa se asentão em estrados, cadeiras ou tanho;

In Japan, women always kneel down, with their feet turned up together behind, with one hand resting on the *tatami*. *As Japoas sempre em baxo com os pés juntos virados pera trás estribando com uma mão sobre o tatami.*

No need to describe what Europeans do. Readers who do not know exactly how Japanese sit should note that the legs are neatly tucked back, shins flush to the *tatami*. Male or female, the legs are folded *straight back under* when sitting formally, with the hands resting symmetrically on their respective thighs, or in front, if the person also bows. Here, Frois describes a slightly informal posture (one arm down) which men never use, because they sit informally with crossed legs (the greater formality of the female way of sitting is probably why Frois made this a female item for contrast). The arm is needed to support the body, because the legs are allowed to stray in parallel a bit to one side.

How do Japanese sit on their legs? Bacon thought the needed flexibility was gained "by the habit of setting a baby down with its knees bent under it, instead of with its legs straight out before it, as seems to us the natural way." In a footnote she added: "that the position of the Japanese in sitting is really unnatural and unhygienic, is shown by recent measurements taken by the surgeons of the Japanese army." (B:JGW): I don't know exactly what measurements proved her point (probably the relatively short legs), *but it was wrong*. To my mind, we might learn something from the Japanese in this regard, for "we," and not the Japanese suffer from bad knees, partly because Western medicine fails to recognize the importance of *opening* the space between the knee-cap and the socket.

2-64 With us, women hold a cup of water in the right hand, and drink from the same;
Antre nós as molheres tomão o pucaro d'agoa com a mão direita e com a mesma o bebem;

Japanese women take up a *sakazuki* [sake cup] with their left hand and drink it with the right. *As japoas tomão o* sacanzzuqi *do vinho com a mão esqerda e bebem-no com a dereita.*

"Our" side does seem the normal human default here and the Japanese one a special custom learned in a particular culture. I have not been able to find any verification of it, but I can think of two logical explanations. First, if Japanese women were not expected to be as sincere as men in their fashion of drinking (i.e., could drink with one hand and pour their own drink) the heavier bottle would be in the right hand and the cup in the left. Second, when Japanese hold cups with both hands, the left one is always under the butt of the cup. This would make it the main hand for *taking* the same and if, when it was passed to the mouth, the right hand lifted it up off the left one, this could conceivably be described as *taking the cup in the left hand and drinking it with the right.*

2-65   European women braid their hair with silk ribbons;
As molheres em Europa transão os cabelos com fitas de seda;

> The Japanese tie them behind in just one place, sometimes with a very dirty rag.
> *As japoas os atão por detrás em hum só lugar, às vezes com hum lenço muito sujo.*

..
The contrast is clear enough – and almost identical with 2-10 – but one wishes Frois was more specific about the class of woman he contrasts. After all, in 2-28 we have the women as uniformly neat as soldiers in full décor. Why should they use dirty rags in their hair? I can only think of two possibilities: 1) Even poor women in Europe were careful to tie their hair with pretty things such as ribbons or colored yarn, whereas women who worked (women and men both worked in Japan, it is strange Frois did not find any contrasts there) in Japan simply tied there hair back with whatever was at hand. The most common item would be a *tenugui,* the piece of cloth already mentioned. Some were probably worn, faded and stained. While not *literally* dirty, i.e., unwashed, they might have *seemed* dirty, i.e., ugly. 2), a less likely possibility is that samurai women whose husbands were off on campaigns had *lucky hair-ties* which couldn't be washed until a loved one returned safely or *faithful hair-ties* waiting for the loved one to untie them or something.

2-66   In Europe, one box of make-up powder would satisfy the demand of an entire country;
Em Europa bastará hum caxão d'alvayade pera todo hum reino;

> In Japan, many Chinese junks full of it come and still this does not suffice.
> *Em Japão vêm muitas somas de chinas carregadas delle e ainda não basta.*

A poetic corollary to contrast 2-15! With noblewomen on horses and sometimes even going to war by the end of the Warring Period (Frois caught the tail of it) the make-up (in Portuguese, *alvaide* = whitening) was lighter than any time before or after (until modern times), but, the demand for the powder, of which there were two types, the very expensive mercury (this expense makes the 200 layers of it applied by Saikaku's character a case of conspicuous consumption) and lead, swiftly grew over the time Frois was in Japan, because the commoners – starting with the wealthy merchant class – began to use it. In a word, it was literally *popular.* So much mercury and lead was imported from China that the most popular powder was called, literally *"Chinese dirt."* The application of these poisons seems dumb – not that we who have given ourselves skin cancer by roasting ourselves in the sun are much brighter – for the danger, as we have seen, was known. What was not known is that it probably was one reason for the high death-rate among the infants of women who were heavy users – 2 of 3 samurai class children died in infancy (LR).

In 1585, I would guess make-up in Europe and Japan alike tended to make women look weak: pallor being their ideal of beauty. This took both cultures away from China, for the Chinese woman traditionally used the white background the better to set off "a coarse big daub" of rouge "on each side of her face," something Ball (B:TC) attributes to a Northern race descending to the South while attempting to maintain their natural appearance. Geo-historical considerations aside, the Chinese usage would create an image of health, contrary to that of the Europeans and Japanese.

2-67 European women do their stitching with copper thimbles on their finger-tips;
As molheres em Europa cozem suas custuras com didais de cobre na ponta do dedo;

> Those of Japan do it with a strip of leather in the palm of their hand or some paper wrapped around mid-finger. *As de Japão com uma tira de couro na palma da mão ou com hum pouco de papel emrolado no meo do dedo.*

Europeans put thimbles on the tip their middle finger of the right hand and push the needle through with each stroke, while in Japan a long needle is held steady with its butt upon the leather or paper for a type of sewing called "grab-needling" (*tsukami-bari*), where the fingertips help fold and push the cloth into the needle, before pulling the needle through from the tip. In the Edo era, a small metal dish was devised for this, where the needle rested against the *concavity* – another contrary yet!

Today, Japanese push the needle through individually as much as they telescope fabric on it – with big jobs done by sewing machine, darning buttons or repairing tears is the most of it – but they still use thimbles that are actually broad-banded rings rather than tiny fingertip-covering cups like ours. *Perhaps the name has something to do with it.* In Japanese, thimbles could hardly be closed on one end when they are called *yubi-nuki*, or "finger-pass-throughs!"

2-68 With us, a knife is used to cut the stitches when a garment is taken apart at the seams;
Antre nós, quando se [quer] descozer hum vestido, cortão-se as custuras com faca;

> Japanese women unlace the thread complete.
> *As molheres de Japão tirão-lhe as linhas inteiras.*

This has nothing to do with fine-tipped fingers and the legendary dexterity of Asian women. It probably has nothing to do with reuse of thread, though that is possible, either. I have taken apart an old kimono, and can testify that this contrast is born of different types of stitching – with the loose (but perfectly straight) Japanese-style stitching, it is simply far easier and faster to pull out the thread than to cut it. (Note that the Portuguese *custuras (costuras)* means both the "seams" and the "stitches".)

endnote II
W*omen*　　　　　　　　　　　　　　　　　　　　　　　女

The reversal of our expectations with respect to the relative freedom of "our" and "their" women makes this chapter an especially attractive part of TRATADO even if the value of the contrast is diminished to the extent that Frois describes Luso-Iberian women, who were especially confined. The reversal occurs because "we" changed sometime between Frois and the End of the Seclusion (1853). The Russian Captain Golownin left us a very finely nuanced description of Japan at the beginning of the 19c and it is little different from what we can gather was the case in 1585:

> Only the princes and the nobility, and the rich who imitate them, keep their wives almost constantly in rooms, to which no person of the other sex, except the nearest relatives, is admitted. This measure, is adopted by the husbands, not so much of jealousy as pride. As for the women of other classes, they may visit their relatives and friends, and appear in the streets and public places with their faces unveiled, but they must not converse with any persons of the other sex, in the absence of their husbands. On the whole, the jealousy of the Japanese cannot be compared to that of other Asiatic nations; I even think that, if female frailty is considered, the Japanese should not be called jealous, but only prudent, or more jealous than the Europeans. (G:MCJ)

Europe, however, was no longer that of Frois's contrast. Sometime after 1585, the segregation of the sexes broke down. Europeans began to think of married life as a partnership, even if the fair sex was still considered the inferior partner. Where Japanese women had been placed in opposition to the more secluded Europeans and Chinese, now, they were placed *between* Asian and Europe. In Mrs. William Busk's collection of Dutch writings on Japan published in 1841 (B:MCJ London), all mention of classes of women disappears and we find only a general fiction, "Japanese women." It was still the case that "the sex . . . approaches more nearly their European condition" than holds true in "other parts of the East" and "are subjected to no jealous seclusion, hold a fair station in society, and share in all the innocent recreations of their fathers and husbands." The fact "their minds . . . are cultivated with as much care as those of the men" is also mentioned. Yet, we *also* find a completely new element of criticism, which we might call *the modern Occidental view of Japanese women:*

> At home, the wife is mistress of the family: but in other respects she is treated rather as a toy for her husband's amusement, than as the rational, confidential partner of his life. She is expected to please him by her accomplishments, and to cheer him with her lively conversation, but never suffered to share his more serious thoughts, or to relieve by participation his anxieties and cares.
> . .

While this popular book (reprinted by the Harper Bro's in New York 1845) was about Japan, the editor writes of "the difference between Asiatic and European civilization" of which "so much . . appears to be intimately connected with, if not actually to result from, the different treatment and condition of woman in the two continents." For the reader who might be surprised to find such a feminist worldview in 1841/45, here is another example, though the contrast is not Japan. It was written by a male New Yorker two decades earlier.

> Under the mild influence of Christianity and the easy sustenance to be procured in our republican states, the condition of women is undoubtedly preferable to that of their sex in any part of the globe. They ought to know that Fredonia [the USA] is women's terrestrial paradise. Here they are the rational companions of men, not their playthings or slaves. (from footnote to Samuel Mitchell's early 19c poem "*Address to the Fredes.*")

As Harriet Martineau pointed out in 1837, the American reality did not exactly live up to this first round of "you've come a long way, baby!" cockle-doodling (see her *Society in America*), but once we start going in this direction, the Japanese cannot help but look backwards. With the reopening of Japan, the extent of freedom enjoyed by Japanese women was re-examined and debated. Alcock, disappointed with not encountering *ladies* to engage in witty conversation with, complained about the "erroneous notions . . . disseminated by the writers on Japan in respect to the position and relations of the wife here." He found upper-class women as secluded as any harem and noticed that "when traveling, or passing from house to house, it is always in a *norimon* [sedan] hermetically closed and surrounded by her husband's attendants." He adds, "I speak of the upper classes; the lower and working orders, here as elsewhere, by the necessity of labor, can not be shut up." (A:COT 1863) Here, he is not quite accurate with his "here as elsewhere," but we get the idea. *The tables have turned.*

~~~~~~

I should add that the treatment of women – or, more precisely, *the assessment* of the treatment of women – in the West, as opposed to the East was no academic matter. *The condition of women became a litmus test for civilization.* America's first Ambassador to Japan, Townsend Harris, wrote something while still en route to Japan that echoes the opinion of Mrs. Busk. After quoting a long and lyrical Cingalese poem to the effect that women are deceivers, he writes:

> In my wanderings in almost every part of the world I have applied one test, which I find to be unvarying, and that is, that the social position of the women in any nation will indicate the amount of its civilization. Therefore, given her social status and you can at once find the mental state of the men. (H:CJTH:1/11?/1856)

Not surprisingly, women, like slaves, were a powerful excuse for colonialist rule. Today, it is easy to laugh at Kipling's phrase "the white man's burden," but try, if you will, to read through his emotional poems on the murder and maltreatment of women in India (not just suttee, but other horrible things) – many of the poems can only be called *feminist*! – and tell yourself that the British should *not* have interfered! (I do not mean to excuse Imperialism, which was 90% selfish, but . .) . But Japan had no worry in that department. Foreigners might quibble on the finer points, but no one denied that women were *much* freer there than in most of the Far East. Isabella Bird's description of the social position of women in neighboring Korea is chilling.

> Daughters have been put to death by their fathers, wives by their husbands, and women have even committed suicide, according to Dallet, when strange men, whether by accident or design have even touched their hands, and quite lately a serving woman gave as reason for her remissness in attempting to save her mistress, who perished in a fire, that in the confusion a man had touched the lady, making her not worth saving! . . .
>
> A man wishing to repair his roof must notify his neighbors, lest by any chance he should see any of their women. After the age of seven, boys and girls part company, and the girls are rigidly secluded . . . Girl children, even among the poor, are so successfully hidden away, that in somewhat extensive Korean journeys I never saw one girl who looked above the age of six, except hanging listlessly about in the woman's rooms . . .
>
> There are no native schools for girls, and though women of the upper classes learn to read the native script [something that takes about ten hours to do], the number of Korean women who can read is estimated at two in a thousand . . .
>
> In the capital a very curious arrangement prevailed. About eight o'clock the great bell tolled a signal for men to retire into their houses, and for women to come out and amuse themselves . . . From its operation were excluded blind men, officials, foreigners' servants, and persons carrying prescriptions to the druggists'. These were often forged for the purpose of escape from durance vile, and a few people got long staffs and personated blind men. At twelve the bell again boomed,

women retired, and men were at liberty to go abroad. A lady of high position told me that she had never seen the streets of Seoul by daylight. . . .

The name bestowed on her by her parents soon after her birth is dropped, and she is known thereafter only as "the wife of so and so," or "the mother of so and so." . . . Silence is regarded as a wife's first duty. During the whole of the marriage day the bride must be mute as a statue. . . . The custom of silence is observed with the greatest rigidity in the higher classes. It may be a week or several months before a husband knows the sound of his wife's voice. . . With the father-in-law the law of silence is even more rigid. The daughter-in-law often passes years without raising her eyes to his, or addressing a word to him. (B:KAN – a long quote for a subject indirectly related to this book, but unlike Bird's *Unbeaten Tracks in Japan*, it is a rare book so I thought I would treat you to it.)

Bird, however, was the first to admit that the Korean women, not knowing any other life, do not "fret or groan under this system, or crave for the freedom which European women enjoy."

One intelligent woman, when I pressed her hard to say what they thought of our customs in the matter, replied, "We think that your husbands don't care for you very much"! (B:KAN)

Japan was already in Korea at the time Bird was there, manipulating the government and doing its best to help shoulder the white man's burden. Her observations show us that Alcock was wrong to cavalierly write that lower-class women were visible in any country (only some servants Bird called *virtual slaves* were visible in Korea, while the *vast majority* of women were visible in Japan). I strongly suspect there were Japanese who cited the condition of women in Korea as one reason for colonizing their neighbor even while Europeans came to hold the view that Japanese women were "their husband's slaves" (S:MQTJ). Even Ms. Bacon, whose JAPANESE GIRLS AND WOMEN is, in many ways splendid, could not help writing that while "Buddhism and Confucianism were elevating and civilizing" they "failed to place the women of Japan upon even as high a plane as they occupied in the old barbaric times" so their only hope was . . . can you guess? . . . *becoming Christian!* There is no small irony in this, considering the fact that Europe was just as Christian in the 16c when Frois found Japanese women more free than women in Europe.

It bears mention that the greatest equality of the sexes – confident and absolutely ebullient girls and women – found by the globe-trotting Bird, were not in the Christian West but in Eastern Tibet: i.e., The Man-tze people, where *"men and women are always seen together,"* where *"a woman can be anything, from a muleteer to a Tu-tze."* (B:YVB) And, to be fair to Bacon, she wrote the above because she was upset that the noblewomen she taught and had deep affection for would be unable to do much if anything with their higher learning. Her usual objectivity lapsed because she was so afraid that her teaching would only hurt them and they would all end up frustrated. Elsewhere, she provided the best analysis of the place of woman in Japan ever written. After describing, *yoshii,* the practice of adopting a man into a *samurai* family to carry on the family name, where the wife usually wears the britches so to speak, she writes:

From the custom of *yoshii,* and its effect upon the wife's position, we see that, in certain cases, Japanese women are treated as equal with men. *It is not because of their sex that they are looked down upon and held in subjugation, but it is because of their almost universal dependence of position.* . . . Wherever the table are turned, and the men are dependents of the women, and even where the women are independent of the men, – there we find the relations of the men to women vastly changed. (B:JGW? my *italics*)

This is an extremely significant point (so, I repeat what has been covered in 2-30). In not a few Eastern cultures – including Japan's closest neighbor – women were viewed as *intrinsically* inferior. (Such a difference doesn't disappear overnight. In Korea (1972 and 1980), I was horrified to find some well-educated men who still thought of women as inferior beings and treated them so. I *never* once met a Japanese man who did this.) But, in Japan, the position of women was not a *given,* it was *ex*trinsic to their nature. After this, Bacon argues for equal inheritance rights and other measures to improve the independence of Japanese women and then goes into depth on a matter Frois neglected and others only broached:

> ..
> The wife of a peasant or merchant is much nearer to her husband's level than is the wife of the Emperor. Apparently, each step up the social ladder is a little higher for the man than it is for the woman, and lifts him a little further above his wife. The peasant and his wife work side by side in the field, put their shoulders to the same wheel, eat together in the same room, at the same time, and whichever of them happens to be the stronger in character governs the house, without regard to sex. (B:JGW)

To this claim, she added personal testimony and more general information on the equality of women in the silk and tea districts where they are the main wage earners and "the equal of the stronger sex." (I would say, rather, that at certain tasks requiring endurance and finesse, women *are* the stronger sex, but her observation stands) and, finally, concludes: "The Japanese peasant woman, when she marries, works side by side with her husband, finds life full of interest out of the simple household work, and, as the years go by, her face shows more individuality, more pleasure in life, less suffering and disappointment, than that of her wealthier and less hard-working sister." (B:JGW) Humorist Douglas Sladen put this into a topsy-turvy context:

> ..
> One of the queerest things about this queer land is the fact that the humbler the wife is socially, the more is she on a footing of equality with her husband. It is the well-born woman who is content to be treated as her husband's inferior in almost everything. She is not allowed to work outside her own garden as her humbler sister may; she may not mix with her husband's friends and enter into conversation with them when he invites them to his house . . . (S:MQTJ)

By describing the above as *queer*, Sladen tells us clearly that *in the West, we expect the opposite.*

~~~~~~

Topsy-turvy is relative. The Iwakura mission toured the USA in the 1870's. The author of the Report expressed their collective shock at what they encountered:

> ..
> Think of the East and the West as lands separated by a mutually insurmountable gap from the start, where each and every more, and even our temperaments are opposite. . . . When our entourage boarded the American boat in Yokohama, it became a unique land, [a place] where our behavior raised their eyebrows and their behavior astounded us in turn. . . . I did my best with [mastering] the many fine points [of their etiquette], but of all of them, the one which seemed the weirdest of all, was the intercourse of men and women, of husband and wife. The way a bride acts toward her mother-in-law or children act toward their patients in Japan is the way a husband here acts toward his wife . . . he brings her trays of food, brushes off her dress . . . helps her up, offers her a seat on the sofa, . . . if the wife is angry, he must curry her affection, or to regain her respect, prostrate himself and apologize and if she still won't listen, stay and even eat outside . . . and with men and women riding together on boats and trains, the able-bodied man rises and gives up his seat to the woman . . . . This [men serving women rather than vice versa] is generally true throughout the West, but it is particularly well developed in England because it is a country with a queen and America because, with its republican government, arguments in favor of male and female equality have taken root. . . . (J/I:IR pt13)

III

OF THE CHILDREN AND THEIR CUSTOMS
do que toca aos mininos e a seus custumes

3-1   Boys in Europe keep their hair trim;
Os meninos em Europa andão trosquiados;

        Those of Japan always let it grow freely up to the age of fifteen.
        Os de Japão até os qinze anos sempre se lhe deixa crecer o cabelo.

The Portuguese term for "children," *meninos* (sometimes spelled *mininos* by Frois) also means "boys," and can include what English calls "babies." To translate, one must guess which is appropriate for the *context,* that is, depend on *knowledge*, not grammar. The chapter title requires the broadest possible term, "children," and this contrast, "boys."

Paintings suggest boys in North Europe wore their hair medium length, sometimes bowl-cut and sometimes as long as the shoulder but seldom longer. But those of South Europe, or the Japanese youths shorn by the Jesuits, show hair that would not have looked out of place in any authoritarian or totalitarian state. (Face it: uniformly short hair has always been a mark of ideological fanaticism and intolerance).

In Japan, a *baby* boy's hair was shaven four to five times a month until he was three at which time there is a ceremony called "hair-placing" (*kami-oki*), after which it is allowed to grow until he is five at which time it is trimmed neatly around the edges in the manner of a bowl-cut. Then it was not cut until the boys coming of age (between ages 11-16); but it was not free in the *wild* sense: Japanese have traditionally considered a shock of loose hair the mark of a vengeful ghost or an outlaw. It was generally bound in a ponytail in the manner of Japanese women (or Chinese men) or bundled higher up at the crown in the case of nobility (*kuge*). In some parts, a *kappa* cut, or page-cut was, like in Europe, not uncommon. Then, at adulthood, the front of the pate was shaven and the remaining hair bound and set as described in 1-6. What intrigues *me* is the contradiction here: tiny children were allowed to do as they wished in Japan, yet we find *their* heads shaved, while older children, who generally had to follow a harsh regime of studies, were allowed to wear theirs in a relatively free style!

Frois's observation is gender-neutral. Valignano's simile was more common: "The boys until age 14 wear their hair long and tied on top of their head *like women*."(1583 *italics* mine). And they shared the mindset, too. As Ribadeneira put it, they valued their hair "as much as the most coquettish [*galanas*] women of Europe prize their red/blond hair [*rojos cabellos*]." (n.100 in V(A):S&A) This was no academic concern for the Jesuits. According to Organtino, the reluctance of young Japanese to give up their hair was a major hindrance to their joining the Jesuit seminary in Kyoto! (Ibid.)

Westernization in the Meiji era again meant cutting this hair, submitting to voluntary cultural castration in order to be considered men by the Occidentals. As Chamberlain noted, cultured people may lament the change and even implore Japanese to keep their own fashions, but *"The Japanese would be blind indeed, did they not see that their best security . . . lies in the determination to be strong, and in the endeavor not to be too different from the rest of mankind; for the mob of Western nations will tolerate eccentricity of appearance no more than will a mob of toughs.* (C:TJ)

3-2 European babies spend a long time in swaddling clothes with their hands kept inside of them; *Os d'Europa andão muito tempo em queiros e com as mãos prezas dentro nelles;*

Japanese wear *kimonos* from the time they are born and their hands are always free. *Os de Japão logo em nacendo lhe vestem* qimões *e sempre andão com as mãos soltas.*

Frois wrote only "Those of Europe/Japan ~) for his subject. By the rules of logic, that would mean using the same subject as that in the previous distich, but that, *in English*, would suggest "boys" rather than "babies," so context rules differently here. Content-wise, there is a slight exaggeration on the Japanese side. Japanese babies did not immediately don adult-style clothing, as the *qimões* (*kimonos*) suggests. They wore robes cut in the same general pattern as kimonos, but thinner and "fastened from behind by two ribbons sewn on either side" (Rodrigues) rather than the girdle-like *obi*. Frois's contrast can be multiplied:

In Europe, we put clothing on a baby;
In Japan, the baby is put on the clothing.

In Europe, babies are dressed one piece of clothing after another;
In Japan, babies are dressed with many layers of clothing, all at one time

In Europe, we stop our babies from moving their limbs by tightly wrapping them up;
In Japan, they allow them to move, slowed down with loose long sleeves covering the hands.

These come from Alice Mabel Bacon's description of Japanese baby dress. The first is possible because a baby can be laid upon an open robe as easily as on a diaper. The second because the parents fit one within another before slipping the baby into them. The third, while somewhat redundant with Frois's contrast, indicates *how* the baby's hands can be free without scratching their faces and getting into their mouths. The result of this is that in Japan, unlike the West, "baby is dressed without a shriek or a wail, as simply and easily as possible," and, Bacon thought, the babies were less irritable. And if the dressing was easy, the *undressing* was easier. Kipling tells us how these "dolls" who "wriggle and laugh" on the backs of their slightly older siblings are

tied up in a blue bed-gown which is tied by a sash, which again ties up the bed-gown of the carrier. Thus if you untie that sash, baby and but little bigger brother are at once perfectly naked. I saw a mother do this, and it was for all the world like the peeling of hard-boiled eggs. (1889: K:KJ)

I am sure Ms. Bacon must have mentioned the biggest remaining question *somewhere*; but I find no *diapers* in my notes. Because the Japanese *tatami* is the ultimate horror to clean, there is probably no contrast to be found, anyway. Japanese *surely* had them. If there is a contrast, it would be with Koreans who had none. They dress their wee ones in robes so short, the slightest bend of the body leaves their privates uncovered, allowing them to go, whenever they please, *without dirtying their clothing.* That is possible because Koreans have hard, seamless floors, Moreover, unlike our (European and Japanese) floors, there is no chill from below, for the flooring is warm in the winter (heated from beneath) so infants can remain open for doing their business year-round.

3-3 In Europe, cradles are used to help children sleep, and carts to teach them to walk; *Em Europa se usa de berços pera os mininos dormirem e carretinhas pera se insinarem a andar;*

Those of Japan have none of that and only use the help given them by nature. *Os de Japão não tem nada disto e somente uzão das ajudas que lhe dá a natureza.*

"Nature" (*natureza*) implies a hands-off policy for the Japanese, but Okada introduces an undated book advising that a wet-nurse cradle the sleeping baby in her bosom for the first 15 days and later stay right by its side. There was also a mandatory night-lamp, hardly "natural." While neither the rocking cradle nor the prison-like crib was found in Japan, there were wicker baskets to hold babies if one could not afford wet-nurses – better a basket under a shade tree than a sweaty back in the sunshine. But these served more to keep a baby than to help it sleep. Today, with baby baskets nearly extinct in Japan, cribs (called *beibi-sahkuru* or, "baby circles") are used during the day-time.

> *In Europe, we think babies should sleep alone in their cradles, cribs or beds.*
> *In Japan, the babies never sleep alone and do not even have their own beds.*

Japanese infants still rarely if ever sleep alone at night. Japanese parents do not feel obliged to teach them to do so. They often keep sleeping with their parents up to grade-school. Neither did "we" in Frois's day, so this is one contrast Frois could not have made.

I have not yet found the cart (or wagon) mentioned by Frois which is charmingly Frenched as *petit chariots*, and will not try to guess what it looked like. The only thing I have ever read about training a child to walk is the following observed by Thunberg in Amsterdam, 1770:

> In my landlord's house I observed a very ingenious method of teaching children to walk. — A ribband was fastened under the child's arms, which passed through a ring that slid on a long iron rod fixed horizontally in the roof, so that the child could walk backwards and forwards along the room, without falling or taking up the time of an attendant. (T:TEAA)

It seems remarkable to me that a device used to encourage children to walk would be forgotten. On the other hand, considering the advantage of a child's *not* walking at a tender age, the loss is not missed.

~~~~~~

3-4 With us, ordinarily, grown women carry babies on their bosom;
Antré nós ordinariamente molheres grandes trazem as crianças ao collo;

In Japan, very little girls go about with the babies almost always on their backs.
Em Japão mininas muito pequenas andão quasi sempre com as crianas aas costas.

In the 20c, every Japanese visitor to the United States returning to Japan reported their close encounters with . . . squirrels! The equivalent topic for 19c Europeans was little children jumping rope, playing ball or shuttlecock with infants on their backs in Japan. An abundance of squirrels may be unique to the US, but little children looking after littler children was hardly a Japanese monopoly. What was the surprise? Was the percent of child-care left to children in Japan particularly high because Japanese women (who could keep what they earned) worked more then did Europeans?

> *Among us, little girls have dolls to carry, hug and kiss.*
> *Japanese little girls have babies on their backs but don't know how to play with dolls*

Still, they were *so* young it amazed "us." A 4, 5 or 6 year-old capable enough to be entrusted with so heavy a responsibility seems miraculous. Lowell, in 1888, resorted to racism to explain it; namely, "That it should be practicable thus to entrust one infant to another proves the precociousness of children . . . that which has less to grow up to, naturally grows up to its limit sooner." (L:SOFE) He is so lyrical: "The youthful nurse, in blissful ignorance of the evidence which her present precocity affords against her future possibilities, pursues her sports with intermittent attention to her charge, whose poor little head lolls about, now on one side and now on the other, in a most distressful manner, an uninterested spectator of the proceedings." (Ibid) In plain English, Asia was doomed because it grew up too fast. Lowell saw the history of the world in that "youthful nurse." It was a world "we" won. Frois and the Jesuits never resorted to *that* much sophistry or racism.

Or, was it the diminutive *size* of the carriers? If so, is this the *cause* for the method of carrying used or the *outcome* of back-style carrying which does not require arm-strength? Sladen, in 1903, used back-carrying to illustrate his claim that *"Japan is the Antipodes as much as Australia,"* yet only a few years later in *More Queer Things about Japan*, noted that babies were "much the same way, shawl-bound to the woman's sides in the streets of South Wales." *There go the Antipodes!*

Europeans think it is natural and good to look directly into each other's eyes.
Japanese think it is rude to do so and tend to avert their eyes or close them.

Why this Faux Frois *here?* I was told by someone I happened to strike a conversation with at a copy machine that there is a psychologist who credits our respective manners of carrying babies for creating our different attitude with respect to eye contact, something discussed in 1-3. When babies are cradled at the breast, there is a lot of eye-contact for the first years of life, whereas there is very little when infants do not spend much time face-to-face with their mother or caretaker. This imprinting lasts for life. *We* find it hard to believe that looking down or closing the eyes as we listen is more polite than looking attentively at the speaker, whereas *they* find it almost impossible to look into our eyes. Indeed, I have seen books instructing Japanese to *stare at a spot between the eyes if it is too hard to look into the other person's eyes as expected by Occidentals!.* Now that less babies are carried piggyback in Japan, we must see if there is any effect on eye-contact!

Note that Frois has chosen ordinary Japanese rather than nobles for this contrast because the nobles, like our upper classes, had grown nurse-maids rather than siblings to look after infants.

3-5   With us, babies [their clothing] has one plain sash tied in front;
Antre nós as crianças trazem hum só ourelo singido e atado diante;

Those of Japan have a mass of ribbons, all tied behind the *kimonos*.
As de Japão trazem nos qimões *hum monte de fitas e todas atadas detrás.*

With babies carried piggyback in Japan, the belts would have to be tied in back if the knot/s were not to come between its belly and its mother's – or older sister's – back. Bows in back are also easier for a parent to untie when a small child squats to go to the toilet. And, without chairs, Japanese had no practice of leaning back, so there was no reason for knots *not* to be in back. This difference carries to adulthood. Frois missed this one, which could have been in Chapter I or II:

We fasten our own belts or tie our sashes in front or slightly to one side;
The Japanese, when properly dressed, have someone else tie their thick belt in back.

But this resemblance with baby-wear is only true for formal clothing. Generally, Japanese belts are tied in front or on the side by the person wearing the clothes.

I do not know why there was such a mass (*monte,* literally "mountain") of ribbons. The two mentioned by Rodrigues is hardly excessive. Period illustrations show women and children sometimes wore multiple thin sashes. I would *guess* a baby's included a red one for warding off bad spirits.

3-6   With us, a child of 4-years still does not know how to eat with his own hands;
Antre nós hum menino de 4 annos ainda não sabe comer com sua mão;

Those of Japan eat by themselves from age three, using *hashi* [chopsticks].
Os de Japão de três anos comem por si mesmos com faxis.

The European side of the contrast is puzzling, for if 6-1, the first item in the Food Chapter is correct, Europeans ate *with* their bare hands, so one would think even a baby would do fine! The hand (*mão*) is, however, singular in case. Was there, perhaps, some tricky one-handed etiquette (such as Indians have to eat rice) to follow we have not heard of?

The Japanese side falls under the rubric of "genius Japanese" contrasts of which we shall see more in this chapter. Frois has Japanese children doing it the hard way, *and* at a younger age. You might think the *hashi* were easier to manipulate than the child's own fingers! In his presentation of "Etiquette at the Table" which begins with the memorable line: "I will not praise Japanese food for it is not good, albeit it is pleasing to the eye, but instead I will describe the clean and peculiar way in which it is served," the Spanish merchant Bernardino de Avila Giron made it clear that the Japanese children weren't just going through the motions with those "two clean sticks, or hashi, as thick as a quill and about a span and a half in length" – "They take these up with four fingers and eat with them, and a child of four summers can remove the bones of a sardine with them." (C:TCJ)

What have these children got that "ours" do not? It seems that the fine chopstick work and the baby-sitting described in 3-4 are describing the same thing, *precocity* – or, viewed from the Japanese perspective, our *retardation*, expressed in the unruliness and inability to learn of little Occidental children. As far as I know, the first person to give a possible reason for this was Alice Mabel Bacon. She hypothesized Japanese babies were less nervous and irritable than American ones because "the poor little weak thing does not have to go through the complicated process of dressing which causes our babies such trials and shrieks every day," (see 3-2) and because it is allowed to cry in peace ("nobody ever makes a noise at a baby, or jiggles or shakes it, to stop its crying"). Bacon wrote at a time where nervousness was both the mark and the bane of high civilization, so one can imagine she had mixed feelings about the significance of the difference, but still, it seems to me, she thought that letting babies be would improve our health as adults. I recall reading more recent studies as to why Chinese tiny tykes are calmer and more attentive than Usanian ones, but cannot recall the results. Maybe that's good. Any short presentation of matters concerning *nature* and *nuture,* both of which can be measured in many ways, is bound to mislead.

But I will add one thing. Lowell's idea of precocity we saw in 3-4 is doubly wrong, for, on the whole, Mongoloids tend to be neotenous, *slow,* rather than fast-maturing. Unless, one is to posit a body/mind split in the rate of development (an interesting theory, I'll admit), we must find other explanations. But, here is one, from the *nuture* side, that belongs right here. In the economic "bubble" days of JAPAN AS NUMBER ONE, the head and founder of Sony hypothesized that the use of chopsticks helped explain the brain gap behind the success of the Far East. Namely, the complexity of the motor function developed neurons in the brain, improving the child's IQ. It's not *what* you eat but *how* you eat that gives you the smarts.

3-7 With us, it is ordinary to whip and castigate children;
Antre nós hé ordinário açoutar e castiga[r os] filhos;

In Japan it is very rare and they are only rarely reprimanded.
Em Jãpao hé cousa mui rara e somente de [r?]aro os reprendem.

Three of the four published translations I have seen chose "son" over the generic "children" here, but I follow the minority. I bet both sexes were whipped in Europe. In 1565, Frois wrote that *children* in Japan are not physically punished and "even children of six or seven were disciplined with words, spoken as seriously as one might speak to a seventy year-old." (carta dated 1565/2/20).

We think we have a right to boss around our children because we are their parents;
They think children should be convinced to do things and reason with them as if they were adult.

Valignano, in 1580: "They are a people universally accustomed to living as they wish, for both men and women are brought up from childhood that they are allowed to behave as they please, without their fathers checking them in the smallest degree, for they neither whip nor scold them." (B:CCJ Boxer tr. *Italics* mine). The idea of Japanese as particularly free souls is not common. Valignano wrote this before having much experience with Japanese. Caron, writing a generation later:

> At school they begin by degrees, by sweetness and not by force, the Masters imprinting a desire in each of them to outdo his fellow . . . The children are so accustomed to this way, that they learn sooner and more then by any correction or whipping; for generous spirits, and an obstinate Nation, such as this is, are not to be forced, but rather won with gentleness and emulation. (C:DOJ)

It is interesting that Valignano thought gentle parenting created willful children and free-minded adults, whereas Caron thought willfulness required gentle teaching. Neither recommends harsh treatment. As the Jesuit policy in teaching was *not to use harsh words*, Valignano and Frois would not have been neutral about this contrast. They would have understood it as one item where "they" excelled "us." The difference lasted. Two centuries later, Thunberg "very seldom heard them rebuked or scolded; and hardly ever saw them flogged or beaten, either in private families or on board of the vessels. While," he adds with no little irony, "in more civilized and enlightened nations, these compliments abound." (T:TEAA) You can bet that the Dutch cabin boys were not so lucky! *Or, was the rod only spared because the Japanese child was not spoiled to begin with?* Valignano mentions willfulness, but he knew it did not go too far, for he *also* expressed surprise that –

> not even the boys use bad language, nor do they fight with slapping and fists like ours, but speak with great courtesy, never losing respect for one another, with such deliberation and gravity that they don't seem children, but serious men. This is true to such a degree that it is unbelievable. (V(A):V&S)

Isabella Bird even worried about the docility of the Japanese child. "They are gentle creatures" she wrote, "but too formal and precocious." Indeed. "I have never seen what we call child's play, that general abandonment to miscellaneous impulses, which consists in struggling, slapping, rolling, jumping, kicking, shouting, laughing and quarrelling!" (B:UTJ) So, what *did* Bird see?

> Two fine boys are very clever in harnessing paper carts to the backs of beetles with gummed traces, so that eight of them draw a load of rice up an inclined plane. You can imagine what the fate of such a load and team would be at home among a number of snatching hands. Here, a number of infants watch the performance with motionless interest, and never need the adjuration, "Don't touch." (B:UTJ)

I have observed the same, and, to tell the truth, would trust the average Japanese 3 or 4 year-old with something breakable before I would trust an average Usanian 6 year-old. How can this be? Mrs. Busk in 1845, gives a seemingly knowledgeable explanation, based on the testimony of the Dutch Meylan: "Children are trained to habits of implicit obedience; which, independent on its beneficial effects on their future character, prevents, in a great measure, the necessity of punishment." (B:MCJ). *Trained? How*? Valignano thought it the natural result of the "concord and quiet" of Japanese domestic life, itself created by the total avoidance of confrontation (see 3-16, below). The favored 19c theory was *heredity*, that Japanese babies were, to use Bacon's words, "born into the world with a head-start" that was increased by "uniformly gentle and courteous treatment they receive."

Let me add that *all* the above (See TT-long for two pages more, including long passages by Morse one including the fine phrase "The Japanese have certainly solved the children problem . . ." and my hypothesis as to how *nature* influences *nature* to create a cycle of corporal punishment . . . etc,) is *still true* today. 20c child psychologists have noted how Japanese mothers squat down and *explain things* at length to recalcitrant children – from what I have overheard, the most common appeal is to the child's conscience by putting it in the place of the other (injured/troubled) party and asking pointed questions, but there are also appeals to a child's pride and its reverse, a sense of shame – where "we" would more likely *demand* obedience. Sad to say, the contrast Frois points out probably has been true for hundreds, possibly thousands of years! One wonders when the West began to go wrong.

Obedience, Conscience, Sin, Shame. (I leave in this one side-track note from *TT-long*, for I think "our" culture is very, very confused about where real morality comes from.) The standard contrast of inner-directed Western morality with outer-directed Japanese morality, with the former being *individual sin-based* and the latter *social shame-based*, is partially correct, but horribly misleading for it neglects the far more important contrast of morality based on *reward and punishment* versus *natural morality* based on having *a conscience*. If the only reason you do not do bad things is because your parents demand you do not do them and you know you will be overpowered or hurt if you disobey, or because the *Bible* says they are "sinful" and you fear the ultimate punishment, your morality is other-based. If, on the other hand, you do not, say, hit another kid in the face because it hurts you to even think of doing so, then you are following your conscience. It is amusing to read of a wee malefactor rationalizing his malfeasance on grounds that the Bible doesn't say anything about not throwing cupcakes at another child's face in KIDS SAY THE DARNDEST THINGS, but that is a perfect description of *the artificial nature of sin-based morality!* (There is nothing in the Ten Commandments about parents not *whipping* their children, either!) Because little children in Japan were treated very gently, and accordingly had consciences, they did not need an artificial construct to compensate, or whips to terrify them into submission if they could not be convinced of the reality of Hell. I think that if a culture must rely on the fear of sin – i.e., believe in Heaven and Hell, which is to say a sort of *"Santa Claus is Coming to Town"* threat for adults to behave – it is a good indication that something has gone wrong with early childhood. Shame, on the other hand, is like the conscience, a natural emotion and, correctly comprehended, is not opposed to but strengthened by having a conscience. (If you do not have a *conscience* you can be embarrassed but not really feel shame.)

3-8   With us, reading and writing are learned from secular teachers;
   Antre nós se aprende a ler e escrever com mestres seqlares;

   In Japan, all children study in the *varelas* [temples] of the bonzes.
   Em Japão todos os meninos aprendem nas varelas *dos bonzos.*

Pangur the white cat, his master and many other diligent monks did help bring books through the Dark Ages but they were not, on the whole, eager to educate people. Faith was first, learning second, and one factor sparking the Reformation in North Europe may have been the fact that the clergy came to lag the laity in learning and thereby lost their respect. The Society of Jesus was to change this in a big way – a bit too late to recover North Europe, but soon enough to save the South for Catholicism – but Frois did not experience that change, for he received his training as a scribe from secular teachers and left Lisbon for the East the year he joined the Society of Jesus at age 16, which, as it happens was the very same year the Jesuits opened their first school, 1548. It was a secondary school in Messina, Italy and by 1585 the Society had opened thirty more primary and secondary schools. I am not sure what percent were primary schools and whether they were open early enough for news to have reached Frois. Regardless, it would have been true that the majority of the schools (and tutors) in Europe were secular and that there was not yet anything as broad-based as the temple-based elementary school system in Japan.

Unfortunately, Frois wrote in such a mercurial age that we can not say with certainty just how far down the social ladder schooling extended (or the percentage of girls) but literacy was, beyond doubt, higher than in the West. Most children apparently attended small temple day-schools in town, but some boarded at the mountain temples from age six or seven and "came down the mountain" as apprentice monks four or five years later.

Buddhism was a major source of letters in Japan. .An esoteric Buddhist abbot was credited with devising one of the phonetic syllabaries and some of Japan's top literary work was written by Buddhist priests. Unlike the case in China where Buddhist monks ended up largely illiterate and all the learning and respect was monopolized by the government scholar-bureaucrats, bonzes in Japan enjoyed a degree of public respect for their literacy and calligraphy. Considering the role of the clergy in preserving literacy through our "dark age" – that is in many ways not so dark, but, like the Tokugawa isolation of Japan, "enlightened" in its own way – it is surprising to me that more of *our* primary education was not likewise in the hands of our religious orders.

3-9   Our children first learn to read and later learn to write;
Os nossos mininos aprendem primeiro a ler e depois a escrever;

> Those of Japan commence with writing and then learn to read.
> *Os de Japão começão primeiro a escrever e depois aprendem a ler.*

Japanese children did indeed write Chinese characters before they could read them. Since most characters have multiple readings in Japanese (eg. 頭 head," is pronounced *atama* for a plain ole head, *zu* as part of a headache=*zutsû* and *tô* when used for counting heads), it takes much more time to master *reading* them than *writing* them, with the exception of the more complex characters, which most people never learn *to write*). Writing also plays a more important role in learning than it does in the West. The thick, brushed line impresses the visual memory deeper than a penned one, and it is important for mastering the order of the strokes. Moreover, such writing is an aesthetically satisfying incentive for the child (We will come back to this in the writing chapter). I don't know how many times I have seen the calligraphy of elementary school children – usually just one or two large brushed characters – on exhibit at the railway/subway station (which is pretty much the center of any town in Japan). Many are just magnificent, for there is a beauty and a power that only repetition can create in art. Framed and exhibited in an art gallery, they would put to shame the largely worthless modern art found in Japan or here. Imagine if you can, samples of our children's writing – or, for that matter any one's writing – on exhibit in art galleries and hanging in homes as art. *Impossible*, isn't it. *Our calligraphy may be an art, but the product is not fine art in the true sense.* It is only *decoration*.

If Frois was not seeking contrast, he might have noted that young pupils in Japan also learn a phonetic syllabary; but with these syllabets (see 10-1) they can read *immediately* – or learn to read as they write. Even Spanish, where what you see is what you get, cannot match this. To *Faux Frois* it,

> *European adults sometimes spell-out words so as to make them incomprehensible to children; Japanese do so to make them clear, for, in Japanese, spelling out is simply saying a word slowly.*

3-10 Our tutors teach catechism, [the lives of] the saints, and virtuous customs to children;
Os nossos mestres insinão a doutrina, santos e vertuosos custumes aos meninos;

> The bonzes teach them to play [musical instruments], sing, game and fence, and practice their abominations on them. *Os bonzos os insinão a tanjer, cantar, jugar, esgrimir e com eles fazem suas abominasões.*

Frois grew up during a time when the Inquisition, having discovered gaps in the knowledge of the Christian doctrine on the part of a majority of adults, encouraged reformers to educate children. The Jesuits were among the first to do so. By the third article of the founding document (1539) of the Society of Jesus, members of the new order were bound to "hold esteemed the instruction of children and the uneducated in the Christine doctrine of the Ten Commandments and other similar rudiments." Before long, they were walking through the streets ringing bells to attract children whom they quickly taught to sing prayers through patient teaching and prizes. Evidently, they really revved them up. Take this testimony from one Diego Xuárez: "It melted my hard heart to see the eagerness with which the children came to doctrine, and they went singing it in the streets and fields, so that almost nothing else was heard. Some women were crying with devotion, and when we asked them why they didn't know the Ten Commandments, they said, "Because they didn't teach it to us like now in the streets." (from N:GIL) Within fifty years, the Jesuits taught most of the higher learning in Europe, but in Frois's time you could say that they sparked the Catholic Reformation child-first. So, you can understand Frois's fury with respect to the more secular education offered by his Buddhist rivals.

The Buddhist temple-schools were a creative space with what we now might consider a progressive curriculum! All those Chinese characters were hard work, but little Japanese, at least, did not have to endure too much catechism. "Gaming," is not only gambling as we might imagine but, encompasses board games such as *shôgi* and *go* (see 14-39), which are, like our chess, games of skill and not intrinsically gambling, though often associated with it. The "abominations" is another matter. When Rodrigues writes that the Jesuits ran schools for the young sons of Christians because of fear that "after studying in these monastery schools they become children of the devil on account of the many bad customs and vices the bonzes teach the children there under their care;" and, worse, that "they not only do not feel these vices to be wrong, but they teach them in such a way that it is considered a virtue to consent to them and a despicable vice to resist and oppose them . . . ," he means one thing: *pederasty*.

Judging from the literature going back a thousand years, there was quite some competition for cute boys. In Japan, as in ancient Greece, grown men unabashedly had young boyfriends with whom they enjoyed sex. Neither were necessarily homosexual in our sense of the word. Usually both were not. An Edo era erotic print by Koigawa Shôsan showing a samurai sodomizing a youth, includes conversation with these words from the older to the younger: *"Let me suck your mouth [tongue-kiss]! For that, I'll even buy you a whore* [a woman] *tonight!"* Risqué poems (*senryu*) – like *Martial's Epigrams* – tell wives not to even *try* competing with hairless young asses, and, better yet, chuckle that even a *wakashû* (literally "young-crowd") – the closest phenomenon to what we call "gay," but invariably transvestite as well – are frightening . . . *when they eat chili peppers!* As the term for a professional catamite, *kagema* or "shade-place" suggests, "male-color" (homosexuality) was nothing to boast about. For bonzes, however, practicing sex with boys was considered far less reprehensible than intercourse with women. They were supposed to avoid "the wide way" (vaginal intercourse) because of the supposedly greater pollution of women, danger of falling into lasting love with the illusory beauty of this world as embodied by women, and for fear of issue, i.e., the social repercussions of fatherhood and adultery – and stick to "the narrow way" (anal intercourse). Like prostitution licensed in order "to prevent the debauching of young Maids and married Women" (Caron) and masturbation, encouraged to preserve female chastity and save men from wasting money and catching sexually transmitted disease, pederasty was considered a relatively harmless vice.

The amount of pederasty in Japan was not exaggerated by the Jesuits. They were only wrong to identify it so completely with Buddhism (4-2). "Bogering boyes" (to borrow Cocks' term) was popular practice. In the *kabuki* days of the 17-18c all the major pleasure quarters had *wakashû*, "young-crowd" houses and not a few female street-walkers found they did better business by impersonating these male female impersonators! Since Confucius and company were not boy-lovers, while Socrates (actually, his love, like a samurai for his boy, was deeper than pederasty) *et al* were, we might

Faux Frois:

Our ancient philosophers were lovers of boys, and all of them would be burned alive today.
Their ancient philosophers were not like that, but loving boys is now thought admirable.

Homosexual relations, like public nudity and male long-hair, was persecuted for the sake of international relations (pleasing the West) and a tradition of a thousand years was driven underground so successfully that the coming out of homosexuality in the West in the late-20c, shocked Japanese who, for the most part, knew nothing about their own culture's bisexual past.

In respect to "our" side, while the Catholic Reformation did indeed crack down on sex (not just between men, but, laudably, against clergy who seduced women who confessed their sins), there were some notable exceptions that suggest the West was by no means innocent of what was charged against Japan. There was a poem *"De laudibus, sodomiae seu pederastiae,"* usually Englished *In Praise of Sodomy*, by an Italian Arch-bishop who dedicated it to a Pope who had orgies with teenage Cardinals (elected because they were his minions) – this going on right about the time Frois arrived in Japan, no less! – I only bring this up these things to complicate matters (see *pages* of notes in *TT-long*) and do not think I have disproved Frois's contrast which, *as a generalization,* holds true.

3-11   Ours as young men do not know how to give a message;
Os de Europa são mancebos e não sabem dar hum recado;

> Japanese children ten years old do so with the judgment and prudence of a 50 year-old. *Os meninos japões de dez annos paresem de 50 no sizo e prudencia com que o dão.*

Japan wins again. This contrast, as with 3-6, 3-13 and 3-14, prove that Frois is not just following an agenda to idealize Europe, but calls it as he sees it. Not long ago, in both the West and Japan, being entrusted with messages was an accepted way for youths to gain status and make connections. While carrying written messages – and filling in the details as necessary – were part of the boy's duty, I believe the ability to recall an invisible, and therefore safe, oral message may be what Frois means here. Our verb "to page" suggests that was the case in the West, too. Okada, who translates *recado* (message) as *kôjô* (oral message) quotes at length instruction for training children from the age of eight to relay messages properly, and notes that "becoming a messenger was considered *the* goal of learning the proprieties." Because the instructions suggested repeating simple greetings a hundred times over so they would become second nature, we can see that *practice* may have had a lot to do with the "judgment and prudence" found in Japan.

3-12   With us, even a man of 20 rarely carries a sword;
Antre nós hé um homem de 20 anos e quasi que ainda não tras espada;
..

> The children of Japan, go about with a *katana* [Japanese sword] and *wakizashi* [dagger] from age 12 or 13. *Os meninos de Japão de 12, 13 anos andão com* catana e vaqizaxi.

In 1547, Alvarez noted that "males customarily carried swords from the tender age of eight years." (B:CCJ) In 1555, Gago claimed it was ten (CARTAS). In 1565, Frois wrote "From a very young age, the boys wear swords and daggers, and when they sleep place them by their pillow"(CARTAS). Valignano dittoed that, and L Abbe d' T improved it, saying they do so "to shew themselves Souldiers in their very sleep." (A:HCJ) This could not have been true for *most* boys in Japan, even in this most warlike age; but it apparently was true for the 5-10% that belonged to the *buke*, or samurai stock and not a few commoners, though they would only wear *one* sword (*two* being a samurai privilege). I think it safe to say that before the modernization of Japan in the late-19c, even wee samurai far younger than "12 or 13" wore the standard "big little" sword set. It is a good thing the swords were sheathed, for looking at their mid-19c photos, one wonders how often they tripped over them!

M & J write that Frois exaggerates, for in 1584, the young ambassadors from Japan to Europe record a visit to a certain Count in Portugal, whose three sons, aged sixteen, fourteen and ten, all wore swords. *Touché?* Not quite. A formal occasion is not the same as wearing them *all the time*, as was the case for little samurai. As Noel Perrin has pointed out, in Japan, the sword was "the only embodiment of honor" that formed part of one's costume. With no signet ring, no jewels, no military decorations, the sword was *the* mark of somebody. "Occasionally a commoner would rise in the world and be granted a sort of life peerage. This was called *myoji-taito,* the privilege of surname and sword." (P:GUG) The swords were, as we have seen in chapter I, part of their clothing.

This contrast reflects not only the utterly martial orientation of the Japanese gentry but the precocious self-control already noted. Young Japanese who could handle chopsticks at 4 and deliver an oral message at 10 could also be entrusted with a lethal weapon. *Why?* Because Japanese children did not fight each other. This was and is largely true right up to the present day. Morse wrote that kite fighting was "the only way I ever saw boys fight among themselves." He also noted that he saw only one street fight in his three years in Japan and he was the only one who watched (and it was only a bit of hair-pulling at that). There was none of that *"fight! fight!"* enthusiasm where all gather round to watch "admiring the punches and regretfully departing when the battle is finished or the police interfere" common to Morse's America and mine (several times per week behind the water-tower near Key Biscayne Elementary in the 1960's). Face it, we *are* barbarians!

There may have been one downside to armed precocity. Valignano, writing about *harakiri*, notes: "To cut the belly in this way is so common in Japan that it sometimes happens that very small children do it in front of their parents when they are angry at them." *That* I find hard to believe.

3-13 Our children show little judgment or grace with respect to our manners;
Os nossos mininos tem pouqo asento e primor nos custumes;

> Those of Japan, in this regard, are so wonderfully perfect in every respect they are admirable. *Os de Japão são nisto estranhamente inteiros, em tanto que poem admirasao.*

Should we ask why "our" children were – and are – so rambunctious? Did "Europe" in Frois's day already have a *youth culture* sufficiently different from tradition to estrange children from their parents and give them an excuse to misbehave? Keith Thomas writes of English children pretty much ignored by adults and running wild, *pissing in the aisles of churches to make ice to skate on*, and so forth. (T:RAD) How typical was this for European children? Was it the result of ebullience? Or was it a reaction to domestic violence? Or, was the importation of sugar, perhaps, already creating hyperactivity? Or should we, rather, ask why the Japanese children were so culture-positive, so ready to try finer things? Ruth Benedict once hypothesized that the *excessive* (her idea, not mine!) artistic activity and ritual observance in Bali derived from the way Balinese mothers continually frightened their children with imaginary ghosts, after which they gleefully cuddled and reassured them so they grew up insecure in the world at large and needed art to feel reassured in a well-ordered little world of their own. I suppose a similar explanation, turning punctilious behavior into abnormality born of neurosis could be made for the children of Frois's Japan. (We have already seen some of this, although Bird and Bacon never go so far as Benedict.) But I think the most likely reason for the goodness of Japanese children is that there is much in the culture that is good for, i.e., satisfies them. (See 3-15)

Then again, it is not only *children* who behave themselves, is it? Valignano, right after expressing his amazement with the docility of Japanese children, pointed out that Japanese in their dress, dining and so forth were remarkably "clean, trim and properly dressed." Indeed: "all of the Japanese have the same order and manner of proceeding, so much so it seems they were all taught in the same school." (V(A):S&A) On November 13, 1857, Heusken, the brilliant young interpreter for the first American Consul to Japan, noted the same, in more detail, with a touch of good humor:

> It seems that the Japanese do everything they must do at the same time, prescribed by law. They take their breakfast, lunch, and dinner exactly at the same hour. They change clothes four times a year on the same day. One day, everybody is busy drying fish; another day is to dry fabrics woven by the women. Apparently they go even further, for today everybody without exception has a cold certainly by order of the government. (H:JJ)

An entire nation literally composed. How could the children fall astray? Morse, after visiting the closest thing to slums in Japan a few years later, ventured that a random sample of even those children would prove "more polite and graceful in manner, less selfish, more considerate for the feelings of others" than their counterparts from upper Fifth Avenue, New York! (M:JDD). With this contrast, too: *no contest.* (We make a mistake to explain behavior by poverty or religion alone.)

~~~~~~

3-14 Our children are, for the most part, embarrassed to act in public performances;
Os nossos mininos, são pola mayor parte pejados em autos públicos e reprezentações;

> Those of Japan are at ease, lively, adorable, and bold in their roles.
> *Os de Japão despejados, libres, e graciosos e muy ayrozos no que representão..*

Why is this? *Isn't stage-fright normal?* If Frois restricted his observation to the children of nobility it might be explained as experience, for judging from Fernao Mendez Pinto's detailed account, they were fond of putting on skits for guests (see 6-1). But there might be more to it. Hundreds of years after Frois, Bacon wrote that "the Japanese girl seems never at a loss, even under unusual circumstances, but bears herself with self-possession in places where young girls in America would be embarrassed and awkward," perhaps because of "regular teaching in the ways of polite society." (B:JGW) That is to say, contrary to our assumption that manners (including polite phrases of speech) are restrictive, they can free those who incorporate them, much as the mastery of a certain type of music (to the exclusion of other possibilities) allows one to improvise freely. Someone – perhaps Eliza Scidmore – called Japanese "a nation of poseurs." If there is anything to that, acting would be nothing out of the ordinary to them. Posing would in no way make the poseur lose his or her composure. The ease with which Japanese *of all ages* perform in front of audiences is still apparent today, is by no means restricted to drama, and suggests the following *Faux Frois:*

> *Europeans freeze up in formal situations and are at ease giving informal opinions.*
> *Japanese have difficulty giving personal opinions but are at ease when performing in public.*

In *informal* situations, or when asked for their *opinions*, Japanese above the age of eight tend to be *more* rather than less uptight than Usanians and, possibly, all Western peoples. Indeed, they see themselves as extremely bashful and even lacking in self-expression compared to "outgoing and brave" foreigners. The Jesuits alternated between praising such bashfulness as discretion and humility and damning it as being secretive. In the early-18c, the extraordinarily objective Golownin gives a fine and long example (which really should be picked up by socio-linguists!) of the reticent style of Japanese argument where "they bring forward their opinions politely, and with many apologies, seeming to doubt the correctness of their own judgment." (G:MCJ) When I think of my countrymen, the countless obnoxiously confident Usanian sound-alikes who *think* they are original – such gentleness and humility seems too good to be true! But, excessive reticence was and still is a problem, for, as even the supreme Japanophile Morse lamented, the Japanese are not only afraid to contradict one another "as it is with us," but "consider it rude to have a different opinion," so all statements are given "submissive agreement" resulting in, "to the uninformed, endless confusion." (M:IGM) There is truth in this lament. Without the unstated agreement to disagree found in the West, lively discussion in much of Japan (Kansai is more like the West and Korea in this respect) is all but impossible while sober.

But in *formal* situations, it is the Western man or woman who is far more likely to be at a loss and claim the cat got their tongue, or blush red as a beat, when asked for a speech at a wedding or to sing a song in front of colleagues, where many if not most Japanese do so with the aplomb of an old pro. In formal or public performance, most Japanese are still as awesome as the children mentioned by Frois. They seem to find what is essentially role-playing – acting out a public *persona* – less stressful than the informal argument most Westerners find relaxing rather than stressful. If this broader difference, or paradox was not mentioned by Frois, it may be because the Iberian culture was also quite performance-oriented.

Or, am I am barking up the wrong tree. Should I have stopped at children doing skits? Are Japanese children more at ease simply because Japanese were spared the rod (3-7)? One thing is certain, the Jesuits were unabashed humanists who, following the Greeks, were so big on plays that they deserve some credit for the 17c being the century of drama in Europe. They doubtless used plays as learning aids in Japan, so Frois's observation probably comes from hands-on experience. Because there is a separate chapter on *Drama*, indicating that Frois did not necessarily stay home, this contrast may instead refer to the dancing and Noh plays samurai children participate in.

~~~~~~

3-15 Children of Europe are raised with many dainty gifts, sweet words, caresses, good food and dress; *Os de Europa são criados com muitos mimos, branduras, bons comeres e vestidos;*

> Those of Japan grow up half-naked, with hardly any gifts, affection or treats.
> *Os de Japão meos nus e quasi que de todos os mimos e dilícias carecem.*

If Japanese were not whipped (3-7), they were not hugged either! Okada quotes a period child-rearing book to the effect that small children should to be "starved by a third and frozen by a tenth." This was thought good for their long-term health. Such advice was probably for the upper classes and wealthy merchant/townsman. The majority of children in Japan, and Europe, were automatically treated to that much! Something of the attitude survives, for even today, primary school children must wear shorts in the winter (*yes, it snows in Tokyo*), and every year a few foreign mothers with children attending Japanese schools write letters to the Japan Times to complain about this "cruelty" and suggest the teachers and administrators follow suit, etc.. Moreover, Japanese still aren't big on hugging each other and don't tell their children that they love them. Then again, adults don't do these things to each other, either.

"Half-naked" encompasses at least four different phenomena. *Health*, as explained above is one; the different *attitude on nudity* we have already discussed, another. *Superstition* is the third: Mrs. Busk's 1841 summary of Dutch observations includes note of the "shabby appearance" of the children, contrasting "most strikingly with the parent's splendid attire;" and it was said to be in order to "preserve them from the blighting effects of the admiration which, if well-dressed, their beauty might excite;" *i.e.*, an instance of "the strange superstition of the evil eye." And, fourth, assuming "half-naked" (*meos nus*) in Portuguese includes the figurative nuance it does in English, we should note that the Japanese by and large *did* let their little children *run wild* – except, as we have already seen, they were wild in moderation, encouraged to make their own little worlds, not modeled, thank goodness, on "our" *Lord of the Flies* model. As Bird put it "I admire the way in which children are taught to be independent in their amusements. Part of the home education is the learning of the rules of the different games, which are absolute, and when there is a doubt, instead of a quarrelsome suspension of the game, the fiat of the senior child decides the matter. They play by themselves, and don't bother adults at every turn." (B:UTJ?) *Even W.C. Fields might have appreciated such children!* Moreover, they were allowed to play for a long time. As Caron noted in Frois's time, school did not begin until they were seven or eight. In Europe, despite "our" relative retardation mentioned in 3-6, the children of the nobility were generally tutored from infancy. And this difference persisted until the 19c. Alcock wrote: "I should say the children of Japan have a merit the tendency of modern education is to deprive ours of at home, namely, they are natural children . . ." (A:COT). And Mrs. Frazer wrote "Here, children are always welcome; they come and go as they like, are spoilt, if love means spoiling, by mother and father, relations and servants; but they grow imperceptibly in the right shape . . ." (F:DWJ)

Today, when Japanese are liable to be identified with *artificial,* this type of observation is good to read. The late 20c obsession in Japan with starting schooling early so children can pass an exam for an elite nursery school so they can pass an exam for an elite kindergarten and so forth, all the way up to the university guaranteed to make them part of the power elite – all this is very new.

So what exactly was it that Frois thought European children had and Japanese did not? The single Portuguese word *mimos* translates as "dainty, delicacy, gift, caress, petting" (one dic.) "dainty gifts," (another dic.). The *branduras* translates as "softness, gentleness" (one dic.) "endearments, loving words" (*carinhosas*) and "tender words" (*palavras meigas*) (my trans. from yet another dic.). I added nouns and adjectives but still doubt the translation covers it. [not all dicts. are in biblio – i promise they're all real]

I believe one thing Frois had in mind was the type of thing I have overheard in Miami: Latin American mothers pouring loving words over their children as one might pour free syrup over pancakes. I do not know if I have ever heard it reproduced and I have a very poor aural memory. Suffice it to say that Anglos only talk that way to their lap-dogs or pampered cats! In the last two decades of the 20c, Usanian parents have started to feel like they must constantly tell their children "I love you," so they majority of Anglo- and African-Americans now have some idea of where Frois's "our" comes from, but I believe they are still midway between the Japanese who do not feel a need to say the obvious and the Latins who constantly use words *for endearment* alone. This is not just about children. A *Faux Frois:*

> *We like to tell others we love them and think it a proper thing to do so;*
> *Japanese think love needs no words and, if it does, it is not love.*

As far as physical caresses go, Japanese will walk a child by the hand, *for it serves a practical use*, but they are just not into *touching for touching's sake:* hugging, stroking and patting. (see 14-30) We take our touching for granted and assume those who do not touch much are "hung up." But consider the opposite possibility. Is it possible that Japanese store up a life-time worth of contact in the first several years when they spend all their time riding on someone and enjoy enough contact in later childhood by continuing to sleep with siblings and parents, not to mention touching in the baths, when different generations soaped one another (though this might be a post-Frois development) that they do not need such reassuring contact? Could it not be that our violence – the need to make up for whipping, emotional outbursts and other not so obvious selfish behavior that create resentment, etc. – *necessitates* so much verbal and physical making-up?

As far as the *gifts* and *treats* go, there were only gifts of money and new clothing every New Year in Japan. There were no birthday or Christmas presents for obvious reasons and lack of close ties with relatives (2-36, 3-20) drastically reduced the number of present-givers. Gifts were plentiful in Japan, but they were of the type cultural anthropologists like to study: they were between adults and confirmed the nature of their social relationships.

But it is misleading to put Japanese children on the side of the have-nots, as in this contrast, without explaining where they enjoyed blessings their counterparts in Europe did not. *Faux Frois:*

Among us, festivals and places of entertainment outside the house always serve adults.
In Japan, there are festivals just for children and many fun places just for serving them.

By festivals, I first mean what Lowell called "the great impersonal anniversaries of the third day of the third moon and the fifth day of the fifth moon" or, as they are usually called today: Girl's Day" and "Boy's Day." In Frois's time, they would have been called Doll-festival (*Hinamatsuri*) and Carp-banner (*Koinobori*), respectively. On 3/3, part of every house becomes a doll house and on 5/5, the sky of every city becomes an aquarium. (Tokio is suddenly transformed into eighty square miles of aquarium." (L:SOFE)) And these aesthetically pleasing festivals are only a start. Children can enjoy visits to shrines and temples where there have always been child-oriented booths on many holidays Everything from soap bubbles – the soap *shabon,* coming from the Portuguese *jabon* – to tiny kinetic toys, such as those Japan would become famous for in the 20c, were available, and cheap. The most common booth today – or at least the most memorable *to me* – is one where children use paper-strung spatulas to catch (and take home) goldfish. It is tricky catching a fish before the wet paper breaks, but the seller always gives the smaller children a hand when necessary, so that everyone gets something. Morse, in 1877, describes *his* favorite, a booth where an old man with a stove sold batter by the cupful to children who could "cook it, and then, scrapping it off, eat it, or give it to their little friends, or feed the baby perched up behind." And, there was another "where children could peep through openings and see pictures of some kind, which were being described by an old man. Again I must repeat that Japan is paradise for children. (M:JDD) I do not know how much of this goes back to 1585, but I cannot believe it sprung up in a century or even two or three.

Still, this does not necessarily contradict Frois's contrast, for when children became old enough to know what's what, the discipline – what we might consider *deprivation* – described by Nitobe in BUSHIDO gradually came to replace the license of the younger child. *There was a fall from Paradise.* There is no contradiction here, either. The inner strength needed for children to study hard and do without, bearing their burden for the sake of a future dream was gained in those exceptionally pleasant years. The one makes the other possible (That is what makes Japanese and Jewish "education-mothers" so formidable). What is hard to say is how many Japanese fell how hard from their children's paradise; i.e., what portion of Japan's children were raised by Spartan *buke* (samurai class) standards at any particular era of Japanese history. Many Japanese hold that Japanese, being, with the exception of a tiny percentage of samurai, a farming people, were raised in a soft, loving egalitarian manner, until forced to copy the West to defend themselves, but my impression is that many of the farming families began to adopt Spartan samurai values in the Tokugawa era or even before then, in Frois's day, and that is one reason they could quickly rise to challenge the West.

3-16 European parents deal directly with their sons/children;
Ois pais em Europa tratão os negocios inmediatamente com seus filhos;

In Japan, everything is done through messages and intermediaries.
Em Japão tudo hé por recados e por terceira pessoa.

"Our" side here seems too natural to require explanation. Valignano wrote at length about the Japanese side. After a paragraph on how prudent and discreet they are in their dealings with others, and how they never mention their troubles, he writes

> For this reason (and also in order not to become heated in their dealings with others), they observe a general custom in Japan of not transacting any important or difficult business face to face with another person, but instead they do it all through messages or a third person. This method is so much in vogue that it is used between fathers and their children, masters and servants, and even between husbands and wives, for they maintain it is only prudent to conduct through a third person such matters which may give rise to anger, objection or quarrels. As a result, they live in such peace and quietness . . . (1583? in C:TCJ)

..
The quote picks up, in my translation (3-7), where Valignano credits this domestic calm with producing nonviolent boys. "With *bushi*," Okada writes, "it was normal for even parents and children to kept a strict distance as if they were strangers." But was it only a samurai thing? The *bushi* (samurai class) may only have intensified and formalized the tendency. Japanese may never (i.e., going back to ancient times) have leveled with one another except when they exploded with anger. Even face-to-face talk was – and still is – generally not eye-to-eye, but down, off to the side, or past one another. Swords or no swords, they avoid confrontation. My hypothesis is that a syntax which weights pronouns in the manner of Japanese will either have speakers who argue ferociously, like Koreans (who share that syntax), or no argument. No matter how many first and second-person pronouns are devised to soften things up, argument in these languages cannot help but come across *ad homininem* because those pronouns are intrinsically all-or-nothing affairs (See my *Orientalism & Occidentalism*, for details). While there are regional variations (the hyperbolized joking confrontations of parts of Kansai seems more like the Korean style of all-out argument), I find myself by and large in agreement with the stereotype.

Reading Valignano, we can see how this contrast lends itself to two contradictory interpretations. It can illustrate how the consensus-loving close-knit Japanese avoid the pitfalls of the "confrontation culture" of the West. Or, it can show that the Japanese are the more atomistic culture, as family members grow up so estranged from one another they must rely on a third party. One modern playwright, Betsuyaku Minoru, apparently saw the paradox. The very first *dogu* (tool/device/dojigger) in his DOGU-ZUKUSHI (*a compleate book of doojiggers* 1984) is the *oitokesama,* a wooden manikin found in the isolated Tohoku (Northeast) region, that could be set down next to a party of two in order to help them in the absence of an actual third party,

> Now, it no longer exists, but the way it was once used is that the *oitokesama* was set down in front, and the two sat side-by-side facing it, and told it everything that they wanted to tell to each other. In this way, everything said to the *oitokesama* was communicated to the other party and it was possible to have a conversation or dialogue, with no "meeting of eyes or shyness" coming between.

Betsuyaku's *dogu* is one of those things about which the Italians say *se non e vero e ben trovato.* Be that as it may – and I write no more (he has four pages on it) for I may try to translate that book some day, and don't wish to give too much away – the *oitokesama* is fine metaphysical proof of the accuracy of Valignano and Frois's contrast. There is, however, one thing still missing in my explanation, the matter of *inequality* and how it is treated. All of the examples given by Valignano involve unequal parties. The deeply Confucian samurai class expected the *inferior* to take great care in what they said to their *superior*. A son could no more remonstrate with a father than a servant could with a master. As Rodrigues explains in his *Treatise on Epistolary Style*, a son could not even address his father directly *in a letter.* He was supposed to do what all vassals did, write him through the auspices of a third party using a level of honorifics suitable for the third party, rather than the father, and the clear (unambiguous) style proper to a "heraldic letter (*hirôjô*) (R(L):TES). While the father could theoretically skip the intermediary, he usually replied through the same so as not to impose himself on his children.   (3-16 translation note: half the translators make it "son," half "children.")

3-17 We take godparents with baptism or confirmation[1];
Antre nós no baptismo ou crisma se tomão padrinhos;

In Japan, one is chosen when a youth gets to wear a sword anew and takes a new name. *Em Japão quando o moço singe de novo espada e muda o nome então o toma.*

Adult baptism is in some ways analogous to purification rites, but includes elements of renunciation, manumission, initiation and adoption. The believer is said to be freed from Satan who owns us from birth, and renounce his or her parents to be adopted into a spiritual family, a concept apparently borrowed by Paul from the procedure of *Emancipatio*, a Roman law for freeing slaves from masters and sons from fathers, or *patria potestas*, who had the legal right of death or life over them. But Iberian children were generally baptized at birth. (Indeed, adult baptism was a capital offense in Catholic countries!) The godfather and godmother were supposed to be "firm believers, able and ready to help the newly baptized – child or adult – on the road of Christian life" (*catechism #1255*). Confirmation was a later ceremony, which generally took place at "the age of discretion," seven or eight in Iberia, fifteen or sixteen in England where a mature adult decision was desired. At this time, the god-parents could be reconfirmed as sponsors or changed.

The Japanese side of the contrast describes a secular coming-of-age ceremony, *genbuku*, which is delightfully Englished by Kenkyûsha's Japanese-English dictionary as "assuming the *toga virilis*." In this ceremony, held when a (samurai class) boy was 12-16, he acquired a valuable sword, adopted an adult style hair-do, over which a "crow-hat-parent," put a "crow-hat" (a tall black phallic-looking thing), and dropped his milk-name for a new one, which usually included a character taken from a posthumous family name (a Buddhist name acquired by any ancestor at death), the name of the crow-hat-parent or a nobleman (acquainted in some way). Rodrigues's description of the ceremony provides an interesting detail:

> The sponsor asks his godson the name he wishes to take, and if he leaves the choice to the sponsor, he writes down three names on paper, and the godson then chooses from them the one he most likes and the sponsor gives his approval. Or else the godson produces a name which he wants or which is common in his family, and the sponsor confirms it as if he had given it to him, and he calls him by this name. (R(C):TIJ)

Has the reader noted how our basic vocabulary forces the use of Christian terms where they do not really belong? Frois avoids calling a Japanese crow-hat-parent a "godparent" or "godfather" but must imply it with his pronoun, while Rodrigues uses "godson" in Cooper's doubtless accurate translation. Rodrigues suggests another *Faux Frois*:

> *Among Europeans, others always choose our names;*
> *Japanese are perfectly free to name themselves.*

Have young Europeans ever been offered a choice? Allowed to help chose their own name? If it were the other way around, would it not become yet one more proof of supposedly special Occidental individualistic tendencies?

Today, there is nothing like the *genbuku* in Japan. Then, again, *genbuku* for most Japanese never was like it was described above. The masses knew nothing of those fancy *crow-hats*. They were more likely to simply shave off the hair in front in the adult style or in earthier parts, to celebrate the wearing of a *loincloth* (*fundoshi-iwai* and *heko-iwai*). In fact, we even had *loincloth-parents* (*heko-oya*) and *loincloth* sons (*hekomusuko*)!

---

1. Confirmation/Chrism? The original is *crism*. Chrism is an unguent of Biblical pedigree. What baptism is to water, it is to oil, olive oil, of course, and it must also contain some balsam (an aromatic resin) of a kind sanctioned by the usage of the church and be blessed by a bishop, or at least by a priest delegated by the Holy See.

3-18   With us, sons accompany their mothers when they go out;
Antre nós os filhos vão acompanhando as mães quando vão fora;

> In Japan, sons rarely or never (when they are full grown) accompany them. *Em Japão raramente ou nunqa (como são grandes)as acompanhão.*

If I am not mistaken, Father Schütte has *sons* accompany the mother *when she goes out*; the French translators have *children* doing the same; Okada conversely has the *mother accompanying when sons goes out;* and Matsuda+Jorissen, escalate that interpretation so we have s*ons, when they go out, having their mother accompany them.* I would waffle were my English only up to it.

At first, I chose the translation where the mother keeps tabs on the sons/children. This allowed me to comment as follows:

> There is something misleading about stressing the independence of Japanese children and their mothers. Valignano, who had mentioned the Spartan upbringing of boys, how they were inured to the elements "going about without hats in the winter as well as summer, wearing clothing open to the cold" – two decades later, rectified, or rather *balanced* the picture, writing, "in contradiction to Maffei" (that is what he wrote before and Maffei translated!), that boys were not separated from their mothers and nurses at a tender age, but "raised at home with much *nobleza* and *servicio,*" that "they suffer in their time great incommodation" to be turned into soldiers. (LIBRO PRIMERO) Alvarez-Taladriz introduces many items showing Japanese children were, "in reality, *muy enmadrados,*" (note 92 to V(A):S&A) that is to say *mother's boys.* "We see them in church, taking the hand, at the breast, or on the back of their mothers, " he writes, citing Frois's HISTORIA among others. The weaning was then, like now – or, until very recently – far later than in Europe. Almeida in 1561 wrote of children who could talk still nursing while being taught catechism. Bacon thought this long nursing the result of Japanese babies being wholly dependent on their mothers for milk. This is interesting for mother's milk has more opiates and that could help explain the greater docility of the infants, but for one thing. Cow milk was not drunken much before pasteurization.

> Maybe it is ridiculous to correlate the length of the nursing period and the degree to which mothers and children stick together later in childhood, but here's a guess: Could the longer nursing period create gentler, more trustworthy children and satisfy mothers so that separation could more naturally occur?

..
But I ended up choosing the less interesting opposite interpretation, that this item would seem to be describing something like 2-34 and 2-35, the relative freedom of the woman, in this case the mother to go out by herself in the respective cultures. In other words, our sons are protecting their mothers.

3-19   With us, a names doesn't change after confirmation;
Antre nós não se muda o nome depois da crisma;

> In Japan, a name changes five or six times in a lifetime.
> *Em Japão pollo discurso da ydade se muda sinco ou seis vezes.*

François Caron wrote that all men had "three names, the children a childish, when they are men a more manly, and becoming old get others suitable to the decays of nature and old age." He might better have put it "at least" three names, or three basic names, for there were any number of possibilities. Rodrigues found ten categories of names, some given, and some taken. Some names changed serially, with better names reflecting higher status replacing previous ones, whereas others were more in the line of pen names or paint names (for artists did it, too), which could be used concurrently.   One can imagine a peasant who stays on the farm would have three names at most, while a samurai or a merchant enjoying many changes of status in a lifetime would have more.   It is a bit of an exaggeration to say with Arthur Hatch (like Caron, quoted in C:TCJ) that "everyone as hee pleaseth may make choyse of his owne name" for some names were granted from above and served as a sort of title. Sometimes it is hard to tell when official names end and nicknames begin. Take this, example, from the diary of the head of the English Factory in Japan: "Sinze, our barkman, brought me a present of a barso wyne and 2 fyshes, desyring me to chang his name, according to order of Japon, which is held a greate honer amongst them. So the China Capt. sayid it was good to call hym Sinemon Dono." (2-14-1617)   *If I am not mistaken, Cinnamon!?*

This contrast is straight-forward enough. What I am amazed at is that Frois failed to list the most obvious contrast involving names. It is so obvious he must have *imagined* he already wrote it down when, in fact, he did not:

> We speak or write our Christian names before our family names;
> They always put their family names before their given ones.

Caron, did not miss this and even included an explanation as to why "they" do it that way. "The surnames are first pronounced, for being their parents were before them, they think it but reasonable that their names should likewise precede." (C:MKJS) Actually, this is the most logical way to make a name, for the same reason the Sino-Japanese system of address (country→state→city→street→number→name) and dating (era→year→month→day) is more logical than ours. We, not they, are in need of an explanation.

3-20   With us, children often visit their relatives' houses and are close to them;
Antre nós os meninos vão muitas vezes a caza dos parentes e lhes são familiares;

In Japan, they rarely go to their houses, and treat them like strangers.
Em Japão hé raro yrem a suas cazas e os tratão como estranhos.

As explained in 2-36, the Japanese stand at the opposite end of the spectrum to Latin culture with its extended families. To the Jesuits, this must have made Japanese seem like cold fish and created a dearth of potential Godparents.

3-21   In Europe, children inherit on the death of their parents;
Em Europa os filhos herdão por morte dos pais;

In Japan, parents retire from life very early to surrender their fortune to their children. *Em Japão os pais se dezerdão muito cedo em vida pera emtregar a eransa aos filhos.*

This can be interpreted in two contrary ways. One is that wealthy parents in Japan, unlike in the West, do not selfishly (and, often, with disastrous consequences when they begin to lose their judgment) hold on to the family fortune and power as long as they can, but share it early enough to improve the lives of their loved ones, and probably improve the family business. That is to say, the parent gives *more* by giving it *earlier*. Even Feudal Lords and Shoguns tended to give up their official position as ruler to their sons, whereas an Occidental potentate would hold out until *the King/Queen is dead! Long live the King/Queen!"* However, it is *also* possible to say that by handing over the business and retiring, the Japanese parents are selfishly getting out of work and onto the dole while they still are well enough to really enjoy themselves. Either way, the Japanese side of the contrast comes off best. So why haven't we done the same? Bacon, who seems to take the latter interpretation, gives a plausible reason.

> The feeling, so strong in America, that dependence is of itself irksome and a thing to be dreaded, is altogether strange to the Japanese mind. The married son does not care to take his wife to a new and independent home of his own, and to support her and her children by his own labor or on his own income, but he takes her to his father's house, and thinks it no shame that his family live upon his parents. But in return, when the parents wish to retire from active life, the son takes upon himself ungrudgingly the burden of their support, and the bread of dependence is never bitter to the parents' lip, for it is given freely. To the time-honored European belief that a young man must be independent and enterprising in early life in order to lay by for old age, the Japanese will answer that children in Japan are taught to love their parents rather than ease and luxury, and that care for the future is not the necessity that it is in Europe and America . . . A Japanese considers his provision for the future made when he has brought up and educated for usefulness a large family of children. He invests his capital in their support and education, secure of bountiful returns in their gratitude and care for his old age. (B:JGW)

In other words, Usanians (and most Occidentals) push their children into being independent all too successfully. Excluding the stereotypical Jewish-American, we are all *A Boy Named Sue*, forced not by our names but by our ideology of standing alone to forego a more intelligent lifestyle.

I am not sure how this contrast holds up today. Japanese probably still give more to their children and vice versa, but Japanese are notoriously *poor* at retiring. Like many Occidentals, work is their everything. This probably was not true in pre-modern times when retirement was a quasi-religious experience, a retreat from the driven world of work into a free world of leisure. I believe the great joy of writing provided by the bottomless well of Chinese characters and the physical pleasure of the brushed letter played a major role in this. Big strokes of jet-black ink on white. Though your eyes dim so you can barely read, *by God you can still write!* And pilgrimages from temple to temple in a narrow land made for easy foot-travel. And the game of *go* (see 14-39), being far more enjoyable than chess, no one with half a brain ever tires of it. And raising – or, rather, training – Chrysanthemum and *bonsai*. Participating in the local festival committees. In my opinion, Japanese had far more fulfilling, truly stimulating leisure activities than we in the West. I say *had* because the mid-20c was so trying a time many Japanese lost their leisure skills.

3-22 For the health of our children, we scarify them and let their blood;
Pera a saude das nossas crianças os sarrafão e lhe tirão sangue;

> In Japan, blood is not drawn, rather, they are treated with clumps of fire.
> *Em Japão [se] lhe não tira, a[ntes] os qurão com botōis de fogo.*

This "scarify," sounds scary! We are reminded of painful rituals to decorate the skin. But, actually, it is a "mild" method of bleeding by making many small puncture wounds – in the 17-18c, spring-loaded devices came to be used – which, with the aid of cupping glasses and syringes took the place of, or supplemented, the more radical venesection. Bleeding, as elaborated in chapter 9, served both to balance over-all body humours (as does Chinese medicine) and to treat local disorders. Since "we" were used to blood, such treatment would not have seemed as horrible as "their" burning.

The Sinosphere preferred burning to blood-letting. It was not because it hurt less. Moxibustion, or treatment by burning a pinch of *moxa* (made from mugwort leaf: see 9-2) set upon the skin is not pleasant. It was just that they did not care for blood. In some ways the two practices were quite similar. *Moxa,* too, was used to treat specific illnesses (hence Frois's "treated/cured"), as well as to build immunity. According to Okada, in Japan, a pellet of moxa was ritually burnt on top of the three-day-old infant's head and, in some parts of Japan, on the navel with a the aim of preventing future sickness (Perhaps this explains why Japanese children came to be so afraid of the thunder gods stealing their exposed navels, presumably by zapping them with lightning!) There was also an annual moxa-treatment ritual, that functioned as booster shots on top of this basic "vaccination." Children in Japan didn't like it anymore than we like shots. In contradiction of 3-7 above, it bears noting that even if children were not whipped, *sometimes* they were threatened with corporal punishment and the method was moxa-treatment!

3-23 With us, only women use paint and powder;
Antre nós as molheres somente uzão de arrebiqe e alvayade;

> With honorable Japanese, boys up to ten also wear some cosmetics when they go out.
> *Antre os Japões honrados quando os meninos até dez anos vão fora, tambem levão alguns posturas.*

The pre-Christian West boasts the Picts whose name says it all. But, the powder European men were supposed to wear in Frois's day was limited to their wigs, and such were only worn by men engaged in legal or other administrative functions in some countries.

Male make-up in Japan was pretty much restricted to boys from the samurai class and above. Okada cites a contemporary Chinese report about "barbarian [i.e., Japanese] boys made up with thick powder like women." Most Japanese fashion has Chinese roots and would not have been worth reporting back to China, so the very fact it is mentioned tells us it surprised more than the Europeans.

In the last decade of the 20c, Japanese boys began to use make-up again. One sees many male *tarento* (minor TV personalities that usually last only a few years until the bloom is off their adolescent cheeks) that can only be described as "cute" and "adorable," rather than handsome and manly like "our" muscular "heart-throbs." These cutie-pies (what else can you call them?) take good care of their hairline, partially pluck and darken their eyebrows and I have even seen eyeliner advertised on television! The object is not to become feminine but to look really good, because young women, though they usually deny it, are picky and want symmetrical finely featured young men.

3-24 With us, youths have sleeves that are narrow and tight about the shoulders;
Antre nós os meninos tem as mangas estreitas e fachadas polos onbros.

> Those of Japan are loose and slit across under the arms.
> *Os de Japão as trazem muito largas, escaladas ao traves por debaxo dos bracos.*

M & J remonstrate that the young Japanese ambassadors from Japan were "delighted" to find the youth in Ebola (Portugal) wearing clothing with "sleeves so broad as not to differ from those of Japan." *Funny.* Such stated delight in encountering the sleeves tells me, rather, that they were rare in Europe and that Frois's observation was valid!

Those slits are still found in some traditional Japanese garments. They are generally not seen, and thus, not remarked upon because even in Japan men do not walk around with their arms held up (笑). If Frois could look up men's nostrils (14-47), he could do the same to their underarms. As far as I know, slits are not particularly associated with *children's* dress; but are common to informal dress. Perhaps adults in the upper classes, who were always formally dressed, did not wear them, whereas their children did and that explains why Frois puts it with children. At least one fashion – resort wear called *jinbei* which does not date back to Frois – takes the slit all the way around the arm, using a mesh or little strings to keep the sleeves from falling off. Underarm slits are very cooling in sultry weather and should join sandals as ecological *who-needs-air-conditioning!* "world clothing."

Actually, "we," adult males at any rate, *did* air-condition our European clothing, too. I do not recall seeing slits under arms but, otherwise, slits in clothing were considered *gallant* from the early Renaissance to well into the 17c. Alvaro Semedo, who met a 1630 expedition to China (Joao Rodrigues and company went to help the Emperor defend the capital and gain brownie points for Macao, but that story is beyond our scope) in the provincial city of Nan-ch'ang, observed that –

> the local Chinese nobles were greatly intrigued by the Portuguese costumes, and they commended and admired all, except the Slashing and pinking of their cloathes, not being able to conceive, why, when a piece of stuffe is whole and new, men should cut it in severall places for ornament." (C:RTI)

I, too, had only thought of this practice as ridiculous, but upon consideration of the function of those underarm slits, it suddenly occurred to me that the European practice was probably long-lived because the foot-soldiers discovered it kept them cool. While these men may not have been as uniformly muscular as our anatomy-besotted artists rendered them, they were doubtless more muscular than average and muscles tend to generate heat, especially when used. *Think of it!* A functional necessity justified as a "cool" fashion!

endnote III

Children

There was one important *possible* child, or rather, *child-rearing* related contrast found in Alcock and Bird, but not in Frois.

> The mothers are not the sole guardians of the infant progeny. It is a very common sight in the streets and shops of Yeddo, to see a little nude Cupid in the arms of a stalwart-looking father, nearly as naked, who walks about with his small burden, evidently handling it with all the gentleness and dexterity of an experienced hand. It does not seem there is any need for a fondling hospital . . . (A:COT)

> Both fathers and mothers take pride in their children. It is most amusing about six every morning to see twelve or fourteen men sitting on a low wall, each with a child under two in his arms, fondling and playing with it, and showing off its intelligence. To judge from appearances, the children form the chief topic at this morning gathering. (B:UTJ)

I would guess from the way he is described, that *the paternal nurse* (as an illustration in Alcock is captioned) struck the 19c visitor as something *odd*. (Morse shows a large boy with infant on back fishing! (M:JDD)) Alcock's words suggest that widowers in Europe would not be able to care for *their* babies and Bird's "amusing" makes it clear that this sort of thing would not be seen in her England. Let's *Faux Frois* it:

> *Among us, it would be laughable to see a grown man caring for a baby;*
> *The Japanese are used to seeing fathers carrying their babies and think little of it.*

Why did neither Frois nor, as far as I know, any of the 16-17c Jesuits, have anything to say about men and child-care? Were Luso-Iberian men *also* paternal nurses, in which case it wouldn't be worth noting? A *note* to Frois's *HISTORIA* provided by his Japanese translators includes a marvelous example, involving none other than Shôgun Hideyoshi, a commoner by birth and upbringing, who had just unified the country. It was recorded by someone in a Korean Embassy that had visited Hideyoshi months before Valignano was far more graciously received (as recorded in detail by Frois). The Korean ambassador complains that instead of proper banquette-style dishes, they had to exchange drinks of *sake* that was murky (Hideyoshi may have preferred this raw, white-colored *sake*, but it was considered inferior to clear *sake*) from earthenware cups, and that they had no time to exchange the proper verbal greetings, much less discuss anything, because

> . . . Hideyoshi suddenly got up and disappeared into the interior [of the castle]. But none of his retainers moved at all. Shortly, a man in plain clothing carrying a baby [Tsurumatsu] came out from the interior and began walking about the great hall. Looking closely we could see it was Hideyoshi . . . Eventually, he called out our country's musicians and had them put on a big show, during which time the infant he held peed on his kimono. . . . Then and there he changed to another kimono. He acted as if no one else was around. It was brazen and shameless behavior. With that banquette, our ambassadors saw their last of Hideyoshi. Hideyoshi gave the Ambassador and Vice-Ambassador 400 silver pieces each and gifts proportionate to their qualifications to the secretaries, translators, and so forth. (J/F:HISTORIA)

Hideyoshi was famous in Japan for being the clown to beat all clowns. He hardly qualifies as a standard example of Japanese male behavior. But, still, as a man of commoner upbringing, I would guess he grew up around men acting like those described by Alcock and Bird hundreds of years later. And, as an eccentric who would behave as he damn well pleased, he brought his peasant behavior right into a banquet.

~~~~~~

In the late-20c, it would seem that things turned upside-down. Many Occidental men – at least, those in countries where women have either been forced to work outside the house, or chosen to spend less time with their children, such as the United States of America – have become part-time house-husbands, while Japanese men became absentee-fathers able to spend only a few minutes per day conversing with their children, if that – which could hardly be otherwise, given their incredibly long commute and work hours. As the customs of decades quickly become traditions, it behooves us to show that things were not always so and need not always remain so. That, I think, is why records of child-friendly Japanese fathers mean a lot.

~~~~~~

I am sure that there are other child-related contrasts that could be added and welcome (for a later edition) contributions from cultural anthropologists. I know, for example, that Japanese children throw their upper baby teeth under their porches and throw the lower baby teeth up over the roof, so the new teeth will grow rapidly in the appropriate direction. Wouldn't it be fun to learn that Europeans threw said teeth in the opposite manner?

IV

OF THE BONZES *AND THEIR CUSTOMS*

da que toca aos bonzos e a seus custumes

4-1   With us, men join religious orders to make penitence and save themselves;
Os homens se metem antre nós em religião pera fazer penitencia e se salvarem;

The bonzes[1] enter religious orders to live in idleness and luxury and escape work.
Os bonzos entrão na religião pera viver em dilícias e descanso e fojir aos trabalhos.

I am not so sure that Frois's description of "our" side is as complimentary as he may have thought it was. Doing something to save one's own tail, *especially one's eternal tail*, is hardly something to boast about, though the good works performed by Jesuits and others seeking salvation are not to be scoffed at, either. Though many of "us" joined because they wanted to help others in *this* world and save them in *that* (though these two altruistic designs occasionally clashed), others, may have been attracted to the religious life by "the promise of leisure and pleasure, derived from communion with fellow religious [clergy] and, if possible, God himself." (DR in (R&A&D:HOT))

On *their* side, Frois follows the party line. In Dialogue 7 of *De Missione*, Leo=Valignano, a Christian cousin of Miguel, confesses that hearing about pious rich people in Europe was very interesting, because "looking at things from the Japanese standard," he had assumed religion was a refuge for people with no fortune or in a bind, but now he realized that "the situation is completely different in the East and West." The young Ambassador Miguel=Valignano is kind enough to give a reason for the gold-digging in Japan.

> If we investigate the difference between the two [Japan and Europe], first, this is because we Japanese suffer from poverty and material want, so that when people seek religion they . . . try to find a monastery with the most wealth . . . if there were another way [for them] to win a large income, honor, a prestigious position, . . . they would never sit tight within the four walls of a monastery. (J/S:DM)

On the other hand, he added, "the [Jesuit] *padres* were not originally people who had nothing, but men who could enjoy a far easier and comfortable life in Europe than in Japan." In a parenthesis, someone (Japanese often do not use brackets so it is hard to tell if it was in the original or added by the translator) wrote that a large fortune is often given up when entering the Company, but that the Jesuit lifestyle in Europe is not a poor one. Frois and Valignano knew well that what they wrote did not apply to *all* Buddhist sects, least of all to Zen, which shared with the Jesuits the distinction of a largely aristocratic membership. But, it is questionable whether they felt Zen was a *bona fide* religion, seeing that many Zen-Buddhists professed belief in *nothing* (see 4-23, below).

This chapter and the next, also about Religion, are the least objective part of the TRATADO. Today, even the most benighted bible-thumper dares not write such harsh things about other religions as Frois and the other Jesuits did. I am not sure if that is to the fundamentalist's credit, either. If you really believe that lack of baptism dooms a soul to Hell, how can you justify *not* engaging in Holy

War against the infidels? I do not for a minute feel people today are kinder or more tolerant than they were in Frois's day. If you accept religious diversity, it is either because you, like me, do not believe in the absolute truth (Truth) of "our" religion (Religion) – you are not Christian in the way most of "us" once were – or, because you are a coward. Yet, there is a kernel of truth in the Jesuits' criticism of the Buddhists: corruption in Japanese Buddhism was indeed rampant. The problem is rather that the Frois conveniently overlooks the equally bad corruption of Christianity in Europe that led to the Reformation and, for that matter, the creation of the Society of Jesus to fight it by example!

1. Bonze. A *bona fide* word in most European languages for Buddhist monks, which is convenient because by using bonze we need not specify monks are "Buddhist." It derives from the Japanese *bôzu*.

4-2 We vow to be clean of soul and chaste of body on joining an order;
Antre nós se profesa logo limpeza da alma e castidade no corpo;

> Their bonzes [pledge themselves] totally to polluting their interior and all the nefarious sins of the flesh. *Os bonzos toda a sujidade interior e todos os pecados nefandos da carne.*

Europeans reading reprints of the stories of Boccaccio – my favorite is the tailing – and new ones by Marguerite de Navarre (1559) might encounter very different monks (and nuns). While stories prove little, they do suggest that, as DR puts it, "it is one thing to make a vow and another to live up to it." In his masterful *The Civilization of Europe in the Renaissance*, John Hale gives documented instances of what we would call rape and child-molestation by clergy. The former was sentenced to be married and the latter executed. Considering the enormous scandal involving Catholic clergy in the United States at the start of the second Millennium – doubtless, fueled by hysteria but not without basis – has given the following words by John Hale new life: "There is a remorseless familiarity about what the sources reveal."

Needless to say, the bonzes pledge themselves to no such thing. For one, Japanese have never been big on pledges. That is an Occidental thing. But, there is no denial that there was a different attitude toward sex on the part of the Christians and the Buddhists. Even St. Francis Xavier, who thought the world of the Japanese, found this habit of "their priests, whom they call bonzes" beyond redemption:

> These men are so given up to the most abominable kind of lust as to make open profession of it. This plague is indeed so common to all here, men and women alike, that the mere custom of it has taken away all their hatred and horror of the crime . . . we find the others listen to us with favor and are well disposed, but the bonzes themselves, when we admonish them to abstain from such filthy lusts, try to turn the edge of what we object to in them by laughter and jokes." (c.1550, C:LLFX)

I wish Xavier had recorded some of the jokes! Seriously. The Jesuits seemed genuinely puzzled to find so much sodomy in Japan and China both because a people thought particularly quick of reason, as were the Chinese and Japanese, ought to have hated sodomy which was, to use Valignano's words, a "vice so abominable and prejudicial *as reason shows*" and because God was not supposed to allow nations that sinned against nature to prosper. Frois, in his *History* of the Church in Japan, time and time again gave instances of God stepping in to punish sinners in *this* world. In Goa, where "we" ruled, sodomites were burnt, but with no one killing sinners for God in China and Japan, *He* was expected to do it himself. Even Gaspar da Cruz, a liberal Franciscan (clearly against slavery), interpreted a disastrous series of earthquakes as "a grievous punishment" against Chinese for allowing this vice (C:TCC in B:SCSC) and the generally rational Valignano claimed the "destruction and wars there are in Japan today, . . shows that the sword of the Justice of God is upon them, castigating this sin, so that the greater part of the men die by the blade and cities and families are leveled and destroyed and all live with continual misery and work." (1583?) Yes, Japanese "lived in much peace under only one king, until a perverse bonze whom they took for a saint and a prophet introduced it among them in the manner that we have seen."

So, not only was sodomy judged "the first bad quality" of Japanese, but the Buddhists were responsible for it. Japanese folk history does indeed *credit* Kôbô (Kôbô-daishi=Kûkai, founder of the esoteric Buddhist sect Shingon (Pure Word) and author of the syllabary-as-poem (10-1 or 10-2) with introducing the practice – his name actually became a synonym for it! – but the idea that it harmed Japan is Christian invention. Older paintings suggests the Japanese hardly needed to import the idea, but that was overlooked by the Jesuits. Blaming the Buddhists rather than checking history was their agenda. Still, the Jesuits could not afford to be philosophical about this. They ran training houses in Japan where young men slept, and they had problems. A 1580 letter of Valignano's shows a rational view. He thought the students mainly sought one another out of despair, straying for consolation and to call attention to their unhappiness due to the harsh treatment by the racist superior Cabral. Seminary rules Valignano helped draw up that same year "stipulated with meticulous care that the students should sleep on tatami mats, separated by little wooden benches, and that a light was to be kept burning all night." (in S:MPMR) Let me add that these students probably slept with their brothers at home and it was more likely there was some touching and masturbation than honest-to-goodness sodomy, which, in Japan, generally presumed pederasty, i.e. an unequal relationship. (see 3-10).

Ironically, the Catholics were on the receiving side of the charges in West Europe. Luther called them Sodomites, and even the generally tolerant Englishman Bulwer wrote that "the ancient Sin of Sodomy" was "in *Italy* nothing more common, and not only tolerated, but held convenient, especially for the Clergy, who are the chief Commanders of these *Ganimedes*, . . ." (B:A) Europe was obviously as *obsessed* with homosexuality as the fundamentalist Christians in the USA, today.

4-3 We make a vow of poverty before God and flee from worldly riches;
Antre nós se promete a Deus voto de pobreza e se foge das riqezas do mundo;

> The bonzes rip off their *dana* [patron/s] and seek to enrich themselves in a thousand ways. *Os bonzos esfolão os dannas e buscão mil modos pera enriquicer.*

Frois is unfair to contrast ideal Christians with worldly Buddhists. His contemporary, the Florentine merchant Francesco Carletti gives us the ideal Buddhist. Between a rare description of what can only be local shamanism and another of "those who adore the lord of the heavens and the earth (Shinto), he describes "the one of Pythagoras," i.e. an austere vegetarian Buddhist sect:

> They all lead a sterile life, in imitation of the founder, who introduced it [to Japan?] They say of him that he never ate anything but cooked rice, and sometimes raw rice, and that to do greater penitence he always wore an iron chain tight against his flesh, where it had made such a sore that it became putrid, generating and nourishing a quantity of worms. And if one of these worms happened to fall to the ground, he would pick it up lovingly and with charity and put it back in the sore, saying: "Why are you fleeing? Are you perhaps lacking something to eat?" (C(W):MVAW)

Actually, the Jesuits, themselves, in collusion with their countrymen, *used* voluntary poverty to sell their religion. Fr. Xavier *insisted* on walking everywhere, and carrying his own things even though he was very sick. When Pinto and his party went to help him, "He wouldn't accept a ride on anybody's horse, so we had to dismount and walk along with him although he wouldn't hear of that either." When they finally reached their destination, an awaiting carrack, "every gun on the ship fired four rounds from bases, falconets and camels, never mind all the rest," so the King of Bungo, who was nearby, "supposed we had been attacked by a pirate fleet." The Portuguese explained to the messenger sent by the king that they were celebrating the safe arrival of "a priest we considered a saintly man, a man for whom the King of Portugal himself had the greatest respect." This astounded the messenger who confessed –

> Our bonzes have told him that this man isn't a saint at all . . . They say they have seen him at different times talking to demons with whom he has dealings and that he uses sorcery to trick the ignorant and gullible. They also say he is not just poor, but so poor that even the lice crawling all over his body are so sickened that they will not taste his flesh. (P(L):TMP) ch 209)

Fleeing lice! For once, the West wins the *I-am-more-austere-than-thou* contest. The messenger tells the King that Fr. Francis was far from the beggar they had imagined because "the ship's captain and all the Portuguese traders assured me that if Fr. Francis asked them to give him the ship and all its cargo, they would gladly hand it over to him there and then, with no questions asked." All of this made the high-minded noblemen and king *adore* Francis to the chagrin of the bonzes, who "lost all credibility" with the king, and were fit to "hang themselves." All this, according to Pinto.

~~~~~~

4-4 We vow obedience to our Superior when we join an order;
Antre nós se profesa e faz voto de obedientia ao Superior;

> The bonzes, do what each wants to, obeying their prelate only when their wishes happen to coincide. *Os bonzos cada um faz o que quer e, per accidens, no que lhe vem hà vontade, obedecem ao prelado.*

Again we have a vow, which is to say, "our" *ideal*, versus "their" *reality* or, rather, our caricature of their reality. If *Tratado* were intended as a learning aid, Frois's hypothetical students would have chuckled at the phrase about wishes agreeing *by accident*.

While the Japanese predilection for disobedience, for following their own wishes, was legend in that era – and one reason given by the racist Cabral for his authoritarian rule before the Bungo Consultation decided on a different course – most Buddhism, with the exception of *some* Zen sects, was not *that* anarchistic. As Blyth puts it, "Zen has much in common with Panglossism, but this is balanced by *the abuse of Buddha and the Patriarchs*. In Western culture we find this freedom only in the history of the Rationalists, where it has almost always been accompanied by a complete lack of poetry, not to speak of religious feeling." (B:MM, *my italics*) In the Zen, Blyth shows us, students are taught to be contrary. It is part of the catechism. In his postscript to Zen and the Zen Classics (vol. 4, *Mumonkan*), Blyth writes: "The best thing about Mumon is his speaking ill of everything and everyone." (Doubtless, Blyth jokingly refers to the opposite policy of the Jesuits to speak *well* of all (*except bonzes*)!)

This does not mean the Zen *practice* was really that wild. But it does mean that if Zen bonzes were asked whether they always did what they themselves wanted to do, they would feel obliged to say *"Yes!"* or *"I try to!!"* This *flaunting of disobedience* and *independence* would have horrified the Jesuits with their Order built upon absolute vows of obedience. But, for the bonzes, doing things out of obedience rather than nature would have been thought demeaning if not sacrilegious. So we may assume that Zen bonzes exaggerated their *badness* as much as the monks of the West exaggerated their *goodness*. Though the contrast in their *behavior* – the real difference – was doubtless far less, I find the contrast between Western religion with its strict (militaristic?) order and more individualistic Eastern religion a welcome contradiction of the Orientalist image of obedient Orientals.

Perhaps, I am being too cautious at stopping with Zen. Japanese in general were not so obsessed with vows as "we" were and the superior-inferior relationship was not thought of in terms of giving and obeying orders, but *asking* and *responding*, *leading* and *following,* or *teaching* and *studying*. While superiors in Japan, like their European counterparts, could be abrupt and did not feel obliged to explain themselves, they knew that they could not behave in a way their inferiors thought was unfair if they hoped to retain their loyalty.

4-5 The temporal possessions of a religious order, among us, is held in common;
Os bens temporais da religião antre nós são comuns;

> The bonzes all have their own property and work for their own gain.
> *Os bonzos todos têm suas propriedades e ganhão pera aqirir.*

A new member of the Society of Jesus gave up (or gave to the Order) all his possessions upon joining. A Jesuit officially owned *nothing*. Anything they earned went straight to the corporation (or was supposed to). Like not a few nonprofit CEO's today, some Jesuits in Europe were said to live as if they were wealthy, but that is another story . . . One reason they did not need to keep any possessions was because once they became a Jesuit they were expected to remain one for life. One would no more think about leaving the Society than one would think of leaving The Family.

Like other Japanese, monks had their own bowls, chopsticks, tea cups, brushes, ink-stones, clothing, bedding, artwork, books . . . and, money. Yes, they were free to leave at any time.
..

4-6 With us, parishioners belong to the entire parish, not to particular clergy;
Antre nòs os freguezes todos são de huma parroch[i]a e não de clerigos partiqulares;

> The bonzes have them divvied up, and each is fed by those in his own charge.
> *Os bonzos os têm repartidos antre si, pera cada hum comer dos que tiver a carrego.*

If Frois's "us" means the Jesuits, the first part of the contrast is doubtless true. Policy is policy. But looking at Europe as a whole, and considering the widespread corruption that made the Society of Jesus stand out like a gem in the dirt, a more cynical appraisal might be "With us, the wealth of the parish belongs to the canon of the cathedral; With them, it is divided among the monks of the temple." In that case, "they" would come out smelling rosy for at least sharing it! But either way, we are talking about incommensurables, for people did not attend temples as they did churches. When they did come, they tossed money into collection boxes called *waniguchi* (crocodile-mouths) that was for all, not individual bonzes. But, Frois has a point. The territoriality of the bonzes who, descending from the temples, went door to door gathering alms (and sniffing out potential funerals? See 4-36) – was legend and this matter of how bonzes made a living was not academic to Jesuits. Frois's *Historia* describes cases where a Christian takeover of a certain district (leaders who became Christian forced it on their vassals) left bonzes without income, and protracted conflict was avoided by paying them enough to allow them to make the transition to another line of work.

4-7 Our clergy condemn people's sins without regard to civilities or circumstance;
Antre nós os religiosos reprendem os pecados do povo sem uzar de respeitos humanos;

> The bonzes court their patrons and praise their sins in order not to lose the income. *Os bonzos grangeão os dannas e lhes louvão os pecados, pera que lhe não tirem a renda.*

Frois contrasts the ideal situation in Europe with sordid reality in Japan, hardly fair when you consider the infamous exchange of sin for money called *indulgences* in the Catholic world. His charge against the Buddhists is identical to that made against the Jesuits by the apostate Fukan Fabian in *Ha-deiusu* (destruction of "deus/deusites: 1620), when he claimed "they invented the game of ringing out the gold and silver they are so crazy about from their patrons" and praised wealthy patrons though they broke the Commandments and were unbelievers, while poking fun at poor men. The Jesuits were among the least corrupt *religioso* and Fabian's blanket criticism is unfair; but, it would be safe to assume some of the Jesuit spiritual advisors on good terms with the nobility of Europe overlooked the sins of their powerful patrons. And I think I know where Frois is coming from. Could not his constant carping on the bonzes' Mammonism reflect his jealousy and his anxiety about "our" lack of income in Japan? Valignano had to *repeatedly* explain the poverty of his beloved church of Japan to the head of the Society. To summarize "the cause and reason why the Christian lords cannot sustain the padres and their churches in Japan:" *First*, with little rent, little personal land, and continual warfare, most lords in Japan have neither income nor wealth, particularly in the mountainous provinces where Christianity made the most headway. *Second*, they have not converted any wealthy lords from the capitol region. And, *third*, Christianity in Japan is very new and the Japanese cannot be expected to give a lot to "foreigners such as us." As the reverse of this, he had to explain how *the Japanese can support so many bonzes.* "There is much difference in their situation and ours." *First*, they began when Japan was prosperous under one king who gave them great support, impossible in this age of warfare. *Second*, they had plentiful family connections and support (rent and land), while we remain outsiders. *Third*, the bonzes can promises salvation without putting "an end to all sensuality" as we do" (polygamy, being the norm for the wealthy). And *fourth*, because, as natives, they can teach children, and know how to pragmatically accommodate themselves to tricky circumstances where we blow it. Considering these handicaps, he concluded, "I say, it is a very great blessing from the Lord, and ought to be taken for something supernatural, that we are suffered to remain on their land." (V(A):S&A)

To my secular mind, sucking up to patrons on the part of bonzes reflected a not-so-bad situation, *where the customer (layman) was king.* This was to change. About fifty years after TRATADO, the Tokugawa government made Buddhist temples responsible for making certain that no one belonged to a proscribed religion (Christian *or* Nichiren Buddhist). Everyone had to belong to a specific sect and be registered at a local temple – which checked that everything added up once every year and reported to the government. This gave the bonzes great power to demand support. As Aramata Hiroshi put it, "finally the Buddhists got control over the living, too." (*Haka-wa Otera . . .* in J/A:NGK) He writes there are even records of some saying things like "if you don't pay up, you might end up under suspicion for being Christian." This not unnaturally gave rise to exorbitant prices for funeral-related services and eventually backfired when the last rulers of the Tokugawa decided to knock Buddhism out of the funeral game and give the right to Shinto and Confucian institutions, not to mention doing away with thousands of temples and melting down Buddhist images to create cannons such as the great cannon of Mito which became a symbol of National=Imperial=Shinto power. After World War II, Buddhism bounced back and retook the lion's share of the dead.

~~~~~~

4-8 Our clergy, out of contempt for this world, do not wear silk clothing;
Os religiosos antre nós, por desprezo do mundo, não usão de vestidos de seda;

> All the bonzes who can, wear silk to parade their worldly pride and vanity.
> *Os bonzos todos os que podem andão vestidos de seda pera maior soberba e ostentasão no mundo.*

If Orientalism means sumptuous Byzantine splendor, then Frois reinforces our "bias;" but if it, rather, suggests the asceticism of yogi and Zen, he contradicts it.

While bonzes did strive to limit their worldly pleasures – as in Europe, sometimes by themselves and sometimes with reinforcement from sumptuary law – they did not want to disgust others with dirty clothing and Japanese Buddhists were one of the most evangelical – if you will allow a Christian term – Buddhists in Asia. They wanted to wear *what worked*. Perhaps, they found that most people prefer the prayers of a bonze whose very clothing shows that fortune smiles upon him over those of a down-and-out beggar And, let's be honest, Buddhist or Christian, attractive clothing and, for that matter, good looks never hurt a preacher-man. Sei Shônagon (born c. 965) put it like this: "A preacher ought to be good looking. For, if we are properly to understand his worthy sentiments, we must keep our eyes on him while he speaks; should we look away, we may forget to listen. Accordingly an ugly preacher may well be the source of sin . . ." (S(M)PBSS) Even Frois, in one of his fine 1565 letters, indirectly supported Shônagon's impertinent observation:

> He was clothed in flowing silk vestments, the under-robe being white and the outer one coloured, and he carried a gold fan in his hand. He was about 45 years of age and the paleness of his face made him look like a German; certainly he was one of the most handsome and engaging men I have ever seen . . . His soft and mellow voice and the gestures which he made during the sermon were all worthy of note. . . . We gained no little profit from this outing, as we learned a great deal about how to preach to the [Japanese] Christians in accordance with their liking and language . . . (in C:TCJ)

Still, the contrast between the Buddhists professed denial of the world and the ostentation of Buddhist high priests was noticed in Japan, too, and became a minor literary theme. The poets Buson and Issa (second and third to Bashô as the top three haiku poets) depict *Their Excellencies* shitting al fresco (called *noguso,* or "field-shit"), dressed in their bright silk and shielded by a servant's umbrella.

~~~~~~

4-9   Among us, good clergy abhor and greatly fear to gain titles and honors;
Antre nós os bons religiosos repugnão e temem muito subir a dignidades e honras.

>The bonzes in Japan are all dying to gain them and spend great sums to that end.
>*Os bonzos em Japão, custão-lhe muito dinheiro e todos morrem por subirem a elas.*

Frois, to his credit, finally qualifies the European side with "good," but his declamation of the bonze side is, like usual, irresponsibly catholic (*todos* = all). Qualifications aside, all nine contrasts in this chapter so far depict "them" as worldly and arrogant and "us" as truly humble. The Jesuits took great stock in their humility. As DR points out, the Society of Jesus policy was "not to accept religious appointments (e,g, benefices)," though they sometimes had to accept positions conferred by "Kings and other powerful leaders." On a micro level, I note our "Luys Froes" signed his letters: *Sieruo inutil de todos* ("I serve uselessly in all"), *Sieruo inutil de todos, y su indigno hermano* ("*ditto,* and your unworthy brother"), etc.; and, as already noted, Valignano, though Visitador of the entire East did not publish his work on Japan with his name on it. Not all Japanese were, however, convinced. Fukan Fabian, the Japanese ex-Jesuit quoted in 4-7 complained: "They (the padres) are always telling people to be humble because pride is the root of all evil and humility the foundation of all good; but, even the King of devils cannot match their own pride, be it their national propensity, or whatever." Possibly reflecting on a run in with Cabral, he further fumed ". . . and because they are such arrogant men, they don't even think Japanese human." (trans. by Elison (E:DD) maybe (LR), but I've seen the Japanese)

But Japanese of all classes did indeed hanker for paper honors. Even secular visitors to Japan, like Kaempfer in the 17c, were surprised at how this was manifest among a groups as unlikely as the blind and the mountain priests (Jammabo):

>If they return home from this hazardous Pilgrimage [climbing a dangerous mountain peak once a year], they repair forthwith, each to the general of his order, who resides in Miaco, make him a

small present in money, which if poor, they must get by begging, and receive from him a more honourable title and higher dignity, which occasions some alteration in their dress, and encreases the respect which must be shown them by their brethen of the same order. So far is ambition from being banish'd out of these religious Societies. (K:HOJ)

Valuing rank and title are bad if one thinks of it as a desire for artificial glory rather than true achievement, but good if you think of it as part of a mindset that valued proven achievement and honor over wealth. One additional point. Given the Japanese sense of honor, where money meant little, but asking for the help of strangers (incurring obligations) meant a lot, begging was a very humiliating act, more so, I think, than it would have been for the religious in the West. So it could be argued that at the very least, these Japanese priests had to swallow their pride and learn to eat humble pie in order to make the world their oyster.

4-10   Our clergy always desire peace and simply cannot stand wars;
Os nossos religiosos sempre desejão a pax e lhe peza sumamente das guerras;

The *Negoro* make war their profession and are hired by lords to fight their battles.
Os nengoros professão guerra e são alugados dos senhores pera yrem pelejar nas batalhas.

While the Jesuits did not do much physical combat, they were not averse to *participating* in "just' wars. In the early 1580's, Valignano contributed gunpowder and other logistical help to Christian rulers in Japan, but soon changed tack, discouraging a plan to convince the governor of the Philippines to send ships and arms to Nagasaki, then under the government of the Jesuits, because Japanese Christians felt safer *not* possessing such might, given the turbulent political situation in his country. *Eventually*, Valignano would make it clear that Christians "were to confine themselves to praying to God for the success of Christian arms." (1592, in B:CCJ), but Frois is premature here, for some Jesuits still relished the possibility of military involvement in Japan. They were not pacifists.

We had "our" own tradition of "fighting monks" of which the Knights of Rhodes are but the most well known. But the Buddhist fighting tradition was indeed much deeper than ours. Martial arts accompanied Buddhism from China as early as the 8c. When Nobunaga razed a Sangakuji temple in 1570, he wiped out a tradition that had lasted for 760 years. Founded in 807, it was one of a number of Tendai sect temples whose fighting bonzes (*sôhei*) opposed the excesses of the warrior-clan politics of the time by sending fighters to help the gentler side. I guess they opposed one warrior too many. The bonzes of the True Word (*Shingon*) sect, headquartered on Mount Negoro also had a tradition of martial arts that predated the Warring Era and at their peak had a coalition of 2000 temples. Valignano mentions them in 1583 in the context of explaining the natural love for arms on the part of the Japanese (i.e., *even* the clergy . . .).   Quick to adopt and make firearms, they played an important role in the some major battles of the Warring era, but they were almost exterminated by Hideyoshi, the great warlord who unified Japan in 1585, no less! Since they comprised one of the hundred-man rifle units, called *negoro-gumi,* for the man who wrested power from Hideyoshi's clan, Tokugawa Ieyasu, some Negoro obviously survived to gain revenge against their nemesis.

None of this is surprising. Religion and war are soul-mates, for true believers (provided their families share their faith or they are single) have no reason whatsoever to fear death. Who better to play the soldier, to serve as mercenaries for people who value life in this world more than life in the next? Be that as it may, with respect to the fighting bonzes of Japan, history is poetic if not just. When Japan began to modernize in the mid-19c and the state dropped its financial support of Buddhism, "the priests, having no income, were advised by the government to enter the army as soldiers!" ("The Daily Evening Bulletin" of San Francisco quoted as an accurate source in L:JIA).

4-11 We struggle with all our might to keep our promises to God;
Antre nós o que se promete a Deus se trabalha de guardar inteiramente

> The bonzes publicly profess not to eat meat or fish, but secretly almost all of them do it, only refraining for fear of being seen, or because they cannot.
> *Os bonzos no de fora profesão não comer carne nem pexe, mas ocultamente quasi todos o comem, senão por temor de serem vistos ou por não poderem.*

About fifty years earlier, Xavier wrote that "formerly the bonzes or bonzesses who had broken one of their five precepts [sex/theft or lying/ homicide/killing any creature/eating the same or drinking wine] were punished with death by the princes and nobles of the place where they lived. . . . But at present, this discipline is entirely relaxed and corrupted; the greater number drink wine, eat meat secretly . . ." (C:LLFX) So, even when the bonzes behaved themselves, the Jesuits attributed it to physical punishment rather than piety. There may be some truth to that charge, too. As we will see in Chapter 6, Buddhist food restrictions are ambiguous, so it is not surprising that only sumptuary laws could assure their compliance. But, Frois only *uses* food for proof the bonzes are hypocrites. This is part of the larger issue of an absence of vows and loyalty in Japan that was lamented by Valignano and others. In *De Missione*, the Ambassador Mancio=Valignano explains the concept of a European vow to Leo. When men are given honor (titles/positions) by their King in Europe, he claims, they pledge their fealty to said King, and this pledge or vow is bound = *religio,* so any disloyalty would be extremely dishonorable, whereas in "our country," Japan, this type of vow does not exist, with the result that, according to the circumstances, one can betray one's lord without dishonor. No Christianity, no dependable relationship. *That* was the message.

Today, even in America with its supposed separation of Church and State, people vow with their hand on the Bible, as if this *religio* were the *sine qua non* for speaking the Truth. In Japan, people simply give their word. All told, "we" Occidentals – here, I include the Islamic World, for Muslims share as high a percent of our memes as chimpanzees do our genes – might be called *a swearing people,* for "we" have long sworn things upon This or That (some very odd things, too, if we think of the etymology of the word "testify!"), while Japanese, and one would presume most people, have no such cultural compulsion (see 10-11 re. notary publics).

4-12 Our clergy, under no circumstances, act as envoys for princes and lords;
Os religiosos antre nós por nenhum cazo andão em recados de principes nem senhores;

> The *tonos* [feudal lords] in Japan use bonzes for envoys and war tacticians.
> *Os* Tonos *em Japão se servem dos bonzos pera recados e* buriaqos *da guerra.*

Actually, the Jesuits "undertook many diplomatic missions on behalf of the Crown of Portugal." (Dauril Aulden *The Making of an Enterprise . .*). Was Frois too low level an operative to have known what was going on? But what about Valignano forbidding Jesuits in Japan "to act as military intelligence agents, or to pass on news of the progress of a campaign, even if it was in the interests of a Christian daimyo against a heathen" (B:CCJ)? Frois had to know that; he recorded it in his *Historia*. Perhaps Frois *meant* that the bonzes are *hired* in that capacity, whereas the Jesuits might *dabble* in the information business, but only as agents of their Society on the behalf of spreading their religion.

Okada points out that each Shogun had his famous bonze envoy or diplomat and that there were actually terms such *shizô* (messenger-bonze) and *jinzô* (encampment-bonze). Were bonzes less likely to be tortured or executed than other envoys? Or were their literary and/or medical skills (4-29) useful? Originally, it would seem that Ippen and the bonzes of his sect, whose name *jishû* stood for the last moments of life 臨命終時, made a vow to remain by dying warriors (when they were not dancing! (see 4-22)) to help them invoke the divine mercy of *Amida* and assure they made it into the Pure Land Paradise. This was similar to the role of Christian priests in "our" armies. Soon, these bonzes came to live "near their lords and aid them in both combat and death." (S(R):WTUD)

4-13   With us, a clergy who gets married becomes an apostate;
Antre nós cazar-se hum religioso hé ficar apostata;

>The bonzes, when they get tired of the religious life, can marry or become soldiers. *Os bonzos, como se enfadão da religião, ou se cazão ou se fazem soldados.*

"Us" here means Catholic *religioso*. Ex-Catholic priest Luther married a former nun about a decade before Frois went to Japan.   Luther felt that enforced celibacy was one reason for clerics' hidden concubines and tolerance of prostitution (H:CER). A few Buddhist sects, like Lutherans, went even farther than Frois notes and permitted marriage while remaining religious. Senryû joke about how these married bonzes both *bore* and *buried* people, or how happy they were to hear their wives crying out *"[I'm] dying! I'm dying!"* when they made love, because such words (a common Japanese love-call) were propitious for their death-related *business*. But this contrast is not primarily about marriage *per se* (if it were, "or soldiers" would not make sense); it is yet another instance of the *vow* vs. *no-vow* contrast. For the Jesuit, a decision to join the Order was *irrevocable*. To quit was to go back on your word, betray the Church and God and your Superiors to whom it was pledged. The same type of stigma was attached to it as one might to a divorce. *Apostate* was and still is a dirty word. For Japanese, however, the religious life was less a life-long commitment than a day-to-day choice. They remained in their temples out of their own free will.

This may be out of order – wrong country, wrong age – but, spending time in Korea in 1972, I recall visiting a mountain temple where a friend of my friend stayed as a monk. My friend said that many, if not most of his friends had spent some time (usually a few months but up to a year) living as a monk. It was part of their life experience. In the West, one is either on the *outside* (visits churches to worship) or the *inside* (one either ministers or becomes a monk/nun).   The closest "we" come to a temporary half-in/half-out religious experience is the relatively short practice we call *a retreat*.

4-14   Within our orders, the succession is made on the basis of election and virtue, not inheritance; *Nas nossas religiões não há socesão por heransa mas por eleisão e vertude;*

>Among the bonzes, the successor is a disciple raised and taught for that purpose since childhood. *Antre os bonzos herda o discípulo que o superior cria de pequeno pera lhe soceder.*

Actually, the Jesuit leadership was dominated by aristocrats (DR). One can't help wondering if Frois, a boy from a humble family who did not rise in the ranks as fast as he should have considering his obvious skills was entirely satisfied with his position, considering the fact that his superior, Valignano, coming from a family with the right Papal connections, despite doing time in jail for seriously injuring a man in a fight, shot up like a rocket to the upper ranks of the Jesuit order, becoming a Visitador in charge of all the East Indies (churches from India Eastward) at age 37 (S:MPMR).   Humble soul that Frois was, perhaps it never bothered him. But, that is unlikely.

The Japanese side sounds like Tibetan Buddhism, where a boy enters the monastery as the Lama-to-be; but in Japan, as Okada notes, a disciple might be chosen from a large number of young bonzes (or bonzes-to-be) on the basis of his apparent intelligence and ability. He was indeed groomed for succession, but it was hardly so arbitrary a process as the contrast implied. Of course, some Zen monasteries took in younger brothers of samurai families, who would give up their inheritance and expected promising opportunities in exchange, so Frois is not all wrong.

4-15 We enter the orders out of devotion and an inner calling to virtue;
Antre nós entrão na relegião por devosão e movimento interior de virtude;

> Bonzes do it to inherit each others wealth and gain worldly glory.
> *Os bonzos entrão por erdarem huns aos outros o fato e terem a gloria neste mundo.*

This is 4-1 all over again. We can be sure people became *religiosos* for many reasons in Europe, not all of which were virtuous, and likewise for Japanese. (I am indebted to DR for the excellent phrase: "an inner calling to virtue." My draft translation, "virtuous interior motives," was *very* lame.)

4-16 Our clergy strive most of all for interior purity and cleanliness;
Os nossos religiosos fazem a principal força na pureza e limpeza interior;

> The bonzes are extremely clean when it comes to their dwellings, gardens and temples, and filthy of soul. *Os bonzos são limpissimos nas cazas, nivas e templos, e abominaveis nas almas.*

"Our" side is getting boring. I almost feel like saying *"yeah, yeah!"* The "they" side is more interesting. Do interior and exterior cleanliness, then, correlate inversely? In 1571, Vilela "could not repress his whole-hearted admiration of the cleanliness and neatness of their persons and surroundings, which he noted as forming a glaring contrast to "the filthiness of their consciences." (B:CCJ) Japanese cleanliness was constantly noted by the missionaries and it was always suspect. In 1565, Almeida, after writing that a Buddhist monastery's kitchen was spotless, added that it was so because it was "a thing very common with the Japanese, being very clean in all their exterior works." He let the dirty *interior* lie quietly between the lines of his letter. Frois in his parallel letter described the same temples as both clean and boasting wood so brilliant that it leaves "our" tapestry of gold, silk and brocade in the shade. He cleverly prefaced his praise with a disclaimer to the effect that they (the Buddhists) have all this loveliness, "solely for their happiness and glory in this world." (I.e. at the expense of neglecting *that* World.) In his *Historia*, Frois later tried the reverse rationalization: lacking hope of salvation and eternal life, the Buddhists concentrate on this world. *Worldly Buddhists* vs *otherworldly Christians*. This stands the classic Orientalist world view on its head.

Christians have long had a problem with external cleanliness and beauty. On the one hand, they profess to despise the world of appearance, but, on the other, as members of the Establishment in the West, they had to keep clean to differentiate themselves from radical or marginal elements. Moreover, with stench associated with the Devil and lack of odor or a good scent (even after death), the mark of a saint, even Christians in hair-shirts probably felt obliged to practice *some* personal hygiene. Obviously they did not practice too hard, for "in Catholic Europe" at least, "lice were regarded as the inseparable companions of monks and soldiers." (B:CCJ) Cleaning might have been included in "good works," but was not in itself considered to be soul work.

In Japan, on the other hand, "cleanliness emphatically came next to godliness." (B:CCJ) The mirror is one of Shintô's main symbols; and keeping it clean was identified with keeping a pure soul. "During impurity, access to any temple, and most acts of religion, are forbidden, and the head must be covered, that the sun's beams may not be defiled by falling upon it." (B:MCJ). As Kaempfer pointed out, "scrupulous adorers" not only must keep physically unpolluted, but "carry things still further, and think it unbecoming to appear in the presence of the Gods, even when the thoughts, or memories of their misfortunes, possess their mind." This is a deeper idea of internal cleanliness than the Christian one which stopped at not thinking dirty thoughts. This idea was evidently not foreign to Japanese Buddhism, either. As mentioned in 1-46, the Wheel of the Law was identified with the moon, likened to a mirror which had to be *kept free of dust*. Buddhism probably *had to* emphasize cleanliness to root in the land of Shinto. Frois and friends did not understand – or, could not accept – that *cleaning* and *reflection* were one, and that Japanese Buddhism and Shinto both aimed for "inward purity of heart" (the first of Shinto's five "chief points," according to Kaempfer). In this respect, the Moslems are closer to Japanese Buddhists and Shintoists than Christians; for they even pluck the hair from their armpits and pubic region (sticky paper for this purpose is apparently sold in the supermarkets today).

The Jesuits' accommodation to the Japanese lifestyle ordered by Valignano included not only the introduction of clean kitchen and dining habits, but more subtle things such as always sending a messenger ahead of time to be certain and give the other party time to clean up as needed and put on clean clothing, and always wearing something clean when visiting. (1583? 1592? in V(A):S&A) If the beautiful and the good were equated in ancient Greece, in Japan, in Japanese today, *kirei* means "clean," "pretty," and "right" – as in "doing it right" (*kirei-ni-shite*). But for all Valignano's apparent awareness of this, "in his "Obediencias" of 1592, he laid down that none but the very sick or aged were to be allowed the frequent use of a *furo* [Japanese bath], and all other personnel, European and Japanese alike, could only take a proper bath once in eight days." Boxer *sighs* "To such ridiculous lengths had the mediaeval Christian reaction against Roman cleanliness and personal hygiene carried the men of the Renaissance." (B:CCJ) I think Valignano's rule had less to do with hygiene *per se,* and more to do with *avoiding sensual pleasure,* for the physical comfort of a good hot bath is not to be reckoned lightly. (To put it the other way around, I suspect Valignano, himself, was a bath-lover.) Presumably, Valignano did allow other less pleasurable means of keeping the body clean enough for Japan.

Perhaps a word more on the phrase "filthy of soul" is needed. It was not just *sodomy* that bothered the Jesuits. It was a general laxity with regard to sex and the genitals. The Buddhists only thought badly of sex in so far as it provoked strong desires and bound one to the sensual world of appearance. Sex *itself* was not sinful and certainly nothing to get excited about. This casual attitude did not only surprise the Jesuits but prudish mid-19c American visitors, such as John Preble, an officer who came with Commodore Perry's squadron in 1854.

> Resting at a temple near Hakodate, he notices a pretty unmarried girl among the crowd. A man comes up to her, whispers, then takes her behind a screen five feet away: Her companions were not slow, to show us, by the most indecent signs in which the old priest joined, what they had gone for. The women laughing heartily as though it were a first-rate joke and no uncommon occurrence to so pervert their Temples. (L:IOJ)

A Buddhist priest – unless of one of the sects that would be the equivalent of our fundamentalist sects – would be above it all. Were he to get huffy-puffy about such things, Japanese might wonder about his spiritual maturity, for a clean soul is calm and laughs off little things like a liaison behind a screen, whereas, an upright Christian *religioso* would have been expected to act outraged, and a bonze who observed such outrage would, then, have been shocked at the priest's passions (a devilish thing) and lack of insight into what matters and what does not.

But to return to the *cleanliness*, the contrast need not be restricted to temples. It was true for most Japanese buildings (like the Chinese, but cleaner, as many have observed) and for the country *as a whole.* Thunberg's complaint of a *lack of weeds for botanizing* (we will find this in ch 11) was later confirmed by Kipling:

> But all I can write will give you no notion of the wantonness of neatness visible in the fields . . . The young rice was transplanted very much as draughts are laid on the board; the tea might have been cropped garden box . . . while the beans ran up to the mustard and stopped as though cut by a rule. (K(C&?):KJ)

~~~

4-17   We are keen to avoid deceit, hypocrisy and adulation;
Antre os nossos se foje muito ao fenjimento e ipocrezia e adulasão;

> The bonzes of Japan live off these, and find them a super way to make a livelihood. *Os bonzos de Japão disto vivem, e o tem por potíssimo meo pera poderem viver.*

Thanks to enmity between Protestants and Catholics (and quarrels between 17c Catholics as well), in the English speaking world, it is "we" – if *we* means the Jesuits – who now have this unjust reputation. The very word "Jesuit" became synonymous with "a dissembling person, a prevaricator" and "black intrigues," and "Jesuitical" with "deceitful, dissembling, practicing equivocation, prevarication, or mental reservation of truth." (OED) To my mind, the reality is complex and the simple-minded ferocity of Calvinism and the Papacy that eventually turned on the Jesuits is what deserves criticism. An attack on equivocation is along the same line as attack on science for being less than certain. Unfortunately, the Jesuits did not equivocate when it came to describing Buddhism. Even gentle St. Xavier showed no Christian mercy for bonzes:

> . . . our greatest enemies are the bonzes, because we expose their falsehoods. . . . They give their word that if anyone goes down into hell he will be delivered by their intervention and labour. We, on the contrary, proved to the people that in hell there is no redemption, ... At last, by the help of God, the bonzes themselves were forced to confess the truth that they could not save anyone . . . but that unless they gave out that they had this power, they would infallibly be reduced to die of hunger. And, indeed, soon after this, the bonzes, . . . experienced great difficulties as to their maintenance, and had to live in a state of degradation. (C:LLFX)

In one sense, Frois and Xavier are right. Most Japanese – even bonzes – were probably not true believers, not confident fanatics as sure of the existence of their God and Heaven as a three year-old is of Santa Claus. Unlike Occidentals – unlike all too many Usanians who *today* would teach Creationism as science – the bonzes were emotionally and intellectually mature and humble enough *to know they did not know everything.* While the Jesuits who went to Japan were sophisticated Christians in the best sense of the word, their sophistication was on behalf of Christianity, which was and is, for better or worse, a very simplistic religion (I include the "better" because of reading Chesterton).

~~~

4-18   Our clergy wear no beard and have tonsures;
Os nossos religiosos trazem a barba rapada e a coroa feita;

> The bonzes shave their heads and beard every 4 days.
> *Os bonzos rapão a cabeça e barba cada 4 dias.*

You might say "our" monk only shaved the part of his head that looked at heaven, while the bonze turned his whole head into a round object, which, in Japan is a similitude for the soul itself.

The frequency of shaving varies. It depended on the sect. The first Occidental observer of Japan, Captain Alvarez wrote: "The bonzes are all shaven with razors; they have rooms built at a short distance from their monasteries, where they go twice a day to perform their ablutions. They heat the necessary water at stoves erected for the purpose, the wood for the fires being given them for the love of God." (C:LLFX)

This is one of Frois's least satisfactory contrasts because there is more similarity than difference. The Jesuits are not included in "ours" here, for they did not shave *their* heads.

~~~~~~

4-19   Among us, clergy wear hats or berets; *Antre nós trazem os religiosos capelos ou barretes;*

> Bonzes generally go about with nothing on their head, but when it's cold they wear baggy barrettes, or *wataboshi*, and others wear caps like the neck and head of a horse, with ears. *Os bonzos o mais do tempo andão sen nada na cabeça e polo frio uzão de barretes como bolsa, ou de* vataxboxis *e outros hum capelo como pescoso e cabeça de cavalo com orelhas.*

Since bonzes, like others, usually wore umbrella-like hats for shade when they went out in the heat, I would guess Frois means *indoors*, for they were never worn indoors while our hats and berets often were. See 2-8 for a description of the *wataboshi* (cotton-hat), which sounds like it might actually *be* the baggy berets. The bonzes' caps tended to have neck-pieces attached, which kept the chill off the nape of the neck. That may explain the horsy simile. Orfanel writes of a "two-pointed hat." (C:TCJ). Perhaps the "ears" appear when the middle part of the rectangular hat settles down leaving the corners protruding a bit! Frois seems to be trying too hard for a contrast that is barely there.

~~~~~~

4-20   Our clergy greatly value modesty and setting a good example.
Os nossos religiosos estimão em muito a honestidade e bom exemplo;

> The bonzes always go about with their legs bare and wear robes so thin they show almost everything in the summer, and no one thinks it bad or embarrassing. *Os bonzos andão sempre em pernas e polo verão com catabiras tão ralas que lhe parese quanto tem, sem disso terem nenhum pejo nem vergonha.*

The genital-sized fig-leaf had grown to insane proportions. "Men of the cloth," indeed. There is no small irony here when you consider the fact that this ridiculous disgust for the body comes from the same civilization that so worships the figure of man that its "masterpieces" even give *God* a muscle-bound body! In Japan and China, where bodies were not idolized in fresco or in oil, no one was the least bothered by thin clothing (the same see-through *katabira* robe mentioned in 1-61) unless, pace Sei Shônagon, the body looked horrible. This contrast may have been thought to depict us as more moral than them, but to me, it only goes to prove our culture was mentally disturbed. Should I add that Frois wrote at a time when the anti-nudity campaign was reaching a zenith in Europe? We had censors objecting to the naked Christ child in the Catholic Netherlands and Frois's King Phillip II draping a scarf around the loins of Cellini's grown Christ, and so forth.

Valignano was the first Jesuit I know to cut the Buddhists some slack on the moral side. In his *Libro* (1601), he qualified his earlier views and admitted that Buddhism had a clean origin, for the Buddha did not practice the dishonesties of Jupiter, Venus and Cupid, so adored by the Romans, and the Buddhists did not have fiestas for Venus, the Priapus and Bacchus, but only ones that are "modest and honest on the exterior." (note in V(A):S&A)   As he wrote this, however, he came down hard on Shintô for having "very impossible, dirty and burlesque histories as was always the case for the histories of the gentile gods."   Someone must have told him about the first god with the part left over and the first goddess with a part missing, and the shuttle-in-the-vagina homicide and clever red arrow flying up from the privy into the same, and the birth of grains from the dying goddess's vagina and so forth! Yes, not only does Shinto have earthy mythology, as most religions with a small "r" do, but was and still is one with the folk tradition of parading large straw or wooden phalluses about in local festivals in Japan. (Christians should not mind *that* as it is about generation, begetting.)

It would be wrong, however, to give the impression of Japan as utterly lacking moral qualms about nudity and sex. In 1840, that is over a decade *before* Perry reopened Japan, the Confucian element in Japanese society prevailed upon the government to crack down on open promiscuity and religion-related sexuality. The pleasure quarters were left as is, but age-old stone phalluses, sculptures of, shall we say, Yin-Yang in action, and the life-size models on their "god-shelves" of courtesans were forced into hiding or destroyed. A large number of the last, according to the journalism of the time, was tossed into a river where they made quite a sight bobbing up and down in the current for, being weighted on the bottom so they wouldn't capsize, the glans penis (particularly large, according to the Japanese aesthetic norm) poked up from the water!.

4-21 Our clergy show great sobriety and temperance with respect to drink, especially wine; *Os nossos religiosos tem muita sobriedade e temperansa no beber,* maxime *vinho;*

> The bonzes, though it is prohibited, are often [encountered?] drunk on the road.
> *Aos bonzos, com lhes ser prohibido, muitas vezes [se achão?] por esses caminhos bebados.*

No comment on our side. A short word will do for theirs. Since poets and others who depended on travel tended to adopt the robe, perhaps paying fees for the necessary credentials, in order to pass through the fief checkpoints more easily, it is a safe bet that many of the drunk bonzes were bonzes in name only. *Not that it matters.* The prohibition in Japanese Buddhism was not absolute. Like meat-eating, drinking is relatively wasteful. Fermentation may help otherwise lost food keep, but taking rice out of its limited circulation to make *sake* from it was, on the whole, an inefficient way to feed a large population. So there had to be some limits imposed and who better to bear them then bonzes who were not supposed to be enjoying this world? But some sometimes drunk. And some drank a lot. Japanese saw and still see nothing wrong with being drunk *per se.* Since there are almost no mean and violent drunks in Japan (6-38 notes), the association of drink with the Devil was simply not there. And, is it not true that *walking around drunk is a religious act in itself*, giving up the hubris of being "captain" of your soul, and letting fate, do as it likes with you?

4-22 Our clergy are not accustomed to singing and playing accompaniment at skits and profane comedies; *Os nossos religiosos não costumão cantar, nem tanjer em autos e farças profanas;*

> The bonzes are old hats at it and accustomed to divert themselves that way.
> *Os bonzos tem isto por suas mangas e nellas se costumão recrear.*

Not only were "our" fathers in Japan not big on performing, but worse, they could be wet-blankets when others wished to. In a letter written by Almeida in 1565, we find a church of Japanese Christians visited by dancing gentiles. In return, they created a dance lauding the Virgin Mary and took it to the gentiles' neighborhood. (*This letter of Almeida's was the first time I ever read of dance exchanges! What a delightful custom!*) On the return trip, they dropped by the church to show off the dance to Father Cosme de Torres, who not only locked the door and refused to see them, but the next day said mass early behind closed doors! He then made them understand how great a disgrace to God, not to mention their *padre,* their behavior had been. A Japanese nobleman took full responsibility, and made *"notable penitencia"* disciplining himself so strongly "that he was left bathed in blood." This sense of personal responsibility greatly impressed Almeida about the quality of the Japanese Christians. He says nothing about whether he felt Cosme de Torres was right to be so strict.

All bonzes were no more performers than they were warriors. But some were. A part of the Pureland (*Sôdo*) sect called the *jishû* was particularly noted for rousing sutra performances, which secular literature reports could attract hundreds of good-looking wives into the temples. Basically, we are talking about a popular proclivity for what might be called Buddhist gospel music. It was centered on vocals, percussion and dancing and was, conveniently, considered enlightening. The trader Caron, in Japan with the Dutch a generation after Frois, gives supporting evidence of a more neutral nature than that given by the Jesuits:

> The best of these [twelve Buddhist] Sects make Taverns of their Temples, which are most commonly built in the pleasantest and best places, sumptuous and well planted with trees and orchards: When the Inhabitants have a minde to rejoyce, they assemble here, and in the presence of their Gods, and company of their Priests, (who are likewise good fellows), they debauch and do those extravagances, which are the concomitants of excess and folly; common whores are permitted to enter and dance, the Priests themselves allowing of this jolity, and a further use, so it be in secret of these immodest females. (C:DOJ)

That this was not meant in criticism is clear from the next sentence: "I never heard that those people trouble themselves to dispute or argue in their religion; neither do they break their heads in converting others to their opinions; but leave every one to the freedom of his own, as indifferent and reasonable, as being infused into him by their Gods." The 1661 edition adds that "anyone who has need for money will readily change his sect for a hundred crowns" but, still, I read this as *approval* rather than criticism. Having witnessed the torture, the massacres and all-round cruelty of the religious wars in Europe, Caron was evidently relieved at Japanese sanity and pragmatism with respect to faith. He also showed up in Japan at the right time, for the Buddhist sects that *had* competed vociferously in Frois's time were quashed, so Japan was a peaceful spiritual free-market.

If some of the Jesuits in Japan were not much on singing and instrumental performance, their Society was, nonetheless, on the forefront of drama-as-a-teaching-device in Europe, and we shall discuss later why it is no accident Frois devoted a chapter of the TRATADO to it.

~~~~~~

4-23 We have faith in the glory and punishment of the future and the immortality of the soul;
Nós temos por fé a glória e pena futura e immortalidade da alma;

> The Zenshû [zen sect] bonzes deny all of this and [claim] there is nothing more than being born and dying. *Os* bonzos Jenxus *negão tudo isto e que não há mais que nacer e morrer.*

Today "we" would be more likely to associate *joy* with Heaven than "glory." The *pena* of the future, suggesting Hell, encompasses both *imprisonment* and *sorrow*, so I chose a word containing both: *punishment*. The "we" means the clergy. I do not know if Frois could have imagined a European like Montaigne (and, doubtless, many who read him), who was unsure about immortality.

Had Frois been writing a book on *similarities* rather than differences, he might have skipped Zen's conspicuously missing spiritual geography altogether, and observed instead that of all Asian people, only some Japanese sects of Buddhism had a Hell – or rather a pandemonium of hells –

horrendous enough to compete with the Christian one! Japanese depictions of Hell are fantastic, more terrifying, and better art than ours. Valignano ascribed the great variety of demons to their being the incorporated divinities of conquered peoples. (S:VMP) Yet, if the Japanese Buddhist Hell was equally full of fire and poking and cutting, etc., how you got there and how long you stayed was another matter. *Faux Frois:*

> *With us, anyone who is not saved by Jesus ends up in Hell forever.*
> *With them, only people who commit major sins go to Hell and for a limited time.*

Is not the Japanese Hell *better* than "ours" from the moral standpoint as well as the aesthetic? Much of the Christian Hell, in my opinion, is *a damnable idea.* Can anyone not *feel for* the poor Japanese and Jesuits, who had to teach the Japanese that all their ancestors and relatives are being punished *forever*? "Seeing their grief, the kind St. Xavier wrote "I can hardly restrain my tears sometimes at seeing men so dear to my heart suffer such intense pain about a thing that is already done with and can never be undone." (C:LLFX) If you ask me, our unforgiving theology itself was Hell on Earth! What a *horrible* belief! If you ask me both the Japanese Christians and St. Xavier were too good for Christianity! For Christ's sake, was "our" God *that* small? Mandatory fixed-punishment is sometimes necessary when time and money does not permit case-by-case judgment, but wasn't *Deus* supposed to be omnipotent? To Catholicism's credit, I should add that since the Second Vatican Council, things have not been so simple.

Frois is right about Zen's belief, or rather absence thereof, though it may be put in a more poetic way: *getting born is dying.* Or to put it in the words of a 19c resident of Concord, *one world at a time.* The Zen-shû, or Zen faith (there is more than one sect of Zen) is one of three main faiths of Buddhism in Japan, the other two being the Pure Land sect, which emphasized egalitarianism and mercy and the Nichiren sect which combined Buddhism with nationalism. Skeptical down to the bone and marked by the practice of meditation with the goal being direct experience of reality rather than paradise, Zen had more appeal to the intellectual upper class than common folk. Because the Jesuits tended to take the high road – try to convert the rulers who could convince their subjects to follow them – in Japan, they quickly discovered they were in competition with Zen. In his HISTORIA, Frois describes a debate between Fr. Lourenço and Shôzaemon, who came walking into their Miaco (Kyoto) church looking for someone who would preach to him. Since Lourenco didn't know how much Shozaemon knew, he began by describing the "great differences" between the Japanese *kami* (Gods) and *hotoke* (Buddhas) and *Deus*. Shozaemon smiled and said it was a waste of time to bother with details about the existence and powers of gods "for all that is a laughable illusion" which "wise and knowledgeable men value not a whit."

Zen bears resemblance to Christian mysticism in both its rigorous practice aiming at unity with the ALL and NOTHING, and in the free behavior of the enlightened. But such an understanding was apparently beyond Frois. He saw Zen temples as places for aristocrats who had no concern whatsoever for their souls and concentrate on one thing: worldly pleasure (J/F:HISTORIA). To a degree, he may have been right. Many of the aristocrats may well have been dilettantes practicing Zen because it was cool (especially with the tea ceremony link). Yet, Joao Rodrigues, writing two decades later, was clearly impressed:

> Their vocation is not to philosophize with the help of books and sermons written by illustrious masters and philosophers . . . . Instead, they give themselves up to contemplating the things of nature . . . Thus, from what they see in things themselves, they attain by their own efforts to a knowledge of the first cause, and putting aside what is evil and imperfect in the mind and reasoning, they reach the natural perfection and being of the first cause. . . . the monks of this sect are of a resolute and determined character, without any indolence, laxity or effeminacy. . . .they do without a great number of things which they consider superfluous and unnecessary. They maintain that a hermitage should first of all be frugal and moderate, with much quietness, peace of soul and exterior modesty. (in C:TCJ)

Rodrigues qualifies his remarks, going on to claim it was so much "hypocrisy;" but I cannot help wondering if he only wrote that to keep from getting in trouble with Rome.[1]

We believe that a man or woman has only one life on this earth which settles our fate forever;
They believe that people are born over and over into higher or lower states depending on their conduct.

Reincarnation is not so perfect a contrast with the Christian belief as the lack of reward and punishment of the Zen faith, but it is better than many contrasts Frois did not forget to make and it was far more representative of the religious belief of *most* Japanese than Zen. And that may be true for Chinese, too. According to Ricci "the pervasiveness of ideas of reincarnation, accounted for the great amount of infanticide in China, since the very poor would kill infants in the hope that they would be reborn soon into a richer family" (S:MPMR). So, *that* sin, too, could be laid at the door of Buddhism, although Ricci took care to blame "our" Pythagoras for inventing the mistaken idea of reincarnation he hoped the Chinese would abandon for the correct religion.

Most upper-class Japanese were probably *agnostic*. Huxley's term fits because Japanese were usually not so black and white about it as our atheists, whose intensity often echoes that of their opposition. This did not just come from Zen Buddhism. Confucianism, which tended toward a sort of deistic animism, was even more influential in Japan. Indeed, Kaempfer, in 1692, described *Siuto* (*judo,* meaning "Confucian-way,") as "the Philosophical Sect" in Japan. Not believing in the transmigration of souls, they "admit of none but temporal rewards, or punishments." They "believe in an *Animam mundi*, an universal Soul, Spirit or power, diffused throughout the whole world which animates all things" but, "admitting no Gods, they have no temples, no forms of worship." This was similar to the belief system of the literati in China described as *Epicurean* by Ricci in 1584 (S:MPMR) and the "free-thinkers" introduced by Golownin in the early-19c, who, I believe, gave birth to the *Inquisitor* chapter of the *Brothers Karamatzov* (see *TT-long* for more on this).

1. Rodrigues and Zen Reading Cooper's *Rodrigues The Interpreter* disabused me of the notion that Rodrigues really did not feel antagonistic to Zen. It also made me wonder if it were not possible that he was helped in his efforts by that missing first book of Frois's which included introductions to Shintô and Zen.

4-24 We profess just one God, one faith, one baptism and one Catholic Church;
Nós profesamos hum só Deus, huma fee, hum baptismo e huma Igreja Catolica;

In Japan, there are thirteen sects and almost all disagree on their faith and devotions. *Em Japão há 13 ceytas e quasi todas discrepão no culto e adorasão.*

Frois *wishes* "our" side were so united! With the Reformation well underway, most of Europe was in a constant state of religious war. "We" contended over infant vs. childhood baptism, predestination vs. salvation by good works, celibacy vs. marriage for clergy, sacred images vs. iconoclasm and, most important, regional vs. Papal control. We are not only talking about armies fighting armies, but numerous gruesome civilian massacres (St. Bartholomew's Day is just one) and the torture and execution of the clergy on both sides. English-reading readers have read plenty about the atrocities of the Spanish Inquisition. How about one from "our" side of the channel?

He left with three other priests for England on April 24. He was asked if the Pope could err. His response was "No." This response was taken as a plea of guilty and he was sentenced to death. He was drawn at Tyburn, where he desired all Catholics to pray for him. He was cut down and disemboweled while still alive. (from WELCOME TO KEEPING CATHOLICS CATHOLIC PAGE XXV)

If there was "one church" it was only "catholic" in the sense that everyone thought their side was the one rightful faith and the others invalid if not criminal. Frois wrote shortly after Phillip (Felipe) II re-conquered the Netherlands. They would soon rebel again. Soon, Lutherans from Holland and England would warn the Japanese against "Papist plots," and, with some help from the Franciscans (who insisted on confronting the Japanese), poison the atmosphere too heavily to permit Christianity to survive in Japan. If we think Frois slow to catch on, even four years *after* TRATADO, when knowledge of the failed Armada should have reached Macao, we find Miguel=Valignano blithely going on and on about the *single aim, single spirit, and singularly perfect unanimity of belief* in the West. (dialog 7 *De Missione*) Did they 1) Wish to keep religious discord in the West a secret? 2) Think that writing something down might help make it come true? 3) Fail to recognize reality because it spoiled their dream?

But let us proceed to the second half of the distich. About Japanese Buddhism, Xavier wrote:

There are nine kinds of sects, all of them different from each other, and both men and women may freely chose whichever one they please, and there is no compulsion to join one sect rather than another. The matter is left for the individual to decide and it is not considered at all strange to find a family in which the husband belongs to one sect, the wife to another and the children to a third. (in C:TCJ)

There were traditionally 13 Buddhist sects in China and 8 in Japan. But that is of no matter. The important observation is that, as Frois wrote, *there was open disagreement* and as Xavier noted, probably without approval, *there was individual religious freedom in Japan* unheard of in Catholic or Protestant Europe (see *TT-long* notes on our mandatory and compulsory religious life). Indeed, members of families of Japanese could simultaneously belong not only to different sects, as he observes, but individually to more than one religion – i.e., Shintô and Buddhism – at once. This did not stop the sects from fighting one another. Xavier also wrote that "little love is lost between" the bonzes who wear gray habits and those that wear black "because black bonzes loathe the gray ones, declaring that they are ignorant and lead bad lives . . ." (Ibid.) But, note: *they did not drag everyone into it and murder each other in the European fashion.*

Frois's contrast emphasizes "our" unity – *there is but one way to go to heaven* – and their disunity – *there are many ways to go to hell.* To Frois, the diversity of Buddhism was a good thing. A passage from his *Historia* immediately following a passage on how hard a time he and Vilela had debating Zen-Buddhists, who wanted concrete rather than logical proof, concludes on a positive note, namely, *it was worth the trouble, for they (Zen-Buddhists) have particularly good-quality minds and later can grasp the truth so much the better,* and "it is a great advantage that Japan has different sects and diverse and opposing beliefs. It made it easier for us to introduce our Lord Deus. If all [the Japanese] solidified around the same religious principles, it would probably have been very difficult to get them to accept our teachings."

What I like about the Jesuits is the way they find *something good in everything*. Whether it is because they want to justify all that happens for the sake of God's reputation or because they were trained in what we now call "positive-thinking" I really can't say! Of course, this wasn't just a Jesuit trait. It was shared to a degree by all good Christians. After Mary Rolandson slaughtered her Amerindian captors and returned to New England civilization, she felt very grateful for the *opportunity* God gave her to suffer and gain brownie points for Heaven. (See her 1682 work, *A True History of the Captivity and Restoration of Mrs. Mary Rolandson, a Minister's Wife in New England*). While Valignano and his able crew in Japan overcame the setbacks of the late 1580's and succeeded in keeping the church membership growing for over two more decades, the heart-wrenching epic of torture and martyrdom that was to put an end to the whole effort was just around the corner. Even though I am very happy that Japanese did not become Christian, it is sad to think about.

4-25   We hate and abominate the devil above all else;
Nós sobre todas as couzas avorrecemos e abominamos ao demonio;

> The bonzes venerate and worship him, build him temples and make him great offerings. *Os bonzos o venerão e adorão e lhe fazem templos e grandes sacreficios.*

..

The Devil. What a concept! Most cultures have no such thing, unless it is a trickster hero/villain of the type of Creation legends we would call *just-so stories.* That is because the idea of a singular Devil is the flip-side of an idea called *God.* If there is just one God and he is accountable for all, one must either admit he has a heartless side or invent something outside of Him. The most influential Kabbalistic text, *The Zobar,* written by the Spanish mystic Moses de Leon in about 1275 found the original "root of evil in God himself" and suggested it became "evil and destructive" only when it broke away from working in harmony with divine Mercy. (A:HOG). With the 1484 Papal Bull *Summa Desiderantes,* the Devil broke away with a vengeance. No longer an abstraction, he took concrete form to the extent that even his freezing-cold forked penis was seriously described! If God was contrasted to the Devil, the Holy Virgin (who, over the Medieval period took over a large portion of religious interest) was now contrasted to the diabolic Witch. With Germany and the other North countries taking the lead, all of Europe, except for Italy, indulged their psychotic fantasies in the trial, torture and execution of thousands if not millions of people that ended in Spain only with Salazar's courageous report of 1611 that found not one *bona fide* – or, should I say, *mala fide?* – witch among 11,300 accused he examined in Spain. The history of the medieval church is a warning to all who would war without real cause. The Church, in battling the heresy of the Manicheans, itself, turned as radically dualistic as a religion could possibly be and (imho) lost its grasp on reality.

Our dualism turned even the gentle Buddha into God's antithesis. In 1569, Vilela wrote "They have a dozen sects and all different one from the other; but, in the end, all give signs of their [common] inventor, who is the devil." But I believe Frois, on the whole less vituperative than Vilela, probably refers in the above contrast to the fact that in Buddhist temples from India to Japan, one *does* often find *the closest thing* to the Devil found in Buddhism. He is called Jemma O, Yama, or Ema. Frois, in a long letter about the temples of Kyoto of 1565 describes a "temple, dedicated to the god and judge of hell" where the walls "are painted the many kinds of torments in hell, with many figures of men and women suffering these pains, and of the demons inflicting them." He further explained that the people "usually repair there to beg the king of hell to deliver them from these torments." (in C:TCJ) What Frois neglects to explain, is why this "king of hell" is *not* The Devil. True, he is, to use the Englished Kaempfer's words, "the severe Judge and sovereign commander of this place of horror and heinousness," but, note: *he is not evil.* He did not lure people or pursue them. He did not delight in bad behavior nor seek to increase it. Sure, he looks terrifying. But this aspect of his character is useful for discouraging bad behavior (indeed, he is used to frighten children in nursery rhymes). Like Saint Peter at the Golden Gate, he only judged people – through a looking-glass of knowledge, according to some and by keeping a ledger according to others – for their sins, and as Commander of the punishing army of demons, made sure they got what was coming to them. Because he was not evil, he could be prayed to. Usually people did this to try to lesson the punishment they thought other people might be undergoing (for it was not eternal) on Jan 16 and July 16, the first day of the waning moon of Spring and Fall in the old calendar when the lids were said to be taken off the cauldrons in Hades and the demons employed for the torture were allowed to take their vacations. Today, you may find Yama on fake Chinese money meant for burning. Had Frois been neutral on religion his contrast might have gone like this:

..

> *Our Devil is cruel and wants to seduce us away from God by causing us to do evil things;*
> *Their Devil is kind, for he wants to frighten people so as to not do any evil and stay good.*

4-26 With us, the temples and offices of the monastery belong to the whole Order;
Antre nós o templo e as oficinas do moesteiro hé da Religião universal;

In Japan, if a bonze becomes disenchanted, he sells off the temple and its offices.
Em Japão se [se?] hum bonzo ali se eemfada, vende o templo e as oficinas e [tudo?]

Yet another contrast of *collectivist=humble us* vs. *individualist=selfish* them. By "offices," Frois means the rights and duties conferred by the authorities to do what the temple does. Perhaps "dispensations" would be better. Okada believes Frois alludes to the fact that when a Buddhist temple lost its backing, or the prelate retired (without a successor?), it was declared a *haidera*, or "derelict temple" and might be bought for use by a different sect. I do not know. I only know that, today, one finds many privately owned Buddhist temples throughout Japan. They are generally passed from parent to child like any other property. That a private property could be "declared a derelict temple" suggests to me a sort of communal ownership specific for religious use: what we would now call zoning.

4-27 Our priests wear a stole to administer the sacraments;
Os nossos sacerdotes uzão da estola pera ministrar sacramentos;

The bonzes wear them for appearance sake when making their visitations.
Os bonzos uzão dela por honra quando vão fora a suas visitasões.

What exactly *is* a stole? To sum a description from an article written by Dean Rose, a parishioner of the Anglican Church of Saint Peter: The stole is a long, two-four inch wide cloth that hangs around the neck and down the front of bishops and priests, but around the neck and across the chest of deacons. It was originally a symbolic towel indicating that a Roman magistrate was sweating or working hard on behalf of society and was worn for public ceremonies. More abstractly, it meant that power also required becoming a servant. A Greco-Latin word, "stole" means "garment" or "cloth" and may be the origin of the phrase "man of the cloth." It was once called an *orarion* (from *orare*, "pray") and indicated the role of priests in leading the prayers in public worship. The white wool reminds us that, like Christ the good shepherd, a bishop must care for the sheep of his flock. "The bishop or priest may kiss this cross before putting on the stole as a symbol that they take on Christ's yoke and carry his cross in the spirit of willingness and love."

The Buddhist equivalent was the *kesa*, a scarf-like cloth generally worn diagonally over their robe like a baldric (belt for a weapon in the West) when going out on official religious duties such as conferencing with other bonzes. It would seem that what Frois is really saying is *We adorn ourselves to pray to God ;they do so to go out and socialize.* But, that is unfair, for getting around *is* the business of bonzes. Frois's *honra* makes it seem that the bonzes dress just to show-off (why I translated "for honor" as "for appearance sake") and not to any deep religious purpose.

4-28 Our priests wear it draped about their necks;
Os nossos sacerdotes a trazem deitada ao pescoso;

The bonzes wear it as a baldric [diagonally], and it is larger and a different shape.
Os bonzos como tiracolo, mais larga e feita doutra feisão.

The *stole* again. This would seem to be for the clergy what the sword was for *The Men* in chapter 1. Funny that the cross is not mentioned. If it were, it might go like this:

Our clergy and many faithful wear a cross around our necks.
They wear nothing, but, then again, Japanese never wear anything around their necks.
..

The fact the priests and bonzes wore something similar enough to be the same "it" in Frois's contrast is far more remarkable than any difference in detail. According to Hendrik Van Loon in his ambitious THE ARTS OF MANKIND, when Rome fell under the cultural influence of "her Oriental possessions "the more austere and more truly Roman toga" was replaced by "ceremonial robes of Asia . . . gorgeous robes of silk, stiff with gold thread" and that we can still "see them being worn by the priests officiating in Roman Catholic churches and reading mass in the former law-courts of a Roman basilica." (V:AM). Could we surmise that Frois's interest in pursuing details of *difference* here derives in part from the all-too-obvious *similarities* between the dress of our respective *religiosos*?

~~~~~~

4-29   Our clergy, if they know how to cure [illness], cure for free out of love for God;
Os nossos religiosos, se sabem qurar, qurão gratis polo amor de Deus;

Most Japanese *medicos* are bonzes who live on their fees.
Os mais dos medicos de Japão são bonzos que vivem de seu estipendio.

Not a few Jesuits did indeed know something about medical care for "Jesuit novices were required to spend time each week working in hospitals"(DR). One of the earliest Jesuits in Japan, surgeon Luis Almeida founded a hospital in South Kyushu and Frois, who was not a doctor of any kind, himself, became what we might call a faith-healer when it was necessary and was remarkably successful. Needless to say, curing was useful propaganda for God and religious men did work wonders, for when the "Doctor" himself believed in his spiritual placebo the placebo effect was heightened. We will have more in Chapter 7, on Medicine. Be that as it may, it is a shame there were not *more* medically trained priests in Europe, for it would have mooted the cruel question of *which to fetch first*, the doctor for the soul or the doctor for the body of the person in critical condition.

Okada writes that while there were bonzes who attended to medical matters in the large temples in Kyoto and Nara, most doctors in Japan shaved their heads and otherwise *looked like* bonzes, so Frois probably assumed (wrongly) they were. Perhaps. But Japanese Buddhism did have a long history of involvement in medicine. It begins in the literature with the fifth chapter of the *Hokkekyô* (*kyô=sutra*) on herbs and their effects and the twenty third chapter on the Herb-King Boddhisattva (yakuôbosatsu) which includes the following: "The Hokke Sutra is good medicine given to all people with disease who, if they believe in it, will recover from their sickness and become both ageless and immortal." As early as 602, a Buddhist priest well-versed in medicine and astronomy came to Japan from Kudara (West Korea.), in 615, a statue of a healing buddha was finished at Hôrinji temple, and, in the 8c, soon after a Chinese bonze with medical knowledge and a perfect nose made it to Japan, we find large temples with rhino bone, dragon bone, ginseng, etc.. Most physicians were herb-doctors (*kuzushi*), generally bonzes, as this medicine required familiarity with a large body of written Chinese and the ability to import what couldn't be grown, but over the Warring Period (1338-1568), a different type of military doctor – a quick-fix artist rather than herb-doctor, who was often not a bonze – began to gain in prestige, so things were more complex when the Jesuits arrived. Bonze, or not, incantation accompanied by dramatic gesture remained part of the treatment and the bonze-doctor continued to practice into the Edo era despite the inroads of new Confucian-based medicine. As *senryû* quipped, the bonze-doctor had it made, as he could always profit by performing the funeral for his own mistake.

4-30 Our clergy, if they were to go about with gilded fans in their hands, would be thought crazy; *Os nossos religiosos se andassem com abanos dourados na mão tê-los hião por doudos;*

> The bonzes, when they preach or go out, have to carry a gilded fan to be dignified.
> *Os bonzos, por honra, quando pregão e vão fora, hão-de levar hum abano dourado na mão.*

These fans belong to a class of fans called either *suebiro*, i.e., "end/tip-open/wide," or *chûkei*, i.e. "middle-open," where the "open" is written not with the most common character but with one meaning "light/bright" which includes connotations of *enlightenment*. But even without this symbolism, these partially open fans reminding one of the opening of a fish-tail palm leaf are, in my humble opinion, a far more elegant symbol of authority than, say, a cross. The fans were used to emphasize points in conversation, as fans still are used with devastating effect by traditional stand-up (or sit-down?) comics called *rakugo-shi,* who pop them open or crack them shut and whack them smartly against their thighs, etc., but, judging from the next distich, this was apparently beneath the dignity of bonzes. Note that Frois is not quite right to give the bonzes *en masse* the right to carry such a fan. Only the higher ranking Buddhist clergy were allowed that honor.

4-31 We stand when we preach and make our gestures by moving our hands;
Nós pregamos em pee e fazemos as acsões com o movimento das mãos;

> The bonzes preach seated, without stirring their hands, and gesture with their heads.
> *Os bonzos pregão assentados, e as acsões, sem bulirem co[m] as mãos, as fazem com a cabeça..*

That "we" should stand while Japanese should sit to preach might seem strange considering the fact that our culture is more dependent on chairs; but it is natural when we consider another of Frois's contrasts (2-60) points out that "we" stand to be formal, while "they" sit.

Europeans *still* express far more with their hands than Japanese. The contrast is greatest with the Southern Europeans who, when they get going, might be said to *talk their hands off*. This might have something to do with "our" more outgoing personalities, but it was not only a natural development of our culture: the use of gesture was taught as part of classical rhetoric or, as we might call it, speech-making. I assumed it might have looked *aggressive* to Japanese, but from what an Edo era anti-Christian folk-historian wrote of Organtino's preaching, *ludicrous* might be more like it: "His voice was like a dove/pigeon's cooing and no one could make out the words and his mannerism was like a bat stretching out its wings, a painful sight." (*Nambanji* in J/E:NBJ)

Japanese moved and *still* move their *heads* so much when they converse that they may be differentiated not only from Europeans but from Koreans or Chinese from a hundred yards away (see14-45). Reading Frois's contrast, I wonder if there may have been less noticed aspects of gesture in Japanese, such as the cocking of the head to indicate doubt, but, as far as I know, we are talking about one thing: *nodding, lots of nodding.* Frois was obviously more interested in evangelizing than religious practice itself or he might also have caught what Kaempfer, a hundred years later, called "a posture very singular in itself, but reckon'd very proper for this sublime way of thinking."

> We meditate while lying down, sitting comfortably on a chair, or kneeling as one does to pray;
> They always meditate seated, legs crossed, with the knees low and the soles of the feet pointing up.

Kaempfer really pegged the posture and its effect:

sitting cross-legg'd, with his hands in the bossom placed so, that the two extremities of the thumbs touch'd one another" was "thought to engage one's mind into so profound a meditation, and to wrap it up so entirely within itself, that the body lies for a while as it were senseless, unattentive, and unmoved by any external objects whatsoever. This profound Enthusiasm is by them call'd Sasen [*zazen*], and the divine truths revealed to such persons Satori." (K:HOJ)

4-32   We preach in Europe wearing a white surplice without a stole;
Nós pregamos com sobrepelix branca em Europa sem estola;

> The bonzes preach with a black *koromo* [a religious habit], a stole and a gilded fan.
> *Os bonzos com* coromo *preto e estola e abano dourado na mão.*

More clothes! Have you, too, had enough? A googled definition of "surplice" is "a loose, full-sleeved white vestment, worn over the cassock (a long, close-fitting tunic, usually black, buttoning up to the neck and reaching the feet) as part of the customary dress of a priest. This is the most basic vestment which belongs to all grades of ordination;" but *color-wise*, the "we" is a bit too pat. Some orders did wear white, but others wore black, grey, brown and off-white. Doubtless the balance-of-color in the 16c was in favor of the white, or Frois would not have so generalized.

The stole, first found in 4-27, was evidently only used for certain services by "us," while the bonze equivalent (also mentioned in 4-27) was more or less standard wear. Orfanel, a Dominican who came to Japan a generation after Frois, described the *koromo* as "a black robe of fine hemp with sleeves so wide and long that they almost reach the ground" (C:TCJ) which is worn over a "very clean white robe" (Ibid.). The word *koromo* is also the traditional generic term for clothing in Japanese.

The religious use of white in Japan was pretty much reserved by Shintô and the mountain wizards, a cross between esoteric Buddhism and Shamanism (with Shintô elements). People on pilgrimages also still wear white. It is part of their orientation toward purity and, today, provides a powerful contrast to the corporative society with its dark suits.

4-33   We preach on pulpits; *Nós pregamos em pulpetos;*

> And the bonzes on chairs like our lecturers. *E os bonzos en cadeiras como dos nossos lentes.*

A pulpit is a platform or stage that assured "we" were high above the audience. In TT-long, I confused it for the stand "we" always stand behind to talk and used the preposition "at." (I am afraid my mind wandered off to the resemblance of the Portuguese to a small Octopus in Spanish (*pulpito*) and . . .).

The chair is another matter. I had imagined the Japanese legless chair, where the seat (with a cushion on it) is flush against the tatami mat. These are offered to old people and foreigners today. Here, too, *I was wrong.* I found a picture of the Buddhist preaching chair, a Chinese design called a *kyokuroku*, in my OJD and it turns out they are rather tall chairs with 1) "X" legs when viewed from the side (which probably means it could be folded up), 2) runners(?) extending between the feet of the front legs and the back legs (one has the support of two parallel lines rather than four points: useful if such a chair sits on mud or snow, I guess), 3) a foot-rest built upon the front runner, 4) a curved back that seems to allow a partial armrest (sorry not to have a picture!) and, 5) a flat seat, which I imagine a cushion was placed on. And the explanation says they were generally vermilion or black lacquer. In short, it seems a remarkably complex chair for a generally chair-less culture!

4-34   We give to others blessed rosaries and the relics of saints, gratis;
Nós damos aos proximos contas bentas e reliqias de santos de graça;

> The bonzes sell a great number and variety of charms written on paper for much money. *Os bonzos grande numero e diversidade de nominas escritas em papel por muito bom dinheiro.*

Perhaps, *the Jesuits* did not sell the religious paraphernalia Frois mentions, but when I think of the sale of *relics* and pushing of *indulgences* and God knows what else in Catholic Europe (a major cause of the Lutheran Reformation) it is hard not to *laugh* aloud. Still, Frois may have a point. The Church received ample funding in Europe, possibly as high as the proverbial ten-percent – when you consider that we chafe at donating even *one* percent of our vastly greater income to foreign aid, one can realize how cheap morality has become – through offerings accepted at the mandatory church services and a variety of direct or indirect rents or taxes; whereas, in Japan, the amount of money tossed into the fixed collection boxes at temples or the bowls of traveling bonzes was miniscule by comparison. The clergy were part of a church with money to spare, while the bonzes had to sell things to eke out a living. Some bonzes (or sects?) may also have gone beyond proper Buddhist behavior with their guaranteed "tickets to paradise" that believers might keep on their body at all times, as Europeans kept their crucifixes, and even worse, as Frois reported to Maffei, "borrow, likewise, money to be repaid with great usury in another world, giving by obligation unto the lender an assurance thereof, the which departing out of this life he may carry with him to hell." (W:HOT?)

Of course, Frois never mentions any of the other ways – more lucrative than charms – by which his Church profitted on the afterlife in Europe. In Spain, and I would guess Portugal, at the time Frois wrote, one had to write a will to be properly buried, and *the law required all wills to request masses*. Needless to say, they were not free. The "Eager for Heaven" chapter of Carlos Eire's *From Madrid to Purgatory* was a real eye-opener for me. During Frois's lifetime, the number of such masses, believed to help speed up one's passage through purgatory, which might otherwise take thousands of years, with time discounted by suffering in this world ("a day of suffering in this life could count for a year or more in purgatory"), inflated from an average of a little more than 100 masses per testator to about 800 masses! Felipe II, who died a year after Frois, requested that all the priests of the Escorial (the royal cathedral *cum* mausoleum) say masses for his soul for nine days (nonstop, I presume), 30,000 such masses be repeated in the shortest time possible by the Franciscan monastery that "could do so with the greatest devotion (to be chosen by his executors)", a high mass, read from the altar directly above the royal mausoleum, "every day until Christ's second coming" (*Anyone, are they still doing it?*) and so forth . . .(E:MP) Not a few men left their entire estate for saying masses. I find myself feeling sorry for God when I read things like this. Can you imagine him sitting up there counting masses?

I cannot help but note that this is the only contrast where Frois mentions relics. A *Japanese* Frois would probably have found *our* practice worth a distich or two of its own:

> In Japan, the remains of a holy man is treated with respect, left whole, or cremated.
> In Europe, a saint is cut up into bits as one would cut up a notorious criminal.

Take Saint Teresa, dead in 1582, dug up in 1585. Two convents had dibs on her, so even before the gradual dismemberment began, we have a Father cutting off her left arm at the order of his superior, in order to compensate the sisters of the convent from which he was removing the body. He hated to do it, but "it was marvelous. Using no more force than would be needed to cut a melon, or some soft cheese, so to speak, he instantly severed the arm at the shoulder joint. Though he had not spent a long time trying to do it, the arm was cleanly separated from the body. (Ribera in E:MP) According to Yepes, "Her bones were white, and her flesh was soft, white and red. The shoulder remained dense and solid, as if she had died a few moments before." (E:MP432~)

> With us, the very idea of fondling parts of the dead is disgusting.
> With them, parts of Saints are kissed and placed over wounds.

When Felipe II lay mortally ill, he asked for and received "the entire knee of the glorious martyr Saint Sebastian, with all its bone and skin," which he kissed and held against his bad knee. He also got "a rib of St. Alban," in some way useful for releasing his soul from purgatory, and "the arm of Saint Vincent Ferrer," possibly because of his connections to "the angel of judgment." (E:MP)

4-35   The friars of St. Francis give some deceased the habit of their Order for free;
  Os frades de S. Francisco dão gratis o abito da sua Ordem a alguns defuntos;

> The bonzes make living men and women buy paper *katabira* [robes] with *hokekyô* [short title of the Lotus Sutra] written on them to wear when they die, and gain a lot from it. *Os bonzos fazem tomar em vida aos homens e molheres humas* catabiras *de papel com o* foqeqio *escrito nelas, pera levarem vestidos quando morrerem e os bonzos ganharem com isso pr[emio].*

Within a century of St. Francis's death, wealthy knights and ladies who made donations to Franciscans were able to be buried in their habits and before long, others (Columbus being one) who shared their millennialism, were also buried in the robes of their secular order and even today, lay Catholics ascribing to the Franciscans' simple life may do this though they no longer believe with the medieval noblemen that doing so might cause St Peter to mistake them for friars and give them a fast track through the traffic jam at the Pearly Gates. I know not why Franciscan robes were thought especially suitable and can only guess that the monks ascetic lifestyle made them most obviously deserving of reward in heaven and the hoods were the better for concealment!

Frois's description of Shogun Nobunaga's cold-blooded execution of everyone related to a political rival (Araki) in his *Historia*, contains an aside on these undergarments worn under the formal dress of 120 women who were crucified. He writes of *secret teachings and histories*, but I would guess it was the *sutra* he mentions above that was written in Chinese characters on robes which brought great offerings and incomes to the bonzes who "took advantage of this fraudulent practice." Frois claimed that only wealthy people could afford such robes (J/F:HISTORIA) "The Sutra on the Lotus of the Wonderful Law" is the full title (*Myôhôrengekyô* or Saddharma Pundarika Sutra). Since the warbling call of the *uguisu* (a little bird) happens to be the short version of the Sutra's title and it was enough to skip the sutra text and just repeat its *name* to invoke its content, the haiku poet Issa joined the bird with his flute to make gospel music with nature! But written language in the Sino-cultural sphere did not need to be evoked to be invoked. The writing could be cast upon the wind, each flutter of a sutra-lettered flag comprising a read; burnt or exploded to float up into heaven or be absorbed into the air; vibrated into heaven by being written around the bonze's hand-drum or upon a temple bell that is struck; "read" to the universe by rotation using human, hydraulic or wind-power; dissolved and drunk, or simply worn, like the robes here mentioned by Frois. Considering the cost of the countless funeral masses said in Iberia – In Eirie's words, "the dead made off with much of the nation's wealth" (E:MP) –it is a shame the Catholics couldn't come up with such labor-saving prayer devices (And some of those wheels could crank out a million prayers a minute! See *TT-long*).

4-36   Our priests hold funeral services for the deceased in churches;
  Os nossos sacerdotes fazem os saimentos aos defuntos nas igrejas;

> The bonzes hold it in the house of the deceased many times over, in order to eat and drink there. *Os bonzos em casa dos defuntos grande numero de vezes, pera comerem e beberem ali.*

Starting with "our" side, let me be rude enough to say that it just so happens that priests did not always stay in church. The 16c Spanish picaresque classic, *The Life of Lazarillo de Torme* is an eye-opener. Hired by a priest who claimed he was, as was proper for a man of the cloth, temperate in food and drink, the perpetually hungry Lazarillo found that "when we went to pray at meetings and wakes, where somebody else was paying, he ate like a wolf and drank more than a quack doctor. And, speaking of wakes, God forgive me, I was never a foe to humanity except on those occasions. Because then we ate well and I stuffed myself. I yearned, I actually prayed to God to kill off one of

His Servants every day." (A(M):LLT) *The Life* is fiction and the wake was at least limited to one-time-per-person, whereas Frois has "them" doing it "many times over." But wait, a highly documented study of the people of Cuenca (a town in La Mancha) by Sara T. Nalle reveals that, after an intense nine-day period of grieving, masses, and grave offerings,

> every day or on Sundays a female member of the deceased's household placed on the grave a gift of bread, wine, and wax which would collected by the priest. Despite the pagan connotations of the practice, the *añal* [annual] was considered a form of suffrage and was not openly condemned in the diocese's constitutions. The añal's function was very different from the ritual funeral banquets that existed at the time in most countries and until recently in some villages of Spain. The wake served to bind the living together in one cathartic dinner; the añal, on the other hand, in a sense prolonged the deceased's life, because for an entire year the dead person continued to be a mouth to feed and a drain on the family budget. (N:GILM)

This was true for the entire 16c. Unlike most pagan offerings, which were eaten by animals or the poor, here, the priests got it! The only difference is that the bonzes in Japan ate at the house of the deceased, whereas the priests apparently gathered theirs wholesale from the graveyards! And, believe me, we are not talking about the priests getting enough for a midnight snack, like we give Santa. By the second half of the 16c, a bonnet maker was giving "six pounds of bread, including a loaf of blessed bread, two maravedis' worth of wine, and two wax tapers" every Sunday and, "on Easter and the feasts of Our Lady, two pounds of stew and the same quantity of wine and wax; and finally, on weekdays, a pound of bread, one maravedi's worth of wine, and a wax tablet." (Ibid) Needless to say, nobles gave more.

Still, *in Japan,* if Frois's *Historia* is true, Christian funerals were a good deal compared to Buddhist ones. Frois pointed out that these services were such a burden on Japanese families that the much cheaper yet attractive Christian alternative was a major draw. Moreover, the missionaries were not averse to burying people for free, and poor people without relatives (for only relatives were allowed to bury or cremate someone), who might otherwise end up dragged to dunghills or the woods at night and left for the dogs to eat – or, worse, still alive and liable to be kicked out from their tenement as they lay mortally ill (so it would not be polluted by their death) – were strongly tempted to convert before dying.

Most funerals are still Buddhist in Japan, as most of ours are still Christian. They are usually held at home. Relatives gather to help with the cooking, cleaning, reception of guests, recording of gifts received, etc.. People sit around, reminisce and occasionally look at the deceased. Everyone lights a joss stick. Bonzes come and go and intone sutras. They surely played a much larger role in these affairs in Frois's time and, not unnaturally, enjoyed the repast. Most bonzes, like most mass-sayers in Iberia probably believed they were doing their work for the repose, or rather *bon voyage* of the soul. Speaking of voyages, here is a fine story from Eliza Scidmore's *Jinricksha Days in Japan.*:

> When the American man-o-war *Oneida* was run down and sank with her officers and crew by the P. and O. steamer *Bombay,* near the mouth of Yeddo Bay, January 23, 1870, our Government made no effort to raise the wreck or search for it, and finally sold it to a Japanese wrecking company for fifteen hundred dollars. The wreckers found many bones of the lost men among the ship's timbers, and when the work was entirely completed, with their voluntary contributions they erected a tablet in the Ikegami [temple] grounds to the memory of the dead, and celebrated there the impressive Buddhist *segaki* (feast of hungry souls), in May, 1889. The great temple was in ceremonial array; seventy-five priests in their richest robes assisted at the mass ... The scriptures were read, a service was chanted, the Sutra repeated, incense burned, the symbolic lotus-leaves cast before the altar .... No other country, no other religion, offers a parallel to this experience ..

Here, pace Shakespeare, we see it is not birth but *death* that makes all men kin. "They" are quick to say mass for anyone. "No other country" is overdoing it, but Scidmore's point is that the Buddhists are *kind.* I would add that when Toby, Alcock's favorite Scotch terrier was buried, sure enough, a "priest of the temple brought water and incense sticks to burn." (A:COT) *Good.*

4-37   For our clergy, yellow is a garish and indecent color;
   Pera os nossos relegiosos a cor amarela hé garrida e indecente;

   The bonzes think yellow or green decent and delight in wearing them.
   Os bonzos a tem por honesta e folgão de se vestir d'amarelo ou de verde.

It is interesting that the West should put down *these* colors in particular: *yellow*, which is close to gold and the color of *our* sun (pictured *red* in Japan) and *green*, the color of plant life! Is it, perhaps, that these colors are not closely associated with the body? Then, again, Frois does not say Europeans, but our *clergy*. In that case, *Is it evidence of "our" failure to find the sacred in Nature?*

In Japan, as was the case with Japanese generally, bonzes wore different colors according to the seasons. The yellow and green traditional Buddhist robes I have seen are, respectively, closer to *manilla* and *moss*, i.e. far from the primary colors one might imagine. In Japan, at least, only esoteric Buddhist high-priests (like "our" colorfully dressed high priests), *hari-krishna* evangelists (now found, together with Jehovah's witnesses, in Japan) and very marginal cults go in for truly bright colors.

4-38   Among us, the clergy of one order do not hate those of another;
   Antre nós não se tem odio humas religiões aas outras;

   The bonzes do, as it adds to their own *isei* [authority] and profit to abhor other sects. *Os bonzos antre si, pera seu yxei e proveito, aborresem as outras ceytas.*

The respective sides of the distich are not really commensurable because the orders to which Frois alludes are all fellow Catholics in broad agreement on the doctrine as interpreted by the Pope – Dominicans, Franciscans and Jesuits all belong to a single, albeit large, sect of Christianity (if Frois included the Protestants, "hate" would be too weak a term for how they felt about one another!) – whereas the bonzes belong to sects as different as (to use contemporary examples) Mormons, Baptists and Catholics. As far as I can see, "we" not only hated but did not permit two sects in a single country, and if it were in "our" power would not have allowed two in the entire world.

Frois begins the chapter 51 (chapter 29 of part 2) of *Historia* noting that "because all of Japan's religious rites were invented by the creator of evil himself, the devil, the bonzes live in a state of perpetual argument with one another and this is not only from enthusiasm about matters of doctrine for even people belonging to the same sect debate each other out of pride or to show-off." The precepts of the Pure Land sect may include Renyo's admonition against bad-mouthing other sects (written about 200 years before *Tratado*) but, in the 16c, even this sect (known by its detractors as Ikkô-shû, or One-way-cult) was aggressively proselytizing and friction was inevitable. So Frois is right about the Japanese side of the contrast. Indeed, he recorded a debate between this sect and the Hokke sect, judged by the atheist Shogun Nobunaga, which ended in the forfeiture of heads and demolishing of a head-temple of the Hokke side that was stumped by the question of what the character 妙 (myô), which Shaka preached for 44 years, meant. The victors did some fan dance and onlookers laughed and tore the robes of the Hokke bonzes and Hokke books that had been brought were shredded on the spot and, to make a long story short, Nobunaga forbade the Hokke sect to engage in argument from then on, not only with the Pure Land sect but with *all* sects! Considering the mean things the Hokke side said about other sects, and the fact that the Hokke sect pioneered the use of force as a means of spreading religion, one feels like applauding, but the truth was that Nobunaga was simply taking advantage of an excuse to do in a powerful rival and he probably did in the wrong side, for the above-mentioned "One-way" Pureland Sect had just "liberated," a large swath of central

Japan (the people, then paid them a tax far less than they paid to their lords) and were spreading like wildfire, and Nobunaga would soon have to fight a ten-year, bloody running battle with them to gain complete control of Japan. (S(R):WTUD)

~~~~~~

4-39 The sorcerers among us are punished and severely disciplined;
Os feiticeiros antre nós são punidos e castigados;

> The *Ikkôshû* and *Yamabushi* are delighted with sorcerers, for being sorcerers.
> *Os bonzos* Ycoxos e Yamabuxis *folgão com eles por serem feticeiros.*

The Yamabushi, literally "mountain warriors," dressed in strange robes and leggings, with strange necklaces, adorned conch trumpets and even weird one-stilt shoes, actually *look* wizard-like to us. They combine elements of esoteric Buddhism and shamanism. After undergoing terrifying ordeals and inhuman austerities in their mountain headquarters (See Frois's *"The Place of Confession"* in C:TCJ), they wander around the country exchanging magic for money. Frois writes that this company, "with curled and straying hair . . . make a profession to find out again things either lost or stolen. . . ." Frois writes that they sold curses as well as blessings, but the detail that I find most interesting is this:

> They set before them a child, whom the devil invadeth, called up thither by charms: of that child then do they all ask that which they are desirous to know. ("Yamabushi" in C:TCJ)

The large Ikkô sect is another matter all together. Their "sorcery" is more like evangelical Christianity practiced under a charismatic leader, where the spiritually charged atmosphere – or mass hysteria, if you prefer – gives rise to faith-healing and other "miracles." The head of the sect was venerated as a reincarnation of Amida, a manifestation of the Buddha. Faith in Amida alone was supposed to be sufficient to save one – again, we are reminded of the evangelical "Jesus saves!" This excerpt from Frois's fellow Japan-hand Vilela's description of "the Ikkô sect" says it all.

> They give this bonze so much money in alms that he controls a large part of the country's wealth [and like so many of our TV preachers, but more brazenly "he publicly maintains many women"] Every year a great festival is held in his [Amidabutsu? The sect leader?] honour, and so many people wait at the gate of the temple to enter that many die in the stampede which results when they open the gates. Such people, however, are considered very lucky to have died in that way and some at their own request are dropped into the crowd around the gates and are thus killed. At night he preaches them a sermon during which they shed many tears . . . (in C:TCJ)

Frois's contrast of "our" disenchanted religion and "their" sorcery-corrupted religion is ironic in that the first popular Christian inroad made in Japan, as described at length by St. Xavier, concerns Portuguese merchants who were unwittingly lodged in "some buildings left without inhabitants, because experience had proved that they were much infested by ghosts." Knowing nothing of this, "For some nights they were continually surprised to find that when they lay down to rest the clothes and the coverings of their beds were pulled off, without their being able to see anyone." To cut a long story short, they also saw "a terrible spectre" and discovered from a servant that "figures of the cross" repelled it. They made such a commotion, their Japanese neighbors heard, and after they told them what happened, "the Japanese confessed that the building had for a long time been infested by a certain evil spirit." The Portuguese told them about the efficacy of the cross and soon

> crosses made either of paper, or wood, or any such substance, were to be seen at the doors of nearly all the houses in the town; the natives, who were often wont to suffer great molestation from the visits of hellish ghosts, making use with great eagerness of the defense against such assaults which had been made known to them. (C:LLFX)

The same sort of event occurred with Ricci fifty years later in China. The Jesuits thought it proved they were holy, but it is more likely the Japanese and Chinese thought: *These water-sprinkling cross-waving fellows are powerful sorcerers!* Could we not say that sorcery and Christianity (or Islam) go hand in hand? Does not religion thrive in a climate of fear, where supernaturalism (by whatever label it chooses to give itself) will snatched upon? Is it purely coincidental that the country where Christians (albeit Protestants) were to make the biggest comeback in the 19-20c, Korea was a sorcery superpower? In 1565, Vilela wrote that Japanese "worship everything. They worship the sun, the moon and the stars. They worship sticks, stones, snakes, foxes, and many other things." This is a view often heard from Japanese intellectuals today, but it is and was a far cry from Korea, where daemons might be found, to quote Bird, "on every roof, ceiling, fireplace, kang [?] and beam."

> They fill the chimney, the shed . . . they are on every shelf and jar. In thousands they waylay the traveller as he leaves his home, beside him, behind him, dancing in front of him, whirring over his head, crying out upon him from earth, air and water. They are numbered in the thousands of billions, and it has been said [by Rev. G.H. Jones] that their ubiquity is an unholy travesty of the Divine Omnipresence . . . This belief . . . keeps the Korean in a perpetual state of nervous apprehension, it surrounds him with indefinite terrors . . . (B:KAHN, much more in TT-long)

Bird was *horrified* by how much of the income of the poor Koreans went to supporting the exorcisms performed by the shamans to relieve them of their fear. I would note that her description is a dead ringer for two other cultures I have read a lot about: the Malays and the Irish, the former mostly Moslem and the latter famously Catholic. From what travelers have written, Japan was simply not *that* spirit-ridden and I think that in 1585, "we" were closer to the three above-mentioned spirit-ridden cultures than to Japan. The strict punishment for witchery found in the West was, after all, *proof* of the depth of "our" belief in what we call superstition in other cultures. Take, for example,

> the case of Margaret Harkett, a sixty year old widow of Hammore, Middlesex, who was executed at Tyburn in 1585. She had picked a basketful of peas in a neighbor's field without permission. Asked to return them, she flung them down in anger; since then, no peas would grow in the field." (T:RDM)

This English *conte* would be amusing had it not ended as it did. At this time, it was usual for mediums in England to try to locate stolen goods for which they would receive 25% – far more than the Jammabo in Japan! Meanwhile, "in France, a decree of Henry III., in 1579, forbade all makers of almanacs to prophesy, directly or indirectly, concerning affairs either of the state or of individuals." (C:CBD) This was not because it was thought to be nonsense but because it was thought to be *diabolic*. Yet, this was also the time when the first rational challenges to the witch-hunts were being published and, soon, the refutations of the concept of witchcraft by several brave Jesuits and one extraordinary Inquisitor (Salazar, mentioned earlier) would put an end to the persecution of witches in Spain. Shortly after that, folk-history in Japan turned the Jesuits into sorcerers themselves. Even Frois might have been amused to see himself (the context suggests his involvement) depicted like this:

> Making handkerchiefs [*tenugui*] look like horses, throwing dust into the air where it turns into birds, making dead trees blossom, turning pebbles into jewels, sitting in the air, hiding in the earth, or instantly creating black clouds to rain or snow . . . (J/E:NBJ)

4-40 The *tabi* [socks] of [Japanese] laymen are black or olive brown;
Os tabis dos sequlares ou são pretos ou almecegados;

> Those of bonzes and noblewomen are white and made of cotton.
> *Os dos bonzos e das fidalgas nobres são branqos feitos de canga.*

Both sides of the above distich are Japanese. If a contrast with Europe is intended, does it mean our clergy and noblewomen wore dark socks/stockings and laymen wore white ones?

4-41 In Europe when a master dies, his servants, crying accompany him as far as the grave;
Em Europa por morte dos senhores os criados chorando os acompanhão ató à cova;

In Japan, some cut their stomachs, and many cut off the tips of their fingers and toss them into the burning pyre. *Em Japão alguns cortão a barriga e muitos as cabeças dos dedos e os deitão no fogo onde os queimão.*

There were many types of funerals in Japan. Frois describes a sumptuous funeral in the capital city of Miyako (Kyoto) with no split bellies nor chopped fingers at great length (C:TCJ). Here, he gives only the most outlandish example. But it was true. English factory director Richard Cox's description of the send-off for a member of the royalty in Hiradox (Nagasaki area) in 1621.

And there was one *bozu*, or prist, hanged hym selfe in a tree hard by the place of funerall, to accompany hym in an other world, for *bozu* may not cutt their bellies, but hang themselves they may. And 3 other of the dead mans servantes would have cutt their bellies, to have accompanid hym to serve hym in an other world as they stidfastly beleeve they might have donne; but the king would not suffer them to doe it. Many others, his friends, cut affe the 2 foremost joyntes of their littell fingers and threw them into the fire to be burned with the corps, thinking it a greate honor to them selves and the least service they could doe to hym . . . (C:TCJ)

The belly-cutting is, as far as I know, uniquely Japanese. The finger joint cutting – today, a monopoly of apologetic *yakuza* – is found in many Pacific island peoples and suggests Japanese are a partly Southern race. Gruesome fare, for sure, but no more bloody and far less outlandish than a good old-fashioned Norse funeral of a type not extant in Frois's time to be sure, described by the diplomat Ibn Fadhlan in 921-2 where the dead chieftain is joined by a favorite slave girl who supposedly volunteered and was treated kindly, feasting and going from tent to tent enjoying sex with many men before taking drugs, drinking, seeing her Master in the Other World, and being strangled under the supervision of an old woman called the Angel of Death after which the ship was burnt to ashes in an hour thanks to strong wind and the interpreter enthusiastically told the envoy that such was a far better send-off to heaven than being buried and slowly eaten by worms in the Arab way. (*Horizon* Spring:1975)

4-42 In Europe, Christians beat their breasts when begging for the mercy of God;
Em Europa os cristãos batendo nos peitos pedimos a Deus misericordia;

In Japan, the gentiles rub very vigorously on their beads.
Em Japão os jentios esfregão as contas muito rijo nas palmas das mãos.

Typically, *Mea culpa, mea culpa, mea maximo culpa!* (Latın), *Por mi culpa, por mı culpa, por me gran culpa!* (Spanish), *Through my fault, through my fault, through my most grievous fault!* is intoned while beating the breast with the right hand and reciting *El Credo* (the Creed) right before saying the words that Christ was crucified. Apparently, this practice was once more widespread.

In the absence of an icon like the crucifix, it would seem that prayer beads played a bigger role in Japanese Buddhism than they did in Christianity. Frois wrote *gentiles* rather than *bonzes* because Japanese Buddhist laymen also had beads. Frois does not kid when he says "vigorously." The grating sound made by the beads of ten or twenty believers in a house I walked by made a roar as deafening as that of the oil-cicada (*abura-semi*) coming from the nearby trees. Perhaps, I recall thinking, *this* is what made the cicada here so loud, *Nichiren* rosaries. While Frois brought up the beads here as a matter of contrast, how amazing this item (more in 5-18) could play so similar a role in two religions as distant to one another as Buddhism and Christianity!

endnote IV

Bonzes

> From the sociological point of view, the whole missionary system, irrespective of sect and creed, represents the skirmishing force of Western civilization in its general attack upon all civilizations of the ancient type . — Lafcadio Hearn (H:JAI)

In *Curious Land: Jesuit Accommodation and the Origins of Sinology*, D.E. Mungello found Ricci "morally, more complex than many historians have described him." He did well by most of the Mosaic commandments but disobeyed his parents in becoming a Jesuit [Didn't Christ welcome such disobedience?] and "showed some highly human equivocation in that most fundamental of Christian commandments – love." *Why?*

> His intolerance and dislike of the Buddhist monks in China was surprising in its intensity. The tendency has been to treat this dislike as part of a quite orthodox Christian opposition to idolatry and it was true that Ricci's dislike for Buddhists as idolaters pales to only moderate dimensions when compared to the standards of his times. Nevertheless, his dislike of Buddhists sharply contrasted with a normally sympathetic attitude toward the Chinese. (M:CL)

Mungello is surprised for the same reason he gave Ricci all the credit for inventing the policy of *accommodation, he fails to give sufficient attention to the Japanese side of the church* (Forgivable when you consider the book's focus was closer to its 1985 title: STUDIA LEIBNITIANA, SUPPLEMENTA 25!). By the time Ricci went to China, the Jesuits had been at war with the Buddhists in Japan for almost four decades and the tradition of respecting the people and their culture yet disrespecting the bonzes was well established. Genius or not, Ricci was part of that *tradition*; and so was Frois.

When, from day one, the Buddhists were attacked for allowing sodomy and infanticide, not to mention worshipping the Devil, they were more than ready to respond. Some sects dispatched preachers who came from afar to take on the new-comers. The trade connection and scientific know-how gave the Jesuits unfair advantage; so some Buddhists played political hardball and tried to get them killed. If soon-to-be Shôgun, the de-facto ruler of Japan, Nobunaga, had not quickly become fond of Frois, our author would probably have been assassinated long before *Tratado* was written, for in 1569, one enemy bonze managed to get the Emperor to sign a death warrant for any Jesuits found in the capitol. Nobunaga gave Frois a safe-pass and "told him, on the eve of his departure, in front of a vast concourse of Kyoto nobility, "Do not worry about either the Emperor or the shogun, because I am in complete control of everything. Only do what I tell you, and you can go where you like."(B:CCIJ) In those heady days when the Jesuits had this advantage over their adversaries, they were arrogant enough to use it. Frois's *Historia gloats*, I repeat *gloats,* over the horrendous destruction of idols on the part of himself and Fr. Coelho in 1582. Considering that cultural terrorism, I sometimes wish Nobunaga let Frois and gang reap the rewards of their rudeness! Then, again, when Nobunaga built Japan's first genuine stone castle (Nijo) in 1569, *he did the same*. Frois observed it:

> As there was no stone available for the work, he ordered many stone idols to be pulled down, and the men tied ropes around the necks of these and dragged them to the site. All this struck terror and amazement in the hearts of the Miyako citizens for they deeply venerated their idols. . . . and as all were eager to please Nobunaga, . . . they smashed the stone altars, toppled over and broke up the *hotoke* (buddhist statues), and carried away the pieces in carts. ("Portrait of a Ruler" chapter in C:TCJ)

While the Christians could not, themselves, do such things in the Miyako, the boondocks were another matter. There was a natural cavern that could only be entered by climbing a dangerous rock mountain on an island off Kyushu. "The Devil," Frois writes, "long ago occupied this terrifying place in order that it could be used for his worship." The bonzes borrowed "the wiles of the Devil" in devising ways up the sheer rock clifts using iron spikes and chain-link hand-holds. As Frois admitted, the extreme difficulty of visiting the site made it a popular place of pilgrimage when Arima belonged to the Pagans. They found the cave to "be close to overflowing with Buddhist idols, all of which were strange figures, very intricate, exquisitely made, so that it would be impossible to think of any better ones than these." Yet, our Christian vandals removed them – burning the ones too large to take out without breaking up – and with the help of their Japanese followers, paraded them back to their quarters where they used them as firewood, basking in the heat of their exploit the whole winter long!

Two things make this *especially* reprehensible. *First*, most of these statues were there because of earlier Christian persecution. It is bad enough to persecute others, but to *pursue* them in that way is *cruel*. Eight years earlier, "because the Japanese are born with such a quick intellect," the local people after hearing only one sermon, turned into a Christian mob and went out burning down temples and destroying idols (and worst of all, some non-Christian retainers were forced to use their own "idols" for firewood). All of this Frois records matter of factly in his *Historia*. And only two years earlier, at Valignano's bidding, the lord of Arima dismantled or destroyed all the Shinto and Buddhist temples – more than forty in all, and some renowned throughout Japan – in his realm and forced the bonzes to convert or emigrate. (S:VMP) Since Shintô was included in that religious cleansing campaign, we can see the action was not just a case of competitive exclusion, either, for Shinto, unlike Buddhism, is not at all like Christianity. Coelho had correctly surmised that some idols were saved and hidden in that cave! And, *second*, that very year, Valignano wrote: "we must show great love for Buddhist bonzes. We should especially refrain from rejoicing at their misfortunes, despising them and others and saying bad things about them. This attitude is particularly disliked by the Japanese; not only does it not raise our prestige, but gives us a bad reputation." The Japanese translators of *Historia* also note that the local tradition of the cave is completely different from Frois's story. What is remembered by Japanese is how some Christians hid out there after the Shimabara insurrection (the war of 1638, where thousands of Christians and oppressed peasants held out in a castle for so long that the Bakufu – Tokugawa government – gave up its plan to try to liberate Luson! ("Liberate" because some Tagalogs had requested it.) and would have escaped had not the departing officials noticed some white smoke coming out of the cave as they departed. They returned and climbed for the Christians. When the Christians had nothing left to throw at their pursuers they cut off and threw the heads of the statues at them and when these ran out they were captured. I like to think the smoke came from a burning idol.

While cultural destruction is a crime and a tragedy, sometimes the little triumphs of "our" benighted crusaders found in Frois' *Historia* are so funny one can't help but laugh aloud. A Buddhist monk shoots into a house in revenge after idols are destroyed and, missing the priests, tells them he will convert if only they don't tell his master and get him in trouble. Of course, they let him and gain a good Christian. A typhoon tosses the head of a popular Kaizodera (a temple for seamen) image into "the really dirty [cesspool beneath the] toilet of one of its biggest believers" and "the next day it was discovered there in the place most fitting for an idol." I am grateful for the amusement, but cannot help saying "Come on, Frois, *grow up!*" But, then, Frois's intellectual formative years (age 16-31) were spent in Goa, a city literally built on religious spoil, parts of destroyed pagodas. Moreover, the mentality of these men was basically one of a being a special agent in enemy territory In Kyoto, literally ringed by hundreds of Buddhist temples, Frois wrote to a friend in Portugal,

> Think of a man from Morocco come to Lisbon, where Christianity prospers, to build a mosque. That is how I stand in the Japanese capital, . . . (M:RPJ)

Still, I cannot help wonder whether Frois, who had by this time surely known some morally impeccable Buddhists, had any qualms about it; or whether the more Japanized Organtino, who was also in the capital for a long time, would have gone along with such mean-hearted behavior. I also wish I could see into Valignano's heart to see whether he pulled the above-mentioned about-face only for the pragmatic reason he gave – the Jesuit image in Japan – or because, after getting to know the heathens better, he had begun to feel ashamed for his and his Society's behavior!

In the end, it was the Christians' turn to cry. The destruction of shrines and temples, and persecution of Buddhist priests, not to mention compelling people under Christian lords to adopt their faith were two of the main reasons given by Nobunaga's successor Hideyoshi for outlawing Christianity, after which martyrdom followed upon martyrdom until Tokugawa Iemitsu's regime took the art of torture to new heights. Horrific details are provided by the far from popish Caron in his 44 page-long description of *the persecution of the Romish Christians.* Since the Christians seemed to welcome such easy executions as crucifixion, beheading and even getting burned at the stake, we find women dragged naked through the street, "ravished and lain with by Ruffians and Villains," or worse, then thrown "into deep tubs full of Snakes and Adders, which crept by several passages into their bodies;" executioners putting out parents eyes "and placing their little Children by them, pinched and plagued them whole daies long, enforcing them with tears of blood to cry to their helpless Fathers and Mothers for an end to their sufferings." Meanwhile, back in Macau, every major martyrdom was treated as a touchdown on the way to winning God's game and fested with "horse-races, fencing matches, fireworks, masquerades, comedies and plays" (B:CCJ?).

Since the object was not so much *killing* Christians as *making them recant*, eventually, a master torturer arose who managed to break them without killing them. Caron claims this Governor *Onemendonne* rooted all Christians out of Hirado/Nagasaki in 45 or 46 days with only one casualty. His method was to take them to Arima's sulfurous "Hell-spring" and continually ladle corrosive hot water over them by day, and keep them awake in cramped huts built over the boiling water at night, while skilled physicians treated them so the torture was as constant as possible without killing them. (C:DOJ) Boxer, speaking of Iemitsu's reign (1623-51) summed it up as follows: "Neither the infamous brutality of the methods which he used to exterminate the Christians, nor the heroic constancy of the sufferers have ever been surpassed in the long and painful history of the martyrdom of man." (B:CCJ)

Lest the chapter leave a bad impression of Japan – for destroying things is not as cruel as killing people – I would like to peg on another observation of Boxer's: "at the martydom of de Angelis and his forty-nine companions at Yedo in December, 1623, no attempt was made to prevent the Jesuit's preaching to the crowd, and to such effect that two of the bystanders rushed forward and vainly begged the presiding judges to let them join the martyrs . . . It is perhaps worth reminding the reader that in contemporary Europe no such evidence of sympathy for the victims would have been permitted among the onlookers [the crowd even sang hymns with them!] at the hanging of the Roman Catholic priests in London, nor at the autos da fé for the Jews in Lisbon." (Ibid) No, our slaughters, in Europe, were carried out more cruelly and, unlike the case where Japanese had reason to fear the take-over of their culture if not state, for no reason other than greed, superstition, religious righteousness and cruelty. While the Portuguese *only* slaughtered Jews now and then, the Spanish, thanks to their age-old struggle with Islam, had a burning agenda to rid Europe of all infidels for good. After Felipe II united most of Europe, including Portugal, under his favorite state, Spain, in 1580, the earlier tolerance (?) whereby Jews were allowed to be baptized and pretend to be Christians and so forth, that had weakened with the coming of the Inquisition to Portugal in 1536, disappeared completely, and all Jews were fair game. Even Neo-Christian *dead* Jews! One such was Jerónimo Dias, a leading physician in Goa whose remains were "exhumed and solemnly burnt . . . in accordance with the posthumous punishment inflicted on crypto jews who escaped the stake in their lifetime" (G:PPI) – this at the same time *Valignano was pushing through his policy of Accommodation in Japan!*

V

OF TEMPLES, IMAGES AND THINGS THAT TOUCH ON THE WORSHIP OF THEIR RELIGION

dos templos. imajens e cousas que tocão ao culto de sua religião

5-1   Our churches are long and narrow; *As nossas igrejas são compridas e estreitas;*

   The temples of Japan are broad and short. *Os templos de Japão largos e curtos.*

Frois's perspective is from the front of the building. To enter a Christian church is to enter a long hall called a *nave* from the end, or *vestibule*, which traditionally was to the West. Since this corresponded to the foot of the cross, a wedding procession that "goes down the aisle" actually goes *up* it. But what matters for this contrast is that it is an aisle, something long and deep.

Buddhist temples, on the other hand, are usually *faced*, as one might face a stage, rather than entered. Like most Japanese traditional buildings, they are open and if there is any aisle it is the veranda that encircles it. One can generally walk *around* that and peer in. Often, that is far enough. Or, one can ring the bell outside from the ground and talk to the priest seated within and go no further, for all can be seen from without. This could be *Faux Froised* as follows:

Our churches have a door that is larger than a house's but smaller than a barn's;
Their temples have doors wider than a barn's for they are as wide as the building itself.

Valignano warns of the importance of guarding this difference while constructing Catholic churches in Japan, lest the church resemble a "devil's temple." (Okada)

As was the case with the last chapter which the title claimed was on *bonzes,* whereas from our perspective, it was on bonzes *and* the clergy of Europe, the title here only mentions the Buddhist "temples." While the Portuguese word *igrejas* has a different root than "church," the translation is clean because both words are only used for Christian places of worship, whereas "temples" as a generic term can be used for other faiths. Japanese are even more discriminating in their vocabulary, for, as with many things, they use completely different terms for native and foreign religions. A small Shinto shrine – a simple wooden building with roof-beams crossing in the fashion of a two-dimensional tepee – is a *yashiro* and a larger one a *jinja*, a Buddhist temple, a *tera* or *otera,* and a church a *kyôkai*. The *kyôkai,* literally "teach-meet" means a society of people sharing a common teaching and, as a building, came to refer specifically to a (Christian) church..

5-2   Ours have choir-lofts, and pews or chairs on which to sit;
   As nossas tem coros altos e banqos ou cadeiras em que se asentão;

   The bonzes pray before their altar seated on *tatami* [mats].
   Os bonzos rezão diante do seu altar asentados nos tatamis.

Pews and chairs were a relatively recent addition. Eastern and Orthodox Christians remain standing throughout the service. The choirs were high in the heart of the church. Could the angel metaphor have made it possible that the singers, though their social position was below that of the priest – and many in the congregation – were they free to occupy an exalted position?

Buddhists seated in a broad room in a temple do not generally pay as much attention to an altar as we do to a preacher on his pulpit. With Zen meditation, one cannot say they "pray," either.

Despite widespread agnosticism in Japan today, almost every Japanese *family* has an altar, whereas it is uncommon for even religious Christians in the USA to have the same. The reason is partly because most Japanese Buddhists did *not* go to temples regularly the way we *attended* church and partly because, after the Christians were kicked out of Japan, the authorities made membership in local Buddhist temples and the owning of a Buddhist altar mandatory in order to keep track of people. I like these little places/furniture for the spirit that serve Shinto (reflection), Confucian ([ancestor] reverence) and Buddhist (prayer) – sometimes in one and sometimes in separate altars.

5-3 We have books put on a common stand for all there to sing together;
Nós temos os libros postos em estante pera todos ali cantarem juntos;

Each bonze has his altar in front of him, and each his book.
Os bonzos tem cada hum diante de si hum banquinho e cada hum seu livro.

Another case of Japanese individualism – or, should we just say, personal usage? This may reflect, as DR opines, the more individual meditation or devotion of the Buddhist as opposed to the emphasis on communion on the part of the Christians sharing in the "body of Christ." It may also have physical causes: 1) the Japanese are not a very touching people; 2) the Japanese had better (i.e. cheaper) printing available; 3) sitting cross-legged does not permit people to get close. But DR has a point, for the singing/chanting by the Japanese is also far less orchestrated.

5-4 Our books are folded and bound with clasps;
Os nossos livros são dobrados e fechados com brochas;

Those of the bonzes' are rolled up and tied with a ribbon.
Os dos bonzos emrolados e atados com huma fita.

Hinged metal clasps held our books tightly together on the open side, making it hard for silverfish to steal the food for thought, or the unauthorized to read, I guess. The last time I saw an old book (an 1871 Bible) with one, the two clasps kept the open side tightly shut but the spine of the book had split in two right down the middle!

The Japanese "ribbons" are finely woven tape-like cords of the same type used as bookmark in Japan. But why was this contrast *here*, rather than Chapter 10, *Of Writing*? Is it because the switch from scroll to book was slower inside temples than on the outside, so the contrast was greater? The flat rectangular secular books in Japan were made of paper much better than "ours" which, like the books we now own, could stay as shut as a sleeping mimosa without a clasp to help!

5-5 Our images are, for the main part, painted retabulo;
As nossas imajens pola maior parte são de retabolos pintados;

The images of the *varelas* [temples: see 3-8] of the Bonzes are all sculpted.
Nas varelas nos bonzos todas as imajens são de vulto.

The *retabulo* is a stand placed behind or above the altar, generally made of ornate wood or marble and containing one or more panels with paintings or low relief generally treating Christ's passion and/or saints. The Buddhist images – and, to Frois's credit, he does not use the prejudicial term of "idol" here – were generally cast or carved in wood. In order to justify this contrast, we must focus on the central images, near the altar. Otherwise, we can find abundant Catholic sculptures and Buddhist paintings.

5-6 We use diverse colors for our images;
Nós uzamos nas imagens de diversas pinturas;

> They gild all of theirs from top to bottom.
> *Elles dourão as suas todas d'alt'abaxo.*

Our images, in retabulo or sculpted, were generally painted in color, as were those of the Classic world. The figures inside the main temple, generally the manifestation of Buddha best reflecting the philosophy of the sect (and/or the founder, himself such a manifestation) are usually gilt but, as Frois knew, the rest usually were not. Guardian demons are red, *Arhat* plain stone, and some saints, as life-like as the fake people "installed" by a modern artist in some mall.

Could Frois mean to suggest that *ours* are not sinful *gilt images*. Think about it. The Old Testament decried not "images," but "*gilt* images.". And, loh and behold, the Japanese ones were just that! Christians have the same problem with gold (and silver) they have with the body. They both love and hate it too much. On the one hand, it is the perfect symbol of truth, incorruptible and, together with the sun, was identified with Christ; on the other hand, its impermanence is material and contradicts faith in the immaterial eternal world. Alchemy in the West might be seen as an attempt to resolve this contradiction, or should we say cultural schizophrenia. In China and Japan, alchemy was so completely absorbed in the matter of longevity, that gold played a far smaller role. Be that as it may, secular Western visitors found the gilt much to their liking. The Englishman Richard Cocks found them "very fresh and glorious to behould." (C:DORC)

The whole idea of images in other religions created by "our" Old Testament is one big mistake. I am delighted to find a best-seller such as Karen Armstrong's *A History of God* get that straight. After quoting a particularly detestable passage of Hosea on sacrificing and blowing kisses to silver calves, she comments:

> This was, of course, a most unfair and reductive description of Canaanite religion. The people of Canaan and Babylon had never believed that their effigies of the gods were themselves divine; they had never bowed down to worship a statue *tout court*. The effigy had been a symbol of divinity. Like their myths about the unimaginable primordial events, it had been devised to direct the attention of the worshipper beyond itself. (A.HOG)

I doubt Frois understood this. And, I wonder how many Christians and Moslems do today.

5-7 All of ours [the images] are proportioned to the human stature;
As nossas são proporcionadas todas hà estatura dos homens;

> Some of theirs are so big that they resemble giants.
> *Algumas das suas tão grandes que paresem jigantes.*

In medieval European paintings, as in paintings throughout the world, important personages were often depicted larger than others around them. Why, then, no huge statues of Jesus or Mary? Did the counter-example of ancient "pagan" sculpture make anything large a "graven idol?" Or was largeness thought rightfully a monopoly of God alone? Secular visitors to Japan, like Cocks, generally approved of the "wonderful bignes" of "The Hudge Collosso" in Kyoto, though one Dutchman could not resist calling it "the mother of all devils." (in C:TCJ/notes) and the Mexican-born Rodrigo de Vivero y Velasco (interim Governor of the Philippines, shipwrecked off the coast of Japan in 1609) concluded that "only the devil could have devised this waste in order to make the Emperor use up his wealth and riches." (in C:TCJ)   Kipling, viewing the *daibutsu* (literally "large Buddha) at Kamakura, penned more fine imagery in a single page than the whole imagist school would ever produce: "Little blue and grey slated figures pass under its shadow, buy two or three joss-sticks, disappear into the shrine, that is the body of the god, come out smiling, and drift away through the shrubberies. A fat carp in a pond sucks at a fallen leaf with just the sound of a wicked worldly little kiss. Then the earth steams and steams in silence, and a gorgeous butterfly, full six inches from wing to wing, cuts through the steam in a zigzag of colour and flickers up to the forehead of the god." And he had what can only be called an epiphany:

> To overcome desire and covetousness of mere gold, which is often very vilely designed, that is conceivable; but why must a man give up the delight of the eye, colour that rejoices, light that cheers, and line that satisfies the innermost deeps of the heart? Ah, if the Bodhisat had only seen his own image. (in C+W:KJ)

While Frois's contrast is couched in neutral terms, his idol-destroying past tells us that he probably felt the Japanese side was *bad*. I cannot help wondering what he would have thought about the fundamentalism in Northwest Europe, which came close to destroying all churches – as Moslems did to all images of the human body – for even churches were considered idolatrous by the purist of the Puritans!

~~~~~~

5-8   Ours are beautiful and inspire devotion;
As nossas são fermozas e que provocão á deva[>o]são;

Theirs are horrid and frightening with figures of flaming demons.
As suas horrendas e temerozas com figuras de diabos abrazados em fogos.

Since "theirs" cannot be both gilt (as in 6 above) *and* burning red, Frois should have said "*some* of theirs." More important, the contrast, though true, could be the other way around:

> Our chief religious image, Jesus, is usually depicted expressing horrible agony upon the cross;
> Their chief religious image, Buddha, is usually shown sitting relaxed with a serene smile.

As the sweet Madonna and Child offset the Passion, the Buddha with his eyes contentedly shut offsets the dreadful bulgy-eyed muscle-bound demons that served to ward-off evil spirits or guard this or that Buddhist treasure. Actually, Frois knew by first-hand experience that some of "theirs" were like "ours," i.e. beautiful. In a letter (Englished by Willis) he wrote: "In the midst of their temples is erected an altar, whereon standeth a wooden idol of Amida, naked from the girdle upward, with holes in his ears after the manner of Italian Gentlewomen, sitting on a wooden rose, goodly to behold." And in another letter, he describes gilt sculptures so brilliant "the sight is enough to blind you with "beautiful faces are so well carved that, but for the fact that it is a temple of Amida, this scene would make a good composition of place for a meditation on the ranks and hierarchies of the angels." (C:TCJ)

Many, if not most of Buddhism's "horrid and frightening" demons are converted local deity, like "our" cynocephalic St. Christopher, whose beastly powers were enlisted on behalf of his new religion (See David Gordon White: DOGMAN). Such demons are peripheral presences for most Buddhist sects but there were sects and temples where they were central. Fishing villages generally prayed to a powerful *tengu*, a long-nosed goblin with mountain, hence wind-influencing ability, who, like St. Christopher was the patron "saint" of travelers. *Tengu are red.* But so is Fûdômyô-ô, literally "the unmoving-light/bright-king" (identified with the Hindi Acala) who was thought to sit fast upon a metal-filled mountain, his countenance glaring like molten ore, with an upraised sword (to severe the deep-seated appetites of the flesh) in hand. There are esoteric Buddhist temples for this god, who was the patron deity for blacksmiths. Yes, he is scary. But his sword, you might note is put to a less bloody and far more edifying use than the indiscriminate slaughters "our" God carried out, according to the Old Testament. Moreover, it should be noted that the red is not just molten power but a charm against evil.

It is about time to qualify Frois's "ours." In 1585, half of "us" were no longer with him. The wholesale destruction of "Catholic idolatry" by Protestants in Switzerland in the 1530's, England in the 1540's, the Netherlands from the mid-1560's and elsewhere make his decimation of the Buddhist art of South Japan seem small peanuts. Here is the tolerant Reformist Erasmus describing an early 1529 outburst in Basel:

> Not a statue had been left in the churches, in porches, on facades, or in the monasteries. Everything frescoed is lost under coats of whitewash. Whatever would burn has been thrown into the pyre, everything else has been hacked into small pieces. Neither value nor artistry prevailed to save anything. On the first of April, the city magistrates approved the outburst . . . (H:CER)

Fearing that the mass destruction would end up destroying all authority, in most of North Europe the attack on Catholic "idolatry" was managed less dramatically by dismantling, storing and selling. Regardless, it is a sad story.

~~~~~~

5-9 We have our bells on very high towers;
Nós temos os sinos em torres muito altas;

> They, low, so close to the ground they may be touched.
> *Elles em baixo muito perto do chão, que lhe chegão com a mão.*

Japan did not have tall structures. Temples with large bells were usually on mountain-sides, on solid ground, yet high enough that the sound would permeate the town below. Our high bells attracted lightning, which was far less of a problem in Japan because the bells were generally lower than the top of the surrounding trees and they were not like bulls-eyes right on top of the building.

Perhaps it bears pointing out that the Chinese were *not* topsy-turvy to us here, for they had bells on the top floor of high pagodas. A 13-story Dragon Pagoda is depicted in Headland's Chinese Mother Goose Rhymes. I suspect that competition with Muslim minarets in West China would have fueled a race for the sky in the towns, something which the Japanese, luckily (considering the earthquakes), never had to engage in. Alternatively, it may reflect the more heavenly orientation of the Chinese.

~~~~~~

5-10 Our bells are tolled and have the clappers attached within;
Os nossos sinos se dobrão e tem o badalo da banda de dentro;

> Those of Japan do not move and are struck from without by a pole like a battering ram. *Os de Japão estão sem se moverem, e tanjen-nos de fora com huma tranca como vayvem.*

When you think about it, our method of tolling bells is matrist, female-active. The ding or the dong called a clapper just hangs there and the concavity does the moving, swinging back and forth until contact is initiated! Actually, that is also how a small hand-bell works, as opposed to the gong where only the striker is moved. Hanging and swinging the huge bells that became common in church towers during medieval times was no easy business and required wheel-like devices the function of which I will not even try to explain. By the early-16c, Europe's great cathedrals boasted 10-ton bells.

We tend to identify large bells with the West, the world's largest *working* bells are actually found in Burma, Korea, and Japan (the 70-ton bell of Chioninji Temple in Kyoto made in 1636 being the largest in Japan today). They are close to the ground and, despite being concave bells rather than gongs, struck in the manner Frois describes for Japan. The striking pole is correspondingly huge. 3-500 pounds and 10-20 feet-long, it is swung back and forth horizontally, building up momentum like a pendulum using a pair or more of ropes attached to each side until, with one final swing, it is launched into the bell like a battering ram, at which time one of the monks letting go sometimes does a backwards flip around the rope (See *TT-long* for Kipling's 1889 masterful description of the pounding of a bell he mistook for an earthquake) .

Shinto Shrines and temples with Shinto connections have yet another type of bell, a gong which visitors (usually after making an offering and a wish but often just for fun) sound very gently by swinging a rope with a knot higher up – they are usually about ten feet up, just under the eaves of the temple. Because one has to put a wave into the rope to get anything more than a muffled sound from the gong, it is ideal for little children to play with: they cannot make enough noise to disturb anyone – speaking of which, Thomas Paine once wrote with respect to the proposal of Camille Jordan to restore the Catholic privilege of Bell-ringing which was taken away by the French Revolution:

> As to bells, they are a public nuisance. If one profession is to have bells, and another has the right to use the instruments of the same kind, or any other noisy instrument, some may choose to meet at the sound of cannon, another at the beat of drum, another at the sound of trumpets, and so on, until the whole becomes a scene of general confusion. (1797? http://www.infidels.org/library/historical/thomas_paine/worship_and_church.html)

While the fact that going to church was mandatory, bells were expensive (people were poor), and, some argue, the vesper bell was first used by conquerors to enforce a curfew, all give credence to Paine's apprehension, his aesthetic sense is not mine. Most people in the West and Japan would, I think, agree that one need not be religious to appreciate bells ringing at dawn, mid-day and dusk. They add a patina of pathos to the natural world and quicken us in ways hard to describe.

~~~~~~

5-11   Our bells toll for festivals, and do it many times;
Os nossos sinos se repiqão polas festas e isto muitas vezes;

>   Theirs never toll for they do not have clappers.
>   *Os seus nunca se ripiqão porque não tem badalos.*

Since the Japanese used bells to mark the time, there *was* repetition, but it wasn't the frantic cling-clanging the clapper makes possible. Still, I recall hearing the bells struck over and over and over on New Year's Eve. I did not count, but the *joya-no-kane*, literally, casting-off-[the last]night-bell which now rings from before-to-after midnight is supposed to sound 108 times. If you live in a hilly area with many echoes, believe me, it sounds like solid bells! It was supposed to purify (or perhaps exorcise?) the 108 sins of mankind and that idea came from China some time before Frois.

But, what did we ring *and* toll "our" bells for? Romans expressed gratitude to the gods for success in battle by ringing bells mounted on chariots in victory parades. Church-bells were first used to summon the faithful to religious services and sound an alarm when danger threatened. The Pope sanctioned their use in 604 and a ceremony for blessing them soon followed. By the 11c, church-towers boasted the large bells we know. These often had poems inscribed in them:

> *Laudo Deum verum plebem voco congrego clerum*
> (I praise the true God, I call the people, I assemble the clergy;)
> *Defunctos ploro, nimbum fugo, festa decoro.*
> (I bewail the dead, I dispense storm clouds, I do honour to feasts.)
> *Funera plango fulmina frango sabbata pango*
> (At obsequies I mourn, the thunderbolts I scatter, I ring in the sabbaths;)
> *Excito lentos dissipo ventos paco cruentos*
> (I hustle the sluggards, I drive away storms, I proclaim peace [after bloodshed].)

Note the Latin rhyme has a peal! Or, in English with a wee couplet in each line: "Men's death I tell by doleful knell; / Lightning and thunder I break asunder; / On Sabbath all to church I call; / The sleepy head I rouse from bed; / The tempest's rage I do assuage; / When cometh harm, I sound alarm." I do not know the date for this poem, but following England's break with the Catholic church, Latin inscriptions such as the above poems or simply *"Ave Maria,"* or *"Sancte, ora pro nobis,"* were replaced by very English doggerel, such as the following complaint, warning and boast respectively, from *Chamber's Book of Days* (C:CBD).

> Of all the bells in Benet I am the best,
> And yet for my casting the parish paid lest.
>
> Repent, I say, be not too late, Thyself al times redy make.
>
> My sound is good, which that you hear,
> Young Bilbie made me sound so clear.

Those English! I think you can see why Catholics liked to stick to Latin! But better is yet to come. Catholic countries had something called a "passing bell," which "was rung slowly when a death was imminent in the parish. When the sick person was near his end the solemn tones of the bell reminded the faithful of their Christian duty of praying for his happy death and for his eternal repose; and after his spirit had departed, the bell tolled out his age – one short stroke for each year . . ." (LR) And, something called "the ringing of the Angelus," which a Catholic trumpets has "nothing resembling it in Jewish and pagan rites." For, "all religions, it is true, have had certain times for prayer; but they have had nothing at all like our Angelus, which consists essentially in the reciting of certain prayers at the sound of a bell at fixed hours." (LR). But more interesting yet, is the existence of a period when bells were *not* tolled. It is from "the end of the Gloria of the Mass on Holy Thursday and the beginning of the Gloria on Holy Saturday, when the Church begins to anticipate joyfully the Resurrection of our Lord." So, *what do these Catholics do with their cuckoo clocks?*

5-12   At our monasteries, there are iron clocks;
Em os nossos moesteiros há relogios de ferro;

The clocks of Japan are only of water.
Os relogios de Japão são somente de agoa.

In the Middle Ages, most clocks in the West used water, too, *for power*. Water-powered clocks had gears but they were only used for moving the fancy automata that put on a show to *tell* the time. In a word, clocks were not for *keeping* time, but *sounding* it. *Clock*, itself comes from OHG *glocka*, OIr *clocc*, meaning "bell." Gears to move hands and dials which could be *read* did not appear until about the 14c and by the mid-15c, most towns had these mechanical clocks. They pretty much had to, both to show they were not lagging other towns and because both the ecclesiastical and secular authorities saw clocks as conducive to good order. By 1585, most European clocks had gained a second-hand and not only monks but hired workers were already following the clock in their chores; but I think we must be careful not to tie these clocks too tightly to the development of capitalism in Europe, for all 16c European visitors found the Japanese and Chinese, who lacked the European-style mechanical clocks, the more industrious workers. The *similarity* Frois forgets to make explicit in this contrast is that the temples, like the churches, were responsible for telling time for all. Indeed, the Chinese character for "time"時 is comprised of the sun/day radical 日 and the character for "temple"寺.

The water clock mentioned by Frois is a "leak-hour," (*rokoku*) in Chinese characters, but the pronunciation was reversed at times and given a native Japanese pronunciation (*tokimori*): the Calendar and Time Department of the Imperial government includes "hour(time)-leak-doctors" (*tokimori-no-hakase* (Okada), though *sand* clocks were quickly gaining ground at the time. These, together with sundials, did the trick for the "hours" and another element, *fire*, also contributed to marking smaller units of time. Rodrigues mentions bonzes using a "very ingenious fire-clock" burning a dry scented powder in "a continuous line of furrows of a determined length, breadth and depth in the form of a square" (C:TCJ) and, within a century, in the pleasure-quarters, a customer's time would be measured by slow-burning sticks of incense. Since incense in Japan was more commonly burnt for the repose of a dead soul (for this reason, the hippie-inspired incense boom in the West did not catch on in the East) senryû about courtesans burning them for dead Johns are particularly poignant.

The Jesuits had the latest European technology with them, and this included the portable clocks invented in the first part of the 16c such as the "Nuremberg Eggs" of Peter Heinlein. They served the Jesuits not so much for keeping time as for proving Western technological superiority (naturally, attributed to Christianity) and keeping in the good grace of the rulers they presented them too.

~~~~~~

5-13 We have twenty four hours between night and day;
Nós temos antre noyte e dia vinte e quatro oras;

> The Japanese have but six hours of night and six of day.
> *Os japões seis oras de noyte e seis de dia somente.*

Until the spread of the geared clock in Europe, "we" had twenty-four uniform hours only twice a year, at equinox, for the twelve hours of day and twelve hours of night divided the actual night or day length, which varied according to the season, into equal units. Japanese still used different length night and day hours in 1585 and that is why Frois wrote "six hours of night and six of day" rather than twelve hours *between* the night and day. I must admit, however, to being confused as to what the church did with its *matins* and *media-dia* and *vesper*, for, to my mind at least, they would not match a system of twenty-four uniform hours (Probably, some observances follow the real sun.).

Actually, the Japanese had the modern system before we did. In the Nara and Heian eras (8-12c), the Court had a system of uniform length hours (*teijihô*), but changed, in the opposite direction as Europe, back *to* the varying length system (*futeijihô*) which better accommodated the common folk who could not afford a good water-clock and had to depend on the sun, i.e. follow the seasonal variance. But, this method was paradoxically, hard on the classes that did have good clocks, for convenient though it may be for marking *dawn* and *dusk*, cutting up hours of a different length every day with good clocks (water or mechanical) was *more* difficult as it requires constant adjustment. Rodrigues described how, with the above-mentioned (5-12) *fire*-clocks, "the furrow is made proportionately longer or shorter according to the length or shortness of the day and night." (Ibid.) When Japanese automata masters copied the new mechanical timepieces, some managed to accomplish the difficult task of making them adjust (in a semi-automatic manner) to the seasonal change.

Were Japanese hours uniform, they could arguably be said to have had the same number of hours as we did, for the *six* hours really subdivide into *twelve* units because each numerical hour marked the *midpoint* of a time-unit called by a Chinese zodiac animal's name, rather than the end of one unit and the start of another as is the case for our hours. This meant that half of the zodiac animal's time was over when the (two-of-our-hours-long) hour struck, and half remained, and if we think of the *before* and *after* portion as separate hours, eg. the *pre-rat* and the *post-rat* hours, the usable units come to a dozen for the day and a dozen for the night. In the older uniform system of the Court, the 12 big hours called *shinkoku* were subdivided into four quarters so one could speak of Rat 1 or Cow 3 and thereby be specific to within 30 minutes! So if Japanese in Frois's time might be said to have had *half* as many hours as we did, they once had *twice* as many!

~~~~~~

5-14   We count hours, one, two, three up to twelve;
        Nós contamos as horas de huma, duas, tres, até doze;

                The Japanese count them in this manner: six, five, 4, 9, 8, 7, 6, etc.
                Os Japõis as contão desta maneira: seis, sinqo, 4, 9, 8, 7, 6, etc.

Here, "our" side is as natural as can be, while the Japanese side is *apparently* unnatural, for it is incomprehensible without an explanation, such as Chamberlain's in the introduction, though he began at *nine* rather than at *six* like Frois. If you recall, there was no 1, 2 or 3, *because the first three strokes of the bell that told time were for the purpose of catching one's attention.* So 1 o'clock is 4, and 6 is 9. Frois probably began with 6 because most people in Japan in Frois's time thought of the dawn as the start of the day. .Judging from the fact that midnight is the rat-hour (or "mouse-hour" if you prefer, for the Chinese term includes both), and said animal leads off the Chinese zodiac, I imagine that once upon a time, midnight was the start of the day, as it has been since I-forget-when in the West. To me, this distich is clear proof that the *Tratado* was intended to be used as a teaching tool and not read without explanation.

~~~~~~

5-15   We adorn our churches with boughs and strew it with rush and narcissus;
        Nós hornamos as igrejas com ramos e as juncamos com junqo ou espadana;

                The Japanese mock this, saying we turn our churches into thickets or gardens.
                Os Japões zonbão disso, dizendo que fazemos das igrejas matos ou ortas.

There is no little irony here, considering the fact Buddhist temples and Shinto shrines long occupied and thereby protected Japan's best old-growth forests, while the Christians went about cutting down the same because it was revered by the native religions of Europe. A church adorned in green: *the oasis in a desert partly of its own making!* Robert Chambers described Palm Sunday when England was still Catholic:

> The flowers and branches designed to be used by the clergy were laid upon the high altar; those to be used by the laity upon the south step of the altar. The priest, arrayed in a red cope, proceeded to consecrate them by a prayer, beginning, "I conjure thee, thou creature of flowers and branches, in the name of God the Father," &c. This was to displace the devil or his influences, if he or they should chance to be lurking in or about the branches. He then prayed – "We humbly beseech thee that thy truth may [here a sign of the cross] sanctify this creature of flowers and branches, and slips of palms, or boughs of trees, which we offer," &c. The flowers and branches [local trees such as box, yew or willow were substituted] were then fumed with frankincense from censers, after which there were prayers and sprinklings with holy water. The flowers and branches being then distributed, the procession commenced . . . When the procession had moved through the town, it returned to church, where mass was performed, the communion taken by the priests, and the branches and flowers offered at the altar. (C:CBD)

There were also funeral garlands for women who died unmarried that were hung in church, and evergreens of Christmas decking churches as well as homes – not until the New Year as we think, but until February! – which periodically were attacked as being of pagan origin as they indeed were.³ But, I think there is a very good chance that Frois is not just talking about Holidays, but the way the churches were decorated *every Sunday*. If you recall, "we" did not have clean floors. How did the church cope with this? In England,

> In the Herball to the Bible, 1587, mention is made of "sedge and rushes, the whiche manie in the countrie doe use in sommer-time to strewe their parlors or churches, as well for coolness as for pleasant smell." The species preferred was the *Calamus aromaticus*, which, when bruised, gives forth an odour resembling that of the myrtle; in the absence of this, inferior kinds were used. Provision was made for strewing the earthen or paved floors of churches with straw or rushes, according to the season of the year. (C:CBD)

The strewing of rush not only in church but everywhere in England was noted by travelers from the continent. I failed to find anything on nature and the Luso-Iberian Catholic church of Frois's time, but the existence of special flower gardens for church flowers and an abundant symbolism of flowers suggests they had a regular place in church, even on the altar (see John S. Stokes, Jr. *God's Flowers* for much, much more.) I would also like to hypothesize that the Christian practice of bringing *fola* into the church, *however it is rationalized*, may reflect the exigencies of the architecture. Western buildings (excluding the open Roman public buildings) tend to have tiny windows. In the event they are large, as DR aptly notes, they "function not to reveal nature, but employ nature (sunlight) to relate a narrative in stained glass." In Japan, the windows are as tall as doors and as wide as the walls are wide. They go from corner post to corner post. The Japanese temple (or house, for that matter) is wide open to nature and/or the artificial nature of the garden. So there is little call to bring it *in*. Even today, Japanese are still not as liable to fill their homes with greenery as we are. The *bonsai* generally sit on the verandas which fringe the house and which become entirely visible when the windows which are bigger than our doors are open. All this holds true for temples as well.

This is not to say the Japanese were completely averse to using greenery for adornment. They stand two cut branches of pine in artistically cut green bamboo vases in front of their houses on New Years Eve (One red pine, one black pine, Yin and Yang, respectively). And, according to Cocks, there was another occasion which was even greener:

> This day is a feast in Japon, of their great profit or god, Shaka, whoe, as they beleeve, died a month past & rose againe this day, being the 8th of their moneth of *Singuach* [*shigatsu*=fourth-month]. Wherevpon they deck all the eaves of their howses w'th greene bowes, in remembrance of his rising from death to life . . . (1617 C:DORC)

Buddha's *death*day was on the equinox but, as far as I know, his birthday, which took place quite a while *before* his death, was not thought of quite in the Easter-like manner Cock's interprets it. Aside from these holidays, the only place in Japan that was identified with greenery was outdoor water-closets, "huts of green-leaved branches" created for Imperial travelers (Kaempfer:1692). Perhaps, this also explains why the Japanese were so shocked with the green church!

5-16 Our candles are thick at the base and thin above;
As nossas candeas são grosas no pee e delgadas em riba;

    Those of Japan are thick above and thin at the base.
    As dos Japões grosas em riba e delgadas no pee.

The West usually made candles from tallow (animal fat) – bee's wax candles were a luxury item – and the dip-drip method of candle-making was common, whereas the Japanese relied on sebiferous trees (mostly the "wax tree" sumac) for vegetable tallow, which was best shaped by hand. The Western method of production explains the shape of our candles, but the Japanese does not. So I'll guess. *First,* Japanese wax runs just enough to look good hanging down from the upper edge, while not covering the surface of the candle, which was often decorated with an auspicious and artistic motif and, second, the Japanese are one of a minority of cultures that almost always puts very wide heads on phallic-looking things (the male member is often depicted as a veritable mushroom) so that the candle just seems natural with a broad top. Note, however, that these candles are not only broader on top but slightly convex when viewed from the side. This gives them a crisp, elegant silhouette that ours, for all their fancy candelabras (another missed contrast: *Japanese have none*), lack.

5-17   Ours have wicks of string;   *As nossas tem pavios de fiado;*

   Theirs of wood and rush stem.   *As suas de pao e miolo de junco.*

We find it hard to *feel* how important candles once were. "The 1579 procession inaugurating the Royal Chapel of the Cathedral [in Seville, Spain], for example, consumed 25,000 pounds of wax candles. Candlemakers thrived when the Inquisition held an auto . . ." (Mary Elizabeth Perry "Crime and Society in Early Modern Seville"   THE LIBRARY OF IBERIAN RESOURCES ONLINE.)   But, here and in the last item, Frois contrasts *expensive candles* used in churches and temples. The candles of the common folk in both countries were cruder. In England – I do not know about Iberia – lard-saturated rush candles provided light for the poor man. Rev. Gilbert White in his *Natural History of Selborne* explains the process of preparing such candles from start to finish. (also in C:CBD)

I am not confident about the exact nature of the Japanese candle referred to. The following observation by Morse suggests it is the central *tube* of the rush which is used:

> The wick consists of a hollow tube of paper; the candlestick has a barb of iron instead of a socket, and the opening in the wick allows the barb to fit into it securely. Such a candlestick, long extinct, was known in England as a "pricket" candlestick. . . . The economy of this shape is seen when the piece of candle burning low is taken off the pricket and adjusted to the top of the new candle, so that not a particle of candle is wasted. (M:JDD)

The reader may find three contrasts with our candles in Morse's short but dense description! But, reading it, still does not explain the wood.   (I did not understand Okada's Chinese quote. Perhaps a thin stick of wood serving as a wick passes through the tube of the rush.)

5-18   We pray advancing our beads to the front;   *Nós rezamos deitando as contas pera diante;*

   They pray drawing theirs always to the back.   *Elles rezão deitando-as sempre pera detras.*

   The roots of "our" beads are debated. I read that monks as early as the 3c in Eastern Christianity used beads, they first appear in a Europe in a 7c tomb of a holy abbess, the more common 33-bead "worry beads" favored in South-east Europe either derive from Christ's age or from Islamic 99-bead prayer strands of which they were a common divisor (the 100th bead marking the 100th name of Allah which only a Camel knows.) and that Islamic traders brought the practice of prayer beads from the East, where the practice was found in Buddhism ever since the Buddha directed a king to thread 108 seeds of the Bodhi tree on a string. Whatever the story is, the early use of beads by the Christians was not what it is now. Serving as talismans against disease, with coral thought particularly efficacious, and adornment when other adornment was forbidden, they were not a little pagan and only were officially *sanctified* while Frois was in Japan, when Pope Pious V decreed St. Dominic (1170-1231) the official inventor of the Rosary. The correct name for a string of Catholic beads is a *chaplet*, but it is usually referred to as a rosary, from *rosarium*, or "rose garden," considered a good place to pray with thorns and red blossoms to evoke the passion and red ones to evoke the holy virgin. Strictly speaking, it is not the *charm,* but a device by which a set number of prayers are recited with the beads helping to keep tally.

The Japanese *juzu,* of course, is used in different ways. Quite aside from the different vector of movement – which a Catholic friend assures me does not hold true for Greeks (Orthodox?) who use one hand and pull the beads as the Japanese do rather than using two hands and pushing them forward – the Buddhists tend to zip along at a syllabet a bead, whereas the Catholics go at a snail's pace, reciting a *Hail Mary* prayer for each bead. But they sure *look* alike! Percival Lowell:

> The resemblance so struck the early Catholic missionaries that they felt obliged to explain the remarkable similarity between the two. With them, ingenuous surprise instantly begot ingenious sophistry. Externally, the likeness was so exact that at first they could not bring themselves to believe that the Buddhist ceremonials had not been filched bodily from the practices of the true faith. Finding, however, no human agency had acted in the matter, they bethought them of introducing, to account for things, a *deus ex machina* in the shape of the devil. They were so pleased with this solution of the difficulty that they imparted it at once with much pride to the natives. You have indeed got, they graciously, if somewhat gratuitously informed them, the outward semblance of the true faith, but you are in fact the victims of an impious fraud. Satan has stolen the insignia of divinity, and is now masquerading in front of you as the deity; your god is really our devil, – a recognition of antipodal inversion truly worthy of the Jesuitical mind! (L:SOFE)

Lowell knew *nothing* of the Jesuits' achievements in Japan, for he continued "perhaps it is not matter for great surprise that they converted but few of their hearers." Actually, they did *far* better than the Christian missionaries in Lowell's era, or *ours,* for that matter. Moreover, I am not certain that Jesuits were really *that* upset about the similarities. True, Xavier, before he even got to Japan, learned of "monasteries" and "habits, with long sleeves almost like our friars", people "praying on their knees as we do at home," while their men of religion "also recite prayers at sunrise, at midday and in the evening," and this "in a language not understood by the common people, just as our priests in Latin," and, finally, that they teach there is "one Supreme God" and a "Purgatory, Paradise and Hell," (LR) etc.; but he seemed to regard it as some distant if benighted, offshoot of Christianity. If the Catholics had any reason to react as Lowell claimed they did, it would have been, perhaps, in reaction to the English, Dutch and German visitors who took every opportunity to exaggerate these similarities (mostly, the use of "idolls") to make Catholics look bad. (The Jesuits, for their part, thought the tendency of popular Buddhism to promise salvation to sinners who simply believed and invoked the names of the Amida or Shaka was "properly the doctrine of Luther." (Valignano:1583) This, in a 1596 *Lettera annua* from our "Luigi Frois" to Rome: "If your powerful God could create the world with just a single word, then why cannot men be saved with another single word?" asked the bonzos to the cristianos, who gave an adequate response. (IBID n48):

If the Devil cleverly modeled Buddhism on Christianity, he did not stop with the Catholics but even had room to include Protestants, although it is true that they do not use prayer beads.

5-19 Our deceased go with their hair as it is when they die;
Os nossos defuntos vão com seus cabelos asi como morrem;

> Those of Japan, men and women, must go shaved.
> *Os de Japão asi homens como molheres hão-de yr rapados.*

Europeans find nothing particularly off-putting about hair. Jesus had long hair and a beard. So do many saints, and angels are all pictured with hairy heads. Blonde hair even took on the positive aspect of purity and light. When the tonsure was invented, it was more for the purpose of distinguishing the humble world-renouncing monks from the proud world-loving aristocrats who happened to cultivate long hair. Or it followed after orders of knight who required full or partial head shaving for the Vigil of Arms that preceded the knighting ceremony because "sacrificing one's hair was seen as a sign of devotion to God." (LR) Or it was done because a ring-like tonsure stood for Christ's crown of thorns or, the corona, according to Isidore of Seville, a crown of authority such as the tiara worn by Hebrew priests, etc.. She also came up with an explanation the first half of which sounds Buddhist: "By this sign, the vices in religion are cut off, and we strip off the crimes of the body like hairs. This renewal fittingly takes place in the mind, but it is shown on the head where the mind is known to reside." Be that as it may, the symbolism never went so far as to tie in with the other world.

All Buddhists knew that hair stood for decoration and the worldly desire = sin that went with it. Hair was not something one would want to take to the other world. Since death was departure from this world, it was like joining an order. Thus, shaving was a sort of cross between an *ordination* (as you may recall, the deceased got a Buddhist name) and a *last-rite*. In 1585, the traditional idea that a person was supposed to have his or her head shaved just *before* dying (and, becoming an apprentice bonze-at-home, get a good earful of sutras on one's deathbed) was in the process of changing to the easier Edo era practice of shaving the dead (who, as a *fictive neophyte* heard the sutras while being borne off to be cremated). Eventually, the shaving itself was often economized to just part of the head or even making a motion as if it were being shaved while intoning the proper words.

Frois's "*go* with their hair" and "*go* shaved" is *ambiguous,* but, as we shall see in 5-22, many Japanese were cremated rather than buried, so he could not be more specific.

5-20   Our caskets are long and narrow;   *Ha nossa tunba hé comprida;*

   Theirs are round, i.e., half a cask.   *E a sua redonda, id est, huma mea pipa.*

"Ours" applies to all classes in most of Europe. "Theirs" refers to the coffins of the commoners in some, possibly most, parts of Japan. Cornwallis, in 1858, describes the Japanese casket as "a sort of tub about three feet high by two and a half in diameter at the top and two feet at the bottom." (C:TJJ) That seems about right; a Japanese source has one meter twenty centimeters.

Sitting coffins (*zakan*) are the most common type for people who bury their dead in clay pots. In Japan, they go back to the Jômon age (10,000 ~300 BC). In the Kôfun, or mound-building age (300-600 AD), more variety is found with stone and wooden boards creating house-like, ship-like, square, rectangular coffins as well. Eventually, most wealthy people ended up with sleep-type (*nekan*) coffins with two layers (i.e. a casket inside). I say "most" because I once read of a luxurious sitting coffin giving the deceased space to be properly seated (the cross-legged meditation position called *agura*, I think). Considering the shaven hair mentioned above, this would let one go out like a saint.

The "half a cask" coffins mentioned by Frois were no longer pottery but wood, which was lighter to transport. All the websites claim they became *the* way for commoners to be taken off for burial or cremation in the Edo era, when they were honestly named "quick-tubs" (*haya-oke*), for they were constructed on-the-spot if it were by specialists in barrel-making (there were no undertakers per se). All viewers of television Easterns are familiar with them and I would guess that many Japanese do not recall how long they survived. As late as 1946, 72% of people cremated in Kyoto were in sitting coffins. This dropped to 55% in 1952. (web LR) With the Westernization of culture, the idea of *death as sleeping* caught on and with cars for transportation, lightness is no longer a problem, so sitting went out. Doubtless it remains in small communities with crematories not made to fit lying coffins.

5-21   Our dead go lying down, with their faces up;
Os nossos defuntos vão deitados com o rosto pera riba;

>   Theirs go seated, bound up with the face placed between the knees.
> *Os seus vão asentados e amarrados com o rosto metido antre os jiolhos.*

"Our" posture is ideal for viewing someone and, perhaps more importantly, as DR notes, "in keeping with the Book of Revelation, Christians have long anticipated that the resurrection of the dead would begin with trumpet calls and other great signs in heaven. Thus, the logic of being buried face up." Of course, "we" did not *look* straight up but *toward the East*, and this was assured by placing the head of the coffin to the West. The wealthy minority who were buried or cremated on their backs in Japan ask for a *Faux Frois:*

> *Our dead lie with their heads to the West so they can better look East for the Awakening.*
> *Their dead who lie, do so with their heads North and faces turned to the West, their Paradise.*

The North was associated with death and the West, which is, after all, where the Sun sets, was the Pure Land Paradise. Here, I think, an argument could be made for the Japanese being linear (East → West) and the Europeans cyclic (East → East)!

The curled-up position Frois describes is that of the true economy-class coffin, for it reduces the volume of the casket making it lighter and easier to carry (two men typically sufficed) and less space-hungry in the graveyard. As far as the details go, on February 20, 1565, Frois wrote "the hands are pressed together like someone praying, and the head bends toward the ground looking at the place the unfortunate soul will be buried." Oliphant wrote that "according to old Arnoldus Montanus [hardly reliable!], the old women are placed in these [caskets/graves] in a sitting posture, *with their hands separated, and their faces turned as though looking over their shoulder"* (*italics mine*: O:EMC) while the men, "seated in a devotional attitude with their hands clasped" are as Frois describes. Either way, it seems to me that the position is basically fetal. With the hair shaved off, we get an image of a baby getting reborn into the womb of the earth. In this connection, I might point out the obviously vulvic tombs found in the parts of Japan that were not completely Buddhified, such as Okinawa. Maybe Buddhism picked up on that and found the posture suitable for they too spoke of rebirth. The only difficulty involved the *stiffs*. People do not usually curl up when they die. Cornwallis in 1849 wrote that "they bend it so it may accommodate itself to the described coffin, the joints being rendered flexible by means of a certain dosia powder[1] which is universally applied to that end after death.."

---

1. *Dosia Powder.* Thanks to Cornwallis, I finally understood where the sand came from that 18c *senryu* have widows throw at the standing part of their dead husbands – embarrassing because such was how men with *jinkyo* (a wasting disease where the bed-ridden men are marked by priapism that poets blamed on good-looking wives) were reputed to die! It must have been that same *dosia* powder! (Whatever *that* is!)

5-22   We inter our dead; *Nós emterramos nossos defuntos;*

>   The Japanese, for the most part, burn them. *Os Japões pola mayor parte os qeimão.*

It puzzles me how Christians, whom one would assume could keep the dead body and soul apart better than, say, animists who find soul everywhere, could come to feel that the corpse needed to be kept entire the easier to be reassembled for the Judgment Day. Apparently, the idea that only burial was sanctioned by the Bible was further justified by taking the *dust to dust* idea literally. The part that goes up in smoke would be cheating the earth of its own. Still, martyrs and people with communicable diseases, etc. were occasionally burnt, and in 1972, the Catholic Church finally came to accept cremation, with the qualification that the ashes be buried and not taken home (as is done in Japan and much of the East) or scattered in the air or sea (wrong elements). Before Christianity, cremation was common in many parts of Europe, but by Frois's time burning was thought of as a punishment and was done to punish the bodies and hence the souls of the executed.

The Japanese changed in the opposite direction. In ancient times, the dead were buried or, especially in the case of the nobility, entombed in mountain caves – one of my favorite *Manyôshû* (c760) poems (#3806) has a brave girl taunt her cowardly lover that if worse comes to worst they can always hide from her father by holing up forever in one of those "stone-forts" – and their spirits were identified with the clouds wafting off such mountains. Buddhism introduced cremation. It allowed descendants to keep clean shards for *memento mori*, and provided a speedy visible demonstration of the immateriality of existence. The smoke of cremation conflated with the animistic clouds born in the mountain caves to remain a favorite topic for the noble poet. A thousand years later, the far-from-noble haiku poet Issa, celebrates surviving yet another serious illness by playing on that trope, though he was not one of the elite who would be cremated: *"New tobacco! / not becoming smoke myself / i take a toke"* (keburi to mo nara-de kotoshi-no tabako kana).

In Frois's time, only the upper 10% or so of the population, if that, would have been cremated, so we can observe how for *this* contrast he chose the burial method of the elite, whereas in the previous contrast he chose that of the commoners in order to better create his contraries.

Today, cremation is the first choice, for Japanese have more money than room and feel more comfortable with a clean burn than the idea of slowly rotting. Most families have small "grave" sites, where a portion of the cremated shards may be interred but a portion is often kept at home. [1]

> *We visit the deceased at the cemetery and only keep the relics of Saints at hand;*
> *They keep shards of their loved ones at home and do not have many relics.*

The finely crafted wooden shrine, usually about the size of a large bathroom mirror-box, which is to say the Buddha-shelf/altar or Kami-shelf/altar, gives a proper place to such remains which rest within a small urn. In this way, the living, and if you believe in them, the dead, may be consoled without going all the way to the cemetery. Now that most of "us" (I hope!) no longer confuse this tender and good custom with "worshipping one's ancestors," we might do well to adopt and adapt such a device for cherishing *our* dead.

---

1. Shards in Japan Since Japanese cremation is not as *hot* as Western cremation, the bones are not completely pulverized. One website points out that when bodies in the sitting position were cremated the bones got all jumbled up, but now they are cremated while lying down, the bones are very clearly laid out and this gave rise to the custom of picking out a few choice bones to keep (the so called throat-buddha (voice-box?) or *nodo-botoke*, in particular). Lest this sound strange, let me add that nothing in Japan comes close to matching the two Capuchin churches in Rome which arrange bones into fanciful flower shapes, chandeliers, and many other whimsical designs! (For a finely nuanced blog discussion of the Capuchin churches and the Catholic perspective on the new possibility of *turning one's loved ones into diamonds* (no joke!) by Fr Jim Tucker (priest of the Diocese of Arlington, in Northern Virginia) *Dappled Things* donjim.blogspot.com/2002_12_01_donjim_archive.html).

5-23   We keep our images and *nominas* inside of our rooms;
   Nos temos nossas imajens e nominas dentro nas camaras;

The Japanese nail them up outside their doors to face the street.
   Os Japões as tem pregadas(!) foro das portas pera a banda a rua.

A *nomina* is "a sack/purse for relics" *or* "a written prayer/sentence[*oráçio*] kept inside of a sack/purse to free us from evil." The best the French translation could do was *"les livres de prières,"* but can you imagine a "prayer book" nailed to a door? The German, by Schutte, a Jesuit, himself, *"Andachtszettel"* or, "devotion-slips[of paper]" is better but they really are "charms" as the Japanese translation (*gofu*) renders them, though Catholic readers may object at the pagan word. But what else can you call it? Inside, even from within a pouch, the *nominas* would *fill the room* like perfume with a blessed and protected atmosphere. But the Japanese, like most people, concentrated their efforts on *keeping out* the bad and *bringing in* the good. This meant paying attention to *the portals*. The gate, door or door-frame were the most common places to stick or nail charms. Kaempfer described a number of these protective devices "printed upon one half sheet of paper."

> The most common is the black-horn'd Giwon . . . the Ox-headed Prince of Heaven, whom they believe to have the power of keeping the family from distempers, and other unlucky accidents, particularly from the Sekbio, or Smallpox, which proves fatal to great numbers of their children. Others fancy they thrive extreamly well, and live happily, under the protection of a countryman of Jeso, whose monstrous frightful picture they paste upon their doors, being hairy all over his body, and carrying a large sword with both hands, which they believe he makes use of to keep off, and as it were to parry all sorts of distempers and misfortunes, endeavoring to get into the house. On the fronts of the new and pretty houses, I have sometimes seen Dragons , or Devil's heads painted with a wide open mouth, large teeth and fiery eyes. (K(S):HOJ)
>
> ..

The Chinese make an even more perfect contrast with "us" in the way they use charms, for they not only post them on the door but sometimes put them on walls *a distance from the house* so strangers could read them and thereby heighten their efficacy! (Something like the 20th century Usanian practice of people praying for others in church.) As DR points out, Frois (and my) inside = us, outside = them equation is a bit too pat, for "Europeans also placed gargoyles, crosses, and other Christian and pagan symbols on the outside of homes, churches and castles to ward off evil spirits."

~~~~~~

5-24 With us, after the funeral, relatives of the deceased go into seclusion;
Antre nós emserrão-se os parentes depois das exequias do defunto;

> In Japan, after the funeral, they give a banquette for the bonzes and others attending.
> *O Japões depois do e ter emterrado dão hum banqete aos bonzos e aos que o acompanharão.*

The Catholic wake was typically held for a couple days *before* the funeral, but in Eastern Europe banquets were held upon the grave, so chances are that in Frois's time there was Japanese-style post-burial eating, drinking and reminiscing in some parts of Europe. Japanese may not have secluded themselves immediately after the funeral, but they probably practiced a measure of seclusion. Today, people who can afford to do so take a long time off work to live in a semi-retired manner and rather than exchanging the usual beautiful greeting cards or visits on the following New Year, they send out a special card ahead of time asking others not to send them greetings.

~~~~~~

5-25 Among us, someone who changes faith is considered a traitor and apostate;
Emtre nós se tem por elche e arrenegado o que muda e lei;

> In Japan, one may change sect as often as one likes without infamy.
> *Em Japão se troca a ceita cada vez que hum qer sem nenhuma infamia.*

The "faith" is the 7th meaning of the "law" (*lei*) in the *Novo Dicionário Aurélio*. The Japanese translations make it *oshie*, or "teachings," Schütte's German and the French translation "his belief/faith" (*seinen Glauben / su croyance*). But it is hard to tell if Frois means the faith = law of a particular order, such as the Society of Jesus or that of the entire Catholic religion as represented by the words of the Pope, who, I might add, is called the *Law-king* (*hôô*) in Japanese!

The Japanese side confirms the greater religious *tolerance* (a good thing!) or *laxity* (a bad thing!) of the Japanese, compared to the, spiritually-speaking, totalitarian West.

5-26   Our baptism is done with many ceremonies and solemnities;
Ho nosso baptismo hé com muitas sirimonias e solenidades;

> In Japan, it suffices to put a book on the head to join any sect.
> *Em Japão basta pôr hum livro na cabeça pera ficar daqela ceita.*

I doubt Japanese actually placed books on their head. Frois really means they lift it up, over and slightly in front of the head, as they would offer something to a superior or receive something from a superior (even out of his presence) in order to show their reverence for the teachings or sutras of that sect. This would be *the public part* of someone's first step to becoming a bonze. There is more going on *in private* – training and tests, head-shaving ceremonies, etc – he missed.

5-27   We ask one omnipotent God for favors in this life and the other;
Nòs pedimos a hum só Deus todo poderoso os bens desta vida e da outra;

> The Japanese ask *kami* [Shinto *god/s*] for temporal good, and *hotoke* [Buddha/s] only for salvation. *Os Japões pedem aos Camis os bens temporaes e aos Fotoqes a salvasão somamente.*

The chapter *"On paying visits"* in Rodrigues's book on Japan gives us a fine window upon the significance of this division. On the New Year's everyone visits the Shinto Shrines and exchange greetings, but the bonzes, who regularly make house calls do not –

> For people regard it as an ill omen for the bonzes to enter their homes at the time of the festive New Year which they wish to begin well so they may live long years. But it is the bonzes' office to teach the way to the next world and the people have no desire to go there too quickly; nor do they wish to speak with the bonzes for their talk is about the things of death. Many people are so superstitious that during these days they will not use certain words which either signify death or have a similar pronunciation . . . (R(C):TIJ)

Shinto for birth and *Buddhism for death, or Shinto for happy occasions* and *Buddhism for sad ones*. In Japan, unlike Europe, both native and imported religion managed to survive by retaining separate niches. Native gods for *this* life and foreign gods for *that*. When Buddhism first came to Japan there was friction, with rulers pushing their favorite, epidemics and other natural disasters taken advantage of to argue that the behavior of one side or the other was being punished, and so forth. But in the end, live-and-let-live won: there was some amalgamation and a division of interests – call it, specialization – and competitive exclusion was avoided! This happened to a degree in Europe (see Flint: THE RISE OF MAGIC) but not so successfully in the long run (see Thomas: THE DECLINE OF MAGIC). Japan's millennium-old system was threatened when the modernizing Japanese leadership gave death, too, to Shintô at the end of the 19c. It was restored after World War II, but the anomaly is brought to our attention every year when debate arises about the propriety of politicians attending the Yasukuni-jinja (head Shinto shrine) observance for those who fought and *died* for their country (right or wrong).

This is the only contrast in these two faith-related chapters that even mentions *Shintô!* A few *Faux Froises* to close the gap:

> *Our priests and educated worshippers generally have read and know the Bible.*
> *Even their priests, if so they can be called, often know nothing of their own Shintô faith.*

That is what is so delightful about Shinto. Its hodgepodge of folk custom is *something,* but it is wonderfully beyond intellectual grasp. Kaempfer notes that they have their "sacred and sublime mysteries" (as do our shriners), but the temples "are not attended by priests and ecclesial persons, but by laymen, who are generally speaking entirely ignorant of the grounds and reasons of the Religion they profess, and wholly unacquainted with the History of the Gods, whom they worship." (K:HOJ) Moreover, Japanese themselves often made fun of their own Shinto mythology *in print* – I have read an Edo era *senryu* that discovers a model of the island of Japan congealing from the primordial sea in a clump of fecal matter floating in a septic tank!

> *Our churches are not in the business of predicting fortunes on any basis.*
> *Their shrines sell* omikuji, *pieces of paper with good and bad fortunes written on them.*

The fortunes are written on pieces of paper folded up tightly which you draw. If you get a great one you may make another contribution; and if you get a bad one, you tie it up on a tree-branch or a fence or something at the shrine and leave it there to get purified so it hopefully won't come true and draw another, hopefully better, one! Trees covered with these look very pretty, but it is probably uncomfortable for them, and I think they would run away if they were only animals.

> *Our God is always in.*
> *Their gods are out for a month every year.*

Japanese (Shinto) gods are bound to caucus in Izumo and wait on the Emperor "'tho in an invisible manner, during the tenth month." (K:HOJ). The subject is a favorite for Edo era haiku poets who found many ways to metaphysically relate the absence of the Gods to the falling leaves, fine fall days and other natural phenomena of the season. Poor Issa has a poem easier for this equally poor writer to relate to: "Poverty my pal / it's high time even you / hit the road!"

> *Our Pope is a man who, with God's guidance, works hard running the only true Religion;*
> *Their Emperor is himself (supposedly) a god who, like their idols just sits and does nothing.*

The Emperor (or Empress, though the 19c introduced a sexist tradition that will, I think, soon change) is directly descended from the top Shintô gods and generally does little other than performing rites such as the first rice-planting, attending sumo matches related to the prognosis for that year's agricultural production, etc.. He was something like the modern English monarch. Scholars, forgive me, but Mrs. Busk's 1841 medley of 17c Dutch writing is too entertaining not to include:

> ..
> He determines the days on which certain religious festivals [of Shinto] are to be celebrated, the colours appropriate to evil spirits, and the like. One other sovereign act, if act it may be called, he daily performs, which would seem to show that, in virtue of his identification with the goddess of the sun, he is considered quite as much the patron divinity as the temporal lord of Japan. He every day passes a certain number of hours seated upon his thrown, perfectly immovable, lest by turning his head he should bring ruin upon that portion of the empire towards which or from which he might happen to direct looks, thus by his complete immobility maintaining the whole realm in a state of undisturbed happiness and tranquility. After he has been seated the requisite number of hours, he resigns his place to his crown, which continues on the throne, as his substitute, during the remainder of the day and the following night. (B:MACJ)

It does, however, help us understand why Frois, with his down-to-earth contrasts based mostly on observation, *avoided all mention of the Emperor!* But he might have caught this:

Our churches have a door, a portal that opens directly into the building;
Their shrines, a pair of pillars with two bars on top at a great distance from the building.

These *torii* mark the boundary between sacred and profane ground. The ends of the crossbars over-reach the pillars and the upper one is especially large and slightly upturned. A simple sketch of one on a map designates a shrine, as a reverse swastika serves for a Buddhist temple. Usually they are either natural wood or bright red!

Our churches have a vertical-horizontal cross on top of the steeple;
Their shrines have no steeple, but the roof-beams cross diagonally like the letter X.

This design seems to hark back to those of ancient times. A 2-D teepee!

Our most celebrated churches took decades if not centuries to build;
Their most famous shrine is torn down and rebuilt every twenty years.

The great shrine of Ise. *Always new, it is the oldest extant shrine (as opposed to ruins) in the world.* The modern pundit Rudolfsky sneers: "Their propensity for destruction is sometimes worked off in rituals: unwilling to wait for lightning to strike or some such sign from the gods, they tear down the Great Ise Shrines every twenty years to rebuild them in their identical image." (R:TKM) I see it as a monument to *the power of mortality*, an expression in architecture of the choice made by the ancestor of the people in Africa (or was it America?) who, asked to chose *the way of stone* or *the way of wood*. An individual stone outlasts a tree, but eventually wears down to nothing, while a tree can survive forever in its offspring. The ancestor chose right and gained the life we now enjoy in turn.

We have no mirrors in our churches;
Their shrines always have mirrors.

Golownin's editor describes the use of the mirror thusly: "On the door of this central building [of the Ise Shrine] hangs a gong, on which every worshipper strikes at his first arrival, to inform the God that he is come to worship him: after which, the votary looks through a window where hangs a mirror, as a symbol that as he sees his own countenance, so does God see his heart and thoughts – and this seems to end the ceremony." (G:MCJ) Oliphant later explains, "Some with a metaphysical turn of mind suppose that God sees into their heart as plainly as they do into the looking glass, and therefore do not pray at all." (O:EMC) A more rational explanation is given by Mori Arinori, the charismatic intellectual who oversaw the hundreds of Japanese students in the USA in the 1870s and returned to become the Minister of Education: "They look in this mirror and examine their own eye, the eye being the index of the soul, the gazer can the more easily determine the honesty of his intentions." (L:JIA) If the mirror found at some of our better zoos says "*You, too, are an animal, and the world's most dangerous one, at that!* the Shinto mirror says, *You, too are a god! This is where you had better look for godliness, within yourself!*

~~~~~~

5-28   Our images are painted on wood;   *As nossas imajens se pintão em pao;*

   Those of theirs on **paper scrolls**.   *E elles as suas em papel emrolado.*

Painting on canvas began in the first half of the 15c in the Low Countries and was not uncommon in South Europe when Frois wrote, but, evidently, it was not the usual medium for painting Christian images. Readers might think the contrast one of *solid permanence* versus *fragile impermanence*. If so, it is not quite right, for the pictures were kept rolled up most of the time so they remain fresh *longer* than ours, which suffer more exposure from constant display. The pictures usually have cloth backing and margins, as well as thin wooden ends on the top and bottom of the scroll (so they can still be rolled up) which not only help the hanging but improve the image, as a frame does.

5-29 Among us, a good retabulo done in oil-color is sometimes worth a lot;
Antre nós val às vezes muito hum bom retabolo d'olios;

In Japan, oil-color is not used and [yet] sometimes a black-ink portrait is worth many thousand cruzados. *Em Japão não se uza d'olios, e val às vezes muitos mil cruzados hum[a] figura em tinta preta.*

While one can find black and white sketches in European art that seem finished (see Rembrandt's simple "portrait of Saskia" or, much later, Turner's incredibly dynamic sketches) today – *after* we have been influenced by Japanese art? – in 1585, such a thing would not have been considered finished works of art, but *studies* preparatory to the real thing, the colored painting. Hence Frois's unstated wonder in the fact that quickly done paintings in black and white could be worth so much.

Though this contrast, couched in terms of "worth," seems secular if not commercial, "our" main *use* of art was religious. The Jesuits believed in multi-media presentation, using architecture and paintings to create a religious mood. Though a black and white painting may be good art, they fail to grab the viewer in the *emotional way* a realistic color painting could. With hundreds of thousands of Christians and over a hundred churches, not to mention requests for a Madonna and child painting coming from all wealthy Japanese with any pretension to culture (as something unlike anything seen in Japanese art, they become a fad item), supply could not keep up with demand. They taught young Japanese to engrave and paint in the Western style. In 1592, Frois observed work by students that was so good even Portuguese shown the pictures thought they came from Rome. "So, with God's help," Frois concludes, "Japan won't lack men who can keep all her churches full of fine images and satisfy the [aesthetic needs of] gentry(*tonotachi*)."

5-30 Our prelates go about on mules; *Os nossos prelados amdão em mulas;*

Their prelates go about in sedans. *Os prelados de Japão em andas.*

The Japanese sedan is a box hanging from a carrying pole, shouldered by two men. As we shall see later, sedans came in many types some of which were appropriate enough for someone of status, for Japanese did not use horse-drawn coaches. True, sedans are not as fast as horse-drawn carriages, but they had springs – the human brain –intelligent enough to read the road and were probably faster than our prelates' mules, for the men took great pride in *their* speed, while mules . . .

But, why *mules*? The Japanese translation *roba* means "donkey" or "ass," as in Abbysinian ass, the humble animal with the mark of the cross Jesus was said to have ridden. My first guess was that this practice was an imitation of Jesus or perhaps to show humility by riding close to the ground, but, Defourneaux, in his book on daily life in Spain in the Golden Age, writes that "persons of quality, who wish to travel comfortably, hire a litter which is carried *by two mules*" (D:DLS – I wish there was a picture: *Imagine each mule like the hull of a catamaran and the man in the center, or is he dragged behind?*) while ordinary folk rode mule-back, with the services of a helper, a *moco de mulas,* or muleteer, as was the case in Japan with horses. The Jesuits apparently chose the later form of travel, as the more humble. Horses on the highway in Iberia were supposedly all rapid runners, reserved for the Royal Mail alone. Don Quixote's bony nag would have met with utter disbelief.

In Japan, the Jesuits usually walked – something associated more with the Franciscans and their vows of poverty in Europe – in order to differentiate themselves from the luxury-loving Buddhist high priests, as their first member and exemplar, Saint Xavier had done.

endnote V

Temples

I have two good stories, both of which I would title *A Matter of Good Faith* which I would share with all who are interested in pursuing religion across cultural borders.

1.

The first comes from the kind and wise Bostonian Edward S. Morse, who found thousands of things to learn from the Japanese, not in their economic heyday, or even after they proved themselves by beating Imperial Russia, but before most of "us" deigned to consider them worth copying. He even found the manner in which packages of seeds are sold to visitors to feed the pigeons that fly down from the roof of the temple worth noting – a footnote added to a later edition of his book suggests he succeeded with this cultural transmission:

> Within twenty years we have vastly improved in this respect, and now one may see flocks of pigeons fed on the Boston Common by men and boys, some of these birds actually alighting on the head, shoulders, or hands of the feeder. (M:JDD)

I love pigeon stories and have collected quite a few, but let's return to the temple and what Morse had to say about it, for the following testimony reveals more about the relationship between Christian missionaries and Buddhism than most entire books do.

> The curious objects one sees in the temple often excite surprise and even contempt. An American missionary journal, reflecting on this subject, held up to derision an object which was seen on the walls of this religious edifice, namely, a framed lithograph of the Pacific mail steamer, City of China. I could not believe it, and so, on this first visit to the temple, I specially searched for it, and found it among the souvenirs and emblems adorning the wall. It was, as described, a cheap, colored lithograph of the steamer, and from its rather soiled appearance I judged it had been there some years. On the glass on one side was an inscription in a few vertical lines. A few days afterwards, I got a student to go to the temple with me and translate the inscription, and this is a free rendering: "This vessel rescued five shipwrecked Japanese sailors and brought them back to their native land. To commemorate this kind act on the part of the foreigner the priests of this temple have secured this picture and placed it among its relics." This was done at the time of bitter feeling against the foreigner and revealed a true Christian spirit on the part of the priests, and this picture is venerated by the Japanese. (M:JDD)

Morse continues, remarking how alike many features at the temple are to "the Catholic cult," as noted by Kaempfer. *Monks and nuns, holy water, incense, rosaries, celibate priests, masses, chants.* "He [Kaempfer] was forced to say *"Diablo simulanti Christum"* (which, if you recall, Lowell borrowed without giving credit). But all that is old hat. The above story of the American Christians is new. The missionaries, not being "Christian" enough to give the temple the benefit of the doubt, as Morse did, put down what they did not understand. They treated the Buddhists in *bad faith.* Morse's terms, "relics" and "venerated," *seem* Orientalist but, in this context, I think they suggest *mementos* and *treasured*. Morse checked out *what really was what* because he treated the Japanese as equals. He did not patronize them or their religion. Inter-religious understanding requires one thing: *good faith..*

2.

The second story comes from Yoshio Markino, who was, as the title of his book puts it, A JAPANESE ARTIST IN LONDON. Not long after moving to England from America, where he had been terribly bullied, he was "a frequent visitor to [the house of a] Mrs. Dryhurst, who introduced me many interesting peoples." (I leave his shocking Japanglish exactly as it was published):

> One day those friends of hers surrounded me and asked me how was about the religions in Japan. That was a very difficult question to me. It is fact that I was at an American Missionary College in Japan and studied the Bible lessons for four years. But among us, the young schoolboys, the Christians were looked down as "not highly educated." I think the main reason was that those terribly ignorant and uneducated American missionaries in Japan were talking and doing too much nonsences. While I was in America when anybody asked me if I were a Christian I always answered negatively to prove that I was not one of those "Uneducated." But to my astonishment I was entirely knocked down. They called me "Pagan," "Heathen," and "Barbarian," and they treated me as if I were not a human. Fancy! that one whose duty is supposed to be "to seek the lost sheep" should act himself not at all humanely!
>
> Now, facing to all my dearly respected friends in Hampstead, I was rather too timid to express my opinion so freely. Besides, it was not my intention to injure the Christian faith in this country. So I shamefully acted myself as a fox. I said: "Japan is a free country for religions. You may find quite numbers of Christians there."
>
> "How pity! How Pity!" were the expressions from every one's mouth.
>
> Some one shouted, "How about your beautiful philosophies, then?"
>
> Mrs. Dryhurst asked me, "Have you ever forgotten Laotze, Confucius, and Mencius?"
>
> I exclaimed, "Ahé, ahé. Wait, wait, wait, wait, wait a second, please."
>
> I could not speak immediately. When those ancient Chinese philosophers' names were mentioned my heart was so stricken with joy, as if one was told the name of a woman to whom he devoted his love . . .
>
> My first words to my friends was, "I am not a Christian."
>
> "You are right," was echoed and re-echoed in their mouth.
>
> Then I confessed how timid I was before them, and they all heartily laughed.

If we find the eclectic mix of religion in Japan a mystery – they find us no less hard to understand. On the one hand, most of "our" intellectuals do not think Christianity is *the* Religion, but only *a* religion. Still, in the United States, at least, an intellectual Christian was and is not yet an oxymoron and even the theist or agnostic usually puts up a Christian front with talk of God, especially if he or she happens to be in politics. As far as I know, Jesse Ventura, the wrestler-turned-governor is the first Usanian politician in history with the guts to come right out and admit he was not Christian and even opine, if so refined a word can be used for his off-cuff remarks, that religion was *a crutch for people too weak to face reality.* (Victorianism was nothing compared to the intellectual cowardice of the politically correct Usanian and we should be grateful for Jesse's guts, even if we don't like his style!)   Please do not misunderstand me. I love the *Orthodoxy* (and even criticism: *The Heretics*) of a Chesterton and admire people who can keep the faith today, even in the USA. So long as they keep it on a high enough level – do not make the mistake of trying to bring down science – I am in no rush to dampen their spirits with my relatively dry brand of reason, and, to tell the truth, I don't mind quaffing a bit of those subtle spirits now and then. Watching the sun rise on Easter morning, I, too, am almost a believer.

Midword

CHINA *VERSUS* JAPAN

> From the great Jesuit scholars of the sixteenth century down to the best sinologists of today, we can see that there was never a more powerful antidote to the temptation of Western ethnocentrism than the study of Chinese civilization.   – Simon Leys

i
battle of the antipodes

Mirror, Mirror on the wall, who is the most other *of them all?* Simon Leys, a sinologist, claims that honor for *his* subject:

> From a Western point of view, China is simply the other pole of the human mind. All the other great cultures are either dead . . . , too exclusively absorbed by the problems of surviving in extreme conditions . . . , or too close to us to present a contrast as total, a revelation as complete, an originality as illuminating as China. (THE BURNING FOREST 1988)

In his opinion, only China allows us to know how much of our heritage is universal and how much reflects "Indo-European idiosyncrasies." Japan, on the other hand, "even when . . . able to challenge the power of the West militarily, . . . never disturbed theologians or philosophers, as it was itself proclaiming that it was marginal, eccentric, and insular."(Ibid.) This generalization should be qualified on two counts. First, just because Japanese have proclaimed themselves "unique among the peoples and cultures of the world" (John Embree, "the anthropologist who wrote a classic study of a Japanese village," also D:WWM) with the implication that they are utterly beyond comprehension, do we need to take them at their word on it? And, second, does the fact (?) a culture is "so peculiarly *sui generis*" (Pre-WW II Japan scholar George Sansom, explaining why he was attracted to Japan. D:WWM) really remove a culture from serious consideration? Because something is unique does not mean it can not challenge us, or must remain beyond our ken, does it?

Another scholar "originally trained in Chinese literature," David Pollack, came to a conclusion as different from Leys' as night and day: "it is difficult to conceive of Japan apart from China; and yet, China seems strangely redundant when we think of Japan." (*The Fracture of Meaning* . . . 1986). And Charles A Moore, "for many years senior professor of philosophy" at the University of Hawaii, asserted that Japan "presents more intellectual and cultural challenges . . . ," no, "more challenges to the "orthodox" points of view of *both* [ital. mine] East and West than . . . any other major tradition." (M:JM 1967). Only Japan, he argues, does not "accept the Socratic dictum that "the unexamined life is unfit to live" and might rather "counter by saying that it is the examined life that is unfit to live, because it is not *life.*" (ibid.) That is to say, *only Japan turns philosophy on its head.*

All parties, then, seem to agree that, compared to China, Japan is *far out*; the only difference is whether that makes it trivial or important!

ii
japan over china

Despite the great prosperity and admirable institutions of government in China, which astounded the first European visitors (See *TT-long* for two pages of notes on what was clearly the wealthiest and, in many ways, *most modern*, economy on earth), most of these 16c visitors who knew both the Chinese and Japanese were more favorably impressed with the latter. Learning that the Japanese "despise riches in comparison with dignity," so even poor nobles were treated with the same dignity as the rich, St. Xavier gushed that he doubted such rectitude could be found "anywhere among Christians." While admitting the Chinese he met in Japan were "in intellect . . . superior to the Japanese," he remained convinced of "the superiority of the Japanese nation over all the others at present discovered in these parts." As Frois put it not long after arriving in the Miyako (the capitol, present day Kyoto) in 1565, "In their culture, deportment, and manners, they excell the Spaniards in so many ways that one is ashamed to tell about it."

China may have given birth to the Chinese character (*ideograph* is a bit of a misnomer), which fueled Europe's search for Universal Letters; but it is the more complex *mixed writing system* of Japan that the Visitador Alessandro Valignano praised as "the most elegant and the most copious tongue in the world; it is more abundant than Latin and expresses concepts better." (C:TCJ) Vilela, Organtino, Frois and others wrote pretty much the same. Valignano was later to qualify his praise of Japanese over Latin (I think not so much because it had been criticized in Europe as because of his experience running a press translating Western books into Japanese; for translation *always* makes obvious the shortcomings of the recipient language); but he reiterated and expanded his praise of Japanese as a language whose very grammar teaches civility.

More important, *the Japanese had guts. More guts than any people the Jesuits had met.*

This was partly because the Jesuits visited right on the tail end of the Warring Era (1338-1568), hundreds of years of civil strife that most Japanese historians consider an anomaly in a millennium of peace. Even the common folk had come to prefer losing their lives to losing their honor and, in Xavier's words, "value arms more than any people I have ever seen," while the Chinese, as Valignano and others would continue to note for centuries, avoid arms like the plague. The following words written by the Marquis de Moge, attaché for the mission of BARON GROS'S EMBASSY TO CHINA AND JAPAN (1858/1860) are risible to most of us today:

> The Japanese know the point of honour. To take his sword from one is an insult. He cannot restore it to the scabbard without having first steeped it in blood. The Chinamen burst into a laugh when they are reproached with running away from the enemy . . . . In all respects, then, the inhabitants of Japan are a superior race to those who people China.

But that was not so before WWII sickened us on war. We thought honor and the courage to uphold it, *everything*. While the Jesuits were concerned about the downside of this bravado – Frois called *pride* their Idol! – the Warriors for Christ admired the Japanese for it as much as did the Marquis de Moge and, likewise, thought less of the Chinese for being meek (*effeminate*, being the usual term). Note that Frois's chapter about Warring & Weapons has 52 contrasts, and that doesn't include the dozens of weapon-related observations found in other chapters (especially ch I, where *weapons*, with clothing, *make the man*). Chinese scholars, like the Chinese themselves, may not think much of military power, but the Christian West has usually given more ear to the strong than the weak. Before Hideyoshi decided to invade China himself, some Jesuits actually tried to convince the Order to invade China with the help of Japanese mercenaries! (A page on this in *TT-long*) If the meek were to inherit the earth, I guess they needed some help.

iii
the chineseness of japan

The first "China vs. *Europe*" listing that I know of – remember, Valignano's short-lived contrast was between "China and *Japan*" – was a long paragraph by the above-mentioned Marquis de Moge.

> In China, the compass is not made to point to the north, but to the south. It has five, not four cardinal points. The left, not the right side, is the place of honour. White, not black, is the suit of woe. Etiquette ordains we should not take off the hat, but put it on, in the presence of a superior, or of anyone whom we wish to honour. Books are printed and read, not from left to right, after our fashion, but from right to left. At dinner, fruit comes first, and soup last. As children learn their lessons aloud, all saying them over at the same time, it is the object of the Chinese schoolmaster not to keep a quiet school, but to make his little congregation as noisy as possible; and silence is punished as proof of idleness. When a man is ennobled for a service done the state, honours so acquired do not descend, as with us, to his posterity, but, strange to say, ascend to his ancestors and ennoble them. They all become, by a retrospective action, dukes and barons and so forth, while the children and descendents of the new-made noble remain undistinguished in the common herd. Pages might be filled with similar contrasts between the habits of Europeans and Chinamen. (M:BGE:1860) [1]

As far as I know, those pages were *not* filled until Dyer Ball's Chamberlain-influenced THINGS CHINESE (1890), in which four pages are given to "Topsyturvydom" (He uses no hyphens.).[2] If Ball follows Chamberlain, not to mention Valignano and Frois *in print*, the Chinese side of most of the dozens of contrasts mentioned precede *in reality*, for "things Japanese" often derive from China. Almost all of the following contrasts in a May 1932 *Ripley's "Believe It Or Not!"* column dealing with China are condensed from Ball and most are previously found in Chamberlain and/or Frois about Japanese.

> He laughs when he is sad and cries when he is glad.
> Wears white instead of black when in mourning.
> Makes the lining of a suit first.
> Shake hands with himself when he meets a friend.
> Removes his shoes instead of his hat when entering a house.
> Wears skirts and puts his vest on over his coat.
> Drinks hot tea to keep cool and carries a fan in cold weather.
> Does not receive a permanent name until he is dead.
> Scratches his foot instead of his head when puzzled.
> He is one year old the day of his birth.
> He mounts a horse from the right side and puts him in the stall backward.
> Builds the roof of his house first.
> His fractions are upside down.
> Whitens his shoes instead of blackening them.[3]

Ripley's horrid caption "the Heathen Chinee is peculiar!" (borrowed from Francis Bret Harte's 1870 poem about a Chinese hustler, *Plain Language from Truthful James*) shows that despite cultural relativism already taking root in academia, most of "us" were shamefully disrespectful of "them." The ethnocentric framing and the lack of proper explanation made the contrasts, in themselves harmless, uniformly degrading to the other and bring to mind the words of Nitobe Inazo,

> "The atmosphere of the Pacific seems to possess the obnoxious power of throwing above the horizon on either side not only an inverted but a perverted image." ("The East and the West" in *The Japanese Nation*. See my *Orientalism & Occidentalism* for a longer quote.)

But the fact that much of what is Japanese is Chinese – as much of what is Western European is Latin (Funny how the Japanese "copied" the Chinese, while our ancestors "inherited" culture from the Greeks and Romans! [4]) – in no way detracts from Japan's antipodal character with respect to the West. China deserves credit for so much of Japan in particular and the world's culture in general that I would never belittle it; but tell me, sinologists, is there a list of Chinese opposites as long as this Japanese list of Luis Frois S.J.? And could "Chinks" possibly replace "Japs" in the following claim made by James Bond's colleague in Tokyo?

The bloody Japs do everything the wrong way round. (YOU ONLY LIVE TWICE)

1. *Moge's China Contrasts*. Most of the contrasts are either self-explanatory or explained elsewhere in this book. Exceptions are the five cardinal points which include a theoretical up-down axis that in no way confuses the directions, which are the same as ours, with the exception of the South being "up" on most maps, as it was once with us, too; the method of awarding titles retrospectively to ancestors, which makes more sense than ours does, because family tradition helps make us what we are and, scholars, in particular, are seldom made in a single generation, while any tradition can easily end in a generation. (In this respect, Valignano, for once, uses contrast to put Europe and Japan *on the same side*, for in his last LIBRO (1601), he notes the absence of hereditary nobility (*nobleza por generacion*) in China (carefully admitting the exception of some of the King's sons) as a natural consequence of titles gained by letters, as opposed to the power of arms, as was the case in Japan, where titles, i.e. hereditary status was passed down the generations from antiquity "in the same manner as do the hidalgos of Spain." (V:LIBRO)

2. *Chinese Topsyturvydom.* Ball's style is clearly influenced by Alcock, Lowell Chamberlain and others who emphasized the topsy-turvyness of Japan, rather than Marquis de Moge's simple mention of "contrasts" (possibly "contradictions" in the French). His Chinese *Topsyturvydom* heading starts off in the pattern we are already familiar with for Japan: "It is the unexpected that one must expect, especially in this land of topsyturvydom. The Chinese are not only remote from us with regard to position on the globe, but they are our opposites in almost every action and thought. It never does to ask how a Chinese would act under certain circumstances . . . he would do the very actions we would never think of performing . . . " (More in TT-long)

3. Odious Contrast: *"Understand it or Not!"* Most of Ripley's contrasts are explained in the notes to this book. A few words in respect to some that are *not*, for as Nitobe Inazo pointed out, *"A mere description without an explanation is likely to lead to a wrong inference."*

Whitewashed shoes. In the summer, such a color would be cool and healthy, almost as good as sandals.

Skirts. Until the 17c, many European men, were still be- skirted, and the Jesuits were, as always, robed.

Hot day, hot tea. Like chili-hot food, it makes you sweat and sweat is cooling . . .

Fan in the winter Heat is best circulated and, if one is warmly dressed, it can get hot in some situations, and sweating can be dangerous in the winter.

Foot scratching Logical enough for someone seated with a foot up as is often true for Chinese – note: the Chinese (unlike the Japanese) always had their feet in clean socks. They are not scratching anything dirty.

Year count The normal "inclusive" way of counting, which is what we use referring to centuries when we call the 1800's "the 19c." To be *one,* then, is to be *in* one's first year of life. The Chinese (and Japanese) did not, however, use the inclusive count as often as our Roman ancestors, whose *"See you in three days!"* meant the day after tomorrow!) In China, but not Japan, individual birthdays were celebrated, but that didn't change the principle of aging with the New Year – a child born on the last day of the year would be two years old the very next day! Again, the Romans thought likewise.

4. "America as Japan" or, *Imitation in the West.* Not only was the West good at imitating=learning, but the West's West, namely the United States of America was especially so. Here is a Chinese writing in the twentieth century.

> "Psychologists divide human talents into three kinds: ability to invent, ability to put to practical use, and ability to imitate. Because America is a late-comer nation, inventive ability is not frequently seen, but America's practical and imitative talents are unusual and unmatched by other nations. No matter what the branch of science, once it is transmitted to the United States, Americans use their talents to imitate it, put it to practical use, and develop it. (LAND WITHOUT GHOSTS (A&L:LWG))"

The Wright brothers were the exception, not the rule. Henry Ford was to the Europeans who invented the automobile what the Japanese in the 1970's and 80's were to "us." Things only changed with the massive brain drain from Europe to the United States after the Nazi rise to power.

iv
the un-chineseness of japan

In *The Voyage of Van Linschoten to the East Indies* (English trans. 1598), a couple pages are dedicated to a just-so story explaining why "touching their traffique, manners, speach, and all their ceremonies" the Japanese "are cleane contrarie unto all other nations, speciallie from those of China, and till this day observe the same as an infallible [orig. *aangeboren,* or "hereditary") law."

Once upon a time, the story began, "a great and mightie familie" in China tried to kill the King of China and usurp his kingdom. They failed and "divers of the principall conspirators" were put to death. Most of the kinsman were allowed to live and given a punishment which for the Chinese "was little better than death," banishment, for "them and all their posteritie for ever out of the countrie, into the Ilands of Iapen, which as then were not inhabited."

> whereby there is so great [envie and] hatred betweene them and the men of China, that they hate each other to the death, and doe all the mischief one unto the other that they can [imagine or devise], even untill this time. The men of Iapen have done much mischief unto the men of China, and many times have fallen upon their coasts, and put all to fire and sword, and now [at this present] have not any conversation with them, but onely they trafficke with the Portingales, and to shew themselves whollie their deadlie enemies, in all their actions they are cleane contrary to the men of China, and to the same end have changed all their customes, ceremonies and [manners of] curtesie from the men of China . . . where the China useth the curtesie of salutation to a man with the head and hand, when they meet together: the Iapens to the contrarie put off their shoes, whereby they shewe them reverence, and as the Chinaes stand up when they minde to recyve any man, and to doe him reverence, they to the contraire set themselves down . . .

After these two partially garbled examples, where Chinese act like Europeans – perhaps twisted from Valignano = Maffei's "*us* vs. *them*" context to better fit his theory – Van Linschoten immediately drops all mention of the Chinese and simply lists strange Japanese customs with occasional reference to Europe ("we"). Montanus retold the legend in 1670, improving the punch-line.

> . . . they so much abhor and loath the Chinese Customs and Fashions, that rather than they would resemble them in their behavior, they have taught themselves such preposterous actions, that they are not onely unlike them, but all the world beside. (M:EEJ)

– but wisely separates the Chinese-Japanese contrasts from the bulk of the European-Japanese contrasts by a few chapters, repeating contradictions where some Japanese traits in the latter contrast repeat Chinese ones in the first. *It is not easy to make black and white contrasts of three cultures!*

v
japan vs. china

When Valignano first wrote about the radical difference in European and Japanese civilization, he did indeed contrast China and Japan:

> In dress, in food, in almost every action they [the Japanese] differ so much from all other races, European or otherwise, that it almost seems as if they were consciously aimed at acting habitually in the opposite way to others, especially the Chinese, to whom they

trace their origin. In everything they try to do just the reverse. The Chinese, for example, have one ruler for their whole empire . . . ; whereas the Japanese have thousands of masters to deal with . . . . In China, no one can carry weapons; here they invariably go about heavily armed. . . . The Chinese will have no friendly relations nor converse with outsiders, while the Japanese are very fond of strangers. The Chinese have the best government imaginable and are sticklers for ordered ways, while here no order or government prevails. In short, they behave in a way quite the reverse of the Chinese and indeed of any other nation. It is clear from all this that Japan constitutes a world apart, and that the people in it act in many original ways new to the rest of mankind. (trans. John J. Coyne in S(C):VMP)

Valignano's contrasts, of which there were over a dozen (which we encounter elsewhere in this book) were basically correct. Nevertheless, they did not remain in his later work, except in so far that they were incorporated into the Europe vs. *Japan* contrasts. Evidently, Valignano's experience in Japan – including a long time with Frois – taught him that the differences between Japan and Europe were so much greater than those with China that contrasting Japan with China was moot and that China and Europe had too "much similarity" (*tiene muchas semejanza con Europa* (Sorry, lost date! I think it is 1601)) to merit the type of topsy-turvy contrast he applied to Japan and Europe.

Moreover, Valignano retained from the Chinese-Japanese contrast the idea that the Japanese are not only different but *want to be* different: that they seem "to study [try] in order to do everything contrary to others" (*que de proposito estudiaron de hacer todo lo contrario de los otros.*). This last line is echoed centuries later by the Hungarian-born English critic and travel writer George Mikes:

the Japanese are human beings like the rest of us, but they will strongly resent this insinuation. They want to be different." (THE LAND OF THE RISING YEN 1970). [1]

If Japanese, then, really are contrary – the antipodes incarnate – the question remaining is *why* this might be so. Here, we come back to their relationship with the Chinese. Frois wrote

. . . albeit the Japans received out of Siam, and China, their superstitions and ceremonies, yet they nevertheless contemn all other nations in comparison with themselves, and standing in their own conceit do far prefer themselves before all other sorts of people in wisdom and policy. (Willes trans. of a Frois letter in his 1577 HISTORY OF TRAVAYLE)

..
Frois' "albeit" – if it is indeed Frois's – is, I think, wrong. It makes more sense to say that *because* of the cultural debt, Japan developed an inferiority complex and compensated with a superiority complex (as Usanians did with their cock-a-doodle poetry vs. England in the 19c which invariably made them, in the words of a British critic "The smartest nation / in all creation."). This, too, would, of course, be a gross oversimplification; but it would make some sense of something real that gave rise to that just-so story introduced by Valignano and van Linschoten. Japanese love to claim that they respect China, but even the extraordinarily objective Russian Golownin noted in the early 19c that "the Japanese even abominate the idea that the Chinese may have been their ancestors; their contempt of that nation goes so far, that when they mean to call any one a rogue or a cheat, they say he is a true Chinese." (G:MCIJ). It makes me wonder – *How would the European psyche have developed had "we" barbarians not managed to over-run Rome and turn the ancients into ourselves?*

1. ***Wanting to be Different.*** The extent to which Japanese differ from others – as all cultures differ from others – and the question as to how much Japanese tend to *emphasize* their difference are different, but not all together different matters. One finds native Americans defining themselves as "what the white man is not" (see Keith Basso's *Portraits of "The Whiteman"* 1979), and one can easily imagine a tendency for the minority peoples in the Sino-cultural sphere to identify themselves in such a manner with respect to China. This tendency could then be expanded to protect/re-create the Japanese identity with respect to the new China, i.e. the West.

vi
japan more chinese than china?

If Western visitors to Japan have tended to regard Japan as the most Eastern place in the world, Japanese have, for the most part, tended to agree with them. This conviction, if it can be so called, in the late-19c fused with the idea of Japan as champion of the East and a political agenda that was not all good, for the Japanese came to push their culture and beliefs upon other Eastern nations as *the* (only) Eastern Way. However, it would be wrong to throw out the whole idea of Japan as quintessentially East simply because of this sad history. If Usanians, despite our long history of discrimination, have come to consider ourselves a "melting pot" of the world's cultures, Japanese intellectuals in the 20c, with equal (imperfect) justification, came to think of their culture as a *cul de sac* of Eastern tradition. *We are more Indian than India*, they claim, for Buddhism that died out there still thrives in Japan. *We are more Chinese than China*, for the Taoism there is hardly so healthy as Zen in Japan, nor the rock gardens so well developed, etc. Nay, this is true for all Asia:

> It is in Japan alone that the historic wealth of Asiatic culture can be consecutively studied through its treasured specimens" (O:IOE)

So boasted Okakura in 1903. This is all the truer today, when the Japanese are so closely identified with many of these things that the Chinese and the few who are aware of China and its civilization (something that may change if the China's economic star keeps rising) must constantly remind Japanophiles where all of it came from! That is why I sometimes go out of the way to point out the Chinese roots of this or that item in this book and will now introduce a long quote from Frois's contemporary, the Florentine merchant Carletti:

> And it is possible to believe beyond any doubt that all these things [printing, making artillery and gun powder] came from them. And I agree to the statement that not only these, but every invention for good or for evil, of beauty or of ugliness, must have come from that region, or, at least it can be affirmed that they have in themselves the knowledge of everything, not having had it from us or from the Greeks or other nations who taught it to us, but from native creators in that huge and very ancient country which, as they say, predates by many millennia the creation of the world described by Moses, and this according to the belief that they hold, which is no less fabulous than false. (C(W):MVAW)

So, long before Professor Needham, China's priority in the arts and sciences was acknowledged. *Or was it?* Carletti's last line, if the translation is accurate, is dis/ingenious to say the least, and seems to be an equivocation intended to save its author from being accused of heresy.
..
But, at the same time, we give China its due, we need to pay closer attention to what Japan has accomplished. The idea of a *cul de sac* does not do it for me. Japan's achievement lies in keeping so much that is so old while introducing so much that is new. Much has been written about Japanese skill at adoption and adaptation of foreign culture. I would say that Europe has done just as much of that, but the difference lies, rather in the fact that "we" tend to roll up the carpet behind us and thereby end up with one, rather than multiple strands of tradition. As pointed out in 1-3+, it is why Japanese still have Japanese (albeit originally Chinese-influenced) robes, while we no longer have our skirts or

togas. It is also why we have one basic image of a pipe, a large roundish bowl, while Japanese have two, a large roundish bowl called a *paipu* and a long-stemmed pipe with a tiny bowl called a *kiseru* (from the Cambodian *khsier*, a pipe=tube). Judging from ship-wrecks, "we" too used to have something like the latter, but our pipes got larger and that was that. The English language maintains a parallel vocabulary of Classical, French and Anglo-Saxon/Germanic words. The Japanese language does the same sort of thing, but more clearly – that is to say, the Chinese, Occidental or Japanese origins of the words remain longer than most of our italics do – for it has more than one syllabary, as will be discussed in Ch 10. What is remarkable is that the Japanese culture does the same with artifacts. Generally, only one type of fashion of clothing or pipe or whatever is popular at a time, but the alternatives remain, tenuously, perhaps, but they do remain, and keeping their original form and name bide their time for as close to forever as you will find in human culture. That is why Japan remains the Far East and that is what I like best about it.

vii
the "true orient"

But forget reality! It is more romantic to view Japan as the font of the East. Frois's contemporary Joao Rodrigues began "This Island of Japon" with a long account of the Proper Names for the nation used both within and without. Some of them, including the most commonly used one today, formalize Japan's extreme location:

> *Nichi-iki* is a dignified name much in use among the Chinese in their books and chronicles. The Chinese pronounce it Jih-yu, and it means Limit of the Sun or of the Orient, where the sun rises and the world begins, for they believe it begins there. . . .

> So to get rid of the ignominious name of the Kingdom of Servants or Slaves, they called the land *Nihon* or *Nippon*, or in the native Japanese *Hi-no-moto*, meaning the beginning or origin of the sun . . . .

> The name certainly fits these islands, for not only are they the most easterly known and form the limit of the Orient (which the ancient geographers placed 180° from the prime meridian passing through the Fortunate Isles [Canary Islands]) but also as far as India and Europe are concerned, Japan is the true Orient, as we have said, where the sun rises before reaching these countries. (R(C):TIJ)

Dig through the earth, then, Rodrigues seems to be saying, and you will come out, not in China, but in Japan!

There are two paradoxes in this schema. First, the Japanese, or at least those living on the Eastern coast, knew well that the sun came from further East and that by being called the Land of the Rising Sun, they are adopting the point of view of another and in that sense, even as they boast, they are belittled. And, second, the only way Japan can become the Far(thest) East is by putting it on the far side of the Eurasian continent depicted as the center of a two-dimensional world, which destroys the idea of topsy-turvy, for that requires a third dimension. One cannot be Farthest East and upside-down.

envoi
What About Marco Polo?

There is someone whose name is better known to most of us than any other traveler mentioned in this book, who went from the Far West to the Far East long before Portuguese ships spanned the globe and the Jesuit order was founded. How does he fit in?

Marco Polo says nothing about *contrary* customs. In fact, the only human artifacts that he clearly took as opposite to the West – although, even here, he did not so express it – was the Sino-Mongolian use of paper for money, which he rightly considered a practical sort of alchemy and "a magnificent palace roofed entirely with fine gold, as we might use lead for our houses and churches" in a place called *Zipangu* (Japan) "an island in the middle of the Ocean, 1,500 miles from the mainland . . . whose inhabitants have white skins and beautiful manners." (trans. Waugh: 1984)

> There is no lack of fabulous items. *Elephant-carrying birds!* Or, historical fact. *The first news to reach Europe of the defeat of the Tartar navy by the Japanese with the help of a typhoon.* And Polo did find a place with a *different* non-human nature: the Malabar Coast (South-West India).

> > Everything there is different from what it is with us and excels both in size and beauty. They have no fruit the same as ours, no beast, no bird. This is the consequence of the extreme heat. (found in G:PPI) [1]

The expression "everything . . is different" has a contrary ring to it, but is not quite the same thing as *opposite*. The only genuine topsy-turvy items in Polo's account are not of an Eastern *versus* Western nature, but between third-party cultures. In Tandifu, a place between Peking and Amoy, he finds virginity was so highly valued a father "signs an agreement with the bridegroom" attesting to it, after which "the relations of both families and certain matrons" test her virginity with a pigeon's egg." We shall skip further details! Let us just say, Richard Burton was vague compared to Polo.

..
> In order to keep their virginity intact, the girls in these parts avoid all violent movement and walk with the tiniest possible steps. (Ibid)

> On the other hand, twenty days into Tibet, Polo finds a culture where

> No man will marry a virgin on the grounds that if a woman has not had several lovers she must be undesirable to men and unloved by the gods. So when foreigners or strangers pitch their tents in the area, as many as forty young girls may be brought by their mothers from the village and offered to them. The more attractive are welcomed and the others go sadly home." (Ibid.) [2]

Marco Polo was as delighted with this last practice as Herodotus was with the Babylonian Marriage Market, and writes more, but my point is made. While Marco Polo may have reached the ends of the Earth, he did not polarize it into East and West. Perhaps this is because his travels progressed Eastward by degree; culturally speaking, he never flipped over, as a man crossing the ocean would.

1. *The Malabar Mystery*. I overlooked this sentence about Malabar when I read Marco Polo and only pegged it down reading it a second time in Gaitonide (G:PPI), who also quotes a pioneering Portuguese apothecary, Tomé Pires on the same Malabar as follows:

> When they are ill, the patients do not eat meat: and have a diet of fish also. The chief remedy is to play the kettledrum and other instruments to the patients for two or three days and they say this does good [we seek quiet repose for the same reason]. If they have fever, they eat fish and keep washing themselves [we avoid the bath] . . . Our people when they have fevers eat fat chickens and drink wine and are cured." (SUMA ORIENTAL, in G:PPI)

Now this may not seem like much – I had to add the brackets to bring out the implied contrasts – but it is possible that the implications are clear enough that a reading could have triggered Valignano's first foray into topsy-turvy territory, a possibility that strengthens when we note the prominent and early appearance of similar medical related detail in his work. Not having read Pires' SUMA ORIENTAL, I can't say how much topsy-turvy is in it, but one more quote found in Gaitonide is suggestive:

> In Malabar, it is the custom for the woman to have her eyes on the bed during the act of coition and for the man to have his on the ceiling, and this is the general practice among great and small, and they consider anything else to be strange and foreign to their condition, and some Portuguese used to this country do not find this ugly."

I dare say if the young Valignano came across that paragraph, it would have stuck in his mind! Gaitonide also mentions a lost book on the riches and greatness of China sent to the Governor of India in 1524. If Malabar is any indication, the book may well have contained contrasts.

2. *Undesirable Virgins*. What began as a short note turned into an essay I couldn't cut. Marco Polo's words bring to mind the discriminatory joke concerning our so-called "hillbillies," where a bride is returned for being a virgin, because "If she hain't good 'nuf for her kinfolk, she shore hain't good 'nuf for us;" but the start of Marco Polo's account suggests something not altogether rare, a culture where perforation of the hymen is regarded as a sort of exorcism, releasing a dangerous spirit, so that it is considered wise to let strangers be the scapegoat. But his account continues:

> The traveler must give the girl a jewel when he leaves to prove she has had a lover. If a girl has twenty jewels, she has had as many lovers. The girls with the most jewels are then chosen as wives because, by common accord, they must be the loveliest. (Ibid.)

Here, we must entertain the possibility of a poor people – sometimes, entire tribes live on the margin – rationalizing a dowry scheme somewhat like what Carletti described in Japan (see note 2-1)! But, not necessarily. Originally, this custom may well have been a marriage-related beauty contest. There is a festival in Tsukuma Japan that goes back to ancient times where the unmarried women parade with pots balanced on their heads, as many pots as they had lovers that year which suggests that much! It was not found elsewhere in Japan, and, being a seasonal event, found its way into haiku. Over two hundred years after Frois died, Kobayashi Issa, the people's haiku poet, took the parade in a new direction altogether:

ima ichido baba mo kabureyo tsukuma nabe
(now, one time, aunties too/even wear them! tsukuma pot)

Tsukuma Festival
(*if you've got it*)

hey, old women!
you, too – why not?
wear your pots!

After noting that the bejeweled women made chaste wives, Marco Polo enthused, "It goes without saying that any young man between the ages of sixteen and twenty-four would be delighted to go to this place."

Additional note. Cultural diversity, poly or polar, is half the Marco Polo story. I was equally impressed by the other half, the *similarities* he discovered, again without comment. Most noticeable of all – and, I fear, a bit sad to contemplate – were a half-dozen accounts of how men in power got more than their fair share of beautiful women and the problems it caused for everyone concerned!

VI

OF THE JAPANESE MODE OF EATING AND DRINKING
do modo do comer e beber dos Japòes

~~~~~~

6-1 We eat everything with our fingers;
Nós comemos todas as couzas com a mão;

The Japanese, men and women, from childhood, eat with two sticks.
Os Japões, homens e molheres, desde crianças, comem com dous paos.

In the 1589 report of the Embassy to Europe, Miguel=Valignano enthusiastically describes the enormous amounts of gold paid by the wealthy in Europe to attend banquettes with equally plentiful silverware. His cousin Leo=Valignano, who remained in Japan, remonstrated: "But, still, aren't they uncleanly? Don't they eat with their fingers?" Miguel replied that most European visitors to Japan are poorly educated sailors and merchants, but that "cultured people in Europe ordinarily use silver forks and spoons to take up food from their plates." (J/S:DM) True, the hands are *sometimes* used, but they are, then, wiped clean on the table-cloth and washed after the meal. With Miguel=Valignano selling Japanese on Europe, we can not be certain just how much, or rather how little these utensils were used; but since Valignano himself earlier wrote "there are no . . . knives, forks or spoons" on the table *in Japan*, some Europeans must not have used their fingers exclusively. Had Frois, having grown up in humble circumstances, not seen any service to speak of? Or did the fork mainly hold down what was cut, while fingers were used to lift food to the mouth, and Frois chose to define "eat" (*comemos*) in terms of the latter action alone? (Boswell later described this in the New Hebrides) Regardless, his failure to mention European utensils here enhances the contrast of *bare* vs. *instrument, crudeness* vs. *culture*" and *clean vs. dirt,* with "our" side coming out uncivilized. In a much earlier letter, Frois had observed the delicacy with which Japanese ate and how they accounted "it great rudeness to touch it [food] with their fingers" (Willis trans). Others, including Valignano, emphasized the cleanliness with which they ate, not letting "even a crumb fall from their plate on to the table," with the implications being that we were, by comparison, sloppy. Since Europeans, with their new-fangled telescopes and guns, even at this early date, considered themselves to be the masters of material culture as well as spiritual, this reversal of fortune at the table must have been a jarring experience. It gave birth to the best passage of Mendez Pinto's PEREGRINATION – and perhaps the best cultural contact story *ever* written. Were it not four pages long, I would quote *every word* of it. I pared it down to two pages for *TT-long*; here, rather than butchering it further, I will simply summarize in a paragraph.

Belchior, the Jesuit's top priest East of India has come to Japan in place of the recently deceased=sainted Xavier and is invited to dinner, along with four other Portuguese, including Pinto, by the King of Bungo, who was considering baptism. The King begs them to eat in the style of their own country, with their hands, *in order to entertain his wife*, which they do to the great amusement of all the Japanese hosts and their own embarrassment at being the butt of many jokes and witticisms. Meanwhile, a fourteen or fifteen year-old daughter of the King asks for and gets permission to put on a play about their guests with a handful of her friends. An hour or so later, she comes back dressed as an old Japanese merchant, white hair and all, and requests permission from the King to trade with the Portuguese, both to help him gain enough money to support his countless children and four wives, etc, and to help the visitors, for his merchandize would help them overcome a great handicap from which they suffered. Obtaining permission, "for the sake of charity," she bows deeply and retires. *Uh-oh, thought Pinto and gang, what is coming next?* After, the old merchant and his children (the Princess's friends) sing something "in sweet voices that were a delight to listen to" (This is, as far as I know, the first time any European admitted to liking any Japanese singing!), and thank the King for allowing them to sell the goods, they unwrap the parcels and out fell . . . *a great pile of wooden hands!* (Buddhists, like Catholics, hang models of cured parts in their temples. Someone must have run to the temple and borrowed them!) The idea, the old merchant explains, is that, by using these, the Portuguese may avoid having their hands stink of fish or meat all the time. Then, the King apologizes and explains that his daughter only dared to put on a play like that "because you are like brothers to her" and the Portuguese, who recognized true nobility when they saw it, good-naturedly said they hope to see her yet as the Queen of Portugal, which "set the girl and her mother off laughing uncontrollably again." (M. Lowery's translation, on the whole good, but I must say, it was amusing to have a Daimyo *and* a princess! Better to leave the former a King.)

In 3-6 we saw why those "sticks" are supposed to make you smart. But there may well be more *significance* in this difference – with the anomalous *fork* and *knife* substituted for Frois's *fingers* – than you ever dreamed. The great Korean essayist I Oryon (sometimes Englished Lee O-Young), expanding Roland Barthes' contrast of "our knife (and of its predatory substitute the fork)" with the chopsticks, "an alimentary instrument which refuses to cut, to pierce, to mutilate" by which food is "no longer a prey to which one does violence" (B(H):EOS), writes that Orientals eating with chopsticks remind one of sparrows picking for grain, whereas Occidentals "tear apart" their food, "like a cat eating a mouse." (Barthes mentioned "pecking" and bird-food, but Lee provides the better metaphor). Why stop with sadism? How about *masochism*? Isabella Bird describes people in inner China who thought the fork must "prick the mouth and make it bleed." (B:YVB:1899) But this sort of fork bashing is not where Lee's main interest lies. Everyone (in the Far East, at least) already *knows* Occidentals are violent. No, Lee goes straight for his Oriental reader's heart-strings:

> Western food – steak, of course, but bread, too – can not be picked up with chopsticks. That is to say that if Asians ate with chopsticks, it means the food was prepared to eat bite-size. The amount of food chopsticks pinch is just the ideal amount for a mouthful. One might even say chopsticks are a scale or measure for food. That food could be eaten without inconvenience, with no need for a fork and knife, is because the person who prepared the food always did so from the eater's point of view. . . . Here is a warm and sympathetic frame of mind only found in the chopstick cultural sphere. (FUROSHIKI BUNKA-NO POSUTO-MODAN 1989 J/I:FPM)

'Tis the *chop*, not the *stick* that matters. The Westerner's implements show a do-it-alone Robinson Crusoe mentality. "With fork and knife in hand, a man gains the freedom to render the world, and solitude," while the Eastern choice reflects people who love people, people chopping for people, who stick together to make a meal. In fact, Lee goes on, "chopsticks") are homophonic with *bridge* (both pronounced *hashi* in Japanese), and not only do they link people horizontally, but *vertically* as well. Unlike the spoon and fork, which infants can master by themselves, the old generation must *teach* the new generation how to eat with chopsticks. *A bridge across the generations.* – While playing at this Oriental/Occidentalism game, let us not forget the contribution *Japanese* – not Chinese or Koreans – made to the chopstick culture. (*Try to guess!* The answer is in the Ch. *Endnote*).

If the Japanese of Pinto's and Frois's day were curious about *our* eating manners, we were curious about theirs, too. Usanians were disappointed to find the first Japanese Embassy of 1860 already skilled in the use of "our" utensils, which they may have practiced using while crossing the ocean; but the Japanese were, nevertheless, kind enough to demonstrate their use during a visit to the National Mint where they graced an "observant America" with a "display of chopstick skill – picking up one pea at a time at high speed with two sticks, for instance" at a luncheon. (A:FJE)

6-2   We ordinarily eat bread of wheat; *Ho nosso comer ordinario hé pão de trigo;*
         The Japanese, rice cooked without salt. *Os Japões arroz cozido sem sal.*

The "we" for Europe is more inclusive than "the Japanese," for commoners in Japan ate as much millet and barley and buckwheat (always as noodles, not bread) as rice, which was, in their case, unpolished. To the poor, good white rice was a luxury item reserved for special occasions or sickness. In that sense, rice was less important though even more highly respected than our "staff of life," which (eaten alone) came to be considered the food of our poor, until the easily grown potato replaced it in some areas (as the yam did in China and Japan).   But if rice was not universally available, it functioned as something common yet valuable in a way that bread (or grain) did not in Europe:

In Europe, we measure a country's wealth in terms of acreage, gold or soldiers;
In Japan, the weight of annual rice production is the measure of its wealth and status.

Eventually, most Japanese could eat rice every day. Rice came to be called the *shushoku*, or "main-food," i.e. *the* staple of the diet. Japanese in the 20c spoke of rice as the *shushoku* of Japanese and bread as the *shushoku* of Occidentals. Among themselves today they speak of people belonging to the "rice-party" (*gohan-ha*) or the bread-party (*pan-ha*)." This idea of allegiance(?) to a single staple is foreign to "us." We take our bread and potatoes or rice for granted and insist upon calling meat the "main-dish." (The only exception is pasta. You don't order a "main dish" of meat-balls with pasta on the side. But, note, pasta came from the East!) Japanese intellectuals have picked up on this with a vengeance. Popular books contrast Rice-eating and Meat-eating Civilizations, i.e., *gentle vegetarians* with *ferocious carnivores*. One book, by Sabata Toyoyuki, titled "Carnivore Thoughts " (*Nikushoku no Shisô*: 1966) not only set pastoral meat culture against paddy-rice culture, but, more importantly did the same for *bread* and rice. Milling grain into powder and baking bread was a far more complex process than cooking rice ("which they boil simply in water" = Carletti). The inhabitants of a medieval community in the West had to pay a miller to turn their grain to flour and, in many cases, a baker to cook it. As Alcock put it in the mid-19c, "boiled rice takes the place of *baker's bread*" (my *italics*) The taxes and inconvenience occasioned by this collectivism were much more onerous than that of a rice culture, where everything could be done at home, and *it was the reaction against this unrelenting oppression that paradoxically gave birth to individualism,* Sabata hypothesized. What a fine come-uppance for the simplistic *Great Irrigation* explanations of "Asian authoritarianism" often encountered in the West! (Note: the same case could be made for our religious totalitarianism giving birth to our need to be "free.")

There is a reason Frois did not make a big deal of our *meat*-eating. While the wealthy middle class devoured a a far greater variety of meat than we do today, the average family in Europe only saw meat once a week, and that usually in the form of a little mince-meat pie (LR). Moreover, the main condiments were generally butter and cheese, not meat. Indeed, the olfactory adjective that the Japanese were to peg on Occidentals was not "bloody," but "butter-stinking (*bata-kusai*)." Only over the last decades of the 20c, has the per-capita meat-consumption in Europe doubled, making the West clearly carnivorous.   This is also true, however, for Japan. When its economy took off in the 1970's, its consumption of animal protein caught up with the West, or some of it, at any rate.   But, in one way, Japanese held the line on tradition. *Faux Frois*:

Our dogs and cats eat meat or meat products.
Their dogs and cats eat rice like they do, or used to do.

Since Japanese rarely reheat rice, there is always a lot left-over. Some elderly Japanese, remembering the old days when every grain was a blessing because the rice often ran out, scold about this waste. But it isn't wasted. I was astonished to see rice as the main food for many Japanese dogs and cats. Some paper-thin and irresistibly aromatic smoked bonito flakes (*katsuo-bushi*) and perhaps the miniscule leftovers of a fish tail or scraps of fish-cake or whatnot convinces them to eat bowls of the stuff! This rice-is-good-for-all-animals mentality, like so many things, would seem to come from China. In the mid-16c century, Gaspar da Cruz, describes how his "nightingales" were fed:

> I kept two males and a female, and they sang in December as if it were April. They fed them with cooked rice wrapped in the yolk of an egg, somewhat on the dry side, which deceives them into thinking they are eating little insects. (TCC in B:SCSC)

6-3   Our tables are there before meals are brought out;
As nossas mezas estão antes que venha o comer postas;

> Theirs come together with the meal from the kitchen.
> *As suas vem juntamente com o comer da cozinha.*

The small Japanese tables were brought out from the kitchen as waitresses carry trays of food. This was a more labor-intensive process than our collective table setting and serving. Bird in 1880, notes "It might not be difficult to provide a dinner for forty, but then it must be forty dinners, i.e. each person must have his separate lacquered table and from four to twelve dishes or bowls containing edibles. I abhor the viands, but I have never seen a coolie taking his midday meal without fresh admiration of the neat and cleanly mode of serving, and the adaptability and elegance of the solitaire dinner service." (B:UTJ) In Japan, today, this is only true for some traditional style restaurants. In Korea, however, food is still often served this way at home. Frois might also have written:

> *We eat around large collective tables.*
> *They eat at small individual tables.*

Again, "we" come out on the collectivist rather than individual side. In medieval Portugal, tables were not the only thing shared. "It must be emphasized" writes Marques, "that each bowl or plate was always used by two guests, seated side by side." He adds that this explains the Portuguese idiom *"comer com aguem no prato,* literally "to eat with someone on the plate" [i.e. from the same plate] "signifying to be very close to someone" (M:DLP). In 1670, Montanus sets the social Occidental against the lone-wolf Japanese:

> Their manner of Diet is also opposite to ours; whereas we delight in Friends and Strangers at our private Tables, or at least admit Relations and Concerns to sit with us, never willing to eat alone; they on the contrary have each their peculiar Boards, where they dine and sup by themselves in a churlish manner . . . (M:EEJ)

As usual, Montanus takes a dry kernel of fact and makes heavily buttered popcorn of it. Perhaps (judging from the present day) the Japanese were not as liable to join strangers in food or conversation as people in some Occidental nations (or in Korea, where people not only engage in talk with strangers but dip into the same soup bowl with their spoons, or did in bars in Pusan 30 years ago), but individual tables were placed in close proximity. There *are* cultures, such as traditional Bali, where eating was so intensely private that members of a family faced their separate corners of the room and strangers were fined for intruding at meal time! Japan was not such a culture. Meals were generally convivial.

6-4   Our tables are high and have tablecloths and napkins;
As nossas mezas são e tem suas toalhas e guardanapos;

> Those of Japan are *urushi'ed* [lacquered] trays, rectangular and low-down, without tablecloths and napkins. *As dos Japões taboleiros vruxados, quadreados, razos, sem guardanapo nem toalha.*

Using Sladen's words to describe the Japanese tables, we get "tea-trays, with legs like dachshunds." (S:MQT). This contrast was no academic matter for Frois. The decision to accommodate themselves to Japan in 1580 meant the Jesuits had to learn to eat in the Japanese style. Schütte S.J. explains why:

> Hitherto, in the fathers and *irmaos* [novices] refractory, the community sat at high tables and made use of tablecloths and napkins. Naturally, these could not be changed and washed after each meal. In the eyes of the Japanese, accustomed to extreme cleanliness, such unchanged table linen was always soiled; in other respects, too, there was a general lack of neatness. All this could be avoided by conforming to the Japanese mode . . . (S:VMP)

Valignano feared the dirtiness of their kitchens and diners was giving the Jesuits a bad reputation among Japanese, "especially all the bonzes . . . who take us for a filthy and unworthy people" ("*Resoluciones del Padre Visitador*," in V(A):S&A) Decades later, Rodrigues reiterated: "they are much amazed at our eating with the hands and wiping them on napkins, which then remain covered with food stains, and this causes them both nausea and disgust." (R:TIJ) These tablecloths and napkins were not only used for hands, but for *knives*. As each person generally brought their own knife to eat with, they had to wipe them clean before they departed. The proper etiquette was to first wipe the knife on the manchets (round bread used for a plate that would be given to the dogs or the poor) and, then, the table-cloth, but such rules were not always followed. (M:DLP) How ironic that the very items the Occidental diner used to stay clean gave "us" the opposite reputation!

The most remarkable thing about this Japanese cleanliness, which surprised 19c observers as much as it did 16c Jesuits, was that it was not a monopoly of the fastidious bourgeoisie, but shared by everyone! In Bishop (the married Bird)'s words, "However dirty the clothing and even the houses of the poorer classes are, I have never seen anything but extreme cleanliness in the cooking and serving of meals, and I have often preferred to spend an hour by the kitchen fire to a dignified solitude in my own room." (B:UTJ)

~~~~~~

6-5 We sit on chairs to we eat with our legs extended;
Nós asentamo-nos em cadeiras pera comer com as pernas estendidas;

> They [sit] on the *tatami* or the ground with their legs crossed.
> *Elles sobre os tatamis ou no chão com as pernas emcruzadas.*

This, too, *mattered*. When the Jesuits asked themselves whether or not to observe Japanese table manners, i.e., how far to accommodate themselves to the culture, it

> reduced itself to whether one was to squat at a low table on ones haunches after the Japanese manner (a radical proposal, this) or sit at a high table as in Europe? If Europeans, for reasons of principle dictated by their task in Japan, decided in future to take their meals squatting on the ground (and every European who has tried to accustom himself to the Japanese method knows what it means), it was only to be expected that such efforts at adaptation would not stop there.

Father Schütte's rare pair of parentheses reflect great sympathy for the excruciating personal sacrifices the Jesuits would have made after Bungo (S:VMP). Some chair-culture visitors to Japan including 20c humorist George Mikes, find this one thing, sitting at tables, an example of carrying "this passion of going Japanese too far." Mikes recounts the night he and some English residents of Tokyo found a friend, "another Englishman – having dinner, squatting on the floor with apparent ease. "'I envy you,' he said. 'The one thing I cannot learn is this squatting.[sic]' 'Quite easy, really,' the other replied, a shade patronizingly, I thought." Now, *the good part:*

We proceeded to the neighboring room, ate our dinner and would have forgotten about him but for his unexpected reappearance. He had wanted to straighten his tired legs – squatting [sic] was easy but not that easy – had lost his balance, rolled over, fallen against the thin paper-wall, burst through it and ended up – with proper British apologies – in my soup." (M:LRY – my *sics*)

One should not quote and criticize; but neither sitting cross-legged in the informal style mentioned in Frois's contrast nor sitting on ones shins in the formal style as suggested in Mikes' story and described by Thunberg as making "a chair of their heels," (T:TEAA) ought to be called *squatting*. A squat is a natural way of *lowering one's buttock*, without a chair to meet it halfway. All people not addicted to chairs do it naturally. It is the natural posture for defecation. Japanese may sometimes gobble down a box lunch *without a table* while squatting, but no Japanese has *ever* squatted *at a table!* These Japanese ways of sitting are proper (i.e. learned), while squatting is far from it. If anything, they are similar to the postures and movements of Bali – where babies were not allowed to crawl! -- which may be expressed in a single word, *rectitude*. Still, there seems to be no way for us to avoid the wrong word here, Schütte (or, his translator) uses it, as does Cooper when he quotes Valignano, who, as a giant, must have suffered greatly: "Their way of sitting causes no less suffering because they kneel on the floor and sit back on their heels, or, as we would say, squat. This is a very restful position for them, but for others it is very wearisome and painful until they gradually become accustomed to it in the course of time." (1583 in C:TCJ) Actually, men begin formal meals in this *seiza*, or "proper-seat" position (see 2-63), but rarely eat entire meals in it. As Thunberg (1775) noted, "being used to this posture, they [the Japanese men] could endure it for a while, but it was easily seen that it proved tiresome to them at length, by their rising up, and sitting for some time like the Europeans." They usually switch to the informal cross-legged style before the meal is over. Women, however, almost never sat cross-legged. As social inferiors, they sat more or less formally all the time.

Valignano, who considered sitting one of the many things one had to relearn *as if they were a child* in this contrary country, realized it went both ways. In *De Missione*, the ambassador Miguel=Valignano and Leo=Valignano, who remained in Japan, had a splendid dialogue, the greater part of which is in *TT-long*. To sum here, Leo noted that Japanese prefer sitting their own way and wondered how it was possible for a body to relax (in Japanese, *settle down*) when the legs were dangling down from a chair. Miguel replies that is a very Japanese thing to say but that Europeans find sitting on folded legs almost unbearable and, moreover that sitting on a chair with the feet on the ground or a foot-rest, is more stable than supporting the weight of the body on the shins alone. Leo remonstrates that Miguel seems to have lost his birthright as a Japanese and turned into a European, but asks what about other cultures. Miguel says, in that case, the Japanese way comes off worse, for the only other truly civilized people, the Chinese, sit on chairs like Europeans. But, after saying that he graciously admits that the Japanese flooring and seating postures are not primitive but elegant and, since the European lifestyle costs more, "we might say that when customs differ, each people have their respective reasons for it, so all customs make perfect sense." (J/S:DM dialogue 9).

Imagine Leo on something even more disconnected from the ground than a chair: *a rotating bar stool!* Might he not feel something akin to the experience of *paling*, a nauseous terror that welled up within a Balinese who didn't know his exact orientation? If a Balinese needed to get out from a car and climb a hill to find his bearing with respect to the mountain and/or sea, would a pre-chair Japanese have had to drop off the bar stool and sit down upon the firm back of mother earth, or rather *tatami*?

6-6 Theirs, either all together – or on three tables; *As suas ou todas juntas – ou em tres mezas;*

Our dishes come out a little at a time. *As nossas yguarias vem pouqas e poquas.*

More proof that the *Tratado* was not in its final form: the order of the contrast is *backward*.

Details of formal three, five and seven-table banquets are provided by Rodrigues. For example, "in the banquettes of three tables, . . . there are twenty dishes and they include four *shiru* [soups, see 6-7 below] . . . with five tables they serve twenty-six dishes, among which are included six *shiru* . . . six tables or trays, there are thirty-two dishes, among which are included eight *shiru*, that is five of fish, one of shell fish and two of meat; one of these is crane . . . (R(C):TIJ) The contrast point would seem to be myriad choice for them, versus an item-after-item, "production line style of eating," for us. Since I have always liked to eat more than one dish at a time – mix my food – I enjoy the Far Eastern freedom to choose, freedom to choreograph ones own meal more than our sequential method. Here, the musical contrast we will see in Ch. 13 is reversed. *They* enjoy polyphony of the palate; *we* plod on, not knowing true harmony. How much do they enjoy it? In the 1980's in Japan, the most popular game show on TV (or *shows* for there were many copy-cats) featured a personality shown eating where challengers would be asked either to guess the *next* dish he or she – usually a very pretty she – would reach for, or, harder yet, the *order* of several or all the items. In Frois's time, this quiz would have necessarily skipped the first couple items in the meal, for people eating formally always began with a few "morsels of rice" followed by a sip of soup repeated thrice over (Avila Giron in C:TCJ). Could this promiscuity have something to do with the implement used for eating? Barthes:

> . . . a chopstick – as its shape sufficiently indicates – has a deitic function: it points to the food, designates the fragment, brings into existence by the very gesture of choice, which is the index; but thereby, instead of ingestion following a kind of mechanical sequence, in which one would be limited to swallowing by little the parts of one and the same dish, the chopstick, designating what it selects (and thus selecting there and then *this* and *that*), introduces into the use of food not an order but a caprice, a certain indolence: in any case, an intelligent and no longer mechanical operation. (B(H):EOS)

When tables are shared, the excitement grows exponentially. While the Occidental, according to Lee O-Young (I O'ryon), eats "every man for himself, the food piled up on his individual plate," Orientals maintain only their rice bowl as home-base while their chopsticks "dance about over the table like a butterfly" picking up this and that. "To beautifully pull off this space-performance, with no conductor and no signal lights," he gushes, "requires a harmonious spirit with heaven, earth and man as one." (J/I:FPM). This sounds idyllic, but living with butterfly eaters is not always easy. The ex-wife of a Japanese acquaintance was a *get-it-while-the-getting-is-good shitamachi* (Liverpool?) Edoite type, while he was a *save-the-best-stuff-for-last* Tohoku (the Ozarks of Japan?) type. Until they divorced, his wife and three daughters – when it comes to food, all children are Edoites – left him without goodies night after night. Every meal was a Tragedy of the Commons with the same victim.

The practice of introducing small amounts of many different things at once and preparing the food ahead of time which is common to chopstick cultures may also explain something Frois forgot to mention:

> *We put only simple meals into boxes and only use them for picnics.*
> *They put elaborate full-course dinners into boxes and even eat them indoors.*

The Chinese cultural sphere's fancy, multi-compartment – a Qing Dynasty Imperial snack box with *18 compartments* partially hollowed out to make the entire box into the Chinese character for "ten-thousand" being the most I know of – lunch-boxes. This tradition is still going strong and makes our paper-bagging and tin lunch boxes seem very, very primitive. Not only carry-out lunches, but cafeteria-style lunches and dinners, and *gourmet banquette food* is often served in these boxes, which are generally lacquer-ware, or, today, imitation lacquer-ware, i.e. plastic.

Even lunch-boxes for children are so complex by the simple standards of the West that Occidental mothers sending their children to Japanese schools find their preparation a major trauma. Their letters to the editors of English language newspapers appear every year, or did when I was there.

6-7   We can eat well enough without soup;   *Nós podemos muito bem comer dem caldo;*

The Japanese can not eat without *shiru* [soup].   *Os Japões não podem comer sem* xiru.

Rodrigues suggests soup was *indispensable* because of the method of serving. With the old style multi-plate banquette, "the food was insipid as it was cut up in portions and brought in on tables, and the only thing hot was the *shiru*, or broth." But that banquette style was already changing in 1585 and by the time Rodrigues wrote the above, some other food was brought out hot. I think the fact Japanese drank little with their meal (*sake* being stronger than beer and no good watered-down like wine, while tea was only drunken after the meal) was crucial: there had to be *something* to wash the food down with.

Today the most common pottage by far is *miso-shiru,* a cloudy fermented bean-curd soup. The ingredients are almost entirely vegetable, but tiny shellfish (*asari* or *chijimi*) in the shell may be added. *Miso* receives as much good press in Japan as wine in France. Hardly a week goes by without the publication of a new study showing this or that new medical benefit – usually anti-carcinogenic – deriving from it, though doctors privately warn about the danger of strokes deriving from its high salt content. But, forget about health. What counts is that *miso* is sacred. Usanians talk about "apple-pie" as a symbol of mother and country, but the claim is weak. If we are asked what we miss most of our mother's cooking, not one in fifty would say "her apple pie." But almost all Japanese *do* say "her *miso-shiru.*" Because there is a much greater difference between each mother's *miso-shiru* and the only other thing almost sure to appear at every meal, the rice, the flavor of that *miso* becomes the most important part of the taste-identity of every Japanese. Abroad, they generally *long* for that soup in a way we who don't have such an emotionally-invested food cannot know. So long as a Japanese can return to sip his mother's miso-shiru, one senses an invisible umbilical cord still passing fluid. I suppose it is something like the flavor of hometown water in the USA.

There is one interesting contradiction about Japanese and "their" *miso-shiru.* The people of the city that was the capitol of Japan, Meaco as Frois called it, did not drink – soup requires the verb *nomu* = "drink" or *suu* = "suck/sip" in Japanese – *miso-shiru*. These Kyotoites only have a very light colored "white" *miso* stew on the first couple days of the year. In his book on the spirit of Kyoto, Umesao Tadao, director of Japan's National Museum of Ethnology writes

I hate *miso-shiru.* I can't eat *takuwan* [radish pickles], much less *umeboshi* [dried plum]. *Sukiyaki*[1] disgusts me.   This kind of Japanese abounds in Kyoto. (U:KNS)

1. Sukiyaki   Selections from Barthes' description of this party dish: "a stew whose every element can be known and recognized, since it is made in front of you;" "garbed in an aesthetic nakedness;" "stew before your eyes;" "an entire minor odyssey of food you are experiencing through your eyes: you are attending the Twilight of the Raw." (B:EOS) By the way, the Japanese pop hit *Sukiyaki* has nothing to do with *sukiyaki.*

6-8   Our service is silver or pewter;
       A nossa baxela hé de prata ou estanho;

That of Japan is vermillion or black *urushi'ed* [lacquered] wood.
A dos Japões feita de pao vruxado, vermelha ou preta.

Perhaps "tin" would be the more precise translation of *estanho* but *tin* today connotes *cheapness*, whereas that was not Frois's intent and pewter is, after all, generally about 95% tin.

Frois may well have explained the benefits of this lacquer-ware in his missing Summary. Unlike ceramics it is light; unlike metals it does not conduct much heat, unlike paint it is permanent and unlike unpainted wood it is waterproof and can be completely cleaned. For these reasons, as Kaempfer was to point out, dishes varnished with the milky juice of the "Urushi, or Varnish-tree" served every one "from the Emperor to the meanest Peasant" and, even at Court, were "preferr'd to those of gold and silver."

My only complaint is that it resembles plastic. Indeed, *today*, most ostensibly lacquered bowls – rarely plates – and spoons in Japan *are* plastic. In a world of slick thin things, we need thick earthenware to retain our material sanity. (It is like realistic painting. I don't care for it today, but probably would have before photography). That my lack of interest in lacquer was not shared in pre-plastic Europe is proven by the fact that it became a household word in 17c England. Called *japan,* the process for making it was *jappaning,* done by *jappaners* who *japanned* it! For a people as pathologically fond of precious metals as we were, this *japan-ware* must have been a tremendous shock, or . . . revelation. To love it was to accept another aesthetic tradition. Read this sentence from "a do-it-yourself of great value to furniture-makers" by John Stalker and George Parker published in 1688 and titled *A Treatise of Jappaning or Varnishing*:

> Let not the Europeans any longer flatter themselves with the empty notions of having surpassed all the world beside in stately Palaces, costly Temples, and sumptuous Fabricks; Ancient and modern Rome must now give place: the Glory of one Country, Japan alone, has exceeded in beauty and magnificence all the pride of the Vatican at this time, and the Pantheon heretofore. (in John M. MacKenzie: ORIENTALISM: History, Theory and the Arts)

The complex art of *urushi* (see Chamberlain = C:TJ = for details!) originated in China, but Japanese artists were and are credited with taking it up to a higher plane. And, unlike China's china, it was never matched by Europe.

~~~~~~

6-9   We use earthenware pots and porringers to prepare our food;
Nós uzamos de panelas e tijelas de barro pera se fazer o comer;

>   The Japanese, cast iron kettles and pans.
>   *Os Japões de tachos e vazos de ferro coado.*

A reversal of our using metal-ware on the table. But I have seen stews slowly boiled in earthen-ware that design-wise seemed ancient in Japan. Indeed, boiling pots are found in the Jomon (10,000-300 BC). Frois lived in a metal-loving region or the Japanese lost and regained the practice.

~~~~~~

6-10   We place tripods with the legs down; *Nos pomos a trempe com os pees pera baxo;*

>   The Japanese, with the legs up. *Os Japões com os pees pera cima.*

Valignano begins a section of his elaboration of Japanese contrariness (1583) with this example, adding that, with the legs-up Japanese tripod, the "ring" was on the bottom. The classic Greeks, who gave tripods, together with pretty slaves, to winning athletes, might have found much of interest in this contrast. But for most modern readers, like me, it is a good thing the contrast stops where it does, for we now have only a vague idea of how these devices also called "trivets," "spiders" and "kettle-holders" were used in the West. Moreover, the tripod is but one of many fascinating cooking devices in Japan. The *irori,* a contraption by which pots are hung over fires still found in old farm houses is too complex to describe, much less contrast. All one can do is picture it (which I hope to do when/if I can afford to get fancy).

6-11   Men in Europe ordinarily eat with their women;
Os homens em Europa comem ordinariamente com suas molheres;

In Japan, it is something very rare, for the tables are also separate.
Em Japão hé cousa mui rara, porque tambem as mezas são divizas.

Though Japanese women were freer than European women in some respects, the two sexes were not considered equal and, among gentry, women were only allowed at the table of men in a serving capacity. With the peasantry, however, husband and wife often ate together, and it was not uncommon for men of any class to eat with their mistresses, at least in private. As the 20c began, this matter of men and women eating together became part of Japan's *national agenda* in its valiant drive to Westernize in order to gain the respect of the world powers. The Imperial family led the way: "The [Crown] Princess [Sada] enters the carriage ahead of him [the Crown Prince] when they drive together, and they habitually take their meals together – an astounding revolution in Japan." (S: MQTJ: 1905)

6-12   Europeans like fish brazed or stewed;   *A jente de Europa se deleita com pexe asado e cozido;*

The Japanese delight even more in eating it raw. *Os Japões folgão muyto mais de o comer cru.*

After Valignano mentions how remarkable it is that things in Japan could be so contrary to those in Europe – yet perfectly reasonable for those who really came to know them – even though Japan was a very civilized place (see the Foreword quotes), here is how he continues:

> What is much more astonishing is that they are so different and even contrary to us, as regards the senses and natural things; this is something I would not dare to affirm if I had not had so much experience among them. Thus, their taste is so different from ours that they generally despise and dislike the things we find most pleasing; on the other hand, we cannot stand the things which they like. (1583 Cooper tr. C:TCJ)

The last phrase in the original reads "we cannot even put in our mouth" (*nosotros no lo podemos meter en la boca*). And the prime example of this was generally raw fish. Mejia in 1584 claimed the Jesuits found eating it "a continual torment" and, as strange as this may sound, thought it edifying for the natives "because they say people who suffer that much to accommodate themselves to them can not but be saintly and come from heaven." If this seems overblown, note that they also believed that "eating it was the reason there were so many lepers in the country." (Alvarez-Taladriz).

Raw, perhaps, but, as a rule, not *as raw* as that eaten today, for it was generally dipped in boiling vinegar (half-way to the herrings of the Dutch) or lightly marinated in a manner that it fermented. The *sushi* we know was not yet developed. That required the creativity of food preparation in the heyday of Edo culture. Be that as it may, before Japan-as-number-one made things Japanese prestigious instead of odd, the prejudice of the West against "raw fish," or *sashimi*, – *sushi*, being thin slices of the fish on rice – not only prevented us from trying it, but even prevented Japanese visitors to the West from eating it. When the 1862 *Bakufu* mission stayed in France, they made *sashimi* and ate it with the 500 bottles of soy sauce they brought along until their "sense of pride . . . forced them to abandon the habit" because they learned a British newspaper compared them to savages in South America. (A:FJE? = LR) One problem was linguistic. As Barthes has pointed out, "for us, rawness is a strong state of food, as is metonymically shown by the intensive seasoning we impose on our steak tartare." (B:EOS) It is more so in his French and the other Latin tongues where rawness is literally "crude" (*cru, crudo, crudité*, etc), with implications of cruelty and savagery. Only Valignano calls it "*pescado salada y fresco*", i.e. "uncooked [[salted?]] and fresh." He must have learned to like it.

6-13   Among us, all fruits are eaten ripe, and only cucumbers green;
Antre nós se comem todas as frutas maduras, e somente os pipinos verdes;

The Japanese [eat] all fruits green, and only cucumbers very yellow and ripe.
Os Japões todas as frutas verdes, e os pipinos somente muito amarelos e maduros.

The Japanese pickled most "fruit," with the apparent exception of, you guessed it, the cucumber! The Portuguese exercised not one iota of influence on Japanese taste in fruit, for the first British ambassador after the Opening, Sir Rutherford Alcock wrote that it was "very difficult to get good peaches to eat" as they were "all habitually plucked unripe" and the Japanese had no idea "what ripe fruit means." Alcock went on at length of the difficulty of trying to train his "market coolie" how to recognize ripeness to no avail. (See *TT-long* for the full quote). About a quarter century later, Morse used another sense to describe the Japanese and their green peaches:

> One can hear a boy bite a peach from across the street, yet in this hard, green state the Japanese seem to prefer them.

> While I am writing this I can see two domestics across the way leaning over a piazza rail eating peaches. The fruit is so green that I can actually hear them as they tear off the bites. They clutch the peaches firmly in their hands as if they were eating the hardest of apples. (M:JDD)

Of all the Japanese fruit, Alcock found only watermelon, persimmon and grapes passable. Strangely, he and Frois overlooked the persimmon, most of which are large and not astringent even though hard and are not only eaten ripe, but post-ripe: dried white with the exuded sugar. Bishop, who agrees with me that the persimmon is "the finest fruit of Japan," found the latter to "taste like a fig."

The difference between fruit in Japan and in the West cannot be described in terms of availability or taste, alone. The attitude toward fruit differs. Most fruit in Japan, until the last two decades of the 20c, was more *gift* than *grocery*. People did not so much eat it with their meals as use it for a gift to present to the host of a house (or office) that one visits. There, it would be peeled and cut neatly up and shared by all. That is why the huge ten-dollar apples and other incredibly expensive fruits sell so well in Japan. It is also seen in abundance at *funeral receptions*. The local green-grocer still derives much of his or her income making baskets of fruit for funeral decoration!

6-14   We cut melons length-wise;   *Nós cortamos o melão ao comprido;*

The Japanese cut them cross-wise.   *Os Japões o cortão ao traves.*

Although Japanese generally cut *melons* like us, length-wise, the *makuwa-uri* (*Cucumis melo var. Makuwa*), which caught Frois's contrast-seeking eyes, was cut cross-wise in thin rings when offered to guests. Logically speaking, it would make sense to cut across all melons that have not been well turned (in the garden) for aesthetic uniformity, and cut length-wise all melons whose ripeness/flavor varies from stem to butt, to ensure each person gets an equal deal. But there may be other matters that come into play. Morse observes that "in serving daikon, a kind of radish, two pieces are always put upon the plate" for one would be *hitokiri*, homophonic for "man-cut," and three, *mikiri*, likewise for "body-cut." So "eggplants and other vegetables, except daikon, must be cut longitudinally and not transversely, because cutting transversely seems cruel." (M:JDD-2) But cutting "transversely" through a *hollow* melon makes a *wagiri*, or ring-cut, and "ring (*wa*)" is is a homophone of "peace/harmony (*wa*)." So *that* was fine. It would not, however have been permissible with a watermelon, for it is solid, flesh-colored and no ring would be made. Speaking of watermelon, I tried to convince a number of grocers to try selling *slices*, or at least dividing them in half, but was always refused. Selling pieces was definitely *not* Japanese they told me. It was an idea that would only fly in American, a society hopelessly infected with selfish individualism (they do not put it quite so plainly, but that was the gist of it). Later, I discovered that in that most purely Japanese time of all, the Secluded Edo era, melons were commonly sold *by the slice* to individuals at a price they could afford. (Since Edo had many times more men than women and most of those men were single, it could hardly have been otherwise!) So much for the stereotypes of pop-Japanology!

6-15   We sniff a melon from the top;   *Nós cheiramos o melão pola cabeça;*

   They from the bottom.   *Elles polo pé.*

See TT-long if you like round-about stories. Here, I will cut to the chase and just tell you why, I believe, this difference makes sense. With our melons, there is a navel-like depression on top which sniffed, does indeed exude far more obvious scent than the bottom. However, *Japanese leave a portion of the stem on the melon for display.* It includes a bit of the main vine as well, so it stands up from the round surface of the melon like the letter "T." The "T" on the "O" not only looks good but is profoundly satisfying for literate people because that "T" is found upside-down in the Chinese character for "melon" (瓜).   Test smell such a melon with its umbilicus still attached and you will find it does not exude any scent to speak of from the top.   If anything, the bottom is a bit more revealing! I should probably stop here and leave well enough alone; but, to tell the truth, I have seen a number of Japanese mothers *sniffing* rather than feeling their baby's diapers, and cannot help but *also* wonder (theory 2) if this bottom-sniffing – in Japan, the bottom of a melon is called its "butt" (*shiri*) – habit might not have been carried over into the grocery store!
..

6-16   We eat it and afterward throw out the rind;
   Nós o comemos, e depois lhe deitamos a casca fora;

   They pare it and throw out the rind before eating.
   Elles o aparão e lhe tirão primeiro a casca fora que o comão.

This is related to what was discussed in 6-1 with respect to chopsticks: people in the Sinosphere tend to completely prepare their food before serving it. The watermelon was an exception; slices were eaten with husk in hand, as we usually eat it. Most melon, not to mention persimmon and pears, are first peeled, and then cut into bite-size pieces. More Faux Frois's might be possible. Vitamins or not, Japanese are not much for skins. Not only do they spit out the inner skins of tangerines (into the peel, which neatly removed forms a receptacle) but squeeze the meat out of grapes.

6-17   We pick green grapes to season our food; *Nós colhemos o agraço pera temperar o comer;*

   They pick them for pickling. *Elles o colhem pera o salgar.*

We once used the juice from green apples and grapes for a condiment called *verjuice*, evidently very sour, for a sour-puss was called *verjuice*. I am unsure how Frois's sour grapes were used. Judging from the Cuban sauces in Miami supermarkets, they were used to season meat for cooking, but the contrast would be enhanced if they were a sweet-sour condiment, for Japanese pickling tends to be heavy on salt – the Portuguese original says "salted." I have never come across these Japanese grape pickles, but working my way back from Japan on Swedish freighters, I discovered how good fruit – lingonberries – could be on meat.

6-18 All of our food, except for bread, is carried out covered;
Todas as nossas yguarias vão cubertas, somente o pão;

> With that of the Japanese, on the contrary, only the rice is covered.
> *As dos Japões pollo comtrairo, e somente o arroz quberto.*

Why was everything of "ours" carried out covered? I think it because we ate almost nothing cold. Most of our dishes were cooked and served hot. The "raw" salads we eat today were yet to be. Bread was an exception. Generally, it was bought at the bakers, as noted previously, so it was not served freshly-made, i.e. hot, like, say, tortillas, which come from the kitchen wrapped in cloth.

The comparison works well because, as we have written, bread and rice are equivalents, the backbone of the meal. Even today, rice is usually set in a covered pot near to the table, so it can be dished out piping hot. But Japanese soup, too, is often carried out covered – the bowl has its own little cover which must be twisted to break the vacuum as it is opened – but that is either a post-Frois development or, as I rather suspect, overlooked it for the sake of a simple, more perfect contrast.

6-19 As much as Europeans are friends of the sweet;
Quanto em Europa são os homens amigos de doce;

> The Japanese are of the salty.
> *Tanto os Japões o são de salgado.*

Okada explains the difference as a result of the fact that salt has long been produced in abundance in Japan, while sugar was an expensive import. *Perhaps*. But the paucity of interest in most ripe fruit that caught Frois's eye makes one wonder whether some other factor may be involved. I crave sweets more when eating bread or noodles than I do with rice, probably because Japanese rice (unlike the *indica* variety popular in the West) *itself* has a relatively high sugar content. Moreover, Japanese *sake* is very sweet, so adult males, at least, got *their* sugar. Isabella Bird's translator Ito, who "invested in sweetmeats everywhere" told her that "all who abstain from sake crave for sugar." (B:UBJ?) Actually, there is a saying to that effect.

The Japanese love for saltiness, in addition to the bread/rice issue mentioned in 6-2, may reflect their low use of other spices. Salt, in the guise of soy sauce and *miso* and pickles must do the trick by itself. But it was also natural for a hard-working people who ate little meat. (Even with their chili peppers, the Koreans likewise overdo salt, while the Eskimos, who ate *only* meat, used *no* salt, for it was in the meat/blood.) Today, people in office jobs sweat far less but keep eating the salty flavor they grew up with. That is why *miso* soup can kill. In some particularly salt-loving provinces in the North of Japan, middle-aged men suffer strokes at rates so high one is reminded of the Swiss whose ridiculously high egg consumption put us on to the relationship of cholesterol to heart-attacks.

There is still much that does not fall into place here. Though Japanese, in accord with Frois, still claim to be astounded by the sweetness of *our* pastry, *their* traditional cakes – if that is what they can be called – that go with tea astound *us* equally, for they are solid sugar! And, their bean-jam tastes *horribly sweet*, although this may be largely because *we are not used to beans-as-jam*. Yet there is one factor, that supports Frois's a broad claim. Japanese do not call things or even people "sweet" (*amai*) in the complimentary sense we do in English (or, Chinese, for that matter!) – it is only used to mean "slut" (*ama'kko*) or, as a predicate adjective, "soft" "shallow" or "a sucker." Owing to our common human nature most metaphors work in most languages, but there are no "sweet" babies or lovers in Japanese! Corollary to this, there are no *sweetie-pies, honeys* or *sugar-buns,* either. Could this lack of a sweet vocabulary in Japanese prove Frois's point? Or, is it only a linguistic quirk?

6-20   Among us, the servants clean up our tables;
Antre nós os pajens alevantão as mezas;

> In Japan, nobles often clean up after themselves.
> *Em Japão os mesmos fidalgos que comem aleva[ntã]o muitas [ve]zes as suas.*

This may be misleading; if Okada is correct, it applies only to etiquette *in a tea-hut,* a place where the host does the serving. He cites a contemporary document instructing that the participants arrange everything on their trays and take them to the entrance/window(?) to the kitchen (*katteguchi*) after the ceremony ends. I suspect that not only Way of the Tea equality, but the fact the *dogu,* or tea-ware, was often the host's most valuable possessions – the equivalent of large diamonds in the West, *but breakable* – may have had something to do with this!

6-21   We wash our hands before and after a meal;
Nos lavamos as mãos no principio e fim da meza;

> The Japanese, since they don't touch their food, have no need to wash them.
> *Os Japões, como não põem a mão no comer, não tem necessidade de as lavar.*

This is one of the relatively rare contrasts including the explanation. The exception for the Japanese is the tea ceremony, where the priceless vessels are taken in hand and respect dictated that hands were washed, much as they are washed entering some Shinto shrines. Today, Japanese restaurants offer a hot wet washcloth-sized rolled towel to wipe ones hands and face before eating. This is an idea adopted from China and is more for refreshing ones senses than cleanliness, for these towels are notoriously germ-ridden. So long as we are on that subject, let me add that according to Marques, with the adoption of the fork, European hygiene would soon worsen, for many would stop washing their hands before their meals (M:DLP).

6-22   We eat our vermicelli hot and cut up;
Nós comemos a aletria quente e cortada;

> [*They*] place it in cold water and eat it very long.
> *[Elles a] metem em agoa fria e a comem muito comprida.*

The cold water referred to is not a condiment but part of the preparation of the noodles. The hot noodles are quickly cooled down to preserve the "hips," that is to say the bite. Long before *insutanto ramen,* Japanese noodles were quicker cooking than most pasta. With the thinner noodles such as the hair-thin *somen,* Okada guesses Frois is referring to here – the Portuguese *comprida* has a *stretched long and thin* feeling, not found in any English word – the line between *al dente* and sogginess is very fine. Most varieties of Japanese noodles may be eaten cold. The Koreans have far more varieties of delicious cold noodles – perhaps because they are heated sufficiently by chili peppers – and sometimes put ice cubes in with them!

It is much easier to eat any type of noodles in the East Asian style, using chopsticks and slurping from a raised bowl, than in our slower and, when you think about it, *ludicrous* method of spooling it on a fork twirling in a spoon! After having experienced the *ease* of eating it the Japanese way, I sometimes feel we should either eat our spaghetti "their" way, or cut it up, as the Portuguese and Spaniards of Frois's day evidently did and have done with it!

6-23 We eat [vermicelli/pasta] with sugar, egg and cinnamon;
Nós a comemos com asuqre e ovos e canela;

They eat it with mustard and chili pepper.
Elles a comem com mostarda e pimenta.

The pasta we are familiar with was yet to be. I knew Latinos, with their rice pudding and bread pudding, had teeth so sweet all grains turn into desert, but *noodles?* This "we" was new to me. M&J back it up with a sentence from De Nola's famous *Book of the Glutton* (*Libro de Guisanos*: 1529). The pasta, after being rinsed in cold water, is "simmered in chicken or meat (?) broth, then seasoned with sugar and goat or lamb milk," and, if this is not enough, served up with sugar and cinnamon sprinkled on!

The Japanese often include sweet *sake* in sauce for *somen* (thin noodles) and, rarely, mandarin orange slices, too – so the contrast was probably not *that* black and white, unless they learned this sweet style of eating noodles from the Portuguese. While Japanese do use mustard with some Chinese dishes (egg-rolls, gyôza dumplings, pork), I have never encountered it with noodles. Could Frois's "mustard," then, be *wasabi,* horse radish, good in the sauce cold buckwheat noodles are dipped in?

6-24 Europeans love chicken, quail, pie and blancmange;
Os de Europa folgão com galinhas, perdizes, pasteis, e manjar branco;

The Japanese, wild-dog, crane, monkey, cat and raw seaweed.
Os Japãos com adibes, grous, bojios, gatos e limos e limos da praya cruz.

M&J, who translate *blancmange* as "creamy white jelly" note that De Nola called it "the king of dishes." *Manjar blanca* was created by boiling a fat and succulent chicken, rice flour, rose-water, sugar, goat's milk, or white almond and saffron, until the chicken looks like melted white cheese, then sprinkling pretty fine sugar upon it. They also note that a 1485 German cookbook does not even mention beef. It was not as popular as pork and poultry. I would guess that in South Europe, fish was more common than pork, too.

This is a lousy contrast, for all but the blancmange are fairly common food in Europe, while only the seaweed was and is common food in Japan. The Japanese items:

Dog. In Korea, dog was eaten by men to gain stamina in the dog days of late summer. In Japan, where there was no central heating, it was considered good warming medicine for making it through the winter. Samurai would present it to inferiors in the early winter. (Okada) Some Koreans still eat it. No Japanese do.

Crane was a banquette food for nobility. Since the bird was a symbol of longevity, it was an auspicious food. Since Frois was lucky enough to know and eat with the rulers of Japan, he was familiar with this extraordinary food. He never had such an opportunity in Europe, or he might have known that the nobility *there* ate not only cranes, but *flamingo* and *peacocks*. Very, very few Japanese ever tasted crane.

Monkey. Japan had and still has a few monkey temples – havens for these macaques, something like what is done on a larger scale in India and the Japanese have never done the cruel things done to monkeys in parts of South East Asia (where, the brains are eaten out of live ones!). But they do raid crops, make love to bitches and kidnap puppies! Japanese farmers doubtless welcomed their hunting and, according to Okada, they were available at a Hunters' Market one station beyond Yotsuya (the edge of Edo). Today, the very idea of eating monkey would *horrify* Japanese.

Cat may be a mistake. Okada believes Frois mistook *tanuki* (racoon dog), weasel or something else for cat. However, considering the fact that cat skin was used for making *shamisen*, and it is unlikely the rest of the cat went to waste, I would bet that *some* cats were eaten by *someone*. The irony here is that, if cat was eaten *anywhere*, it was in Europe! According to M & J, De Nola's famous book included a recipe for *roasted cat*. "After removing the hair (singed?), the cat (Pyrenees wild cats are best) is wrapped in hempen cloth and buried in the ground overnight, then (?) garlic and oil is rubbed in, and the cat roasted, after which it is carried (whole?) to the table like rabbit or veal." The author also advised that "the brain not be eaten, lest the diner become crazy in the head." (Note: this cookbook by the chef of Rey Hernando de Napoles was *the* best-selling book of 16c Spain!)

Raw seaweed. Finally, an everyday food. But one rarely comes across "sea-weed" (*kaiso* actually sea-*grass*) in Japan. Japanese no more eat "sea-weed" than we eat "land-weed." They eat *nori, ishinori, konbu, wakame, mozu, hijiki,* etc.. Most of these are processed or cooked, but many varieties of raw "seaweed" whose names are only known by gourmets are served on a *sashimi* platter. Frois's *limos da praya*, or "scum/slime/ ooze of the beach" suggests two of the six varieties above-mentioned, for they really are slimy. Today, *seaweed* in Portuguese is "alga" and *sea-grass* "sargaço."

Montanus, hyping Valignano, wrote:

And that we account delicate, dainty or a well-seasoned Dish, that they spit out, and their Stomacks rise at: In like manner, what they highly commend, and seems to have a most delicious gust, that we as much abhor. (M:EEJ)

With Frois's examples, such a claim would fall flat, for he forgets to include European items likely to have disgusted Japanese. Meat ground-up and *stuffed into intestine* (sausage), stuff *squirted from cow*, *sheep or goat tits* (milk), left to age and harden (cheese) – that type of thing. Here, I can't help thinking of a different contrast altogether. Europe and Japan *versus* China. *We in Europe and Japan eat some things but not others; In China, they eat everything!* (For two more pages on China, on how we prepared peacock, etc. see *TT-long*).

~~~~~~

6-25   We eat trout lightly broiled or stewed/baked/boiled;
Nós comemos as trutas asadas brandamente ou cozidas;

They spit them on wood and roast them until they are burnt.
Elles as espetão em paos e poem a asar até ficarem torradas.

In the old country hotel where I spent my first few months in Japan, the smoke always gave away breakfast and I can remember my father explaining "they never *cook* fish, they always *burn* it! As most of the blackened part was on the skin-side of the slices, and the heavily salted skin might be discarded anyway, this was not so crazy as it might seem. A sympathetic view would be that Japanese have learned how to barbecue on a plain gas range (Honest to goodness, they do it on the stove!). From reading Frois, we can see they had centuries of practice at it, and had only to adapt themselves to gas. With the traditional fire, the end of the spit for the trout was stuck diagonally into the sand around the fire/coals so the fish, head up, leaned over the heat. This was more commonly done for the smaller *ayu*, or sweetfish, than trout, but Frois probably did not want to introduce a new fish to his imagined audience. The contrast is also weak, for baking and roasting are hardly contrary. This is better:

We drop lobsters alive into boiling water but don't eat them until they are good and dead;
They cut up fish alive and eat them while they still quiver with life.

It is pretty shocking to see a fish with its diced up meat arranged upon it – like the yellow of a devilled egg returned to the white – with its tail still flickering with life. Apparently (I have not seen it), the slices were sometimes left tenuously in place and a drop of vinegar applied to the fish's eyes to induce a convulsion and pull the slices apart. It is puzzling to find such a "cruel and disgusting spectacle" (de Hubner, cited in L:IOJ) in Buddhist Japan, where the traditional poets went on and on about the sinful occupation of the cormorant-fisherman! (In defense of the Japanese, let me say that fish are not very sensitive animals. Once, I caught a large mackerel, hammered it on the head, cut off fillets on both sides flush to the backbone and tossed the skeletal remnant into the water, where it immediately revived and swam off!) But I do not know if Japanese ate sashimi like this in 1585.

6-26   With us, wine is chilled;
Antre nós se esfria o vinho;

> In Japan, it is heated for drinking practically all year round.
> *Em Japão, pera se beber, quasi todo ano se aqenta.*

Imagine coming home for *a hot one* rather than a cool one! In the absence of ice, it is easier to heat something than to cool it. But ice was as available in Japan as in Europe. Issa even mentions an ice-seller shivering at the first sign of fall – when the demand for his product would drop. *Sake* lovers explain how the heat brings out this or that quality of the *sake*, but I believe the wariness Japanese had, and still have for all cold drinks was probably the main incentive. To me, nothing tastes more refreshing than good cold *sake* (the one with a resinous scent called *masuzake*) in a cedar cup with a pinch of salt on the corner. *Corner?*

> Our cups always have circular rims;
> Some of theirs are completely square.

As far as I know, drinking from square cups is a far rarer phenomenon than warm drinks. I am not certain whether these cups evolved from high-sided square trays for *sake* cups sometimes used at banquettes in Frois's day, or from square *measures* adopted for cups; but suspect that one reason they are used on celebratory occasions today is because their name, *masu,* happens to be a homophone for "increase!" But, to return to the subject of Frois's contrast, twenty years after *Tratado*, Rodrigues complicates the picture. The "true and ancient custom," he writes, was for warm wine "to be drunk from the ninth day of the ninth moon until the third day of the third moon, except for the first wine which is brought out on New Year visits, . . . For the rest of the year cold wine should be drunk, although nowadays this is neither usual nor definite because everybody now drinks warm wine all the year round." (R(C):TIJ) He also noted that the Chinese drank "warm wine throughout the year;" but did not mention that in mid-16c France, the custom of drinking wine warmed by the fireplace or diluted with warm water was popular, or that wine was sometimes warmed by dropping hot pieces of toast, white hot pieces of iron, gold or, in the case of the poor, burning coals into it! (M&J) Be that as it may, Frois had the big picture right.

6-27   Our wine is of grapes;   *Ho nosso vinho hé de uvas;*

> Theirs is all of rice.   *O seu hé todo de arroz.*

I would add another contrast:

> Our wine, red, white or pink is clear;
> Theirs comes in two types, clear and cloudy.

The latter is called *nigorishû* or "murky *sake.*" It is usually translated as "raw sake," but does not taste as raw or sour as Korean *makali* or Mexican *pulque,* both of which I love. Once, I suspect, it was the most common type of *sake,* but it is rarely drunken today. Japanese, like most people, tend to go for clear alcohol if given a choice. The last time I went to Korea, beer was beating the pants off *makali* and my Korean friends thought me terribly old-fashioned to prefer *makali.*

6-28   We drink with one hand; *Nós bebemos com huma mão;*

They always drink with two. *Elles sempre bebem com duas.*

Men, that is (see 2-64). Although Japanese *sake* cups were bigger than Chinese ones, they were still usually smaller than ours. There was no physical reason for using two hands when two fingers suffice. To receive something with both hands shows it is not taken lightly and to continue to cup it while drinking, I think, was an unconscious token of sincerity (see 1-34). Just a guess, but if I am not mistaken, Japanese used two hands with superiors or equals with whom they were not on familiar terms but slacked off with others, except at a tea hut, where all were equal before the tea. Today, two-handed *sake* drinking is as polite as it is rare. I imagine it most common with the old-fashioned *yakuza.*

Frois's contrast also concerns only the receiving end. He might have complemented it with a contrast on *pouring*:

We pour wine with our arm bent in a natural manner;
They pour theirs with both arms held straight out and rigid.

This idea of propriety through stiffness – straight arms rather than bent ones – is still understood in Japan, but adhered to less dramatically than in Korea, where the straight right arm was braced by a straight left arm with the hand clasping the wrist of the right arm as recently as 1980 (when I was there).

6-29   We drink seated on chairs; *Nós quando bebemos, estamos asentados em cadeiras;*

They, setting on their knees. *Elles postos de jiolhos.*

Again, *formal* drinking where men sit "back on their feet with their knees pointing forward." (Rodrigues) Men did not always drink like that – they also sat cross-legged – and today seldom do.

6-30   We drink from cups of silver, glass or porcelain;
Antre nós se bebe por copos de prata ou vidro ou porcelina;

The Japanese from *sakazuki* of wood or clay *kawarake* [unglazed earthenware].
Os Japões por sacanzuqi de pao, ou cavaraque de barro.

A *sakazuki* is a *sake* cup. It is the shape of a martini glass, but, generally smaller than a shot-glass, though sumo tournament champions down their *sake* from cups as large as a garbage can lid. Frois is both right and wrong to describe them simply as *wood or clay.*

Rodrigues mentions *sakazuki* made of "gold, silver, unicorn, or rhinoceros horn, red sandalwood," "the very large red and beautiful beaks of certain birds found in China, very fine red scented wood with delicate work on the outside, while the inside where the wine is poured is overlaid with silver" as well as porcelain, "the meanest of them all." (R(C):TIJ) His paragraph-long descriptions of "five kinds of cups which they use when they entertain guests with wine [sake]," reveal far more precious material than Frois might lead us to anticipate, and more remarkable yet, a three-legged cedar "salver" or tray shaped in "imitation of a jagged seashore with its entrances and exits like the bays and capes of a shore, . . . painted entirely blue, or the colour of the sea, and decorated with various patterns of flowers or small trees, especially the pine which grows along the coast . . ." (Ibid) that held up to five gilded earthenware cups.

Yet, Frois's contrast of "our" luxurious items with apparently crude materials on the Japanese side is an excellent one *once you know what he is driving at*, or should be driving at. The wooden and unglazed clay cups such as those he mentions are *always new* and *only used once*. This, and their primal appearance made them appropriate for the New Years and other ancient ceremonies. Some reports say the Emperor used such cups because everything he used was used only once, then destroyed so no one else could use them. Indirect confirmation comes from the December 8, 1857 notes of the first American Consul to Japan, Townsend Harris: "The dinner sent to me was placed on some forty to fifty trays made of unpainted wood. . . . I was told that the trays and other utensils, after having been used by me, could never be used by another person, and therefore they were made of unvarnished wood, this being the custom of Japan when presenting food to persons of exalted rank, etc., etc. (H:JJ) The poor man, who had long suffered from a strong appetite, but weak digestion, was sick that day, and, torture of tortures, "unable to eat a morsel" from all those trays! Perhaps I should add for the consolation of poor Harris's soul that those who are most commonly served in unglazed pottery don't eat it either. I refer to the offerings left on the "god-shelves" of the household shrine.

Even Rodrigues, for all his evident appreciation of the naturalism of the tea ceremony and its apparently simple, but incredibly expensive *dogu,* had no sympathy for these throw-away items. The unglazed pottery was literally worthless, he complained, "there is a great number of them on sale . . . and they are so cheap that they are hardly worth anything at all." Moreover, "this sort of new earthenware cup is dry and therefore sticks a good deal to the lips, people who are not careful sometimes find themselves in trouble because they cannot easily unstick them; before they drink, they first of all must moisten their lips . . ." (A good Japanese drinker barely touches a cup to his lips. He moves his whole head back lightly as the cup meets his lips rather than turning the cup edge in his mouth as we do. Someone who drank with the proper alacrity might not need to wet his lips. Evidently, for all his smarts, Rodrigues was not a good drinker in the Japanese style.). His last word on the unglazed *kawarake* was "Whence can be seen the power of ancient customs and notions of countries that could well use precious and convenient things which do not have such drawbacks, but instead leave them aside in favour of those of little worth, whose use offers such difficulties." (R(C):TIJ)

For us "worth" was and still is largely dependent on either the substance from which an item is made or the name value of its maker. The idea of using service of cheap substance made by unknown craftsmen and of little monetary value on important occasions escapes us. Japanese were appreciative of gold and silver, but they were *also* fond of something we failed to find value in: *material evoking our connection to the primal elements.*

6-31 With us, no one drinks more than he himself wants to, without being persuaded by others; *Antre nós não bebe cada hum mais que aquilo que qer, sem persuasão dos outros;*

Japanese are so demanding they make some throw up and others drunk.
Em Japão se importunão tanto, que a huns fazem arrevesar e a outros embebedar-se.

Forced drinking in Japan was the child of pushiness and pride. Rodrigues observed that men took pride in their drinking ability and would not refuse when challenged to a drinking match, "because they regard it just as if they were fighting a battle or duel." Moreover, there were professional instigators, "woman dancers and singers and other types of depraved people, who, when they drink, challenge whomsoever they wish to partake as well; they take the cup from which they have drunk and give it to a person, and pride prevents his refusing to accept it and drink from it." Sometimes this escalates until some "challenge others to drink wine from hand-basins and other large vessels." Moreover, "thousands of kinds" of tasty appetizers were concocted "as incentives" for drink. He found it "astonishing to note the various devices and means, which the devil has taught them to encourage much wine drinking, and those who drink next to nothing are often obliged to partake. There are cases in which such people cannot avoid doing so, nor will any excuse be accepted, so they are obliged to drink even when it is injurious to their health." (R(C):TIJ)

So Frois was right about Japan. But Europe may have been a bit less angelic than he paints it. M&J quote a February 12, 1528 letter of Erasmus of Rotterdam criticizing a banquette where he was forced to drink and Thomas Coryat (*Coryat's Crudities*, vol.I,II:1611) on how a wine-glass full of wine would be given to a man in Germany, who would be, then considered impolite unless he drank it down to the other's health and handed it back (Even without reading such evidence, can anyone imagine Occidental drunks not being pushy?). Yet, I think it is true that despite the generally mild nature of the Japanese, even today there is a stronger tendency for drinking men to *push drinks* on others in Japan than in the USA at least. This is doubly bad for Japanese because so high a proportion of the population has a degree of alcohol intolerance. A late-19c traveler, who evidently did not know this, mistook it for a peculiar property of *sake,* declaring its "first effect is to loosen the tongue and limber the joints; its second to turn the whole body flaming red" (S:JDJ) Even that is not quite accurate, for many if not most Japanese turn beet red *after only a sip*, that is *before* loosening their tongues. Not surprisingly, the Japanese themselves have long been aware that pushing drinks on people is bad. About 250 years before *Tratado*, the Buddhist priest Kenko wrote "I cannot imagine why people find it so enjoyable to push liquor on you the first thing, on every occasion, and force you to drink it." After describing the many agonies of a hang-over, its disastrous effects on one's work, and the cruelty of the practice of pushing drinks, he concludes "If it were reported that such a custom, unknown among ourselves, existed in some foreign country, we should certainly find it peculiar and even incredible . . . Buddha taught that a man who takes liquor and forces another to drink will be reborn a thousand times without hands. . . (K(K):EI)

Kenkô was wrong to make it purely a matter of private morals. Considering the various types of exchanges of multiple cups, sequential drinking from single cups (something the Chinese never do, according to Rodrigues), etc. – we can see that half of the forced drinking problem was systematic rather than individual. *First*, there was a tradition, still expressed in song today, of drinking as manly and manliness as Japanese, so, one man can turn to another who wishes not to drink and chide him: "And you call yourself a Japanese!" *Second*, there were customary *ways of drinking*, similar to that Coryat described for Germany, requiring the exchange of drinks or the partaking of a cup that was passed from man to man. The Japanese government made refusal of such offers (and the substitution of tea) officially acceptable shortly after the country reopened in the mid 19c (more in *TT-long*).

There is a paradox which deserves note. While the open drunkenness and lavish banquettes, i.e. parties, found in Japan were attributed by the Jesuits to the pagan propensity to favor flesh over soul, the same Jesuits and other observers from Xavier on unanimously agreed the Japanese were, *generally*, moderate eaters and drinkers. Valignano's last word on the subject was that even the wealthy and the grandees of Japan are more parsimonious eaters than most Europeans. The Japanese are "content with few things, which is something that puts to shame the Christians of Europe, who, parting from the teachings of *Jesucristo,* go looking for so many inventions=discoveries of food to satisfy the palate (that more seem to live to eat than to eat to live), and justly, in punishment for over-eating, suffer from many and grave illnesses, and also shorten their lives."(1601 in V(A):S&A)

6-32   To us, it would be nauseating to drink from a bowl that held chicken, fish or meat;
Antre nós beber pola tijela de caldo, de pexe ou carne se teria por nojo;

> In Japan, it is common to empty one's *shiru-goki* [soup-bowl] and drink from it.
> *Em Japão hé muito uzado despejar o xiru goqi e beber por elle.*

I have known Japanese to drink their tea this way, but not *sake*. Okada writes it must have been common in Frois's day and documents it with two episodes from a journal whose name Englishes as "drunk-sleep-smile/laugh," one of which tells of drinking 4 servings of dessert sake, each from a larger bowl, the last being the rice bowl! Another way to put this would be:

We flavor our food with a little wine;
They flavor their wine with a little food.

For some reason, *sake* tastes alright like this, while wine does not. I have even drunk *sake* in the shell of a crab after eating out the inside. The after-taste of crab eggs is said to enhance the *sake!*

6-33   Our everyday drinking water has to be cold and clear;
Antre nós a agoa que se bebe antre-dia á-de ser fria e clara;

> For the Japanese, it has to be hot and have tea powder frothed up with a bamboo whisk [in it]. *A dos Japões à de serqente e à-de levar pós de chá batidos com huma escova de cana.*

While cocoa, an invention of nuns in Mexico, would become very popular in another decade or two, Iberia was and would remain the cold drink capitol of Europe. According to Defourneaux, there was a great demand for orange juice, strawberry water and orgeat (almond and orange), things generally tastiest cool. "Great quantities of snow were taken during the winter from the Sierra, which is some 40 kilometers from Madrid, and deposited in 'snow-pits' . . . [and] sold in turn for cold drinks and sherbets." (D:DLS) Presumably, this predilection for cold extended to water.

In Japan, tea was *de rigor* at temples, despite the fact they tended to include mountain springs. Frois describes only one way of making tea – to quote Bishop, with "the appearance and consistency of pea-soup" – with the expensive bright green powder now identified with the tea ceremony, which was once drunken with meals by the well-to-do. Usually, tea was made from leaves lightly steeped. A more generally valid contrast would have specified that in much of Japan, *water has to be drunken hot as tea, barley tea or noodle cooking water.*" I write "much of Japan" for there was regional variation, as pointed out by Rodrigues. To the East of Kanto, "they drank cold water even in the winter." (R(C):TIJ) Frois knew the half of Japan closest to Korea, where even the horse were rarely allowed to drink water (They were fed on "brown slush as hot as they can drink it, composed of beans, chopped millet stalks, rice husks, and bran, with the water in which they have been boiled. (Bird:K)) did not know the Kanto (=Edo=Tokyo area). But even in Edo, cold water was probably viewed with trepidation by many. In the "Tokio" chapter of her 1891 book, Skidmore chuckled "The Japanese seldom drink water, although they splash, dabble, or soak in it half the time." (S:JDJ) I think this is because Japanese think it important to keep the belly warm. Many if not most Japanese of middle age and up have, until recent years, worn belly-wraps around the clock. Many still do. Perhaps the risk of disease had something to do with this, for even if Japan had a good water supply and effective recycling of human waste, the populated area was very crowded and the summer hot. In the words of an old *senryu*: "water, sir, / is poison!" says the vender / of watermelons" (*mizu-wa doku de gozarimasu to suika-uri*). Since we all know how hard watermelon is to digest, it is not hard to imagine how cold water was viewed!

As it turns out, much of Europe in 1585 was like Japan and Korea, rather than the Spanish and Portuguese, with one important difference. Beer and wine, rather than tea, was drunken instead of water, all day long. A century or two later, tea was cheaper in the West. Industrial workers in crowded cities who could not afford to drink enough to avoid drinking polluted water, benefited from its anti-bacterial properties. As one Cambridge professor put it, they were saved, together with the industrial revolution that might have collapsed had they fled back into the country, by the tea-break. (See *TT-long* for a 3 page discussion, and Andrew Barr's excellent *Drink: A Social History Of America* for how we got from hard liquor to the water fountain in the USA.)

6-34   Among us, the burnt rice at the bottom of the pot is thrown out or given to the dogs;
Antre nós o arros qeimado do fundo do tacho se deita for a ou se dá aos cães;

In Japan it becomes the after-dinner fruit or is thrown into the hot water drunk at the end. *Em Japão hé fruta de sobremeza ou se deita na agoa q[ente] que se bebe no cabo.*

"After-dinner fruit" would appear to be the start of what we now call "dessert!"

Okada explains that the Japanese practice is due to the respect paid by Japanese to every last grain of rice. In this era, where each lord's holdings were described in terms of its potential rice harvest rather than acreage, rice had indeed become more than a food; but it wasn't yet the sacred=imperial=Japanese object that neo-nationalist myth-makers would create centuries later. Indeed, I question the Okada's assumption that all the rice was always eaten. Many Japanese may well have felt it better to leave rice for servants or pets or fertilizer. Otherwise, how could Bird note a superstition like "for children to eat the charred rice which sometimes remains at the bottom of the rice-pot is to ensure their marriage to persons scarred with small-pox?" (B:UTJ) It was also a matter of taste and mouthfeel. I know Japanese who *like* the crispy "burnt" part (which is to rice what toast is to bread). Sometimes it comes out cracker-like, tasty even for this Westerner. Perhaps, too, Japanese who were not from the part (North) with the superstition recorded by Bird, were allowed to scrap off and eat it as children, as we lick mixing bowls, and this psychologically endears it to them as adults.

  While Japanese can still get excited about their rice – and I, too, defend rice-nationalism because paddies mean *frogs and ducks* – most of the rice at the bottom of the cooker or, worse, the bowl, no longer religiously consumed or superstitiously avoided, goes to *wan-chan* and *nyan-chan*, the dogs and cats of the house, as mentioned before. Despite the dear price of rice in Japan, one is amazed to see more old rice than pet-food in their feeding bowls!

6-35   With us, the drinking commences as soon as [the meal] starts;
Antre nós logo depois do principio se começa a beber;

In Japan, they start bringing out the wine toward the end of the meal.
Os Japões, quasi no cabo da meza emtão começa a vir o vinho.

Japanese also drank *before* eating. Sladen in 1905 wrote "a man who is fond of his cups drinks heavily before dinner, and not afterwards, as he does in England," and I would bet that custom was the same in 1585. Frois only contrasts drinking *as part of a formal meal*. But even formal culinary events may have offered more variety. Kaempfer, toward the end of the 17c, describe a delicious 8-dish course, where "after every one of these dishes, they made us drink a dish of Sacki, as good as ever I tasted." It is possible they broke out the drink early for the foreigners, but I doubt it. Probably, because sake is relatively sweet, like an after-dinner wine, it is best after things. And, why not after each dish rather than at the very end? Cruz, describing Japan's ancient model for decorum, the Chinese:

> They also had a very tiny gilt porcelain [cup] that carried one mouthful [*bocado*] of wine, and had a waiter for it by the table. They drank so little because for each mouthful of food they had to take a mouthful of drink, and for that the cup is so tiny. (Note: *bocado* is more like a "bite" than a "mouthful," – for the mouth is not filled – but "a bite of food and a bite of wine" does not work. (C:TCC)

Was Frois so busy contrasting the crude Japanese sake cup and yucky manner of drinking with the more elegant West, that he forgot to contrast the thimble-sized *sake* cup with our huge mugs? Or, did Japanese, drinking from their dishes and, according to Giron rice-bowl tops, rarely use the tiny cups we know?

6-36 We do not drink out of the porcelain in which we eat our soup or rice without washing it;
Antre nós na porselana em que se comeo caldo ou arroz não se bebe por ella sem se lavar;

> The Japanese dump out the *shiru* [soup] from the rice *goki* [bowl] and then drink hot water from it. *Os Japões, deitando xiru no goqi do arroz, bebem depois a agoa qente por elle.*

Porcelain, from the Portuguese (from the shiny *cowry shell*) got to England in the 16c, whereas *china* did not until the 17c, so I use the former word though it reads poorly. This contrast is the water equivalent of 6-32, where *sake* was drunk from the same. One contrast naming both liquids would have sufficed. If 6-32 was about the etiquette of formal dinners, this one is about everyday meals, when *sake* was rarely drunken. Unlike the French with their wine, Japanese, like most Usanians today, generally *drank to drink.* This was inevitable in Japan because of the high percentage of people allergic to alcohol. In the United States, it is because of a lingering prejudice against alcohol and fear of addiction in a society that does not have, and so, does not believe in, self-control.

6-37 Our quills for the teeth are very short;
As nossas penas pera os dentes são muyto curtas;

> The sticks for the teeth of the Japanese at times surpass a palm [8-9"] in length. *Os paos pera os dentes dos Japões passão às vezes dum palmo.*

To us, today, this might seem a trivial contrast, but in the 16c toothpicks were considered *fashionable accessories* by some of "us." Googling brought me a *picture* of a 16c silver tooth-pick that looks like a miniature screwdriver with a big jewel embedded in its butt and a finely engraved silver cover; *knowledge* that 16c teeth from Europe occasionally show a notable loss of enamel accompanied by scratch marks as a result of metal toothpick usage, which this made "us" similar to our ancestors, for "grooves on the approximal surfaces of molars in Paleolithic persons are attributed to the sustained use of bone needle tooth picks;" and, less importantly, that the nine-day queen of Henry VIII Lady Jane Grey collected "a motley assortment of fish-shaped toothpicks" and Shakespeare's character Clown (*The Winter's Tale*) recognized "a great man . . . by the picking on's teeth" or perhaps by the fact (?) *the toothpick in its jeweld case might be dispalyed in the hatband* (!?). The only thing I could find on the Spanish or Portuguese toothpick in particular was *a line in Cervantes* (ch.44) *"Poor gentleman of good family! always cockering up his honour, dining miserably and in secret, and making a hypocrite of the toothpick with which he sallies out into the street after eating nothing to oblige him to use it!"* (trans. Ormsby). Since *George Gascoigne's foolish traveller* –

an "Italianated character" (or fop) – "*came home in 1572 with a toothpick hanging out of his mouth,*" we can assume the habit came from the South side of Europe.

Okada writes that Japanese toothpicks were generally between three and fourteen inches in length. The short ones, called "fingernail toothpicks" (*tsuma-yoji*), used today in Japan, caught on much later. Japanese toothpicks are cut rectangular rather than round and almost always made of bamboo. Anyone who has used both prefers theirs. But the Japanese can keep the sucking noise that traditionally (?) accompanies the use of said toothpick!

~~~~~~

6-38 Among us, to be drunk is offensive and to a man's discredit;
Antre nós hé grande injuria e descredito embebedar-se hum homem;

In Japan, they are proud of it and asked: "How is your Tono [master]?" reply "He's drunk." *Em Japão se prezão disso, e perguntando: "Que faz o Tono?" dizem: "Está bebado."*

True, the Iberians may not have drunken much. Even in the more decadent mid-17c, the Countess d' Aulnoy noted their dryness: "One could not enrage them [the Spaniards] more then to accuse them of being drunk" (D:DLS). But all of Europe? As M & J point out, the writing of the time singled out the French and Germans for being big drinkers. Still, they admit, even the liberal Erasmus and Montague found drunkenness ignominious if not immoral (though the latter's attitude is more complex than that might indicate). Yes, Montaigne thought drunkenness was "a particularly gross and brutish vice" because men lose their rational facilities; but he *also* admitted not all men forget themselves when they drink and joked that the Germans whose aim was "to swallow rather than to taste" have "much the better part of the bargain" for "their pleasure is . . . plentiful and right at hand," while the French style of drinking "at two meals and moderately, for fear of your health, is to restrain the god's favor too much." After all, "the ancients spent whole nights at this exercise and often added the days . . ." ("Of drunkenness" M(F):MEM) And, shortly after Montaigne wrote, about the time Frois wrote *Tratado*, even the hitherto sober "English in their long wars in the Netherlands first learnt to drown themselves with immoderate drinking and by drinking other people's healths impair their own." (Camden's *History of Queen Elizabeth* quoted in *Curiousities of Literature* v5, London 1823). Tom Nash, in *Pierce Pennilesse* (1595), wrote that this *Sin* of "superfluity in drink" that came from the *Low-Countries* was previously "held in that highest degree of hatred that might be" and

Then if we had seen a man go wallowing in the streets, or lain sleeping under the board, we should have spet at him, and warned all our friends out of his company. (in *Curiousities*)

His "previously" describes Frois's "us." While laws were passed to try to stem the rising flood of spirit, they failed. Pepys & co. a couple centuries later drank until they spewed or dropped. Still, no one (unless it be Rabelais, indirectly) came out clearly and asked: *"Why not? Why, the hell, not!"* The Christian West insisted drunkenness was *bad.* In that sense, the spirit of Frois's contrast holds true for *all* of Europe.

In Japan, on the other hand, Rodrigues writes, "all the banquets, revelries and recreations are aimed at persuading them by various means to drink too much wine until they end up drunk and many of them completely lose their senses. The Chinese and the Japanese do not consider drunkenness in banquets and revelries as something wrong." (R(C):TIJ) And, what about those who live between China and Japan? Bishop in 1897: "I should say that drunkenness is an outstanding feature in Korea. . . . If a man drinks rice wine til he loses his reason, no one regards him as a beast. A great dignitary even may roll on the floor drunk at the end of a meal, at which he has eaten to repletion, without losing caste, and on becoming sober receives the congratulations of inferiors on being rich enough to afford such a luxury."

Despite the Confucian stress on propriety (or, is drunkenness needed as an escape *because of* it?), the Sinosphere *still* doesn't think it *wrong*. And *why should they?* If it is wrong to lose our senses, then we sin every day, *by sleeping.* If the Ancients in the West were not ashamed to get drunk, and the Ten Commandments say nothing, what is the problem? More than anything else, it would seem to be *our character.* With a few notable exceptions, visitors to Japan have pronounced them pleasant drunks compared to us. (See *TT-long* for another page, i.e. a more finely nuanced discussion).

~~~~~~

6-39 We esteem things of milk, cheese, butter and marrow;
Nos estimamos couzas de leite, queijo e manteiga e tutanos

> The Japanese abhor all this and it smells very bad to them.
> *Os Japões abominão tudo isto e cheira-lhe muito mal.*

Eating raw fish is no big thing. Many mammals do it. But squeezing a substance from the living body of another species and eating it? We are the only mammals to act like ants with their aphids! Van Linschoten gives a reason for the Japanese distaste for dairy products:

> they doe likewise refuse to eate Milke, as wee doe bloud, saying that Milke although it is white, yet it is verie bloude. (L:VJHVL)

Philosophy lost. Today, most Japanese like all milk products that are not sour. I should add that coming to Japan in the early 1970's, nothing Japanese I ate shocked me half so much as how men in bars *ate butter*: thick slices of it with two or three raisins embedded in each, eaten with tooth-picks as appetizers. *We* may be called "butter-stinky" (*bata-kusai*), but only Japanese actually *eat* the stuff!

While I, like any Occidental who is not vegetarian, love sucking the marrow from bones, it puzzled me that Frois put an item so minor as marrow together with dairy products until I read enough 16c recipes to realize this marrow was thought of as a "dainty" and served as a thickener and flavor enhancer for pottage, broth, stuffing, tarts, pies, cakes, puddings and other pastries. Obviously, the sweets and the meats had much more in common in those days than today.

~~~~~~

6-40 We season our food with diverse spices;
Nós temperamos o comer com diversos adubos;

> The Japanese with *miso* [bean-paste], which has rice and rotten grain blended with salt. *Os Japões com* miso, *que hé arroz e graos podres misturados com sal.*

Yes we did; and, many of those spices came from "the East Indies" – they helped get the Jesuits *to* Japan, but they were not *in* Japan.

Japanese *miso,* or at least most modern Japanese *miso* is boring, i.e., lacks bite, doesn't stink enough (compared to Korean *miso,* which I love) to my mind; – Frois's "rotten" rather than *fermented* grain suggests that the *miso* at that time might have been nastier=better than it is now! That Frois does not mention the main ingredient of *miso*, namely *soy beans* (mentioned in the contemporary Nipo dict.) suggests, once again, that the contrasts are meant to be explained, or for the enjoyment of those in the know. Be that as it may, *miso* and the condensed liquid *miso* called *shôyu* (soy sauce) aside, traditional Japanese *cooking* is indeed far from spicy. Some Chinese and/or Portuguese-influenced confectionary includes cinnamon, and stews in some parts of Japan include sugar (usually as sweet cooking *sake*) and chili pepper, which (6-23) was already used in 1585, but that was about it.

After the dishes are cooked, however, spices could be added. Besides 7-flavor red pepper (*shichimi togarashi*) invented to keep people doing waterfall prayers (you let the cold water fall on your head as you pray) warm and *sohsu*, or "sauce" (a Worchester-like sauce) put on dishes of a Chinese or Western origin both clearly post-dating Frois, there is a finely ground brown-green Chinese pepper, *sansho*, which numbs the tip of the tongue and is most commonly used with eel, a sweet miso which is delicious on cooked egg-plant or tofu, peppery hot sesame oil and vinegar for some Chinese dishes, and my favorite, *wasabi*. Most people feel it in the nose, between the eyes, or inside the forehead, but I am one of a minority who feel a sharp pang an inch or so inside the crown of the head!

..

~~~~~~

6-41 We avoid [eating] dog, and eat cows;
Nós fujimos de cãis e comemos vaqa;

They avoid cows, and eat dogs decorously, as medicine.
Elles fojem da vaqa e comem lindamente os cãis por mezinha.

Dogs again (see 6-24)! Frois knows what will disgust us. The clear mention of *mezina,* or "medicine" indicates he *knew* dog was not *usually* eaten but only indulged in by some men in their "medicine-eating" (*kusurigui*) when Buddhist guilt at taking life was overridden by health, and, I think, appetite. On this, our second time around, let me add that dog was not the only meat at the early winter medical barbecue. "Mountain whale" (wild boar) and "autumnal/red-leaves" (venison) were also eaten (and maybe horse, perhaps as winter-cherry[blossom], for it is called *sakura* meat – it is velvet to the tongue and very sweet compared to goat which always tastes like a petting zoo). Is this use of euphemism and ceremony why Frois writes *lindamente* (decorously)? Most Japanese had mixed feelings on eating dogs and there may have been periods when they abstained completely. When Kaempfer visited a hundred years after Frois, thanks to the "reigning Emperor," (the dog-Shôgun Tsunayoshi) Japan was a veritable Dog Paradise, with mandatory shelters for sick dogs on every street, laws against abusing or insulting them, capital punishment for killing them, and the obligation to bury them up in the mountains. This about sums up a lengthy quote in *TT-long*; the closing joke must be savored in full:

A Japanese, as he was carrying up the dead carcass of a Dog to the top of a mountain, in order to its burial, grew impatient, grumbled and cursed the Emperor's birthday and whimsical commands. His companion, tho' sensible of the justice of his complaints, bid him hold his tongue and be quiet, and instead of swearing and cursing, return thanks to the Gods, that the Emperor was not born in the Sign of the Horse, because in that case the load wou'd have been much heavier. (K:THJ)

Though beef, as already noted, was not eaten on a modern scale by European peasants, it was much more part of the diet of the wealthy classes than was dog in Japan. Moreover, Europeans were not completely innocent of eating man's best friend. Keith Thomas notes that in hard times in early 17c England "dog's flesh was thought 'a dainty dish' in many houses, and cat's meat was turned into 'good pottage" (T:MNW). 20 years in Japan and I *never* encountered any dog meat or even heard of anyone eating it. But Koreans still do – or did until the Seoul Olympics turned it into an international hullabaloo – using ample sesame leaves to mask the doggy flavor (They told me it was *lamb* or *goat,* until I wondered aloud part way through the meal). In Korea, unlike Japan, dog was "extensively bred for the table." (B:KAHN). But Japanese not only ate less dog than there neighbor, they ate less mammal meat, period. Kaempfer, despite noting the scarcity of "*desart* [wild] places" for wild four-footed Beasts to "increase and multiply," gave the official reason for the low meat consumption as Buddhism: "Pythagoras's doctrine of the transmigration of the Soul being receiv'd almost universally, the natives eat no Flesh-meat, and living, as they do, chiefly on Vegetables, they know how to improve the ground to much better advantage, than by turning it into meadows and pastures for the breeding of Cattle." Koreans were also Buddhist, but shared the Tibetan propensity to eat meat (the larger the animal, the better, for more can be fed with the sacrifice of a single soul).

Religion aside, the example of Frois and company did convince Japanese to try beef. Etchu Tetsuya writes "the Japanese taboo on beef-eating gradually disappeared after the Europeans established themselves in Japan." Avila Giron, who came to Japan about the time Frois died, "related how the price of beef had skyrocketed over the years. He claimed that the reason for the high cost was that all the citizens of Nagasaki had begun to eat beef." Japanese accounts concur on the popularity of beef. Matsunaga Teitoku (1571-1653), a linked-verse poet sometimes called the first haiku poet, wrote in *Nagusamegusa* that "around the time when Christianity was introduced to Japan, even people in the Kyoto region referred to beef as *waka* and ate it as a highly prized delicacy." (Etchu Tetsuya EUROPEAN INFLUENCE ON THE "CULTURE OF FOOD" IN NAGASAKI trans. Fumiko F. Earns www.uwosh.edu/home_pages/ faculty_staff/earns/etchu.html). But, *because of the association with Christianity*, the eating of beef had been outlawed again before Kaempfer visited.

Even today, Japanese are not big meat-eaters, nor are they vegetarian (in food, like religion, they are not extremists). The West has the lion's share of vegetarians, with England and its mad cows leading the herd.

6-42 To us, putrid fish gut is something abominable;
Antre nós as tripas podres do pexe se tem por abominasão;

  The Japanese use it for *sakana* [*appetizers*] and like it a lot.
  Os Japões uzão dellas por sacana *e folgão muito com ellas.*

Once, Japanese salted and aged many varieties of fish tripe and roe. Today, *shiokara,* or salt-tripe almost invariably means the fermented guts of the squid, though (if I recall correctly) strips of squid are often mixed in. There is, however, another far more expensive fermented tripe, *konowata,* sea cucumber guts. This *konowata* was one of the tribute items delivered annually to the Imperial Court for hundreds, possibly thousands of years and is considered as one of the three top gourmet foods in Japan, though some Japanese who have not learned to like them compare the taste to s__t.

6-43 Among us, making loud noises while we eat or gulping down wine is considered gross;
Antre nós mascar muito alto o comer e escorropichar o vinho hé tido por sujidade.

  The Japanese think they are both just dandy.
  Os Japõis antre si huma e outra couza o tem por primor.

The noise Japanese make while eating has long upset Western visitors. Men in particular often chew with their mouths open, amplifying each bite of the *daikon* pickle (the loudest culprit), making smacking sounds with open mouths – the "tongue-drum" noise a sign that the food is being relished as "lip-smacking" is, at least in the idiom, for "us" – slurp up noodles and drink down whatever is not hot enough to prevent it in audible gulps. In the case of the "wine," Frois means either the formal way a tiny *sake* cup is downed in a single movement (the toast, *kanpai!* means "drain/dry-cup") – rather than sipped – or the atrocious practice of chugalugging.

Today, there is disagreement about the appropriateness of making excessive noise chewing, but slurping is still proper and gulping is, shall we say, popular. It serves as *the* main subliminal (but very obvious to a foreigner) part of beer, sports-drink or soft-drink advertisements in Japan. The *gokugokugoku* (to use Japanese mimesis for *glug, glug, glug*) sound is so loud one feels that a microphone is embedded in the actor's Adam's Apple – usually a large and active one shown bobbing up and down in synch with the noise. This is soon followed by an even louder *ahh!* of thirst-quenched ecstasy, which mercifully gives way to triumphant music or some clever catch-phrase.

6-44   We praise the wine of our hosts by showing them a gracious and happy countenance;
Nós louvamos o vinho dos ospedes com lhe mostrar gracioso e alegre rosto;

The Japanese praise [their host's *sake*] with a face so sour, they seem to be crying. *Os Japões o louvão mostrando tão roim cara que parese que chorão.*

Sour is the best I could do for *Roim,* or *Ruim,* which means *perverse* and *prejudicial* as well as "broken down," "crumbling," etc. What Japanese actually *do*, even today, is *grimace*. We think a good drink should be mellow. In their hearts, most Japanese would probably agree. But, strength is a desired characteristic of a drink, so a grimace showing it hit the spot is the traditional way to express gratitude for one. From the grimaces some actors make on television, you would think they had their first taste of 100-proof rotgut rather than a beer!

6-45   At our tables we converse, but we do not sing or dance;
Nas nossas mezas practica-sse, mas não se canta nem balha;

The Japanese don't converse until almost the end of the meal, warmed up, they dance and sing. *Os Japões até quasi o fim da meza não practicão, mas qentes balhão e cantão.*

This rings true. Japanese do need to be warmed up, that is drink a bit before they find their tongues. Needless to say(?), they do not dance and sing every day at their meals. This is not your average household dinner, *but a party*. After a half an hour of sitting without moving on *tatami*, it feels good to move a little. Moreover, the songs and dance of traditional Japan, unlike most of Europe, are easily performed by individuals with no back-up, yet still satisfy (more in the *Drama* chapter). At a memorable "Forget the Year Party" (*bonenkai*) for the Japan Translation Center in 1978, one older secretary took a tiny bivalve (*chijimi* or *asari*) from her soup and rhythmically clicked the shells together while singing something to the effect that she was a young and innocent little thing, while a country boy (a young salesman who once mistakenly used honorifics with respect to his own boss while speaking to an outside third-party on the phone) took a liter-size beer bottle in hand to indicate his complementary part while dancing. I doubt anyone dared to dance quite like that for Frois and the other Jesuits!

6-46   Among us, the guest goes to give thanks to the host;
Antre nós o comvidado vai dar graças ao que o comvidou;

In Japan, the host goes to give thanks to the guest.
Em Japão o que comvidou vai dar graças ao convidado.

Okada writes "this is exaggerated for the sake of contrast, but probably refers to tea ceremony etiquette." Not long after the Bungo Consultation, the Jesuits were instructed to have "in all the houses . . . a special room near the entrance door for the preparation of the *chanoyu*, the ceremonial tea," which "could not be omitted even in mission stations" and make certain to have "a tea attendant, the *chanoyusha*," who "was to be continuously on duty,"(LR maybe Valignano's 1581 *Advertimentos* in S:VMP?) and so forth, with an aim to being ready for any visitor at any time. So they had an official interest in that etiquette. Etiquette does not require explanation. But, logical reasons for the Japanese side are wanted, I think I have them. 1) It is better to give (a party) than to receive. 2) Transportation in Japan being as slow as it was (see ch.8), the guest deserves thanks for coming. 3) Many Japanese were, as I happen to be, homebodies preferring to receive visitors than go out. In this case, it is only natural that we thank them. (It is why I *never* allow guests to wash dishes.)

6-47 We esteem fried fish;
Antre nós hé stimado ho p[eix] e frito;

> They do not like it, but love fried sea-weed. *Elles[delle]não gostão e folgão com limos fritos do mar.*

The Luso-Iberians are still big fried fish. Japanese roast or boil it, but even today rarely fry it except in *tempura* (from *tempora* = "Lent") something adopted and adapted from the Portuguese. Deep-fried *konbu* (kelp, also called *kobu*) is still found today; and I would describe it as the seaweed equivalent of a thick potato-chip. But it is just one of a tremendous variety of fried or dried snacks and a far cry from the presence it was when it was hawked in the street. But why didn't Frois give seaweed a whole contrast? Say,

> *In Europe, we eat many kinds of vegetables that grow on land and only use seaweed for fertilizer; In Japan, they not only eat a dozen types of seaweed but pay more than for land vegetables.*

Maybe *some* seaweed was eaten here and there in Europe, but usually such exceptions did not stop Frois . . . Seaweed is not only a vital source of iodine, but of many other trace elements whose value we are only beginning to appreciate. Even today, many varieties are served in many ways and seaweed is almost as popular as it was when Bird wrote: "Seaweed is a common article of diet, and is dried and carried everywhere into the interior. I have scarcely seen a coolie make a meal of which it was not a part, either boiled, fried, pickled, raw, or in soup." (1880 B:UTJ)

6-48 Fishing, among us, is a recreation for honorable people;
O pescar antre nós o tem as pessoas honradas por desenfadamento;

> In Japan, it is thought a lowly activity and work for the base.
> *Em Japão se tem por cousa baxa e obra de jente vil.*

In Japan's oldest anthology of poetry, the *Manyôshû* (c.760), there are a few poems about noble poets going fishing where they meet goddesses in the guise of fishing girls. But nothing like the *Compleat Angler* tradition of the West would evolve. One reason why is suggested by another poem in the same anthology, Okura's Chinese style lament for his illness, where he whines that there are old yet still well cormorant fishers, despite the sinful nature of *their* livelihood, while his ever-so-innocent Buddhist self is the one getting the bad karma. In the 20c, however, the number of Japanese anglers multiplied as fast as good streams were ruined by the developers and civil engineers, with the comical result – unbelievable crowding (more fishermen than fish) – seen in photo magazines.

Traditionally, almost all fishing in Japan was done from fishing boats, as work. A mid-19c century observation by an American who participated in the transport of the first Japanese embassy to the United States gives an idea of how much was done: "The fish caught in the bay are generally more remarkable for beauty of form and color, than for delicacy of flavor; but there was no limit of the number of fishing boats constantly employed in the capture of the finny tribe, seeming almost to equal that of the unwary victims." (A:FJE)

6-49 The diligence with which we clean our teeth after eating;
A diligencia que nós pomos em alimpar os dentes depois de comer,

> The Japanese show in the morning cleaning them before washing their faces.
> *Dessa uzão os Japões pola menhã de os alinparem antes de lavar o rosto.*

Among the rules for dental health devised by Johannes Arculanus in the 15c, we find "Clean teeth immediately after meals with a toothpick;" "After picking, rinse with wine and sage or wine, mastich, gallia, moschata, cubeb, juniper seeds, root of cyprus, and rosemary leaves;" and "The teeth must be rubbed with a dentifrice before bed *or in the morning*." Things are not quite as clean-cut as Frois makes them and probably never were.

6-50   Among us, the animals eat the plants' leaves and leave the roots;
Antre nós os animais comem as folhas das ervas e deixão as raizes;

> In Japan, for some months of the year, the poor people eat the roots and leave the leaves. *Em Japão alguns mezes do ano a jente pobre come as raizes a deixa as folhas.*

This *ridiculous* contrast of grazing livestock and the dirt-poor ("water-drinkers = *mizu-nomi* to use the Japanese idiom) would seem to refer to the last crops of the year, the turnips and huge radishes called *daikon*, which, pickled, were the main (sometimes only) condiment in a poor man's *miso* soup in the winter. When they are being put up, there are simply too many leaves to eat – and, more important, digest! – so they are turned into mulch or used to dangle their roots from drying poles, as a person might be dangled by his or her hair. If my metaphor seems outrageous, believe me, it is nothing compared with what other Western visitors have written about these big roots. First, Kaempfer:

> Turneps grow very plentifully in the Country, and exceeding large ones. Of all the produce of the fields they perhaps contribute most to the sustenance of the Natives. But the fields being manur'd with human dung, they smell so strong, that Foreigners, chiefly Europeans, cannot bear them. The natives eat them raw, boil'd, or pickel'd. (K:THJ 1690)

> Provisions of this nasty composition [manure based on human waste] are kept in large tubs, or tuns, which are buried even with the ground, in their villages and fields, and being not cover'd, afford full as ungrateful and putrid a smell of radishes (which is the common food of the country people) to tender noses, as the neatness and beauty of the road is agreeable to the eyes. (Ibid)

To wit, Kaempfer blames shit for the strong flavor of *daikon* (he means *daikon* when he writes "turneps") and, elsewhere, turns around and blames *daikon* for the strong smell of the shit! (The latter is *true*. Eat a lot of it and your offal smells woefully raw!). Even Morse, who appreciated more about Japan than anyone except, perhaps, Lafcadio Hearn, had hard words for this "curious kind of radish."

> It is eaten raw as a relish, and is also fermented and converted into something resembling sauerkraut, and, as a friend with me expressed it, was odiferous enough to drive a dog out of a tanyard. You recognize the odor as it is being transported through the streets, and it is hardly less offensive to encounter than the offal carriers. (M:JDD)

Personally, I *love* the various kinds of pickled daikon and think of them as Japan's gift to the world, so it surprised me not to find a single kind word for it from the European visitors. Even the cosmopolitan Isabella Bird had nothing but invective for the *daikon*:

> I have left to the last the vegetable *par excellence,* the celebrated *daikon* (Raphinus sativus), from which every traveler and resident suffers. It is a plant of renown – it deserves the honorific! It has made many a grown man flee! It is grown and used everywhere by the lower classes to give sipidity to their otherwise tasteless food. Its leaves, something like those of a turnip, are a beautiful green, and enliven the fields in early winter. Its root is pure white, tolerably even, and looks like an immensely magnified radish, as thick as an average arm, and from one to over two feet long. In this state it is comparatively innocuous. It is slightly dried and then pickled in brine, with rice bran. It is very porous, and absorbs a good deal of the pickle in the three months in which it lies in it, and then has a smell so awful that it is difficult to remain in a house in which it is being eaten. It is the worst smell that I know of except that of a skunk! (B:UTJ 1880)

Chamberlain, more fairly, describes it "as great a terror to the noses of most foreigners as European cheese is to the noses of most Japanese." Exactly! *Cheese.* What we like most as adults are those tastes we must acquire. They must run a different route through a finer part of our brain than the strawberries any child will like from the start. The sassy Edoite yellow *takuan* and the mellow rusty *nara-zuke* of the ancient capitol are, flavor-wise, as *good* in their own way as any fine *adult* cheese and as low calorie as dill pickle. (I know I should have shortened this item but I just couldn't cut a thing!)

~~~~~~

6-51   Among us, it would be insulting to eat or send someone a gift of rotten meat or fish;
Antre nós comer ou mandar prezentes de carne ou pexe podre seria afronta;

> In Japan, they eat it, and are not embarrassed to present it, foul smell and all.
> *Em Japão se come, e, asi fedendo, se manda sem pejo.*

The Portuguese can *also* be read "they eat it, and stinking of it, deliver it without shame." At any rate, *we get it.*

I assumed Frois meant *kusaya,* coyly defined by Kenkyûsha's Japanese-English dictionary as "a horse-mackerel dipped in salt water and dried in the sun, which has a very characteristic odor." *Characteristic?* It smells like rank carrion. What a hound will roll on. I tried roasting some once and the odor remained in my kitchen for two weeks! But, before you think the Japanese are crazy, remember that most Japanese do not like it, while half of the people in Norway (in the Occident, right?) eat their *even more putrid fish* that smells so bad you look for the maggots (I ate it for my first-time-across-the-equator hazing while a work-away on a Scandinavian freighter, and needed every ounce of that half bottle of vodka consumed in advance to get it down!). Because Japanese food is, on the whole, mild, many Japanese do not like strong odors, period, *even if they are Japanese odors.* The fermented beans *natto,* which I love – which Japanese expect all non-Japanese to hate – is disliked by about half of the Japanese! (unlike most other strange flavors, *natto* is unique in that people either love or hate it from their very first taste!)

But Okada does not mention *kusaya* and thinks Frois means *sushi* which, at that time, was aged – i.e. allowed to ferment – for four or five days in the Fall or Spring, or a day or two in the summer. (Like *natto,* one had to literally sleep with it to make it in the cold of winter!) A haiku by Issa even describes the *noises* it made while fermenting! I suspect Okada is right and I am wrong, for the name *kusaya* has "stink" (*kusai*) in it and was probably not a common gift, while *sushi* was.

~~~~~~

6-52   In Europe, it would be vulgar for a respected citizen to sell wine like a cheap tavern at his house. *Em Europa seria baxeza vender hum cidadão honrado vinho atavernado em sua casa;*

> In Japan, highly respected citizens sell and measure it out with their own hands.
> *Em Jāpao o vemdem e medem por sua mão os cidadões muito honrados.*

Most *sake* was sold by *dosô,* money-lenders with earthen rooms protected against fire and well fortified against thieves. Up to 300 of these stores were in operation in Kyoto and 200 in Nara at the time (OJD). The question is whether Frois's "respected citizen" means the owners of the largest of these stores *had become* major merchants who gained some social respect (not much one would think, for *warriors* and *scholars* were theoretically more admired), or, as Okada guesses, major merchants joined the game, selling *sake* alongside of these *dosô.*

"At his house?" Since *most* Japanese stores were and are literally the front of the owner's house, *does this mean that even then, European stores and homes were generally separate?*

"With his own hands?" The hands-on way of doing things is found even today in Japanese companies where the good boss wants to directly meet guests and treat them specially by doing deferential things an Occidental might prefer to leave to a lower employee. Does Europe lie closer to the North African(?), Near Eastern(?) idea of men not doing manual work if they can avoid it, but, rather than compare the respected citizen who gets his hands dirty in Japan with their less diligent counterparts in Europe, Frois makes them seem crass by introducing the difference in a contrast involving alcohol?

6-53 Europeans like to raise chickens, ducks [and rabbits?];
Em Europa folgão de criar galinhas, adens [coelhos e patos?] etc.;

>The Japanese don't like to do this, except for raising roosters to delight the children. *Os Japões com nada disto folgão, somente com galos pera os meninos folgarem.*

Remember, this is a chapter on food, not pets. With most hunting grounds monopolized by the wealthy in Europe, I would guess most meat the common-folk got to eat was what they raised.

Ducks, at least, were quite common around country houses in Issa's time. They make quite a contribution to the paddies by aerating the water and eating insects. Were they only kept in parts Frois missed? Or, despite their clipped wings, were they were not closely enough managed for Frois to consider them honest-to-goodness domestic animals? Roosters were indeed Japan's pride. Fighting was not so important as it was in South East Asia, but the beauty of the long tails for which they were bred and their diligent time-keeping was much appreciated. I had never identified them particularly with children. Perhaps Frois is referring to the practice of noble families, something I know little about. Were I Frois, the contrast would be:

>*Europeans keep chickens, ducks and other animals they eat.*
>*The Japanese only keep roosters and bugs for their songs and for their fighting.*

Come to think of it, the Japanese also ate a number of types of bugs (most commonly *grasshoppers*, and most rarely, for medicine, *cicada*) – not those kept for the above-mentioned reasons. How strange Frois neglects them in this chapter while twice mentioning "dog" in others.

6-54 In Europe, pastry is made from flour;
Em Europa a fabrica do pastel hé da masa;

>In Japan, they throw out the meat of an orange, and with the peel and what is stuffed inside it make a pie. *Em Japão se tira o amago da laranja e com a casqua e o que lhe metem dentro fiqa pastel.*

Sweet *miso* (fermented bean-curd) stuffed inside a de-meated *yuzu,* or citron (also called a "Chinese lemon") – not *orange* – then lightly braised is called *yuzumiso* or *yûmiso*. Today, it is sold in Japanese-style pastry shops (*wagashiya*). The scent of the citron skin is heavenly. It is not as common as pastry made from pounded glutinous sweet-rice filled with sweetened bean-paste.

Frois overlooked a much larger difference. Japanese generally did not eat dessert. A few years after *Tratado,* Miguel=Valignano notes the *"surprising variety of pastry comprising dessert"* in Europe. Dessert was evidently identified with plenty, for the discussion closed with this: "To sum up the food situation in a word, our Japanese food fits our narrow and skinny [infertile] land, while Europe's is understandable given its rich soil. Considering this, there is absolutely no reason to dispute [argue the superiority or inferiority of] our diets. (1589 J/S:DM)

Japanese were intrigued with European baking as they were with all "our" food. While the making of bread (still called *pan* in Japanese, after the Portuguese/Spanish), was eventually forbidden because it "symbolized the flesh of Christ" (Etchu Tetsuya: Ibid 6-41), some types of Portuguese pastries survived and evolved (flan called *pujin, a* pound cake called *kasutera* = bolo de Castella and a star-shaped colorful candy called *konpeitô*) Today, not only do Japanese enjoy pastry, but they enjoy what is on the whole *far better* pastry (especially the cakes) than what can be bought in the USA. However, they still rarely eat it after meals. They eat them with coffee in coffee-shops or take them to friends' houses or offices, and eat them together, as was the case with fruit.

6-55 In Europe, wild pig [boar] is eaten well cooked; *Em Europa se come o porco do mato cozido;*

The Japanese eat it raw, in thin slices. *Os Japões o comem cru em talhadas.*

The Japanese translations of *cozido* are "boiled," but I follow father Schütte with "well-cooked" (*gekocht*) rather than choosing between the various possible translations of *cozido* here.

Since I have never heard of this meat fermented, it is evident from what Frois writes here that *sashimi* in the modern sense of the word as *fresh and raw slices* of meat was already eaten and how remarkable land animals, not sea animals, should take the lead, especially swine, though all Japanese *porco* was wild boar, presumably clean and suitable for raw consumption because there were no domestic swine for it to mix with! Even so, pork was probably rarely eaten by most people and then more commonly as part of a stew. Because the Jesuits rubbed shoulders with the nobility, I can only guess some boar taken in a fancy hunt were sliced up pretty much on the spot..

When we consider the incredibly diverse swine-culture of their Chinese neighbors, the Japanese forbearance of this succulent animal the English essayist Lamb later turned into gastronomic pornography, is nothing short of miraculous.

..

6-56 With us, missing salt for the meal is but a small inconvenience;
Antre nós carecer de sal pera comer hé pouqo incomviniente;

Japanese without salt bloat and become sick.
Os Japões se carecem de sal inchão ou adoecem.

Being salt-less was considered so excruciating an experience in Japan that there was a custom of fasting from salt (*shiodachi*) while petitioning Shinto or Buddhist gods. Okada hazards the guess that Japanese ate so much salt on a regular basis that a disruption was felt as *withdrawal*. I would add that the difference probably owes a lot to the fact that "we" automatically eat salt in "our" bread and meat, so we never really lack salt even if there is no salt-shaker on the table. Also, hot steam baths meant that more sweat – and with it salt – was lost in Japan. But there is no question that the Japanese are more salt-conscious than Europeans. One reason today is that all school-children read about the warlord Kenshin (1530-1578), who sent salt to fellow warlord and nemesis Shingen, who was blockaded by other rivals, because real warriors fought with weapons and not food. Also, according to the Tobacco and Salt Museum, "by comparison with other heavily populated parts of the world, Japan has always been at a disadvantage, for it has no known rock-salt deposits or other terrestrial salt sources, while its relatively low median temperatures and heavy rainfall make reliance on natural evaporation impracticable." In other words, salt was valuable because it was scarce. *Did the name of the Museum just mentioned catch your eye?* For 90 years, until 1997, Japan Tobacco Inc. had a monopoly of the salt market. Be that as it may, the placement of big scoops of salt around a building to purify it and the throwing of salt by a sumo wrestler before a match shows that, in Japan, there is something nobler about salt than the mere "salary" we identify with it. I don't know about Frois's *bloating* claim.

6-57   We ordinarily think their *shiru* [soup] salty;   *Nós ordinariamente temos o seu* xiro *por salgado;*

And they [think] ours insipid.   *E elles o nosso caldo por ensoso.*

A simple illustration of the relativity of senses discovered by Valignano. If a reader would like to *experience* it, or imagine how one could have a different taste, try drinking some tap-water just after eating raw egg. You will find the water tastes absurdly sweet.

6-58   In Portugal, rice cooked without salt is used as medicine to bind the bowels;
Em Portugal se come arroz cozido sem sal por mezinha para estancar as camaras;

For the Japanese, rice cooked without salt is their regular food as bread is for us.
Pera os Japões o arroz cozido sem sal hé seu continuo mantimento como antre nós o pão.

So that is why the lack of salt in the rice was worth including in contrast 6-2! It is also worth mentioning parenthetically that our medical profession continued to *believe* in saltlessness for bowel disorders (diarrhea and mal-absorption) until the advent of the space age, when they *finally* discovered that some salt added to the sugar-water *helps* rather than hurts it get absorbed. This horribly belated discovery – *after* the first heart transplant! – proves how little modern medicine knows about the body's most basic operations, and shows why we still need to keep one eye open to folk-medicine (Oriental and Occidental). *There had to be traditions where the importance of mixing salt and sugar were already known.*   Still, because we had salt in other things, salt-less rice might have been beneficial and Japanese also practiced the *shiodachi* (salt-fast) for certain diseases.

"Our" practice of always salting rice, however, is ridiculous. The rice of South Europe is fat and sweet like *Japonica* rather than the skinny and less tasty *Indica*. If I am not mistaken, even the Indians, whose rice is less tasty, generally do not salt it (though the wealthy may add saffron and I imagine coconut and sugar is added in some places) but are content to enjoy the flavor of the rice *with* the curries and other condiments.   What made "us" incapable of combining our flavors as we chewed? And most of us are *still* like that. We insist on putting butter or salt or soy sauce *on the rice* and letting it soak in so the rice is flavored before reaching the mouth rather than putting a bit of a spicy side dish on it just before taking a mouthful or alternating mouthfuls of rice and side-dish. As someone who began in "our" mode and switched to theirs, I can testify that "we" are missing out, *for it is a richer experience to enjoy separate flavors mixing in the mouth than to have them dulled by mixing ahead of time.* To claim rice is "flavorless" and must be salted or buttered up is to confess to an improperly developed personal gastronomy.   Or could there perhaps be a deeper reason, some ancestral memories that might explain the strange fear otherwise cultivated people of European descent still have for leaving their rice alone?

To the Dominican fathers of the Goan Inquisition, of course, this process of acculturation was always unacceptable. Any sign that Hindu customs were being followed in a Christian house were enough to get the entire family and their servants arrested and put to torture. A list was drawn up by the Inquisition of banned Indian practices . . . . . Included in this list are such shockingly heretical practices as 'cooking rice without salt as the Hindus are accustomed to do' . . . . . (William Dalrymple: *White Mughals* 2002)

6-59   Among us, mullet is highly esteemed;
Antre nós as tainhas são estimadas;

In Japan it is thought repugnant food fit for the poor.
Em Japão lhe tem asco e são pera jente baxa.

Mullet has a way of going either way, *baitfish* (as in Miami, where I grew up) or *delicacy* (as per the Greeks). The roe is esteemed in Japan and probably was in Frois's time, too. So many mullet were caught and the poor, doubtless got the part of the mullet in less demand. That is, at any rate, my theory about how mullet got a low reputation.

Despite a half-dozen contrasts involving fish, Frois forgot the most interesting one of all: the deadly *fugu* (globe/blow/swell-fish). It is possible that what might be called the blow-fish *cult* evolved *after* 1585, as a sort of thrill-seeking by men who missed not risking their lives after the centuries of wars finally ended. If so, it sunk in its roots very quickly, for Kaempfer, in 1692 wrote *pages* on it. "The Japanese reckon" the *mabuku*, or true blowfish, "a very delicate Fish, and they are very fond of it." They know that "the Head, Guts, bones, and all the garbage must be thrown away, and the Flesh carefully wash'd and clean'd before it is fit to eat. And yet many People die of it, for want, as they say, of thoroughly washing and cleaning it. (K(S):HOJ) Indeed. A famous saying has it that "only a fool would eat blowfish, or *not* eat it!" and *senryû* mention the wisdom of washing it *at your friend's house* – for the poison is so powerful the tiniest trace remaining might contaminate the sink. To *Frois* this fish,

> *We never willingly eat food that might kill us;*
> *They not only do so, but think it very gallant.*

Kaempfer also mentions a regulation on the books of many fiefs, which may be Froised as follows:

> *Our laws do not deny certain foods to certain occupations.*
> *Theirs deny the blowfish to soldiers and all meat to the bonzes.*

The life of a samurai was deemed too valuable to gamble with. I would add that the blowfish was considered uniquely good for warming the body. Issa, who made fear of the cold his trademark – even explaining his short neck as being permanent hunched up against the cold! – was a big fan of blowfish for that reason, and wrote dozens of haiku about half of which concern the expression on the face of the blowfish, which he fancied to see on many of his compatriots and vice versa.. I will introduce them in another book (*Swellfish Soup*). Here, we shall simply Frois:

> *In Europe, we think any warm soup is warming.*
> *In Japan, only soup made from the blowfish is believed to have special warming properties.*

The cynic might add, yes, sweating from fear! Another blowfish, introduced by Kaempfer, is "call'd Kitamakura, which signifies North Cushion [pillow]. I could not learn the reason of this Appellation. The same Name is given to a Person that sleeps with his head turn'd to the North. The poison of this sort is absolutely mortal, no washing or cleaning will take it off. It is therefore never ask'd for, but by those who intend to make away with themselves." A hundred years later, Thunberg got the reason, more or less: "it being the custom with these people, to turn the heads of those that are dying towards the north." Less, because the head was to the North but the face was turned to the West. In English, we might name that blowfish *As-good-as-dead*.

> *Among us, no one would buy a fish to take the life Deus entrusted them with.*
> *The Japanese think eating a certain blowfish is a capital way to go to hell.*

6-60 Among us, belching at the table in the presence of guests is thought uncouth;
Antre nós dar arrotos à meza diante dos ospedes se tem por mao insino;

> In Japan, it is very common, and no one is fazed by it.
> *Em Japão hé muito corrente e nenhum cazo fazem disso.*

More vulgarity to be added to 6-31/38/43. Later, Thunberg was to remonstrate: "the Japanese have the bad custom of very frequently breaking wind upwards, and [it] is by no means thought indecent as in Europe; in other matters, they are as nice as other polished nations;" and Alcock note more objectively that: "it takes a long habit before Europeans can bear the frequent and loud eructations, as evidence of a good meal, without a strong mental protest." Ball's remarks on *Noises, etc.* within his "Etiquette" heading of *Things Chinese* took into account historical perspective:

> Guttural sounds, hawking, clearing the throat, spitting, using the fingers to blow the nose, and eructations, are not necessarily considered impolite by the Chinese. It must be remembered that they look upon such things in a quite different way than we do nowadays. We say nowadays, for it is not more than a few centuries ago that a book was published in England containing, among other things, directions on how to blow the nose neatly with the fingers. But we will not offer any more remarks on such a nauseating subject. (B:TC)

Since Frois was writing "a few centuries ago," such perspective does not contradict Frois, but Ball's point is well taken. Moreover, it shows that this habit of belching (something I never heard) may have come from China. Could it have gotten to China via the Silk Road? I ask because, as far as I know, though Japanese and Chinese may have traditionally been allowed to burp to show their appreciation for good food, but I do not believe it was ever *de rigor* as (I have been told it was) in the Near East.

Let me try to do the impossible, i.e., put burping into a more graceful context by quoting a haiku+explanation from my book *Rise, Ye Sea Slugs!*

海鼠食べられて噯となり出づる　高沢良一
namako taberarete okubi to nari izuru – Takasawa Yoshikazu
(sea cucumber eating/ate[respectful passive] eructation-as/into becomes leaves/comes-out)

eating *namako*
indulgence that ends
in a fine burp

I called the sea cucumber the Japanese name *namako* here rather than "sea slug" as in most of the poems (actually, it is about sea *cucumber*, but the word is too long and lacks the proper metaphorical feel) because I realized that no amount of explanation can make the burp as sweet as it is in the original with the creature clearly identified. The added "indulgence" is my way to recover the politeness of the conjugation of the verb (eat). So said, I had only known the vulgar sounding *geppu,* until reading this haiku, which uses a more formal word for "burp," namely *okubi,* which is written with a single Chinese character, also new to me, comprised of two parts, "mouth+love." In fact, one pronunciation of the word is *ai,* the same as "love." Takasawa wrote me that the burp arises because (he/the slug?) ate mud-like stuff. So, is the burp on behalf of both of them, the poet and his food?
..

endnote VI

F*ood*

~~~~~~

To me, the most interesting difference in our customary manner of eating and that of the Japanese is *the way meals start and finish*. We have traditionally opened "our" meals with a prayer said by one person who is either the host (at home, the *pater familia*), or the person indicated by the host. The content is Christian and concrete, mentioning God and/or Jesus and giving thanks for specific things. "They," the Japanese, cut out all the extraneous detail, giving us *a grace in a word*, said by each person, alone or together to open their meal: *Itadakimasu*. "[I humbly/gratefully] accept=take=eat." (G:O&O)

> *We begin our meals with a prayer thanking god.*
> *They begin by thanking no one in particular.*
>
> *We have one person say the grace for all.*
> *They each say their own, which is only one word.*

Personally, I do not care for "our" way. Talking to God may be fine for many Christians, but it seems childish and, let me be honest, corny, to one who is not even a believer. On the other hand, it feels good to have *something* to open a meal with (What is the opposite of a *sense of closure?* a sense of *aperture?!*). So, call me odd, but I always say *Itadakimasu!* no matter where I am. The Japanese also have a grace in a word for *finishing* their meals: *gochisôsama-deshita*, mentioning the host (in the abstract, by prefixes and suffixes alone) running about (= *preparing the meal*, say the philologists). No one thinks much about what it means, but it is a splendid way to say *"Thanks!"* and close one's meal.

> *We start our meals with various long graces depending on the occasion.*
> *They have standard graces of just one word both to start and end their meals.*

I believe that Japanese Christians introduced the practice of saying grace at the end of meals as well as the beginning, but am afraid I have lost my sources. The Japanese practice probably goes far back in Japanese history, because Japanese are almost religious about *beginnings* and *endings*: they bind up them up neatly in words. Whenever people leave home (or a cluster of homes if it is a tight-knit neighborhood), one says *"Itte-kimasu* ([I am] going-[and will] comeback)!" And the person/s remaining shout back *"Itte-rasshai* (go-[and]comeback[politely expressed])!" and when you come back you shout *Tada ima!* (Just now!) and they shout in reply, *"Okaeri* (Welcome back)!"

> *We have nothing in particular to say whenever we go out and return to our homes.*
> *They have a word or two they always say without fail.*

Oops, no food there. During the Seclusion, the Japanese invented *another* splendid way to start a meal, to give a fresh sense of opening. This was not necessarily the reason for the invention – which is *the answer to the question* I asked in my annotation of the first contrast of the chapter – but the *result* was to get every cheap bowl of noodles off on a refreshing start.

> *Our restaurants use service of silver or stainless steel that is washed and reused.*
> *Theirs often use chopsticks that are only used once and thrown away.*
>
> *Our utensils come ready to use.*
> *They sometimes must break their chopsticks apart before they can use them.*

The disposable chopstick has received a lot of criticism from Western environmentalists. I once read a Letter to the Editor where a conceited young Yank promised to cram the disposable chopsticks up the nose of anyone caught eating with them who *dared* to talk about ecology! Coming from the representative of a culture using twice the energy per capita (despite having an equal income) of the Japanese, that cannot even pass a decent gas tax, gives people *bonuses* for flying a lot instead of rewarding those who stay put, allows its population to keep growing (Japanese are less prolific), and eats higher up the food chain than all but the Argentineans (who have abundant grass pasture) – do *"we" have a right to talk?* The crisp crack of a disposable chopstick, its woody texture and scent, bring the user back to the real world, the material world the ecologist, of all people, must love.

True, there is some waste. But, it is surely less than that caused by the plastic utensils served at all too many cafeterias in the USA – and these do not take us back to our roots as do the chopsticks – and it may well be no less harmful than the detergent and energy needed for hot water to wash our utensils. Moreover, old chopsticks may always be recycled as fuel for baths (in old Edo), garden aids (stuck into the soil of pots lacking holes, they prevent root-rot) or toys. If a mountain gorilla can tear off dozens of branches of leaves to make a bed every night, surely a human can afford to use tiny twig-sized sticks to eat with several times a day! What, one wonders, does our politically correct ecologist do for toilet paper!?

"Our" biggest food-related problem with Japan in the last quarter of the 20c was not, however, disposable chopsticks. It was *whales*. Until the middle of this century, the contrast might have been:

> *We only kill whales for the oil and throw away most of the rest.*
> *They use all of the whale and find it very filling food.*

Needless to say, their behavior was admirable and ours was not. During the Occupation, General MacArthur *encouraged* the Japanese to go out and get whales so that the people could get enough animal protein to stay healthy. But, thirty years later, we suddenly said, *Whoa!*

Conservation of cetacean resources? Yes. *But that wasn't all.* If it were, "we" would not have continued to raise a stink about Minke whales, *for there are plenty of them.* The Japanese, not illogically, responded, *you eat cows, why can't we eat whales?* Let's face it, "we" see the cetacean as an especially intelligent and good-natured creature *worthy of special treatment,* not accorded to cows and pigs. But, did we honestly admit that? *No.* "We" are not good at complex moral issues and admitting degrees of intelligence *terrifies us*, so we did not, and still do not admit that is what it was about. It's easier to pretend *a whale is a whale is a whale* is scarce, even when it is a lie. In the USA, if the national executive of the Japan-American Citizen's League did not exaggerate, anti-Japanese bias arising from our teaching about "cruel" and "barbaric" Japanese whale-killers even gave rise to prejudice against Japanese-American children (in L:IOJ) In Japan, on the other hand, comic books with multi-million reader circulations featured stories about how the anti-whaling *mafia* in the USA attacked Japan to take the world's attention off Vietnam. (Meanwhile, polls of Japanese students showed America as more feared than the Soviet Union.) When research showed that low bad-cholesterol and high good-cholesterol properties of marine mammal meat – which explains why a solid animal diet didn't hurt the Eskimos – some Japanese cynically wrote, *Watch and see how long before those self-serving whites start eating whales!*

The whale-eater's anger is understandable, but the Japanese mass media stressed racism too much. It failed to pay attention to Greenpeace's actions against Norwegian, Soviet and Spanish, (all Caucasian) whaling vessels, and professed outrage at "whites" out to trash non-white food-cultures. The distrust spawned by this sorry exchange, which I did my damndest to make more civil, bodes poorly for the future, where diminishing marine resources and a growing global population ensure a continuing Tragedy of the Commons, particularly over food issues.

VII

OF JAPANESE OFFENSIVE AND

DEFENSIVE WEAPONS & OF WAR

das armas ofensivas e defensivas dos Japõis – & da guerra

7-1   We use swords; *Nós uzamos de espadas;*

And the Japanese cutlasses. *E os Japóes de traçados.*

Our *espada* = sword = epee is double-edged, sharp-pointed and absolutely straight, while their *traçado* = cutlass = saber is single-edged; slicing-sharp; and slightly curved. Because the edge and point are covered elsewhere (1-21 and 7-7, respectively), I *guess* the intended contrast is straight *vs* curve here. This is a good example of why description beats names.

For us, the difference between a sword and cutlass means nothing. But Frois's day was the heyday of the fencing instructor and more noblemen died in duels than in the constant warfare.

7-2   Our hilt is [long] enough to fit a hand;
Ho nosso puho [hé] quanto cabe [a] mão;

Theirs exceed a palm and, sometimes, 3.
O seu passa de hum palmo, e às vezes de 3.

One hand for "our" sword and two for theirs. The reasons have already been discussed in 1-34. Naturally, it follows that ours has a short hilt and theirs a long one, long enough that the position of the hands on the hilt may vary, like in baseball, golf, or pole-vaulting. Avila Giron wrote that the length of the Japanese sword blade and hilt maintain "a due proportion." (C:TCJ) If 1:8 was our ideal ratio for a human head:body, the *katana* was 1:6. (To me, they appear 1:5. Perhaps Giron meant the *tang* (the metal part of the hilt which is not seen on a completely dressed sword).)

7-3   We carry our swords on baldrics; *Os nossos trazem a espada em talabartes;*

They, [with a] hooklet in/on the sash. *Elles em hum ganchinho na sinta.*

The *talabarte,* or baldric, is a sling-style belt that goes over one shoulder. Judging from some old paintings, the low side of the baldric tended to be lower than the Japanese *obi* belt, so that our swords often hung way down on the thigh. Did the mercenaries often pictured so think it debonair?

The samurai's 3 (later 4-5) inch-wide sash called a *katana-jime,* or sword-holder, was once used together with the classic dangling *tachi* (long sword) noted in 1-25+. Since Frois does not mention the two strings or straps used for *dangling* a sword horizontally, I guess differently from Okada that Frois refers to the practice of sticking scabbards through *obi* sashes and the *ganchinho* means the *kaerizuno*, a hook-like piece of metal or horn bound to the scabbard to keep it from slipping through the sash. Either way, the contrast intended here is probably between *specialized equipment* (a diagonal belt for girding swords) and the *adaptation* of an ordinary sash worn around the waist.

7-4 We wear our sword on one side and our dagger on the other;
Os nossos trazem a espada de huma banda e a adaga da outra;

        The Japanese always wear their sword and dagger on the left.
        Os Japões trazem a espada e adaga sempre da parte esqerda.

The most common short sword was called a *wakizashi* or "stick-in-the-side (of the belt)," so it was doubtless carried on the side, but the handle could stick out diagonally over the belly.

7-5 Our daggers are short;
As nossas adagas são curtas;

        Some of theirs are longer than half a *katana* [sword].
        Algumas das suas são mayores que mea catana.

The linguistic confusion here will be cleared up in 7-11. Frois seems to call the second blade a *dagger* by definition.

7-6 Gloves hang from our swords; *Nas nossas espadas se perdurão as luvas;*

        From theirs, a cord that serves for nothing. *E elles hum cordão que não serve de nada.*

Armored gloves were worn when fighting in Europe. In Frois's time, they were no longer as heavily armored as the Medieval gauntlet, but they were not yet abandoned.

The Japanese item may be the *sageo,* lit. "dangle-string." A "sword knot" tied the scabbard firmly to the upper outside *obi* during military campaigns, but the cord ordinarily just dangled.

7-7 The people of Europe are used to stabbing swordplay; *A jente de Europa custuma jugar de ponta;*

        The Japanese in no case do it. *Os Japões por nehum cazo.*

Stabbers and *slashers*. Is stabbing *extroverted* whereas slashing is *introverted?* Would a criminal psychologist find a basic difference in those who did one or the other? Or, do weapons come first and mentality follows, i.e., "ours" boast sharper points and theirs sharper edges? Whatever it is, the difference is reflected in our idiom: we get "stabbed in the back;" they "back-cut/sliced" (*uragiri*).

European Medieval swordplay was mostly hacking, this changed in the Renaissance and, with the invention of the thin rapier that evolved into the yet lighter épée while Frois was in Japan and, soon, to the remarkable foil (imagine, a square cross-section!), thrusting was *de rigor*. Frois's, "play at point" (to literally translate *jugar de ponta*) is strangely apt, for it seems to predict where we were heading, for, believe it or not, "we" were soon to create *a rule of right-away* where noble duelers took turns attacking to prevent a tie (simultaneously stabbing each other) and this, according to my lost internet source, was to greatly reduce casualties in dueling.

Frois's "in no case" is an exaggeration. The most famous swordsman and strategist in Japanese history, Miyamoto Musashi, who was born in 1584 or 5, included stab strokes in his *Water*

Book of instructions for sword-fighting. Still, stabbing was never a first resort in Japan, except, perhaps, for assassination. In that case, the classic – or at least classic *modern* – style in Japan is to grip a short sword or knife with one hand, put the other behind the butt of the handle and holding that against one's own body, throw oneself directly against the target. But that is hardly sword*play*.

7-8   Among us, lords are presented with swords of very good iron;
Antre nós se dão aos senhores de presente espadas de muito bom ferro.

In Japan, they are given wooden swords with sword-belts of *nuno* [cloth].
Em Japão lhe oferecem espadas de pao com talabartes de nuno.

From ancient times, Japanese rulers wore wooden swords called *tsukuridachi, kidachi* or *kodachi* for ceremonies. In Frois's time, the *shogun* might wear one to a (war) strategy meeting. Perhaps this follows the primitive-as-festive idea discussed in 6-30. Japanese also had *bokuto,* blunt wooden swords that served for exercise and were sometimes used in matches between heads of schools (heavy oak, they could kill) and *shinai,* the equivalent/opposite of our square-edged (post-Frois) foil, tubular swords comprising strips of bamboo, bound around at broad intervals with strips of leather, that collide with extraordinarily pleasant-sounding whacks. Even today, one-on-one *shinai* matches are part of physical education (*kendô* classes for both sexes) in all public schools in Japan. These *Xinai* were in the 1604 Japanese Portuguese Dictionary (NIPO), so they probably predated Frois.

The more interesting Japanese ceremonial weapon would be the *hamaya, head-less* demon-destroying *arrows,* which ordinary people – in both a private and company capacity – still bring back from the Shrines as talismans to undo a bad event or year and hope for better fortune in the new year.

7-9   We only put swords in our scabbards;
Nas nossas bainhas não se mete mais que a espada;

Those of Japan have a place for a knife and a *kôgai* that serves for nothing.
Nas dos Japões de huma parte a faca e da outra o congay que não serve de nada.

This *kôgai* goes back almost as far as the above-mentioned wooden sword. It was an ivory or silver bar (one English language sword site calls it a "skewer") almost as long and somewhat thicker than a chopstick, rounded at one end and used by nobles from ancient times to scratch their scalp or re-arrange their hair after putting on their armor. A *one-tooth comb*?! Sometimes the tip was slightly notched, like a crochet needle, "which made them look like ear-wax removers, but they were not used for that, rather for poking a bad horse" says one old source (OJD). This anachronism remaining on the scabbard but seldom used, was defined by the 1604 NIPO as "a metal object like a tiny knife made of black lacquer or gilt copper stuck in one side of the scabbard." Women found it made a stylish hair pin. Soon it revived: split in two, it became a *wari-kôgai,* portable chopsticks for the samurai of peacetime!

7-10   Our swords, though new, if they are very good, are worth a lot;
As nossas espadas, ainda que sejão novas, se são muito boas, valem muito;

Those of Japan, although new, have no value, and the very old ones are expensive. *As de Japão, ainda que novas, não tem valia, e as muito velhas são de preço.*

Our side is simple. Needless to say, a new sword is less likely to be nicked than an old one and worth more. *Their* side is more complex. New swords were hardly worthless, but the older ones were treasured both for their history and because the greatest swords were made before 1450, while the master swordsmiths *still made their own iron from scratch* (later, it was mass-produced in mills). Valignano, in 1583, mentions three Japanese items as the equivalent of what jewels are to Europeans: certain tea utensils, simple black-and-white *sumi-e* paintings, and swords. He mentions swords worth thousands of *ducados* (millions of dollars in today's prices). Alvarez-Taladriz quotes Vivero on a sword worth a hundred thousand *ducado*. A sword by the 13c swordsmith Kanemitsu came to be called *Ikkoku Kanemitsu*, or "[worth] one-country-Kanemitsu!" because its owner refused a request for it by the Shogun Tokugawa Hideyoshi, though it might cost his entire province (Tôsa, the island now famous for drumming). The Shogun's emissary liked his guts and he kept both. Since swords have to be proven, there are logical reasons for favoring old over new, but logic probably does not mean much here.

7-11   We wear no more than one sword and one dagger at most;
   Antre nós, quando muito, não se uza de trazer mais que huma espada e adaga;

>   The Japanese sometimes wear two swords and a *wakizashi* in the belt.
>   *Os Japões às vezes duas catanas e hum* vaqizaxi *na cinta.*

We had exceptions. The man who slyly won the last judicial duel in France (1547) by cutting his opponent's ham-string wore several daggers the better to reach one if said opponent, a powerful wrestler, tried to grab him! And, pictures show "our" mercenaries so loaded with arms they looked like porcupines. But there were more Japanese who wore three blades than Europeans. With "two swords and a *wakizashi*" we might assume the latter is the dagger. Actually, it is hard to say, for the *wakizashi* had a cutting blade one to two feet in length, while the "small swords (*kogatana, tanto*)," had blades sticking out less than a foot beyond their sword-guards.

7-12   Our knives generally have wooden studs;
   As nossas facas ordinariamente tem as tachas de pao.

>   Those of Japan have hilts of copper or another metal.
>   *As de Japão tem hum punho de cobre ou de outro metal.*

The Japanese knives are the "small-swords" already mentioned. Is it strange we have rivets of wood rather than metal and that they should have metal handles? This contrast loses me.

7-13   We cut with a knife either inward, or from left to right;
   Nós cortamos com a faca ou pera dentro ou da parte esqerda pera a dereita;

>   The Japanese always cut outward.
>   *Os Japões cortão sempre pera diante.*

Left to right for a right-handed person is not very different from cutting away from oneself. So the contrast is imperfect. But, I know what he is getting at. Once, a Japanese, astounded to find me whittling by pulling the knife with my fingers toward my thumb, warned: "[That's] dangerous! We always cut away from ourselves." Usanians all learn – or are supposed to learn – not to point a gun at themselves or others even if it is unloaded; Japanese apparently have a rule about pointing away with a cutting instrument. E.J. Harrison describes the etiquette of showing a good sword to a guest:

>   The sword would then be handled with the back toward the guest . . . the weapon was drawn from the scabbard and admired inch by inch, but not to the full length, unless the owner pressed his guest to do so, when, with much apology, the sword was entirely drawn and held away from the other persons present. (THE CULT OF COLD STEEL in N:MAR)

How pleasant to find the directions here contrary to the case with saws or weaponless fighting; it is never mentioned by pop-Japanologists, for an inward *pulling* West and an outward *pushing* Japan would contradict the vectors of the accepted stereotype of our respective characters.

7-14 Our beads for prayer are always made on a lathe, and our crosses, too;
As nossas contas pera rezar se fazem sempre em torno, e as cruzes tambem;

> The Japanese often make them with a knife, as well finished as by a lathe.
> *Os Japões as fazem muitas vezes com faqa tam bem feitas como em torno.*

The Japanese had lathes. A "*million* miniature wooden pagodas" (my *italics*) each containing "four Buddhist incantations printed on a long strip of paper" – i.e., tiny *stupa* – were "mass-produced on lathes" at the request of the Empress in 764. (P:GUG). Needless to say, there were devices to turn out beads 800 years later. But making items for religious use was itself a type of devotion. People carved everything from statues of the Goddess of Mercy to prayer beads. (But how were beads *held* when carving?)

7-15 We, for the most part, cut our nails with scissors;
Nós cortamos pola mayor parte as unhas com tizouras;

> The Japanese always cut them with a knife.
> *Os Japões as cortão sempre com faca.*

It is hard to say whether this was because Japanese scissors were that poor or because Japanese blades were *that* sharp! Since we *are* in a chapter on weapons and war, perhaps Frois means the latter. I think that was the point about 7-14, too, that Japanese are a knife-loving and knife-using people!

7-16 The leaves and twigs we take from trees to decorate our presents;
As folhas e ramos que tomamos das arvores pera emramar os prezeentes;

> The Japanese make artificially with their *kogatana* [knives].
> *Fazem os Japões artificiais com suas congatanas.*

Japanese did not simply whittle replicas. Their foliage, if that is what it stood for, resembles the tinder sticks of boy or girl-scouts, but the shavings are much finer and longer, so they curl like ribbon. This suggests the Ainu influence on Japanese culture, for the "hairy Ainu" are the world's most prolific shavers of wood. Isabella Bird wrote that "wands, with shavings depending from the upper end" were the "Aino Gods" and stuck in the walls, by windows, on a shelf, that is to say both adorned and charmed their dwellings. (B:UTJ v2)

7-17 Our spearheads are long and broad; *As nossas lanças tem os ferros compridos e largos;*

> Theirs, short and thin. *E as suas curtos e estreitos.*

The Japanese had *many* types of spears and Frois only compares the most common variety which did indeed have a very small blade. A big blade is fearsome to behold, but if thrusting through armor, or simply stabbing a body, is the main intent, a thin blade can generate far more pressure per square-inch. Our spears, as suggested by the name in Portuguese, apparently owed much to the heavy *lances* of the knight, designed more to knock a man off a horse than to pierce the armor.

7-18   Ours [our spears] are smooth, of the color of the wood itself;
As nossas são lizas com a cor propria do pao;

>Theirs have shafts that are *urushi* [lacquer(ed)] or gilt.
As suas ou são vruxadas *ou algumas delas douradas nas asteas.*

A reversal of the more usual *painted Europe* and *bare Japan*? Were "our" spears used for jousting, thought of as expendable, unlike our swords, which were heavily adorned? Spear shafts were natural wood color in Japan, too, until the Warring Era (1338-1568), when black lacquer, mother-of-pearl and vermillion – the last as a privilege for battle exploits – became current (Okada).

7-19   We use halberds; *Nós uzamos de partezanas;*

>They, *naginata* in the shape of a sickle. *Elles de nanguinatas que são da feisão de fouces.*

Our *halberds* were ferocious-looking hybrids with a long spear shaft with a sharp spear-point at the tip, under which an axe-head juts out (angled in such a way as to add some slice to the hack) on one side and a prong or hook on the back of the axe-head on the other. Their *naginata* was more like a curved sword on a long shaft. Classic *naginata* were about 40% blade and looked like sickles. Because of the gun, they were on the wane in Frois's time. Soon, the blade shrank to knife-length and became the official weapon for noblewomen – in the TV Easterns they whirl them about like huge batons – to practice with and use in defense of their lords and castles.

7-20   We use bombards; *Nós uzamos de partezanas;*

>They have no more than arquebuses. *Elles as não tem, mas uzão de espingardas.*

The *bombard* was originally a stone *thrower* but came to mean cannon/mortars that shot stones or large shot weighing up to 200 pounds. I hesitate to choose which Frois intends. The OED's *bombard* citations reveal how hated it was: "to discharge a bumbard, to batter or murder with bumbards." The person firing it was a *bombadier*.

At last minute, I dropped the archaic "musket" (though it should be OK for translating *espingardas*), for the obsolete "arquebus," the most common word used with respect to old Japanese guns, which were indeed "hackbuts!" (see 7-52) as they were Englished by a Tudor Royal Proclamation in the very year the first guns came to Japan – 1543, when three Portuguese "rovers" on a Chinese trading ship landed in Tanegashima, Japan. Two had *arquebuses* "and at the moment when Lord Tokita, the feudal master of Tanegashima, saw one of them take aim and fire at a duck, the gun enters Japanese history." (Noel Perrin: GIVING UP THE GUN) Within a year, his chief swordsmith had made ten guns and within a decade gunsmiths all over Japan were making thousands. Pinto, who always exaggerates on the side of the truth, claimed there were 300,000 by 1556. Let us just say, that Japan quickly had more guns than any country in Europe (more detail in *TT-long*). Moreover, Japanese did not *just* copy the *espingardas*. "They increased the caliber of the guns to increase each bullet's effectiveness, and they ordered waterproof lacquered cases to carry the matchlocks and their gunpowder in," and refined "the comparatively rude Portuguese firing mechanism – developing, for example, a helical main spring and an adjustable trigger pull" as well as a "gun accessory – unknown, as far as I am aware, in Europe – which enabled the matchlock to be fired in the rain." (Ibid P:GUG)

But Frois is right, the Japanese did not show equal progress with *large* firearms. Some good cannons were made, but all were field weapons: for whatever reasons, the Japanese never made decent shore batteries or armature for ships.

7-21   We carry our powder-horns on a shoulder-belt;   *Nós trazemos o polvarinho ao tiracolo;*

   They carry them about the neck like a relic.   *Elles ao pescoso como relicairo.*

The Japanese powder-horn, called a "mouth-drug-holder" (*kuchigusuri-ire*) or a satchel (literally: "torso-rampant," why I do not know!) was indeed dangled from the neck, but they were also secured to the chest and did not bounce around.   Japanese may have had to ford more rivers than Europeans.   I assumed they would be made from the plentiful bamboo; but internet photos show a beautiful array of hard-wood, lacquered, bamboo and horn "powder-horns" *far* finer (aesthetically developed) than our comparatively folksy horns!

7-22   Our bows are medium [in size] and made of wood;   *Os nossos arcos são medianos e de pau;*

   And theirs, very large [and] made of bamboo.   *Os seus muito grandes feitos de cana.*

With Robin Hood as my namesake, I am very aware of the English long bow, though they were not nearly as long as the 7-8 foot Japanese bow,   originally all wood, mostly catalpa or spindle tree, but later including bamboo.   The lamination technology for making good composite bamboo bows is difficult, but still far less interesting than two functional facts Frois overlooked:

We hold our bows in the middle when we shoot them;
Japanese bows have their grip about one third of the way from bottom of the bow.

Shooting right-handed, we rest the arrow on the left-side of the bow;
They place the arrow on the right-side of the bow so it rests upon their thumb.

There are other longbows, bamboo bows and laminated bows in the world.   But as far as I know, only the Japanese shoot in this way, permitting long bows to clear a horse's back.   It is amazing Japanese did not copy the stronger and far more compact Mongolian bow, as they later did European firearms.   Since a bow dance is still done by the Sumo grand-champion, which takes full advantage of the uniquely *wobbly nature* of the unstrung Japanese bow, the answer may be that the Japanese just had too much affection for their strange weapon.   Had Japanese bows been more powerful – like those of the Mongols (or Caribs of my Florida) I wonder if they would have shown so much interest in guns.

7-23   Our arrows are wooden;   *As nossas frechas são de pao;*

   And theirs also [like the bows] of bamboo.   *As suas tambem de cana.*

Okada points out that willow arrows were also used up to the Heian Era (Think of it: *I shot an arrow in the air / and where it fell, a tree grows there!*).   This bamboo is not the same plant used to make bows. The bow is made with strips of real bamboo, while arrows are made from *yadake* ("arrow-bamboo") that I'd call *cane*.   Considering that Frois gives the type of feathers used in *helmets* a contrast (7-29), he might have taken a closer look at the fletching as well as the shaft:

The feathers on our arrows are slightly out of line with the shaft to make it spin and go straighter.
Theirs are perfectly straight but spin it by being convex on one side and concave on the other.

That is too say their feathers are warped and, rotating toward the convex side, work on the principle of some of the earliest airplane wings!   Arrows were sold as sets, a clockwise-rotating *haya* and counter-clockwise *otoya*.   If, it turns out that all European arrows spin in a single direction, this would give us something rare in this weak chapter, a true contrary and not just a difference.

7-24   Among us, arrows are dispatched with the archer clothed;
Antre nós se despedem as frechas estando o que as tira vestido;

> In Japan, someone who shoots a bow must half remove his *kimono* to bare his arm.
> *Em Japão quem tira com arco á-de despir meo* qimão *pera ficar com hum braço nu.*

The Japanese practice is clearly the stranger of the two, but I do not think it as incredible as the fact the arrow is not shot from mid-bow (as per my *Faux Frois* in 7-22). One wonders if Frois was not distracted from more careful observation by the bare left shoulder and some of the chest of the archer. This is not so bothersome a matter for the archers as might be imagined, for Japanese can yank in their arm and shoot their fist out through the lapel of their kimono while shrugging their shoulder in a split-second! It takes loose sleeves, a broad armpit and practice. Still, to see people lined up at a *kyûdo* gallery, all with one arm/shoulder bare (except for the arm-guard) is weird. *Why, you ask yourself, don't they just wear something with tight sleeves?*

7-25   Among us, no one yells out when shooting a bow;
Antre nós se tira com arco sem fazer nenhum rujido com a boca;

> The Japanese have to give a big shout when they release an arrow.
> *Os Japões em despidindo a frecha hão-de dar hum grande grito.*

Our side needs no explanation. *Theirs* is remarkable. And, it is also true for sword-fighting (7-51) and the modern martial arts of judo and karate. *Why do "they" do it?* Some say "to throw off the guard of the enemy for just an instant when the sharp cry (almost a *yelp*) interferes with their cognition." I recall reading, perhaps in *The Japanese Brain* (Tsunoda), that Japanese heard such a yell on the verbal (left) side of the brain, as significant, unlike other people who processed it in the right as mere noise, so it had more effect on them. That might matter for face-to-face combat, matches or even hunting (freezing deer or boar?) but why do it for archery in a gallery? Some think it functions like exhaling quickly when weight-lifting, i.e., provides a clear physical benefit; but, Japanese do not yell as the bow is *drawn*, but only as it is *released*. Some think it a sort of psyching up, where each blow/shout increases one's excitement level until the adrenaline is sky-high. Again, that makes no sense for the calm "Zen of archery." Be that as it may, there is even a word for it, *kiai,* literally "spirit-meet." To put *kiai* into something (*kiai-o irete* is "to do something with spirit." To lose to someone's *kiai* is to be overawed (*kiai-make*), or psyched-out by them.

7-26   We use either round, gilt escutcheons or leather bucklers;
Antre nós se uza d'esqudos, rodelas douradas e adargas de couro;

> The Japanese, in place of these, use a piece of board flat like a door.
> *Os Japões em lugar disto uzão de hum pedaço de taboa raza como porta.*

Since our swords were wielded with one hand, it made sense to hold a small shield in the other. These *rondache* or bucklers were not just round but slightly rounded (convex), the better to protect the hand. I can see polished steel to blind someone but why would one *want* "gilt" shields?

The Japanese were not without their small shields, too, but the door-like shields doubtless stood out for the European. In Japanese, these were called "wall-shields," for lined up, they made a protective barrier for arrows. With the adoption of firearms, they were replaced by bundles of bamboo which could deflect most musket balls.(Okada) But, they must have come back after the gun was banned, for even today, Japanese riot police (Koreans and Chinese, too!) still use 5 or 6-foot long, narrow shields, often improved with plexiglas windows that offer excellent protection from stones.

~~~~~~

7-27   Our armor is very heavy; *As nossas armas são muito pezadas.*

   That of the Japanese very light. *As dos Japões muito leves.*

The plate armor of our knights was notoriously heavy. Sometimes knights had to be hoisted into the saddle using a block and pulley. It had lightened up by 1585, but was still heavy by Japanese standards which because of the needs of smaller horses and superior design and manufacture held the line at about 25 pounds.

~~~~~~

7-28   Our armor suits are all made of steel-plate.
   As nossas armas brancas são todas de aso;

   Theirs are made of scales of horn and leather laced together with silk cord.
   As suas feitas de laminas de corno ou de couro tecidas com retros.

The Japanese *lamina* was bound slightly overlapping like fish scales or shingles. Japan also used metal to produce "more varieties of mail than all the rest of the world put together" (George Stone in P:GUG) and "we" also had something similar to "theirs," *coats of mail* (neither chain-mail, nor plate).

~~~~~~

7-29   The plumes on our helmets are white or beige and very beautiful;
   As nossas prumas dos elmos são brancas ou pardas muito fermozas;

   Those of the Japanese are the longest tail feathers of roosters.
   As dos Japões são de penas de galo das mais compridas do rabo.

Our fluffy plumes *stood up.* Perhaps, the long cock-tails *dangling* behind the Japanese helmet was, to the European mind, as silly as wearing a cap backwards. Japanese roosters have the longest tails in the world – check *Guinness!* Japanese identified the cock with a martial spirit though, compared to the Chinese and Malay, they were not much into cock-fighting.

~~~~~~

7-30   Ours [helmets] have visors; *Os nossos levão vizeiras;*

   The Japanese [ones] a demi-mask of a devil. *Os Japões mea cara de diabo no rosto.*

The visor is the eye-slit piece (The colander-like mask covering the face, a *ventail*). Our knights in armor look *artificial* if not *robotic.* Japanese visors have slightly larger oblique eye holes. The Shogun and major Lords often have crescent-moon horns on their forehead and hair, but the lower half of the helmet, done in *black* metal with nostrils and maleficent mouths (open wider at each edge than in the middle) are what terrifies and creates the definitely *diabolical* effect.

~~~~~~

7-31   Our helmets are round; *Os nossos capacetes são redondos;*

   Theirs have ears and necks made of plates. *Os seus tem orelhas e pescoços de laminas.*

These "ears" stick out like a bat's, but since "we" also had neck-pieces called "beavers" and gorgets, the contrast, if it is one of a *unit* vs. *pieces*, would seem to be of small degree. I find *shoulders* much more interesting, for "ours" are less angular than football pads, while the large shoulder fins on some Japanese armor reminds one of the classic Cadillac.

~~~~~~

7-32   We must wear thick clothing beneath to put on armor;
Antre nós, pera se hum armar á-de vestir debaxo couza de pano groso;

       The Japanese, when they wear armor, are naked as when their mother bore them.
       Os Japões, quando vestem as armas, despem-se nus como suas mãis os parirão.

Unlike our large sheets of steel, Japanese armor (7-28, above) was not egg-frying hot like "ours," so no insulation was needed. Moreover, the Japanese armor allowed ventilation – Japanese had muggy weather – that might be taken advantage of in such a pristine condition, though I doubt they would be without loincloths! One more contrast which Frois probably knew nothing about:

       Our knights often go to war with the handkerchief of their patroness.
       Theirs keep a dirty picture within the helmet to keep them from harm.

Apparently, there was a superstition going back to ancient China that pictures of men and women in coitus had charm value. Some believe they prevented desecration of the grave for they were found in ancient caskets. Perhaps they were only there because the deceased liked sex. But they were also placed in boxes of books to keep the silverfish away. *A good rationalization for a man to buy dirty books, huh!* Then, they were said to help one achieve military success. This, too, cynics laughed at. No, it is just because the armor was a sacred thing for the samurai, so no one other than a thief would dare open one's armor chest. What better place for a man to keep his pornography than in his armor? All of this has been argued back and forth for hundreds if not thousands of years, and I have no idea how many men actually went to war with these "charms."

~~~~~~

7-33   Among us, it seems one cannot go to war, unless fully armored;
Antre nós não yr hum todo armado parese que não vay à guerra;

       In Japan, it suffices to wear an armored collar to say that one goes armored.
       Em Japão basta pôr hum colarinho ao pescoço pera se dizer que vai armado.

Apparently neck-plates (*shikoro*) were the *sine qua non* for doing battle. It makes sense when one considers the fact that war in Japan was largely a matter of *taking heads* – they even had arrows with tips designed to do this! The word *kubi*, or "neck," in Japanese also means a cut off "head" (versus an attached head, or *atama).* We get *fired*; Japanese get *necked* (*kubi ni naru*). So it is not surprising they wore impressive neck-pieces (some which required a key to open!), if nothing else.

~~~~~~

7-34   We play fifes, drums and royal trumpets in battle;
Antre nós se tanje na guerra pifaro e atanbor ou trombetas reais;

       The Japanese have no more than some raucous whelks that sound very bad.
       Os Japões não tem mais que huns buzios rouqenhos que soão muito mal.

We march into battle to the soaring intonation of the trumpet, whereas they sound their more monotonous conchs, the same shell (actually a large whelk) used by mountain priests. Since the Japanese had no brass, this was the closest they could come to the aggressive tooting which has become identified with armies around the world. Okada notes that Japanese also used drums, military bells and gongs. Perhaps, these were not played in parades, as in the West, so he never heard them.

7-35   We carry rectangular battle standards by hand;
Antre nós se levão as bandeiras do campo nas mãos, quadradas;

>The Japanese each carry their very long, thin ones on bamboo poles fastened on their backs. *Os Japões levão cada hum sua, metidas nas costas em huma cana muito comprida.*

Frois's Portuguese, with the "rectangular" at the end of the sentence, is poor. All the other translations have the *"very long and thin"* (*muito comprida*) modify the bamboo poles, but I suspect a comma is missing and Frois meant to describe the standards/flags, as that would make the more perfect contrast and we do not need to be told the obvious fact that bamboo is long and thin. Because "we" must *hold* our standards, we require "standard-bearers," whereas Japanese (each samurai on horseback) may each (*cada hum sua*) carry a standard. Judging from a genre of painting called "battle-pictures," the Japanese battlefield was awash in these standards, or rather, vertical banners. This allows modern movie producers to turn mass battles into extraordinarily colorful pageants.

7-36   We have sergeants, squad heads, decurions, and centurians;
Antre nós há sarjentos, cabos d'esquadra, decurios e senturiões;

>The Japanese do not care for any of this.
Os Japõis totalmente se não qurão nada disto.

Not only did Japanese have no perfect equivalent to "our" hierarchy but were not so well organized or obedient to a strict chain of command as "we" were. Yet, Japan had a far larger military class than Europe – 5-10% of the population vs. 1%. Moreover, each warrior had peasants along to serve him and there were large contingents of spear and, in 1585, rifle-bearing footmen. These armies were an order in magnitude larger than those of Europe. How all that was organized successfully is a mystery to me! (I assume it followed the same structure found *outside* the military.) One thing is certain, the warlords who unified Japan when Frois was there, executed complex maneuvers which required a chain of command of one sort or another.

When Japan modernized in the 19c, it adopted Western military ranks, yet, even today, they are not quite as familiar to the average Japanese as they are to us. Corporate ranks largely meaningless to us, on the other hand, are complex and familiar to all in Japan. I had great trouble finding English equivalents for these various "ranks" to use on name cards for Japanese companies.

7-37   We fight on horseback;
Antre nós se peleja a cavalo;

>The Japanese dismount when they have to fight.
Os Japões se apeão quando hão-de pelejar.

We will discuss *the riding gap* in the next chapter. Suffice it to say the Japanese were far from Mongols and had little interest in improving their horsemanship, for fighting by sword, on foot, one-against-one was considered *the* manly way to fight in Japan. In Europe, the men fought and sported with many weapons on horseback. In the *De Missione* report, "Miguel=Valignano" describes "dusty" tournaments held inside of private courtyards and explains to his doubting listeners, who saw it as "a sure way to die" rather than entertainment, that casualties were far fewer than one might imagine because a rope made lanes between the horses to prevent head-on collisions, the armor was strong enough to resist bullets, but, just to be safe, the lances had dull tips and were made of easily breakable wood. (The knights would break one, get a replacement, break another, . . .). But, "nothing was so thrilling to the spectator" as the fancy horsemanship, "with the horse moving at [the rider's] will, moving every which way," demonstrated by knights fighting with sword and shield in hand. The knights also shot reed arrows tipped with clay balls or oranges at each other. Imagine the knights "sometimes chasing, sometimes being chased, bending their bodies to avoid the missiles, deflecting them or making other such movements to spectacularly entertain the onlookers." (J/S:DM dialog. 11)

7-38 Our kings and captains pay a salary to soldiers;
Os nossos reis e capitãis pagão soldo aos soldados

> In Japan, everyone must pay for his own food, drink and dress as long as the war goes on. *Em Japão cada hum á-de comer, beber e vestir hà sua custa emquanto anda na guerra.*

Not only are European soldiers paid, or at least fed, but veterans got fine stipends for their service, and the amount might even be appealed, explains "Miguel." Moreover, nobles and knights who personally contributed to a war effort were given correspondingly great rewards including positions of authority. Some Jesuits thought the lack of proper payment was one cause of the disloyalty endemic to Japan (see 7-42), while others saw this self-responsibility as a clever way for the Japanese Lord to quickly conscript and field an extraordinarily large force in comparison to his low income and limited wealth (Valignano noted that the lords in Japan are often "so poor in wealth and rent that they don't even seem to be gentry (*senores*)" (V(A):S&A pg 8) but still "resemble kings in Europe for being very powerful in people," *i.e. military man-power.* Indeed. In 1614, Tokugawa Ieyasu commanded a force of 200,000 men for his Osaka "summer campaign." This figure far exceeds those in the closest parallel in Europe, the Thirty Years' War (Boxer note, in C:MKJS). Could it be said that most soldiers in Europe were mercenaries, while most soldiers in Japan were closer to what we might call national guard and draftees? Depending how you look at it either system could be considered more feudal or more modern.

7-39 We fight to take places, cities, villages and their riches;
Antre nós se peleja por tomar lugares, cidades e vilas e suas riqezas;

> In Japan, the fighting is almost always to take wheat, rice and barley.
> *A peleja quasi sempre em Japão hé pera se tomar o trigo, arroz e cevada.*

The European defensive tactic of burning fields to deny them to the enemy while retreating might have made a more elegant contrast on "our" side.

Crops may not have been the aim of war in Japan as Frois claims, except in the sense that a provinces wealth was measured in terms of grain production, but they were taken enough that the practice of *karita*, or "reap-field" – taking grain for one's own soldiers while depriving the enemy of food – was common enough to be forbidden by the Shoguns and there are even Chinese documents discriminating between Chinese and Japanese "wou'ko" (*wako*) pirate raids, by identifying the latter as the ones so poor they waste time stealing grain (as opposed to gold and other real treasures). I cannot help but wonder if there was a sort of "rice-raid" tradition, – like the pony-raids of the Amerindian – in at least the Southwest part of Japan where Frois spent some of his time!

7-40 With us, horses, dromedaries and [bactrian] camels carry the soldiers' gear;
Antre nós, cavalos, dromedarios, camelos, etc., levão o fato aos soldados;

> In Japan, each soldier's *hyakushos* [peasants] carry his gear and food on their backs. *Em Japão os fiaxos de cada hum lhe levão seu fato e mantimento aas costas.*

Camels? Spain was once occupied by the Berbers, who rode only camels and no horses. Evidently, the camel was conscripted by the triumphant Iberians but only for the less prestigious role of a carrier. (Note also that Mohammed's army rode camels and had less than 200 horses for 10,000 men. The Arabian horses largely came from Iberia where they later returned. The history goes round and round and round!)

The Japanese "soldiers" here are *samurai*. The contrast, while correct, is misleading if one thinks the Japanese practice was specifically military. Civilians also depended more on human than nonhuman animal power for transportation in Japan.

7-41 Among us, killing oneself is considered a grave sin;
Antre nós se tem por pecado gravissimo matar-se hum a si mesmo;

> The Japanese in war, when they can do no more, cut their belly to show their guts.
> *Os Japões na guerra, quando não podem mais, cortar a barriga hé grão valentia.*

If we define "us" to extend back to our Classical world, the contrast is less absolute. Who doesn't know of the proverbial Roman soldier falling on his sword? But this practice was by no means limited to warfare in Japan. The "voluntary taking of one's life to avoid disgrace, and blot out entirely or partially the stain on an honorable name" (B:JG&W) may have originated in battle as a way to prove one's bravery and avoid execution at the hands of the enemy. Since suicide might be thus interpreted as bravery or cowardice, the Japanese came to do it in such a difficult way (self-disemboweling) that it could only be interpreted as the former! Or, it may go back further to the widespread cultural practice of suicide-as-revenge (saddling another with one's spirit). But, be the roots what they may, the Japanese came to make a special institution of suicide, where it served as a way to take responsibility for ones wrong-doing *by oneself,* thereby preventing the laws of collective responsibility from exterminating one's entire line. As outlandish as this practice may seem, "we" had it, too. Montaigne, in his essay "Custom of Cea", not only details *whole Spanish towns* committing suicide rather than submitting to the Romans – this reminiscent of what sometimes happened when Japanese castles were over-run – but a very close parallel to the above-mentioned "special institution."

> In the time of Tiberius, condemned men awaiting execution lost their property and were denied the right of sepulture; those who anticipated it by killing themselves were buried and could make their will." (M(F):CEM)

Yet, many if not most of the many suicides recorded in Cocks' diary and Kaempfer's History of Japan (especially the diary-like "Affairs at Nagasaki" chapter) are done for no reason other than chagrin or despair, as was what must be the most incredible suicide of all history, reported by Caron (details in *TT-long*), by a young woman who farted in her master's presence. It is hard to say why Japanese could kill themselves so easily. Theoretically, any people who believe in a pleasant afterlife or rebirth and have no specific strictures forbidding suicide, should do so at the drop of a hat, and Frois in 1565 describes small groups of cultists who loaded their sleeves with stones and jumped into the sea merely to get to paradise more quickly.

Today, one still reads of Japanese committing suicide to take responsibility for scandals, but, on the whole, there is little to differentiate Japanese suicide from that in the West, particularly when the "West" includes Eastern European countries with double the suicide rate of Japan, as well as Catholic nations with suspiciously low rates. The biggest difference would seem to be in the way suicides are treated as a concept, how they are depicted on television. Plays and movies about the 47 Ronin (masterless samurai) who end up committing *seppuku* (formal *harakiri*) en masse are shown every year as a sort of *morality play.* These samurai pretend to lead dissolute lives, putting their own families through hell and enduring themselves every insult in the books to eventually assemble and take revenge upon a man whose insult resulted in their beloved master's forced suicide, a venture in which they succeed and, having broken the new laws of an era that no longer allowed such vendettas (this was a century after Frois), themselves, had to commit suicide. I applaud such a play for we need to be reminded that there are things more important than living. But, considering the sacrifices made by the heroes' families and the parallels with people working themselves to death for the sake of heartless companies, I can understand why not a few Japanese *detest* the play and the "feudal" (a word with very bad implications to most Japanese today) values it represents.

Paradoxically, doctor-assisted suicide has, if anything, met stronger resistance in Japan than in most of the West. The main reason for the lack of organs to transplant which sends many Japanese abroad for surgery is the reluctance of Japanese doctors to allow even brain-dead patients to die. Since WW II, Japanese have done a back-flip on the sanctity of human life (aside from abortion, where there is a question as to whether the life is yet human). They *claim* that, unlike the West, where men became accustomed to controlling the deaths of animals and, by extension men, their tradition of Buddhism does not allow this, and the idea of *brain-death* itself is a Western invention depending on the separation of soul and body, which is alien to their animistic souls. I think the main issues are actually that, *first*, the tradition of forced suicide makes Japanese rightfully aware of the dangers inherent to euthanasia, and *second*, Japanese doctors are, as everyone else in Japan, simply afraid of taking responsibility, for responsibility in Japan is something absolute and doctors, understandably, fear it.

~~~~~~

7-42   With us, treason is rare and reprehensible.
      Antre nós a treisão hé couza rara e mui estranhada;

> In Japan, it is so common it is almost never criticized.
> *Em Japão hé tão comum que já quasi nada se estranha.*

Apparently, the main reason for treason in Japan was not so much a lack of pecuniary incentives to remain loyal (7-38) – after all, as Xavier and others noted, honor meant more to the Japanese than wealth – but the unsettled nature of the era revealed the arbitrary nature of authority and encouraged the capricious recourse to capital punishment that made even persons *suspecting themselves to be under suspicion* liable to break and run for a new master to save the hides of their families and themselves. Ironically, the quick recourse to capital punishment itself was largely due to fear that the retainer, *suspecting he might be suspected,* might betray his master, or a servant kill his master and commit suicide. Miguel=Valignano discusses this at length in *De Mission*, contrasting the mercurial situation in Japan with that in Europe, where people of all social levels could rest assured of fair trials and even a peasant could sue a King for his rights, where everyone knew and accepted their proper place as if they were members of a big family because retainers had fixed roles for which they were well trained from infancy, unlike in Japan, where servants were both vertically and horizontally mobile and, thus, could hardly be content with their proper places. In Europe, the King was beloved of all, lords were "loved and respected like parents" and "treated their subjects with mercy as if they were their very own children," and rulers and ruled alike rested easily knowing, as "Mancio=Valignano" points out, that "their authority could be expected to pass safely down the generations as it had reached them from ages immemorial," unlike in Japan, "where all was extremely inconstant, where clans' fortunes rose and fell, where no position, no person, and no family was not exposed to extreme danger." In this secure place called Europe – *Machiavelli? Never heard of him!* – no one feared treachery.

The constant change, the mutability, the impermanence, the uncertainty of life in Japan (ultimately blamed on their Buddhist rivals) was *the* most constantly reiterated theme in Jesuit letters to Rome. Of course, the prescription for a cure was a good dose of Christianity. The Tokugawa government was soon to make a more rational choice, however, *Confucianism,* and would in two or three generations be more stable than any Christian government in Europe.

7-43 With us, it is the supreme infamy to be an executioner;
Antre nós hé sumo vituperio ser algoz;

> In Japan, any nobleman can kill someone for justice, and they take pride in it.
> *Em Japão, matar a hum por justiça qualquer fidalgo o faz e se preza disso.*

"Our" image of an executioner is indeed a grim one. What executioner is depicted without a hood over his head?

On the other hand, as Frois's contemporary Avila de Giron wrote in a rarely caustic vein: "Name a Japanese and you name an executioner – and they say it is cruel to punish children!" (C:TCJ) This was true. *First,* there was perfunctory execution, when a maleficent was cut-down on the spot. Needless to say, lords who exercised this prerogative too much were not liked. *Second,* there was formal execution where a lord might choose to do so to show off his arm and test his sword – get in the first sword-test, if it were – or, for the satisfaction, because damage had been done to him. *Third,* there was *seppuku,* where someone ordered to disembowel himself, might ask (or order) someone else to do him the honor of seconding him, i.e. cutting off his head. Since, the kindest cuts – made for someone who was not really interested in showing his guts, but just saving his name or family by properly taking responsibility – came as soon as the short sword touched the belly, this assistance (*kaishaku*) is better called *euthanasia* than execution. Since no one would want a weak assist (Poor Mishima! His failed to part his heavily muscled neck at a stroke) to be asked to assist would indeed be an honor and accepting a good deed, because a samurai wished to die at the hand of someone he respected.

Morse, sensing an anomaly between the gentle men he knew and this seemingly sadistic behavior, explains the *second* type of execution by linking it to the *third*, kindest type. He milked "Mr. Machida, the sword merchant" for information, and learned that although the professional executioners were of the [despised] Eta class, a gentleman had a good reason for wanting "to try the temper of his blade by executing a criminal." Namely, "beheading a criminal gives a man practice" in case "any of his friends had to commit hara-kiri" and he were to be called to give the *coup de grace*.

7-44 The *cambala* [yak hair] that in India serves gentiles and moors as fans,
As cambalas que na India servem a jentios e mouros de abanos,

> The Japanese use for the wigs around their helmets.
> *Os Japões uzão dellas pera cabeleiras ao redor dos capacetes.*

When you think about it, a swishing tail is not just a fly-shoo but a fan. As described in 2-5, the Japanese imported the yak tail hair from China. A talismanic element may be involved with the helmets for this hair is seen on everything from spearheads to fly-flaps called *hossu* often seen in the hand of Zen patriarchs, which signify the one thing we really need, *something to guard against the various types of desires that swarm the mind like flies.* Did the helmet wearer feel said hair, like the broom tied on the mast-tip of Dutch warships, was an appropriate symbol for ridding the land of pesky rivals?

7-45 Our razors are thick and flat; *As nossas navalhas são grosas e razas;*

> Theirs are slim and curve on one edge. *As suas delgadas e curvas de huma banda.*

Okada mentions an old tale called "The (Buddhist) priest and the acolyte (和尚と小僧) where the razor serves as a simile for *ayu,* or "sweet-fish," a small river fish with a lithe and slightly curved silhouette.

7-46   We grind ours with oil on hard stone;
As nossas se amolão com azeite em pedra dura;

      The Japanese grind theirs on soft stone, with water.
      Os Japões amolão as suas em pedra mole e com agoa.

Worldwide, water was the more common lubricant and even the Greeks who rubbed oil on their bodies used waterstones. Without a lubricant, natural stones tend to clog. "Ours" were helped by mineral oil (perhaps diluted with petroleum, also called "rock-oil" in Chinese), while "theirs" was best soaked in water for ten minutes or so before using. With waterstones, there is an interesting paradox: since much of the abrasion comes from floating particles, a soft stone which releases many will sharpen fastest, but also hollow out fastest and need to be planed back in shape. Modern artificial sharpening stones are the most contrary of all, for they generally work best dry.

7-47   Among us, only barbers shave; *Antre nós os barbeiros somente rapão.*

      In Japan, almost everyone knows how to do it. *Em Japão quasi todos o sabem fazer.*

As suggested in 7-14, 15 and 16, above, Japanese blades were sharper than "ours." They could apparently even shave with their short swords! Doubtless their cutting culture was equally advanced, with more professional sharpeners (*togishi*) offering door-to-door service, and a greater appreciation for maintenance than was the case in Europe. Finally, using a brush to write meant that most Japanese had to have had far better control of fine, unsupported hand movements than most Europeans.

7-48   We cannot shave our beards without going to the barber;
Antre nós se hum não for ao barbeiro não pode rapar a barba;

      [In Japan] Many *bonzes* and laymen shave their beards and heads by themselves.
      Muitos bonzos e sequlares rapão a barba e cabeça por si mesmos.

7-49   Among us, soldiers carry the match in their left hand;
Antre [nós] os soldados trazem o murrão no braço esqerdo.

      The Japanese with their right.
      Os Japões no direito.

The Japanese for *murrão* is *hinawa*, or "fire-string," a clearer indication of what we are talking about than the English "match." It was a fuse-like smoldering string, kept ready for firing a musket. The dictionary Englishes it as both "fuse" and "match." Since we identify a burning string with a *fuse*, that was my first choice for translation; but, considering the fact these "matches" were not necessarily the matches we imagine ("match" once even meant "lamp!") and that the rifles were and are still called "matchlocks" (as opposed to the later *flintlock*), I went with the second word though I almost went back on myself after reading the following translation of the end to a shameful raid in South China honestly recorded by Pinto:

> So everyone ran down to the beach and got back to the junk without any opposition whatsoever. We were all very rich and very happy. We had also captured a lot of beautiful girls for our use later on and it was pitiful to see them coming along in groups of four and five, *hands tied up with musket fuses,* the girls all weeping and our men all singing and laughing. (my *italics,* L:PFMP)

7-50   Our matches are made of twine; *Os nossos murrões são de fiado;*

   Theirs, of paper and bamboo husks. *Os seus de papel ou cascas de cana.*

This is a difference, but hardly a contradiction. (For a real difference, we need to wait for the flintlock, a 17c European invention possibly inspired by the flint and steel mechanical lighters Japanese nicotine addicts devised the better to light up at night.)

7-51   We can fence without yelling;
Antre nós esgrimi-sse sem falar;

   The Japanese must give a shout with every blow and parry.
   Os Japões a cada talho ou reves hão-de dar hum grito

We have discussed this fully in 7-25. What an experience it is hearing a *kendo* class – preferably high-school girls – practicing with their bamboo *shinai* swords. Someone should make a symphony of it: *Scream! Whack! Scream! Scream! Whack!*

7-52   Our Swiss soldiers discharge their arquebuses from the shoulder;
Os nossos soldados na Suisea desparão as espingardas no onbro;

   The Japanese place [the butt of the rifle] in their faces, like someone aiming at enemies. *Os Japões a poem no rosto como quem aponta a inimigos*

The "our" here has two possible meanings. *First*, for over a hundred years, squads of Swiss mercenary arquebusiers were engaged all over Europe by anyone with the money to hire them. From the way they turn up everywhere, I would not be surprised to learn that at their peak they commanded the majority of small-arms in Europe. *Second*, a unit of mercenaries was engaged by Pope Julius II in 1505 and have served as the Papal Swiss Guard ever since.

Why did Japanese not use their shoulders? The butts of their guns were short.. *Why?* Did they want the gun in front of the face to keep the exploding powder further from the ears? Or was it easier to aim? Did the Swiss, then, *not* aim? Or, is Frois's expression "like aiming at enemies" the idiom for a sniper? If so, did we have snipers that shot differently than the Swiss? I have read of our arquebusiers marching along, their faces all black from the powder. If so, how could the Japanese bear to be yet closer to the chamber? And considering the fact that a kick in the shoulder hurts, how did Japanese survive getting kicked in the face? *I do not know any of this.* I only know the guns remained that way for a long time, for over 200 years later, Golownin observed:

   The butt ends are very small, and they do not put them to their shoulder to fire, but lay them to their right cheek and so take aim." (G:MCJ)

endnote VII

War

For all the piddly detailed contrasts, I feel many more basic items were missed here. For a start, how about this:

We do not ask for the names of people before we fight them in a war.
Their nobles and even many gentry insist upon knowing who they fight before drawing their sword.

In the traditional battles of Japanese clans, there was a complex etiquette of doing battle where every samurai acted in a manner found only among a far smaller number of knights in Europe. Announcing (*na-nori*) was an important part of this. It was probably true in parts of Europe, too, a couple hundred years earlier (before the cream of French chivalry was shot to pieces). But even then, it couldn't have been as common a practice as it was in Japan or we would have a name for it.

We fight wars outside of our countries.
Japanese are happy to fight at home.

Frois could have written this, for Hideyoshi's attempt to conquer the world (beginning with Korea) happened *after* TRATADO (from 1592). But I suppose that Frois might have replied that the wars of the Spanish against the Dutch and English and others were also civil war inside of a single Empire rightly ruled by the Pope and his representative King (Phillip II, of course).

We only launch an attack after proclaiming the legal justification and having it duly recorded;
They have no such system and simply attack without proper justification whenever they want.

As ludicrous as it may seem, all the invasions and massacres carried out in the Americas were done legally, recorded by notary publics as described in 10-11. Japanese had their reasons, of course, but were not so hypocritical about it.

We raise various dogs to be mean and train them to hunt, attack and tear up our enemies.
They think it an unnatural thing, worse than cannibalism to teach dogs to eat humans.

The Iberians did not only use dogs in battle but to murder the defenseless. In the Americas, they played a special role in the extermination of the *Berdache,* or third sex, an accepted gender found among most native people. No doubt "we" would have sicced them on the abomination-loving bonzes in China and Japan if given half a chance! That does not speak well for "our" side. But even this is detail. Let us delve into the bigger picture.

If the *De Missione* report on the situation in Europe is taken at face value, the biggest contrast of all in the 1580s was the fact that "We enjoy domestic peace; while the Japanese are constantly at war." This was true for Japan and *Luso-Iberia* (for the Portuguese and Spanish took their wars elsewhere in Europe!). But, what irony! "We" brought the seeds of peace to Japan. If it were not for those guns, it is unlikely even the wily steel-nerved Nobunaga could have defeated his more powerful traditional rivals and the warring might have continued for hundreds of years. As it was, in less than a century, even Europeans described a situation exactly opposite of that described in *De Missione*: Now, *They were at peace and we at war.* Yet, fast-forward another 250 years and things flip over again. After WW II, "we" simplistically turned the losers into an *inherently warlike people,* one so dangerous the Occupying Authority had to have a special Constitution denying their right to self-defense:

The Japanese people forever renounce war as a sovereign right of the nation. (Article 9)

Helen Mears deserves plaudits for her long (and, unfortunately boring) MIRROR FOR AMERICANS (1948), which, almost alone, took America and the West to task for this self-serving stereotyping that continued for decades. I see no need to elaborate upon her general argument that the kettle was calling the pot black: *Americans were and are every bit as militaristic as Japanese.* But I think we do need to think about how and why Japanese changed. Remember, Japan was universally praised in the West for its fine behavior when it beat a leading Western military power, Russia. Unless everything I have read is wrong, it was a *good* war for Japan, a good war objectively speaking, and one Japan should remember with pride. They were provoked and responded by beating the Russians fair and square and on top of that, to quote Sladen, "their demands were marvelously moderate." Unlike the case with WW II, Japan treated prisoners better than International standards required. It is easy for us to say that they were only trying to put on a good face, but this was no little war. It was perhaps the largest war in history up to that time. In a war like that, no nation can put on an act on all fronts. The Japanese were *that* good, period.

How, then, do we explain the Rape of Nanking, medical experiments, forced name-changing (in Korea, everyone had to adopt Japanese names)? Part of the problem was prejudice toward their neighbors on the part of the Japanese that were already observed by the 16c European visitors. The Japanese, as already pointed out, shared the European belief that military prowess and courage gave one the right to rule (though they might not agree with it so baldly stated) and despise the meek. They were "one of the boys" from the get-go. That is why Hideyoshi could think of conquering Korea and China. Sure, Japanese were happy to accept some of our scientific justification (social Darwinism) for self-serving behavior, but I do not for a minute go along with the idea that they had to "imitate the white man" to learn to mistreat "natives," something they did even at the same time as they behaved like gentlemen in the War with Russia. What about the Bantam March? *We asked for it.* Generations of Japanese emigrants were brutalized by whites, especially on the West Coast of Usania, and the size of the Japanese navy was unfairly limited by the international (Euro-American) community. *Read the contemporary literature.* There is no question about it. "We" tried to block the rising power of a non-christian, non-white nation and the Japanese, not surprisingly (with the help of the same yellow press we had and same nationalist types) responded as you might expect, *with hate.* At the same time, the increased size of the draft brought in raw recruits removed by class and by generations from *bushido*-style chivalry. They went through the same desensitizing drills "our" marines do and many became monsters . . . But not *all.* Read K'tut Tantri's *Revolt in Paradise.* Read about the Japanese guard who surreptitiously let her out of her cell in Jakarta to see the moon.

~~~~~~

In one sense, *Article 9* is very Japanese. The Japanese have, after all, disarmed *themselves* in the past. *More than once.* First, after obtaining the greatest small arms fire-power in the entire world (7-20), the Japanese "gave up the gun." Frois, in his *Historia,* gives us the first inklings of the renunciation when, in 1586, Hideyoshi "to protect his own self from any stray bullets, forbid the ownership of guns under pain of the penalty of death in the several countries neighboring his palace." Two years later, he initiated his more famous sword-hunt, taking all real weapons away from the hitherto armed peasantry, so only the samurai portion of the population was armed. And, as battles slowly petered out in the first fifty years of the Tokugawa era (1600-1868), guns disappeared. It is not quite correct to say that the samurai all returned to their swords, because many never left them – the riflemen had mostly been peasants or bonzes. Guns were not absolutely outlawed, but the government licensed so few to be made that they stopped multiplying and evolving. They were not, like Christianity totally wiped out. The parades observed by the Dutch invariably included many rows of colorful old-fashioned arquebus bearers.

Eventually, even the samurai's swords would have their turn. After giving the historical and romantic context of "this magical weapon," Chamberlain explains what happened to the samurai's custom of always wearing two swords, dating back to the Warring Era, that is to say at least 500 years:

> It was abolished by an edict issued on the 28th March, 1876, and taking effect from the 1st January, 1877. The edict was obeyed by this strangely docile people without a blow being struck, and the curio-shops displayed heaps of swords which, a few months before, the owners would have less willingly have parted with than with life itself. Shortly afterwards, a second edict appeared, rescinding the first and leaving *any one* at liberty to wear what swords he pleased. But as the privilege of a class distinction was thus obliterated, none cared to take advantage of the permission, and the two-sworded Japanese gentleman is now extinct. (C:TJ)

Strangely docile? *I would call it brains.* Wearing Western clothing and making a money in the world became the mark of an honorable man and the Edict made it official. In that brave new world, sword-waving became a prerogative of the military machine. A generation later, The Occupation expressed the same surprise at the docility of Japanese. What did we expect? *Again, I would call it brains.* The ability to recognize changed circumstances and act on it.

In the first decade after the Black Boats pushed open their nation, samurai assassins 1), revenging real (Westerners not observing proper quarantine rules because of the unequal treaty brought in cholera that killed hundreds of thousands) or imagined slights (accidents of etiquette), or 2), hoping to create a confrontation to topple the government and create a tougher anti-foreign one, or 3), ideological xenophobes terrified the new foreign community and earned a measure of respect for Japanese as a people not to be messed with.

Eventually cooler heads prevailed and Japan concentrated on development. The traveler-writers arrived. Japan was very popular as a queer place, *but no longer respected.* Prefacing his "Peace Edition" of MORE QUEER THINGS ABOUT JAPAN, written shortly after the Ruso-Japanese War ended, Douglas Sladen admitted he previously thought of the Japanese navy in their "little white men-of-war built by Armstrong" and their British Navy look-alike uniforms as "a mere parade" and "attached even less importance to the Japanese Tommies, five feet high, who were marched and countermarched in Italian uniforms by German instructors." *Sladen saw toy-soldiers; and he was not alone.* "The British merchants of Yokohama were never tired of telling you how the Japanese had been dispersed at Shimonoseki by a taste of cold steel." But he was wrong. *It was those 47 Ronin* (masterless samurai, pretending to be resigned to being losers but really just biding their time to take revenge) *all over again.* After Sladen learned of the bravery of the Japanese soldiers fighting Russia, who did not hesitate to die for their country as a martyr dies for his faith without drugs like the Dervish or "promises of Paradise like the Mahommedan [sic] who is fighting against infidels," he confessed:

> I laugh now when I think of what a lot of venerable myths we hoarded up; but I do not laugh, I almost shed tears of respect and sympathy, when I remember that ever since I have known the Japanese up to the beginning of the present war they have possessed their souls in patient, content to be branded as a toy nation – almost as a nation of cowards – until, as Minerva sprang fully armed out of the head of Jupiter, they leapt upon the astonished Russians, a nation armed cap-a-pie, a type of martial wisdom. (S:MQTJ)

That is to say, the coming of the Black Ships placed the Japanese under a *moratorium.* I would guess that Douglas Sladen, as a writer (who, like most writers, probably had to bide his time as a poor man before finally making it), knew first-hand the collective hell the Japanese went through. Hence, the wet eyes. Still, one has to question why he and others were so blind to Japan's potential clout. I do not know how many 19c references I have read of Captain Golownin's evaluation of the Japanese as *unfit for modern warfare.* Between 1811 and 1813, he discovered what Perry and the first English and American Ambassadors would rediscover: *flimsy fake forts* and described a people so long at peace that they would rely on a charade for protection and, by character, timid, rather than aggressive like many Westerners. Indeed, he wrote that "it requires at least a century to introduce an innovation into their military system" where "strict observance of ancient order and rules is their unalterable tactics [sic]." But, he also made it clear he was talking about Japan in "a state of peace." But, what none of those references noted was that elsewhere, in his book, this fair-minded and insightful Russian captain made it clear that the Japanese were, nonetheless highly disciplined, determined *and could take on the world at any time if they decided to do so.*

> If the Japanese government desired to have a navy, it would be easy to build one upon the European system, and to bring it to the greatest perfection. They need only to invite into their country two or three good naval architects and some naval officers. They have good ports, all the necessary materials, a number of able carpenters, and very active and enterprising sailors. The people in general are quick of comprehension, and ready at learning. It requires no little boldness to put out to sea in such vessels as they now have. . . . We were frequently witnesses of the activity of the Japanese sailors; it is wonderful with what dexterity they manage their great boats in the violent surf . . .

Golownin liked and admired the Japanese on many counts, but he feared an increase in the number of world powers and wrote that Japan's neighbors "must thank providence for having inspired the Japanese lawgivers" to promote isolation "and should give them no inducement to change their policy for that of Europe." He predicted that if the Japanese had a sovereign like Peter the Great, her "numerous, ingenious, and industrious people, who are capable of every thing and much inclined to imitate all that is foreign" would "become in a few years, the sovereign of the eastern ocean." In that case, he wrote, even the West coast of America would be under Japanese influence. And if the Japanese were to "adopt our policy as a model, we should then see the Chinese obliged to do the same." He was a bit off on China – unless we include late 20c developments. He feared "we" would eventually "compel them" to do this.

> Attacks, for example, like that of Chowostoff [his misbehavior in the North was the reason Golownin was held by the Japanese], often repeated, would probably induce them to think of a means to repel a handful of vagabonds who disturbed a nation. This might lead them to build ships of war on the model of those of Europe; these ships might increase to fleets, and then it is probable the good success of this measure would lead them also to adopt the other scientific methods, which are so applicable to the destruction of the human race. In this manner all the inventions of Europe might gradually take root in Japan, even without the creative spirit of a Peter . . . The Japanese certainly would not be in want of teachers if they would only invite them; *I therefore believe that this just and upright people must, by no means, be provoked* . . . I do not mean to affirm that the Japanese and the Chinese might form themselves on the European model, and become dangerous to us now; but we must take care to avoid giving cause to our posterity to despise our memory. (G:MCIJ *my italics*)

Golownin's editor writes that the "extreme readiness" of the Japanese "in acquiring European knowledge is certified" by none other than our "father Luigi Froes, in 'Lettere del Giappone'" where he attests to the talent for learning on the part of the Japanese exceeded that of Europeans. Be that as it may, Golownin's warning was paid no heed. *"We" provoked Japan.* And, wouldn't you know it, Golownin's own nation was the first big loser! And, I dare say, the whole world has suffered for it. Had Russia only heeded their own Captain Golownin's advice and not forced Japan to fight, the chain of events leading to the Bolshevik take-over and, a bit more indirectly, to Hitler's Germany – would not have happened.

To be fair to both the Europeans and the Japanese, we should point out that they were not by any means the only war addicts in East Asia, either.

In the 16c, wars involving *hundreds of thousands* of people and casualties likewise in the *hundreds of thousands* – in at least one case, if Pinto is to be believed, costing the lives of thousands of elephants (not in battle, but eaten during a siege!) – were endemic in South-east Asia. Pinto, who lost no opportunity to point out the cruelty of his own countrymen, tells nonfiction tales of siege and rapine, revenge and sadism that curdle the blood which have nothing to do with the Japanese or "us." The Burmese, whose bravery would later be praised by Kipling, and others whose names I can't recall (probably Thai and Cambodian kingdoms) were *every bit* as ferocious as our Far East and Far West exemplars. Here is but one of the cruelties visited upon Prome after the city's fall. Let us note that Pinto writes nothing this horrid about warfare in Japan:

> When this was over, he [the Burmese tyrant] went to stand at a window overlooking a courtyard where they brought the bodies of more than two thousand children that had been lying in the streets, and right there in front of him he had them cut into very small pieces, rolled in rice chaff and grass, and fed to the elephants. (P(C):TMP ch155)
>
> And to crown it all, on the following day, which was Saint Bartholomew's Day, he had all the noblemen who had been taken alive – and there must have been more than three hundred of them – impaled on *caloetes* [an Indian term used by Pinto], and in that manner, impaled like suckling pigs, they too [we have skipped other atrocities] were thrown into the river. So that the means used by this tyrant to punish these unfortunate people were so unheard of, that "we Portuguese all went about gasping in horror." Believe me, Pinto knew *that* was saying a lot!

VIII

of Horses
Do que toca aos cavalos

~~~~~~

8-1   Our horses are very beautiful; *Os nossos cavalos são muito fermozos;*
          The horses of Japan are much inferior to them. *Os de Japão lhe são muito inferiores.*

We tend to connect Greece and Italy with all things classic, but when it comes to *horses* Spain has the pedigree. They are in the Iliad and Greek's first equestrian Xenophon (430 BC) thought "gifted Iberian horses" without equal as a war-horse. Long *the* horse for battle and portrait for most of the kings of Europe, as Frois wrote, Phillip (Felipe) II, was busy restoring it into *the perfect horse* as described in classical texts. We are not only talking performance and character but *features*; the horse had to *look* noble and beautiful. Hence, the *"convexo"* profile was restored – i.e., the snout of the Arab horse which had bred with the Andalusian (Southern Spanish) when the Berbers occupied *Hispania* was a bit concave, or turned up and this upset the classicist who thought all noses human or equine should be Roman! The purest result of the King's project, now called an Andalusia in the USA and a *Pura Raza Española* (PRE) horse by the Spanish government, figures heavily in approximately 80% of the bloodlines of all modern breeds!

With respect to Japanese horses, Frois's was a typical European opinion. His contemporary, Giron writes cruelly: "According to our standards, their horses are not at all good and the very best one in all Japan is only fit to carry firewood." (C:TCJ). Bartolli, restating Frois in his *History of the Society of Jesus* snickers that next to the magnificent Arab, "even the best horses in the Imperial [Hideyoshi's] stable were but hacks." Most Europeans, Iberian or not, in whatever century one chooses concur. In 1878, the Englishwoman Isabella Bird was scathing:

> The Japanese horse is a mean, sorry brute, a grudging, ungenerous animal, trying to human patience and temper, with three *movements* (not by any means to be confounded with paces) – a drag, a roll, and a scramble . . . The traveling is the nearest approach to "a ride on a rail" as I have ever made. I have ridden or rather sat upon seventy-six horses, all horrible. They all stumble. The loins of some are higher than their shoulders, so that one slips forwards, and the back bones of all are ridgy. Their hind feet grow into points which turn up, and their hind legs all turn outwards, like those of a cat, from carrying heavy burdens at an early age. (B:UTJ)

Brinkley, author of an incredible encyclopedia on Japan published in 1901, admitted the "mishapen ponies" showed "hardiness and endurance" but would not admit them to be worthy of the name "war-horse" because they were "so deficient in stature and massiveness that when mounted by a man in voluminous armour they looked painfully puny" (in C:TCJ). Brinkley's emphasis on the horses' respective fitness or unfitness for war is correct. In 1585, the Spanish government controlled horses as modern governments control advanced weaponry and the Portuguese horse-traders were the equivalent of "our" international arms traders. The only somewhat favorable comment I know comes from the English merchant, Captain John Saris, writing only decades after Frois: "Their horses are not tall, but of the size of our middling Nags, short and well trust, small headed and very full of mettle, in my opinion, farre excelling the Spanish Jennet in pride and stomacke." (C:TCJ)

Even today, most equestrians in the West are so infatuated with *appearance*, so biased about what makes a good horse, that not only have they little interest in Japanese horses, but few appreciate the world's oldest genuine horse-centered culture, the Mongols. Go East, cowboy, if you would see the real thing! Get out into the country where little children ride before they walk! (The Mongolians are kind, lively people and offer some very reasonable horse-tours on their "misshapen ponies." So if you must travel . . .)

8-2   Ours, running, [still] stop on the spot;   *Os nossos correndo parão hà risca;*
Theirs are horribly uncontrollable;   *Os seos são muito dezenfreados.*

Frois does not exaggerate on either account. The Iberian horse "was designed with a short back, strong loins, able to move off quickly from a standstill (for the bullring), stop quickly and change direction. The Spanish Andalusian has a capacity for lightning acceleration and yet stopping dead in his tracks." (EVOLUTION AND HISTORY OF THE SPANISH (PRE) ANDALUSIAN – www. preandalusians.com/)

Even the long and tame centuries of Seclusion did nothing to improve Japanese horses whose unmanageability was a common complaint of 19c European visitors. Bird has *dozens of pages* of invective scattered in her thousands of pages of writing on Japan – and as far as horses go, identical – Korea. Her first meeting with "the terrible Japanese pack-horse" – which was also generally the only horse a visitor rode – was dramatic. Excited by the crowd that always gathered when she passed through, the "horribly fierce looking creatures" went berserk and broke their "head rope." Her mount

> proceeded down the street mainly on his hind feet, squealing, and striking savagely with his fore feet . . . jumped over all ditches, attacked all foot-passengers with his teeth, and behaved so like a wild animal that not all my previous acquaintance with the idiosyncrasies of horses enabled me to cope with him. (B:UTJ)

When she and her interpreter, who had been thrown, pulled into a post for a change of horse, the stallions were so provoked by the other horses they threw the interpreter again and even the horsewoman herself, by cleverly rearing up right when she was in the process of dismounting, then dashing at her "with his teeth and fore feet." Yet two letters and a hundred miles later, she is on the back of a more "wicked" horse yet, one who tried to side-kick her when she touched the saddle, "made dashes with his tethered head at flies, . . . attempted to dislodge flies on his nose with his hind hoof, executed capers which involved a total disappearance of everything in front of the saddle . . . " They even changed her opinion on horse psychology. "I used to think that horses were made vicious either by being teased or by violence in breaking; but this does not account for the malignity of the Japanese horses, for the people are so much afraid of them that they treat them with great respect; they are not beaten or kicked, are spoken to in soothing tones, and on the whole live better than their masters. Perhaps this is the secret of their villainy – 'Jeshurun waxed fat and kicked.'" Later she found a problem with the breaking-in process which involved "atrocious cruelty" and didn't blame horses for their tricks, such as "lying down in fords, throwing themselves down head foremost and rolling over pack and rider," etc..

But the need to dismount before passing or being passed by a superior in Japan probably contributed to the lack of concern for improving equine transportation, for it made the horse *all but useless for rapid transportation* and, more importantly, with almost all horses in Japan not so much *ridden* as led about by one or two footmen – because not as many people could ride and because many who could feared the responsibility in the case of accident – there was little demand for horses trained to respond in the way we expect horse's to respond, anyway. Kaempfer writes:

> The Japanese look upon our European way of sitting on horseback, and holding the bridle oneself as warlike, and properly becoming a soldier . . . they seldom or never use it in their journies. It is more frequent among people of quality in cities, where they go a visiting one another. But even

then the rider (who makes but a sorry appearance when sitting after our manner,) holds the bridle meerly for form, the horse being nevertheless led by one, and sometimes two footmen, who walk on each side of the head, holding it by the bit." (K(S):HOJ)

Where it *did* matter, horses were trained well enough. In the Shinto rite of shooting arrows (*yabusame*) at a small target at a dead run (gallop) without a hand on the rein and spectators standing dangerously close, or, competitively shooting running dogs (with padded arrows) in a crowded field of competitors, etc. would be impossible with the frightful mounts we have been reading about.

8-3 Ours allow one to ride on their rumps; *Os nossos consentem cavalgar nas ancas*;

   Those of Japan are not so trained. *Os de Japão não o tem por custume.*

Apparently, Europeans were not adverse to putting two people on a horse – and the body of the Iberian horse being relatively short encouraged use of the rump – while pony-sized Japanese horses were not built for more than one rider.

8-4 Ours proceed abreast of one another; *[Dos] nossos vai hum apar doutro paseando;*

   Those of Japan always go one after another. *Os de Japão sempre hum detraz doutro.*

I wish I could *ask* Frois to explain this one. Are the roads too narrow because, carts are scarce so most roads are made for foot traffic in Japan? For one versed in classical Japanese literature, all this is a comical reversal, for "horses" – or rather ponies – in Japanese poetry *always* race across the fields side-by-side (*koma narabete*)! If Frois is right, Japan changed since ancient times.

8-5 With ours, the tail is extended for beauty's sake; *[Aos] nossos se entende o rabo pera fermozura;*

   With theirs, it is bound in a knot. *Aos seus lhe atão com nós o rabo.*

Japanese tails were usually fixed in this manner on formal occasions when a Chinese-style saddle was used and was called "China-tail" (*kara-o*). The knotted tail was actually stuffed into a sack which was then bound to the tail. Gosh, if I had a knot tied in my tail, I might be unruly, too!

8-6 The manes of our horses, if long, are the best ornament;
As comas dos nossos cavalos, quanto mais compridas, hé mayor ornamento;

   With horses in Japan, the mane is cut and rice straw attached here and there to what remains in order to enhance the horse's *isei* [presence]. *Aos de Japão lhe cortão as comas, e no que fica lhe vão atando de lugar a lugar humas palhas de trigo pera mais* yxei *do cavalo.*

With respect to hair, we evidently had the same standard for equine and feminine beauty, whereas the Japanese had different ones. The inclusion of two contrasts involving hair is not surprising for the Iberian horses were bread for thick and silky hair.

The *palhas de trigo* (grain straw) here means rice-straw, which does not have the humble connotation it does in English but was auspicious for its association with plenty. Okada cites literature suggesting Japanese had two main styles for manes, *nogami*, meaning "field" or "wild-hair," which resembles the European one, and the *karihôshi*, or "shaved-priest" style suggested by Frois. Substyles include one where the bristles stick out like a clipped hedge, and *keppatsu* (bound-hair=hairdo), clipped to about 6 inches in length, and bound into 33 little nubs, or made into "nine-heads," etc..

8-7   Our horses are all shod with iron horse-shoes and nails;
Os nossos cavalos todos se ferrão com cravos e ferraduras.

Those of Japan are not; instead they wear straw shoes that last but half a league.
Os de Japão a nenhum, antes lhe calsão sapatos de palha que lhe durão mea legoa.

According to the Japanese emissary to Europe, Miguel=Valignano, who assures the Japanese who stayed at home that shoeing did not draw blood or hurt a horse as they might imagine (*One wonders about the man who drove the first nail into a horse's hoof!*), Europeans "worked iron into shoes" so that "the horse's trail could be more easily followed," – a new one to me! – and, *also,* in order that the shoe would "last for many rides." Apparently, the unwillingness of Japanese to immediately try horseshoes *troubled* the Jesuits because Miguel's statement ends as follows:

> Europeans really wanting to know other peoples' customs, gladly learn technology and inventions from one another, and find this intercourse not the least bit shameful. But, with the Japanese, the bad habit of finding this [learning from others] shameful is very strong. Japanese, no matter what it is, unless it is something they themselves thought up, whether they have it or not, tend to be ashamed and fear adopting it from foreigners. ([*De Missione,* dial.10.(J/S:DM)

This is deliciously ironic considering the stereotype of the humble Japanese copier and the conceited do-it-himself Occidental. Eventually, the superiority of iron shoes on rocky surfaces and ice convinced some samurai to try to copy the Portuguese, but a century after *De Missione*, Kaempfer, writing of travel preparation, makes it clear that "our European Iron horse-shoes" were still unknown!

> Shoes, or slippers, for horses and footmen. These are twisted of straw, with ropes, likewise of straw, hanging down from them, whereby they are tied about the horses' feet . . . They are soon worn out in stony slippery roads, and must often be chang'd for new ones. For this purpose, the men that look after the horses always carry a competent stock along with them, . . . tho' they are met with in every village, and even offerd them to sale by poor young children begging along the road. Hence it may be said, that this country hath more farriers, than perhaps any other, tho' in fact it hath none at all. (K:HOJ)

In 1858, Oliphant found something more poetic to say about the straw shoes his horse's feet were "swaddled in."

> . . . whenever one shoe was worn out or kicked off, another was immediately tied on; hence arises the custom in Japan of measuring distances by horses' shoes. Here you ask in how many horse shoes will I reach the residence of the Spiritual Emperor? which, after all, does not differ very much from the old problem of how many cows' tails will reach the moon. (O:EEM)

At that time, horseshoes were still virtually unknown and caused quite a sensation. (See Harris's and Heusken's journals). But Japan had changed from the time when Miguel=Valignano wrote and the generally advanced nature of Western technology was admitted, so the improvement was quickly adopted and, today, Japanese horses all wear horseshoes.

8-8   With us, a lackey takes the halter in front;
Antre nós leva o moço d'esporas o cabresto diante;

In Japan, depending on the road, they carry straw shoes for the horses.
Em Japão, segundo os caminhos são, vão carregados de sapatos de palha pera o cavalo.

There is no exact equivalent of the Portuguese "boy of spurs." Since Europeans usually did their own riding, could Frois be talking of someone who accompanies a sumpter-horse (carrying supplies for military officers) called a "bât-boy?" Or, an "ostler" (parking valet for a horse) at an inn?

For a general term, "footman" seemed best, but considering that the Japanese shoe carriers generally ran, a "lackey," defined by OED as "a running footman, a valet," seemed best.

The straw shoes of the pack-horses were usually "ty'd to the portmantles" (both sides of the rear of the saddles), but mounted gentleman doubtless preferred to have lackeys carry them. In Japanese, too, there is an abundance of terms, some specific to the person, some to the shoes.

8-9   With us, the bits have their gag and rings for inside the mouth;
Antre nós o freo tem sua lingueta e argolinhas pera dentro da boca;

> In Japan, they have no more than an iron [bar] passing through the mouth.
> *Em Japão não tem mais que hum ferro atravesado na boca.*

Riding and driving bits in the West were not only complex but very diverse. Horse people can guess what Frois sketches whereas the rest of us will not get it even if it were to be described in detail.

Again, as explained in 8-2, above, the demand for such control just wasn't there in Japan.

8-10   We mount with the left foot; *Nós cavalgamos com o pee esqerdo;*
> The Japanese with the right. *Os Japões com o dereito.*

It would be clearer to speak of mounting the left or right *side* of the horse, for it is unclear from the above whether the foot in question goes into the stirrup or over the horse. (Hence in one version of Valignano's SUMARIO, it is reversed!) Luckily, others make it clear. Montanus: "Having the spirit of Contradictions so much, that as we Mounting on the left side, they get up on the right side of a Horse."

"Our" way makes sense because the stronger right arm can grasp the saddle to help lift and because most people naturally roll better from that direction when high-jumping. Perhaps their high stirrups play a role, too, though Okada has a simple explanation: the samurai held his bow in his left hand and rein in his right hand, which could *also* grasp a saddle. Today, bowless Japanese mount from the left apparently proving ours the "natural" way and theirs the result of extenuating circumstances Even so, the Japanese are not alone. The editor for the English translation of Golownin (G:MCJ) gave this contrast as an example of "the points in which they [the Japanese] differ from, and also those in which they agree with other nations, with whom they have had no possible intercourse." He suggests another reason to boot: "They mount a horse on the offside, like the Arabians; the reason assigned for which is that in an action so noble and manly, it is wrong to rest upon the left foot." Apparently, Arabs noticed which foot went *into the stirrup first*. Mounting is also the only one of Frois's contrasts found in the *five* horse-related items noted by Chamberlain in his "Topsy-turvy" essay:

> The whole method of treating horses is the opposite of ours. A Japanese (of the old school) mounts his horse on the right side, all parts of the harness are fastened on the right side, the mane is made to hang on the left side; when the horse is brought home, its head is placed where its tail ought to be, and the animal is fed from a tub at the stable door. (C:TJ)

It is surprising Frois did *not* note the location of the head and tail, for this was the *first* thing every 19c visitor noted. See Alcock, the first British Consul,

> ... the horse's head was where his tail would be in an English stable, that is facing the entrance. It certainly seems a much more rational thing to be able to go up to your horse's head, when [where?] he has an opportunity of recognizing you, rather than to his heels, with a preliminary chance of a kick and a broken leg. (A:COT)

And Ms. Bacon, first foreign teacher for the daughters of the Imperial Line, respectively, on this most charming contrast:

Horses here are put into their stalls wrong end foremost, so that I never go into the stable without thinking of the nursery rhyme, ---

"See! See! What shall I see?
A horse's head where its tail should be." (B:JI)

Perhaps, I thought, the Iberians did not always stable their horses like the English did, in which case Frois's lacuna is forgivable. But, in 1609, Rodrigo de Vivera y Velasco wrote: "Each horse is tethered with two chains, their croups toward the wall and their heads facing the entrance to the stables so that there might be no danger of their kicking anybody." (C:TCJ) Perhaps Frois just didn't frequent stables. I doubt if most of us today can guess which way the head and tail went in our respective cultures! But, now, that my attention has been caught, I cannot help but recall the French objéct-poet Ponge's fixation on the horse's magnificent high-heeled "courtesan buttocks." Our culture apparently preferred to see a horse's ass to its head! Actually, there are reasons for our way, too. My equestrian sister says facing *in* rather than *out* prevented horses from swiping each other's food and from "being cheeky" to incoming horses. But the modern West would appear to no longer have a single way. Remember Mr. Ed, the talking horse? Did his facing the camera convince any Usanians in the middle of the 20c to place the head where the tail ought to be? Be that as it may, nowadays, most stalls are big enough a horse can face any damn way he/she pleases, and some people feed them from an inside window and others hang a bucket from the front of the stall in what was – unknown to them – the Japanese style. *The world of horses, like that of humans, is becoming grey.*

8-11 Our reins are of leather and very well made;
As nossas redeas são de couro muyto bem feitas;

Theirs are of strips of *nuno* [cloth], colored and twisted.
As suas hé huma tira de nono *pintada e emrolada.*

Ancient reins were generally white, dark blue and pale blue twisted hemp made into a triple braid (Okada). The braid kept the twisted cloth from untwisting. The contrast suggests that Japanese reins are *not* well made; unlikely, for I cannot recall finding any poorly made products in Japan of old.

8-12 We have a full saddle and full-length stirrups;
Nós temos sela e estribos são hà bastarda;

In Japan, one always rides with short stirrups.
Em Japão não se cavalga senão só a jineta.

When small horses run, extended stirrups can get in the way of their legs. But Japanese stirrups seem even shorter than necessary. Obviously, short is good for standing up to see over a field, shooting a bow over a horse's head, etc. The *jineta* style (*genette* in French) was identified with crack cavalry in Europe (and jockeys today). The dictionary always includes "bent knees" in the definition, but short stirrups imply that, so I did not add it in translation. However, we can turn this around and say most Europeans, as they are weak-kneed for lack of squatting, must keep their stirrups lower than would be optimal for riders with more powerful legs and have more support from a full saddle as well.

8-13 Our stirrups are iron, open in front;
Os nossos estribos são de ferro, abertos por diante;

Theirs are wooden, closed in front, and long and thin like moorish shoes;
Os seus de pao, fechados por diante, muito compridos, como sapatos de mouro.

While the 15c Portuguese King Don Duarte in his pioneering book on horse-gear and horsemanship (*Livro da Ensynanca de Bem Cavalgar toda Sela*) included an idea of his own for stirrups with a closed front (M&J), our stirrups were almost without exception open (Hence heeled shoes).

The Japanese once used open (loop) stirrups adopted from the Chinese that were not so different from "ours." These were often combined with a toe-bag. Some had a hard "tongue" – i.e., a sole – extending lengthwise for added support. Some "tongues" were no longer than the bag and only supported the toes, some supported the front half and, eventually, most came to support the entire sole, which made sense for Japanese footwear for riding had soft bottoms. The bag and the loop were then dispensed with entirely. This was possible because the sole support does not so much *close* in front as loop up and over. The end of the tip loops back a bit further than the ball of the foot, and is where the stirrup strap attaches (⊂----). The open sides – or side, for the inner side was often covered – has the advantage of allowing "the rider to get his foot loose with ease in case of a fall." (K(S):HOJ).

With the exception of horses ridden for traditional rites, Japanese today use Occidental style stirrups when they ride. However, when Japanese children ride stilts, which are called "bamboo-horses," *they still do so with their whole feet resting on the supports* – as was the case with the old stirrups – toes facing *directly into the stilt-legs* rather than sideways to the stilts in "our" manner.

8-14   We use spurs. *Nós usamos de esporas;*

> They don't use them. They only use the *wara* [straw →brush?] on a very short segmented cane. *Elles não, somente de* vara, *que hé da cana de nós muito curtos.*

I believe we are talking about *sasa, i.e.* bamboo grass and that Frois means the clump of leaves left on it when he writes his favorite word for a crude artifact, *vara* or, "straw."

8-15   The bow of our saddles is completely closed in front;
Ho arsão das nossas selas hé todo fechado por diamte.

> Those in Japan have a hole to cling to.
> *Ho de Japão tem hum buraco pera se apegarem nelle.*

We are talking about a handhold under the front edge of a Japanese saddle – not a raised saddle horn, or pommel, but a space, or "hole." If the standard European saddle (a fiction: see Kaempfer's remarks in 8-32) has an inverted "lazy U" shape, the Japanese saddle is more like an inverted "V," or, to use Bird's perfect expression, "fashioned like a saw-horse" I am not certain when the handhold was used. I imagine it would help a passenger (not controlling the horse but just sitting) on hilly terrain . .

8-16   We use cruppers, caparison and golden studs on the trappings;
Antre nós se uza de retrancas e caparazões e nominas;

> The horse of Japan do not have them, and only use a tiger skin with the hair-side out as a caparison. *Os de Japão o não tem, somente uzão de caparazão de pelle de tigre pera fora.*

Would automobile parts interest a pre-motoring reader? I fear detailing these trappings may likewise bore the post-equestrian reader. How many of us care to know that *cruppers* are bands that circle the rump to make certain the saddle and whatnot don't work forward? Or, that the *caparison* is a richly decorated cloth that could extend from ear-tip to hoof and was sometimes leather and used for defensive armor? The "golden studs on the trappings" are, however, interesting for the fact that in the original Portuguese, they are called *nominas;* this is *the same word* we saw meant a written charm, a pouch for relics, straps wrapped around the arms for praying (i.e., *phylactery* in 5-23). Maybe . . .

Horses were generally less sumptuously dressed in Japan. It goes without saying that tiger skins (there being no tigers in Japan) were rare and only found on the horses of the Shôgun and some of the nobility! Japanese horses appearing in festivals are another story altogether. Note this 1626 procession described by the Dutch East India Company's envoy to the "ziogoon" (Shogun), Conraedt Cramer, as Englished by Ogilby.

> . . . [The 24 nobles were] bravely mounted on gallant horses, proud of their little heads, short ears, and gaunt yet well trussed bodies, insomuch that the meanest their seemed to excel the most generous and bravest steed that ever Europe boasted or bred. Their saddles were all waxed or gilded; the seat embroidered with silver or gold or else spread over with tiger skins; their manes, like ours were curiously plaited with silk, silver and gold ribands. Their caparisans, that covered their breasts and haunches were a kind of network of crimson silk, full of tufts, and dangling with the motion of the wind; on their foreheads a golden horn, resembling our painted unicorns . . (in B:MCJ)

The decorations may reflect some European influence. I leave it partly because, after Saris, these are the only kind words I've found for Japanese horses!

In 1692, Kaempfer observed something else on ordinary Japanese horses: "a net-work of small but strong strings to defend" the head and "particularly the eyes, from flies, which are very troublesome to them." Is Frois not a bit more likely to spot things *we have* that *they do not have* more often than the *vice versa*?

～～～～～～～～～～～～～～～～～～～～～～～～～～～～

8-17   Ours [saddles? bags?] are made of leather and wool; *As nossas [ressas?] tem couro e lã;*

> Theirs wood and *urushi* [lacquer].   *As suas pao e* vruxi.

Schütte writes "*ressas*" in brackets and calls it a correction (on the manuscript). "Ressas" does not, however, mean "saddles." The modern Portuguese version (1993) guesses it probably means *redeas*, or "reins;" but that would not jive with the description of reins in 8-11 above; and who can imagine wooden or lacquered reins! All the other translations simply go with "saddle." The materials described seem correct and, at least on the Japanese side, it is perfect. I do, however, suggest another possibility: *saddle-bags* or *trunks*, for Japanese horses carried wooden lacquered boxes. Whatever the case, Japanese used little leather for they ate less of the meat the hide originally housed. The exception was the *shamisen* made from cat-skin, whereas our stringed instruments were made of wood.

～～～～～～～～～～～～～～～～～～～～～～～～～～～～

8-18   Our stables are always put behind or below the house;
As nossas estrebarias se poem sempre detras ou debaxo das cazas;

> Those in Japan are built in front of the house.
> *As de Japão se fazem na dianteira das cazas.*

Okada cites a contemporary document describing two stables at the residence of a magistrate, with one between the living room and reception room and another by the East gate, facing West. (貞丈雑記). Since a good house would face East or South and a reception room would clearly be in the front . . . I think Okada is right that this reflects the high value the samurai placed on their horses, yet, 11-19 (the respective locations of the human water closets) suggests another possible explanation.
..

～～～～～～～～～～～～～～～～～～～～～～～～～～～～

8-19   In the houses of gentry in Europe, guests are first greeted upon coming inside;
Nas cazas dos senhores em Europa se agazalhão primeiro os ospedes nas salas;

> In Japan, the first reception is in the stable.
> *Em Japão o primeiro recebimento hé nas estrebarias.*

For guests and horses alike the Japanese method seems more efficient and friendlier. Since horse-lovers will always take you back to their stables to show off, one might as well *get it over with* while having your own horse "parked" and groomed down. Okada cites a 1586 report of a noble, who visiting Hideyoshi, enjoyed entertainment (dancing girls and other such expected at a party!) in the stable before anything else. Speaking of Hideyoshi (who, as we have seen elsewhere (?), was thought to resemble a monkey), in the New Year holiday season, the horses had a visitor of their own: *a monkey*. The performing monkey was auspicious as a charm for all because its name *saru* means "leave" (all the bad spirits and bad luck should then hit the road) and for other reasons to be elaborated in 14-24, its most serious *job* was blessing horses, warding off disease and injury and ensuring their good behavior. Can you imagine a performing monkey visiting a stable *behind* a residence?

8-20   Our horses are cleaned with curry-combs; *Os nossos se alimpão com almofaças;*

Those of Japan by hand or with some cords. *Os seus com a mão ou com humas cordas.*

Okada writes there was a wooden comb used in Japan called an *akatori,* or "crud-remover," but apparently hands and cords were more common. I imagine a rough cord used by two grooms would work well, but have yet to find a picture of it.

8-21   Our horses have mangers; *Os nossos tem manjedouras;*

Those of Japan eat in buckets. *Os de Japão comem em selhas.*

The Portuguese word for what the Japanese horses eat from, *selha,* is tricky. It is defined as a "round wooden *vaso* (container?) with low sides." Okada writes they generally had handles and were used to carry fish to market. He also wonders if the contrast was not between individual "hay-buckets" for European horses and collective hay troughs for Japanese horses. (Some Japanese trays were definitely trough-size, for I have seen old citations where people sleep in them.) But, Alcock later contrasts our stable with its "*fixed* mangers" with the Japanese stable where they "*hang* their food from the roof in a bucket." (A:COT) So it may well be that *built-in* versus *portable* was Frois's intended contrast, rather than Okada's *single* versus *collective* schema.

The "manger" (*manjedouras* or "feeders" in Portuguese) is a pleasant puzzler in English – most English native speakers only know it today from the Nativity scene and have a blurry and ambiguous picture of a trough with straw acting as a cradle *and/or* the whole stable or barn where Jesus and his parents slept! – but the biggest dictionary can only tell Japanese it is a "straw-bucket." In English, a manger is a manger *whatever it is*, but what happens in translation is another story! Take this sweet episode recorded by *A Diplomatist's Wife in Japan*:

I did not realize the intense difficulty of translating our thoughts into Japanese till the day after our Christmas tree, when O'Matsu came to me looking very puzzled, and said she would like to ask a question: why did Imai San (the gentleman who made the little address about the meaning of Christmas) say such a dreadful thing about "Jesu Sama"? He had said that Jesu Sama was put into a bucket, such a thing as ponies have their food in! That seemed very horrible and undignified to her. I tried to explain that in Palestine the animals did not eat in buckets; but I saw that I made very little impression. Imai San was a man, and a Japanese, and evidently my Bible history carried no weight in comparison with his. A day or two after this, I sent all the maids and children down to the convent in Tsukiji, where my friends the nuns had made a beautiful *creche* for their children. Here, in lifelike figures, were the Mother and the Babe, Joseph and the Shepherds, and the crib with its straw, all the scene splendidly decorated with pine branches and imitation snow and gold paper stars. O'Matsu came back beaming. "I understand it all now," she told me; "eyes speak better than words. Buckets, indeed!" and she laughed triumphantly . . . (F:DWJ:1899)

8-22 Ours often lie down in their master's stable;
Os nossos nas estrebarias dos senhores deitão-se muytas vezes;

> Those of Japan almost always, day and night, tied about the belly [tethered] high up. *Os de Japão estão quasi sempre de noite e de dia atados pola barriga em alto.*

The verb *atado* (tied/fastened) in the original is insufficient to explain what is what. Had Frois written in English, might it not be *hoisted up by the belly*? I have found two references bearing upon this. Alcock noted that "When not eating . . . their head is often tied up rather above the level of the neck, without any freedom or power of moving from right to left, merely to keep them quiet, which is great cruelty, and all to save a lazy groom the trouble of cleaning them if they lie down." For reasons obvious from the next contrast (8-23), Alcock's reason may be wrong. Bird, observed the same *in Korea* where "At the inn stables they [the ponies] are not only chained down to the troughs by chains short enough to prevent them from raising their heads, but are partially slung at night to the heavy beams of the roof." She noted they were "never allowed to lie down" but confessed "I know not whether the partial slinging of them to the crossbeams is to relieve their legs or to make fighting more difficult." (B:K&HN). Leaving aside the unsettled *why*, I do know one thing: *horses like to lie down* and, if given a chance, even dig out craters to make comfortable beds to lie in.

8-23 Our stables are made on the ground; *As nossas estrebarias se fazem no chão;*

> Theirs have to be covered with planks. *As suas hão-de ter sobrado de taboas.*

A stable at the entrance of a Kyoto mansion Frois visited in 1565 was made of *sugi*, the fragrant smelling Japanese cedar, whose wood is used for shrines (Shinto), temples (Buddhist) and other valuable architecture. Frois noted the only part of the floors that were *not* wooden – where there were rush mats – was for the human attendants! (in Okada J/F(O):T) I have no idea *why* wood was favored and can only guess that fear of fleas and ticks may have played a role.

8-24 The horses of Europe urinate on the ground of the stable;
Os cavalos d'Europa ourinão no chão nas estrebarias.

> The horses of Japan have their urine taken by long *hishaku* [ladles]. *Aos cavalos em Japão tomão-lhe a ourina em fixaqus compridos.*

There were two kinds of long-handled ladles in stables, the *umabishaku* for scooping up water to wash the horse and the *baribishaku* for receiving the horse's stale. While horses drop their dung on the run, they must set-up (move their legs apart) to stale, so an attentive groom would be able to pick up the ladle in time. The handles were about 5-feet long, the scoop 9 inches across and 10 deep (Okada). One would think carefully collected urine would be put to good use, but see contrast 11-22!

8-25 We have mules and jennies, zebras, asses and beasts-of-burden;
Antre nós há mulos e mulas, zebras, asnos e azemalas.

> In Japan, they have none of these.
> *Em Japão não há nenhuma de couza destas.*

Precise translation was impossible. *Azêmola,* says a Portuguese-English dictionary, is a "pack-mule," a creature not in my English language dictionaries, or a "beast of burden," which puzzled me until I found it might mean old and decrepit horses that are put to work. But, then again, it could be a draft-horse. *Asno* can be a donkey or an ass (both are *Equus asinus*) or an onager, possible here, considering the fact the zebra is included! Should the *mulos* and *mulas* become *he-mule* and *she-mule*? Only a lover of all horses versed in old Portuguese and English can sort out this mess!

8-26 With us only jenny-mules have long saddle-cloths;
Antre nós as mulas somente trazem gualdrapas de pano compridas;

> The horses of nobles in Japan have round-edged hides, and those of others are of straw. *Os cavalos dos fidalgos em Japão as trazem couro redondas e outras de palha.*

Remember the *mula* in 2-50 and the pillows that turned out to be saddle pads? If I am not mistaken, the saddle-cloths above are the same. Were "our" cloths long for she-mules because they side-kicked or because all legs were thought unseemly when a woman (or a priest?) was mounted?

The straw was woven mat, cool in the summer. The French *couvertures de toile* suggests the point of the contrast might be that such items are for working beasts and not for high-class horses.

8-27 For us, it would be ridiculous for a nobleman to ride with a halter on his horse and its cord in hand; *Antre nós seria couza rediqulosa yr hum fidalgo com o cabresto no cavalo e corda na mão;*

> The King [1] of Bungo and his sons often go about in this manner. *No regno de Bungo os filhos d'el-Rey andão muitas vezes desta maneira.*

Ridiculous if one's idea of riding is active, but not if you don't mind sitting back and enjoying the ride. Evidently, a good horse (there must have been some in Japan) could be trusted to do right without using the reins. To my mind, this style of riding reflects a laid-back attitude on the part of the Bungo nobility. The cord (properly a *longe*?), may well be what Consul Harris described as "a third rein" for the groom to lead the horse. (H:JTH) "Rein" suggests it was attached to the halter in a manner that made it more servable *as a rein* than would be the case for our halters and *longes*.

1. The King of Bungo. Bungo, a Christian stronghold thanks to the conversion of the King, was the choice part of Kyushu, the Southern Island which fronts on Korea. Here, Frois uses the term "king" (*regno* and *rei*). In his HISTORIA, I would guess he speaks only of rulers [*kokunushi* = "country-master" in Japanese – I cannot attest to the Portuguese term yet since I read the HISTORIA in Japanese (in such a situation involving terms, more of the original should be supplied, but, sob! seldom is)] because Frois explains why "king" is no longer appropriate in the prologue to the missing first volume of the series, where it serves as the ninth of ten examples of *how terms can confuse us in translation*. In Japan, it is commonly written there are 66 reigns, but their rulers' power is limited. Thus, there is only one King of Japan in the meaning Europeans give the word. However, Frois admitted there were some exceptionally powerful rulers who might have merited the name "king," and, we may assume, the King of Bungo (who began his rule before Nobunaga conquered most of Japan) was one of them.

8-28 When we run or mount a horse, we use one hand for the reins;
Antre nós, quando se corre ou cavalga, se leva a redea em huma só mão;

> In Japan, they have to hold both reins.
> *Em Japão se á-de levar em ambas de duas.*

In his *Journal*, the first American Ambassador to Japan, Townsend Harris was undiplomatically blunt:

> The Japanese are no horsemen; both hands are employed in holding the reins; they have no martingale, the horse therefore carries his head very high with his nose stuck out straight. They therefore have no command over him. (H:CJTH or, I mistook it for Heusken, his sec. H(V&W): JJ)

Readers who know what a Martingale is can make sense of this. I can not. Miguel=Valignano boasts of European horsemanship in a manner reflecting Frois's contrast: "It is amazing to see how European horses, well-trained and taught good habits, smoothly respond to commands to do this or that movement or run in circles, with the rider holding the reins with only one hand." (J/S:DM 1589)

~~~~~~

8-29   Our horses are only bled; *Os cavalos emtre nós se sangrão somente;*

> In Japan, they are often bled and, also, clumps of fire are put under their chins.
> *Em Japão se sangrão muitas vezes e lhe poem grandes botões de fogo debaxo dos qeixos.*

"Ours" were bled, both for specific disorders and to clarify the blood and prevent illness. I do not know about Spain and Portugal in Frois's time, but an Englishman, William Dade, "recommended making an incision on the necks of horses and drawing blood on the first day of April to make them stay healthy 'the whole year'" (*English Almanacs and Animal Health Care in the Seventeenth Century* by Louise Hill Curth); and farriers (smiths who shoed *and* doctored horses) had a bloodletting tool called a fleam "with several shafts that fold into a case much like a pocketknife" each with "a different size cutting blade, constructed at right angles to the shaft."

The Japanese only practiced phlebotomy for the relief of local symptoms. Okada writes that when Frois probably means treatment by needles (*shinjutsu*). This was not the same as the acupuncture we are now familiar with, for it tended to be applied directly to the trouble spot. It could draw a little blood, but was not blood-letting. However, Frois mentions a lancet being used to bleed horses in Japan in 9-3, and I cannot imagine Frois could not tell the difference between a scalpel and a needle. Moreover, what may be the first written report of veterinary acupuncture, (from the West Zhou dynasty of 1111 BC-771 BC), refers to "jugular phlebotomy to treat some febrile diseases of horses." ("Sustainable Medicine for Veterinarians in the New Millennium" Jen-Hsou Lin, Leang-Shin Wu, Philip AM Rogers)

The "fire," or *moxibustion* treatment ("point cautery"), is described in 3-22 and in the next chapter. Here, let me just note that the treatment was primarily preventative – perhaps it stimulates the immune system – and done on a calendrical, *i.e.* ritual basis. In the 19c, Usanian Consul Harris observed that "Every month the horse is burned in his belly in a quincunx, – i.e., as the spots are placed to mark five on dice; then he is burned in the roof of his mouth in the same manner. He thought it might explain the infamously bad temper of Japanese horses.

~~~~~~

8-30   In Europe, the reins are loosened for running and tightened to stop;
Em Europa afloxão as redeas ao cavalo pera correr e as apertão pera parar;

> In Japan, they are loosened to stop and tightened to run.
> *Em Japão as afloxão pera parar e as apertão pera correr.*

The Japanese side of the contrast seems incredible. After all, common sense tells us to give a horse his head to let him go and pull back to stop him. But once we get to running, we *do* tend to pull in the reins so the horse does not over do it: so, there *is* an association between tightness and speed which a horse might be trained on. Paradoxically, at the very time Frois was writing, the revival of classic dressage, the *Haute Ecole* or "high School" of riding was being taught at academies throughout Europe. Indeed, the existence of tight-reined riding in Europe was pointed out just four years after *Tratado* by Miguel=Valignano: "Europeans generally follow one of two equestrian modes. The first is called *stapedium*, in this the reins are tightly held and the steps are quick . . . (*De Missione*). This school taught riding with the taut reins still used for dressage today. From what my equestrian sister says, I gather it is like driving a car with hard steering rather than soft. You and the horse can feel each other better.

In respect to stopping, when we sit still we *do* let the reins go slack. The association is there, too. As strange as it may seem, the Japanese way is ideal in one respect: if a horse stops when reins go slack, it would not wander when its rider fell or driver fainted. *It is like a safety device.* And, again, my equestrian sister says "a good dressage horse will usually stop if the reins are released, for the lack of information. But," she adds, "you don't need to do *anything* with the reins to stop a good horse. All you have to do is shift your weight slightly back and they read you." *Butt-readers, huh?*

8-31 We only use oxen to till the earth; *Entre nós se lavrão as terras somente com bois;*
In Japan they use oxen or horses. *Em Japão com bois ou cavalos.*

Even without mentioning North/West Europe where, according to the histories we all read in high school, new types of harnesses had been invented in the Middle Ages that, in combination with the three-field rotational system, made *horses* so productive tillers that we achieved the superfluities of life necessary to spark the Renaissance and move Europe ahead of the rest of the world, etc. etc., even without all this, looking only at Iberia, Frois was *wrong*. The oxen *had* indeed been the traditional draft animal of the Classical world as shown by the word (*boustrophedon*) for writing lines back and forth (right-to-left-right-left . . .). And it was still "the normal work animal" in 1500 (*Land and Society in Golden Age Castile* by David E. Vassberg THE LIBRARY OF IBERIAN RESOURCES ONLINE). But, over the course of Frois's century, the rising population pressure and taxes forced towns to open new fields for plowing – or, rather wrest away pastures from the sheep herders, as many saw it – and use mules which moved twice as fast as oxen, which was important for plowing and commuting from town to field and field to field and, additionally, were more suitable for use in "vineyards and orchards, where a yoke of horned animals was not only difficult to maneuver, but also a potential danger to tender vines and branches" (Ibid). The first anti-mule tract, "impassioned denunciation of the mule." was printed in 1568 (More on these "adulterous and sterile bastards" in TT-long), so we must assume the use was widespread before 1585. Finally, "by 1600, the mule had become the most widely used agricultural work animal, except in certain isolated or backward areas, mainly in the mountains." (Ibid) A better contrast might have been:

In Europe, we harness more than one animal per plow;
In Japan, they never use more than one animal at a time.

8-32 The packsaddles of Europe are made of cloth and straw; *As albardas d'Europa são de pano e palha;*
Those of Japan are made of wood. *As de Japão são de pao.*

This is the last mention of saddles. Frois neglects the most interesting contrast involving packsaddles: how they were *ridden*. A hundred years later, Kaempfer observed that on both sides of the Japanese packsaddle loom side-trunks (portmantles) carrying light and voluminous luggage and behind, helping to fasten those trunks together is a stronger back-trunk (*atozuki*) for valuables made of "thick strong grey paper." Here is the choice part:

the middle cavity between the two trunks, fill'd up with some soft stuff, is the travelers seat, where he sits, as it were upon a flat table, otherwise commodiously enough, and either crossleg'd or with his legs extended hanging down by the Horse's neck . . . (K(S):HOJ:1692)

The "soft stuff" makes it clear that Frois is not describing the entire saddles but the frames. Bird, in the 19c, seconds, and even mentions *straw*: "The pack-saddle is composed of two packs of straw eight inches thick, faced with red, and connected before and behind by strong oak arches gaily painted or decorated." (B:UTJ) As to how they were ridden, Kaempfer wrote that the traveler must be careful to remain in the center, lest he "make the Horse fall, or else the side trunks and rider." Bird, explains why: "The saddle is merely balanced, not girded on, and the animals are so sleepy, slow-footed, and stumbling, with a lurching, swinging gate like a camel's, that riding one is really a feat." (B:UTJ) The Western visitor had to learn t*o rest his or her feet on the horse's neck* (a haiku found and lost on winter travel mentions welcome heat from the horse absorbed through the traveler's soles.):

> *We always ride on a horse with our legs hanging down.*
> *They travel with their legs crossed sitting high on the horse like an Arab on a camel.*

Normally, this was, as might be expected, at a slow camel-like pace. But Morse, up in Hokkaido, observed an interesting exception: "When the Ainus ride they sit cross-legged and perched up high on the saddle, and whenever I saw them they were going at full gallop." (M:JDD) That is the strangest riding I have ever heard of, and stranger yet when you consider that "It is *vulgar* and *low* to ride fast in Japan." (Alcock A:COT)   Only drunks, officials on urgent business, or people up to mischief ever risked galloping on purpose. More generally:

> *With us, when we are on a horse we usually actively ride it;*
> *They usually travel sitting like luggage on a packsaddle while led by teamsters.*

Kaempfer noted another contrast incidental to the different gear. Because of the side trunks, in Japan, *"the traveler mounts the horse . . . not on the side as we Europeans do, but by the horse's breast, which is very troublesome for stiff legs."* (K(S):HOJ) Note that Kaempfer was not searching for differences; he also described the "plain wooden saddle" of Japan as "not unlike the packsaddles of Swedish Posthorses [and, say M & J, the aubardá of Majorca]." and wrote that from a global perspective, "the saddling of their horses differs but little from ours. Their saddles come nearer our German saddles, than those of any Asiatic Nation." (Ibid.)

~~~~~~

8-33   We don't carry a load without a crupper; Antre não se leva carrega sem atafal.

   In Echizen they don't use one. *Em Yechijen não se uza delle.*

The French translation calls the *atafal* a crupper, but from the description in a Portuguese-Portuguese dictionary, I get the idea it might be the "breeches" mentioned in 8-16. At any rate, in Echizen, there is nothing behind to keep the saddle from sliding forward during a quick stop or going downhill etc.. This is a bit weird because, first *we already know* Japanese horses have nothing back there (or was 8-16 only meant to be about horses on parade?) and second, is it really fair to contrast *one province* of Japan against "Europe?"

~~~~~~

8-34   Our pack-horses wear bells and rattles;
   Antre nós os cavalos de carrega levão chocalhos ou cascaveis;

   In Japan, they wear jingles like those on tambourines.
   Em Japão levão soalhas como de pandeiros.

Okada surmises the Japanese side may refer to *gyôyô*, leaf-like trinkets (literally "apricot-leaf" for the shape) that hung behind Chinese-style saddles (and, judging from similar trinkets I have heard on a Mongolian dancer, make a tinkling sound), or *kanrei,* hollow donut-like bronze bells strung up 3-4 to a ring that hit together like chimes worn by ancient *haniwa* (buried clay funereal) horses. "Maybe at this time, they or something like them, were still being used." (J/F(O):T) Kaempfer wrote a hundred years later about "small bells" hung from "the neck, breast and other parts" of Japanese horses. I think he liked details enough to have described the bells had they been significantly different and would guess that the German original might have turned into "bells" in English for lack of a better word.   *Aurelio* defines "soalha" as each one of the plates (*placas*) on a tambourine." So Frois did not really even have to mention the instrument.

One might expect something louder on the Japanese side, for up to the late 19c, an accidental death could easily result in an execution – but, I may be reading the protected world of the Tokugawa into Frois's far wilder Japan. Or, maybe, they were so slow that jingles sufficed. I think the more interesting contrast, though not yet necessarily true in 1585, was this:

We think nothing of galloping down a street with no one announcing our coming..
They wouldn't think of going any speed without a footman running ahead or shouting to clear the way.

19c visitors wrote that, without a man running out in front to clear the way, they could never go faster than a walk. Mrs. Hugh Frazer gives the funniest description of what it was like to ride in Japan: "I found constant excitement in watching our groom racing along in front of the horses, lifting fat babies out of the middle of the road where they sat confidingly, leading deaf old women politely to one side, and apparently saving a life once in every ten yards." (F:DWJ)

8-35   With us, bulls are savage and huge; *Antre nós os touros são bravos e grandes;*

In Japan, they are small and gentle. *Em Japão peqenos e mansos.*

The chapter title is belied. We have horses *plus*. Frois's bull is *bravo* and *grande*. Our word "brave" comes from the Latin for "barbarous." The Spanish *Rio Bravo*, or Wild River, like Frois's Portuguese usage, is closer to the roots of the term. With the bull-fight to consider, it will not do for "our" – that is, the Iberian bull – to be gentle. In Mexico D.F., I was *horrified* to see a gentle bull who did not want to fight *licking the television camera* before he was poked over and over by the picadors until he saw red and briefly behaved as he was expected to. Now (3yrs ago), living in Florida, on a farm with cattle, I note the huge bull is *very gentle*, while the cows can be downright rough and even *mean* to the calves of others. I doubt that all European breeds of bulls were *bravo*. And, I would caution you not to touch the horns of a Japanese ox (water buffalo?), for they do shrug and accidents happen.

8-36   In Europe the carriers load the beast and go empty-handed themselves;
Em Europa os almocreves carregão as bestas e elles vão vazios;

Those of Japan pity the beasts and, at times, carry a third of the cargo on their shoulders. *Os de Japão, por se doerem das bestas, levão às vezes hum terço da carrega às cos[tas].*

Isabella Bird's 19c observation concurs:

I have not seen any overloading or ill-treatment; they are neither kicked, nor beaten, nor threatened in rough tones, and when they die they are decently buried, and have stones placed over their graves. It might be well if the end of a worn-out horse were somewhat accelerated, but this is mainly a Buddhist region, and the aversion to taking animal life is very strong. (B:UTJ)

It is also possible that the calcium-deficient grass of Japan would have made the horses more liable to leg injuries when tired (Japanese race horses broke bones at a *tremendous* rate in the 1980's).

8-37   In Europe, beasts are loaded by eye;
Em Europa o fato que se carrega nas bestas hé a olho;

In many kingdoms of Japan, they do not want to carry anything without weighing it.
Em muitos reinos de Japão não o qerem levar senão a pezo.

Who can say whether this is due to a Japanese tendency to be exacting (and I would expect the same in Germany and Sweden), or the same compassion mentioned in 8-36? I think the off-the-cuff estimates of professional carriers would be good enough but, even today, no matter the matter, it is incredibly hard to get a *guestimate* or a rough answer out of a Japanese; they usually *insist* on making you wait until they find the precise figure so, if you are a so-and-so person, like me, you sometimes wish you never asked. I couldn't resist the direct translation "by eye," and trust the reader can guess its meaning "by feel" or "rough estimate."

8-38 Among us, an unsaddled horse is led about by one man by the halter;
Antre nós hum cavalo sem sela leva-o hum homem polo cabresto.

> In Japan, a Lord's horse, though it be very gentle, has to be led about by one man with a cord in front and another with another [cord] behind, like a stayed bull.
> *Em Japão os cavalos dos Tonos, ainda que sejão muito mansos, á-os de levar hum homem com huma corda por diante e outro com outra por detras, como touro em cordas.*

"The master's horse was treated especially carefully," writes Okada. Even a gentle horse can react when bitten by a horse-fly, so it doesn't hurt to be careful in a country of frail dwellings and crowded streets where dereliction of duty could cost a man his head.

..

8-39 Our girths fasten on the flank below the saddle;
As silhas dos nossos cavalos se apertão a huma ilharga debaxo da sela;

> Those of Japan fasten above the front saddle-bow.
> *As de Japão se atão em sima no arção dianteiro.*

Part of this may be because of the larger stature of our horses. But it also may have to do with the different manner of cinching up the girth. Japanese have long excelled in all forms of binding and fastening. Kaempfer was impressed with the way the horses could be loaded up or "unsaddled and unladen in an instant." (Remember the baby clothes?) After taking off the bed-cloths, "they need but untie a latchet or two . . . and the whole baggage falls down at once." He wrote the "latchets, thongs, and girths . . . are broad and strong, made of cotton . . . with oblong, cylindrical pieces of wood at both ends, which are of great use to strain the latchets, and to tie things hard." (K(S):HOJ) With the greater leverage possible due to those pieces of wood, the girth would not need to be worked the way we must work it to cinch up and could then fasten in a position other than the flank. However, as we have already noted, the saddles were not paradigms of stability. Perhaps, a cross between Japanese fastening convenience and European overall design would have been ideal.

endnotes VIII

Horses

On a quick reading, this seemed like a lot on horses. But, as I proceeded, it became clear that Frois put too much weight on describing gear minutia for one type of riding and missed travel-related items. If one read only Frois and not Kaempfer, one would imagine Bashô (born 1644) sitting astride a horse, alone, when it suddenly ate that Rose of Sharon by the roadside, as recorded in his famous haiku. Now, you should see him being *led by a "horse-boy," sitting up high, perhaps cross-legged* on his mount, brush and paper in hand. Not only did Frois overlook these contrasts I added to note 8-32, but he completely neglected the whole area of wheeled cart and human-borne sedan-related transportation!

> *Among us, gentlemen most commonly get around by horse or donkey.*
> *In Japan, they are usually carried about in boxes borne by men.*

These boxes came in two basic types, cheap "baskets" (*kago:*) dangled from a single plain pole and expensive "riding-things" (*norimono*) with poles on both sides, "the bigness and length of which were "determin'd by the political laws of the Empire, proportionable to every one's quality" (K(S):HOJ). The latter had various types of windows. For a man of Volkswagen rank to be carried about in a Cadillac could get a man "a severe reprimand if not a considerable fine in the bargain," but women were allowed to show off as they pleased regardless of their husband's rank! Human-carried *sedans/litters/chairs* came to only a few parts of Europe, while Frois was in Japan, but let me be bold:

> *Our sedans have their carrying poles on the bottom side and are lifted by hand..*
> *Theirs always have the carrying poles on the top and are supported by the shoulder.*

> *Our sedans have two carrying poles to lift up like a liter.*
> *Theirs have only one so the compartment must hang.*

> *Our chairs are always wooden and solidly attached to the poles.*
> *Their cheapest sedans are baskets which sway below the poles.*

With centuries of history behind them in Japan, the sedans (mostly one-pole) were taken for granted. In Europe where they were new and never expanded beyond a number of crowded metropolitan areas, they were a luxury. A fop might "hail a chair" to visit the playhouse, but the use of the hands rather shoulders for carrying restricted the European sedan to short trips. Even Caucasians with their thicker forearms and stronger hands than Mongolians could not overcome that difference, and of course, there was the more abundant horse and horse-drawn carriages. Today, with more female paramedics, in the Occident, it might make sense to redesign litters to be carried by shoulder-pole.

> *In Europe, carriages are a popular form of rapid transportation and always drawn by horses.*
> *In Japan, there are no carriages but slow ones drawn by oxen.*

If "we" failed to develop human-powered transport, "they" neglected animal transport. "Our" coach was invented in Kocs, Hungary in the 15c. While coaches and carriages and 2-wheel carts with springs – items for transporting people rather than goods – did not serve everyman until the 17c, reading *De Missione* (where Leo=Valignano imagined how good it might be to lounge about with six or eight friends while going down the road in a big coach), we can see they were common enough in the late 16c to have merited a mention by Frois, especially considering he was not adverse to contrasts involving the nobility alone. Leo did have his doubts about how teams of four or more horses could be controlled, but was assured that it was nothing, for "European horses are by nature very placid and have been road-trained . . . And, not only that, you cannot forget the knowledge and skill of the driver who sits up on a seat over the thill [look that up in your dictionary!], and holding the reins with one hand and a whip in the other, splendidly drives. (J/S:DM) Then, we are told of the gorgeousness of it all – the palatial decoration of the coaches, how teams of horses were chosen for the color-effect . . . Leo asks "How many of these splendid coaches are in Europe anyway?" and he is told by Miguel=Valignano that there are three thousand in Rome alone, for in Europe there are an infinite number of horses and moreover they are so beautiful, especially in Spain, the horses of Napoli and Mantua . . . ." One wonders if any of today's evangelists from Usania boast about the automobiles of their wealthy nation.

In Japan, the closest equivalent were the ox-wagons, or "lumbering bullock-carts" to use Chamberlain's phrase, which were not for zipping about so much as for taking noblewomen out cherry-blossom viewing or for processions, where they seem more like floats in a parade. Here, again, is Cramer describing that parade in 1626. Following those unicorn horses (see 8-16), there were

> three rich coaches, each drawn by two black bulls, covered with red silken nets and led by four footmen in white liveries; these coaches were each four fathoms high, two long and one broad, being adorned with waxen figures, and enameled with gold; on each side there were three windows . . . which were hung with rich curtains; the entry behind opened like the gate of a prince's palace, steps , ascending with turrets on each side, the windows beneath shaded with black wax, the rounds of the wheels gilded, the spokes neatly turned and inlaid with gold and mother-of-pearl, which, moving, cast beams like a looking-glass reflecting the sun, a novel and most glorious sight. . . . These coaches or rather towers . . . carried in state the dayro's [same as *daimyo* or, feudal lord] principal wives. (in B:MCJ)

Frois can *not*, however, be faulted for not mentioning the device we now associate with transportation in the Far East, the *rickshaw,* or, *jinrikisha* (*jin-riki-sha*: literally, "person-power-car/t"). Depending on the source, this single or double seat between two broad-diameter light wheels with two pulling shafts and a cross-bar was invented by three Japanese in 1869, or by an American missionary, or by a British chaplain (the names of all parties are given)! At any rate, it quickly became popular in parts of South Asia too crowded for horses. Alice Mabel Bacon, whose fine insight on *Japanese Girls and Women* has been borrowed many times already and whose *Japanese Interior* will help us in chapter 12, had a great deal to say about *jinrikisha,* or rather, *her* jinrikisha *man*. If it is the nature of women to fall in love with horses, it would seem that a man serving in the same capacity was, likewise, liable to be adored. She first seemed to notice his legs:

> The garden was crowded with visitors, from the jinrikisha man in blue blouse and with symmetrical brown legs, to the fine lady in paint and powder, silk and crape, pattering along on her high, lacquered clogs. All were gazing at the flowers lost in admiration. (B:JGW)

This was an age when the adoration of well-turned male legs was still strong enough that there were people who *loathed* trousers for hiding them. Toward the end of her book, Bacon was still enthralled by them. She gave her jinrikisha man and his body two entire pages of which half is in *TT-long*. Here I give what fits:

> When you have ridden for miles and miles, by night and by day, through rain and sleet and hottest sunshine, behind a man who has used every power of body and mind in your service, you cannot but have a strong feeling of affection toward him, and of pride in him as well. It is something the feeling that one has for a good saddle-horse, but more developed. You rejoice in his strength and speed, put forth so willingly in your service; in his picturesque, dark blue costume with your monogram embroidered on the back; in his handsomely turned ankles; . . . (B:JG&W)

IX

OF DISEASES, DOCTORS AND MEDICINES
das doenças, medicos e mezinhas

9-1   Among us, scrofula, stones, gout and the pest occur frequently;
Antre nós alporcas, dor de pedra, podagra e peste hé couza frequente;

All of these diseases are rare in Japan.
Todas estas doenças em Japão são raras.

Scrofula: Swollen lymph glands, often, but not always, associated with gonorrhea. In 1569, the year Frois convinced the warlord Nobunaga to give him *carte blanc* to preach in the capital, Charles the IX of France touched and presumably cured 2,092 scrofula sufferers. And this kept going on for centuries, even in England where such miracle-working was otherwise denigrated as Catholic. *Stones:* Including not just *renal calculosis* (kidney stones) but other types of calculae. Perhaps prostate cancer was included, for the European rate is ten times that of the Japanese. *Gout:* The Portuguese term *podagra* is still used by doctors and apparently means gout especially hard on the legs, perhaps from too much meat and not enough diuretics, like tea. *Pest:* Bubonic fever. From the fleas on rats that multiplied because Europeans killed too many cats and snakes (the latter being by far the better mouse-trap for it gobbles up baby mice in their dens). You might call it the revenge of the pre-Christian religions for "our" un-ecological behavior (See the long snake note in *TT-long*).

This contrast is naively egoistic. We tend to be far more aware of our own diseases than those of others! I cannot help but wonder what diseases a Japanese might find rare in Europe. One might be *senki*, a complex disease often mentioned in haiku and senryu and usually translated as "lumbago", where the legs may be put out of commission like gout, but which also causes severe pain in the groin and often enlarges the testicles. It was usually particularly bad in the winter. In the 20c, about half of all Japanese claim to have stiff neck and shoulders (Call it the national ailment – is "ours" heartburn?), but I am not certain this should be mentioned next to the serious diseases Frois gives.

9-2   We use bleeding; *Nós uzamos de sangrias;*

The Japanese use burning pellets[1] of herbs. *Os Japões de botões de fogo com ervas.*

"Phlebotomy clears the mind, strengthens the memory, cleanses the stomach, dries up the brain, warms the marrow, sharpens hearing, stops tears, encourages discrimination, develops the senses, promotes digestion, produces a musical voice, ..." (G:PPI) In so far that bleeding involved cutting, it seems the very model of Western medicine, but the *principle* of balancing humors to improve the health generally agrees with what we tend to call Eastern medicine. Metaphorically, the justification for bleeding would be "the more one draws upon the stagnant water from the well, the more fresh water it produces . . ." (*Varietes chirurgicales* (Renaissance France) in G:PPI).   Yet, there is always an equal but opposite metaphor. Nieuhoff takes it from the mouth of the Chinese, who, like their protégés, the Japanese, did not countenance "breathing a vein," preferring to "reduce the fermented Blood by cooling Medicines, to a good Temper; for (as they say) if Broth boyls in a Pot, we must not pour it out, but command to take away the Fire under it. (N(O):EC)

Burning moxa (Artemisia/mugwort) is less drastic than bleeding. As Kaempfer writes, moxa burns slowly so "the pain is not very considerable, and falls short of that which is occasion'd by other Causticks." To the extent it was used *as a cure* for instant local relief, it could be called Western. "It seems to be considered a universal specific" wrote Alcock, "even the accoucheur calls in its aid, and is directed to burn 'three cones on the little toe of the right foot to facilitate delivery.'" (A:COT) Unfortunately, the Japanese and the Chinese Physicians did not always agree about *where* to burn for various complaints, so that "if their different opinions were to be brought together," Kaempfer writes, "I believe, that in some distempers there would be scarce any one part of the human body left, but that some of them would single out as the most proper to be burnt with success." Indeed, visitors from the 17-19c found scarred backs the rule rather than the exception. Isabella Bird pointed out that, like blood-letting, moxibustion was performed as preventive medicine as well as cures. "Here, these little mugwort cones are to be found in most houses, and people are burned in the Spring, just as in England blood-letting was formerly customary at the same season." (B:UTJ) And it was not just England: "the physician to Charles IX and Henry III of France prescribed preventive bleedings monthly in young people and six times a year in the old" (G:PPI)

We should not laugh at our ancestors. Both practices may well have more than a placebo effect. Studies have shown a longevity reward for giving blood accruing even to men who do not suffer from *hemochromatosis* (too much iron) and even if moxa may not effect your system as described, it could heighten immunity, as bee-stings do.

1. ***Frois Explains the* Botões**   In the prologue to his missing Summary (first book of his *Historia*), Frois cites the expression he uses here for burning pellets or cones, *botoes de fogo*, as an example of terms that are misleading without proper explanation. Apparently, *botoes* conjured up images of larger and more painful caustic remedies used in Europe, so that where "it is written that three or four thousand *botoes* of fire are placed on the body to cure someone suffering from eye problems or rheumatism, one should know it is commonplace in Japan and take it the same way as the other things [items misunderstood because of incommensurable vocabulary and insufficient knowledge]." The so-called *botoes* are really "little balls" (*bolinhas*, mistranscribed as *lourinhas*) about "the size of large pomegranate seeds," and that "once fifteen or twenty" of these has been piled up and burnt "in the same place, almost no pain is felt, because that place has been well mortified" (Kaempher mentions that moxa hurts the first few times, because the skin must be broken in, and that this was called *kawakiri*, or skin-cutting, a term subsequently used for a high initial tax). And, finally, Frois's clincher: "I myself, have tried this Japanese [cure] for various aches and pains and eye disease, and had over three thousand [pellets] put on my back and knees" (J/F:Historia). I.e., Frois was experiencing, not Orientalizing.

~~~~~~

9-3   Our men ordinarily bleed their arms;
   Os homens antre nós se custumão ordinariamente sangrar nos braços;

   The Japanese use leeches or cut their foreheads with a knife and the horses with a lancet.   *Os Japões com sanbixugas ou c[om] faca na testa, e aos cavalos com lanceta.*

For standard phlebotomy (venesection) – whether *derivative* (near the lesion) or *revulsive* (on the far side of the body from the same) – "we" opened one or more of the larger external veins. The arms were accessible and, compared to the lower limbs or the neck, better for regulating the speed of the blood-flow, which was considered important (some diseases responded better if it was rapid enough to visibly effect the system, perhaps even induce fainting). Like the Japanese, the Jesuits were not big on this practice "for the Church had eschewed blood ever since the famous Council of Tours in the year 1163 – *'Ecclesia abhorret a sanguine'* – yet, writes Wolfgang Michel (On the Reception of Western Medicine in Seventeenth Century Japan), sick Jesuits in Japan did travel long distances to Nagasaki for treatment.

Leeches in Japan? They may actually have been *more* popular in parts of *Europe*. In England, "a leecher" was synonymous with a physician, the art of healing was called "leechcraft" and the medical/physic finger (next to baby-finger) the "leechfinger." And it didn't stop in Frois's century. The biggest leeching boom was in 19c France. "In the year 1833 alone, 41,500,000 leeches were imported into France and only nine or ten million exported." (G:HOM) The leeches were eventually driven to extinction in some countries. Now, medical leeches are most commonly used for sucking blood through reattached digits. My chance experience with leeches in the wild taught me that they are *absolutely* painless (unlike our needless which sting, ache or both) and I would prefer we use them to draw all blood! (They were infected with something and I had scabs for a year or more, but that is besides the point.)

The forehead bleeding refers to a Chinese practice carried out with a "three-corner-needle" or a *fleam,* upon the crown and occipital part of the head (since the crowns are shaven, Frois made it the forehead?) for removing bad blood, but it was not so common a practice as venesecting arms in the West and probably was only used for certain maladies. Otherwise, Valignano (and others) would not have written: "they never bleed a person." (in C:TCJ 1582? 83?)

9-4   We use clysters and syringes;   *Nós uzamos de cristeis ou siringas;*
      They, in no case, use this remedy.   *Elles por nenhum cazo uzão deste remedio.*

Is it not ironic that Japan, with its more open tradition of homosexual, i.e. anal, sex should deny, and Europe welcome the enema? A "clyster" was a suppository "to cleanse the bowels or afford nutrition." (OED) Reading this makes us reflect that the "syringe" *entered* holes long before it *made* them (shots came in the 19c). It was also used to baptize babies *in utero!*

The Japanese did occasionally clean themselves out, but it was from the top down. Valignano writes, in a rare contrast not found in the TRATADO, that "their purges are sweet-smelling and gentle – in this they certainly have an advantage over us for our purges are evil-smelling and harsh." (1583? in C:TCJ) Ribadeniera, a Franciscan, even wrote of "candied pills" to administer purges. (in C:TCJ) Apparently, Japanese did not need enemas because their purges were better. The plethora of advertisements for "figs" (*ichijiku*) on TV in Japan, suggests they now use enemas as much as "we" do. Could Western-style toilets and diet have anything to do with this? (Note: 16c China had enemas.)

9-5   With us, the doctors write prescriptions for pharmacists;
      Antre nós receitão os medicos pera as boticas.
      The doctors of Japan prescribe medicine from their own houses.
      [Os]medicos de Japão mandão as mezinhas de sua caza.

For better or worse, "our" medicine was already specialized. Doctors in Japan were still called *kuzushi,* or "medicine-masters" and, true to their name, fulfilled their own prescriptions. This does not necessarily mean they grew, gathered and made all of it. Much was bought from merchants, but they did keep a stock. When Almeida, a Jesuit who had been a surgeon and probably a wealthy merchant took over a clinic at the Our Lady of Mercy hospital in Bungo (Kyushu) in 1559, he quickly set up a pharmacy and because it depended on fluent reading of Chinese books (and ordering Chinese medicines from abroad), put a Japanese Jesuit who was a former Buddhist monk in charge.

In 1577, Frois, himself, was pressured into playing doctor and giving out medicine – his own! The man next door to Frois's inn was gravely ill and the inn owner begged him to help. Frois demurred, *"If it's for the soul, I have some very good medicine . . ."* But, in the end, gave in and sent him a little powdered *pedra de basar* (*bezoar*: Persian for "antidote" made from many types of animal innards, but most notably from stones found in the stomachs of Persian sheep), which, as luck would have it, made him feel great, making Frois "a famous doctor" and filled the Inn with everything from sick infants to cripples on crutches overnight.

9-6 Our doctors take the pulse of men and women first from the right arm, then from the left;
Os nossos medicos tomão o pulso a homens e molheres primeiro no braço dereito, despois no esquerdo.

The Japanese [take] the men from the left first and the women from the right first.
Os Japões aos homens primeiro no esquerdo e aas molheres primeiro no dereito.

This fe/male difference, writes Okada, comes from Oriental yin-yang philosophy. When the print on the third digit of the index finger was read to diagnose an infant's disease, it would be on the left hand of a male and right hand of the female. And this pattern of the sinister male and dexterous female was not restricted to medicine. Male-left, female-right also applied for the use of one or another fingertip to sign documents or make oaths with a bloody fingerprint. As far as I know, both genders meditated with the left leg crossed over the right, but considering the superiority of the male in so many areas of the society, and the generally favorable connotation of right, this is puzzling.

9-7 Our doctors look at urine to learn more about an illness;
Os nossos medicos vêm as ourinas pera terem mais noticia da infirmidade;

The Japanese, in no case, look at it.
Os Japões por nenhum cazo as vêm.

It is hard to over-estimate the importance of urine as a diagnostic tool for early modern Western medicine. Physicians in Renaissance art are commonly portrayed holding a vial of urine. One wonders all medical doctors did not end up being called *urologists*, or as a 1637 critique had it "pisse-prophets"! (S:SCP)

Urine which is milky on the surface, dark at the bottom and clear in the middle is a sign of dropsy. But ruddy urine in a dropsical patient is a sign of death (normally it betokens health). [this, an example of *prognosis* as well as *diagnosis*.]

Where the urine is frothing high up, it shows there is more pain on the left, for the left side is colder than the right. (G:PPI, my brackets)

Gaitonide quotes two entire pages of this from Talbot's *Medicine In Medieval England.* Urology (I almost wrote *uromancy!*) survived the Renaissance intact. A paragraph in *Aubrey's Brief Lives* tells about a Dr. William Butler, who was three years younger than Frois:

A Serving man brought his Master's water to Doctor Butler, being then in his Studie (with turn'd Barres) but would not bee spoken with. After much fruitlesse importunity the man tolde the doctor he was resolved he should see his Master's water; he would not be turned away, threw it on the Dr's head. This humour pleased the Dr., and he went to the Gent, and cured him. (A(D):AL)

Southern Barbarian Medicine, as Portuguese medicine was called, brought the custom of looking at urine to Japan. Okada points out that Luis Almeida, the surgeon Jesuit already mentioned, checked the urine of the fief-lord of the Goto islands according to his October 20, 1566 letter. Presumably, this is the first recorded use of this diagnostic tool, that was common by the time Japan was opened in the 19c, in the Orient.

9-8 The body of a European, being delicate, is very slow to heal;
A carnadura dos de Europa, por ser dilicada, vai sarando muito devagar;

That of the Japanese, being robust, heals much better and faster from grave wounds, burns, abscesses and accidents. *A dos Japõis, por ser robusta, de graves feridas, qebraduras, postemas e dezastres, sarão muito milhor e mais depresa.*

Frois's contemporary Mexia, likewise wrote: "When they fall sick, they recover in a very short time without taking hardly any medicine." (in C:TCJ) Are these, together with statements by European visitors about the light diet of the Japanese, the first indication of the concept of the *underliving* oriental, who is constitutionally tougher and can survive on less than the Occidental? Is this just a-grass-is-greener-on-the-other-side-of-the-fence type of thing, or a fact owing to the Japanese having a better diet, body-friendly clothing? Today, Japanese lead the world in length of hospital stays, so it might suggest Frois's robust race has undergone a change. Or, it might just be they can afford to stay in hospitals because of they have reasonable health insurance. (Unlike the USA).

How does this fit with 1-1? It would seem "a good build" (*boa estatura*) is not necessarily a robust one (Muscles being more expensive to maintain?). Are "we" Europeans, then, the original thoroughbred, fast but delicate? What, then, about the classical idea that beauty was by nature useful?

9-9 We sew up wounds;
Antre nós se cozem as feridas;

> The Japanese put a little sticky paper on them.
> *Os Japões lhe poem hum pouqo de papel grudado.*

In Japan, despite the practice of acupuncture, wounds were not yet sewn up. If we wonder at their slowness to do so, considering all those sword wounds one might expect, we may wonder equally about why it took us so long in the 20c to stop doing unnecessary stitching where good adhesive band-aids do perfectly well. Okada suggests the "glue" (*grudado* was not a noun so I used one of its adjective forms, "sticky") was really *medical ointment*. Chances are it functioned as *both*.

9-10 All the treatment we do with cloth, *Toda a qura [que] fazemos com panos,*

> The Japanese do with paper. *Fazem os Japões com papeis.*

Japanese could use paper and not cloth for treating wounds for the same reason they could use it to wipe up after or during sex. It could be as soft as gauze yet not break into little bits that could enter wounds and cause infection. I would not be surprised to learn the paper also had the advantage of breaking down in time, *i.e.* the equivalent of the modern vanishing-stitches.

9-11 We burn abscesses with fire;
Antre nós qeimão-se as postemas com fogo;

> The Japanese would rather die than use our harsh surgical methods.
> *Os Japões antes morrerão que uzar dos nossos remedios asperos da surugia.*

If Hindi purified dead bodies by burning them, "we" burned ourselves alive to purify parts of them, not realizing that the trauma incurred was as often or not as deadly as the infection. Our burning was not confined to cautery (applying hot irons) either. Scalding oil was poured into gun-shot wounds in order to remove their poison. When the oil ran out in a battle in 1537, Ambroise Pare, "the father of modern surgery" – who once bled the same patient 27 times in 4 days – found that those who had to settle for "a digestive of eggs, oil of roses, and turpentine" actually healed faster. Still, it took a century for the practice to die out. Now, we know that maggots beat all of these medicines.

Frois does not write rhetorically; there surely were Japanese patients at the Bungo hospital who refused Almeida's advice on this and died; as there were surely others that refused it and, for that reason lived.

9-12   When our sick have no appetite, we work hard to make them eat;
Aos nossos doentes, se tem fastio, trabalha-se com elles pera que comão por força;

The Japanese think this cruel, and the sick with no appetite are allowed to die. *Os Japõis o tem por crueza, e se o doente tem fastio deixão-no asi morrer.*

"We" forced food for the body on people the same way we forced food for the soul, i.e. religion, on them. One wonders if anthropologists can find a correlation behind this analogy! Eating, especially eating rich food, was thought to reduce the efficacy of Chinese medicine, and what is eaten without an appetite, or even in the face of nausea, may only exhaust the malfunctioning gastro-enteric system by increasing putrefaction and flatulence, hastening a person's death, where fasting may allow organs to recoup enough to make eating beneficial. So, there may also have been a practical side to allowing people to follow their natural inclination. Where the reason for lack of appetite is trauma, forcing food might make sense. But let's consider a more general *Faux Frois*:

We think death something horrible that should be delayed as far as possible;
They claim to be embarrassed by living too long and do not fear death.

Frois might not agree with the "we," for Westerners of deep faith did not necessarily think of death as horrible, unless they had reason to fear for their future. But, would it be right to say that forcing the sick to eat suggests that we, as a culture, had mixed feelings about death, and on the whole, placed our bets on this life? To me, the fact that Japanese faced death with equanimity even when they were not members of faiths as fanatical as 16c Christianity (with a Heaven that was almost tangible) is as laudable as it is incredible. We talk of when death was natural in the West, and give examples of content people dying in bed surrounded by family. But comparing the attitude of the Japanese expressed in their countless fine death poems, with what I have read of the West, I would have to question whether most people were *ever* really at home with death in our civilization.

2. *At Home With Death.* From Madrid To Purgatory presents the Spanish "culture of death," and tells how Felipe II, "spent his final days much as had his father Charles, contemplating death with his own coffin at his bedside." (E:MP) The faith of these men is impressive. At the same time, I find the details of their belief and the trappings of the final act terribly immature. Maudlin Felipe clutching the relics of saints as he dies reminds me of the antics of the turn-of-the-century actress Sarah Bernhardt, who made a practice of sleeping in her coffin. Such drama does not suggest true equanimity but a death fetish. It seems to me that "we" have never out-grown our childish fear of death (Remember going through a period when you feared death so much it gave you nightmares?) and I find that both endearing and disgusting, refreshingly naïve and pathetic to witness.

9-13   Our sick lie on cots or beds with bedspreads, quilts and pillows;
Os nossos doentes estão em catres ou leitos com lensões, colchões e traveseiros;

The Japanese on a mat on the floor with a *makura* [pillow] of wood and their *kimono* over them. *Os Japões sobre huma esteira no chão com huma maqura de pao e o seu quimão em riba.*

This is simply an ordinary sleeping arrangement described elsewhere in separate contrasts regarding the bed, bed-spreads and pillows. Perhaps, Frois felt repetition was worthwhile for the *soft* vs. *hard*, *luxury* vs. *spartan* contrasts might be better felt in the context of the sickbed. The *kimono* suggests a winter sickbed, for, as explained elsewhere, there were kimono-futons. If it were outside (a field hospital), the mat would lie on the "ground" rather than "floor." *Chão* can mean either one. A later topsy-turvy statement of Japanese sleeping in their clothing by L' Abbe de T. that is too general to be true for all, but true enough and well put:

We Undress ourselves before we go to Bed; they, on the contrary, lie constantly upon Mats in their Cloaths. (A:HCJ)

9-14 In Europe, hens and squabs are used for medicine for the sick;
Em Europa se têm as galinhas e frangãos por mezinha pera os doentes;

> The Japanese think these are poison and give them fish and salted radish.
> *Os Japões tem isto por pesonha e mandão-lhe dar pexe e rabão salgado.*

Valignano wrote "everything which we would give a sick person, they forbid, and what we would forbid, they give them. And so they regard hens, chickens [tabooed for being domestic], sweet things and practically all the foods we would give patients as being unwholesome for them; on their part, they prescribe fresh and salted fish, sea-snails and other bitter, salty things, and they find from experience they do patients good." (1583 in C:TCJ) The "unwholesome" is no less than *cosa pestilencial!* (V(A):S&A) A small portion of slightly fermented pickles – for that is what the "salted radish" is – like red wine and un-pasteurized cheese, can fight bad bacteria and work to prevent run-away putrefaction in the digestive tract. L'Abbe, after repeating Valignano's contrasts (the same as 9-2, 12 and this 14), concludes with a shiver that, "by those methods which in our Opinion wou'd kill all our Sick in Europe; they recover, and live usually longer than we" (A:HCJ); while Montanus, exaggerating as usual, writes: "and as we have our Physick well prepar'd, the ascerbity or other ill tastes taken off with Correctives, they take them simple in their own likeness, able to kill our Horses . . ." (M:EEJ)

I recall some awfully bitter medicine in Japan, but it was not that it was particularly bitter by nature; it was bitter because it was not enclosed in pills. It was taken in powder form – one folds a small square of paper, pours it onto the tongue and drinks it down quickly, taking care not to breathe!

9-15 We pull our teeth with forceps, tongs and parrot-beak pliers;
Nos tiramos os dentes com botiqão, alsaprema, biqo de papgayo, etc.;

> The Japanese use a chisel and a mallet, a bow and arrow attached to a tooth and iron nail-pullers. *Os Japões com escopro e macete ou com arqo e frecha atada no dente ou com troqes [torques?] de ferreiro.*

It is fun to imagine a tooth tied by a 10-foot string to an arrow which is shot from a bow, but as Okada suggests, the bow and arrow is probably a bow-drill.

9-16 Our seasonings and medicines are pounded in mortars;
Os nossas speciarias e mezinhas se pizão em gral ou almofaris;

In Japan, it is ground in a copper *navicula* with an iron wheel between both hands.
Em Japão se moem em huma naveta de cobre com huma roda de ferro antre ambas as [mãos].

Navicula, which means small boat is, properly speaking, a sun dial where the prick (?) mimics a mast for what we might call a ship-of-time clock. I hope the reader will pardon my acting like Humpty-Dumpty and enlisting it to mean what I want it to mean! The Japanese *yagen* it refers to is a single-grooved, slightly curved (concave) oblong mortar upon which a single wheel that serves as a pestle is held with a hand grasping the axle on each side. I cannot recall whether the wheel rotates around the axle which the hands grasp firmly or the axle, solidly attached to the wheel, rotates in the palms as the hands are moved back and forth while pressing down. Because the wheel is operated by two hands at the end of straight arms it can do more work than our mortar and pestle with its *twisting*, *grinding* and pounding. *Considering the small use made of wheels for transportation in Japan, what fun to find the wheel used here!* (It came with Chinese medicine from China) Since the wheel was identified with Buddhist law in Japan, I dare say it would also put some spirit into the medicine!

9-17 Among us pearls and pearlets, are used for personal ornament;
Antre nós se uza das perulas e aljofre pera ornamento das pesoas.

> In Japan they only serve for being crushed to make medicine.
> *Em Japão, não serve mais que de se moer pera fazer mezinhas.*

Considering the uses Europe had for various stones found in other animals, this use of pearls by the Japanese is hardly surprising. In Chinese-style medicine, it served to relax the spirit, settle the soul, brighten the eyes, and cure deafness (Okada). That is to say, it was considered good for the nerves. Considering the fact it contains zinc and selenium and other trace elements, I do not doubt it. If I am not mistaken, pulverized cicada shares some of its properties. But, the strangeness in Frois's contrast is in the fact that pearls were not much valued for adornment and, thus, were destroyed to be ingested. If we are looking for an interesting medical contrast, it would be this:

> In Europe, we pay a high price for mummia pitch or powder made from ancient bodies;
> In Japan, eating such a substance even for medicine would be thought ghoulish or insane.

Mummy was a medicine in great demand since the days of the Crusades. It is easy to understand why, for tar/bitumen/pitch has marvelous medical properties (especially for dermatological problems where the healing is obvious). At first, tar itself (called *mummia* from Persian or *mûmîya* from Arabic) was used, but when natural asphalt ran short, that found in the hollows of corpses and finally the corpses themselves were used. Exporting corpses to Europe was big business in the 16c and, not unnaturally, fraud was rife. When French physician Guy de la Fonteine investigated the mummy trade in Alexandria in 1564, he found fresh corpses were being dug up to satisfy the demand this patent medicine. (See Brian Fagan: *"Mummies or the Restless Dead"* in *Horizon* (Summer 1975))

9-18 Among us, if a doctor does not pass an exam, he is penalized and cannot practice;
Antre nós, se um medico não for examinado, tem pena e não pode qurar;

> In Japan, whoever would make a living can become a doctor.
> *Em Japão, pera ganharem a vida, quem quer uza de ser medico.*

Certification has always been a mixed blessing for all but the wealthy. In 1589 London, there were just 38 licensed physicians for 120,000 people and about twice as many druggists, who functioned as general practitioners would today (T:RDM). The doctor-to-patient ratio proves that the exam system was more for the purpose of protecting the livelihood of doctors than the lives of the population. The heavy use of obfuscating Latin terms by the druggists was, likewise, purposefully done to prevent competition from folk practitioners and keep the prices of drugs artificially high. (Nicholas Culpepper, a truly conscientious herb-medicine specialist who fought to break that monopoly and return medicine to the folk in the mid 17c is one of my heroes). Perhaps the best thing that can be said about the monopoly of physicians, is that it saved many people from being killed by their medical care!

In Japan, too, the risk was known. There is an old saying that "a hundred men must die to make a good doctor." That brings a whole other nuance to the term "medical *practice.*" (Nowadays, we just aren't so honest about it. Wherever I have lived, people without connections often get tired and inexperienced interns that do little better than Frois's "anyone.")

9-19 Among us, for a man to suffer from the pox is always a dirty and shameful thing;
Antre nós adoecer hum homem de huma mula sempre hé cousa suja e vergonhoza;

> The Japanese men and women think it nothing out of the ordinary and are not ashamed of it. *Os Japões homens e molheres o tem por couza corrente e nada se pejão disso.*

Whether it came from the Americas or Africa, one thing is certain, Christians spread syphilis around the world. How convenient to have "proof" sex is sinful and a way to catch sinners and mark them for life all in one! This contrast is of a type we have become familiar with: it shows Japanese as not ashamed of things we are. In *not* bringing out the opposite instances, Frois reveals unspoken bias to the effect that only Christians are moral enough to feel shame. For example, he might have added "they would be ashamed to use their hands" in 6-1, when eating with hands was contrasted to using chopsticks, or, he might have contrasted European women who walked with their feet straight or even with their toes pointing *out*, to pigeon-toed Japanese who would have found that wanton behavior. But, perhaps I am being unfair. It is always easier to recognize lack of shame in others with regard to things one feels strongly about, than to discover things others find shameful that one would not even give second thought to: the *balance of shame* always falls in one's own favor. Be that as it may, the 9-19 contrast is correct as far as it goes, but it would be more interesting to add this:

We treat lepers in our hospitals and do not feel that their disease makes them any less human. They will have nothing to do with lepers and keep them away from all society as if they were beasts.

Japanese may not have been ashamed of sexually transmitted diseases, but they have long been terrified of *all* incurable and visually distressing disease. That is to say, they were more sensitive to the mark *as* sin than the mark *of* sin (You may notice that bad people often are punished by visible blemishes in TV dramas). They remained, until very recently unrelenting in their attitude about leprosy, preserving a far more stringent segregation than found in the West. Though the Japanese in Frois's time may not have been particularly ashamed about *catching* a sexual disease, the affect on their appearance would have troubled them and caused them to seek treatment before the disease played out its full course.

Both of these diseases must have weighed heavily upon Frois's mind because the Jesuit hospitals in Japan had been forced to reverse their policies with respect to them. When Almeida ran the clinic in Funai (in the realm of Bungo), the hospital had three wings, one of which was for incurable diseases and included many lepers and some incurable syphilitics. It was so popular, patients, few of whom were Christian, came from all over Japan. Rome was not at all happy with this, for, if I understand Jacquees Proust (P:ETPJ) correctly, the policies set by the ecumenical councils allowed for assistance of the poor but not "medical activity" *per se,* much less going all out like this! For a couple decades, the hospital operations were hushed up. Proust writes that "from 1562 onward there was no mention of any *medical* activity in Jesuits' letters from Japan." In Valignano's *Sumario* of 1583, he pretends nothing ever happened and suggests each region create a "house of charity" and a "hospital to take in poor and sick Christians, and also children whom the mothers customarily kill." He also recommended that the incurable, especially lepers be excluded because the Japanese found them repugnant. This was definitely a wise move from the point of view of winning support in Japan. But it is also the only instance I know of where the admirable policy of Accommodation decided by the Bungo Consultation of 1580 clearly backfired (at least to our moral sense). The free treatment of the poor, including gentiles, that Almeida had championed was also no longer permitted and admission restricted to "Christians from honorable and noble families." (P:ETPJ)

When AIDS exploded in our midst, Japanese had already become Western and modern and even conservative in the sense that the bourgeoisie usually is and most people had come to think of homosexuality as part of a corrupt, individualistic, sexually promiscuous Occident. Perhaps because AIDS was associated with what was considered immoral behavior and was (and still is) incurable, Japan's reaction against it was greater than was the case in the USA, even with "our" gloating "We-told-you-so!" fundamentalists. Turning 9-19 on its head, AIDS became a far *more* shameful thing in Japan than in the West. People were terrified to reveal they had it or even to get tested (The many infections through contaminated blood was the responsibility of the companies, but fear of talking out on the part of victims and their doctors delayed the response.) and were Japanese not the world's greatest producer and user of condoms, AIDS might have spread like wildfire.

endnote IX

Medicine

Compared to the equestrian arts, architecture or ship-building, our medicine does not come off as significantly more diverse or advanced than that of Japan, or for that matter, other Eastern nations. This was because it wasn't. *Not yet.* In Goa, we find that the viceroys, arch-bishops and Portuguese aristocracy preferred to be treated by the Hindi Vaidyas rather than their own physicians (G:PPI). Even the 1589 Report of the Embassy to Europe, with its constant boasting about superior European development has nothing to say about the medical science. *De Missione* does, however, have something to say about the *accessibility* of health *care*. In the context of introducing something called *societas* – what Americans now call non-profit corporations – such as the *Mons pietatis,* known as the "Mountain of Piety" (*Monte di pieta*) for the purpose of lending money to the indigent, *xenodochium,* or public inns for foreign travelers, *brephortrophium,* for the care of orphans, and *gynaeceum*, a sort of half-way house for raising the level of living and thereby reforming wayward women, Valignano=Miguel describes the *nosocomium,* or hospital,

> among which there are some with every kind of medicine and every type of equipment that give cheerful and free, complete medical care to people suffering from any complaint. Because there are many types of disease, there are many types of hospitals, or they are divided into wards, within are themselves well ordered, clean and take every consideration for the care of the patient . . . (J/S:DM)

If Sir Thomas More's *Utopia* had not already been written, one might think it all Miguel's invention. Christianity got all the credit, of course, – nothing is mentioned about Islam setting the example for the public hospital. Valignano=Leo responds:

> Such places would certainly be extremely beneficial. Because of them, many sins common in our country can probably be avoided in Europe. Sins such as ravishing virgins here and raising whorehouses there, using medicine, or rather poison for abortion, after which the mother murders her own dear child, and, furthermore, leaving sick men and other unfortunates to suffer and die on the road, . . . (J/S:DM)

While Japan did not have as many such societies as Europe, the claim probably goes too far. Not all of Christendom was taking care of everyone half so well as the wealthiest cities, whose riches may well have been the cause of poverty elsewhere, and the Tokugawa government, without the help of Christianity, thank you, would soon establish a thorough system to assist sick or injured travelers – each neighborhood had a place and a budget for so many days of care and send-off money.

> *Europeans believe miasma (pestilential airs) from swamps and dumps bring influenza;*
> *The Japanese imagine there is a demon, who sneaks over the roofs, that brings it.*

> *In Europe, someone in mortal danger usually sends for a priest, first;*
> *In Japan, they always call for a doctor before the clergy.*

Frois might have accomplished much more with this chapter. I think of the cultural side of disease such as the above *Faux Froises* which need no explanation. But, more than anything else, I would have liked Frois, with his Christianity as "medicine for the soul," to have taken as much notice of *how the best Japanese died* as he did of funeral customs. Here is something that took place when Frois was in Japan. Call it secular hagiography if you wish, but it really pulls at my heartstrings.

A warrior called Akaboshi was a vassal to Ryuzoji Takanobu (1529-84). The latter suspected Akaboshi of wishing to rebel against him and so took two of his children, a girl of eight years and a boy whose age is not given, as hostages. Takanobu eventually crucified them. The soldier in charge of the execution turned the children westward (toward paradise), his eyes brimming with tears. Before dying, the boy Shinroku, asked, "Where is my homeland?" "Toward the east," answered the soldier, whereupon the child replied with this poem:

Please don't face me	*Waga omote*
toward the west	*nishi ni na mukeso*
lest I should turn	*Akaboshi no*
my back upon my father	*oya ni ushiro o*
Akaboshi	*miseji to omoeba*

(From Yoell Hoffmann: *Japanese Death Poems*, Tuttle, 1986). The original poem is more poetic for, in Japanese syntax, the father comes earlier and the poem ends on the main idea: *"lest I should turn my back."* At the risk of sounding sacrilegious: Didn't this boy show a higher level of moral development than someone who cowardly cried out *"My Father, why do you forsake me?"*

Although I am not a Christian and am delighted that Japan, in the end, escaped being converted, I feel sorry for what happened to any useful medical knowledge Almeida brought to Japan, just as I feel sorry for the whole Jesuit mission and many if not most of the believers there. All that genuine good will and knowledge and even that explicit program of cultural accommodation of the likes Christianity had never seen and never would again until the Second Vatican took it even further to include religion in the mid-20c. *Poof!* On the basis of an extensive search of Japanese sources which found "not a single reference to any Western work on medicine, surgery, anatomy, pharmacy is known in any manuscript dating from the long period between the advent of the Iberians in 1549 and their final expulsion in 1638," Wolfgang Michel came to the sad conclusion that the Southern Barbarian (*namban*) hospital wrote its history entirely on water: "Given the destruction of the mission hospital in Funai, the mounting persecution of Christians and also resistance within the Society of Jesus, there was no stable basis anymore for an effective interchange. . . I do not believe the Japanese ever came to practice "southern-barbarian-style surgery" in the sense of a paradigm that could be passed on or handed down to succeeding generations [as is popularly believed]." (M:MSB) Western medicine had to be reintroduced by the Dutch and Germans in the 17c.

Meanwhile, the Jesuits in South America discovered *quinine*. Judging from their interest and readiness to learn about Chinese drugs, I would guess they were taught by a native of Peru. As *the first specific drug for a specific illness*, it gave a strong incentive for scientists to search for other cures. Brought to Europe in 1632 and in 1644 it became *the first medicine subjected to empirical testing* at the instruction of the Pope (so Rome was not entirely anti-medicine). Neuberger writes "it did for medicine what gunpowder had done for war" (G:HOM) and by quickly curing a protracted fever which the standard humor-correcting medicines/blood-letting had not affected "was the end of Galenism in medical practice." (Reader, do you realize how *significant* that is in the history of medicine?) It also played a role in one of the most shameful episodes in English history. Known as *Jesuit's Bark* or *Jesuit's powder*, it was rumored to be an insidious poison the Jesuits brought to Europe "for the purpose of exterminating all those who had thrown off their allegiance to Rome." (See the quotes in *TT-long* about he London hysteria of the 1678 that ended up getting 35 people, including 8 Jesuits executed).

If involvement in medicine sometimes got the Jesuits in trouble, it was a plus for their missions in Asia and absolutely vital in the Americas where measles and small pox and other deadly deceases from the old world killed most of the natives. This horrible tragedy that coincided with, and especially, *preceded,* the coming of the Jesuits, destroyed the credibility of the shamans and gave "our" *Black-robes* their opportunity.   While they were thinking of saving souls, the natives were thinking of saving themselves. Even baptism was thought of as charm against these horrible diseases and the relative immunity of the Jesuits to these diseases (together, I suspect, with their lack of fear of death) that permitted them to nurse the sick, doubtless enhanced their and their God's reputation. In the penultimate chapter of *Disease, Depopulation and Culture Change in Northwestern New Spain 1518-1764,* Daniel T. Reff points out:

> Most of the medicines, herbs, rosaries and potions used by the Jesuits probably had little or no intrinsic value. However, the very fact they were used and combined with basic clinical care [getting decent food and water, kept in clean bedding, helped with body functions, protected from animals (and from committing suicide) given encouragement] meant that at least some survived that otherwise would have died. Modern medical practitioners and researchers have known for some time that clinical care can have an enormous impact on mortality rates. [After this, Reff gives examples.] (*the bracketed comments are mine* – R:DPC)

So even clinical (as opposed to medical) care can help! That helps explain a lot. Reff also notes that while the Jesuits had *a good explanation* (God's punishment for believing in the wrong gods, etc.) and *attractive public rites* to help people cope with these lethal diseases, in some cases where disease hit the natives hard *after* they were baptized, the Jesuits and their religion was blamed and baptism came to be thought of as a death sentence.   So, the total picture was complex, though on the whole, it worked out favorably for the missionaries.

In Japan, the importance of disease and, hence, the medical care offered by the Jesuits, was far less than in the New World, but I think it safe to say that medicine and the mission were inexorably married (though the relationship was sometimes strained) wherever the Jesuits went. And, in a more recent book, *Plagues, Priests and Demons* (Cambridge University Press 2005), Reff demonstrates the similar relationship of epidemic disease and successful proselytizing in the Americas and in the earlier rise of Christianity *in Europe*, or, at least the similarity of the Christian accounts of both.

~~~~~~

As true for all chapters, we have enjoyed many entertaining differences. But none seem as interesting as one *similarity,* a quirk in history, I happened across recently. I had long known *we* danced. I had read of "our" Dancing Mania, St. Vitus's Dance, *Danse de St. Guy,* St. Anthony's Fire, etc., attributed to mass hysteria, outbreaks of religiosity and, more convincingly, to ergotism (mold (fungus) on old grain with toxic and, apparently, psychedelic properties, that tends to accompany famine (when people will eat what they can find) and diphtheria and influenza and other diseases (caused by famine which lowers immunity and causing a worse famine by taking people out of the fields), but I had not heard of *theirs*.

> In 1134, following strong rains that caused flooding, Kyoto suffered a famine, and its residents fell victim to an epidemic . . . In 1153-4, . . . it was another disease, perhaps smallpox that mowed down the inhabitants. In the spring of 1154, crowds of people overwhelmed by adversity went to Murasakino Shrine . . . to rid themselves of the demons that had apparently caused the disease. The ancient Japanese thought that illness was caused by evil spirits possessing the body and that these spirits could be exorcised by dancing. Men and women, commoners, nobles, and outcasts all gathered . . . and danced, accompanied by flutes, bells and tambourines . . . Young servants of the shrine, dressed in ceremonial robes, performed acrobatics while the crowd danced and stamped their feet on the ground to expel the demons. The dances lasted day and night. The people seemed to have gone mad, perhaps hoping their madness would cure both fear and illness. (Souyri S(R):WTUD)

X

THE WRITING OF THE JAPANESE AND THEIR BOOKS,
do escrever dos Japões e de seus livros, papel e tinta e cartas
PAPER, INK AND EPISTLES

10-1   We write with twenty two letters;
Nós escrevemos com vinte e duas letras;

        They write with 48 *kana* abc and with infinite characters of diverse letters.
        Elles com 48 no abc de cana *e com infinitos caracteres em diversas letras.*

The alphabet used by Romance languages In 1585 was four letters short of 26. It lacked *j*, which was written with an *i, u,* with a *v, k* with a *q,* and *w.* The letters in the Japanese *abc,* to use Frois's term for what is properly called a "syllabary," are called *kana* (as opposed to *kanji,* or Chinese characters). Consonants invariably come with a vowel pegged on, e.g. "*ka, ki, ku, ke, ko,*" yet each is a single letter, か、き、く、け、こ, respectively. I call them *syllabets.* The vowels, on the other hand, can be written by themselves (a=あ, i=い, e=え, o=お, u=う in the Japanese order) and are remarkably similar to those of Latinate tongues, both in number and pronunciation (as in *Buenos Aires.*) Had Frois been a modern student of ancient tongues, he might have written,

     Our ancestors first invented stand-alone consonants and only later made letters for vowels;
     Their ancestors first invented stand-alone vowels and they still have no consonant letters.

In the early-19c, Golownin wrote that "every Japanese, however low his rank, knows how to write in this last character [the letters of the syllabary, as opposed to Chinese characters]. They were exceedingly astonished to find that of four Russian sailors not one should be able to write." (G:MCIJ) If your language is lucky enough to be sound-poor, a syllabary is far easier to master than an alphabet. Children can be reading and writing with few spelling mistakes in weeks if not *days!* The difference between the simple Japanese syllabets and "our" letters would have been at a minimum for Latin languages which are relatively easy to spell, but the pronunciation *of the name* of a given consonant is not necessarily the same as the bit of phoneme heard when pronouncing a word. With Japanese, each syllabet in a word is pronounced exactly like its name, so *spelling out a word only means saying it more slowly than usual.* Froising this, we get:

     With us, parents sometimes spell out words to make them harder for children to understand;
     In Japan, parents sometimes spell out words to make them easier for the child to hear.

I once heard a Japanese expert on America and its popular music explain on Japan's national public radio (NHK) that Tammy Wynette spells out D.I.V.O.R.C.E. and "C.U.S.T.O.D.Y. to "make these difficult words" *easier* (I repeat "easier"!) for her little child to catch! Our respective concepts of spelling out are indeed contrary. But, there is one aspect of the Japanese syllabary that is, indeed, more complex than ours and this was as true in 1585 as it is today:

     We only have one way to write our alphabet.
     They have two very different common ways to write their syllabets, and many more difficult ways.

By this, I do not only mean printed style versus cursive style, but what appear to be completely different syllabaries. The letters of one are soft and rounded, that of the other so hard-edged one might think it was designed for writing with a stylus or preparing print-blocks. Look at this haiku by Keigu in the alphabeticized, *hiragana,* and *katakana* versions and original mixed system:

> *anonamakokayakutsundeorukamoshirenu*　　　*keigu*　　(called *romaji*, or "roman-letters" by Japanese)
> あのなまこかやくつんでおるかもしれぬ　　けいぐ　(soft: most common letters in most writing)
> アノナマコカヤクツンデオルカモシレヌ　　ケイグ　(stiff, used for foreign and scientific words)
> あのナマコ火薬詰んでおるかも知れぬ！　　敬愚　　(mix of letters, including *kanji*: easy to read)

My haiku pen name, Keigu, is a pun on the closing of a letter, "respectful-tool" = 敬具, where the last character, "tool" = 具 is changed to "fool(ish)" = 愚. More commonly, a single name pronunciation-wise, may be written in *dozens* of ways by various characters. For example, using the paltry MS-Word standard cache alone, there are over a hundred ways to write the name *pronounced* "Kenji": 賢治、健二、健治、健次、健司、賢二、憲治、謙治、賢司、謙二, etc. But to return to the haiku and what it shows, Frois should have caught and included this:

> *We separate our words by spaces to read them more easily;*
> *The Japanese do not separate their words at all.*

A mixture of characters and syllabets creates easily readable clusters in the otherwise unbroken space. When Japanese is Romanized, we must make separate words clear. For example, my haiku – meaning: *that sea slug / it just might be tamped / with dynamite* – reads better like this:

> *ano namako kayaku tsundeoru ka mo shirenu.*

Since Frois does not mention what makes *kana* (syllabets) different from "our" alphabet, and the slight difference in number (22 *vs* 48) is far from contrary, the real contrast would seem to be between *a finite number of letters* and those "*infinite characters,*" (Mexia 1598 in Cooper) which I'll treat in the next contrast.

..

~~~~~~

10-2　 We study many arts and sciences through our books;
　　　　Nós estudamos diversas artes e scientias por nossos livros.

> They spend their entire lives mastering their characters.
> *Elles toda a vida gastão em conhecer o corasão dos caracteres.*

Okada notes that Rodrigues's *Arte de Lingoa de Iapam* (1604-8) claims that a total of 209,770 Chinese characters can be found! One of those "0"s probably does not belong, for estimates of "the total number of Chinese characters ever used from antiquity to present (including variant and dialect characters . . .) range up to 80,000 (Samuel Martin 1972:83)" (Hannas: 97). Rodrigues himself wrote elsewhere that "there are as many as 70,000 or 80,000 of these letters and characters" but added that "it is generally enough to know about 10,000 characters or a little less, because if these are known, many others can be understood by their composition." Rodrigues means *for a learned man*, like himself. Half that many sufficed for most people (and, today, half again of that). In a sense, characters are more like *words* than letters. The more difficult ones, *like our more difficult words,* are simply not missed by most people. Of course, more time is required to master them. In *De Missione,* Miguel=Valignano mentions that in Europe twenty-three letters (I don't know which letter was added) suffice, and that, learning them, "they can read and write naturally and very easily." Indeed, Japanese children in church schools are learning to "read and write" European tongues *in one or two months* adds Leno=Valignano. This is followed by what may be the first long complaint about the effort wasted on Chinese characters compared to the alphabet. Even the difficulty of writing homophonic Japanese vocabulary with the syllabet alone is considered – Miguel claims the diligent fathers can devise a system of accents and other signs to supplement the syllabet. (This would work for a few homographs that are accented differently, but most homophones are exact, so it would not help).

There are studies confirming the Jesuits' impression of Japanese writing as wasteful. (For details, see *TT-long*.) But I agree with Chamberlain, who found "the oft-repeated assertion that the ideographs waste years of school life" dubious because "the Japanese lad of fifteen is abreast of his English contemporary in every way."(C:TJ) And I would go further and point out that the reason Japanese were able to learn written Western tongues so rapidly was *because* learning Chinese characters improved their intelligence. But, the other side has another more sophisticated argument that was, as far as I know, first hypothesized by Alice Mabel Bacon, namely, that the years of study needed to master the written language "leave comparatively little time for the conducting of any continuous thought of one's own account, and so we find in Japanese scholars – whether boys or girls – quickness of apprehension, retentive memories, industry and method in their study of their lessons, but not much originality of thought." (B:JG&W) This idea, which Hannas made into a book (*Asia's Orthographic Dilemma*), without knowing of Bacon, is dubious, for our time is not so limited and because, to my experience, the best way to memorize is by inventing stories, which is to say exercising originality of thought! (i.e., rote learning is not necessarily contrary to creative growth). Moreover, I find the large initial investment *worth it*, for characters promote a large vocabulary – I can read far more specialized terms in Japanese than in English! – and, therefore, is more efficient in the long run. Be that as it may, nothing has been *proven* either way. That is why, I am irked by the confident putdowns of Chinese characters in Japanese by alphabet-lovers. Best-selling author Jared Diamond, wise indeed when it comes to *birdsong*, is full of it when he claims Japanese use Chinese characters "in preference to efficient alphabets" because of the prestige of Chinese things which he compares to "designer jeans." (*Guns, Germs and Steel*). Note: There are *many* compelling reasons Japan continues to use Chinese characters. Because of their phonemic poverty and enormous number of homophones, Japanese have more reason than the Chinese themselves to stick with the characters. Much Japanese is unreadable by phonetic character alone. A large portion of one of the world's most wonderful literature – would be rendered unreadable. Diamond seems to have affection for a diverse ecology and so-called primitive languages, yet, for some reason, he shows absolutely no sensitivity for Japan's wonderful system of writing, which shared with Chinese another not easily calculated value:

> *With us, even a word written by a calligrapher would not, by itself, be thought of as art.*
> *With them, a single character written in a second can be hung up like a painting and enjoyed.*

10-3 We write across, from the left-hand to the right;
Nós escrevemos ao través, da mão esqerda pera a dereita;

> They do so vertically and always from the right-hand to the left.
> *Elles ao comprido, e sempre da mão dereita pera a esqerda.*

On January 14, 1549, Xavier sent a list of Japanese "characters" to John III, King of Portugal which "the Japanese write in a very different manner from other nations, beginning at the top of the page and writing downwards to the bottom." He also noted that the Japanese covert Paul, responding to the question of why *they* did not write as *we* do, replied "Why, rather, do not you write as we do? The head of a man is at the top and his feet at the bottom, and so it is proper that when men write it should be straight down from top to bottom." (C:LLFX) Acosta, in his *Historie of the Indies*, has a paragraph-length chapter on *the direction of writing*, which ends on this fine relative note: "To conclude, we finde foure different kindes of writings, some writte from the right to the left, others from the left to the right, some from the toppe to the bottome and others from the foote to the toppe, wherein wee may discover the diversity of mans iudgement." (A:NMH) But the *reason* he gives for vertical writing is ridiculous:

The *Chinois* write neither like the Greeks [left to right] nor like the Hebrews [right to left], but from the toppe to the bottome, for as they be no letters but whole wordes, and that every character signifieth a thing, they have no neede to assemble the parts one with an other, and therefore they may well write from the toppe to the bottome. Those of *Mexico,* for the same cause did not write in line, from one side to another, but contrarie to the *Chinois,* beginning below, they mounted vpward. (Ibid 1604)

But there might be *something* here. A "thing" is best expressed by a vertical presence, for a horizontal one would be merely a backdrop, a horizon. This is why, I believe, Japanese haiku can be written in one line more effectively than they can be in English. Be that as it may, Japanese also write horizontally, left to right, as we do, and horizontally right to left, mostly on Buddhist plaques (names of temples) and, most visibly, on the right-side of commercial vehicles so the writing flows from the front to the back on the right side of the vehicle as well as the left! This variety of directions is stimulating. Returning to the Occident after twenty years in Japan, I sometimes feel how someone used to a color TV might feel going back to black and white. One-way-horizontal alone is a terrible *bore.*

Letters in any language are written from the upper-left hand corner. It is how human's (right-handed humans, anyway) naturally draw and may even have to do with how they read faces. Vertical lines should flow from *left to right* rather than *right to left,* as is the common practice. A technical reason that no longer matters – try writing vertically on top of a scroll of writing paper held in the left hand while pulling it open toward the right – made this happen. Unfortunately, it means that books of horizontal English footnotes and vertical Japanese text do not mix today. There is *one* interesting reversal corollary to contrast 10-3. Speed-readers, alone, read like their Antipode:

With us, a fast reader skims pages of horizontal text vertically,
With them, vertical text is skimmed horizontally.

10-4   Where the last pages of our books are,   *Onde as derradeiras folhas dos nossos libros*

Theirs begin.   *Ali começo os seus.*

If it were not for the unfortunate reversal mentioned above, this difference would not have been, and what Acosta wrote about Hebrew = "The Hebrewes contrariwise beganne at the right to the left, and therefore their bookes beganne where ours did end" = would be equally true for Japanese, for the direction of a book follows that of the lines. When Japanese write books in horizontal lines (common for books including Western language, equations and anything else horizontal), the front and the back of the book are the same as ours. But such books were not found in Frois's time. There is, moreover, one more difference associated with the direction we read. *Faux Frois:*

Europeans tend to turn pages from the top;
Japanese from the bottom.

I once drew my hands moving to turn the pages of a book for a *meta*-flipbook, but I failed to notice that reading direction changed the way we flip the pages of our books, until I read a book by my friend, Tsurugaya Shinichi, describing how he first noticed the difference from a painting of a French girl reading by the painter Kuroda Seiki, then confirmed it watching an unwitting Occidental working with him, . . . *me!* I tended to turn pages from the upper right hand corner, or "heaven/sky" (in the language of Japanese printers); further investigation made it a certainty. Tsurugaya notes it comes naturally from the direction we turn. (I would add, *coupled with our handedness* – left-handed readers in our respective cultures should tend to turn pages like right-handed readers in our antipodes.) And he surmises the different movement and position of our fingers helps explain the tendency for the chapter or book-title to be written on the head of the pages in Western books and the foot of the pages in Japanese books. (『書を読んで羊を失う』鶴ケ谷真一)

10-5 We hold printing in high regard;
Nós temos ha impresão por cousa singular;

> They almost always use manual script because their printing is worthless. *Elles quasi em tudo uzão da escritura da mão, porque a sua impresão não presta.*

Block-printing in Japan goes back about 800 years before Frois. Moveable type, which Gutenberg had reinvented in Europe, had also come over from Korea, but it was rarely used and Frois doubtless has in mind the wood-blocks that were carved individually by hand. It is hard to say if Frois's *escritura* means the hand-written style of the wood-block printed pages or manual copying. Because of the volume of printed books available in Japan, I assume he means the first. But it was not an either-or thing. Rodrigues (in C:TCJ) described Japan wood-block printing in detail:

> First of all, they take a sheet of paper the same size as the proposed book and carefully write on it in the desired style, with the required number of lines, spaces and everything else. Then they glue this sheet face down on the block and with great skill cut away the blank paper, leaving only the blank letters . . . They then carve these letters on the block with iron instruments . . . They are so dexterous in this art that they can cut a block in about the same time that we can compose a page.

Considering the fact that pulling out type from among thousands of choices would take more time than choosing from 22 (or 44 if we include our capital letters), speed might have been a major reason Japanese did *not* prefer moveable type! As Rodrigues suggests, it might have been as fast to carve blocks as to set type. But I feel aesthetics was more important. In Japanese, aesthetically pleasing script literally *flowed* from letter to letter in ways not easily broken up into type (depending which letter came next and the space available a different link would be needed) and all of this flowed organically about the contours of the pictures. Compared to this, our best illuminated manuscripts were child's play (see the note on our calligraphy in *TT-long*). So, who says printing is better?

10-6 We write with pens of geese and birds [crows?];
Nós escrevemos com penas de pato ou de aves [de corvos?];

> They use brushes like those of an artist made of the hair of horse and rabbit on a bamboo handle. *Elles com pinceis de pintores feitos de cabelos de lebre e o cabo de cana.*

In Frois's time, a pen in English was a feather ("the rauen wyll not gyue his blacke pennes for the pecockes paynted fethers"), a flight-feather (pinion), a short, rudimentary feather, the quill or barrel of a feather, a quill-like pipe, a quill shaped like a spoon for taking snuff, the internal feather-like shell of squid, the midrib of a leaf . . . also described by the OED as "a quill feather or part of one, with the quill or barrel pointed and split into two nibs at its lower end, so as to form an instrument for writing." A 1748 usage example from a letter of one Lady Luxburough includes "A curse against crow-pens!" This suggests that Father Schütte's guess of *corvos* for an illegible word is correct. Doubtless, other birds were also used. The Japanese animals named are, likewise, only a small sampling of the menagerie called upon to give their hair for what was a far more versatile instrument:

> As for the brush (. . .), it has its gestures, as if it were the finger,; but whereas our old pens knew only clogging or loosening and could only, moreover, scratch the paper always in the same direction, the brush can slide, twist, lift off, the stroke being made, so to speak, in the volume of the air; it has the carnal, lubrified flexibility of the hand. (B:EOS)

Barthes aside, most of "us" feel the brush is a crude, inefficient way to write; but the truth is that the physical and aesthetic satisfaction of the brush far, far exceeds that of the pen.

10-7   Our ink is liquid;
  A nossa tinta hé liqida;

> Theirs a bar which they grind when they [would] write.
> *A sua hé em pãis e moe-se quando se escreve.*

This *liquid* vs. *solid* difference goes back several millennia. Both the ancient Egyptians and the ancient Chinese burnt vegetable oils for bases of their ink, but the former kept the result suspended in *liquid* while the later kept it in a *solidified* form (*Why the difference? Can a chemist explain?*). Japanese ink, or *sumi,* is, indeed, usually made *by the writer*, who grinds the bar on the tool Frois roughly describes in his *next* contrast, thus maintaining control over the dilution of the ink. Sometimes servants, wives or children did the grinding. (I once observed a top landscape painter in Korea fast at work – a brush between each finger! – as his daughter ground his paints just fast enough to keep ahead of him). The pigment is amazingly concentrated.   Although I have never measured it, nor have I seen it sold with the promise to make so many liters of ink, my impression is that one ink-stick the size of a small candy-bar makes gallons of ink and one is more likely to lose the stick than to ever use it up. Rodrigues writes that "the best kind is made from the smoke of sesame oil . . . which adheres to a vessel, and from this they make paste." These, then, are stamped with information, fine names and "decorated with various flowers, serpents and figures from legends . . . they add some musk while making the best sort so that it will smell sweetly when they write with it." Some were "small, others long and others round in standard shapes" (R(C):TIJ).   Rarely, gold powder was mixed in the ink-stick or the entire stick molded into something. (A *sumi-e* painter to whom I mailed a real cicada sprayed gold sent me in return an ink bar resembling a cicada, covered with a light gilt!)

Advantages may be found in this inconvenience of making one's own ink. Morse, noted that "If one is in a rage and is inclined to dash off an angry letter, he has sufficient time to cool off in getting ready to write it." (M:JDD); but the lack of ready writing instruments made life hard for poets, carpenters, whoever had to make some notes on the spur of the moment.   For this they had portable equipment called *yatate,* a tube decorated with an "infinite" variety of designs with a small writing brush, "and attached to the top at right angles, . . a receptacle for a wad of cotton saturated with fluid ink." (ibid) Today, people who like traditional writing instruments but are too lazy to grind ink may buy it ready-made in bottles. And, if that is still too inconvenient (an inkstone ramp is still needed to wipe the brush), there are brushes with squeezable rubber handles full of ink, i.e., fountain-*brushes* rather than fountain-*pens*!
  ..

10-8   Our inkwells are made of horn and round; *Os nossos tinteiros são de corno, redondos.*

  Theirs of slabs of stone. *Os seus de pedra comprida.*

In English, an inkwell used to be called an "inkhorn." Containers meant not only to be dipped into but to keep ink are, naturally, deep.

The adjective *comprida* ("long and thin"), describing the Japanese stone in the original, I turned to "slabs," which are, in Rodrigues's words, of "suitable smooth marmoreal stone" (R(C):TIJ). They are usually rectangular, oval, or in-between and are, perhaps, ten times longer than deep, with "a raised rim around the edge and a reservoir in the middle where the ink is ground. At one end, of this there is a small well, gracefully carved, wherein they pour the water with which the ink is mixed . . . This is rather like the stone or palette in which artists prepare and mix the colours that they use in painting. (Ibid.) The most magnificent inkstand I know turns that small well into a grotto-like reservoir with the elixir of immortality from the Other World below the cosmic Mt. Feng-lai. Today, most inkstands have no separate well *per se,* but a graduated slope, resembling a boat-launching ramp.

10-9 Our inkwells come with lids and quill wipers; *Os nossos tinteiros tem cubertura e poidouros;*
Those of Japan do not. *Os de Japão nada disto.*

This is because, as mentioned already, our inkwells were also for *keeping* ink, whereas theirs were enlisted anew each time and the last of the ink dumped (or sucked up by the ink sprite captured in detail by the mind's eye of blind Borges). But Japanese were not lacking in accessories as the contrast might suggest. As Rodrigues notes, they "place all their writing instruments in a beautiful lacquered box made for that purpose." (Read Cooper's translation of *This Island of Japan* – I dare not quote more here!)

10-10 Our papers are of only four or five varieties; *Os nosso papel hé de 4 ou sinco layas somente;*
Those of Japan surpass fifty. *O de Japão pasa de sincoenta.*

The Europeans were paper-poor, the Japanese, as part of the Chinese cultural sphere, paper-rich. (In China, Marco Polo was amazed to find *even money was paper*, "made from bark collected from mulberry trees on whose leaves the silk worms feed," and that "throughout the empire this paper money is used in every transaction." Polo considered this sheer *alchemy*.

Japanese paper was made from dozens of plants. There were probably more varieties of tissue paper alone than Europe had varieties of all paper. Alcock mentioned "an infinite variety of paper" and sent *sixty-seven* different kinds to a World Fair. (A:COT)

10-11 We use only the mark of a notary public for official documents;
Nós em as escrituras publicas somente uzamos do sinal de tabalião publico;
The Japanese, besides their signatures, each make their own marks on their letters.
Os Japões, alem do nome, cada hum faz seu partiqular sinal em suas cartas.

Reading about 15-16c notary publics, I think of the old adage about the pen being mightier than the sword. The notary public not only attested to the fact that someone swore something was true, but supplied the documents that served in the capacity of those that today come from law offices and courts. In other words, the notary was both lawyer and judge and in that capacity generally grew very wealthy – the person who bought himself the most posthumous masses (11,038 in 1595) in La Mancha, Vicar M Juan de Viana, was an inquisition notary reporter. As "reporter," the "all-purpose scribe and contract lawyer" was sent all over by the Crown to take testimony and make official what would otherwise be hearsay. It was as important for a town to have a notary as a priest, for until he wrote it down *nothing happened*, officially speaking. Even a conquistador off in the Americas about to enter into a battle had to proclaim his reasons for war and have a *bona fide* notary there to "duly record" it (See James M. O'toole: *Cortez's Notary*) One might say the notary had as much power to establish the truth for *this* world as the priest had with respect to the *next*. Who knows how all this ever got started, but ours was a society of *truth-swearing* and *litigation*, two things that seem to go together.

The existence or non-existence of the notary public himself might have made a contrast, for Japanese had no exact equivalent then, and still do not today. But, to proceed to Frois's contrast, the Japanese *sinal* (sign/mark/signature) would mean a personal seal, like what may be seen stamped on prints and paintings, but larger and more script-like, called a kaô or "flower-stamp/chop." Documents could be signed and stamped (just below the signature), or just stamped, but they were seldom just signed. Rodrigues wrote that the *Chinese* stamps sometimes even gave the rank of its owner in the royal household and that the seal was *everything* to a magistrate, for it was his "stamp of office," and nothing they did had validity without it. To lose it was to lose one's office, and "they are accustomed to having this seal carried in front of them in a chest slung from a pole borne by two men, and they cover it with a sunshade of yellow silk out of reverence for the king whom it represents." (R(C):TIJ) In Japan, it never went *that* far, but Rodrigues couldn't help mentioning it anyway, and neither can I!

10-12 With us, the mark of the notary public never changes;
Antre nós o sinal do tabalião publico nunca se muda;

In Japan, they change marks whenever they want to.
Em Japão se mudão estes sinais cada vez que hum quer.

Again, since there were no notary publics in Japan, it is hard to know exactly what and how many Japanese are "they." Anyone big enough to have a chop with clout, I guess. With us, I assume the same thing could be said for our signature. In general, it is assumed to remain the same for life. That was definitely not the case with Japanese chops, which were changed when they were promoted, as might be expected because they often changed their names at the same time. Because they generally had more than one seal at a time, they could use different combinations for different letters. Okada guessed that great men had an average of about twenty "official" chops (fancy kaô, literally *flower-stamp*) over the course of their lives.

10-13 With us, all paper is made from rags; *Antre nós todo papel se faz de pedaços de pano velhos.*
In Japan, all is made from tree bark. *Em Japão todo se faz de cascas de arvores.*

More trees, more types of paper? Frois's "trees" should include some shrubs, for hemp paper was well known. Alcock found this tree bark paper tougher than any in Europe: "Even the fine kinds can only be torn with difficulty, and the stronger qualities defy every effort. Indeed it supplies the place of linen and cambric . . . They are not unacquainted with the process of manufacturing paper from cotton rags – indeed, I believe they would make paper out of old shoes – but the former are little used, because the bark is preferred." (A:COT) He goes on to mention foreigners taking advantage of this by buying up Japanese rags, which soon rose in price, for export.

10-14 With our letters, we cannot fully express our ideas but through long explanations;
As nossas cartas não podem manifestar os conceytos senão por grande leitura;

Those of Japan are extremely short yet very comprehensive.
As de Japão são brevissimas e muito compendiozas.

Francois Caron (1600-73), of the Dutch East-India Company wrote that terse writing was common to Chineses, Japanners, Correes and Torquains[?]: "A man that can contract much matter into a few lines, and intelligible, which is that which they all practice, is greatly esteemed amongst them; for such they employ to write their Letters, Petitions and the like to great persons; and truly it is admirable to see how full of substance, and with how few words these sort of writing is penned. (C:TCJ) We would seem to be talking, then, about the telegraphic Chinese style of writing used by men. Women in Japan often used a style that was every bit as prolix as "ours."

10-15 With us, writing between the lines would be uncouth;
Antre nós escrever antre as regras seria mao insino;

In Japan, they always *waza-to* [on purpose][1] write between the lines.
Nas cartas de Japão vaza to se escreve sempre antre as regras.

While an unglossed manuscript was considered green in the Medieval West – some supposedly scribbled glosses on their own new manuscripts to make them seem respectable – these generally kept strictly to the margins. Not so in Japan. Okada mentions a number of types of recognized *gyôkan-gaki*, or "line-between-writing" in Japan. There is the *otte-gaki*, or "chasing-writing" something like our postscript.; the *kaeshi-gaki* or "return writing," where one person's letter is returned with the reply between the lines — the *nao-nao-gaki*, or "this-too-this-too-writing," which simply adds more detail, . . . And, I would add, last minute additions, for I have occasionally seen such squeezed between the lines of books printed in the 19c!

Had I not read Okada's notes, I might have mistaken this writing between the lines for the use of phonetic syllabary written small, next to Chinese characters to supply their pronunciation in the case of hard-to-read names, unique usage, or for the sake of poor readers, in which case they may be placed by all *kanji*. These wonderful little trainer-wheels, called *furigana*, a godsend for punsters because they permit one to play with Chinese characters, have reaped scornful comment from some in the East and the West. "I doubt there is any other language that cannot be understood unless you use two lines at once to write it out . . . I envision a procession of black bugs. Why do we have to allow those disgusting bugs to crawl around the sides of our sentences." (Yamamoto Yuzo, found in Inoue Hisashi's *Shiban Bunpô?*) "One hesitates for an epithet to describe a system of writing which is so complex that it needs the aid of another system to explain it." (Sansom in 1928, in Unger: *5th Generation Fallacy*)

1. **Translation**. Yet another *vaza to!* Maybe someone could count up the *vaza to* and *vaza vaza* in this book! Note how it is always applied to the Japanese, making it seem that their contrariness is deliberate.

~~~~~~

10-16 Our letters are folded; *As nossas cartas vão dobradas;*

        Japanese ones, rolled up. *As dos Japões emroladas.*

While Japanese are big on *origami*, or "fold-paper" art, letters were generally not folded. It is hard to say why rolls were preferred. The availability of strong yet cheap tubes in the form of bamboo? The feeling it was not good to crease letters, breaking up the beautiful writing? Or, could there have been bad-luck associations due to the verb fold being homophonic with cutting through or killing? Regardless, literature has examples of letters being folded up and stuffed into the bosom for carrying, so the difference was not absolute. When Japan began to modernize and send mail by the packet, Morse writes that the old style letter boxes big enough to fit a number of rolls were abandoned as too bulky and letters written on paper attached to a roll, "were torn off, [loosely] wound up again, flattened by smoothing with the hand, and slid into a long, narrow envelope." (M:JDD)

~~~~~~

[10-16a] We give the year in which we write a letter;
    Antre nós se põe a era em que se escreve;

        The Japanese only the day of the month when it is sent.
        Os Japões o dia somente da lua em que se manda.

Frois forgot to number this one that was evidently squeezed in. The "year" is my figurative translation of *era*, in the original. For the Jesuits, the year was an essential element of dating. Spread around the world, their letters took years – sometimes decades – to reach their destinations. In Japan, letters arrived within hours or at most days from the time they were mailed. So the day was sufficient. But, most European letters presumably did not need a month, much less year. Did Christians desiring to be perpetually reminded of their "Savior," *make a point of writing the year,* and having written it, added the month, so that full dating became habitual? Formal Japanese letters were, of course, dated.

10-17 The christian era never changes from the birth of Christ until the end of the world;
A era dos christãos nunca se altera do nacimento de Christo até o fim do mundo;

        Eras in Japan change six or 7 times in the lifetime of a king.
        A era de Japão se muda seis e 7 vezes na vida de hum rey

In Japan, the years went back to *Start,* Year One, whenever an Emperor died, secular rule changed, major policy changes were made, a major disaster occurred (i.e. for the sake of better luck!), etc.. The official right to change the era rested with the Emperor, but the power often rested elsewhere. If names could be changed at appropriate junctures in people's lives, why not *Time*, the years, months and days Bashô was soon to call "our fellow travelers," do likewise? Still, the changes were occasionally too frequent. In the six decades before the *Tratado* was written, new eras began in 1521, 28, 32, 55, 58, 70 and 73. And just before the Meiji Reformation (1868), in 1844, 48, 54, 60, 61, 64 and 65. This *is* ridiculous. In 1869, the *gengo* system was modified so that the era would only change with the inauguration of a new Emperor (which was a separate parallel system, the *dai*, anyway).

    I beg to disagree with the Occidentals who feel that maintaining this separate system is "useless" or even bad, for the connection with the Emperor. *I* prefer they keep it, if for nothing else to remind the world that Christianity is *not* "different from the others", and there is more than one way of marking time. With the short-run calendar, for example, "our" year 2005 is Heisei 17. The Japanese newspapers generally put both year dates on the top of each page. I guess the double dating is wasteful, *but so what?* The biggest difficulty, true inconvenience, concerns the long run – even most Japanese have to use Christian dating to keep track of when was when back then, for some sort of perpetual calendar is needed. Even, here, however, there are advantages to the Japanese system, for there are all sorts of eras within eras and varieties of eras and whatnot that make a sort of verbal Venn diagram of Japanese history which, I think, is useful for the more studious part of the population. Unfortunately, it is not ideal for world-history.

    Despite these constant return-to-start eras, Japanese were not completely cyclic in their long-term concept of time. This is obvious from a classic poem that hopes a lord's realm will last for ages while *pebbles grow into mossy boulders* (the growing pebbles may have originated from reference to coral). There was also a Japanese long-count going back to the ascension of the first Emperor using the ancient Chronicle. On New Year's Day of Meiji 26 (1893) young Shiki (proud of his samurai past and one of the last to cut his hair) wrote: "origin two-thousand five-hundred fifty three year's spring," which is supposed to be a haiku (*kigen ni-sen go-hyaku go-ju-san nen-no-haru*) and maybe is because he was the father of modern haiku. With a bit of poetic license we have:

        nippon banzai!

        upspring the year!
        two-thousand five-hundred fifty
        three years here!

    So long as most of the world uses Christian dating, the Japanese do well to use it, too. But this is no reason to give up their *gengo* system. In culture-ecology, too, diversity has value of its own. At the very least, we from cultures that have long used the Christian era, should not take for granted the accident called history that has made "ours" the *de facto* World Calendar. We should feel *regret* for the cultural sacrifice we force others to make and apologize for it sometimes. Others are conscious of our unintended cultural aggression. When, in 1634, the Dutch (who disclaimed religious affiliation the better to press their trade) were ordered out of Hirado to join the Portuguese on Dejima, a tiny fan-shaped island just off Nagasaki, built artificially only seven years earlier, it was the Christian era that provided the pretext for the crackdown. The authorities noticed that "you write the date of Christ's birth over the doors and on the tops of your houses, in the sight of everyone in our land" and ordered them to "demolish forthwith all your dwellings which bear the above-mentioned date (without exceptions)" (in intro to C:MKJS)

I only wish Japanese *also* kept their lunar calendar I feel more comfortable reading letters or diary entries written hundreds of years ago when I know whether they were written under a new moon or a full one than more recent ones where such information is lacking. This calendar was superb, for it kept account of the solar cycle as well as the moon. To my mind, a pure lunar calendar is bad, for it fails to keep account of the reality of the seasonal year (reflecting a culture that fails to appreciate the ecology of the natural world), whereas a purely solar calendar is bad for ignoring the moon (reflecting a culture that fails to appreciate the emotional side of life). We *need* a mixed calendar.

10-18 Our letters are sent sealed with wax or lacquer;
As nossas cartas vão mutradas com sera ou com lachre;

Those of Japan have a little ink put on the flap.
Nas de Japão se põe huma pequena de tinta sobre a cha[ncela?]

Another way to have translated *sera* and *lachre* would have been "bee's wax and sealing wax." The latter, by Frois's time, may have been "a mixture of shellac, rosin and turpentine, prepared for the purpose of receiving the impression of seals." (OED)

Japanese actually had more ways of sealing letters than Europeans did. Okada mentions "glue-sealing, twist-sealing, knot-sealing, cut-sealing, fold-sealing and so forth". But they did not drop and stamp warm sealing wax. The symbolic closure Frois refers to was achieved by making an ink mark: either an initial, a diagonal line or a diagonal line with a small line crossing it to make a sign resembling the syllabet *me* (✗), which stood for "*shime*" or "closed=tight=done," in such a manner that half is on the flap and half on the envelope. Today, it is common to stamp or initial documents in the same way, with the mark crossing the divide to make what is, to use printing terms, a registration mark. You will find a large version of the *shime* here and there in this book, for I like it.

Let me add a contemporary difference in what computer software allows in English and Japanese.

We type words into our computers and learn if they are spelled right or wrong.
They type words into their computer and are offered many choices none of which are right or wrong.

The *enormous choice* necessary because of the Chinese characters also allows for other symbols. For example, in Japanese it is as easy as pie to type in "pai" and chose to make it Π. Or to type in "manji," the character for a Buddhist temple, and chose: 卍 (Can we could learn the difference in direction and *keep the good swastika*, as the Japanese have? Or do we lack the brains to make the distinction?), or — > and chose → or ⇒ or, better yet, "ue" meaning "above" lets us choose ↑ and "shita" or "below" yields ↓ both of which are very useful for computer discussion boards (bbs's), and "mugen" for unlimited yields us ∞. (If we were but conscious of such possibilities, we could easily do this in English by expanding the *spell-check* function to include more choices for certain words. One can also get to a larger cache of symbols by typing in the Japanese for "symbol", rather than relying on the "Insert" tab alone. My favorite is the Russian "da" (д): it makes a fine nose for little beasties.)

10-19   Our letters are sent done up in packets;
  As nossas se mandão feitas em maços;

   Theirs are sent in oblong lacquered boxes made for that purpose.
   As suas metidas em humas caxinhas compridas vruxadas feitas pera aquilo.

This is not a description of individual letter coverings but of the way *batches* of letters were transported by the couriers. Letters in Japan were put into special waterproof containers called *fubako* or *fuminohako* (letter-boxes) rather than simply bundled together.

10-20   In Europe, paper is beaten flat with an iron mallet upon a smooth stone;
   Em Europa batem o papel em plaino com maço de ferro sobre pedra liza;

   In Japan, they roll it up on a pole and beat it with two more.
   Em Japão o emrolão em um pão redondo e ali o batem com outros dous paus

   Is a method which involves rolling more sophisticated than mere beating?   What is the diameter of the *pau redondo* or "round/cylindrical stick" on the Japanese side? I wish I knew more.

10-21   We wipe ink off our pens upon black clothing;
   Nós alimpamos as penas da tinta nos vestidos pretos;

   Japanese suck them clean with their mouths.
   Os Japões as alimpão chupando-as com a boca.

   Here, I first followed Okada, having "us" use a black *cloth* to wipe off the pens, but after seeing Father Schütte's translation had a rare parenthetical exclamation mark – the only one I have found, so far – added to his translation, thought *"Oops!"* and, re-reading carefully, saw what was happening! The "black-robes," as Jesuits were sometimes called, had found a good use for their vestment. Someone who wrote as much as Frois probably never had to re-dye his robes!

   The Japanese side seems just as funny.   Japanese (and Chinese) did and still do put their pens in their mouths. The most common pen-in-the-mouth poems treat the hardship of being a scholar, which is to say, having to chew your icy frozen pen (which says a lot about the temperature of your humble hut) before starting work. Less common in poetry, but more common in reality is this gentle practice as described by poet Tachibana Akemi (1812-68) in his *Poems of Solitary Delights*: "What a delight it is / When I find a good brush, / Steep it hard in water, /Lick it on my tongue / And give it its first try." (trans. Geoffrey Bownas & Anthony Thwaite: *The Penguin Book of Japanese Verse* (pardon my de-parsing!)) The tip of a new brush is rock-hard, for the hair is given a permanent to hold and show its shape (the bristles come to a perfect point) and must be soaked into softness. Speaking of *steeping,* the process of breaking in a brush, like the English one of making tea, is delicate and full of details that only matter if you do it. Any post-use sucking that is done is done *after* the ink has pretty well been cleaned off by brushing it dry, and is more to smooth out the hairs and leave the brush with a sharp point again. Little, if any ink is imbibed and it may have more to do with perfection of form than cleaning *per se.*

1. Jesuits Writing. One could probably fill a book with anecdotes about *writing Jesuits,* for they *wrote* and *wrote* and *wrote.* an anecdote about St. Robert Bellarmine:

> "Bellarmine wrote with a quill; he used to cheat with that quill, in a way I would not really recommend to any of us. St. Ignatius of Loyola made a wise rule that Jesuits should not work more than two hours straight without taking a little break—get up and stretch, get a cup of coffee, whatever. Bellarmine kept that rule, but in his own way. Every two hours he would flip the pen up and catch it, then keep on writing." (John Patrick Donnelly, S.J. *St. Robert Bellarmine Who Was He? What Can He Teach Us?* www1.bellarmine.edu/strobert/about/lecture.asp)

10-22 We write our letters on desks or tables;
Nós escrevemos nossas cartas sobre mezas ou taboas;

> The Japanese write them on the fingers of the left hand.
> *Os Japões as escrevem sobre os dedos da mão esquerda.*

Japanese have very good little desks (see 10-28) and used them to write on notebooks, but letter writers generally held a scroll of paper in their left hand, a brush in their right, and wrote on the convex side of the paper one line at a time with the roll providing the backing. Even with the roll between, the left hand is involved in the writing process. Perhaps writing on paper held by hand releases a certain sensibility not found when we write upon a desk, or the floor, where formal Japanese calligraphy is also done. There, too, we find an important contrast Frois missed:

We rest the butt of our hand upon the paper while we write.
They suspend their hand in the air, writing without support.

The brush is lightly gripped and dangles down like a pendulum. As Bacon pointed out,

> To write, with a brush dipped in India ink, upon soft paper, the hand entirely without support, is an art that seldom can be acquired by a grown person, but when learned in childhood it gives great deftness in whatever other art may be subsequently studied. This is perhaps the reason why Japanese value a good handwriting more highly than any other accomplishment, for it denotes the manual dexterity that is the secret to success in all the arts, and one who writes the Chinese characters well and rapidly can quickly learn to do anything else with the fingers. (B:JGW?)

I would guess that this skill is like a second language or fiddle-playing, where the top levels of skill require that we start by seven or eight, ten at the latest. If you have a child . . .

10-23 `We seal [a mistake for "open" ?] our letters with scissors;
Nós fechamos [abrimos?] nossas cartas com tezouras;

> They [un?]seal theirs with knives.
> *Elles as fechão [abrem?]com facas*

The original has a mistake. Instead of "open," Frois writes "seal." The knife is a small one with a very sharp tip generally called a *sasuga* (literally "stab-sword"), and they served as what we now call a letter-opener – kept in the writing-box with the inkstone ink-stick, water vessel, etc.. This is similar to 2-68, where the same contrast is made for cutting *thread*. If Japanese now use a scissors for cutting thread, we use a knife-like letter-opener. As far as the third scissors and knife contrast, 7-15, goes, the contrast is moot, for both of us now prefer nail-clippers to scissors *or* knives. Three similar differences and three different outcomes. But, why so many scissors/knife contrasts?

10-24 We scatter sand on our paper; *Nós deitamos area em nosso papel;*

> Their ink is instantly absorbed [by the paper]. *No seu logo se a tinta sume.*

Here, the Japanese way sounds familiar; and it is what "we" did that is foreign to most of us!

10-25 Our letters are very small; *A nossa letra hé muito peqenina;*

> Theirs are larger than our capital letters. *A sua hé mayor que a nossa de cabidula.*

This was not so much due to our respective letters, as to the different writing devices. Now that brushes are only used for signing art gallery registers and writing old-style New Year's greetings, Japanese script is written by ball-point or printed the same size as ours, despite – in the case of characters – holding ten times the visual information!

After writing my first draft of the last paragraph, I saw something that made this contrast *far* more meaningful to me: one of only two extant copies of Valignano's 1601 *Libro* (V:LIBRO) in the British Library. I knew quills wrote well enough for, like everyone else, I had seen pictures of old documents with calligraphy that put my messy writing to shame; but I had never seen anything to prepare me for what I saw that day. *The writing was so small I could barely read it!* The capital letters were smaller than *my* handwritten small letters! Imagine, if you will, a *manuscript* with lettering the size of the print on one of those tiny pocket-books one no longer sees. *The lines were often thinner than that of the finest ballpoint!*

I can understand how Japanese do *their* bold brushwork. But I can not begin to see how *we* did *this!* The human cost must have been tremendous. Presumably, paper, transportation and ink were more important than the eyes and hands of Valignano's scribes. No wonder Frois, who spent most of his life serving as a scribe for his superiors as well as writing a multi-volume history and perhaps the most ample letters ever written, had painful arthritis by the time he was fifty! His hands must have been horribly deformed by the time he died and God knows what condition his eyes (for which he burned *moxa*) were in!

10-26 A stanza of our poems comprises 4, 6 or 8 lines;
A sentensa das nossas trovas se inclue em 4, 6 ou 8 regras;

All the songs of Japan comprise two lines, unrhymed.
Todas as cantigas do Japão se incluem em dous versos somente sem consonantia.

The name for Japanese classical verse, *waka*, literally breaks down into "peace=japanese + song" and poets were said to "sing" poetry, rather than to "make" or "write" it. Frois's use of *cantigas* for Japanese poems apparently reflects knowledge of this. While Japanese poetry, unlike Chinese poetry, did not use *obvious* end-rhyme, it is going too far to say, as Frois does, that there was no *consonancia* ("unrhymed" being a loose translation). There is ample alliteration and not a little internal rhyme, largely "vowel-rhyme." Eg., my favorite *Shin-Kokinshû* (c.1205) blast against the Wind, admittedly more rhymeful than most, includes an ABAB rhyme-scheme: *hana chirasu ka<u>ze no</u> yadori wa dare **ga shiru** / ware ni oshi<u>eyo</u> yukite **uramimu**.* And there is the *ware/dare/kaze* in it too. (My Learical translation: Pray, tell me / where to find / the dwelling place / of master wind! / i'll give him / a piece of my mind / i will / that spoiler of flowers / the wind!)

Many old Japanese songs were longer than two lines, but the 5-7-5 / 7-7 (or 17 / 14, because the rhythm of each line varied) syllabet arrangement was typical.

10-27 We read very rapidly; *Ho nosso ler hé muito depresa;*

They do so **pausing, and in jumps.** *O seu pauzado e em saltinhos.*

Despite the fact that the pronunciation of many characters depends upon context that is sometimes not grasped until the word is passed, most Japanese can read as quickly as we do, *when they read silently.* Because there are more cases in Japanese than English where thought must be given to pronunciation, reading aloud does take a bit more work. So, I would prefer *this* contrast:

We find it is easier to read aloud and often move our lips when reading in silence;
They are completely at home reading silently but struggle to read aloud.

In English, and perhaps all European tongues, we find the poor reader has great difficulty keeping his or her mouth closed. In Japan, I have not noted this. However, there are so many possible pronunciations for some words that reading correctly aloud requires knowledge and thought.

Frois may be thinking about how Japanese read the pseudo-Chinese writing called *kanbun*. This is indeed one of the strangest and cleverest (or, *most idiotic*, depending upon your mood!) ways to read that has ever been invented, for the Japanese mark the edges of the lines, written entirely in Chinese characters, with a number of signs which indicate how to *change the previous word-order, i.e.,* grammaticize the original *as one reads*. They are, then, translating, or rather *doing simultaneous interpretation* of a sort called *kaeri-yomi,* or "return-read." This does indeed require pauses to figure out *what was what* interspersed with jumps, especially when/if vocalizing. Not only was the word order changed but the reader had to supply the part of Japanese the telegraphic Chinese does not make explicit! This *kanbun* is of intellectual interest because it shows how well/poorly Chinese characters *by themselves* allow communication between exotic tongues.

~~~~~~

10-28 We write sitting in chairs at high tables;
Nos escrevemos em mezas altas, asentados em cadeiras;

They, do it on low stands, seated on the floor or on *tatami* [mats].
Elles em banqinhos baxos asentados no chão ou sobre os tatamis.

English lacks a word for a small table. Nothing for the Portuguese *banqinho* seemed right. The item in mind is the traditional Japanese desk, a tiny table with folding legs and, sometimes, an adjustable angle writing surface, one of the few examples of furniture in Japan. Today, such desks are rarely seen, for Japanese use Western-style desks. Indeed, I would bet that since the latter half of the 20c, Japan could boast more desks per capita than any nation in the world. Even where their children do not have their own bedroom, they *always* have their own desk.

~~~~~~

10-29 In Europe, books are bound by sewing together the paper at the edge;
Em Europa emquadernão os livros cozendo o papel polas bordas;

In Japan, they are sewn at some points and the folds left as they are.
Em Japão cozen-nos polas pontas e as dobras ficão soltas.

In the West, the spine is tightly bound and even glued, as we all know. I doubt that any reader who has not seen a Japanese book could guess how they are bound by Frois's description! Imagine a long, long strip of paper folded back and forth on itself like an accordion. Then imagine it sewn on one side only. Not right at the edge but, loosely, a half an inch or so from the edge where the spine would be if there were a spine, which there never was. The other side is just left as is. Since the leaves are not cut with these books, one can remove the thread and pull the entire book out into one long piece of paper written on one side only! Here, it is hard to say whether Frois refers to the folds of the leaves on the side of the book opposite to where the spine would be or those on the sewn side, for both are "left as is."

endnote X

Writing   書

This chapter is very unsatisfying for the word-lover because Frois really restricts himself to *the writing system* and fails to introduce any of the topsy-turvy grammar which Percival Lowell suggests in *The Soul of The East* in 1888.

> He [the Occidental] discovers that this people talk, so to speak, backwards; that before he can hope to comprehend them, or make himself understood in return, he must learn to present his thoughts arranged in inverse order from the one in which they naturally suggest themselves to his mind. His sentences must all be turned inside out. He finds himself lost in a labyrinth of language. The same seems to be true of the thoughts it embodies. (L:SOE)

The Romance languages, especially Spanish and Portuguese are more flexible about the order of the major parts of speech than English, so the word-order reversal (the Japanese object *before* the verb) is less clear-cut and Frois can be forgiven for skipping it, but he might at least have noted the opposite order of our *smaller parts* of speech (pre/post-positions and particles):

> Our "the," "a," "on," "with," "by," "to" etc. all come before the words they indicate;
> Theirs never do because they all come after them.

After all, the use of *pre*positions rather than *post*positions holds equally for Germanic and Romance languages. As for the oft-remarked, seldom-used personal pronouns in Japanese, it so happens the Latin tongues, unlike English, can do without them (partly because it is apparent from the conjugation, and partly because these languages, like Japanese, tend to have polysyllabic words and thus are long where human breath is of the same length everywhere). So Frois did not find a difference there, while an Englishman surely would have. But Frois might *at least* have mentioned this:

> We have but one word to indicate ourselves with and two to indicate the other person.
> They have a dozen ways to say "I" and almost as many to say "you."

Frois did catch some important language-related differences and put them into the miscellany in the last chapter of the *Tratado*. There is one on the different manner of using *honorifics* (14-20), one about a different attitude toward *clarity* and *obscurity* (14-36), a the respective *body-language* between unequal parties (14-45) and the *posture for delivering messages* (14-44). Excuse me for jumping the gun, but had Frois put the second item mentioned into *writing* terms, it might have come out like this:

> We admire neatly written letters and our calligraphy with its ornament is very precise;
> They admire writing that is so messy that not one in a hundred who read can read it!

Japanese calligraphy, even more so than Chinese, can be so impressionistic as to verge on the abstract. At the same time, they generally follow various abbreviated script patterns (and which can be made out by very studious people. But when it comes to writing meant to be hung up as art (as *kakemono*), very few people have any idea what it says. This is a constant cause of embarrassment for interpreters who are asked *"What does that say?"* by foreigners visiting Japan. Speaking of question marks, Frois forgot this, too:

> *We have interrogatory marks, exclamation marks and quotation marks;*
> *They have none of these..*

The Japanese generally ask questions by affixing the interrogatory *particle* "ka" (か) to the end of the sentence. So, there is usually no need to use a question mark. A *yo* (よ)or *zo* (ぞ)or *ze* (ぜ), etc. suffix expresses our "!" phonetically. Still, questions and exclamations can be made without such particles and so today, our marks are *also* used, and more freely than we use them, for Japanese do not hesitate to line up multiple exclamation marks for greater emphasis!! Some conjunction-like particles at the tail of a statement replace quotation marks (though some indication of voice is occasionally given) and our boring "he said" "she said" crap. This makes Japanese superb for novels.

> *We have capital letters which we always use at the beginning of sentences and for proper names;*
> *They have no capital letters, but sometimes bracket names.*

How could Frois have missed this one? While I can see how our capital letters help indicate the start of a new sentence, I do like the idea of the equality of letters, as found in Japanese, because it doesn't allow one to capitalize ones own *God* while not so honoring the *gods* of others. With no capital letters, Japanese has no small ones, too. Still, Japanese do write letters small sometimes in order to create some of their limited number of (slightly) complex phonemes such as "myo = みょ" or "kyo = きょ" where a tiny "yo = ょ" syllabet is put next to larger *mi* = み or "*ki* = き" syllabets.

> *In Europe, old books are not written in the common tongue but in Latin, Greek or Arabic.*
> *In Japan, people can read books written hundreds of years before, without a translation.*

I do not have a very good grasp of the written culture at the time Frois was in Japan. It was evidently widespread but, following centuries of warring, it is hard to imagine it could have been prospering. Yet, I know that heavily illustrated stories (*kanazôshi*) thrived and, if nothing else, the demand for news – keeping up with all that change – may have placed a premium on literacy. Anyway, with peace, letters of all types flourished and a couple hundred years later, Edo boasted *walking libraries* (*kashihonya*) going door-to-door with as many books as a man can carry (specially selected with an eye for that day's customers) and door-to-door joke-sellers (*kangaemono*) who left written jokes (mostly riddles) in the entrance and returned later to accept payment *if you liked them*. That tells us something. Golownin says the guards kept them awake until they got used to their reading aloud in sing-song voices all night (What were they reading? Anyone?) and he describes something still true, the way everyone – including his guards – spent *days* writing letters for New Year's greetings. He did not say that being a diligent writer was the secret of being a popular prostitute at the Yoshiwara, that not a few prostitutes were poets . . . (But, then, it is amazing how much Golownin, in captivity, managed to find out! I have no right to complain about what he *didn't* write!) The long and the short of it is that when Japan was "opened" in the mid-19c, it was probably the most literate country in the world. Tested literacy was not the basis for achieving posts in the government as in China but, largely owing to the efforts of the Buddhist clergy, the level of *popular* literacy was higher. It seems to me that something we might call *the joy of letters* permeated the society. *Before the modern T-shirt, where but Japan was there clothing with poems written on it?* (Kimono with poems or part of poems on them were popular in the Edo era). The much maligned Japanese system of writing has, I believe, been a source of more *satisfaction* than any other writing system I know of.

> *In Europe, we can read aloud whatever is written down;*
> *In Japan, much that is written down can not be read aloud.*

To me, this is the most important difference between "our" writing system and "theirs." *Ours is, at heart, an adjunct of the spoken language.* It may tend to use fancier words – don't you *hate* to read essays by university students stuffed with so much polysyllabic Latin the sentences require a plunger to flush! – but, at heart, it is one and the same thing. In Japan, we who write are asked to give talks (on anything under the sun), but we are seldom asked to "give a reading" of our books because far more is lost than would be gained (by intonation).   I think Chamberlain had it right:

> The influence of writing on speech – never entirely absent in any country possessing letters – is particularly strong under the Chinese system. We mean that the writing here does not merely serve to transcribe words: – it actually originates new ones, the slave in fact becoming the master.

Chamberlain was there just in time to see the Japanese translators taking full advantage of the Chinese characters to coin words by the hundred to "designate objects, ideas, appliances, and institutions recently borrowed from Europe." He noted that

> Some of these new compounds pass from books into common speech; but many remain exclusively attached to the written language, or are at least intelligible only by reference to the latter, while at the same time they endow it with a clearness and above all a terseness to which the colloquial can never attain. (C:TJ)

To my mind, the best part of all has nothing to do with *practicality*. It has to do with *pleasure*. By having simultaneous use of Chinese characters and a phonetic letters, one can pun to one's heart's content.. It is not just having both, but an attitude, for even when the Chinese characters served in the capacity of phonetic letters, Japanese scribes played around.   The first poem in Japan's oldest anthology of poetry, the *Manyôshû*, which is about an Emperor approaching a young woman, starts with lines about her *having a pretty scoop and basket*, which I think means "you have the female=basket and scoop=male pair, but how about yourself, my girl?" ("Scoop" has the etymological feeling of being a *digging-skewer,* so it is more male in Japanese than in English.). Here is how the words (*mi-bukushi mochi*) meaning "pretty scoop carrying," as pronounced, are written and their literal meaning:

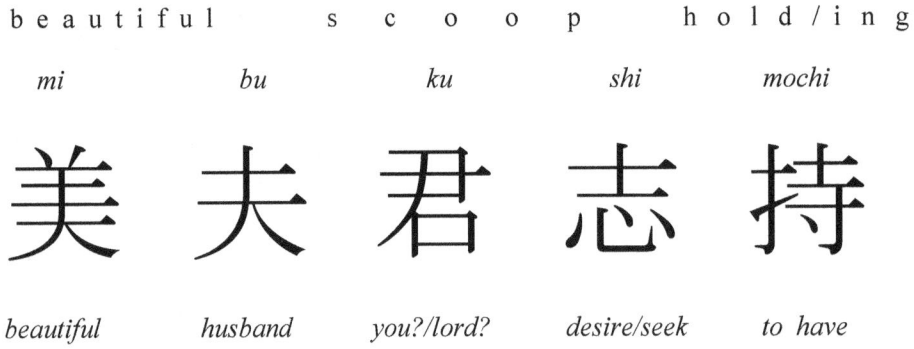

In old Japanese (or Chinese) "beautiful" could modify either sex, so I did not change it to "handsome," but I think you can get the idea: the amanuensis (or *transcriber –* I do not know) has scooped *the intent of the poem* while phonetically rendering it. Other Chinese characters could have been used to record the sound, but someone *chose* to have fun.   This is an exceptional example, but the principle is true for much Japanese writing: you get far more using your eyes than you can with your ears alone. As the Japanese linguist Suzuki Takao puts it – *Occidental language is radio, Japanese is television.*

XI

OF HOUSES, BUILDINGS, GARDENS AND FRUITS
das cazas, fabricas, jardins e frutas

11-1   Our houses are tall and of many stories;
As nossas cazas são altas e de muitos sobrados;

   Those of Japan, for the most part, low and single-story.
As de Japão polla mayor parte baxas e terreas.

This is true. But, why? *Earthquakes*? South Europe is also on faulty ground. *Cosmology*? Some say Japanese are earth-bound souls and see no need to reach for the sky as we, with our Heaven-dwelling God, do, i.e., *We are vertically oriented; They horizontal.* But this is too simple. "High" is as metaphorically lofty in Japanese as it is in English: our churches may stick up, but theirs are generally higher because they are placed on mountain sides. I believe something less dramatic, *climate*, is largely responsible for the difference. Sultry summers want an open house. As Chamberlain noted, "the side of the house, composed at night of wooden sliding doors called *amado*, is stowed away in boxes during the day-time. In the summer, everything is thus open to the outside air. ("Architecture" in C:TJ) In a word, it had "no *continuous* [corner to corner] *walls.*" And, there was no internal wall to speak of, either. Even when a room had one, in Kaempfer's words, "the least kick would break it to pieces." (K(S):HOJ) This meant there would be little support available for a second floor. Moreover, tall buildings would block the little sunlight available during the monsoon for drying the tatami and *futon*. Even with the floor-frames raised a foot or so over the ground for the sake of ventilation, mildew and fleas (11, below) were an ever present threat. In order to block the rain yet leave ventilation, the eaves must be large, so little sunlight can get in from overhead. The potted plants, that most Japanese kept and still keep *outside* rather than inside like our *house*plants, and the inner-gardens of the wealthy would all suffer from multi-story dwellings. For these reasons, Japan, despite being one of the world's most notorious construction states, has pioneered something called "sunshine laws" to ensure new development does not take away that vital drying power called sunlight.
..

11-2   Our [houses are made] of stone and lime; *As nossas de pedra e cal;*

   Theirs of wood, bamboo, straw and mud. *As suas de paos, canas, palha e terra.*

Not long ago, "lime" (*cal*) meant plaster – a mixture of lime and sand, so I retained the old usage in translation. This contrast is, obviously, far from absolute. Wood was not uncommon in Northern Europe. The large stav churches not only are wooden but, with the raised corners on the roofs look very oriental! Moreover, lime, albeit in a different manner, was occasionally used in Japan. Almeida, writing in 1565 of the short-lived castle of Tamon in Nara, described "whiter and smoother walls than ever I saw in Christendom. For they mix no sand with the lime, but only knead it with a special kind of white paper which they make for this purpose. . . To enter in this town (for so I may call it) and to walk about its streets seems to be like entering Paradise. (in B:CCJ)

Be that as it may, wood was indeed *the* main material for Japanese building. From the 16-20c, Japanese architecture *as a whole* was often put down for lacking grandeur (no tall buildings) and being imitative (Chinese). But the fine quality was obvious from the start. "Indeed," writes Rodrigues, "in the view of responsible people, who have seen various parts of Europe, Japanese construction in wood does not appear to be surpassed or even equaled elsewhere."(R(C):TIJ) Almeida, in the same letter quoted above was overcome by the high quality: "It does not appear to be the work of human hands. For not only are they constructed of cedarwood, whose delicious odor delights the senses of all that enter, but all the verandahs are built of single beams about seven feet long. . . . The ceiling of these buildings looks like a single piece of wood, since no join is visible even if you look very closely. I cannot write of the other decorations for words fail me." (B:CCJ) Frois, likewise, found Nobunaga's Azuchi Castle, which "looks as if it were built of strong stone and mortar" but was actually "constructed entirely of wood" to be "in a word . . . beautiful, excellent and brilliant," and (partly because of being on a hill) "looks as if it reaches to the clouds." (C:TCJ) To come back down to earth – or, rather, the *bamboo, straw* and *mud* part of the contrast – Rodrigues: "It [the wood] provided the pillars and beams, while grates of bamboo provided the ribs for clay-like mud strengthened with straw to stick on and make what walls there were." He even cited the Old Testament in support of adding that straw (R(C):TIJ). Actually, Japanese *did* have some very good stone walls independent of houses, both the natural type made by farmers and some monumental works dating back to ancient times, but bricks were virtually unknown and should have been in the contrast. They did not make it to Japan until modern times. A 19c Japanese visitor to England described buildings with "exteriors . . . made up of cornered blocks like pillows piled on top of each other." (LR)

> *In Europe, we think of a house as something permanent, rooted in place like a tree;*
> *In Japan, they think nothing of moving them around and some have moved more than once.*

That *Faux Frois* is based on Rodrigues, who noted that *mobility* was a benefit conferred by wood because it was light. Even, "populous towns" could be moved entire! (R(C):TIJ) Douglas Sladen, centuries later, quipped "the thing which surprised me most was that he did not build it a little smaller, and carry it to work with him like an umbrella." (S:MQTJ)

11-3 Ours have foundations buried under the ground;
As nossas tem alicesses fundos debaxo da terra;

> Those of Japan have a stone under each *hashira* [pillar], and they [the stones] are above the ground. *As de Japão huma só pedra debaxo de cada* faxira *e estas em riba da terra.*

To us, a pillar is round, not square. Perhaps that is why Frois chose to use the Japanese word. The *hashira* are large square beams standing at each corner and both ends of the center of the roof. All but the smallest houses also had a central *hashira* which usually retained at least part of its natural features – some were (and still are) completely natural – reassuringly powerful piece of unpainted, polished natural wood that can be seen and felt inside the house. The butt of each *hashira* resting on its stone – the bottom half of which is slightly under-ground – is visible from the outside. Usually cedar, it neither rots nor attracts termites; and, there is something metaphysically cheering about knowing *exactly what you stand upon*. Moreover, the building is more stable for *not* being attached to the ground. Describing a "*daimio's* house," Douglas Sladen justifies the seeming paradox:

> It had no foundations, but stood on a stone platform, with a sort of ball-bearings, like a bicycle. Even lofty pagodas will stand earthquakes if they are treated like this. You can see how the principle acts if you watch a woman with a cup of boiling tea in an express train. She lets the cup follow the swaying of the carriage, and the Japanese style of building lets the house follow the swaying of the earthquake. It must be very unpleasant to be in one during a good earthquake. (S:MQT)

The *hashira* that rest on these stones – or, in the case of large structures, a large stone platform – are the very soul of the house. After they are set up, a ceremony is held. Cocks, on 12-28-1615 described how "they brought in all the pr'sentes sent and sett them in ranke before the middell post of the howse, & out of eache one took somthing of the best & offred it at the foote of the post, & powred wyne vpon eache severall p'rcell, . . ." Frois missed something here:

> We build our houses from the ground up, finishing with the roof;
> The Japanese build houses from the top down, starting with the roof.

That is to say, the roof was raised over the *hashira* before the rest of the interior was made – as Chinese did it – a smart move when one considers the rain.

11-4 Our doors, for the most part, move upon stiles;
As nossas portas pola mayor parte andão sobre couceiras;

Those of Japan, almost always run upon *shikii* [sill/s].
As de Japão quasi todas são corrediças sobre xiqis.

Frois could have explained "our" doors better by writing that they "rotate" or "swing" (rather than simply *andam* = move/go) *around* the stile or door-post – or more simply, "with hinges" – as opposed to the way Japanese doors "run" or, better yet, "slide" upon sills." Be that as it may, there is no question that the sliding door saves space and contributes toward temperature control because it does not push in or pull out air. That is why it, and not the rotating door is favored for modern buildings.

Our doors and windows usually move in different ways from one another.
Japanese doors and windows almost always slide on their sills in the same way

Japanese windows, whether door-size or, more rarely, small, slide upon horizontal sills, just like their doors. I do not know how many of ours were hinged and how many slid in Frois's time, but either way, they were not like doors (Our veranda openings are a special case, both window and door).

11-5 Our partitions are stone, lime or brick; *Os nossos repartimentos são de pedra e cal ou tijolo;*

Those of Japan are paper doors. *Os de Japão de portas de papel.*

Japanese houses generally have no internal walls. The house is divided by lightly framed, sliding doors of paper. In English and Portuguese, the items described in 11-4 and 11-5 are both "doors." Japanese actually use different terms. The outside front-door is called a *to*, the translucent paper inner-door and veranda doors are called *shōji* and the generally opaque and lightly ornamented room-partitions *fusuma*. The *fusuma* are grooved above as well as below in such a manner that they can easily be lifted up from the tracks and turn two, three or four rooms into one without a single partition. Here is Alice Mabel Bacon in 1891 on the significance of paper doors/walls:

> No thick walls and long passageways separate the nursery from the grown people's apartments, but the thin paper partitions make it possible for the mother to know always what her children are doing, whether they are good and gentle with their nurses, or irritable and passionate. (B:JGW)

Since these partitions are often kept open, on a summer day one can see right through a traditional Japanese house – indeed a syphilitic nose was called a *natsu-yashiki,* or "summer mansion," for that reason! Kaempfer, in the 17c, recognized smart design when he saw it and claimed that it was "very healthful to live in these houses" where "a free passage is left for the air to strike through the whole house." (K:HOJ) Chamberlain, with his "draughts insidiously pouring in through innumerable chinks and crannies" might beg to differ, but a house opened up in this way is not only healthy but beautiful, for it gives one the spacey feeling of a temple, or the woods cleared of yucky underbrush. Even a small house can feel roomier than a large one partitioned into individual rooms. Of course, there is a downside to this: *a lack of privacy*. But, as Morse writes, we forget that "privacy is only necessary in the midst of vulgar and impertinent people, – a class of which Japan has the minimum, and the so-called civilized races – the English and American particularly – have the maximum." (M:JH&S)   Point well taken, but even in Japan, people snore; babies, occasionally, cry. Young children play loudly. Some of us do want *quiet* now and then. I wonder what Morse would think of the modern Japanese office, where this open tradition means dozens of people per room, desk to desk, not even a partial cubicle between them, bombarded with loud telephone beeps, conversations and even shouts.

Assuming we could get used to the loss of privacy, would Japanese houses work in the West? Morse had to conclude it was "obviously absurd to suggest" such a structure "as a model for our own houses." *Why?* Because

> its fragile and delicate fittings if adopted by us, would be reduced to a mass of kindlings in a week, by the rude knocks it would receive; and as for exposing on our public thoroughfares the delicate labyrinth of carvings often seen on panel and post in Japan, the widespread vandalism of our country would render futile all such attempts to civilize and refine. (Ibid)

Over a hundred years later, nothing has changed. What is it that makes "us" so rough we must treat ourselves like children?

11-6   Our roofs are tile;
Os nossos telhados são de telha.

> Those of Japan for the most part of wood, straw and bamboo.
> *Os de Japão pola mayor parte de taboas, palha ou canas.*

The straw roofs on Japanese farm-houses resemble those of England. They seem an extension of the landscape, sometimes a veritable garden. Morse described ridge-poles of many of the roofs in the north of Japan covered with red lilies, and around Tokyo, blue iris. (M:JDD2) This was no primitive thatching. Many types of grasses and reeds used.   Light and dark colored straws were often alternatively laid so that the cleanly cut eaves (up to 3 feet thick!) were decorative. As Morse noted, they offered *superb* insulation and came in a great variety – especially the central ridge design – of regional styles, far more interesting than the "stiff, straight" and monotonous "ridge-pole and eaves" where *if you have seen one you have seen them all*, in the United States. Compare Morse, with his open mind, to Loti, who was too Occi-centric to see the individuality in Japan and claimed that "one gets bored with the endless monotony of the little Japanese streets, with the thousands of identical little grey houses, all of them wide open as though to show off their identical interiors, the same little white mats, the same little smoke-boxes, the same little ancestral shrines." (in L:IOJ)

Straw or not (the houses of the nobles in Japan generally had tile roofs – Frois conveniently forgot that to heighten his contrast.), Japanese roofs were *very* heavy. *Why?* Sladen thought it was because "if the roof were light the commonest typhoon would play kites with it." But, "What, then of earthquakes?" he asked his Man Sunday. "He answered, with the wisdom of the wise, that in earthquakes the roof does not kill the people in the house, but the people in the street." Kaempfer came closer to the truth in 1692, when he wrote that heavy roofs were good for earthquakes, "because they observe, that in the case of violent shock, the pressure of the upper part of the house upon the lower, which is built much lighter, keeps the whole from being overthrown." (K(S): HOJ) His *reason* right, but not the *principle*. Only Morse got that down pat – or, at least it sounds right to me: "the inertia of the roof is such that it does not move, while the building itself may be swaying. In balancing a cane on the finger some difficulty is experienced. If a heavy book could be fastened to the top of the cane, it would be much easier to balance it, and the hand could be moved rapidly back and forth a few inches without the book moving at all. (M:JDD) Combined with the loose foundations (11-3), we now have the whole earthquake strategy. Basically, Japanese houses are top-heavy, while ours are bottom-heavy, just the opposite from what might *seem* the case from Frois's contrast of tiles and straw!

11-7 Our rooms are of wood, well finished and polished;
As nossas camaras de madeira mui lavrada e polida;

> Theirs for *chanoyu* [the tea ceremony] of wood just like it came from the woods, in order to imitate nature. *As suas de* chanoyu, *com a maeira asi como vem do mato, pera ymitar a natureza.*

Since "meeting to drink *cha*" was for "the quiet and restful contemplation of the things of nature in the wilderness and desert," Rodrigues wrote, "all the material of this place [the *sukiya*, or tea hut], is entirely adapted for this purpose and for eremitical solitude in the form of rude huts made naturally with rough wood and bark from the forest, as if they had been formed by nature or in the usual style of those people who dwell in woods or the wilderness." (R(C):TIJ) This sort of taste is understandable among literatae (and that includes many samurai) who respected sage-poets who lived pure lives in the mountains. What is more impressive is that the taste spread beyond the tea huts. As Kaempfer noted, Japanese ceilings generally showed off the natural grain of the wood and only rarely pasted it over with colored wallpaper (as Koreans do). The tea ceremony sensibility apparently succeeded in becoming the Japanese sensibility, the national aesthetic. Morse, would have loved to spread Japanese good taste to other parts of the world, but he also realized how hopeless it is to teach it. *Viz* the concluding paragraph to his *Japanese Homes and Their Surroundings*:

> I do not expect to do much good in thus pointing out what I believe are better methods, resting on more refined standards. There are some, I am sure, who will approve; but the throng – are won by tawdry glint and tinsel; who make possible by admiration and purchase, the horrors of much that is made for house-furnishing and adornment – will, with characteristic obtuseness, call all else but themselves and their own ways heathen and barbarous.

11-8 Our rooms generally have windows of great clarity;
As nossas camaras tem jeralmente jenelas com muita claridade;

> The *zashiki* [parlor] of *chanoyu* [the tea ceremony] are windowless and dark.
> *Os zaxiqis de* chanoyu *sem jenelas e esquros.*

This contrast is completely correct – the tea hut was a closed space, which screened out the world at large – yet misleading because, *generally speaking*, it is the Japanese house whose walls are all window, while European houses, by comparison, have little port-holes to peek out at the outside world. The only really dark dwellings in old Japan were the snowed-under houses of the snow-country and the huts of the Ainu (They were so dark, that to our loss, Morse could not make out the details within!) So the real contrast here is not about ordinary rooms, but *taste* with respect to the design of rooms used for important socializing. The sensory overload of one of our drawing rooms versus the voluntary deprivation of the tea room. Or, rather, the choice of a very few objects to focus on. But the visual aspect may have been only part of it. Small windows let in less noise. The quiet tea-house allowed for very quiet person-to-person communion. And, it was a democratic place, where the usual rank-related formalities were suspended. All in all, the Jesuit brotherhood highly appreciated these retreats, these tiny shrines to quiet and calmness, and many high-ranking Japanese Christians were *Way of the Tea* aficionados.

Frois wrote in the Age of the Tea Ceremony. In 1587, Hideyoshi summoned all the tea-lovers of the nation to an unprecedented ten-day tea party (!) Judging from his character, I think it may not have been a party for many but a duty: *Come with all your priceless curios or else!* Much about this event with gaudy (?) tea ceremonies in baths and whatnot betrayed the very idea of *chanoyu* as most understood it. Meanwhile, the patron saint of the tea ceremony as we know it today, Sen no Rikyu (1522-1591), took up the simplicity "commanded by the poverty of the country, exhausted by ages of warfare . . . and raised it into a canon of taste" (C:TJ) before the same Hideyoshi had him put to death for reasons partly justified (*lése majesty*) and deserving a longer treatment than I can possibly give here, so I won't, other than to say that it is pleasant to think of Rikyu as *the world's first martyr for aesthetics* (as Socrates was for philosophy).

~~~~~~

11-9   We treasure gems, pieces of gold and silver;
Nós fazemos tezouro de pedraria e peças d'ouro e prata;

> The Japanese [treasure] old caldrons, old, cracked porcelain, clay vases, etc.
> *Os Japões de caldeirões velhos, porselanas velhas e qebradas, vazos de barro etc.*

All of the Japanese items are related to the tea ceremony (see 14-21). Rodrigues, in the early 17c, describes the *dogu* (implements) aptly: "The vessels and dishes used in this gathering are not of gold, silver, or any other precious metal, nor are they richly and finely wrought; instead they are made of clay or iron without any polish, embellishment or anything which might incite the appetite to desire them for their beauty and lustre." The fact that these earthenware utensils can be "worth ten, twenty or thirty thousand cruzados or even more . . . will appear as madness and barbarity to other nations that come to hear of it." (R(C):TIJ) Decades earlier, Valignano was shown a tea caddy bought for fourteen thousand ducats, "for which, in all truth, I would not have given more than one or two maravedis." Indeed, he thought "it would only serve us as a water jar for a bird." (SUMARIO 1583) Yet he also developed the relativity of gems and *dogu* at considerable length, pointing out that it took the fine eyes of connoisseurs to recognize the one in a thousand that was good "as our silversmiths, who can recognize and distinguish false and real jewels; and it doesn't seem this understanding can ever be achieved by a European, for no matter how long we look, we cannot even begin to understand what comprises the value or the difference." (LR)

Two things might be added. *First*, the Portuguese and Spaniards, doubtless with inside Japanese help, *did* manage to make "vast sums" (B:JCC) at this time by importing old pottery from the Philippines (especially caddies reputed to be especially good at keeping tea fresh in the humid season). Taladriz-Alvarez states the pottery earned more than any other Philippine export and the amazed Spaniards at first thought some superstition must be the cause of the high demand. (V(A):S&A). And, *second*, many specific cups and caddies mentioned by the Jesuits are still famous today. If time tells, unlike the contemporaneous Tulip craze, the *dogu* were for real. Today, we are far more appreciative of the value of *dogu* because of developments in the world of art since Valignano's time. Rare gems and *curios* were collected then, but art work *per se* generally was not. Churches commissioned religious scenes, the rich commissioned portraits of themselves and their possessions, and the publishers were just beginning to commission illustrations. The bourgeoisie bought paintings, hangings and sculptures *as decorations*, but most people did not value handicraft as we do today – at least the Spanish did not, because if they did, they would not have kept melting down American art for the gold and silver content alone. Now that we have an established concept of artwork, *dogu* would no longer be compared with gems. However, *dogu* do complicate matters by comprising two very different categories of art. On the one hand, there is the *dogu* made by a famous Japanese or Chinese artesian. On the other, there is that made by the naïve hands, skilled by repetition, of an un-named workman, possibly a child, *valued by the fiat of a connoisseur*. It would be interesting to know what percentage of the *dogu* held in Western collections comes from which type and how much we paid for them.

11-10   Our [houses?] are decorated with tissue, Gaudameci and Flemish tapestry;
As nossas [cazas?] se ornão com tapeçaria e godomecis e panos de Frandes;

> Those of Japan with *byôbu* [folding-screen/s] of paper, golden or of black ink.
> *As de Japão com beobus de papel dourados ou de tinta preta.*

Let me be blunt. "Our" decorations are just too rich and, subject-wise, too anthropomorphic(?) for my taste. Ridiculously ornate palaces make me close my eyes and shudder to think of the personality of the people who *wanted* such interiors. So I am not the right person to describe us. Lisa Jardine has a good summary of what this stuff meant. After introducing the lavish material ("Granadan silk threads in sixty three different shades of colour," "seven types of gold thread and three types of silver thread," etc.) and the financing ("the Fugger bank had advanced all the money . . . and had then acted as brokers for its sale") that went into royal tapestry, she writes:

> Tapestries have not endured as recognized 'works of art' into our own period. In the fifteenth and sixteenth centuries they were a particularly ostentatious art-form, perfectly suited to the requirements of wealthy clients of the time: they combined exquisite design and workmanship with extremely labor-intensive (and therefore valuable) craft skills; they rendered any room in which they were hung instantaneously sumptuous; they kept large ill-insulated rooms warm and draught-free; . . . Furthermore, they had the advantage over frescos and paintings that they were highly portable and could readily travel with their owner . . . They carried his renown along with the luggage . . . (*Worldly Goods – A New History of the Renaissance:* Nan A. Talese. Doubleday: 1996)

All of Frois's items might be loosely translated as *tapestry*. Dictionaries suggest *tapeçaria* might be cloth woven with gold or silver threads which the English called "tissue." The Flemish art called "cloth" (*panos*) by Frois is what we identify with painting-like tapestry today, and Guadameci, an ancient tapestry from Gadamés, Tripoli, gilt painted leather. Perhaps the intended contrast is between cloth that *hangs* and screens that *stand*. Or, it might be an extension of the last two contrasts, in the sense that paper is less substantial, or to use Jardine's adjective, *sumptuous,* than tapestry.

The *byôbu* screens almost always had six panels. Frois's writing is so sketchy one might assume the paper is solid gold or black, but actually both gold dust and black ink were commonly used to paint scenes or poetry, and Nobunaga had given such a screen – a very valuable black and white landscape of the capitol (Kyoto) – to Valignano in addition to talking tea with him. But these folding screens are more than mere decoration. They share the wall-making function of the *shôji* and *fusuma* described in the notes to 11-5, above. Portable, they provide temporary private spaces or back-drops for audiences. Korean *nihonjinron* essayist Lee O-Young contrasts the "screen-cultures" of the Far East he identifies with the free and fluid privacy of these screens with the solid-wall culture of the West, where a fixed concept of privacy begins in the cradle and ends in the basement fixations of the underground man of Dostoevsky (Yes, Russia is "West" to the Far Eastern intellectual. Wouldn't that get the Slavophile's goat!). One must quote Lee to do justice to his "post-modern" essay-style:

> The function and characteristic of a *byôbu* lies in its separation of the wall from the building. That is, the concept of the wall as unmovable has been made moveable, and given birth to its own independent culture. While Westerners made more and thicker walls for the sake of individual privacy, the people of the Eastern Trio [China, Japan and Korea], made the wall lighter and thinner in order to liberate it. Then, walls, instead of restricting people, fell under our free control. This became a reality because of none other than the *byôbu*. . . . In the *byôbu* cultural sphere, the individual and the group, the self and the other are not an antagonistic black and white choice. There is fusion and . . . expansion and closure depending on the circumstance of each situation. For this reason, the first-person singular of the Eastern Trio, unlike the absolutely unmoving West's, changes . . . This is not to deny the individual. It is only to say that while each panel of the *byôbu* is independent [physically of one piece and as artwork sufficient onto itself], they stand up so well *because* they link together six, ten or twelve panels at a time. (J/I:FPM:1989)

Cross-cultural metaphysics aside, *byôbu* are still used in Japanese homes and restaurants – where they separate parties but not the noise. If they are not found everywhere, it is because the very folds which allow them to stand take up too much of the high-priced room, so the plain, ugly Western partition, or *sukurinu* (screen) is now more common. Forgetting current reality, I'll Frois Lee:

> *The houses in Europe have thick and unmoving walls;*
> *Those of Japan have paper walls that move about.*
>
> *Our partitions are straight and require stands or legs;*
> *Theirs zig-zag and stand up straight without those things.*

The wall most commonly mentioned by boastful Japanese *nihonjinron* of the 1970's and early 1980's was not the endoskeleton of a dwelling. It was the exoskeleton of the city. The standard line was that the West had castles and walled castle towns because meat-eating nomads that they were, war was the norm and people had to be constantly on guard, while Japan, being a peaceful country of farmers, didn't need walls. And this was, then, extrapolated to the Japanese house open to the outside, because the occupants were not in a state of war with nature, in contrast to the small-windowed Western house-as-my-castle (which is to say *fortress*). This view of walls (not to mention our respective people) is a bit too pat and, as with many contrasts, it helps to have a third view to complicate the picture. Japanese might be amused to read what pioneer of fired adobe dwellings, Nader Khalili, wrote about walls *and the West*. "If we look at the West and its literature, we can see that it has always tried to tear down the walls." Occidentals don't like to be fenced in. Whereas "in the East, walls have an entirely different meaning. In Persian, "neighbors are called *hamsayeh,* people who share the shade of the same wall."

> ... a neighborhood starts with a wall, united in shade. Each side can take advantage of the shade. One in the morning and the other in the afternoon.. In the East, a wall is built to break the wind, to create privacy, and to have the shade. (CERAMIC HOUSES AND EARTH ARCHITECTURE 1986/1999 Cal-Earth Press)

The climate is, of course, the main reason for this "Eastern" wall loving. For ". . the walls grow much faster than trees here [in Persia], and give better shade for less water. . ." (Ibid) How, then, would Khalili compare/contrast his culture *with Japan?*

~~~~~~

11-11 Ours are decorated with carpets and rugs; <small>As nossas se ornão com alcatifas e tapetas;</small>
        Theirs with straw mats. <small>As suas com colchões de palha.</small>

With carpets or rugs, we think *decoration*. Or we did before wall-to-wall became taken for granted. Rodrigues wrote of *tatami* mats "so close to each other that there were no gaps at all between them, just as if they were floorboards." (R:TCJ) Were floorboards considered decoration? I do know that the floors in Japan are not decorated *with* tatami. They *are* tatami. Frois *should have* written:

> *We cover our hard floors with soft rugs;*
> *They never cover their floors, because the floors themselves are soft straw mats.*

These mats are not mats in the sense we imagine, for they are over three inches thick. Frois missed this:

> *We fit our floor rugs to the dimensions of the room.*
> *They fit their rooms to the dimensions of their straw mats.*
>
> *With us, no two houses have exactly the same floor space;*
> *Japanese houses come in standard sizes, in multiples of their mats called* ma.

I may be unfair to Frois, for *tatami* was just then becoming common in all rooms rather than just where people sat. But Rodrigues, who wrote twenty years later, noted "all the houses are built according to certain measurements on account of the mats or *tatami* with which they are laid . . ." They are "woven of common straw and rushes, faced with a closely wrought mat of rice-straw" (Ibid) and approximately 3 x 6 feet. (S:JDJ) Even today, the floor space of an dwelling for rent is given in terms of these standardized mats. My last abode was *roku-ma*, or *6-mat*. Amazing as this may seem, this standardization that began with the mats extends to other areas. The length of the mat, 180 centimeters, is also the height of "paper doors" of all types, the length of all closets and many beds. It is impressive to see a country so literally united, but at 6'2," I find the units not only inconvenient but, "as tall Saxons and Celts have found to their cost many times," downright dangerous. "H.M.'s Consul at Kanagawa fairly tried the strength of his skull against the sharp edge of the traversing beam," continues Alcock, "and measured his length backward on the ground under a blow that might have killed a weaker man." (A:COT) I am reminded of Piet Hein's *grook:* "Small people often overrate / the charm of being tall / which is that you appreciate / the charm [and safety!] of being small." But, to be fair to said beams, I should add that Alcock, in a footnote, credited one of them with saving the life of another tall Englishman by parrying the sword-blow of a would-be assassin. If the 180 centimeter high beams are not all bad, the tatami that created them is not all good either. Tatami is beautiful, soft, light and easier to keep clean than carpet, but has a problem, or two, according to Sladen:

> In a common lodging house they are an Alsatia for fleas. To a flea, a Japanese mat is a fortress with thousands of doors. He burrows in it like a rabbit. The mats have the further disadvantage that the house is theirs and not yours. As your heels would be bad for it, you have to leave your boots on the doorstep of your own house. (S:MQT)

About the fleas, he is right (See *TT-long* for details) The "boots on the doorstep" is wrong, for Japanese homes have no doorsteps, they have *porticos*, ante-chambers of various sizes, and that is where you leave your shoes, where deliverymen bring and wait for things. It is a liminal zone, neither truly inside nor out – but certainly out of the elements. If *tatami* cause any in-and-out problems, it is the opposite of what Sladen imagined. After all, it is *more* comfortable to have one's shoes *off* than to have them on. The problem is rather that the need to keep dirt out of the house *is hard on children*. Morse touched upon it indirectly in a paragraph on Japanese cleanliness: "Children of the poorest classes play in front of the house, but, instead of enjoying their fun on the ground, a straw matting is spread for them." (M:JDD) That would be a drag. But all in all *tatami* is child-friendly. Montanus exaggerated a little when he claimed *tatami* was "stuft like a quilt, which indeed are rather their Couches or Beds, where lay themselves down," but it is true that Children cannot get concussions by simply falling down, as they can on a hard floor.

~~~~~~

11-12 Ours [are decorated] with leather chests, Flemish coffers and cedar cabinets;
As nossas com arcas emcouradas e cofres de Frandes, ou arcas de cedro;

> Those of Japan with black baskets made of cow hide.
> *As de Japão com cestos pretos feitos de pelles de vacas.*

On the Japanese side, it is surprising to find even this black basket – according to Okada, probably woven with a wisteria warp and hide-strip weave, then lightly lacquered – for Japanese rooms generally have a large closet (*oshi-ire*: literally "stuff-in"), which includes a shelved area and boxes for storage, so quality space may be saved for humans rather than furniture. Partly because of my difficulty with the translation above – Should it be a leather *trunk*, Flemish *chest*, etc.? – the italicized phrase in the following words of wisdom (Japanese philosophy according to a Dutch friend of Alcock) delight me to no end:

> You build houses ten times as large as is necessary for your accommodation, and more than your income can keep up . . . merely that you may have room to stow away *an endless succession of ugly square and oblong pieces of timber*, tortured into various shapes and uses. We build houses to live in, not for ostentation, and still less as warehouses for useless things. (A:COT)

Alcock was extremely drawn to the Japanese way for its social benefits: without the enormous first expense of marriage, an enormous "upholsterer's bill," not to mention the cost of upkeep, young men could get married on an income of £ 400 per year. "If," he remorsefully muses, "European joints could only be made supple enough to enable their owners" to live in the Japanese way, more poor people could get married. Not only could they get married, but the poor woman could be freed to go out and work, for lacking the etiquette that, in Bacon's words, "gives a Japanese woman something to do" in her empty home that "has about as much in it as a paper lantern," (B:JGW) a Western woman in a Japanese house would have time on her hands instead of wax.

Furniture "conspicuous by its absence," as Chamberlain put it ("Architecture" C:TJ), would seem to be uniquely Japanese. Korean rooms are dominated by heavy wooden chests and cabinets profusely inlaid with mother of pearl – this furniture to them what cattle are in some cultures, a representation of wealth (and important part of marriage gifts), while the Chinese had chairs.

11-13 The people of Europe sleep up high on beds or cots;
A jente d'Europa dormem em alto em leitos ou catres.

> Those of Japan sleep low down upon the *tatami* with which the house is matted.
> *A de Japão em baxo sobre os tatamis com que a caza estaa esteirada.*

Many Japanese (40%) still do. The practice is very good for the little folk, who not only need not fear falling *out* of bed, but are at liberty to crawl *in* and take a nap any time they want to. I patted myself on the back for that observation, then found Alice Mabel Bacon had beat me to it by over a hundred years: "Babies never fall out of bed, because there are no beds; they never tip themselves over in chairs for a similar reason." (B:AJI)

11-14 Our beds are always extended;
As nossas camas estão sempre estendidas nos leitos;

> Those of Japan are always rolled up and hidden out of sight during the day.
> *As de Japão sempre de dia emroladas e escondidas onde se não vejão.*

Perhaps futon have grown thicker since 1585, for today, *futon* are usually not *rolled* up, but *folded* in three and put away into the *oshi-ire* closet. In good weather, the *futon* are "hung over balconies to air, coming back damper than ever, if the servants forget to bring them in before sunset." (S:JDJ) They – the *futon*, not the servants – are also thoroughly beaten. This is still true. Every modern apartment must have a place for *futon* to be aired and beaten.

11-15 Our pillows are made of feathers, linen or cotton, soft, long and thin;
As nossas almofadas são de prumagem, canh[g?]a ou algodão, moles e compridas;

> Those of Japan are made of wood, and just one [type?], a palm in length.
> *As de Japão de pao, e huma somente, de comprimento de hum palmo.*

Hard, narrow, and high as a double-pillow, Westerners found Japanese pillows a literal pain in the neck. In Mr. Sladen's words, "hair, like Macbeth, has murdered sleep." He noticed an identical pillow in Africa (Mashonaland) and claimed it "looks like a door-scraper with a top taken from a cripple's crutch." Like Morse, he recognized it was intended to help the elaborate hairdos last, but he did not notice that "In hot weather the air circulates about the neck, and this is very agreeable." (M:JDD) While the pillows of the common folk were generally *all* wood, according to a note in Golownin (G:MCJ), "the higher or richer classes make use of a very neat box, about eleven inches high, to the lid of which an oval [actually *tubular*] cushion is affixed, from six to eight inches in length, and from two to three in breadth. This box contains articles which they make use of at the toilette, such as razors, scissars, pomatum, tooth-brushes, powder, &c." Imagine: *pillow as a medicine cabinet!*

It is hard to say whether Frois means there was at most one pillow used in a bed (which is true, for they do not stack up) or mentions only one type of pillow to heighten the contrast. There were *also* hollow lacquered woven bamboo pillows which may still be found in old inns. Although more giving than solid wood, they are still too hard for most Westerners and young Japanese. All one can say is that either we are very soft-headed, or the Japanese of yesteryear must have been a very hard-headed people indeed! All of the "forms of pillow in common use" sketched by Morse – who also mentions pillows with wooden ends and basket-work middle, portable folding pillows, as well as rarer porcelain (!) pillows – show short tubular cushions "stuffed with buckwheat hulls" tied by a single string to the top of the wooden blocks. (M:JHS&S) So, it would seem that a quarter century after the Black Ships of Perry, most Japanese were already sleeping in the mode of the upper classes.

Our pillows are put into one or two pillow cases.
Their pillows have no cases but only a piece of paper tied into place.

The same string that ties the small conical cushion on top of the wooden stand secures the paper. With the death of the traditional hairstyle, the top part of the traditional pillow, the tubular cushion alone survived. Enlarged and conical, rather than flat, like ours, they are hard enough to still give "us" trouble. Here is Ponting reporting from *The Lotus Land Japan* in 1922: "Though I have spent many months at Japanese inns, I have never mastered the knack of keeping it [the pillow] from rolling off the futon and letting my head down with a bump. Invariably, I had to put my large camera-case at the head of the bed to keep it in place – much to the amusement of the *neisan* [*nesan* = sister = young lady] who saw it.

Today, the covering on traditional tubular pillows is cloth, often with lace near the outer edges, and extends most of the way around the pillow, leaving the ends of the pillow completely open to the air. About half of the pillows are now the shape of ours, but they tend to be cooler with barley hulls, macaroni-like bits of plastic and other airy stuffing. If we only had the brains to learn from "them," our air conditioners could be given a vacation.

~~~~~~

11-16 In Europe, pavilions, canopies and curtains of damask and silk are used;
Em Europa se uza de pavolhões, esparaveis e cortinas de damasqo e seda;

In Japan, in the summer [they use] **kaya** [mosquito net tent] of very thin *nuno* [cloth] or of **paper**. *Em Japão pollo verão de* cayas *muito ralas de* nuno *ou de papel.*

This is very funny if you get it. Frois compares "our" luxurious bed accessories with their dry goods item. But, he *knows* the humble *kaya* is *by far* the more valuable device, worth more than its weight in gold, for it permits one to sleep. A summer vesper in Japan is, if I may borrow from a haiku by Issa, an announcement that one has crossed the border and entered *Mosquito Country!"* (*kane naru ya ka-no kuni-ni koyo-koyo-to*). Alcock, who minced no words concerning his hatred for "these Poisoners of the human race, and Destroyers of all peace" on the eve of his dispatch to Japan, later found said net a happy example of the "perfect genius" Japanese have "for attaining the most useful ends with the smallest expenditure of material, and by the simplest means." At the various inns where he spent the night when traveling (partly to test the freedom of travel granted by treaty), he attests

> We should have been devoured by the musquitoes had the landlords not come to our rescue by the simplest of all contrivances, a musquito curtain, open at the bottom, made up in the shape of a parallelogram, is let down over the mat (6 feet by 3) selected by the sleeper, a cord is run from each of the four upper corners (into which a sort of eyelet hole has been worked), and four nails driven in to enable a servant to suspend it. Under this, the persecuted martyr creeps, tucking in the sides and ends under his cotton quilt or mat . . . (A:COT)

Originally, Japanese relied completely on smudge. The *Chronicles of Japan* (*Nihon Shoki* c.720) reports mosquito-net sewers coming over from part of ancient Korea. Needless to say, only the nobility used them and even they used smudge as well for there wasn't enough netting for the retainers. Nets only began to spread about the time Frois arrived and became common a hundred or two hundred years later. This was not accomplished by imports. Making a mosquito net became a woman's once-in-a-lifetime work, like a man's making a house and women gathered to stitch together lengths of netting, much like the roof-raisings of men. (In Kumamoto prefecture's Tamano county, they brought in a mortar and a cat, who is hit on the head because it had to meow to complete the ceremony!)

Today, most Japanese have adopted the modern Occidental solution of fitting mosquito nets to the windows, which is to say *screens*. These screens are all-too-often an ugly swimming-pool blue because that is supposed to look literally cool. But some people stick by their nets. The hemp ones are said to suck the moisture not only out of the air but from the *futon*. That is, to function as dehumidifiers.

~~~~~~

11-17 Among us, it would be below a nobleman to sweep his room;
Antre nós seria baxeza varrer hum fidalgo sua camara;

> Japanese gentry do so and think it very dandy.
> *Os senhores Japões ho uzão e o tem antre si por primor.*

With the advent of the witch, the broom became so thoroughly identified with women in Europe we cannot blame men for fearing to touch them, right? The Chinese character for a wife (妻) has a woman (女) with a broom over her head, so you might think all men in the Sinosphere would avoid the broom like the plague. At first, I thought the broom might be a confined to the tea hut which Frois has taken so much advantage of. But, look what Golownin has to say about Inns:

> ‥
> It is a whimsical rule that the guests must leave the apartments as clean as when they entered them; so that no person ever quits an inn, until he has seen his apartment put into proper order. well swept, and washed if necessary. In short, it would be considered an act, not only of impoliteness, but even of ingratitude, if the smallest speck of dirt was to be left behind. So precise are the Japanese in this respect, that even the Dutch, when permitted to traffic there were deemed deficient in neatness. (G:MCJ)

‥
If men traveled alone . . . Then, again, Frois may be referring to the annual Beat-out-the-dust Day (*susubarai*), which *everyone* participated in *with gusto*. In this case, they would be literally *sweeping up*, for the rafters are only cleaned on this one day, when dust clouds were reputed to hang over the entire city, as they do after festivals in Chinese cities because of all the firecrackers. Even today, every year, everyone must pitch in and clean at the office, and television news shows us battalions of dust-masked priests and volunteers from the congregation doing what looks like a search-and-destroy mission against enormous temples using brooms and dusters with handles as long as pool-cleaning poles. These annual offensives are generally commanded by men.

~~~~~~

11-18 We wipe our faces with fine towels;
Nós alimpamos o rosto com toalhas delgadas;

> They *waza-to* [chose to] wipe them with rags or hemp hards.
> *Elles vaza to com liteiros ou tomentos muito grosos.*

This contrast is given in the prologue to Frois's missing summary at the end of the discussion on handkerchiefs and tissue paper. However, Frois has already contrasted handkerchiefs in 1-50."

This seems a poor contrast for this section on facilities. It would seem the "cleaning" of rooms got Frois to thinking of personal hygiene. The contrast would seem to be that "they" prefer to wipe their faces with *rough* material, while we preferred *fine*. Does this reflect a different attitude toward skin-care? Scourging *vs* Polishing? Was "our" skin too delicate to permit the former approach? The modern washcloth suggests, however, that we have come to follow the Japanese way.

~~~~~~

11-19 Our lavatories must be behind the house, hidden. *As nossas latrinas ão-de estar detras das cazas escondidas.*

Theirs are in front, patent to all. *As suas na dianteira, patentes a todos.*

Here, Okada writes, Frois, desperate for contrast, is back to the homes of the commoners, for they were the ones that often had the outhouse in front (Not right by the door, but off to the side a bit, by the household garden.) The better houses, like those in Europe, had theirs out of sight in the North-side (nether regions) of the house. Be that as it may, this practice had its merits. *First*, the toilet would be closer when one returns home. *Second*, it might bring in "fertilizer" (see 21, below). And, *third*, who says the front must be the best part of a house, anyway? The nobility's outhouses were inside an interior garden, a little paradise – there was an "upper" one and "lower" one, the former for only the lord and very favored guests, and the latter for the women of the house (Don't ask me where the other people went!). Toilets or not, the rear of the house was attractive (it had the decorative 'natural' garden) and the front, aside from the gate, nothing much. This was hard for "us" to understand, for we put our best everything out front. According to Consul Harris, the fact that "the most honorable rooms are in the rear" in Japan led to cultural misunderstanding when visiting Westerners thought they were placed in these rooms "merely to prevent their seeing anything of the people, etc." (H:CJTH).

I think the reason Frois chooses to start his discussion of toilets and excrement with this observation is because of his long stay in Miyako (Kyoto), a city which was famously upfront about collecting and recycling human waste. Kyoto even boasted public toilets *in front of shops on the Main Avenue* and at many of the cross-roads. Polymath Aramata Hiroshi in his long essay into the origin of ancient, traditional and Western style toilets in Japan, took the odor into consideration, and called these "toilet-urge-enticing devices." (J/A:NGK) – I am reminded of the sign by the public toilet photographed in the Peoples Republic of China: *"Don't be selfish* [i.e. keep it for home], *use this!"* (This would not necessarily mean waiting until one gets home either. In *Everyday Things In Modern Japan*, Susan Henley mentions 19c travelers carrying containers for their urine, which they would exchange for food or money.) The Kyoto area was, and still is, known for its many fine leafy vegetables – they even have a type of cabbage (*Kyôna*) with a head large enough to feed a small village! This meant urine, with its phosphate, was in particularly high demand. As Aramata notes, people from Edo were as astounded as any foreigner to see urinals out in front of the outhouses proper, in full view of passersby in Kyoto. This *was* indeed "patent" in the original meaning of the word: *to stand wide open.* And what shocked them even more was the fact that women also used them, *standing,* hiked up kimonos, with their buttocks bent out slightly over the troughs. And these were not only servants, supposedly even the wives of wealthy merchants joined in! About a hundred years after Frois, the *senryu* poets – largely from Edo, for its largely male population found consolation for their loneliness in black humor – could not resist taking a dig at the urine capitol of Japan and its women, who were otherwise considered paragons of womanhood.

wc's galore

there are no signs
saying "Urination Forbidden!"
in old Kyoto

shôben-muyô-fuda wa nai kyô-no-machi

perfection lost

Kyoto women
have a wee flaw – they stand
to make water

kyô-onna tatte tareru ga sukoshi kizu

11-20 We seated; *Nós asentados;*
        And they squatting. *E elles em cocoras.*

This refers to the style of doing the "big," as Japanese call what Usanians call "number two." Just as Frois missed the chance to comment on the direction of horses in their stalls he missed a big one here:

We face out to defecate;
They face in.

I cannot recall if this aligns us with out horses or puts us at odds with them. It does put the Japanese in a more defenseless position, but also makes embarrassment less likely.

We urinate and defecate together;
They use separate toilets.

It goes without saying that *their* way is ideal for collecting fertilizers. Japanese bathrooms were suitably designed for this. In the late-18c, Thunberg described a Japanese bathroom as follows:

> Every house has its *privy;* in the floor of which there is an oblong aperture, and it is over this aperture that the Japanese sit. At the side of the wall is a kind of box, inclining obliquely outwards, into which they discharge their urine... (T:TEAA)

Said hole is flush with the floor and one does not make any contact with its edges. (Since sitting implies contact of buttocks with seat, the "sit" may be a poor translation from Thunberg's German.) These logistics – i.e., the distance from standing to the floor in the case of men – meant that even where fertilizers are no longer collected, most Japanese homes with traditional hole-toilets also have urinals, which, judging from this description, either did not exist or were not common in Europe until relatively recently.

When somebody not used to squatting squats, he or she finds it both tiring and unstable. After the husband of the *gaijin* couple in *The Japan Times* cartoonist Roger Dahl's "Zero Gravity" boasts that he has fulfilled their agreed upon daily quota of "aerobic calisthenics," she asks: "Since when does using a Japanese-style public toilet facility qualify as a full aerobic workout?" He replies "Since prolonged breath-holding was combined with the deep-knee-bend." (date lost) *This is no exaggeration.* It is hard for neophytes to squat for more than a minute or two and, because their heels fail to settle on the floor, they must occasionally grab the walls or pipes in order not to fall-over. Old generation Japanese can read a book while squatting at their business as well as we can sitting on the pot and, for their part are amazed to hear *we* can do the same, for, as they note, correctly, potty seats can cut off blood-circulation. "We," as a culture, do not understand squatting. Alcock tries:

> A Japanese quite at his ease, and *sans gene,* as naturally drops on his heels and squats, with no more a support to his person than his legs or heel can afford, as an Englishman drops into a chair when he is tired. // As soon as the babe leaves its mother's breast, the first thing it learns is not to walk or to run, but to squat on its heels in this baboon fashion. (A:COT)

Alcock's artist did not look close enough, for the illustration entitled "How Japanese Rest" mistakenly shows raised heels. If you are *balancing* on the balls of your feet, you know not squat about squat, for the whole point of *true* squatting is to *gain*, not lose, stability. The feet of the accomplished squatter, heels and all, rest square on the ground. The trick to gaining the ability to squat like this depends upon getting the upper part of your foot to come closer to your shin and your knee-joints open. Health-wise, the more natural squat (for nature does not always have chairs) surely provides more benefits. A recent rise in constipation in Japan is blamed on the Western toilet and very few Japanese have bad knees. Or, did Westerners adopt seats *because* they had bad knees? Frois was not very toilet-minded or he might have had more, such as:

> *We use water;*
> *They use sand.*

Or did we use water in Frois's day?

> *We do not take particular measures to reduce noise;*
> *They spread leaves in the urinal.*

The use of feathers was also tried but they had the disconcerting habit of floating up to greet you.

> *We leave the toilet door open after use;*
> *Theirs is always closed.*

I am not sure where I got the above one from and suspect it may only apply to post flush-toilet Usania.

~~~~~~

11-21 We pay for someone to carry our night-soil away;
Nós damos dinheiro a quem nos leve o esterco f[or]ja;

> In Japan, they buy it and give rice and money for it.
> *Em Japão o comprão e dão arroz e dinheiro por elle.*

A straight exchange was common for buckets of urine, while ordure was usually bought and the food-stuff was more in the way of a bonus. In Osaka and Kyoto, these waste products comprised a considerable portion of the family income. Even store clerks were reimbursed for their contribution. For a store owner with ten employees, it could amount to 20-30% of each employee's income! In Edo, on the other hand, the landlord sold the night-soil – with the urine mostly drained off (wasted) – and retained the proceeds for themselves. In parts of Japan, if enough men (over 4, perhaps) lived in a small room, *they could pay their entire rent with their waste,* which is to say, they could stay for free! (J/A:NGK). Kaempfer described at length (see TT-long, where this section is 4 ½ pages) the care taken "that the filth of travelers be not lost" (1692) in the country-side and initiated centuries of complaint about the stench of the tubs where "this nasty composition" was kept. To be precise about that stench, it was, "as ungrateful and putrid a smell of radishes (which is the common food of country people) to tender noses, as the neatness and beauty of the road is agreeable to the eyes." (K(S):HOJ) Alcock, summarized the 18c observations of Thunberg like this: "Japan would be a very good country to be fed in, but those who live in it ought not to have noses as well as mouths, or be in any way endowed with olfactory nerves." Thunberg, himself, put it like this:

> We were, . . . whenever we passed through any village, subject to an inconvenience which embittered all our pleasures, and obliged us to keep the windows of our norimons [*norimono* = sedan] shut. A privy, which is necessary for every house, is always built in the Japanese villages towards the street, and at the side of the mansion-house; it is open downwards, so that passengers may discharge their water from the outside into a large jar, which is sunk on the inside into the earth. The stench arising . . . was frequently, in hot weather, so strong and insupportable, that no plug introduced into the nose could dispute the passage with it, and no perfumes were sufficient entirely to disperse it. (T:TEAA)

Japanese villages generally had "only one street" of a length that "frequently surpasses all belief: most of them are three quarters of a mile in length, and some of them so long it requires several hours to walk through them." Moreover, "some also stand so close together that they are discriminated from each other only by a bridge or rivulet, and their name." That is to say, we are not talking about a passing inconvenience but a constant one! Thunberg also found the liquid fertilizer hard on the eyes, it made them "red, sore and running." Elsewhere he blamed the eye problems on "the smoke from charcoal within the houses, and the stench proceeding from the jars of urine." Obviously, *stench* does not effect eyes, but a high concentration of ammonia might! Stench problems aside, the Japanese arrangement made, far more sense than ours. Morse, alone, in 1877, recognized it as more rather than less hygienic than our practices:

Somewhat astonished at learning that the death-rate of Tokyo was lower than that of Boston, I made some inquiries about health matters. I learned that dysentery and cholera infantum are never known here . . . But those diseases which at home are attributed to bad drainage, imperfect closets [toilet systems], and the like seem to be unknown or rare, and this freedom from such complaints is probably due to the fact that all excrementitious matter is carried out of the city by men who utilize it for their farms and rice-fields. With us, this sewage is allowed to flow into our coves and harbors, polluting the water and killing all aquatic life; and the stenches arising from the decomposition and filth are swept over the community to the misery of all. . . . It seems incredible that in a vast city like Tokyo this service should be performed by hundreds of men who have their regular routes. The buckets are suspended on carrying-sticks and the weight of these full buckets would tax a giant. (M:JDD)

Morse may have exaggerated the difference between Japan and the USA, for only three years after he made the above observation, 103 of 222 cities surveyed in the United States put night-soil to agricultural use! And, even as late as the 1970's, about 30% of our farm villages still did (according to "New Age" magazine, Feb. 1982). In one sense, however, there surely was a difference. I doubt if *any* of our systems were *ever* as thorough and efficient as those of Japan. If they were, we too would have been *paid* for waste, rather than paying for it to be removed, right? A "pay toilet" would pay the user. The long and short of it was that "we" thought of soil as something to be used up or at best maintained, whereas the Japanese thought of it as something to be enriched with offal and junk fish, which was also used in abundance for manure. *There is good reason for it, too.* "Without manure they do not cultivate; the soil is not rich in productive materials, as it is mostly of volcanic origin. A Japanese saying is, "A new field gives but a small crop." (M:JDD) I cannot help but recall something written by the right-wing intellectual, Watanabe Shoichi. Waxing ecstatically for page after page on the subject of those *old* fields, that big farming in America – trying to open the market – could never understand, he described the Japanese farmer's deep attachment to his land, *for it had been literally created from the bowels of his ancestors* . . . Deep shit, indeed! Then there was a column by Jeremy Angel called "Flush toilets and the Dearth of Night Soil" in The Daily Yomiuri (1995/2/9). The carpenter who built his house, described his studies at an agricultural college 30 years earlier: "Part of our practical education was to wander the countryside, dipping fingers into such pits, and licking them to determine the age and quality of the contents – a bit like wine tasting?"

Japanese tend to think they have the patent on shit, but everything written above could be repeated for China. Long before Morse, indeed about thirty-five years before TRATADO, Pereira, a merchant who endured a long captivity in China, wrote:

The country is so well inhabited, that no one foot of ground is left untilled . . . These countrymen by art do that in tillage, which we are constrained to do by force. Here be sold the voidings of close-stools, although there wanteth not the dung of beasts: and the excrements of man are good merchandise throughout all China. The dung-farmers seek in every street by exchange to buy this dirty ware for herbs and wood. The custom is very good for keeping the city clean. (B:SCSC)

As Boxer points out, Pereira was doubtless thinking of Europe where chamber-pots and close-stools were dumped out windows and there were no houses of office. (language from a 1706 book published in London cited by Boxer) Coincidentally, the *via* for the oldest surviving draft of Pereria's account "hurriedly copied by the children of the seminary attached to the College of Sao Paolo at Goa at the end of 1561" is endorsed by none other than our Frois! Cruz, who further detailed the trade, wrote, "nothing is ever lost in this country be it ever so vile; for the bones as well of dogs as of other beasts, they do use, making toys, and carving them instead of ivory, they inlay them in tables, beds and other fair things . . ." And Pinto, the third of the great China visitors of the mid-16c, used excrement to example "how greed can lead men to seize upon the vilest, filthiest things to make profit," but ends up crediting it for increasing the number of crops by a third! (3 rather than 2 a year).

Note: Roadside fertilizer gathering rest-stops were also found in ancient Mexico (Bernal Diaz, in TT-long).

11-22 In Europe, horse dung is thrown into vegetable gardens, and that of man into garbage dumps;
Em Europa o estero dos cavalos se deita nas ortas e o da jente nos monturos.

In Japan, horse dung is thrown in garbage dumps and man's into vegetable gardens.
Em Japão o dos cavalos nos monturas e nas ortas ho da jente.

An enormous English book called *A Compleat Body Of Husbandry* (1770) details the use of half a dozen types of ordure used as manure in Europe including that of horses, cows, sheep, hogs, pigeons, poultry and . . . man. The last was used in "some parts of England, and in many Places Abroad," such as the "Vineyards of Languedoc" and "in Flanders," where it was "regularly sold" for fertilizer for "Corn" (i.e. grain) crops. Frois can be forgiven for overlooking its use for, unlike the case in Japan, it was used "oftener than is thought," which is to say it was "a Practice every where carry'd on clandestinely for nobody would care to buy that Farmer's Corn, who should be known to use it." The first sentence of the opening paragraph to the section on night-soil gives valuable insight into how "we" thought: "There is something disgustful in the Thought of using the Excrements of our own Species for the Dressing of Lands, as it is putting them again down our Mouths: but this particular type of Dung, is not without its Efficacy . . ."

It is unlikely the Europeans copied the practice of using human ordure from the Japanese or Chinese, because the method of preparation was completely different. *There*, as we have seen, it was wet. In Europe, it was spread "for a time upon a Bed of Mould [mulch?], and let to be exposed to the Sun" to dry it out, lessen its smell and its overly "hot" quality (The "heat" or "very rich" nature of our ordure was judged the result of our eating high up the food-chain – a meat diet with alcohol being especially likely to ferment). But even treated, it was considered "a filthy ore, and . . . the least manageable of all others, the most offensive to the servants employ'd in spreading it, as well as to the thoughts of those who are to feed upon the Corn that rises from its Richness."

If human excrement was not totally ignored by European husbandry, horse dung was *not* really thrown away in Japan, either. It may not have been sold in the city but thrown on a heap, but that heap was surely *used by someone* for something. It is mentioned in OJD as a fertilizer and I have read of warriors using it to cook food in their helmets, which would suggest that it served the poor in the same capacity. Moreover, it is debatable to what extent the Japanese actually had *monturas* ([garbage]mounds) in the sense we understand them. Haiku mention sweep-piles (*hakidome*) and specific piles of shell-fish shells, disposable chopsticks, or flower petals. But all of these are *small and temporary*, honest-to-goodness dumps are hard to find. Morse in the late-19c noted that

> In country village and city alike the houses of the rich and poor are never rendered unsightly by garbage, ash piles, and rubbish; one never sees those large communal piles of ashes clam shells and the like that are often encountered in the outskirts of our quiet country villages. In refined Cambridge . . . This land was so disfigured by a certain type of rubbish that for years it was facetiously called the "tin canyon"! The Japanese in some mysterious way manage to bury, burn, or utilize their waste and rubbish so that it is never in existence. (M:JDD)

A century after TRATADO, Kaempfer wrote: "The Inspectors for repairing the highway are at no great trouble to get people to clean them; for whatever makes the roads dirty and nasty, is of some use to the neighboring country people, so that they rather strive, who should first carry it away." In this respect, he specifically mentions horse dung, saying it does not "lie long upon the ground but it is soon taken up by poor country children and serves to manure the fields." Evidently, horse (and cow) dung was not as prestigious (?) as human offal, but only cow piss was clearly not used, for an old Japanese proverb equates *"the lectures of parents and cow piss: long and good for nothing!"* Thunberg adds that this cleaning, or rather gleaning work was mainly done by old men and children, and "very readily, . . without stooping, with a shell (*Haliotis tuberculata*) which resembled a spoon, and was fastened to a stick. The gatherings were put into a basket and carried on the left arm." (T:TEAA)

In view of the overwhelming evidence that the wasteless economy of old Japan came from China, there is one Sino-Japanese difference I constantly came across in 19c writings by Europeans (and soon thereafter by Japanese) that just does not make sense. Namely, the Chinese are depicted as a dirty people living in pigsty conditions, while the Japanese are credited with being the cleanest people in the world, not just for their renowned daily bath but for the fact that even the poor lived in a neat manner. Efficiency & *neatness* seem like a reasonable pair. But efficiency & *slovenliness* seem an odd combination. One wonders how the Chinese managed both.

11-23   We lock our chests with iron locks;
Nós fechamos as arcas com fechaduras de ferro;

> They their baskets with cords, paper seals and Chinese padlocks.
> *Elles seus sestos com cordas e mutras de papel ou cadeados da China.*

The contrast seems one of solid protection with something far less. Doubtless, our locks were substantial. "We" even had large, ridiculously complex "masterpiece locks" that were never used, made simply to gain accreditation as master locksmiths. This was even reflected in out respective literary trope. Locks barely figured in Japanese metaphor, while it was a very common metaphor in "ours" and, if Japan had its keeper of the barriers or the gate, we had our "keeper of the keys." The Pope was "the keeper of the keys to heaven." According to the Schlage.com website,

> Several centuries ago, in Spain, there was a great distrust of locks. To be safe, the householders of a block hired a watchman to patrol the neighborhood and carry the keys to their dwellings. To enter or leave a house, the resident clapped his hands vigorously to summon the watchman with his key, so, all comings and goings became a matter of public record and there was little chance for "hanky panky" in old Madrid.

Distrust of locks? Yes. Copies of keys could be made by the residents which could be passed on to lovers . . . This goes back to the seclusion of women discussed in chapter 2. Reading Casanova, I can only think that the effect was counter-productive, and they might have done as well to have done away with them entirely and joined the Japanese with their cords and paper seals!

The Chinese padlock Frois mentions is a "shrimp-lock" – a bent piece of metal shaped like a shrimp stuck into a main piece. I would guess the intended contrast is a built-in lock for us, versus attached outside locks for them, but it is hard to tell. What I can say is that *serious locking up was just not a key part of the Japanese culture.* If women in many parts of Europe were given bundles of keys upon marriage (for inside the house at any rate!), a Japanese woman received a cooking ladle. Even when Japanese doors *were* locked, it was generally by a bar, *from the inside only.* When the family went out, say, cherry-blossom-viewing, someone always remained as the *rusuban*, an "absence guard." But, even this was less to guard against robbery than to have someone there in case of fire or earthquake. When Europeans came again in the 19c, they found Japan was still virtually lockless (We will come back to Morse on this in 14-7). Frois might better have written,

> We have many locks and lock many things;
> Japanese have few locks and rarely lock anything, even their houses.

Even water closets generally had no locks, so people coughed before opening the door.

11-24   We use secret compartments in our chests; *Nós uzamos de escaninos nas arcas;*

> And they, *kakego* [drawers] in their baskets. *E elles de caquegos nos cestos.*

Judging from 11-23, Frois is still talking security or lack thereof. Japanese tended to trust to the conscience of others and rarely locked up things (14-7). *Kakego* today generally refers to a nest of boxes, one within another, like those Russian eggs, but the Japanese-Portuguese dictionary of 1604 calls them *hikidashi,* or "drawers." At any rate, they are more accessible than "our" hidden safe. While I *chose* "chest," the translation for our side could as well have been "trunks" or "boxes," so long as they are imagined hard and rectangular, for the Portuguese *arca* is one with "the ark," literally, a "box-boat." This suggests a more general contrast Frois missed, which Lee O-Young based his *Furoshiki Bunka no Posuto-Modan* book on:

> We put things into solid containers, or fill up soft ones of a predetermined size;
> They wrap up things in furoshiki.*[a pretty square piece of cloth] to fit the size of the thing.*

In the Sinosphere, a cloth rather than a container of fixed size is used to carry things about – things are first set on it, then opposing corners are tied diagonally, two at a time. Professor Lee claims this "primary opposition" of cultural codes, i.e., "putting in" (the box principle) versus "wrapping up" (the clothing principle) goes back to primeval times, and boasts that the greater versatility of the *furoshiki* – which brings to mind morphing robot toys (largely a Japanese invention) – makes the Far East fitter for the Post-Modern poliverse. The Ark, suggests Lee, is too square to save us in modern times!

~~~~~~

11-25 Our carpenters work standing up; *Os nossos carpinteiros trabalhão em pé;*
Theirs, for the most part, remain seated. *Os seus pola mayor parte sempre asentados.*

Materials may play a role in this. You *go to* the stone and bricks, but wood is light enough to be carried into the workshop. But that is not all. For "us," sitting is thought to impede all physical work but key-stroking and paper-pushing. But sitting can actually allow *more* work to be done. Not only does it save energy wasted on standing, but it frees up the *feet* to join in the work. We are surprised to see people doing handiwork with their feet. As Percival Lowell put it "from the tips of his fingers to the tips of his toes, *in whose use he is surprisingly proficient*, he (the Far Oriental) is the artist all over." (my italics: L:SOE) Ah, but they are only normal. People *all over the globe* used to use their feet in that way. *We are surprisingly inept.* The only feet we allow to develop their potential are those belonging to people missing arms (See Ricky Jay's *Learned Pigs and Fireproof Women*). Today, most carpenters in Japan feed their table saws, standing. But people working on sheet metal and other things not using large tables, may still be seen seated on their *tatami* with their feet out, fast at work.

~~~~~~

11-26 Our gimlets open up holes by arm power;
As nossas virrumas vão abrindo os buracos à força de braços;

Those of Japan are always given a [a twist? a blow?] with a mallet.
As de Japões vão-lhe sempre dando com hum macete em [schütte =volta? rdg = golpe?].

A gimlet is a capital "T" shaped twist-drill. A good example would be a simple cork-opener, which once was called a gimlet. Since the spiral starts close to the tip, we can start screwing from the outset applying a bit of downward pressure and torque, using nothing but arm-power.

The Japanese gimlet was not spiral. Indeed, the first screws had just arrived in Japan (within the arquebuses!) and would not find other uses for quite a while (after all, ours only served for pumps and presses for their first 500 years). Their gimlets used a different method to bore, *sharp edges*. The *mitsume-giri* had three edges and the *yotsume-giri,* four. That is to say, the triangular or square cross-section resembles that of "our" fencing blades, or *foils*. I have used one of the four-edged gimlets and was surprised at how quickly it worked not only to bore but to enlarge holes. The only hard part was the first half-inch, where a hammer helped to drive it in far enough to gain purchase. Since I did not find the twisting that difficult, I guess the missing word is not *volta,* or a "turn," but *golpe* or some other word meaning a "blow."

11-27 In Europe, we don't feed carpenters or their helpers;
Em Europa não se dá de comer aos carpinteiros nem a [seus] criados;

> In Japan, they eat where they work, and their boys, who do nothing [are also fed].
> *Em Japão comem aonde trabalhão, e [tambem]aos seus moços, que no fazem nada[, se da de comer].*

This is still true in Japan. Carpenters may bring some snacks of their own or go out for a soft drink; but the lady of the house usually brings out trays of food and tea. Today, one might think, it saves their valuable time, as they are employed by the day. But, carpenters were not paid much in Frois's time. Alice Mabel Bacon provides a more plausible reason for the practice:

> So rigid are the requirements of Japanese hospitality that no guest is ever allowed to leave a house without having been pressed to partake of food, if it be only tea and cake. Even tradesmen or messengers who come to the house must be offered tea, and if carpenters, gardeners or workmen of any kind are employed about the house, tea must be served in the middle of the afternoon with a light lunch, and tea sent out to them often during their day's work. (B:JGW)

Another factor may be considered together with this hospitality. Bacon herself gave much of her chapter on "domestic service" to it: Japanese were fundamentally more democratic than we were, when it came to their attitude toward servants and other people doing menial work.

> In explaining to my scholars, who were reading "Little Lord Fauntleroy" in English, a passage where a footman is spoken of as having nearly disgraced himself by laughing at some quaint saying of the young lord, my peeresses were amazed beyond measure to learn that in Europe and America a servant is expected never to show any interest in, or knowledge of, the conversation of his betters, never to speak unless addressed, and never to smile under any circumstances. Doubtless, in their shrewd little brains, they formed their opinion of a civilization imposing such barbarous restraints upon one class of persons. (B:JGW)

In Japan, servants were allowed and expected to have their own minds. How ironic that our standard image of an Oriental servant as subservient is exactly what *we,* ourselves, demanded. *"Even in the treaty ports, where contact with foreigners has given to the Japanese attendants the silent and repressed air that we regard as the standard manner for a servant, they have not resigned their right of private judgement, but, if faithful and honest, seek the best of their employer, even if his best good involves disobedience of his orders,"* writes Bacon. Sladen also marveled at this:

> No Japanese servant will ever condescend to be turned into as human machine. Even in the most perfectly appointed house he retains his individuality, although her may fall upon his hands and knees when he enters your presence. But he evidently believes in the Horatian maxim of his country, "Give genius a chance," for he persists in using his own brains instead of those of his master or mistress. (S:MQT)

As Sladen points out, if you are not a worrier who insists on doing things the way you expect them to be done, such a thinking servant is a treasure. But, what is disconcerting about all this is "our" attitude. Whether excused by the contract mentality of Usania or aristocratic conceit of Europe, such a denial of human dignity is hard to stomach. (See 14-20 for my paradoxical theory as to why this difference may have come to be) Granted, a worker is not the same as a servant, and I may have wandered a bit too much in my explanation.

11-28 Our adze is large and broad and does a lot of work;
A nosa emxó hé grande e larga e faz muita obra;

> The adzes of the Japanese seem like toys.
> *As emxós dos Japões parecem couza de brinqo.*

"Our" adze (or *adz*) is basically a short-handled sharp-edged narrow-blade hoe – or, when two-sided, an anchor-like device – for working wood. "Their" adze has a handle so long and thin it looks like a cane held upside-down. Made from a single bent piece of iron, it is far more svelte than its stocky-looking Western counterpart. But, toy? *Hardly*. Aesthetics aside, I cannot speak for their relative merits and demerits except to venture that the Jesuits could not do much with them because the small diameter and round cross-section of the handle would not permit one to force himself upon the instrument in the manner "we" are used to. This would not trouble the Japanese carpenter for his lumber would already be straight and he would naturally pull the blade in such a way as to require little torque or prying. That is to say, he would not need to do *muita obra* (much work) to work. The OJD defines the Japanese *teono* as a tool to make roughly cut lumber even. Such a use seems a bit more limited, but still close enough to what "ours" do not to merit a contrast. I think the most significant difference is on a different level altogether.

> *In Europe, an adze is just a tool for the carpenter and the cooper.*
> *In Japan, an adze is the very symbol of carpentry and they even have rituals for them.*

The *teono-hajime,* or "adze-start" was a ceremony done to start construction of a house or ship and to start the carpenter's work in the New Year.

With this, Frois contrasts his last tool in the book. I am puzzled that he never discovered the difference in saws or planes (*push* vs *pull*-cut, as per my *Foreword*) and snail-like markers (we measured, they snapped an inked or powdered string at an angle), both of which impressed me.

~~~~~~

11-29 In Europe, the house is built as the wood/lumber is worked;
Em Europa, asi como se lavra a madeira, asi se vai logo pondo na fabrica;

In Japan, they first work [the lumber for] the entire house, then erect it very quickly.
Em Japão se lavra primeiro a caza toda e depois brevissimamente a alevantão.

The "very quickly" is elsewhere specified by Frois as "three or four days," and Carletti as two days." It is still true today. A carpenter spends most of his days *at his home* planning, marking, cutting and otherwise preparing parts for assembly. If you are friends of the carpenter and visit him, you know how busy he is. Otherwise, you get a very different impression of construction in Japan. Since the ground of the site is usually broken – and the foundations laid (today, there is always some foundation, for Japanese *wallow* in concrete) – long before the parts are ready, you feel *those incompetents are taking forever!* Then, you come home from the office one day to find the house finished! Such construction minimizes the window of vulnerability for a half-finished house in an earthquake and typhoon-prone nation. Still, Kaempfer writes something that indicates one part of Europe – if one thinks of it as Europe – brought prefabricated housing even further than the well-prepared lumber of Japan. After noting that parts of the infamously haphazard Edo were regularly laid out "entirely owing to the accidents of fire" which allowed "builders" to make the new streets according to a plan, we find this eye-opener:

> Many of these places, which have been thus destroy'd by fire, lie still waste, the houses being not built here with that dispatch, as they are at Moscow, where they sell them ready made, so that there needs nothing but to remove and set them up, where they are wanted, without lime, clay, or nails, any time after the fire. (K(S):HJ)

Chamberlain writes something I find incredible that suggests what might have slowed down the Japanese carpenters enough to prevent them from impressing Kaempfer, although my prefabricating carpenter friend does not do it today:

> When building a house, the Japanese construct the roof first; then, having numbered the pieces, they break it up again, and keep it until the substructure is finished. (C:TJ)

11-30 With us, when the figures painted are many, the delight for the eyes is more;
Antre nós, quando as figuras pintadas são muitas, deleitão mais à vista;

In Japan, the less the figures, the more they are appreciated.
Em Japão quanto menos figuras tanto lhe são mais aceitas.

As Okada writes, "at this time, *fûzoku-e* (genre pictures) full of people on screens (*byôbu*) were fashionable. Apparently, to enhance his contrast with Western paintings, Frois is thinking only of *sumi-e* (black ink paintings)." There were indeed depictions of folk-life, although not quite so heavily peopled as those by the Flemish painters, battle-scenes crowded with warriors and horses, although most men tended to be shown in the mass, rather than treated as individual "figures," horrific yet entertaining panoramas of the pandemonium of Buddhist hell, and, of course, celebrities: sumo wrestlers, courtesans, and soon (within fifty years) *kabuki* stars. But, all of these were, I think, considered decoration and not treasured as art, as the black and white *sumi-e* was. While color had been abundantly used in classical Japanese painting, the new warrior culture, with its ideal of strength and discipline respected bold strokes of black and white ink. The Zen tradition became *haute culture*.

In Valignano's SUMARIO, *sumi-e* comes right after the *dogu* (tea utensils) as an example of something simple and (to the Portuguese eye) virtually worthless, that commands a high price. Valignano mentions "a paper painted with a birdy and a little tree [too bad English has no diminutive for *arbolito*!] of black ink, which done by the hand of a known ancient master brings four and ten-thousand ducados [14,000? 410,000? 4x10,000?]." Frois writes about the very picture, by a Chinese master, describing the tree more accurately as "dry/withered" (i.e. leafless for winter, or *dead*) in his *Historia*, for Hideyoshi's desire for it and a tea utensil were held responsible for the execution of a Japanese Christian "Lucas," apparently a saintly man much beloved by his community, when a killing by a half-brother of his gave the authorities the pretext to do so (If *imitation* is the best compliment, *murder* is worst). Decades later, Rodrigues emphasized the importance of minimalism in Japan even beyond Frois: "Although they copy nature in their paintings, they do not like a multitude and crowd of things in their pictures, but prefer to portray, even in a sumptuous and lovely palace, just a few solitary things with due proportion between them . . .". (in C:TCJ)

Frois's word *figuras* is problematic. They may mean *people*. The tendency of the West to literally anthropomorphize its God – that ridiculous enormous *hand* sticking out of a cloud! Is it Michelangelo's "right hand of God" the same one my catechism said Jesus rose up from the dead to "sit on?" – and idolize humans by covering walls with absurdly muscular images does indeed contrast with the nature-painting tradition of the Sinosphere (While the Islamic world managed to contradict *both* with pure geometry! How ironic that "figure," or "figures" (*figuras*) came to mean both *bodies* and *numbers*!) But Frois may be talking about rich versus paltry content, rather than *human* figures (For a page more on human figures, see TT-long), alone. Occidental artists could not bear empty space. Like the literary hack who is paid by the word, you would think they were paid by the number of items crammed into their work, with a bonus paid for the color. Rembrandt and others made studies that bear some resemblance to Japanese art, but (correct me if I am wrong) even the artists who did these sketches apparently did not think of them as pictures worthy of framing, hanging and gazing at. We didn't really *get it* until the 19c. When Lowell writes in *The Soul of the Far East*, "Far Eastern pictures are epigrams rather than descriptions," he acknowledges that the sketch is equally a work of art. The artist's "brush strokes" he wrote, "are very few in number, but each one tells. . . . The force of it grows on you as you gaze. Each stroke expresses surprisingly much, and suggests more." The reason for this are 1) The random yet not chaotic artlessness born naturally from speed; 2) The greater information or "grain" – voluptuousness, sensuality – found in each brush stroke; and, 3) The mastery inherent in the practiced stroke, which Lowell thought "requires heredity to explain." To *Faux Frois* this, respectively:

Among us, artists take days if not months to paint a picture;
In Japan, they can complete a picture in seconds.

We admire the way things are reproduced in our pictures;
They delight in the texture of the brush mark itself.

We write and paint with different instruments upon different materials;
They paint using the very same things they do their writing with.

The dexterity learned with Chinese characters and the mastery of *stroke* marking Far Eastern painting are one and the same. One could say, *they paint writing and write painting.* I wonder if the resultant minimalism gave birth to Zen in China, rather than the vice versa, as is commonly held.

~~~~~~

11-31 We take care to plant in our gardens trees that bear fruit;
Nós de preposito plantamos em noss[os] ja[r]dins arvores que dem fructo;

> The Japanese prize most in their *niwa* (garden/s) those that bear only flowers.
> *Os Japões estimão em mais em suas nivas as que dão somente flores.*

The Iberians in general and the Jesuits in particular seem to have been *very* fruit-conscious. They continually use the metaphor of "bearing fruit" when writing of their Christian mission. Cruz enthused on Chinese fruit – including three major types of oranges – and a fruit related to the lichee which one could never eat enough of. In *De Missione*, Miguel=Valignano boasted that in a single orchard in Lisbon there were no less than 76 varieties of pears! (J/S:DM) dial.17) No wonder Columbus described the shape of the earth – it was supposed to rise up high at the equator, or rather around the garden of Eden – as a pear!

But Japanese? They preferred food for the eyes in their gardens. And what really surprised the Jesuits was not so much the absence of fruit and abundance of flowering trees in Japanese gardens as the fact that the very tree types they cultivated for and identified with fruit were, in Japan, feted for their bloom. If "we" (in our Latinate or Germanic tongues) don't specify we are talking about a *tree,* the word "cherry," or "plum," alone, presumes the *fruit*. In Japan, on the other hand, these trees are synonymous with their bloom – so a plum (*ume*) or cherry (*sakura*) means the blossoms of the same, and, in the case of the cherry, even the generic term for blossoms/floweres, *hana,* can refer to the tree! To specify the fruit of the cherry, on the other hand, a longer word (*sakuranbo*) is needed! While Frois's contrast is fine as is, we could use some more specific to flowers:

> *In Europe, we walk about looking at and gathering the flowers of spring.*
> *In Japan, they find one flower, or rather a blossoming tree and sit under it for hours.*

> *In Europe, we only write poems to people;*
> *In Japan, they sometimes write them to trees and hang them from their branches.*

For more on blossom-viewing, please see my soon-to-be published *Cherry Blossom Epiphany*.

~~~~~~

11-32 We use fireplaces;
Nós uzamos de chiminés;

> The Japanese, at covered *kotatsu* [tables] in the middle of the house.
> *E os Japões de cotacçus cubertos no meo da caza.*

With *kotatsu,* "covered" goes without saying. Heat from live coals is kept within the skirts of the cloth or quilting that goes over the table and extends down to the floor and beyond. If central heating is a rug, the *kotatsu* is a pair of slippers, which does the same thing more efficiently and better, if you, like me, prefer a cool head. Speaking of slippers, you must, however, have clean socks or the stench is horrible! Otherwise, the *kotatsu* is delightful. The great traveler Bird – who had been around the British isles and the American Rockies (among other places) before visiting Japan – put the *kotatsu* into international perspective. With "the whole" of a Japanese house "being merely a porous screen from the inclemency of the weather . . . the invitation to creep under the kotatsu is as welcome as the "sit-in" of the Scotch Highlands or the "put your feet in the stove" of Colorado." (B:UTJ)

I had always thought the device a purely Japanese invention, but Okada writes it is *Chinese*. Regardless, it is the Japanese who have developed it into the most splendid heater in existence, the *hori-kotatsu*, where a pit is made in the floor – a *tatami* mat is removed and replaced when the *kotatsu* is put away – so one may dangle one's legs under the table while seated warm at floor level, and the modern version, the *denki-kotatsu*, where a small electrical heater is attached to the bottom of the table.

1. Fireplaces: When Frois wrote, English also conflated "chimney" and "fireplace." Pardon my modernized translation. I assume we always envision a fireplace connected to a chimney.

~~~~~~

11-33 In Europe, the sawyers are hired, and not the saw;
Em Europa se alugão os serradores e não a serra;

> In Japan, each saw costs as much per day as each one of the sawyers.
> *Em Japão tanto jornal leva a serra por dia como cada hum dos serradores.*

"Our" side is the opposite of 12-21, where we hire a boat but *not the men* who come with it. The Japan side of both contrasts, however, is similar, for the men and the tool/vessel are separately hired. It would seem the Japanese liked itemized bills.

~~~~~~

11-34 The lawn of our patios is appreciated for people to sit on;
A relva em nossos pateos hé estimada pera se asentar a jente;

> In Japan, all the grass on the grounds is *vaza to* [deliberately] denuded.
> *Em Japão vazato se há toda a erva de arrancar dos terreiros.*

All grass – except for bamboo, mungo grass (called *ryunohige:*dragon-whisker) and such "grasses" not made for walking on – is *weed* to the Japanese. The very word is the same. What English calls "weed-pulling" is *kusa-tori*, or "*grass*-taking." When pressed to explain their tendency to denude the ground, most Japanese will they say their compulsive weed-killing is to prevent mosquitoes and other harmful bugs (*gaichu*) from "boiling up" (*wakideru*) during the humid season and allow more air to circulate, preventing houses from rotting, but I feel this lack of sympathy toward all things not growing in pots, gardens or crops doubtless derives from a farmer's control mentality. It is certainly true that in the USA, too, farmers have been known to raze the trees around their houses simply to gain more field and more view of it. Moreover, Japanese crops, unlike those of Europe, were in perpetual danger of being re-taken. This, writes Watsuji Tetsuro, means everything:

> Japan's most difficult season, the one which determined its architecture, the scorching heat of the dog-days, is just when vegetation proliferates and this means a fight to the death with weeds. To neglect this battle is as good as giving up farming all together. And, it is just this battle with weeds that is unnecessary in Europe. Once the ground is cultivated, the land remains submissive to humans. It doesn't try to revert to wilderness at every turn. So farm work lacks the element of battle with nature. You sow your wheat or hay and wait for it to grow up. . . . even if some weeds are found between the grain, the weeds are weaker. Eventually, harvest comes. You might say there is no need for defense, just the offensive plowing, sowing and harvesting. (*Fudoron:* 1935)

The result? The people of the Mediterranean – the font of Western culture – are naturally lazy. I threw caution to the wind and took this idea further in my 1984 book, *Han-Nihonjinron* (J/G:HNR), where I suggested that the Western idea of casting oneself into the hands of fate was to *do nothing* – like that Lilly in God's hands – while, to the Japanese, it was *work-as-usual*, for, in weed-paradise, *work was taken for granted*. I justified this stereotyping of our respective views of following fate as a tool for deconstructing the hoary stereotypes of an *active West* and *passive East*.

I disliked the mud my Japanese landlord forced me to walk through by putting weed-killer on the grass I allowed to grow in front of my rented house; but the Japanese approach, for all its problems, beats the modern Usanian one which wastes more irreplaceable fossil fuel on lawn-mowers and leaf-blowers – not to mention irrigation – than people in most of the world use to live on, while lowering the quality of "our" own life by *destroying* the quiet.

keeping the sabbath

lawn-mow sunday
only thunder brings us
peace and quiet!

How, one wonders, did the Portuguese of Frois's time keep *their* lawns mowed? Or did they manage to find grasses that didn't need clipping? (Were long handled scythes used? Were sheep brought in? Or were armies of servants on their knees clipping away?)

11-35 In Europe streets are low in the middle for the water to run there;
Em Europa são as ruas baxas no meo pera por ali correr a agoa;

In Japan, the middle is high, and it is low by the houses for it to run alongside.
Em Japão no meo altas, e baxas junto das cazas pera correr ao[no?]longo dell[as].

Thunberg wrote "the roads in this country are broad and furnished with two ditches, to carry off the water, and in good order all year round." The very fact he mentioned *two* ditches implies that in the late-18c, "we" still had only *one*. Here is a clear case where "we" are the party to have changed our ways, for most roads in the West with visible ditches today have the ditches on the side rather than the middle. In Texas, (another country altogether), country roads may go *under* rather than over small streams – you clean off your tires coming into the LBJ ranch! – but I have never seen one with a gulley going *down it* as Frois describes. Okada cites a Japanese source indicating that Kyoto streets were especially high in the middle. Frois may have missed a much larger difference. Thunberg:

> Their care for good order, and the convenience of travellers, has even gone so far, that those who travel up the country always keep to the left, and those that come from the capital to the right; a regulation which would be of the greatest utility in Europe, enlightened as it is, where they frequently travel upon the roads with less discretion and decorum. (T:TEAA)

The *second* time I read this, I realized that Thunberg has given us the recipe for a head-on collision! Actually, *he* is heading to the capital on the left-hand side of the road and those coming toward him from the capital are on *his* right. (Since Thunberg was a careful on his physical observations, I suspect a mistranslation into English.) Another interesting contradiction that post-dated Frois were the mile posts. Thurnberg noted that "all the miles are measured from one point only of the kingdom, viz. from Niponbas [Nihonbashi], or the bridge in the capital of the country, Jedo." This was true from 1603. In *Japan-think America-think* (1992), Robert Collins writes:

> AMERICA-THINK measures distances between cities and towns from "city limits" to "city limits."
>
> JAPAN-THINK measures distances between cities and towns from arbitrarily selected "city centers" to "city centers." (One can go thirty miles *in* Tokyo until getting *to* Tokyo – a historic area "downtown" called Nihonbashi.) (C:JA)

11-36   In Europe, one enters a house from level ground;
  Em Europa se emtra nas cazas por terra chã;

> In Japan, they make bridges with some wood or stones to pass [over into the house]. *Em Japão lhe fazem pontes com alguns paos ou pedras pera pasarem.*

Frois is explaining 11-35. These "bridges" let the drainage flow down the street unobstructed. Needless to say, the entrance-bridges also provided an aesthetic opportunity.

11-37   In Europe, doors open directly upon the street;
  Em Europa saem as portas da caza patentes pera a rua;

> In Japan, [they open] into their yard or *niwa* [garden], to avoid facing the street. *Em Japão pera seu qintal ou* niva, *proqurando não estar fronteira hà rua.*

The hard-to-translate *patentes* of the original implies that by opening "directly" upon the street, "our" doors show what lies within the house to anyone who might be looking from the street.

The gate and the door are still generally separate in Japan, even for small houses with miniscule yards. One can think of the space between as insulation needed because the doors themselves are not very strong and the houses are left wide open all day in the summer. Also, it is a matter of custom. For someone used to it, stepping right out into the street, and vice versa, would be too fast a transition to and fro the outside world. I, for one, appreciate that speed-bump.

But Frois's contrast only concerns *the houses of the gentry.* Many if not most of the homes of the townsmen and almost all boarding houses in Japan had no front garden. A note by Golownin's editor describes the Japan of the rest, that is the poor majority, of us (when I lived in Japan, I was poor and so I include *myself,* here.): "In their houses, the street door always stands open; but there is a jealousy [jalousie] or blind put up at the entrance, formed of small net work, which prevents the inmates from being seen, without impeding their sight. (G:MCJ3) Besides the blind, which is usually completely open for the bottom three feet or so, the Japanese take measures to prevent dust and heat from blowing in from the street: they regularly dash or sprinkle water in front of their homes.

11-38   In Europe, pools are made with clean rectangular, walls;
  Em Europa se fazem tanqes de parede quadrados e limpos;

> In Japan, they make ponds or cisterns with crevices, small inlets and with rocks and little islands in the middle; and this is dug in the ground. *Em Japão fazem humas lagoaszinhas ou balsas com recantos e emseadas peqenas, com penedos e ilhaszinhas no meo, e isto cavado no chão.*

There is a world of difference in aesthetic taste expressed here. Raised geometrical perfection versus sunken natural scenic beauty. It is the Japanese and not the Europeans who long for the Garden of Eden, the land the farmer betrayed. Today, the Far Eastern pond – for the credit hardly belongs to Japan alone – may well be more common throughout the world than the rectangular ones which most people identify with industrial use or something equally ugly: swimming aimlessly back-and-forth.

The Japanese youth who toured the West while Frois wrote his TRATADO were less impressed with the rectangular, clean walls (they do not mention them) than with another aspect of Western waterworks Frois happens to neglect. Miguel – here, I do not feel Valignano took the lead! – goes on and on for pages about the gardens with the innumerable devices for squirting people with "spears of water," so, "in the final event, there is not a single place in the gardens where you are safe from a water-attack!" (J/S(V):DM) The emissaries were, after-all young, and like today, where the Japanese flock to Disneyland . . . – Seriously, we all know about Versailles, but here we are talking about the grounds of the Count of Tuscany half a century earlier. These water-tricks and the countless fountains were explained, as everything else, as proof of Europe's great wealth. Still, one can't help wondering if the wise Valignano felt the childishness of his Western Civilization as he dialogued Miguel's report.

Annotating this contrast was hard because almost everything I can find on garden history begins with the geometric excesses of the 17c and follows with the Chinese-English idea of natural irregularity. We are not told that both the triumphant un-natural geometric paradise *and* the refreshing wilderness (equally contrived, but, like those in the Far East, not obvious) were found in 16c Europe. Duerr and Brueghel's evident love for natural scenes must already have been reflected in at least some of "our" gardens. Of course, many of "us" did not care for wilderness – "Van Mander sourly remarked that the artist [Brueghel] 'in passing the Alps' in his journey to Italy, 'swallowed the mountains and crags to vomit them up on his return on his canvases and panels.'" (H:CER). Moreover, we usually did not put sages into the wilderness, as the Chinese and Japanese did. We identified the woods with the "wild man." Still, the wild man of Giambologna's gigantic sculpture Allegory of the Apennines (1579) looks intelligent and I have found *one* appreciation of the natural (besides Rodrigues on the Zen garden, as quoted elsewhere):

> an author in 1575 explains that the paths in a country house garden are 'as pleasant to walk on as a seashore when the tide is out.' (H:CER)

It goes without saying that the taste of the majority of Frois's compatriots favored the rectangularity he noted. Another *Faux Frois* based on what Francis Bacon wrote about *his* ponds which (like many English things) belatedly reflected the continental style of Frois's time.

> *Our pools have pretty tiles that may be seen at the bottom because the water is clear.*
> *They have no tiles and the only sight is fish near the surface for the water is too dark to see below.*

~~~~~~

11-39 We work hard that our trees grow straight upward;
Antre nós se trabalha muito que as arvores vão direitas pera cima;

> In Japan, they *waza to* [deliberately] hang stones from the branches to make them become bent. *Em Japão vazato lhe pindurão pedras nos ramos pera as fazer yr tortas*

Since most trees want to grow straight up, "our" side of the contrast brings to mind the little boy who informed Art Linkletter that *he taught the rooster a trick*. "And what might that be?" asks our host. The little boy gulps: "I taught the rooster to chase the hens." But, to Japanese, "our" trees would have looked strange, like they'd been tampered with. "The generally weak wind in Europe," writes Watsuji in 1935,

> is apparent in the shape of the trees. They are straight and orderly as botanical specimen. The umbrella[cone]-shaped pine and pencil-shaped cypress are especially noteworthy. Perfectly composed, bun-like pines are not only found in parks but growing in fields and on mountains. . . . For us – we to whom the very word *pine* invariably calls to mind kinked trunks and lopsided limbs – this symmetrical shape seems extremely artificial. . . . Considering further, this shape seems artificial because we are used to seeing the irregular tree forms of our native land. In our country, it is regular forms that can only be artificially produced. But, that, for the tree *is* a natural shape, and an irregular shape unnatural. So, in our country, the *artificial* and the *rational* are conflated, while in Europe the *natural* and the *rational* are. (J/W:F)

This faith in the rationality/logicality/reasonability (all these meanings are inherent in *gôri-teki,* which I translated as "rational") of nature deriving from mild wind, then, led the West to search for rules inside of nature and *voila!* Science here we come! While strong winds may have created the irregularity of Japanese pines out in the mountains, Watsuji might have given his countrymen a bit more credit for their work to make domestic trees look natural. Alcock was impressed:

> It is perfectly astonishing to see the amount of industry and perseverance which the Japanese must have devoted to the production of these plants. There were some little fir trees, not more than a foot in height, and yet I counted upward of fifty ties, by means of which the shoots were bent backward and forward in a zigzag way. (A:COT)

I would say that Japanese trees show *more character* than "ours," but some people feel the result is stunted, ugly. *The Barbarian in Asia*, if I may describe Michaeux by his very apt title, wrote that "the trees are sickly, puny, meager, rising feebly, growing with difficulty, fighting against adversity, and tortured as soon as possible by man to appear still more dwarfish and miserable." In *The Lotus and the Robot*, Arthur Koestler found a display of the stick-supported trees "looks like a procession of invalids walking on crutches." Even monk Kenkô, the 14c doyen of subdued taste in Japan might have agreed, for he found the behavior of a man who threw away all his bonsai after realizing that deformed men were "ugly and repulsive" "quite understandable" (trans. Keene). In this contrast, Frois used the word *tortas.* The root of this word for "bent" or "crooked" is one with *tortured*.

But pine growing on the side of a mountain in the face of a brisk wind *do* grow like that. And, their slow and tortured growth – especially the paucity of limbs – actually contributes to their incredible longevity. Granted, this is not naturally found except in the mountains or on a seashore, but if your idea of paradise is a sage one (a Chinese-style mountain-peak landscape) how could such limbs seem deformed or cruel? It also bears noting that shape – bending for the sake of appearance – is but half of the idea. The hanging stones (or other ties) are also meant to prevent the limbs from growing away from us. There is a magic to tall trees "reaching the sky," but there is something equally precious about low branches on large trees, where a life far larger than ours remains within our pitifully low human reach, literally touchable. When such a cherries bloom, we can walk around with our head in the clouds. *We can experience trees as a bird would.* But, high or low, big or small, the main effect and justification for the domestic tree is aesthetic. Some may see the the Sino-Japanese tree as Golownin's editor did; i.e. "old, distorted and deformed;" I, for one, find a very pleasing *cubism*, a cubism that satisfies more than Picasso, the much older cubism found in mountain trees and the art of Sesshu. And, related to this free-and-tall contrast another Frois skipped:

> *In Europe, the only tiny trees are seedlings which are encouraged to grow into large trees.*
> *In Japan, there are trees as small as a palm in height that are older than any living human.*

Frois forgot to mention *bonsai.* Why? Why? Why? I cannot imagine anyone overlooking something *so* different, *so* incredible, *so* adorable and *so* old!

Frois's contrast wants one important qualification. If the wind-warped tree represents the aesthetics of Taoism, the straight cedar stands tall for Shintô, the traditional Way of the Gods. Today, Japanese usually write it 杉. But, once, it was more common to write 真木 (*maki*) meaning "true-tree." Japanese revere these trees, even putting huge braided holy ropes, or festoons, around large individuals (completely untouched, ramrod straight cedars). Japan has always had a straight side, too.

11-40 We wash our hands and face are washed in silver or ceramic basins;
Antre nós se lavão as mãos e o rosto em bacios d'agoasmãos de prata ou porselana;

> In Japan, they are washed in a wooden *tarai* [tub], at best *urishi'd* [lacquered].
> *Em Japão se lava em hum* taray *de pao quando muito* vruxado

European face-washing basins were intricately decorated affairs, whereas a *tarai* is a plain item, made like a barrel, of slats reinforced with soft metal bands. Small ones are not only used to wash ones face and hands, but to scoop out water from the bath to wash oneself. Speaking of which, Frois caught a small contrast with respect to washing but may have missed a large one.

We use soap to wash inside of the bath;
They wash outside of the bath and rinse off before getting into it.

Or, was this a difference that did not yet exist in the 16c? But if Frois misses some contrasts that (rightly or wrongly) seem obvious, he never misses an opportunity to point out that *lacquer*. It is almost as if lacquer by itself – or, rather, *by not being a valuable metal* – was enough to make *anything* contrary! All told, lacquer appears in a dozen or so contrasts. While such a use of it implies its relative lack of value next to the gold or silver, Frois elsewhere expresses his fondness for lacquer-ware, and the Mission churches used a decorated form of it called *makie* (designs which included some gold glitter) to make picture frames for the images of Jesus and Mary and bible stands. But the greatest supporter of *urushi* was Chamberlain, who gave it five pages in his THINGS JAPANESE! The article includes the "mysterious but undoubtedly authentic" fact "that lacquer dries most quickly in a damp atmosphere." And if the room is dark "so much the more quickly will the lacquer harden." That makes it somewhat like cement, which reputedly cures best under water. But Chamberlain's best line is this: "Appreciation of lacquer is a taste which has to be acquired, grows upon one, and places the best lacquer in the category of almost sacred things." Marco Polo's Zipangu as El Dorado turned out to be, rather, the Land of Lacquer, *Uruxi*, or, as lacquer was called in English, "Japan!"

Frois's contrast is a bit disingenuous because, Okada points out, the Japanese had their own fancy toilet ware. These lacquered vessels with *makie* paintings were not, however, for washing the *face*. They were for washing the *hands* and included a very clever device, "horns" to catch and hold back the wide ends of the sleeves so they would not get wet!

..

~~~~~~

11-41 We pour water on our hands from the spout of a jug in a thin stream bit by bit;
Nos deitamos a agoa às mãos polos biqos dos gumis, que saya delgada e pouqa;

> They pour it out in a torrent from a wooden pail.
> *Elles por qubos de pao que deitão hum torno muito groso.*

And, not only for washing our hands: water came out of our fountains and wine from our wine-skins in pee-like streams. Should anything be read into this?

For once, *De Missione's* central concept has been overturned. Here, Japan would seem to be the one with resources to spare. Water, at any rate was abundant.

Today, we and Japanese generally use the same type of basin or sink. There are only two places where we wash our hands in different ways. First, when entering a shrine in Japan, we find something rarely used for anything but stew in the Occident, *ladles* to scoop out water to wash our hands. Second, most Japanese flush-toilets let you stick your fingers into the water refilling the tank, which is designed to flow in a little stream through the air above the tank. Not only does it save water, but does not require one to touch any handles, so it is hygienic. Of course, you may still have to grasp a door-handle to leave the rest-room! (I fear that sanitary engineering East and West is an utter farce!)

~~~~~~

11-42 In Europe, our roofs are ordinarily clean;
Em Europa [est[ão] ordinariamente nossos telhados limpos;

> Those of Japan are loaded with stones, wood and bamboo for wind [protection].
> *Em Japão carreg[ados de] pedras e paos e canas pera o vento.*

Much of Japan is Chicago. The same gusts of wind that make crooked trees can blow off the straw from a poor man's roof. But for all the huffing and puffing, honest-to-god tornados and even hurricane force winds – which would make such stones dangerous – are *very* rare. Big stones are still found on some remaining straw roofs and more recent corrugated tin atrocities. Not all are there for wind protection alone. According to Okada, stones and lumber were often *stored* on the roof! The main roof of finely laid straw was usually too sharply sloped for stones to rest and heavy enough by itself. So the roofs referred to here are those of tiny shacks, and a sort of awning-like extension that may be found on many larger roofs.

~~~~~~

11-43   Our pines, for the most part, bear fruit;
   Os nossos pinheiros pola mayor parte dão fructo;

   In Japan, while there are countless pines with nut-sized cones, they are worthless.
   Em Japão, com aver infinitos, dão pinhas como nozes, que não prestão.

Almost worthless. Kaempfer says "pine-nuts" were "gather'd for fewel." (K:HOJ) and I have come across many haiku and senryu about their being used to roast clams (somewhat suspicious because the pine cone was a conceit for the male gonads (*fuguri*) and the clams . . . – need I say?).

The East coast of the USA with a climate similar to Japan's, likewise does not boast pines with edible pinions. That type of pine may be found in the West with its European style climate of dry summers and wet winters.

~~~~~~

11-44   Our cherry trees bear very delicious and beautiful cherries;
   As nossas sireijeiras dão mui gostozas e fermozas sirejas;

   Those of Japan bear many small, bitter cherries and many beautiful flowers, which the Japanese appreciate. *As de Japão dão muito peqenas e amargozas sireijas e muito fermozas flores que os Japões estimão.*

How interesting that Frois would describe "our" cherries, meaning the fruit, as *beautiful* as well as tasty. I never thought of fruit on the tree as food for the eyes.

If there is fruit on the Japanese cherry tree, I've never seen it. Those "small bitter berries" grow after the blossoms fall, and who looks up then? Until something the Japanese call the "cherry-peach" (*sakura-momo*) was imported in the 19c, there were *no* real fruit-bearing cherries in Japan. On the other hand, clusters of Japanese flowering cherries now bring delight to people in the West. We, too, it would seem, don't mind tree-flowers. But there is no question that we are less aware of them then Japanese. Could it be a linguistic problem?

   To Europeans, a flower is something growing on the ground or close to it.
   To the Japanese, a flower is a flower is a flower though it be a huge tree.

For more on blossom-viewing, again, please see my *Cherry Blossom Epiphany* (740 pages!)

   We think that a flower is better for blooming a long time because we can enjoy it more;
   They claim that the faster a flower falls the more attractive it is, and the more admirable.

~~~~~~

11-45   With us, when one picks a rose or fragrant carnation, we first smell it and then look;
   Antre nós, quando se toma huma roza ou cravo cheirozo, primeiro o cheiramos e depois a vemos;

   The Japanese, paying no attention to the smell, only delight in the sight.
   Os Japões, sem terem conta com o cheiro, se deleitão somente na vista.

Unless the Jesuits imported roses and tested them on their converts, this seems a trick contrast, for the closest native Japanese equivalents (a briar rose and a pink) of what I translated as "rose" and "carnation" are practically without scent. The cherry is also scentless, but the Japanese pay almost as much attention to the scent of the official bloom of the New Year, the plum flower, as we pay to that of the rose. The difference is that the rose was literally brought to the nose or vice-versa, while the scent of plum bloom filled the air, all the way to the hazy moon, if the poets are to be believed.

~~~~~~

11-46 We have many roses, [flowers?], carnations and herbs fragrant and very aromatic;
Antre nós há muitas rozas, fl[ores], cravos e ervas cheirozas e mui odorifeiras.

     In Japan, very few of these have a fragrance.
     Em Japão mui pouqas destas couzas tem cheiro.

Logic-wise, the "flowers" makes no sense. Schütte leaves it as is, so do the Japanese, but the French translators kindly kill it. Maybe Frois himself had a line through it which was eaten by the silverfish with the rest of the missing part of the word.

Besides the plum blossom already mentioned, the jasmine, mandarin orange blossom, orchard, chrysanthemum and violet all delight the nose. We do not have Japanese bending over to smell them, but they did note their scent. Issa had the violet growing wherever the micturition of the goddess of Spring overflowed – a perfect metaphor considering the fact that the scent of the flower in question was considered by some (Ben Franklin, at least) to be the smell of ideal urine (as opposed to what asparagus does to you, and creatable by a liberal intake of pine-nuts!). A Japanese friend, YM, after discussing the various references to scent in Japanese literature came to the conclusion that Frois had a faulty nose and that *the reason the cult of the rose did not develop in Japan was because they enjoyed a much greater variety of scent.* An interesting reversal, but considering 11-45, I have my doubts.

I must admit to being curious about a bigger contrast Frois missed. Unless I am mistaken:

We have flower gardens where many flowers boast their color and scent;
They have only chrysanthemum, which are more like pets or peony or water lilies by themselves.

We have flower-beds near our houses;
They keep most of what few flowers they have in pots or ponds.

In THINGS CHINESE, Ball notes that "the Chinese have no flowers-beds on land, but their flower-beds are in the water." All of the above-mentioned Japanese flower culture comes from China.

~~~~~~

11-47 To the people of Europe, fragrant waters, like of rose, of angelica, etc. are very pleasant;
Hà jente de Europa são mui aceitas agoas cheirozas, como rozada, de flor de angeres etc.;

     The Japanese are not pleased with any of these scents.
     Aos Japões não lhe agrada nada nenhum cheiro destes.

I think most readers will be familiar with rose-water. Rabelais (in Engl. translation) mentions "spirit of roses, orange-flower-water and Angelica." (OED) Father Schütte and the French translators both guess that the *flor de angeres* means orange blossoms. But I doubt Japanese would have disliked *that* scent (While the blossoms and the skin are not the same, Japanese do, after all, put the peels of certain oranges into bath-water). Since Frois elsewhere has no trouble spelling *orange*, and there was an "Angelica water" also called Angel-water (OED), I follow the Japanese translations, both of which go for "flower of angel/s," or Angelica, defined in English as med. L. = *herba angelica* the 'angelic herb,' or 'root of the Holy Ghost,' so named . . . on account of its repute against poison and pestilence, prob. from the fragrant smell and aromatic taste of its root. . . . (OED)

The Japanese were not used to scents sweeter than the incenses they were familiar with. In a word, scents that bear resemblance to what we call perfume or cologne today. A whiff of rose water (see 14-53), to a Japanese aesthete, would be the equivalent of a sip of Rosé table wine to a lover of dry Bordeaux! Even today, Japanese feel Westerners use far too powerful perfume and attribute it to "our" having such strong body odors, bathing less, or being overbearing individuals who don't mind stinking up other people's noses.

I feel there is a broad range of delicate smells which Japanese enjoy that most of "us" know nothing about. These are mostly eatable plants such as *udo, seri, mitsuba* and *myôga*. Chances are you do not know them unless you have lived in Japan.

~~~~~~

11-48 Among us, the scent of benzoin, daisy, etc. is highly esteemed;
Antre nós se estima muito o cheiro de beijoim, de boninas etc.;

> The Japanese think them too strong and cannot suffer them, much less like them.
> *Os Japões o tem por forte e não o podem sofrer nem lhe ag[rad]a.*

My English dictionary calls this benzoin "frankincense of Java," and the Chinese characters used to write it are "easy-breath-scent." (安息香 *ansokuko* in Japanese) The characters meaning "easy" or "relaxed" and "breath" without the "scent" mean *a rest*, and placed before the character for "day," rather than "scent," mean the "sabbath" (安息日 *ansokubi*). I thought it might be named for its effect on those who smell it or for its use in church, but my OJD gives the Persian *arsak* for the etymology. But this does not mean the Chinese characters were *only* chosen to match the sound. Most likely the Chinese person who named it, unlike the Japanese mentioned by Frois, found it relaxing.

In his final LIBRO (1601), Valignano qualified "Maffei's" (i.e. his own (!) earlier) remarks to the effect that Japanese senses were contrary to ours, so that what we thought smelled *good* they thought smelled *bad* and vice versa, by adding that they were not "not discontented with all of our scents, but only the strong ones like Benzoin." That this correction – not needed, of course, by Frois, who sticking to particulars did not err (though I find the Japanese daisy *stinks* and wonder . . .) – went unpublished/unnoticed in Europe is shown by the topsy-turvy hyperbole of Montanus:

> Whatever is most sweet, fragrant and odiferous to us of *Europe*, seems to them as abominable as the stench of Carrion, or whatever else is odious. (M:EEJ: 1670)

It seems to me that Frois has favored scent with far more contrasts than a modern writer would. *Why?* One guess would be that the Jesuits, forbidden to engage in carnal pursuits sublimated their libido into their probiscus. Another would be to deny that Frois has favored scent and point out that *we* have pretty much given up our noses because our eyes and ears are so over-stimulated in the electronic world. A third would be to hypothesize a particular Luso-Iberian interest in scent learned from their neighbors who designed gardens that would smell good in the moonlight, for the importance of scents

> was a concept of central importance in Islamic thought, Muslims who to whom it was a central concept in Islamic thought, an idea which derived from the Hadith, attributed to the Prophet: 'Scent is the food for the soul, and the soul is the vehicle of the faculties of man.' (William Dalrymple *White Mughals.* Viking 2002)

endnote XI
Home & garden

I will not try to find all the house and garden items Frois (and I) may have missed in the course of this chapter, but just give my three personal home favorites – one to heat the body, one to cool it and one for the delight of the soul: the *hibachi, dakikago* and *tokonoma* – for my garden favorite, *kare sansui* (dry rock garden) please see TT-long.

A *hibachi*, literally "fire-kettle" or "fire-pot" is, according to the dictionary, a "charcoal brazier." Here is Ms. Bacon:

> Our *hibachi* is made of a section of a tree trunk, smoothed into a regular oval and hollowed out in the middle. . . . Into the hollowed center is set a copper pan. This is filled with light straw ashes, a little earthenware inverted tripod is pressed down into the ashes so only the three points stick up, and then in the centre, between the three points, a charcoal fire is made. This smolders away quietly under the tea kettle placed on the tripod, and gives out neither smoke nor gas. The arrangement is far superior to an alcohol lamp, as well as much cheaper, and why we do not use it in America I cannot imagine, except we are not bright enough to think of such a simple thing . . ."
> (B:AJI 1893)

These fires could be carefully *buried in the ashes* (which seem like a fine silt) and be waiting for you in the morning. I suspect the biggest problem for "us" would have been obtaining the right type of charcoal. That is not so simple. You can not just stick in the type of stuff you would roast a weenie with, for you would fill your room with smoke. There are charcoals of all different colors, scents, burn-speed, sound (!) and shape. (A good traditional charcoal maker in Japan is a National Living Cultural Treasure.) While tea or sake may be steeped or heated, and the faint light would have been useful for the long winter night, the main purpose of the *hibachi* was, I think heating hands. Bacon's was a section of hollowed-out tree trunk, but ceramic or metal *hibachi* were more common, so that the *Faux Frois* image I get is this:

> *We put kettles and pots on our fires.*
> *They put fires in their kettles and pots.*

I borrowed the phrase following "they" from the turn of the century humorist Douglas Sladen, who further describes them as "exactly the Italian *scaldino*, a hoop-handles saucepan for holding charcoal embers." (*"Japan, the Italy of the East"* chapter in S:MQT) He describes the fire as "a shovelful of charcoal ash, with a smouldering ember in the middle like a cuckoo's egg," and declares that "Finger-stoves would be a proper name for them." (*"Topsy-Turvy Tokyo"* chapter in Ibid.)

> *We have our guests take a seat by the fireplace of which there is generally one.*
> *They bring in a cushion and a fireplace for each guest.*

But when Sladen writes that "in winter, out of the sun, no Italian or Japanese is ever warm beyond the tips of his fingers," (Ibid), he forgets about the *hibachi's* rival the *kotatsu* (11-32), a superb leg-warmer. Some people, mostly elderly, still enjoy *hibachi* today. And, I can't say that I blame them, for old people do get cold fingers and poking at coals that brighten up and even sputter back at you is so much more satisfying than switching a heater on and off! You might say the *hibachi* keeps you company.

The *dakikago* literally translates as a "hug-basket" or "embracing-basket." It is long, hollow tubular basket of woven bamboo. It came from China originally, but is known in the West as a "dutch-wife." In the sultry summers, they kept ones limbs apart and off the bed so there could be greater ventilation and transpiration. Today, they would still be important and sold in every department store if we took the environment seriously and restricted AC use, but pardon my preaching. *Faux Frois* is more fun:

> We carry produce in baskets but do not take them to bed with us.
> The Japanese not only take them to bed but embrace them while they sleep.

Its other names were "bamboo-wife," "bamboo-slave," and *she* gave birth to countless haiku in the days when haiku were part of the mirth-filled body of *haikai*. Here are a few gathered by Shiki:

an old relationship	*together for the dog-days*	*who's complaining!*
making up after a year apart, me and my hug-basket	my bamboo wife without you, how could i make it through the night!	so quiet she's a bit too cool my bamboo wife
a pinch in the night	*a cool hug*	*too bad she can't fan!*
is my bamboo wife jealous of beauties who come in my dreams?	summer's when we get the hots for bamboo wives	is this sweat-rot? we need some cooling wind my bamboo wife!
from vanity to vanity	*no sweat last night!*	*cool and empty*
a hug basket and a mistress – yesterday versus today	a hug-basket now, even my dreams are all cool	ah, hug-basket your heart so very close to the fall

(the Japanese originals with the authors' names – and no titles, of course – are in Shiki's BUNRUI-HAIKU ZENSHU *vol.5*)

If air-conditioning should ever be outlawed, we may *all* rediscover our *bamboo wives*, or, now that we are in a more egalitarian society, gender-wise at any rate, *bamboo husbands*, too.

The *tokonoma.* With winter cold and summer heat vanquished by clever traditional engineering, it is time to consider the third item, the one that is good year round and benefits the soul:

> We put sculptures on stands and hang as many pictures as we please on any wall.
> They only display artwork one item at a time in an alcove built into one wall of the house.

The alcove is called a *tokonoma.* It is a small space, longer up and down than across, located directly behind the seat of honor in the living room. If Japanese culture had invented nothing else, this shrine for art built into every traditional house would be a great contribution to world civilization. It used to extend from the ceiling down almost to the floor, but now sometimes begins at about desk level. We put all sorts of things on the top of a hearth, but this display space is for *bona fide* art alone. If we eat meals in serial and they do so promiscuously (6-6), the opposite can be said about artwork. We crowd pictures together on walls; the Japanese traditionally did not hang up their entire collection (or even a part of it) at once, but regularly changed the single item on display in the *tokonoma.* This isolation of the object assures it gets attention. And the change of display guarantees we don't take it for granted. Or, in Morse's measured words:

The principle of constant exposure is certainly wrong: a good picture is all the more enjoyable if it is not forever staring one in the face. (M:JH&S)

If Morse spoke for the Japanese way, A JAPANESE PAINTER IN LONDON, Yoshio Markino, wrote a few words in defense of "ours." When another Japanese commiserated, "I say Markino, don't you feel it is more like a shop than a drawing-room when you go to the English house? They put all their properties on their drawing rooms," Markino, as a true Anglophile, defended *us*:

> I love both way, Japanese as well as English. It is only different taste, that is all. Certainly it is very artistic taste to have only one genuine Kakemono [hung scroll-picture] on the Tokonoma, and it concentrates all our eyes there. It gives me a very pleasant feeling. But on the other hand, I don't object the English idea at all. When they are arranged beautifully it is awfully nice. Besides, we must think how long could we live in this world. Suppose one had more than five hundred pictures, and he was keeping them in Japanese way, how many times could he see the same picture in his life. How pity to hide some pictures or curios which he so dearly loves. When I think this point, I like the English way quite well. (M:JAL 1910: Chatto and Windus decided not to correct his "quaint English.")

Ideally, one would be wealthy enough to have a gallery room for dozens of pictures *and* a drawing room done in the more subdued Japanese way.

> *We keep the same tapestries hanging up year round;*
> *They change their hanging painting every season or, in some places every week.*

As the Japanese knew, seasonally adjusted decoration satisfies something in us, perhaps the soul we had when we lived outdoors. Theoretically, a wall full of paintings could be re-hung with every change of season, but it is impractical. A *tokonoma* encourages it. This does not mean no paintings of snow in the summer. There is no need to be simplistic. One might prefer a snow-capped mountain in the summer *for the cooling effect*. A clear link with the season is ensured anyway, by a simple flower arrangement in a vase some other device that usually stands on the base of the alcove (or, if it is small, the ledge of the niche) as a complement or offering for the painting – usually black and white calligraphy – hanging above and behind it. The two objects do not compete for attention. The effect is that of a single multi-media work and is not like our practice of hanging different pictures on facing walls or side by side on a wall. Morse also noted that filling up all wall space with pictures meant that most would not enjoy proper light. He did not think we should have to *endure* this.

> Why not modify our rooms, and have a bay or recess, – an alcove in the best possible light, – in which one or two good pictures may be properly hung, with fitting accompaniments in the way of a few flowers, or a bit of pottery or bronze? We have never modified the interior arrangement of our house in the slightest degree from the time when it was shaped in the most economical way as a shelter in which to eat, sleep, and die, – a rectangular kennel, with necessary holes for light, and necessary holes to get in and out by. At the same time, its inmates were saturated with a religion so austere and sombre that the possession of a picture was for a long time looked upon as savoring of worldliness and vanity, unless, indeed, the subject suggested the other world by a vision of hexapodous angels, or of the transient resting-place to that world in the guise of a tombstone and willows, or an immediate departure thereto in the shape of a death-bed scene. (M: JH&S)

In other words, Morse argues that "we" thought of art like most of the Justices of the US Supreme Court thought of pornography when arguing *Fanny Hill*: it had to have a socially redeeming value, and failing that, was judged sinful and therefore intolerable. And like the new rich, now that we can indulge ourselves, we overdo it. We have too much desire and too little taste. The *tokonoma* would be a good way to train ourselves, but for the contradiction already noted by Morse, the worse one's taste, the least likely we are to realize it. Moreover, most Americans no longer even concede there is such a thing as Taste with a capital T. Today, there is only *Your* taste and *Mine*. Even a Ruskin would not make a dent on our democratic denseness. In the end, it is hard to say whether the *tokonoma* is the cause or the result of the good taste it epitomizes and the same thing could be said for the entire interior. Most Western visitors to Japan in the 19c never failed to admit that, *taken in mass, the Japanese have better taste than we do.* Morse put it in terms of "some" versus "the throng."

> With us, the wealthy have a monopoly on good taste.
> In Japan, the poor people are often as discriminating as the rich.

The Jesuits wrote that the really dissolute poor found in the West were not seen in China and Japan. They were delighted to find *all* the people in Japan were remarkably clean, and wrote about it many times. But they did not comment on their equally remarkable aesthetic taste. Is it because *almost all Europeans at that time had no artistic taste* to speak of and simply equated the brilliant, the sumptuous, and the richly adorned with beauty and the realistically depicted with art? Our idea of art was, and still is, *high end*. It costs bundles. Alice Mabel Bacon put it bluntly:

> It seems as easy for the Japanese to make things pretty and in good taste, even when they are cheap and only used by the poorer people, as it is for American mills and workers to turn out endless varieties of attempts at decoration, – all so hideous that a poor person must be content, either to be surrounded by the worst possible taste, or to purchase only such furnishings as are entirely without decoration of any kind. "Cheap" and "nasty" have come to be almost synonymous words with us, for the reason that taste in decoration is so rare that it commands a monopoly price, and can only be procured by the wealthy. In Japan this is not the case . . . (B:JGW 1890)

What I find unique and valuable in Bacon's appraisal is that she does not think that "our" poor *necessarily* have bad taste. Not *all* of them are "won by tawdry tint" (as Morse puts it) so much as *forced* into it. Yet she does admit that our poor were not as aesthetically advanced as theirs. A few years later, in a fine chapter called "the instinct of beauty" in her lesser known book, A JAPANESE INTERIOR, Bacon notes that "the Japanese artisan" cannot help but make beautiful things "whether he makes anything pecuniarily by it or not," and opines –

> I cannot get at the bottom of the whole thing, or find out how much this instinct of beauty is the cause, and how much the effect, of the gentleness and attractiveness of the common people here, but certain it is, that in this country there is no need of the various missions (flower missions and the like) which have been started in England and America to cultivate the aesthetic sense of the poor in the great cities; for here every poor man's table service is dainty and delicate in the highest degree . . . and as he sits at his work he usually has somewhere about the room a vase of beautifully arranged flowers. One of our workmen would starve on what supports him and his family, and yet the Japanese laborer has his aesthetic nature fully developed, and its gratification within his reach at all times. With him "the life is more than meat," it is beauty as well, and this love of beauty has upon him such a civilizing effect that some people are led to think that the lower classes in Japan do not need Christianity . . . (B:JI)

Note. The flowers were not *bought* beautifully arranged. The poor man or woman *did it.* As Menpes the painter wrote, at about the same time as Bacon,

> It would be no exaggeration to say that if a common coolie were given an addressed envelope to stamp, he would take great pains to place that little coloured patch in relation to the name and address in order to form a decorative pattern. . . . The whole of Japan is one perfect bit of placing." (M:JRC)

In her earlier book, Bacon explained matter-of-factly that artwork could be bought in Japan with "the money that in this country must be spent in beds, tables and chairs;" but, here, she admits she can not really comprehend the phenomenon. Menpes, I think, *does*. Still, the last words to Bacon's paragraph are precious. As a Christian, perhaps thinking of easy divorce, abortion and such, she found the Japanese lower classes *less* moral than our lower classes, yet she also *knew* they stole and killed less and were:

> . . . more gentle, more contented, more civilized I should say, except the word "civilization" is so difficult to define and to understand, that I do not know what it means now as well as I did when I left home. (B:JI)

XII

OF BOATS, THEIR CUSTOMS AND DÔGU [TOOLS]
das embarqasões e seus custumes e dogus

12-1 We have *naos,* galleons, caravels, galleys, pinnace, *catures,* brigatines, etc.;
Antre nós há naos, galiões, caravelas, galés, fustas, catures, bargantins, etc.;

In Japan, there are none of these.
Em Japão penitus não há nada disto.

Plenty versus *poverty* in ships. Frois's homeland boasted over a century of excellence at sea and these boats were both the symbol and the result of this pioneering. It didn't come easy. When Prince Henry the Navigator (Infante Dom Henrique) died in 1460, he left his friends and acquaintances with a huge debt. Eventually, it paid off. By leading the way in the Age of Exploration, Portugal (and, by the time Frois wrote, Spain) not only gained the prestige which the USA got for making it to the moon, but enormous material benefits that made them the envy of Europe. And those boats generated far more wealth than we generally imagine, for most of the precious metal robbed from the "New World" did not cross the Atlantic but the Pacific, where it was traded for spices which, while not necessarily worth their weight in gold, would sell in Europe for much, much more than the gold (or copper or silver) used to buy them. The ships mentioned by Frois are:

The *nao.* Stretch-jet of European shipping and representative "southern barbarian boat" (*nambansen*). This three-mast, three or four-deck ship with a beautiful name (from the Greek word for temple, *naos*) was a plumped up *caravel* (below). As Portugal's mainstay for shipping in the East Indies, it ferried hundreds of people and goods back and forth from Macao to Japan. The *nao* was lightly armed compared to its look-alike *galleon,* but still out-gunned anything in the East (see 12-9).

A *galleon's* guns were legend. In *De Missione,* Valignano=Miguel mention "the most popular type of galleon" made in the days of "the world-famous Portuguese King Sebastian" (the warrior king who saved Europe from the Turks), which "has one large cannon for every day of the year." Valignano=Mancio cuts in later and adds that in the Republic of Venice – sometimes "Europe" was more than Luso-Iberia – they had one with 500 big guns! Even a Hollywood movie producer could not reproduce such fire-power! Shorter and higher than galleys, they carried on most of the trade with the Americas (With all those English pirates out there, what but a battleship would do?)

The lateen sail *caravels* are what got the West around the world. Lateen sails were found on small boats in the Mediterranean for centuries (maybe millennia). Triangular, they let a boat tack into the wind but, for some reason, Europeans were hooked on square sails and only the concerted efforts of Prince Henrique, who knew well that our Muslim rivals got around far better than us with lateen sails got us to try them. The two or three-mast *caravel* was light, strongly built, and streamlined, for the cabins were put fore and aft and the central deck was low and clear. *It was against the law to sell them to foreigners.* Considering the expense of development, and the fact they were strategic weapons, that was understandable. If I understand correctly, even with Spain and Portugal united under one king in the late 16c, Spain had beg Portugal to sell them caravels (F(M&J:T).

Galleys had one to three rows, or banks, of oars of varying length (all the oar-holes later served for guns). The longest were made possible by what I think is a European invention, the *apostis* "a framework standing out on each side of the hull and running parallel to it; a strong external timber, in which the thowls, against which the oars were rowed, were set." This added leverage allowed the use of oars of 30-50 feet (about a third inboard) pulled by 3-7 men who sat on steps (*alla scaloccio*). 208 of such hyper-long oared, single-bank galleys took on the Muslims in Lepanto. Though mostly confined to the Mediterranean, combined with sails, they also served for North Africa trade.

As for the rest, the *cature*, was a small war-boat used in the Indian sea, the *fusta* (pinnace: French) a triangular-sailed ship, and the brigantine (bargantine/burgantino) a square-sailed two-masted ship; (F(O):T) and Frois's Japanese side, being only "none of these," requires no explanation.

~~~~~~

12-2   Our boats have ribs and decks;   *As nosssas embarqasões tem cavernas e cuberta;*
           Those of Japan do not.   *As dos Japões não.*

This is getting to sound like old Chinese definitions of the *sea cucumber*. It has *no* head *no* tail, *no* eyes, *no* bones, *no* scales ... So, what *does* a Japanese boat have? Let me just say *it is more like an insect, all shell, while the more sea-worthy European vessel had a solid endoskeleton.* For this reason, the size of the Japanese ship was severely limited. So was its functionality. Its construction was sturdy as hell, but "the form and rig ... have never altered in historic times." (H. Warrington Smyth, *Mast & Sail in Europe and Asia* (1906))

Lest "we" get *uppity* (the perfect adjective for the Occident for the last few centuries, right?) it should be pointed out that the *Chinese* sea-going junks of the early 15c, of which the largest type (over 400 feet in length and a 165 feet wide) dwarfed the Western ships of the Age of Exploration, were more advanced than ours, for, like the bamboo, or more appropriately, the whale, they had water-tight bulwark compartments – something the West "invented" in the late-18c, dating back to at least two centuries – holes in the prow to dampen rocking movement in heavy seas, a balanced rudder (equal parts before and after the stern post), a large after-hang, centerboards and leeboards, flat sails and other modern aspects. H. Warrington Smyth, summed it up well: the junk was long ahead of us in "scientific fore-and-aft sailing." They got around, too. "When our forefathers paddled along shore in open boats, the Chinaman sailed to East Africa in five-masters." (Smyth) And, they had colonies in New Zealand (more in TT-long, or see Louise Levathes: *When China Ruled the Seas – the treasure fleet of the dragon throne 1405-1433*; and Gavin Menzies: *1421, The Year China Discovered the World*).

So what prevented these Chinese from discovering the West? *Politics*. In *Guns, Germs and Steel*, Jared Diamond theorizes that progress in Europe was unstoppable because of European diversity, whereas China's unity – the government ordered the explorer-traders to stop sailing – allowed otherwise unstoppable Progress to be nipped in the bud. Indeed, the Japanese would give up the gun after unifying; but the DE MISSIONE report of 1589 opined that political *disorder* in Japan, as opposed to Europe where Christian fellowship held all together amicably, was the only thing holding Japan back. There would seem to be a fine tight-rope to walk between order and disorder. Umesao Tadao, a Japanese anthropologist not cited by Diamond wrote such an *Eco-History of Civilization* (*Bunmei no Setai-shi*: 1974), which explains the success of the Far East and Far West in terms of their being close enough to major ancient civilizations arising on the Euro-Asian Continent, but far enough removed from the center to avoid being constantly over-run by migrations from droughts in the dry center of the continental mass, so that stability needed for long-term development was possible.

~~~~~~

12-3   Many of our boats operate by sail alone;   *Das nossas embarqasões muitas se servem somente de vela;*
           Those of Japan are all rowed/sculled.   *As de Japõo todas se remão.*

M & J write that Frois, because he is proud of his nation's *sailing* tradition, exaggerates by claiming that most Portuguese ships relied *only* on sails. But "many" (*muitos*) is hardly *all*. Frois's contrast stands. Generally speaking, Japanese did not rely on sails as much as Europeans. Their boats, had sails, but they were relatively small and poor at going into the wind. Moreover, they often operated near convoluted rocky coasts and islands with fickle wind and water currents, so man-power was indeed commonly resorted to.

Portuguese sailing technology not only made them the first Europeans to round Africa, reach America (Columbus may not have been Portuguese, but we should be more aware that financial support was not all he got from Luso-Iberia.) and make it around the world, opening up new geography, but, R. Hooykaas opines, it helped instigate the renaissance of *learning*. By proving the Ancients did not know everything, that there were people living in the Torrid Zone which was supposed to be too hot for life, that people really did live in the Antipodes, etc., the explorers opened up minds to a new world of empirical science. Even the lines from early-16c Iberian poets quoted in his *Humanism and the Voyages of Discovery in 16th Century Portuguese Science and Literature* sparkle with intellectual energy. Too bad that even as they wrote, intellectual freedom was eroded by religious censors (the first index of proscribed books was in 1546) and most men chose to make a living by fighting with arms or the word of God, rather than by thinking and creating. King Sebastian even outlawed all interest – now, *that* is fundamentalism! – from 1557 until 1578 when he died. Without capitol – who would lend for no interest! – business dried up. By 1570, a quarter of the adults in Spain were clerical – close to a million people, over half the adult population of England! (M(B):HIC) "An edict of 1558 forbade the import of foreign books, and in 1559 Spanish students were forbidden to study abroad, except at specially exempted institutions." (http://nick.frejol.org/writings/siglo-de-oro.live) In a sense, Spain secluded itself *before Japan* did and, I think, pulled Portugal down with it.

12-4 Ours are treated on the outside with pitch or *galagala* so they don't take in water;
As nossas se consertão por fora com breu ou galagala pera não fazerem agoa;

Those of Japan [do it] with only the good fit of the planks, without any other bitumin. *As de Japão com somente a boa juntura das tab[o]as sem outro bitume.*

Bitumin, ("originally, a kind of mineral pitch found in Palestine and Babylon" = OED) *impregnates*, *varnishes* and *cements*. Frois would seem to use it in a generic sense, including pitch, *galagala* (a Malaysian word for a mixture of tar and resin) etc. While Japanese did not treat the whole surface, they used *some* caulking; and the precision of their workmanship was assisted by the radically straight lines of Japanese naval architecture. *Curved* vs. *Straight*. Frois overlooked *that* contrast. Kaempfer, a hundred years later, pegged it: "The body of the ship is not built roundish, as our European ones, but that part which stands below the surface of the water, runs almost in a straight line towards the keel." (K:HOJ)

12-5 Our small boats are high in the stern and low in the bow;
As nossas peqenas são altas de popa e baxas da proa;

Those of Japan are high in the bow and low in the stern.
As dos Japões altas da proa e baxas da popa.

In comparison to modern boats, the height of the poop on the European boats of all sizes in this age *is amazing*. Frois has a reason for confining his contrast to small-craft, i.e., skiff and gondola-like boats. Large Japanese vessels also had amazingly high sterns, but their poop-deck was more of an extension *out over* the stern (in the traditional Chinese manner) than the top of a multi-deck aft-cabin, as was the case with ours.

A high bow seems more natural for slicing through waves without taking in excessive water. And, lacking true decks and bilges, the Japanese would want to keep water *completely out,* rather than taking it on and having it run out the scuppers as is common in the West. On the other hand, a high stern seems ideal for navigation, for a steersman can not see over a high bow, and all on the poop would be left very high and dry.

12-6 Ours have sails of cloth; *A nossas tem velas de pano;*

All their sails are straw. *As suas todas velas de palha.*

Frois's "all" exaggerates. While most Japanese small-craft may have still used woven straw-mat for sails, cotton cloth was already common and soon to largely replace the mat. I suspect, however, that Frois was still thinking small boats and the smallest of the small would have been the last to make the switch . . . somewhere in my head, I can picture one of those *funa-bikuni* (boating nuns), taking a customer aboard and lowering her straw-mat-sail for their bed! Come to think of it, fishermen probably made a practice of sleeping on their sails. I joke, but mat actually made fine sailing because a stiff sail actually worked better, so long as it was not square, as the Japanese ones were. Almost all the fast and sea-worthy Chinese ships – including the celebrated Hong Kong cargo boat – used mat sails, as did *most* boats *around the world.* Why make threads to weave with when you can go straight from straw/fiber? Most Japanese boats only switched to cloth after Matsu Migieimon, in 1785, discovered a way to prepare cotton thread and weave it into strong, taut and light one-piece sails. This *sudare-ori* "canvas belt"(?) style-sail survives to this day. (http://www.koti.jp/marco/)

12-7 Our rope is hemp, sago palm or *cairo;* *A nossa cordoalha hé de linho, gamute ou cairo;*

Theirs are straw. *A sua de palha.*

Straw again! What do Japanese *not* make of it? It seems strange Chamberlain failed to give it a section in *Things Japanese.* Here, Frois mentions only the most common rope. Japanese had others.

"Our" hemp, it goes without saying, is tough (I do not know if they got it in Manila yet, but the Jesuits were there, so . . .), the sago palm, or *gamute,* is from the Malay *gomûti* and is a particularly elastic fiber and *cairo* comes from coconut husk fiber and has nothing to do with Egypt. According to the French translators, *kaïr* comes from the Malay-Tamil word *kayuru*, meaning "cord/rope" and was especially common in the Maldives. In his novel *Waga Tomo Furoisu* (My Friend Frois), Inoue Hisashi's Frois gives a whole paragraph of a letter over to describing the wonders of the palm-tree which stands high despite roots that don't spread out and are useful in every part, from fronds used for hats, sap used for wine, nets and rope from the bark, oil for cooking and medicine from the nuts, ladles from nut-shells, fuel from husks . . . He calls it *the money-bearing tree* and claims the Jesuits own plots of them, which they leave to the natives to run and that he is set to buy and set up a new one, the earnings of which will go toward supporting the Nippon (Japan) Mission . . .

12-8 Our anchors are of iron; *As nossas ancoras de ferro;*

Theirs of wood. *As suas de pao..*

The wooden anchors sank because they had stones tied to them and a cross-bar helped keep the single barb pointing down. Ours, I thought, had a minimum of two barbs, or flukes, so it surprises me Frois does not make that contrast, too. There were probably some four-fluke (Chinese-style) iron anchors already in use in Japan. A hundred years later, Kaempfer wrote that "the anchors are of Iron, and the cables twisted of straw, and stronger than one would imagine." So wood soon turned to metal but straw remained king!

12-9   Our *navios* [fighting vessels] have prows with rams or beaks;
Os nossos navios tem na proa ou esporão ou goroupes;

>   The *fune* [ship/s] of Japan have open bows not much suited for battle.
>   *As funes de Japão são polas proas abertas e muito pouqo guerreiras.*

Like mountain rams, our ships were made for butting heads or stabbing below the belt, if the chance offered itself (the "beak" was at the waterline or slightly lower).

On the other hand, the unsuitability of the Japanese boat for war is legend. Japan had one famous ancient "naval battle" that sent the whole Heikei clan to the bottom of the sea where their warriors left their faces on the shell of the crab called *heikei-gani*. Actually, the boats did not so much battle each other as serve as water-borne *stages* for men who jumped back and forth from boat to boat to fight as they fought on land. In other words, they had no *ramming*, or *fire-power* to speak of. The Japan Sea was used for fishing and trade, not fighting. Of course, there were exceptions. Only a few years before *Tratado*, Nobunaga used iron-clad ships to cut off supplies to Buddhist monks he was besieging in Osaka (L:EJ). But Japanese had not been in a state of constant attack-or-be-attacked naval warfare as the states of Europe were with each other and their neighbors. Some Japanese *countries* (they only became fiefdoms about the time the *Tratado* was written) could *field* a large number of boats in a worst comes to worst situation, but they were more Dunkirk-like affairs depending on the many fishing and trading ships. In 1585, as far as I know, there were no navies to speak of in Japan.

In Europe, warring and shipping was synonymous. There were books like Padre Fernando Oliveira's *Arte da Guerra do Mar* (1555), *The Art of War at Sea*. The title of Dialogue 14 of *De Missione*, cited in 12-1 with respect to Galleons, was not "On the Ships of Europe" but *About the Ordinary Way Naval Battles Are Carried Out In Europe*. To Europeans, a word like "battle-ship" would have been redundant. *Ship = Battle.* True, Europe had to war to defend itself: it took a coalition of Spain and Venice to beat the Saracens (Ottoman Turks) at Lepanto in 1571 (Not that this stopped the Turks for good – King Sebastian was defeated in a crusade against the Moors in 1587 (the Battle of Alcacer Kebir), and the Ottoman Turks kept invading Europe until they reached Vienna in 1683.) But real battles were not enough, "we" also enjoyed putting on enormously costly mock battles.

The Japanese were well aware of their disadvantage at sea. Frois, in his *Historia*, records a conversation with Hideyoshi, Shogun of the newly united Japan, where he talks openly of his intention to conquer Korea and China and requests *two large warships, with experienced Portuguese crew*. He even offered to buy them and pay more than the going wages for the crew. Had the Portuguese gone along, the history of the world might be different for Hideyoshi's invasion of Korea (1592-7) was largely lost at sea. Koreans, though vanquished on land, managed to cut the Japanese supply lines and prevent re-enforcements from arriving. But it is dubious whether even the two *nao* would have helped, for Admiral Yi Sun, in what may be the greatest feat of naval history – performed on two major naval fronts, no less, – sank the Japanese fleet with a squadron of newly invented turtle-boats – a whole fleet of Monitors and Merrimacs centuries ahead of their time – with fire and under-water rams!

12-10   Our seamen, when rowing, are seated and quiet;
Os nossos marinheiros emquanto remão vão asentados e calados;

>   Those of Japan stand and almost always sing as they go.
>   *Os de Japão im pee e quasi sempre vão cantando.*

Sitting *vs.* standing. So, *which is the better position to row?* Captain Sarris, in 1613, observed something that only a captain would observe, namely, that by performing "their worke standing as ours doe sitting . . . they take the lesse roome." (in S:MQTJ) I believe that a standing position should also be less tiring than the sitting one used by Europeans, for continual exercise with a bent body tires the internal organs; the effect bears resemblance to that of absorbing body-blows in boxing. In Southeast Asia, we see skinny old women sculling produce to market, quickly. By sculling, I mean moving the oars without removing them from the water (That we do not have it in the Olympics proves Western bias even today!). It is less tiring than our rowing, which, by the way, the Japanese did not do.

Quiet *vs.* Singing. *"Row, row, row your boat!"* Seriously, I thought we sang too. We did, after all, have our sea-chanties. But we must not have done it very much, for Kaempfer, who came from North Europe seconded Frois: "They row according to the air of a song, or the tune of some words, or other noise, which serves at the same time to direct and regulate their work and to encourage one another." And, significantly, he didn't write *like in this or that part of Europe*, here, as he often did. And, this contrast was indirectly confirmed by the Japanese diplomatic mission that visited the United States in 1871 when they noticed Amerindians who sang as they paddled. Back in Japan, Morse observed they put "quite as much energy into the grunts as they did into the sculling" and found "the noise they made sounded like the exhaust of some compound and wheezy engine;" elsewhere he heard some tolerable singing though he did not go so far as Bird who called it "impressive and melancholy." Note, she did not care equally for the coarse, guttural grunt of the cart-men. Physiologically speaking, it is *right* – beneficial – to let out a rush of air while making a sudden strenuous effort. (It contracts the groin muscles preventing hernia and, in some way I can feel but do not understand, protects against lower-back strain). And, as Morse pointed out, vocalizing with the rhythm of one's work (whether scullers or gold-beaters or fish-choppers), helps to lighten the burden of our labor.

My impression of late-20c Japanese blue-collar work was *very* different. Blue collar workers are, on the average, sassier than white-collar workers, and I like that; but they are still too damned quiet and serious as they go about their tasks! Heavy momentary exertion still makes them vocalize, but otherwise they keep their mouths shut. I never heard a woman singing as she worked and only heard one young man do so – a house-mate who was a budding opera singer. On the year-end office-cleaning day at the publisher I worked for, I was always the only one singing as I scrubbed. While Japanese never were a culture which would refuse to work unless there were a band accompanying them (such cultures were once not rare!) they did sing while doing collective work – My man Issa once felt guilty about napping to the accompaniment of the rice-planting song. Indeed, in large fields, bands played when they planted. But now, I find Japanese manual work depressing, for they think singing frivolous or are embarrassed to sing sober. Hearing me sing as I work, someone will say in a patronizingly sweet tone of voice *"Robin-tte yôki da ne"* which might be Englished "Aren't you the cheerful one!" (In that sense, I thought of contemporary Japanese culture (white-collar at any rate) as *sick*.)

~~~~~~

12-11   Our oars are all made from one piece of wood;   *Os nossos remos são todos de hum pao;*

          Those of Japan from two pieces.   *Os de Japão de dous ped[aços].*

Not *all* of Japan's oars/sculls/paddles are two-piece. Frois is probably contrasting the largest type of oar here. Kaempfer describes such an oar as "being not at all streight, like our European oars, but somewhat bent, with a moveable joint in the middle, which yielding to the violent pression of the water, facilitates the taking of them up. The timber pieces and boards are fasten'd together in their joints and extremities, with hooks and bands of copper." I would, rather, say that the upper third of the shaft is splinted to the lower part to allow some *give* and the replacement of either half. Eliza Skidmore gives us a picture of them working in Yokohama: ". . . voluble boatmen keep up a steady *bzz, bzz, whizz, whizz,* to the strokes of their crooked, wobbling oars as they scull in and out." (S:JDJ)

Like many things, the idea for two-piece oars came from China. H. Warrington Smyth (ibid) describes the arrangement on a Hong Kong cargo-boat, "one of the finest sailing lighters in the world."

> To this not only the large deep rudder, but a couple of vast sculling oars, one upon each quarter, contribute. This form of propulsion is the usual one for big heavy craft in China. The long oar, *usually in two pieces*, is pivoted on the quarter or stern, the fore end being held in place by a strong lanyard to the deck. Any number of the crew can work on each oar, giving to it the motion known to seamen as sculling. A vessel of several hundred tons can be propelled in this way at from three to four knots. Its great advantage is that it is perfectly quiet, not exhausting, and the oar being in line with the boat, it is peculiarly applicable to crowded anchorages or narrow waterways. The motion is really that of the gondolier when his blade is brought aft to clear an obstruction.

12-12 Our oars have blades that are removable and broad;
Os nossos remos tem as pas postiças e são largas;

> The blades in Japan are the same wood [as the handle] and long and narrow.
> *As de Japão são do mesmo pao e estreitas.*

Now who has the single and who the double oar? Frois uses the same *remos*, but probably refers to something different. Because I cannot find anything about removable blades for "us," I would have assumed Frois meant to write "rudder" (*leme* – note: the "l" and "r" in Portuguese are often confused) rather than *remos* (oars) had the next contrast not continued with rowing contrasts.

12-13 When our sailors row they lift the oars clear of the water;
Os nossos marinheiros quando remão alevantão os remos fora d'agoa;

> Those of Japan are continually rowing under the water.
> *Os de Japão vão sempre remando por debaxo do mar.*

The Japanese side of the contrast here perfectly defines *sculling* proper, which was done on the side by teams and stern by a lone sculler. Kaempfer defines it from a different angle: "They do not row after our European manner, extending their Oars streight forwards, and cutting just the surface of the water, but let them fall down into the water almost perpendicularly." (K(S):HOJ) He also notes it is "just like *stirring up* the water." (Okada) If Captain Saris found it saved space on ship-board, Kaempfer noted it saved space *in the water* as well, enabling boats to pass each other in narrow passages and Morse also notes something that must have stared Frois in the face so hard that he blanked out:

> The sailors are fine, muscular-looking fellows; wearing nothing but a breech-cloth, they are as brown as russet apples. In rowing the boat they push instead of pulling the oars, and consequently face the bow of the boat. (M:JDD)

Push versus *pull!* The best oar contrast yet. Just the opposite of the case for carpentry. Japanese also faced the side – and when sculling alone at the stern were had to look over their shoulder, but with the feet askance to one side, even then they could see where they were going, unlike our style of rowing which may be true to life, for it only lets us see where we have come from but not where we will go, but *practically speaking*, is dangerous. (For a whole page on the debate on the efficiency of *rowing* versus *sculling* initiated by Chamberlain, see *TT-long*).

12-14 On our boats we are very cautious about fire;
Nas nossas embarqasões se tem grande tento no fogo;

> On Japanese boats, though there's straw everywhere, they take no care of fire.
> *Nas de Japão, com ser tudo palha, sobre o fogo não há nenhuma guarda.*

So that's why *snuff* and chewing tobacco was so big for sailors in the West! They were not permitted to smoke. On 16c Spanish boats, according to Peréz-Mallaína,

> The cooking fire was the only light that was permitted on board without being enclosed in a metal or glass lantern. During storms, the cooking fire was put out after sunset. At night, the only light that remained was the one that illuminated the compass box and one lantern shared among those on guard. Despite these precautions, there were many disastrous fires, but perhaps none like that in September 1561 [two years before Frois arrived in Japan], which destroyed twenty-three ships moored in the port of Seville. The origin of the fire was in the tomfoolery of a sailor, who eased his boredom by setting cats on fire [And I had thought burning cats was English!] . . . (P(P):SMS)

Obviously, regulations are no substitute for the quality or lack of quality of the man-power. You could no more imagine something like that happening on a Japanese ship then, than today!

Did Japanese, who tended to stay near shore and lived in tinder-box houses, think that boats, with less paper and surrounded by water, were comparatively safe places for fire? Or, was it because most Japanese ships were not full of gun powder?

12-15 With us, honorable people are always favored with the poop;
Antre nós por primor vai sempre a jente honrada na popa;

> In Japan, the nobility rides on the bow, where they are often completely soaked.
> *Em Japão a jente nobre vai na proa onde [às] vezes se molha arrezoadamente.*

I played a bit with "our" translation. "Favored with the poop" should be "ride on the poop because it is cool/classy/dandy" (Yes, *primor,* again!). Metaphor can favor either first or last, as the classier location for big shots. With a ship, the bow should offer the clearest view, but it *also* was not only wet but the roughest ride. Was the samurai spirit of the Japanese upper class not daunted with such practical matters? One reason for the high poop in Western vessels is, as noted before, for the steersman (or watch) to better see over the bow. That would put the honorable people closer to the controls. Did the Luso-Iberians with their sail-loving kings like it that way? And, finally, if most pooping was done directly into the sea, was the poop not the best place to poop from?

12-16 Our boats have round masts; *As nossas embarqasões tem o masto redondo;*

> Their *fune* [boat/s] square ones. *As* funes *quadrados.*

If square sections were good, I would think tree-trunks would grow square. Unlike trees, which encounter the wind from all angles, boats do not sail backwards, so I can at least imagine a mast with a half circle cross-section. But *square* or *rectangular*! Since "square mast" also means a mast with square sails, my first reaction on reading Frois was to suspect a mistake, though "our" sails were not "round." But it turned out that square masts are not uncommon on modern sailboats. They are said to be easier to make than round or octagonal ones, and "stiffer for their size and you can make them hollow if you want," as one boat designer put it! A Japanese website dedicated to the relatively small Japanese transport boat the *maruko-bune* of Biwako, Japan's largest lake confirms that the Japanese-style of mast was the same length as the boat and . . *square*. Square was said to be stronger!

12-17 We never demast our boats;
As nossas embarqasões nunqa se dezemmasteão;

> The Japanese, when they are going to row immediately remove the mast.
> *Os Japões, como vão a remo, logo tirão o masto fora.*

I don't know about that "never." In a storm, "our" masts were sometimes cut down ("We cut the masts down with as much care as possible, but we still weren't able to stop the mainmast from falling on top of fourteen men, including five Portuguese, and splattering their brains and guts all over the place." (Pinto) But, Frois means as a regular part of sailing. As Kaempfer wrote, the mast of the typical merchant vessel was "the same length with the ship" and "wound up by pulleys and again let down upon the deck, when the ship comes to anchor." This "roof, or upper deck" was "flattish," and in rainy weather the mast was let down upon it "and the sail extended over it for sailors, and the people employed in the ship's service to take shelter under it, and to sleep at night." (K(S):HOJ) Well, that suggests *one* reason for a square mast, it wouldn't roll over on a sleeping sailor!

12-18 Our boats have topsails, mizzens and foresails; *As nossas tem gaveas, mezenas e traqetes;*

Their *fune* [boats] none of them. *As funes nada disto.*

The *gavea* is actually the "main topsail," but a loose translation suffices. One might even skip the names altogether and just say, our ships have *zillions* of sails, theirs usually just *one*. The caravel had only 3, but the *ñao* and galleons boasted 10 or more.

Like ancient Egyptian or Viking ships, the Japanese merchant ships had one square sail. The pleasure boats also had only one sail with one boom on *top* of the sail and none on the bottom-side, so the sail was shaped like a triangle standing on its head – the exact opposite of the typical modern sailboat, but not opposite to the Portuguese ships, for they too had the booms on top. This would be safer when *jibing*. It is interesting that Frois used the Japanese generic term for boat, *fune,* as if to suggest it is, or should be, a *type* of boat.

12-19 Our boats travel by day and by night;
As nossas embarqasões caminhão de dia e de noyte;

Those of Japan stop in port at night and travel by day.
As de Japão tomão porto de noyte e caminhão de dia.

In the 20c, long distance trucking in Japan was almost all done at night and Japanese fishing boats operating in concert with mother (factory) ships remained away from port longer than anyone; but it seems coastal shipping or fishing operations in Frois's time were strictly *day-work*. Frois chose coastal traffic for the contrast. Japanese ships still traded as far away as South China and the Philippines but within a half century what slight sea-worthiness the Japanese ships had became criminal. "By the laws of the Empire, their ships must not be built strong enough to bear the shocks and tossing of huge raging waves," wrote Kaempfer, who explained the primary guarantee was a requirement that a wide opening in the stern originally made for easier management of the rudder but bad on the high sea be retained in all vessels. In short, *a hole in the poop kept a whole nation plugged up!* We laugh; but laws like this closed a coastline that measures in the tens of thousands of miles. Improbable as it may seem, Morse found an equivalent in Cuba, "where the ears of a cat are cut off to prevent it from roaming in the cane fields. The sudden showers that fall in the tropics are annoying to cats, inasmuch as the rain gets into their ears, and this they particularly loathe. The result is that cats remain near the house, so that in case of a shower they can make a quick dash for protection." (M:JDD)

12-20 Ours often keep moving without taking any account of the rain;
As nossas muitas vezes caminhão sem terem conta com chuva;

Those of Japan do not have to go when the sky isn't clear.
As de Japão em que o [tempo] não estaa claro não hão de caminhar.

As Kaempfer pointed out, the poop was not the only problem, "the deck is built so loose that it will let the [rain] water run through before the mast hath been taken down and the ship cover'd, partly with mats, partly with sails." Knowing this, Kaempfer writes, we can't accuse the Japanese captains of "fear and cowardice" for the manner in which they repair to the nearest harbor at the slightest pretext. Again, Frois contrasts coastal shipping. The decks on the dozens if not hundreds of boats that still ventured across the high sea at the time *Tratado* was written had to be waterproofed.

Apparently, the straw-mat sails got heavy and hard to operate when it rained. That, too, may explain why Japanese preferred to avoid the rain. It also suggests that the all-weather mat-sail boats from other countries either used different straw or wove it differently.

12-21   With us, when a small boat is hired, the boatmen are not separate;
Antre nós, quando se freta huma embarqasão peqena, não se divide dos marinheiros;

>   In Japan, you pay as much for the boatman as for the *fune* [boat].
>   *Em Japão tanto se dá polo frete da* fune *como por hum marinheiro.*

Again! We have seen the same in the last chapter with respect to the sawyers and their saw. Here, a charge for a seaman seems odd to us. In the other case, the charge for the *saw* seemed odd. In either case, we evidently expect to pay for the big thing, and have the smaller come with it.

12-22   With us, a ship's carrying capacity is measured by its hull;
Antre nós se faz conta do que levará o navio polo casqo;

>   In Japan, by counting the sections of the **sail**.
>   *Em Japão pola conta das esteiras da vella.*

Frois means *classes* of ship rather than capacity *per se*, which was measured in tonnage in the West and "stones" of rice – thought of as a numerical quantity, rather than a weight – in Japan, where estates and fiefs were also ranked for prestige and taxes according to the same unit representing the output of the harvest. Japanese sails were not measured in their equivalent to our square-feet or yards, but *in units of a given area*, so you have the *10-section sail* class and the *20-section* sail class and so on. We are talking mats, the same we saw was the case for houses.

12-23   We have carpenters specifically for ships;
Antre nós há carpinteiro detriminado pera o navio;

>   In Japan, *fune* [boat] masters are almost always carpenters.
>   *Os Japões oficiaes da* fune *quasi todos são carpinteiros.*

Okada writes tellingly, "this says there were apparently no specialists in ship-building, but the Japanese-Portuguese Dictionary (1604) has a heading for *funa-daiku* = "ship-carpenter." I would guess Frois happened to be familiar with provinces with comparatively few specialists. Considering the angularity of Japanese boats, however, I can well imagine that most were made by house-builders!

12-24   With us, someone who receives cargo aboard a boat hands over a freight bill to its owner who stays on land; *Antre nós quem recebe a fazenda no navio deixa conhecimento ao dono que fiqa em terra;*

>   In Japan, the man handing over the cargo also gives a freight bill to the carrier.
>   *Em Japão o que emtrega a fazenda dá tambem conhecimento della a quem a leva.*

With regional powers being actively checked, partly through control of trade, by the Shoguns, did carriers have to be careful to have proof of exactly what was being carried and for whom?

12-25 Our ships' flags are square;
As nossas bandeiras dos navios são quadradas;

> Theirs is a thin strip of cloth put on a bamboo pole.
> *As suas são huma tira de pano comprida, toda enfiada em hum banbu.*

This is almost a perfect repeat of 7-35, with the *battle standards*. But, look at the Portuguese! For once, he uses *banbu* rather than *cana!* Did he feel it proper because the poles were larger? According to the OED, the Portuguese generally called very large cane *mambu* after the native Concan (?) word in the 16c. This may be one of the first *bamboos* with a "b" in Portuguese.

Japanese ship "flags" came in two basic types. The one I think Frois means might better be called a banner. If our banners run horizontally, Japanese banners run vertically. Today, they work perfectly for advertising hung from the corners or standing by the entrance of buildings. These are strung on, or fastened by loops to the edge of a pole, have a small stick at the top edge and sometimes at the bottom, too. They may flutter, but do not flap in the breeze, serving identification purposes well.

12-26 On our boats, nothing placed aboard becomes an augur [of disaster];
As nossas embarqasões não tem agouro em couza que nellas se meta;

> The Japanese have great fear of carrying temple bells.
> *Hos Japões o tem grandissimo em levar sinos das varelas.*

In the Far East, large bells were considered dangerous cargo popular with the Dragon God/s at the bottom of the sea, who would capsize boats to get them. *Why bells?* There is an old Chinese tale about a jealous female dragon and a bell but I forget the details . . . If logic is allowed: *a large bell might actually be a strong draw for lightning!* Okada points out that horses and oxen and other 4-legged animals were also taboo, for they were considered impure, and all impure items were jinxes.

"Our" side, reflecting the Christian party-line, was *probably* optimistic for many of the Luso-Iberian explorers and crew, and *surely* wrong for the West as a whole. Up to the 20c, seamen in the North Sea believed it was better to leave men to drown than to save them, for that would anger the Sea God who was already smacking his or her lips, right? On Spanish ships, sailors were advised to "let out a great yell" as they fell to call attention to their going overboard and indicate which side it was, not to mention scaring off any shark that happened to be in the vicinity (Alonso de Chaves in P(P):SMS); moreover, they did not particularly mind carrying women, whereas in North Europe, the presence of a *woman* aboard was believed to either incur the jealousy of the boat, which might just commit suicide against a reef or anger the feminine spirit of the deep into throwing up huge waves (The great Russian Ballad, *Stenka Rasin* has that great line about tossing a Princess overboard to placate a stormy Mother Volga). So, if relics and miracles are considered, the Iberian culture seems the least modern, but when it comes to old superstitions, the Northern cultures were the more old-fashioned. This was not only true for seamen. Keith Thomas, writing of the generally superstitious mindset of the English, provides these gems

> In 1593, it was feared that the plague in London would get worse because a heron perched on top of St Peter's, Cornhill, and stayed there all afternoon.

> In 1604, the House of Commons rejected a bill after the speech of its Puritan sponsor had been interrupted by the flight of a jackdaw through the Chamber – an indisputably bad omen. (T:MNW)

12-27 We think things like mermaids/sirens and mermen/men of the sea are tall tales;
Nós temos por patranhas toda a couza de serenas ou homens marinhos;

> The Japanese think there is a kingdom of lizards under the sea, that they are rational and can save them. *Elles tem que debaxo do mar há reino de lagartos e que são racionais e se salvão.*

Frois contrasts a simple world explained as *all but dead* by Christians, who believed a lot about a little, with a richer, enchanted world where most people believed less about a lot more. As mentioned in 12-26, not all the West was *that* disenchanted. Frois makes an ironic choice in his examples, for one export item the allegedly superstitious people of the Far East made for export to the gullible West was none other than mermaids and mermen! But there is truth in the contrast, for "we" had to *pretend* to disbelief: any sailor who made too big of a fuss about The Old Man of the Sea might have been thrown into it (or burned) by his more fundamentalist compatriots, while Japanese fishermen continued to supplicant their age-old sea gods, which were, indeed, Dragons:

> Our dragons are full of fire have hooked tails, embody hellishness and kidnap maidens.
> Their dragons are watery spirits considered benign unless angered who control the weather.

While Japanese fishing villages really did support their temples and shrines with dragon and other maritime connections, they were by no means as openly religious – to the Christian mind, *superstitious* – as the Chinese whose seamen were famous for their loud invocations "by the song of gongs" (M:BGE:1860) Indeed, the Japanese traditionally prided themselves on *not* raising a ruckus to the Heavens like their cowardly neighbors (if I correctly understand the intent of the long-controversial classical phrase denoting Japan as the *koto-age-wa senu kuni* (word-raise not do country)). Am I rude to mention that St. Xavier famously performed a two day-long non-stop prayer which was credited with saving the ship he was on from being sunk in a typhoon?

A truly fair contrast would not have put the "lizards" against mermen and mermaids. If the dragons, elemental spirits, or, rather, spirited elements of Taoism that found their way to Japan, perhaps replacing and/or incorporating the serpent-centered part of their ancient beliefs were "tall tales" or "superstition," then what is "our" rational God (and son and holy ghost) who can save us? To me, the dragon looks like a far more convincing denizen of space than "our" muscle-bound bearded fellow! Or, leaving God out of it, we may note that, Frois aside, the Iberian sailors' still had faith in something far more subtle than God, a host of guardian spirits harking back to pre-Christian times, as we know from the prayers of sailors collected by the commissioner in Vera Cruz, Mexico in 1586 at the instigation of the Inquisitor General of Mexico for burning because of their superstitious content. Peréz-Mallaína gives us a number (not marked as such, but probably burnt) including:

> *Prayer to St. Elmo*: Holy Body, true friend of mariners, we want you to help us, and always to appear at night before us.
>
> *Prayer to Our Lady of Barameda:* Now that we have passed your sandbar, be pleased to have us return and pass over it again, with a good and safe voyage.
>
> *Prayer to St. Clare:* That she be pleased to give us clear skies night and day and bring us good weather and keep us from bad shoals, and bad fleets and bad company, and that she be pleased to bring us safely to good harbor, Our Father, Ave Maria. (P:PSMS)

Other prayers were to St. Nicholas, the Four Evangelists and Our Lady of Fair Seas. On top of this, "to avoid the evil eye, the crew members wore around their necks the well known "figs," that is, small amulets shaped like hands with the thumb placed between the index finger and the middle finger, which have been found in abundance in the remains of shipwrecks." (Ibid) In other words, if the cross didn't work, "we" could always try giving bad spirits the bird!

12-28 On our boats, we always carry water for the long haul;
Nos nossos navios se leva sempre agoa pera muito tempo

> The *fune* [boat/s] of Japan each carry only two days of water.
> *Aas funes dos Japões quasi cada dous dias fazem agoada.*

This is a variation on 12-19, above, day-sailing. But, one wonders why Japanese didn't consider the possibility of being swept out to sea or marooned somewhere.

12-29 When our sails tear, we sew them up immediately;
Antre nós se a vela vai rota logo hé cozida;

> In Japan, they go on with them torn or coming apart and pay no attention to it.
> *Em Japão vai sempre ro[ta] ou descozida sem se ter conta com isso.*

Since the Japanese straw sails are made in sections, as mentioned in 12-22 above, a stitch in time wouldn't make much difference. Moreover, it is probable some of those openings were, unknown to Frois, *deliberate*. After changing to cotton, it was common for sails to be –

– made of long, narrow strips of thin cloth laced together, leaving an interspace of three or four inches. The sails are very large and these interspaces relieve the pressure in high winds. (M:JDD)

– laced together vertically, leaving a decorative lacing six inches wide between each two widths. Instead of reefing in a strong wind, a width is unlaced, so as to reduce the canvas vertically, not horizontally. (B:UTJ)

Chances are that this practice was a carry-over from Frois's time. Further description of cloth sails is found in the last sentence of two beautiful paragraphs of *A Diplomatist's Wife in Japan*. "Every fishing-boat from every village" took advantage of "a liberating breeze" to head out to sea.

> The peculiar warm sheen of the junk sails, square above and round below, made in long strips, seamed and held together in a thousand lovely patterns by the interlacing ropes strained against the breeze, gave the impression of a web of silver against the blue; and the calm majesty of the silky rush on the water's surface made me feel our great coal-fed, screw-driven liner was a blot on the universe, and had no title to travel with that fair company." (F:DWJ)

12-30 With our *fustas* [pinnace] and *catures,* we embark and disembark at the bow.
Nas nossas fustas e catures se embarqão e dezembarqão polla proa;

> With the boats of Japan, the stern quickly swings around to land and one embarks and disembarks from there. *As embarqasões de Japão virão logo a popa pera a terra e por ali se embarqão e dezembarqão.*

To pick a couple of many ships for a contrast seems rather silly. If it were only true for all, we could put it against 12-15 and note that the important people must either walk to the other end of the boat or get off *last*. A better contrast was out there, too. I will *Faux Frois* a Chamberlain (adding the unwritten side, ours):

In Europe, boats are hauled up on the beach bow first.
In Japan, *Boats are hauled* [up] *on the beach stern first.* (C:TJ)

This is exactly what proper people do with shoes in the porticos of Japan: they leave them facing outwards to be ready for the next trip. If we "come and go," the Japanese "go and come" (*itte-kuru*). They like to be ready to *go*.

endnote XII

Boats 船

Since I have little more to say on boats *per se*, let me add a bit more about the Seclusion that put a period to the Jesuit endeavor in Japan and the dreams of the Japanese. As explained already, the Seclusion made the poor sea-going vessels even more dangerous. Excluding a few merchant ships licensed to trade with Ryukyu (Okinawa), Korea and Ezo (the Ainu land that is now Hokkaido and includes islands occupied by the Soviet Union → Russia?), Japan got out of the offshore boat game altogether. Kaempfer noted that this was not so bad as it seemed to the West:

> Another objection that could be made, is, that a Country must still be unhappy, whose inhabitants are kept, as it were, prisoners within the limits thereof, and denied all manner of commerce and communication with their neighbors . . . [but] these many and different islands [of Japan] are, with regard to the whole Empire, what different Countries and Provinces are with regard to the whole globe: Differing in soil and situation, they were to produce various necessaries of life. And indeed, there is scarce any thing that can be wished for, but what is produced in some Province, in some island or other . . . (K(S):HOJ)

More important, self-isolated Japan was not closed in spirit. The dreams of its people spanned the world. As a result, Japan had one boat which the West lacked. And, from the point of view of the land-lubber, *that* Japanese boat was better than all of the rest of the world's boats put together. I refer to the *takara-bune,* or "treasure ship" of the popular imagination. This boat was believed to carry magical treasures, secular ones like hats to make you invisible, mallets to make wishes come true, bottomless bags of gold to spring out wherever a hammer is struck (I am a bit confused about the relationship of bag and hammer), scales useful for weighing the thoughts of others, keys to open any door, rhinoceros-horn cups [1] to alert you to, or even purify, any poison, religious ones like the wheel of law, the umbrella of heaven (to float you into paradise, I guess) etc. . . . (treasures usually come in sets of 8, a number symbolizing plenty and 8 sacred mountain peaks each connected with a religious treasure in India) and the Seven Chinese gods of prosperity. These Gods and most of the treasures just mentioned were imported but some (the *scales*, perhaps, for the homophone *omoi* for "thought" and "weight.") may have been added by the Japanese artists who made prints of this boat to put under the pillow on New Year's Night in the hope of having an auspicious dream on that night.

I do not know if the treasure ship of the Japanese imagination began with the enormous boats of the Chinese treasure fleet or, both were inspired by older Chinese legend. Could it be called an artistically sublimated or healthily domesticated cargo cult? I will try to have this worked out for *The Fifth Season* (the New Year volume of my *In Praise of Olde Haiku* (IPOOH) series which should be ready by 2005) for there is an entire chapter dedicated to this pleasant fiction.

1. Rhinoceros Horn Cup Before coming to Japan, Thunberg happened to encounter the rhinoceros-horn cups in South Africa, where the magic was taken literally, for

> it was generally believed, that goblets made of these horns in a turner's lathe would discover a poisonous draught that was put into them, by making the liquid ferment till it ran quite out of the goblet. Such horns as were taken from a young rhinocerous calf that had not yet copulated were said to be best . . . of these goblets are made, which set in gold and silver, and made presents of to kings . . ." (T:TEAA 1773)

A medical doctor, he experimented with horns taken from two-horn rhinocerae "both wrought into goblets, and unwrought, both old and young horns, with several types of poisons, weak as well as strong" but "observed not the least motion or effervescence." Only "a solution of corrosive sublimate, aqua phagaedenica" or the like gave rise to "a few bubbles, produced by the air, which had been inclosed in the pores of the horn, and which was now disengaged from it." [More odd stuff in TT-long].

XIII

OF THE PLAYS, SKITS, DANCE, SINGING AND MUSICAL INSTRUMENTS OF JAPAN

dos autos, farças, danças, cantar e instromentos da muzica de japão

13-1 Our plays are ordinarily performed at night;
Os nossos autos ordinariamente se fazem de noyte;

> The Japanese perform them almost all the time, day [add. and night].
> *Os Japões quasi os fazem sempre de dia – [e de noite.]*

Autos, the term used by Frois, were one-act plays. Content-wise, they included the religious, topical, comical and fantastic. Structure-wise, they were pretty much the only serious drama he could have seen, because five-act tragedies and comedies had fallen afoul of the Catholic Church and were long forgotten in the Portugal of his youth. But classical drama was already well into the process of revival in Italy and the Jesuits with their humanist schools – already 70 schools in 1556 – probably did more than anyone to revive it in Luso-Iberia.

> For the same reasons Pascal denounced theater – its capacity to move the emotions of its spectators with a lifelike replica of human existence – the Jesuits embraced theater as a pedagogical tool. Through a humanistic marriage of the heroic, secular virtues of antiquity and Christian morality, they created images both appealing to a larger public in their human drama and edifying in their intended effect. Dramatic reenactment could, through the power of declamation, gesture, and set machinery, put into living motion the kind of exalted religious images prized in painting and sculpture. (adapted from Larry F. Norman, "The Theatrical Baroque," in The Theatrical Baroque (Chicago: The David and Alfred Smart Museum/University of Chicago, 2001 www.fathom.com/course/10701023/session1.html)

> Jesuit theater began as simple dialogues but soon evolved into elaborate and complex spectacles involving music and dance. Both tragedies and comedies following classical models were produced. The average Jesuit college presented two principal public plays a year. (LR)

> The mixture of theater and religion reached its zenith with the founding of the Jesuits' houses in Seville. Many Jesuits used theater and drama to teach virtue and dramatize the life of Jesus and the saints. Students who were taught in the Jesuits' schools became stars in the acting companies in sixteenth and early seventeenth-century Spain . . . Great emphasis, too, was placed on good, clear speaking, and this was further fostered by the famous and novel Jesuit practice of producing school plays in Greek and Latin on sacred or classical subjects. The idea came not from Italy but from Portugal . . . (STUDIES IN SALESIAN SPIRITUALITY Elisabeth Stopp)

These *comedias* were generally acted out in the courts of houses, and the first permanent theatre in Madrid was not erected until 1579 (M:HIC). The difference in location – the Japanese had halls for drama, comic story-telling, etc. – partly explains the different hours, but a different attitude toward the night (14-13) may be equally important.

The Japanese equivalent of the *auto* is almost certainly *Noh* which was at the peak of its popularity when Frois wrote. *Noh* was defined as an *auto* in the Japanese-Portuguese Dictionary (NIPO in J/F(O):T). It had at least two acts, but could have three times that many because one act seldom went more than an hour without a comic interlude, and could go on for a whole afternoon or evening, i.e. 5

or 6 hours. As a high art, *Noh* captured the interest of the rulers at the same time the Way of Tea did. A couple hundred years later, it was still performed, in the words of Okakura, on a stage "of hard, unpainted wood, with a single pine tree somewhat conventionally portrayed on the background" thus, suggesting "a grand monotony" to heighten the "infinite suggestiveness" of this "short epic drama" (O:IOE), which, Eliza Scidmore noted, might be "a trilogy, occupying four or five hours of three successive days." (S:JDJ)   Still, Noh was so high an art it was probably above the interest of many Japanese.   Luckily, there was more drama out there. I do not know if there was yet anything as powerful as the *kabuki* Alcock brings to life by conveying a Dutch resident's testimony about a young woman, who, like the proverbial soap opera addict of the late-20c, came to work still sobbing for the fate of a poor lover stabbed by a jealous husband (A:COT):

> 'Why you little fool, it is all sham; he has not been killed at all, the fine gallant, and is most likely very busy eating his rice.' 'Oh, no, he *is* killed indeed, I *saw* the sword go into his body as he fell.'

13-2   Among us, one actor with a mask makes a very slow appearance;
Antre nós sai hum reprezentador com mascara muito devagar;

> In Japan, two or three with bare faces appear very quickly and place themselves before each other in the posture of fighting cocks. *Em Japão saem dous ou tres com o rosto descuberto muito depresa e poem-se huns defronte dos outros na postura em que estão galos pera pelejar.*

M & J write that Frois is mistaken about Europe (for a number of actors generally took the stage at once) unless he means someone who first took the stage to explain the play or to narrate a prologue.   The French translation supplements (?) Frois by having "our" actors make their entrance "one by one" (*un à un*).   Okada guesses Frois refers to the Kyôgen (translated as *farza* = farce by the NIPO dictionary) intermezzo, for Noh is generally masked.   Frois's contrast would seem to be of how dramas began.   It just so happens that Kyôgen served not only as an *intermezzo* but a sort of *antipasto*.   In the 19c, Ms. Scidmore describes a pre-Noh Kyôgen entrance as follows:

> The actors enter at a gait that out-struts the most exaggerated stage stride ever seen, the body held rigid as a statue, and the foot, never wholly lifted, sliding slowly along the polished floor. (S:JDJ)

How a super strut can also be a slow slide is beyond me.   This would seem to be the origin of MJ's "moon-walk."   Old Japan abounded in stylized movement and its strange walking was by no means limited to the stage.   Was *this* what Frois saw as game cocks sizing each other up?

13-3   Our plays are in verse; *Os nossos autos são em trovas;*
   Theirs are all in prose. *Os seus todos em proza.*

In Spain, lyrical poetry and drama went hand in hand. Latins find rhyming easy for having less phonemes to match and used a wide range of versification in their drama, including Byron's beloved *ottava rima*. The wealth of sound in English allows rhyme, but only with considerable effort, which makes them sound too *obvious* for spoken drama, so English used little of it and might be counted on the Japanese side of the contrast here.   Still, there is no way most Japanese drama can be defined as prose, if prose means normal speech.   It is as far from that as our opera is from speech.   The soon-to-come Kabuki dialogue (style-wise, hardly pulled from a hat) is largely 7 and 5-syllabet, as is most Japanese song and poetry, and the lines of Noh are *yôkyoku*, by definition a type of song.   But must *the* poetry *vs.* prose *battle be confined to words?*   Here is a better contrast:

> *We move about on the stage in a more or less normal fashion.*
> *They move about in odd ways only found on the stage.*

That is to say, if we look at the *walk* instead of the *talk*, the contrast clearly reverses and it is *we* who are prosaic and *they* poetic. As Menpes put it, *"You would never see a man walk in the street as he would on the stage. And, then, the tone of voice, bearing, and attitude – everything about the man is changed."* (M:JRC) Menpes also quotes, Danjiro, the greatest *kabuki* actor of his day to the effect that the poses of Western actors "suggested to me badly modeled statues."

13-4 Ours often vary and others are created from scratch;
Os nossos se varião muitas vezes e outros se fazem de novo;

Theirs are entirely determined from the start, with no [room for] variation.
Os seus são já ab initio detriminados em tudo sem se variar.

This is the drama version of 1-3+ (changing fashions in Europe and lack of change in Japan). The flourishing 16c Portuguese poetry and drama not only revived classics but showed great attentiveness to contemporary themes: the lyric poet (Luis de Camoas 1524-80) wrote "the greatest Virgilian epic of the Iberian peninsula," in 10 *ottava rima* cantos about Vasco de Gama's expedition to India! In Japan, on the other hand, *Noh's* Shakespeare, Zeami, died in 1443, a 100 years before the first Portuguese reached Japan, and Noh had become *the* drama of Japan by the time Frois arrived on the scene. Just as opera in the West soon came to stick to a score of classics, the Japanese stuck to theirs. Japanese critics usually blame the "closed" Tokugawa Era for creating a *revere-the-tradition* tradition, or should I say "copy the canon" mindset; but thanks to Frois, we can see that *in drama* it was true over a decade *before* that conservative era began.

Not that it is a bad thing to repeat. We in the West today tend to validate invention as "creative" and consider it "ours." We may even profess surprise at people enjoying themselves by going to see the same old plays year after year. Sometimes, we are told (by the anthropologist trying to be helpful) it is the slight embellishments that hold the audience's attention. Or we may be told the idea is to see *how this or that actor did this or that*. The point, usually missed, is that we do not *need* such apologetics. We are talking about *a performance*. We who listen to the same classical tune – no, even pop tune! – over and over again, or see the same opera dozens of times (I use the royal "we" – like Ulysses Grant, I personally have trouble sitting through an opera *even once*) should not find that so hard to understand! In the case of *Noh*, I would guess that the difficulty of catching (even for the Japanese) all of the lines, historical innuendo and puns make each performance a new, richer experience for the viewer.

Still, that single play by the Japanese princess and her friends that Pinto treated us to (6-1) is enough to suggest that the Japanese could be *impromptu* and there may well have been some creative drama around the fringes missed by Frois.

13-5 Ours, being plays, not tragedies, are not divided in acts;
Os nossos, sendo autos e não tragedias, não se dividem em senas;

Theirs are always seen divided into [acts], the first, 2nd, 3rd, etc.
Os seus vem sempre repartidos em primeiro, 2°, 3° etc.

Again, Frois refers to the *auto,* making a contrast that was soon to become moot. As far as the *"etc."* goes, Chamberlain writes that "Japanese plays (*kabuki*) are apt to run to extreme length, – five, seven, twelve, even as many as sixteen acts." Alcock mentions Japanese spending "a whole day seeing either a succession of plays, or one interminable piece of ancient history, and wars and battles innumerable." And, Morse describes a play that "began at half-past six in the morning and continued in a series of acts until nine o'clock at night." Others, he wrote, took *several days* to finish and "I was told that some plays in China require a month or two for a complete performance." (M:JDD) These quotes may concern different types of drama and be hundreds of years out of date, but they all suggest a different attitude toward drama than "ours." There may also be a method to this madness all the above visitors failed to catch. It may be that the plays in Japan were that long *because* they were broken up in a manner not to be found in the West until the age of television! Here are the 18c Dutch findings (Siebold, perhaps?) as presented by Mrs. Busk.

> Three different pieces are frequently represented on the same day; not the entire pieces successively, but interchangeably in parts; first the first act of one, then the same of a second, and after this of a third; then the second act of the first play, and successively . . . preceding in this way till all the three are completed. Thus any of the audience who wish only to see one of these pieces . . . may withdraw while the pieces they do not care to see take their turn of representation, and come back refreshed to witness the next act of their favorite drama. (B:MCJ)

Perhaps the comic interlude found between acts in a Noh play which was itself a mini-act gave rise to the idea of presenting plays in this way. The Japanese intermezzo, then, would conversely be a thread of common difference weaving together a potpourri of plays. There may also be a fashion factor here. "Japanese ladies" took advantage of the breaks to "repeatedly change their attire in the course of the afternoon and evening." (Ibid) Even today, Japanese women still show a strong proclivity to redressing. Wedding receptions average 3 dress changes and some have as many as 5 (only by the bride, though). All of this in itself, would seem to reflect an attitude that *life is a play*.

13-6   Our characters come out from inside a separate house where they can't be seen;
    As nossas figuras saem de dentro de outra caza donde se não vem;

> The Japanese are near the stage, behind curtains of *fune* boat/s.
> *Os Japões estão perto[?] do teatro metidos em cortinas de* fune.

The *playhouse* as we know it was not yet perfected in Europe. The stage was outside and the dressing room in a separate "house," or, in good weather, a patio. Japanese, with their broad, wide open architecture did have playhouses with various devices (most post-dating Frois) to keep performers hidden while waiting for their call. Frois's "curtains of boat/s" (*cortinas de fune*) have everyone stymied. Okada guesses he means an *age-maku*, an entrance curtain that raises up in a manner suggestive of the sail of a boat (that could be hoisted up to the upper boom, there being no lower boom with Japanese boats). From the illustrations of dressing rooms I have seen, *my guess* is that Frois means that the rectangular tent-like tops, with open sides, resembles the protected space for parties on the pleasure-craft that plied the rivers of Japan. Later, with the development of *kabuki*, Japanese actors would come to walk up a "flower-road" *through the audience*, or *pit* each time they set afoot on the stage, but that is another story (more in *TT-long*). In that case, we would have a difference that might be expressed as *bounded* vs *unbounded* stages or *inclusion* vs *seclusion* of the actors.

13-7   Our plays are performed in the spoken tongue;
    Os nossos autos se reprezentão em practica;

> Theirs, almost always singing – or dancing.
> *Os seus quasi sempre cantando – ou bailhando.*

Frois's *practica* for our side means "talk" and most talk is dialogue, though some may be soliloquy. While the first recognized performance of the genre of drama that was to mark the Tokugawa era, *ka-bu-ki,* or "sing-dance-technique," did not take place until 1594, such *song and dance* was long part of all traditions of Japanese drama of which Noh, popular at the time, has more narrative than dialogue. To the Japanese way of thinking, Frois contradicts his assertion in 13-3 that Japanese plays are in prose, for what is sung in Japanese *is* song and song is poetry (5-7 and 7-7 syllabet meter). Since the Japanese did not follow life as "we" did, poetry or not, our realistic "spoken" dramas impressed them as much as our perspective drawing. Miguel=Valignano in *De Missione*:

> Reciting their lines in male or female roles, people use many different voices depending on the topic, sometimes delighted, sometimes crying, sometimes pained, sometimes forsaken; that is to say, they can change their voices to reflect any mood. It was so skillful as to be beyond technique and I think must have come from a natural born talent. Indeed, they don't raise their voices tensely like they are singing as is ordinarily done in our country. (J/S:DM)

A few hundred years later, Ms Scidmore found the "high-pitched, falsetto sounds" of the Japanese actors horrendous and noted that "many performers have ruined and lost their voices, and even burst blood-vessels, in the long-continued, unnatural strain of their recitatives." (S:JDJ) Luckily for these performers, Noh is "full of semi-articulate sounds," such as "the soughing of the wind amongst the pine boughs, the dropping of water, or the tolling of distant bells, the stifling of sobs, the clash and clang of war, echoes of the weavers beating the new web against the wooden beam, the cry of crickets, and all the manifold voices of night and nature, where pause is more significant than pitch." (Okakura) While this sound/pause was going on, the actor-reciters could rest their voices and allow dance to tell, or rather, suggest the story. Here, I cannot help giving a contrast:

> *Our actors use or exaggerate their natural pitch to express emotion;*
> *Their actors express all moods the same way and only change their intensity.*

While the tail-end of the verb in Japanese allows for marvelous tonal expression of emotion – so much so it taught me how to talk with cats (see HAN-CHAN'S DREAM when it is published!) – the Japanese sentence *as a whole* is as flat as Florida. Singing out the whole sentence in slow motion a word at a time, the usual clarity of the tail-end – and with it the individual emotional significance – is completely lost. In other words, the whole thing is so ridiculously emotional that only visual elements or the expressed meanings of the words tell you what the particular emotion is! At least, that is *my* impression of Noh and Kabuki.

..

13-8 For us, it would be disturbing and an insult for one to make noise during the performance of a play; *Antre nós seria perturbasão e injuria estar hum bonzeando emquanto se faz o auto.*

> In Japan, it praises and decorates the actor for there to be onlookers making great hisses/hoots/shouts. *Em Japão hé decoro e ornamento do que se reprezenta estarem alguns de fora dando humas grandes apupadas.*

Apparently the practice of shouting out encouragement and appreciation for the actors later found in *kabuki* had already begun. In Japanese drama, the words are so slowly drawn out that a shout could cut clean through crosswise and hardly even nick a syllable. Outside of drama, in Japanese folk (festival and farm) singing, a shrill chorus of voices, usually female, often cuts in. If it is sassy it is all the more appreciated and increases the total energy level of the performance, much in the same way call-backs improve the total sound effect of a Southern black Baptist congregation in America. There is even a word for it in Japanese, *hayashi*. Until reading Frois, I assumed a Latin drama performance would be full of the same, for flamenco is famous for it. Or, do I read wrong and Frois means only that the Japanese voices indicating praise or simply excitement sound like what "we" would do to show our disgust? The fact Usanians whistle with approval whereas most Latins do so where "we" would *boo*, shows how tricky such cross-cultural comparison is. Had Frois been a 17-18c Englishman, he might have written, instead:

> *We express ourselves in the galleries using an instrument called a cat-call which we buy.*
> *They show their enthusiasm during performances entirely through their own devices.*

The OED defines the *cat-call* as "a squeaking instrument or kind of whistle used esp. in playhouses to express impatience or disapprobation." On the whole, the intent was bad – supporting Frois's contrast where "we" identified noise during performances with criticism – but reading Addison's essay *The Cat-Call* (see *TT-long* for the best of it) one gets the feeling that the gallery had so much fun with it that the *cat-call* may well have been used in good humor at the appropriate turns of the play. So, the English, at one time, may have ever so slightly approached the Japanese in their attitude toward theater.

13-9 Our masks cover the chin all the way down to below the beard;
Antre nós as mascaras cobrem o qeixo da barba todo por baxo;

> Those of Japan are so small that even when playing a woman, the beard can always be seen below. *As de Japão são tão peqenas que o que emtra por figura de molher, ficão-lhe sempre parecendo por baxo as barbas.*

Noh masks are tiny. They are not intended to actually disguise the actor, but just to give the audience enough to go on. If Japanese painters did not yet paint good perspective, they could be *very* realistic in three dimensions: they made statues showing each pore of the skin, with carefully implanted real hair. The *noh* mask, then, is representative of an *aesthetic choice* to be impressionistic or symbolic rather than realistic as in Europe, where, according to Miguel=Valignano the backdrops and other props were so *real* that even actual events might be expressed *just as they were*. (J/S:DM)

But remove the mask and *noh* is stranger yet: "these buckram figures, moving with the solemnity of condemned men, utter their lines like automata, not a muscle nor an eyelash moving, nor a flicker of expression crossing the unmasked countenance" writes Scidmore (S:JDJ), who might have been surprised to know that 50 years later a Japanese novelist would write that *Western* chorus and opera singers looked like *singing-machine* with their mouths opening wide and moving straight up and down like that. The funny thing is that Tanizaki Junichiro (*Inei Raisan*) is as right as Scidmore. Formal Western singing *is* very weird looking. The mouth movement resembles string operated puppets, and with them doing it in perfect unison, it looks even scarier. Only the folk tradition, *in both cultures,* lets us see humans singing naturally. But, speaking of puppets, Frois missed a big one:

> *With us, the puppeteer or puppeteers must always remain out of sight.*
> *The Japanese puppeteers often remain in plain view on the stage.*

Like the beard below the mask, we are not supposed to see the puppeteer. This is not so difficult as it might sound, for the puppeteers dressed completely in black. The same pure black clothing, including a black hood was adopted in kabuki by helpers called *kurogo* (blacklings?), who held light up to the protagonist's face or moved props around before the eyes of the audience.

13-10 Our comedies and tragedies are accompanied by soft-sounding musical instruments;
Nas nossas [c]omedias ou tragedias se introduzem suaves instrumentos de muzica;

> In Japan, by goblet-shaped drums, a drum with two sticks and fife of bamboo.
> *Em Japão huns atabalinhos da feisão de calix e hum atabale com dous paos e hum pifaro de cana.*

Unlike our accompaniment, Japanese instruments functioned more like the sound-track of a modern thriller movie: they could get very intense and dominate tense moments.

The first type of drum is called a *tsutsumi* (wrap [drum]?) and looks like a long hourglass, or two champagne glasses cut through mid-stem and welded stem to stem. The membranes are laced with chords that cross from membrane to membrane so they may be squeezed – thanks to the narrow waist very tightly. In other words, it is a *talking-drum*. Japanese, not having a tonal language, cannot use it to talk with. *So why do they have this rare type of instrument, that Europe never made?* Because the condensed emotion expressed at the tail of a Japanese sentence makes obvious what Europeans only theorize about: the unarguable emotional significance of *rising* and *falling* tone. The *tsutsumi*, like a bongo, is played by hand. The second type of drum is just a drum (*taiko,* but called *ôkawa* (big-skin) in Noh). Hit on the head it is capable of a thunder-clap. However, those sticks Frois mentions spend much time mincing out rhythm on the side of the drum, too. Both drums were used to speed up or slow down time. Since the *taiko* drums have toured around the world, I assume readers are familiar with the way Japanese do that by telescoping or un-telescoping a simple beat. The fife was indeed played by blowing over a hole from the side and its naturally shrill quality, which makes it a favorite for military bands in the West, achieves a new level in the sound-world of the Japanese. A Japanese fifer doesn't blow, he *blasts*. This blasting has two characteristics not often found in Western music. First, it is not only worked up to, in the Western manner where sound crescendos, but often *begins* in its full fury. That is to say, it is explosive. It *hits* as strong gusts of wind often do. And, second, the fifer does not stop when the sound threatens to break, but enjoys blasting it up and over its limits. This critical break is played upon like a surfer rides a wave, and the thrill to the initiated – or, those with an ear for it – is pretty much the same.

13-11 In our dances, they move to the sound of the tambourine, but do not sing;
Nas nossas danças fazem mudanças ao som do tamburil, mas não cantão;

> With Japanese dances, they always have to sing to the sound of the drums.
> *Nas dos Japãos se há sempre de cantar ao som do atabaqe.*

I am not sure exactly what Frois means by "our dances." The Japanese dance would probably be the *bon-odori,* or "bon-dance." Today, the singing for the bon dance is either recorded or done by a few people using microphones. I do not yet know if people sang as they danced, but there is indeed always a singing voice prominent in the music that is danced.

13-12 Ours carry bells and proceed straight ahead;
Os nossos trazem cascaveis e andão dereitos;

> Those of Japan have fans in their hands, and always proceed like [?] people who have lost or go looking for something that is lost on the ground. *Os de Japão abanos nas mãos e andão sempre como [?] ou como pessaos que olhando pera o chão andão buscando o que perderão.*

Our "bells" would probably be *jingles* if we only had such a word. The straight ahead would seem to indicate dancing as part of a procession rather than a social dance. With a Japanese *bon odori,* the dancers circle a stationary band. Frois seems to be taking a close look at the slow forward progress which does include alternate right and left movement where the body is often bent (sometimes one is reminded of judo) slightly forward – in other words, Japanese do indeed look like Frois says they do. The fan is good to have for cooling off between dances and playing with. Doing the *tanko-bushi,* a coal-mining *bon dance* number, I enjoy turning my fan into a shovel.
..

13-13 Our dances are performed during the day; *As nossas danças se fazem de dia;*

> Theirs almost always at night. *E as suas quasi sempre de noyte.*

Almost the opposite of 13-1, for "we" went to plays at night. M & J take issue with this contrast, citing instances of night dancing in Europe going back to 1451 in Lisbon and point out that dance was the rage in Portugal, with the 15-16c called "the era that danced the night away," largely as a result of profits from overseas. Frois may, however, be talking not about such social dances, but *performances* of dance commensurable to the Japanese *mai* of the dancing girls In that case, Frois can be faulted for completely neglecting *participatory dance* in the respective cultures.

> *We go to dances in any season of the year.*
> *The Japanese only dance in the hottest part of the summer or early fall.*

The dance is part of the Festival of the Dead. The *bon* lanterns to light the way for the souls, the heat and the nature of drum-centered music – I don't know why, but drumbeats die in the day-light – make the night the only time for such dancing.   And how about the next examples?

> *Among us, we have dances for men and women to dance with each other as couples.*
> *In Japan, there are no dances for couples and the very idea seems absurd.*

> *Among us it is considered perfectly proper for men and women to touch when dancing.*
> *Among the Japanese, for men and women to touch when dancing would be degrading.*

When Miguel=Valignano mentions the existence of mixed dancing in *De Missione*, Leo immediately remonstrated that it *certainly reduces Europe's prestige in his estimation*, to which Miguel replied that if the cheerful and open spirit of the dance were not enough, a mature character and properly serious demeanor on the part of the dancers made such a worry (Public sexuality? Seduction? Jealousy? Or, just men mixing with women?) beside the point. You have to know how strongly women are honored and protected in Europe, to appreciate why this (apparently scandalous and demeaning activity) is safe, he added, going on to explain how the slightest suspicion about a woman's being compromised can lead to a bloodbath, *with judicial permission, of course* (lawful Europe vs. lawless Japan being the catechism). Surprisingly little had changed when ambassadors for the first Japanese mission West since the *Missione* attended a dance at U.S.A. Secretary (of War?) Cass's house in the 19c:

> Upon enquiring, we were told that this was a "dance." As we watched the various movements of the dancers, I could not help smiling at the way the very large skirts, called crinolines, which the ladies wore, increased in volume until they became of enormous proportions when the dancers attained their top speed. . . . This continues until midnight. . . . our wonder at the strange performance became so great that we began to doubt whether we were not on another planet. . . . It seems very funny indeed to us, as dancing in our country is done by professional girls only and is not at all a man's pastime. (A:FJE)

Chamberlain gives us a far less diplomatic description of "our" dancing reflected in the eyes of the Japanese: "A plain-spoken writer in an excellent illustrated periodical entitled *Fuzoku Gwaho* [customs report], says that, whereas his imagination had painted a civilized ball-room as a vision of fairy-land, its reality reminded him of nothing so much as lampreys wriggling up to the surface of the water, and (*passez-lui le mot*) fleas hopping out of a bed." ("Dances" in C:TJ) Morse tied in the lack of "the marching habit" in Japan with their never dancing together. Conversely, we were the more collectivist in our movement. A Chinese who observed Americans in the first half of the 20c put it like this: *"Westerners walk together like a formation of geese; Chinese are like scattered ducks."* (A&L:LWG) Yet, today – thanks to the militarization in the mid-20c? – Japan and China are ballroom dance powerhouses.

~~~~~~

13-14   European dancing has much movement of the feet;
   Ho dançar d'Europa hé de muitos movimentos dos pés;

> That of Japan is more solemn and, for the most part done with the hands.
> *Ho de Japão hé mais grave e fá-los pola mayor parte com as mãos.*

Chamberlain, not knowing *Tratado*, stated the same with envious economy: "Europeans dance with their feet, – not to say their legs – Japanese mainly with their arms." (C:TJ) Okada, who quotes this, together with Chamberlain's next sentence – "The dress or rather undress of a European *corps de ballet* would take away the breath of the least prudish Oriental" – follows up with a *reason* for the difference: "[Our] clothing is probably the reason the legs are not normally moved a lot in Japanese dance." *Perhaps*. But, the naked Hawaiians did most of *their* dances with their hands, too. My guess is that the emphasis on arms is a Far Eastern and Pacific phenomena that has more to do with living on mats which would be destroyed by Occidental dance. Okada himself, probably does not much care for "our" dance because his translation, unlike Frois's original, makes the leg movement (but not the Japanese hands) *imperative*, i.e. "[you] must move [your] legs a lot." (*ugokasanakerebanaranai*)! But to return to Frois's contemporaries. After apologizing for making too much of European dance, "for comparing different cultures and contrasting their customs, making one base and adoring the other is bound to bring on a reaction, and I have no intention of putting down Japan," Miguel=Valignano writes, "but if, by any chance, one [culture] were by the will of God, or by all of the races' common assent, or criticism . . ." Here, either de Sande's Latin or the Japanese translation peters out of meaning (at any rate, I can't make sense of it) ; but Miguel, continuing, soon makes sense again: "taking dance for example, excluding a few things that might be somewhat unsuitable from the standpoint of Europeans, it shouldn't be too difficult for our country's dance to adopt the good parts of European dance and embody the true nature of dance." Leo=Valignano pops in and asks: "What are those somewhat unsuitable things?" Miguel's reply:

> There are two main points. First, when someone from our country dances, he generally wears the mask of an unfortunate dead woman with wildly tangled hair, or similarly, a mask representing a soul that has left someone's body when he performs, so that instead of the cheerful thrill of dance [as in the West], it seems to produce pain and melancholy. And second, the dancing person now and then stops suddenly in mid-dance and howls, to which the audience replies with similar howls. For this reason, Japanese dance seems like a noisy and confused shrieking contest rather than something lively and interesting. If the Japanese could only get rid of those depressing masks and dance in beautiful costume to music in a scale used by Europeans, they would easily be able to achieve the European level of dance. But it is a fine thing for each country's unique customs to remain. (dialog. 11 J/S:DM)

The two points mentioned concern only a small fraction of Japanese dance. But that fraction happens to be the most *active* part of Japanese dance. Only the crazy, the demonically possessed whirl about and leap wildly like Europeans do in their dance. Naturally, Japanese felt "going round and round" to quick music in the European style was "too savage to bear." Details aside, Miguel=Valignano is dealing with a problem salient even today in Japan: *the relationship of Japanese culture to a Western-biased "world culture."* The same assertions followed by contradictory reassurance of cultural relativity, the same tendency to bend toward the West rather than to hold up something new and challenge the West . . . It is both delightful and depressing to find such thought over 400 years ago. But to return to Frois's contrast, it was indeed true that our dances were far more active than the Japanese ones. Yet, it was not all so sweet and cheerful as depicted. If the *De Missione* ambassadors reported anything like the Zarabanda of the Corpus Christi Celebration, representing "the abortions of Hell" which, the Jesuit priest Mariana warned, inflamed "even very honest people" (STUDIES IN SALESIAN SPIRITUALITY Elisabeth Stopp) Valignano chose not to include it:

13-15 Among us, music of diverse voices is sonorous and sweet;
Antre nós a muzica de diversas vozes hé sonora e suave;

> That of Japan, as all screech in just one voice, is the most horrendous that can be made. *A de Japão, como todos se esganisão em huma só vox, hé a mais horrenda que se pode dar.*

Two issues – that should have been two separate contrasts – are conflated here: *harmony* and *smooth voices*. The former in its fully developed form, *i.e.* polyphony, is often credited to the West, and proudly ascribed to the growth of polyvalent modern culture or the analytical scientific mindset, etc.. Actually, it is traditional in Mongolia and much of continental Asia. The Far West was only a Johnny-come-lately. Polyphony did not reach Japan, either, and the Japanese never discovered it for themselves (see 13-18). Then, again, they did not *need* it as much as "we" did. The individual Japanese voice, human or instrumental, is *far* more complex than those of the West. It is as richly textured as a bark-covered kinky tree branch, whereas ours is smooth and featureless as a dowel. Morse:

> Later I learned from a [Japanese] student that our music was not music at all to them. He couldn't understand why we cut it off by jerks; to him it was "Jig, jig, jig, jig, jig, jigger, jig, jig"! (M:JDD)

For that reason, one can derive infinitely more pleasure from singing Japanese songs – *a cappella* and alone – than "ours" (*karaoke* could never have started in the West). For religious and philosophical (Platonian?) reasons, we pursued sweetness and suavity of voice to the exclusion of all nitty-gritty sound, until we ended up with polished perfection, which we then fled by combining our "dowels" into more complex structures, i.e., polyphonic melodies or dressing them with melodic instrumental music. Morse is the only Westerner I know of who came to realize this:

> We heard the most wonderful music of the flute by a Japanese court musician. . . . The enjoyment for us consisted in the delicious contrasts between note after note. The notes were long and of exquisite purity. It was a revelation to us. With harmony one gets these effects in our music, but in Japanese music there is no harmony, only melody. (M:JDD)

Listening to that and other music that was "certainly very weird and very impressive," Morse recognized that "here was a chance for some one to secure ideas in regard to the power of music in a new direction" and, about two-hundred pages later, he naturally went where Valignano had gone before, acknowledging that experience could change our reason: "As their pictorial art was incomprehensible to us at the onset, and yet at further acquaintance and study we discovered in it transcendent merit, so it seemed to me that a study of Japanese music might reveal merits we little suspected" and he studied a form of Japanese singing called *utai* ("singing"). While I like Japanese folksong and music, I must admit, *I* don't care for *utai* and was not surprised to find Morse concluded it was "not singing, but inflectional declamation, not unlike the conversation of the countrymen of Yorkshire."

Most Westerners did not even *try* to appreciate Japanese music of any type and give a uniformly negative opinion of it. Samuel Johnson once wrote that "of all the noises, I think classical music the least disagreeable." All Western visitors to Japan from Frois to Chamberlain – even Morse at first – unanimously thought that of all noises, Japanese music was the *most* disagreeable. Fiddles and opera have endured their fair share of insult, *but never in history has any music been so harshly and repeatedly put down as Japanese music has.* Why? Is Japanese music uniquely horrid? After all, there are hundreds, if not thousands of musics in the world. Perhaps, the fact that the Japanese culture so delighted the *eyes* of the West made our *ears* doubly disturbed not to get equal satisfaction – How can a people who sweep us off our feet in the plastic arts fail to do so in the acoustic ones? How, also, can something *that different* be disliked? Distilling over a page of ferocious criticism in *TT-long*:

> . . . it is quite a trial to listen to it for a quarter of an hour; but to please the Japanese we are obliged to listen to it for many hours. (Mexia S.J., writing about the same time as Frois. In C:TCJ)

> They say the Japanese teach them [uguisu warblers] to sing beautifully, which is the more extraordinary if true, as they certainly do *not* teach themselves; and, if I had not lived among the Chinese, I should have said they had the least conception of either harmony or melody of any race yet discovered. The discord they both make, when they set themselve to make what they call music, is something that baffles all description. Marrow bones and cleavers are melodious by comparison. . ." A:COT 1863)

Of course, pathology is as legitimate a study as physiology. Those, therefore, who wish to investigate more minutely the ways and means by which injury is inflicted on sensitive ears should consult the authorities enumerated below . . . ("Music" heading in Chamberlain: C:TJ: 1890)

Still, we must credit Chamberlain for *eventually* admitting to the other side of the equation, that "Dislikes are bound to be mutual" and *they* did not care for our music, either. He provided proof. Witnessing an Italian opera, the Japanese were "seized with a wild fit of hilarity at the high notes of the prima donna, and started laughing so hard "their sides shook, and tears rolled down their cheeks; and they stuffed their sleeves into their mouths, as we might our pocket-handkerchiefs, in a vain endeavor to contain themselves." (Ibid) One can well imagine how surprising those arias where the prima sounds like she is either being continuously goosed or has managed to cross a howling spider-monkey, a laughing hyena and a clucking hen, must have been to the Japanese!

13-16 In all the nations of Europe, we find full-throated singing;
Antre as naçoes d'Europa em todas há garganta;

Among the Japanese no one sings like that.
Antre os Japões nenhum gargantea.

There is a dilemma here for the translator. The temptation is to write *warble* or *quaver* for that is how the verb *gargantear* is translated by the Portuguese- or Spanish-English dictionaries. Moreover, a *garganteo* is "a tremulous modulation of the voice." But Japanese folk music (as opposed to that of the Imperial court) actually uses the grain of the voice *more* than Europeans do. They *do* warble, *i.e.* make fine trembling modulations. Indeed, female professional singers were called *uguisu,* a type of *warbler* usually translated as "nightingale" because the song was considered the sweetest of all birds (Today, women manning the loudspeakers in politicians' sound-trucks are usually called the same!). A *Mutamagawa* senryu provides a self-description by the Japanese: "when a warbler loses its teeth [the edge on her voice], the voice of a cicada." The latter would be an older women. So, if warbling was not something "we" had and Japanese did not, it occurred to me that Frois might be referring to *vibrato* (not the delicate quiver of young Dolly Parton, or the cat-in-heat rasp of Janis Joplin, but the mechanically uniform sounding steady tremolo of a singer trained in formal European style singing). That, however, seemed too restrictive – who says everyone sang that way in Europe? – so I wondered aloud to a Mexican friend, M, who swears that the Spanish equivalent of *gargantear*, means to use the full throat to *really* sing. It is possible, for singing well in Portuguese and Spanish is not to have a *voice* of honey, but "a good throat." Is it not possible that Frois, thinking of Japanese nasality, meant that Japanese had no *throat*=voice to speak of? After all, our classical critics describe good voices as "round" throughout its ranges and unsullied by or lost in the nose or throat.

In my opinion (which will infuriate you if you are a music-school-type), European art-music – including opera *appoppogio* and all – represents *the impoverishment of the voice* and country music's George Jones and blue-grass's Ralph Stanley, who retain some of the real soul in our music, are worth a thousand Pavalottis. The *vibrato* is a wretched standardization of the more interesting irregularity of natural warbling, a move back from the truly plaintive call of the cricket to the droning cicada. The rest of the world may not be able to equal the range of octaves of a top opera singer or break a glass, but it can use the voice in a far more complex manner, so complex, indeed, that many of the nuances defeat all efforts to write it down. Most of us have simply lost the ears to comprehend a rich and complex grain of voice and hear it as primitive cacophony. Isabella Bird was an exception. Despite finding Japanese vocal performances "excruciating," and "agonizing," and even complaining that the minor scale was "a source of pain" to her (as an ebullient Christian, she doubtless liked inanely cheerful major notes), she gamely kept her ears uncovered long enough to give us the best description of Japanese traditional singing ever written: "It seemed to me to consist of a hyena-like howl, long and high (a high voice being equivalent to a good voice), varied by frequent guttural, half-suppressed sounds, a bleat, or more respectfully, "an impure shake," which is very delicious to a musically-educated Japanese audience which is both scientific and highly critical, but eminently distressing to European ears." (B:UTJ)

With all of the people I have quoted, an unstated bias toward upper-class Music exaggerates the Japanese-European difference in taste. None of the Western commentators represent the folk-view. The folk never got to Japan or never wrote of it. In *The Resolver* (trans. 1635) Scipio Du Pleis wrote much the same thing about *our* folk that most Occidentals, including Frois, did about the Japanese:

> Q – Wherefore is it, that the most part of those which are ignorant of Musicke, are more pleased with hearing an onely voyce shrill and tuneable, then to a Musicke accomplished with all his parts?
>
> A – It is with the ignorant vulgar in the Art of Painting which are taken more with fresh colours in pictures . . . then with . . . Michael Angelo, where all the proportions are curiously observed, and [rather] makes more business of a petulant and bawling advocate then of him which observes with moderation all the precepts of Rhetorick; likewise those which understand nothing of musick, love better to hear often a long squealing voyce, then a perfect and harmonious comfort.

13-17 To us, the music of the clavichord, viola, flute, organ and *doçaina* are very sweet;
Antre nós hé suavissima e melodia de cravo, viola, frautas, orgãos, doçainas etc.;

To the Japanese, all our instruments sound harsh and unpleasant.
Aos Japões, todos nossos instrumentos lhe são insuaves e desgostozos.

"Sweet" in the original is "soft." The *doçaina* is a type of bagpipe popular from the 12c-17c. I cannot for the life of me imagine a *suavissima*-sounding bagpipe, so I left the original word!

After touching on European-Japanese differences in visual sense (See "black and white" 1-30), Valignano wrote, "And the contrariety of our hearing is no less, for our vocal and instrumental music commonly injure their ears, and they are extremely happy with their own music which really torments our hearing." Montanus rephrases, noting that what music is "most Ravishing and Grateful to us" grates their ears "so much, that they will stop them with their fingers," while L' Abbe says straightforwardly that our music holds no charm for them while "theirs to us is nothing else, but an ungrateful Noise of Kettles and Frying Pans." *All this relativity is nice, but it is a bit too perfect*, for not a few Japanese found our music sweet from the beginning. The rulers of Japan, Nobunaga and Hideyoshi apparently listened with pleasure (V(A):S&A, note 73) and Frois's colleague Organtino was convinced there was so much appreciation for the organ and other European instruments in his district that if he only had "organs and other musical instruments, and enough singers" he could "convert all of Miyako [Kyoto] and Sakai in only a year." (Ibid. and S:VMP). Coelho, in a 1582 letter about Nobunaga's visit to Organtino's seminary testifies "of all the things introduced into Japan so far, the playing of organs, harpsichords and viols pleases the Japanese most" and explained that these things acted "as bait" to attract the pagans. (in C:TCJ) Mexia, however, wrote Japanese didn't care for organs. One wonders if Organtino, true to his name was so superb an organ player that even Japanese liked to hear him! Seriously, in 1590, Frois, himself, recorded the musical success of the newly returned Embassy. "Listening to the group sing and perform on the various instruments brought back from abroad, every one was delighted and surprised at the harmony and the correspondence maintained among the various instruments." (HISTORIA/v86) The youths had learned to play a variety of instruments and perform in four-part harmony while staying in Europe! Reading this, we can't help wondering if Western music could have made sufficient inroads to influence the course of Japanese music had Japan not closed.

The Japanese, at least, were open-minded. Here is what Chamberlain wrote in the late 19c.about classical (Occidental art) music taking root in Japan:

May this happen here before another century elapses, and then may all the *samisen, kotos,* and other native instruments of music be turned into firewood to warm the poor, when – if at no previous period of their existence – they will subserve a purpose indisputably useful! (C:TJ)

13-18 We greatly appreciate the consonance and harmony of our organ music.
A consonansia e proporsão da nossa muzica de canto d'orgão¹ estimamos em muito;

> The Japanese find it *kashimashi* [noisy, clamorous] and do not enjoy it.
> *Os Japões a tem por caxi maxi e não gostão nada della.*

Speaking of the 16c, Jacques Barzun writes "The period was one of musical expansion – larger choirs in churches, bigger and better organs, larger "families" of instruments and more numerous players in town bands." (*From Dawn to Decadence*) On the positive side, he quotes Thomas More's *Utopia* where "music takes the impression of whatever is represented, affects and kindles the passions, and works the sentiments deep into the hearts of the hearers;" and, on the negative, Erasmus (1513), who regrets that "in college or monastery it is still the same music, nothing but music. Words nowadays mean nothing. . . . Money must be raised to buy organs and train boys to squeal." The *De Missione* ambassadors reflected the Jesuits' favorable view toward music. After Miguel=Valignano introduces nine European musical instruments, including ones with names that sound like parts of the human body or diseases to me – *tibia* (a type of flute) and *fistula* (reed instrument?) – and claims that they sound good when played together properly, Leno=Valignano, responds that hearing you play them the other night was very refreshing even for us (stay-at-home Japanese), "but we just couldn't feel that sweetness of which you speak." To this, Miguel, sounding very Valignano, replies:

> It shows how hard it is to shake custom and how powerful the effect of not being used to something is. And this same thing goes for singing. Since you are not yet used to the harmony of European harmony, you cannot know the true joy and melodiousness of it. But, as our ears are already used to it, there is nothing so pleasant to hear. (J/S:DM)

Then, Miguel describes the different types of voices of harmonizing and boasts of its complexity as an art in a manner suggesting deep appreciation: "Vocalizing all of that, fitting it with the instrumentals, while preserving the rules of music, or sometimes going up higher, beyond the rules . . ." That "going beyond" to me at any rate, means the joy of improvisation. Such a "perfect art," he continues, is a "lofty" one, "born of freemen distributing [?] and adjusting their respective voices" and, now, "diligently studied from childhood," it is making continued progress. Meanwhile, Japanese song is "monotone, with no divisions of voice." Actually, Japanese do have one type of accidental harmony. In a large temple, with fifty or more people sing-songing the sutra in their natural tone of voice, each pausing to take his or her breath whenever they naturally run out, and perhaps partially synchronizing this subconsciously to the periodic chime, an effect similar but far more relaxing to the staggered singing of "Row, Row, Row, Your Boat" is achieved. I, at least, find it more interesting than our more orchestrated chants. But, Japan has never known anything approaching even the simple harmony one finds in any choir, many blue-grass songs, or a barbershop quartet.

1. Translation. *Canto d'orgão* is literally "song of [the] organ;" At first, I thought it might be songs made to be sung with the organ, but I could not confirm this and went along with the other translators. The German translation filled out the meaning of the consonance and proportion part: *symphony of tone* and the *harmony (accord)* of the music," but no one really defines what would seem to be the name for a genre of music.

13-19 Ordinarily, with us, the music of the nobility is gentler than that of mean folk;
Ordinariamente antre nós a muzica dos fidalgos hé mais suave que a [da] jente baxa;

> That of the Japanese nobility, we cannot bear to hear, and that of seamen pleases us. *A dos fidalgos Japões, nós não a podemos ouvir, e a dos marinheiros [hé]-nos aceyta.*

Since Europe decided that *smooth was classy* and thought nothing sounded better than castrated boys, that would, indeed, be the case. The first *castrato* (in the guise of the Spanish "falsettist" Padre Soto) on record at the Sistine Chapel was 1562 (About 15 years after Frois left Europe for the Far East). It was a common practice in the 16c – not just in Spain and Italy but in Germany and France, too – because the elaborate *a cappella* (in chapel) style pioneered in the previous century demanded more complexity than mere boys could hack, and the voice was preferred to that of falsettos and women (who were also forbidden to sing in church). *But what delicious irony* – the devilish practice of castration to create music thought to be angelic, unnaturally deforming bodies because the natural falsetto was considered false and detested by the pure of heart! Dating at least as far back as the 2c in Rome and continued in Constantinople, the practice was not invented at this time, but, like so many things, part of the revival called the Renaissance. Italy was most castrato-positive and almost never used the word. They were called *musico* or *virtuoso* and treated with corresponding respect. Throughout Europe they came to be treated like superstars and to act like superstars (weird dressing, ridiculously intense rivalries, tantrums, etc.). This popularity peaked in the 17c. There is no need to go on about *castratos*. My point is only that "our" upper-class's unnatural desire for *sweet* and *smooth* (but ornamented) sound was so powerful that the boy-voice became synonymous with Music.

The nobility in Frois's Japan was basically military class, with subdued Zen taste. The stark music of Noh was appreciated. The court music, something called *gagaku,* is less subdued in that more instruments come into play, yet sounds bad even to me. Nakata Taizo, a Japanese *gagaku* aficionado describes the combination of three instruments like this: "When all sound together a Cosmos can be heard / Imagined by those now distant Elegant in the flickering candle of time."(http://www.gagaku.net/index.ENG.html) But, I fear I would agree with Edward Yong, who had to provide 10 minutes of Japanese Court Music for a college play based on Rashomon and confessed

> If anyone who attends the production thinks what I'm playing sounds absolutely horrid, tuneless, dissonant and out of tune, you're absolutely right. That's how Japanese court music sounds. In fact, what I'm playing is already a more tonal and tuneful version – I can perceive neither tonality nor melody in the original stuff. . . . When I first read accounts of the western missionaries having to sit through endless hours of Japanese court music and complaining that they'd not heard anything so horrible in their lives, I thought they were just ignorant Westerners who couldn't appreciate the beauty of Asian things, even though they said they wished they were back in Cathay (China) where the music was tuneful and entertaining. Then I heard Gagaku, and I realized they were right. . . . There is, however, one undoubted advantage in Japanese Court Music. There are people who can hear no melody in Chinese Classical Music. Such a person should attend a concert of Gagaku, with all the traditional instruments and dances , and then attend one of Chinese music the next night. If, after their horrid wailing, he can still find no melody in our Chinese dances and songs, he must give up looking for a tune in anything. . . . Apparently, Japanese Court Music is supposed to be a descendant of T'ang Chinese Court Music, . . . I find it hard to believe the Chinese could have ever had such hair-raisingly awful music, and that when the Japanese in the 9th Century were aping Chinese culture, they tried to imitate the Chinese stuff and didn't quite get it right. There's no other explanation for it. (infernoxv.blogspot.com/2004_01_01_infernoxv_archive.html)

By definition, *gagaku* was refined and graceful, respectable music as opposed to the vulgar music of the folk. As anthropologist Robert Garfias notes, its very name (雅楽) suggests the Confucian concept of good wholesome music to keep the elements in balance, though it really derives from a different strand of Chinese music associated with court banquets (宴楽). The Kunaicho (The Imperial Household Agency) writes that "the Japanese singing style and vocal arrangements for Gagaku are composed of advanced musical techniques, and have not only had a direct affect on the creation and development of modern-day music, but Gagaku itself also has the potential to develop in many aspects, as a global art form." Put more cynically, it is strange enough to have caught the attention of avant-garde musicians seeking the non-linear and whatnot on the one hand yet belongs to a tradition old enough to make it a living anachronism, *a coelacanth of music.*

By music of the seamen, Frois probably means the working chants mentioned in 12-10. Some were honest-to-goodness folk-songs – chanties as opposed to chants. Morse found the most pleasant ones in the extreme North and South of Japan. He thought them almost identical to what Russian sailors sung. I think they would be the 3-beat ballads musicologists tend to identify with the horseback riding peoples of Asia and I would, with Bird, associate with the "extreme plaintiveness" of much Korean music ("partly due probably to the unlimited quavering on one note") and, to be bolder, with *all* minor-key folk music as described by Joseph Needham in his *River of Time*. The philosophers (Plato or Confucius) reason that sweet and happy (i.e. *proper*) music make people feel thus, but the people themselves tend to favor a homeopathic approach: *sad music to cure sadness*.

13-20   In Europe, children sing an octave higher than men;[1]
Em Europa os meninos cantão 8 pontos mais alto que os homens;

In Japan, they all hit the same note, shrieking[2] so our sopranos would be out of work.[3] *Em Japão todos em ygual ponto esganiçando-sse no ponto em que o tipre [tiple?] estaa descansado.*

This is partly because Japanese do not harmonize but sing a single melody in a single key as already noted. It also may have something to do with the fact that the physiology of sexual difference is less radically developed in Japanese, and other East Asia people so that male voices are generally not so low (obviously Tibetan throats are another story!!) and it is possible for everyone to sing along.

1. Men?   I was tempted to write "adult," but such a word was little used until the mid-17c in English and probably not much in Portuguese, either. (We sometimes say that the concept of a *child* and *childhood* is a modern invention, but these predate the *adult* and *adulthood*!) Also, as it is possible Frois might be thinking "male," I prefer to leave the generic men, but is it *grown-up*?

2. Shriek?   The same "screechy" sound we found in 13-15 here is better as "shriek." Cooper (C:TCJ) renders it "shouts" here, where he made it "howls" in 13-15.

3. Soprano?   The last half of the Japanese part of the contrast has some translators scratching their heads. Frois does confuse his "l" and "r" (or Portuguese has changed) from time to time, so most translators have chosen "tiple," a word meaning "soprano." The modern Portuguese translation, alone, renders it "timbre," so that the means "until they lose their timbre" (actually "until the timbre is resting"), using timbre, or "tone." But, "soprano" or "tone," there is still an idiom to guess about: "soprano/tone would be *descansado*". Cooper translates "In Japan, everybody sings in the same octave, shouting on a note suitable for a soprano. (My italics C:TCJ) The French translation is similar, making ". . . the note one that, with us would be easy for a soprano." (*notes où un soprano est à l'aise chez nous.*) Okada, on the other hand, "There, the soprano *is on a [can take a?] vacation/ break.*" (*soko de wa sopurano wa oyasumi de aru.*). I think *his* rhetoric means, "there, a soprano would be *out of a job*, for they all shriek on the same high note." He adds in a note that Frois was probably thinking of a boy-soprano. Matsuda & Jorissen follow Okada, who follows Schütte, (*die dem Sopram bequem est*). Schütte also added a wee bit in mid-sentence that includes the word "falsetto." [a falsetto that takes off from where a soprano rests[?], or, so overpowering a falsetto that a soprano would only be drowned out?] I chose to follow the German/Japanese interpretation over the English and French, for it has that humorous twist. But strictly looking at the grammar, I was tempted to follow the others, who may well be correct. If you wish to take that interpretation, I would suggest using an English idiom: "on a note that would be a breeze for a soprano." Finally, I wonder whether a third interpretation may not be possible in which the other (most common) meaning of *ponto[punto]*, "point," is taken, so that it reads: "shrieking *at the point where [even] sopranos leave off."* That is to say, shrieking so shrill as to suggest an *alto*.

13-21   Our guitars have six strings, not counting the doubles, and are played with the fingers;
As nossas violas tem seis cordas afora as dobradas, e tanjen-se com a mão;

Those of Japan four, and they are played with a sort of comb.
As de Japão 4 e tamjen-se com huma maneira de pentes.

The German translation waffles with "stringed-instrument" (*saiteninstrumente*), while French boldly went for the "guitar," which has a longer classical pedigree than one might imagine, though its earliest usage example in the OED is in 1621. Other lutes are not necessarily 6-string and lack the waist found on the viola, so *guitar* it is.

The 4-string Japanese instrument is a *biwa,* a beautiful teardrop-shaped lute – with the back round and the front flat, sound-holes modeled after heavenly bodies (crescent and/or circle) and a neck that bends back in a right angle at the top. Like the folk *shamisen* (that would soon become the more popular instrument), it is powerfully plucked – or, rather, *struck* – a *biwa* player is called a *biwa-uchi:* "*biwa*-striker" – with an enormous plectrum, usually ivory, the size and the shape of a thin hatchet head. (Frois wrote "comb" because combs used to be very high-backed and the over-all shape resembles the plectrum). There are things only a handful of fingers can manage. For example, a single pick can not simultaneously pluck 4-strings. But a large and heavy pick, which is indeed a good contrast with delicate finger tips, is useful in more ways than one might imagine. *First,* it prevents the acoustic leakage: the vibration that would be lost with fingers or a lighter pick, improving high notes in particular. *Second,* the length translates a small movement of the wrist into a large one at the end of the pick: a lot of action for little work. And *third,* it can serve as a defensive weapon – against a snowball in a haiku of Issa's, but, more commonly (at least in pulp fiction and Easterns!) to cut the throat of another or oneself (I doubt most were that sharp or too many strings would be cut, but the fiction is a pleasant one). The large plectrum may be a Japanese invention, for the Chinese, from whom the *biwa* was adopted, pluck with their fingers (anyone?).

~~~~~~

13-22   Among us, the nobility takes pride in playing the guitar;
Antre nós a jente nobre se preza de tanjer violas;

>   In Japan, it is the office of the blind, as with the accordionists in Europe.
> *Em Japão hé oficio dos cegos como em Europa os samfonineiros.*

If Japanese noblemen and samurai were expected to be proficient at letters and the tea-ceremony as well as swordsmanship, Portuguese knights became infatuated with the troubadour art of singing ones own poems to the accompaniment of ones own plucking, something previously left to their poets and pages. For almost two centuries, write M & J, they had come to prefer music and other parlor games to tournaments and hunting, so that Prince (later, King) Don Duarte of Portugal, in the early 15c chastised the knights for becoming effeminate in his book on horsemanship. Indeed, the attention given to riding was spurred by the desire to restore the nation's manliness. But, continue M & J, the guitar/lute craze by no means stopped with the nobility. In the 16c it was popular everywhere people gathered as an instrument of solo accompaniment. (J/F(M&J:T)

In Japan, the lute was indeed identified with blind musicians. My dictionary (OJD) says they were called *biwa-hôji,* or priests of the *biwa.* And they put on a religious front – the costume and shaved head – although they were rarely actual Buddhist priests. Their specialty was not the love songs – or hymns, for the church in Portugal was not adverse to the *viola* – of the Portuguese nobility, but *almost entirely historical legend*, and that generally the same one, the Heikei-monogatari, or *Tales of the Heikei*, which tell of the tragic downfall of an old and beloved, highly aesthetic noble clan at the hands of a more warlike younger one. The *biwa* was not, however, *only* played by the blind. John Saris, head of the East India Company's first trading fleet to visit Japan (Nagasaki, 28 years after TRATADO) describes what would appear to be that instrument used in a manner more like we associate with the *shamisen* on the occasion of a courtesy call on shipboard by the King of Hirado:

> The king's women seemed to be somewhat bashful, but he willed them to bee frolicke. They sang diuers songs, and played vpon certain instruments (where-of one did much resemble our lute) being bellyed like it, but longer in the necke, and fretted like ours, but had only foure gut strings. Their fingring with the left hand like ours, very nimbly, but the right hand striketh with an iuory bone, as we vse to play upon a citterne[1] with a quill. They delighted themselues much with their musicke, keeping time with their hands and playing and singing by booke, prickt on line and space, resembling much ours heere. (Included with the Letters of Will Adams in S:MQTJ)

The "delighted *themselves*" would seem to be tongue-in-cheek, for Cooper, who quotes the same passage (with only the *u*'s corrected to *v*'s), writes Saris also wrote he found "musique after the Countrey fashion" to be "harsh to our hearings." (C:TCJ) The best part of Saris's letter, however, is where he "daue leaue to diuers women of the better sort to come into my Cabbin, where the picture of *Venus,* with her sonne *Cupid,* did hang somewhat wantonly set out in a large frame. They, thinking it to be our ladie and her sonne, fell downe and worshipped it, with shewes of great deuotion, telling me in a whispering manner (that some of their companions which were not so, might not heare) that they were *Christianos:* whereby we percieued them to be Christians, conuerted by the *Portugall* Iesuits." This picture story is particularly funny when you learn that when Saris returned to England, he had *a stock of pornographic books and paintings* that "were discovered and publically burnt on 10 January 1615." (L:IOJ) Ian Littlewood calls Saris "a clod" for not following Will Adam's advice and thus losing out on the chance to establish a trading base in Japan. This may (or may not) be fair, but I wish Saris had stayed in Japan longer and written a book about it, for he was a damn good reporter. He did mention one more concert:

> The old King came aboord againe and brought with him diuerse women to be frolicke. These women were actors of comedies, which passe there from iland to iland to play, as our players doe here from towne to towne, hauing seuerall shifts of apparell for the better grace of the manner acted: which for the most part are of Warre, Loue, and such like. (Ibid)

I included these long quotations because they show how someone not looking for contrast may find similarity ("*as we use to* play upon a citterne,"¹ "*resembling much ours* heere," "*as our players doe* here") in the same field where another of narrower experience finds only difference.

1. Citterne. A *Cithern/Cittern* according to the OED was "an instrument of the guitar kind, but strung with wire, and played with a plectrum or quill. The method of playing takes us closer to the Japanese one. In England it often had a grotesquely carved head and hung in barber-shops and the Tyrolese form is called (why I know not!) a zither. I found one mention of it in a 16ᵗʰ century Iberian context. "Their [the parish churches in Cuenca Spain in the 1520's] sanctity was violated by criminals who, exploiting their right to asylum in a church, lodged themselves inside, gambled, brought in women, played the *cittern*, and used the temple as a hideout from which they could attack their enemies with impunity." (Sara T. Nalle *God in La Mancha: Religious Reform and the People of Cuenca,* 1500-1650 THE LIBRARY OF IBERIAN RESOUCES ONLINE)

13-23 Our clavichords have four strings and are played with keys;
Os nossos cravos tem 4 cordas e tamjen-se polas teclas;

> Those of Japan have a dozen strings and are played with wooden picks made for that. *Os de Japão tem 12 cordas e tanjem-nos com humas unhas de pao feitas pera isso.*

The European instrument is a proto-piano, of which there were many types before the huge modern piano came into being. The number of strings makes me want to call it a keyed-up dulcimer, because we have already been told it sounds sweet (17, above).

The Japanese *koto,* a long zither that looks like a crate for an alligator is played by both sexes, but despite the considerable strength needed to depress the strings (to vary the tension) and carry the instrument, it has traditionally been *the* instrument for proper young women to play (perhaps because, like a piano, it stays home?). In 18c Edo, *senryu* joke about the *koto* as an instrument played and appreciated by such women. The *koto* comes with them when they get married, after which it grows cobwebs, for no husband has any interest in listening to them except when he is a captive audience, i.e. *too drunk to flee!* In that case, he may even use it for a *samisen,* that is to say:

i'll be damned!
a drunk in a blither dances
to a . . . zither!

baka na koto namayoi koto de odoru nari

I imagine the harp was similarly regarded in Europe. Yet, sweetness is not intrinsic to the instrument. As there are bluesmen who bounce bottles of beer on their macho pianos, there are *koto* players who really rock out. I have seen Korean women jamming so ferociously they seemed to be fighting! But the general sweet tinkling (?) quality of the *koto* – the one that makes it the darling of the environmental=background music today – made it the instrument that least bothered Occidentals. My favorite is the 1-string, for it is both easier and harder than playing anything else. There were various sizes and types of *koto* with various numbers of strings, but they generally settled upon 13 by the time Japan was opened again. I would think the fact *each string had its own, extremely tall bridge* (which, to me, bear some resemblance to the Eiffel Tower!) would be worth a contrast, but let me stick to Frois's. The *picks* he mentions are, in Japan, almost always used. They deserve a contrast, too:

> *Our clavichords are played with flat picks squeezed between the finger-tips;*
> *Theirs are played with picks called talons that are tubular and fit over the fingers*

13-24 Among us, the blind are very pacific;
Antre nós os cegos são muito pacíficos;

In Japan, [they are] very pugnacious, carrying staffs and *wakizashi* [dagger/s], and are real paramours. *Em Japão muito brigozosos, trazem bastões e* vaquizaxis, *e são muito namorados.*

The blind in Japan have always worked as musicians, masseurs, pimps and money-lenders. In their latter capacity, some numbered among the wealthiest individuals in Japan. In the Edo era, some even bought – that is, *freed* – high-level courtesans, something that cost the equivalent of millions of dollars today. And, as is true for the rich anywhere in the world, they were popular with the women. The Portuguese (*namorados*) I translated as *"real paramours,"* – it could as easily have been "real ladies men," real womanizers, or love-makers. In his capacity as a pimp, the blindman was regarded as an extraordinary judge of what we might call woman-flesh. A hundred years post-Frois, *Yanagidaru senryu* will quip that "for women / none has a better eye / than the blind boss" (*onna ni isso me no aru zatônobo*). But the most incredible thing about the blind was their organization that dated back centuries. In Alcock's words, the "two sects of the blind . . [are] founded by two great celebrities of Japanese history – one the third son of a Mikado who wept himself blind for the death of his mistress, and the other by a defeated general in the civil wars, who tore out his eyes that he might not be provoked to take the life of a generous victor . ." With organization came special privileges and monopolies. The organization is a complex pyramidal "common-wealth" with "their General" residing in Miaco (Kyoto, the capital). Like most Buddhist sects, they did not hesitate to guard their turf in that rambunctious age when the Jesuits arrived in Japan, and if the violence naturally arising between organizations was not enough, the blind had a reputation for being sharply tempered and nursing a grudge. With all their money and women to protect, those canes came in handy as cudgels, especially in the dark when they were the only one who could "see" what was happening.

> *blind vengeance*
>
> in jealous rage
> the head returns home
> with bated cane
>
> *yaku zatô tsue o koroshite kaeru nari*

The original is better, for the pun is double. In Japanese, to bate one's breath is not only to hold it to keep quiet, but idiomatically to "kill" it. For fairness sake, I should point out that not *all* blind got respect in Japan. Blind singer-prostitutes, the *goze,* are usually *beaten* in *senryu*. Superstition said it was good luck to hit the *goze* one slept with!

13-25 Noblemen in Europe sleep at night and play by day;
Os fidalgos em Europa dormen de noyte e folgão de dia;

> The Japanese noblemen sleep by day and have their parties and play at night.
> *Os Japões fidalgos dormem de dia e tem suas festas e folguedos à noyte.*

As Sir Thomas Browne (1605-82) wrote, we should go to bed with and rise with the sun *as God intended,* for to do otherwise was "to play the part of our Antipodes." If the Far East is antipodal to us, as far as nobles go, Browne was wrong! From ancient times, noblemen in Japan played the roving Tom at night while poets sat still and viewed the moon. But I did not know the upper class had a *generally* nocturnal lifestyle until reading a 1563 letter, where Frois gives a long description of what amounted to a friendly round-the-clock siege by the nobility of South Japan, who came –

> each day to hear mass at the house at three o'clock at night: because it is the custom of these gentlemen [*senores*] to sleep very little at night; and they waited until four when father Cosme d' Torres came to give it . . . And because, after being baptized they hadn't had the opportunity . . . to hear the mystery's of the mass and of the sacrament of the Eucharist, one night they were with brother Juan Fernandez from three to five . . . another time they called for him at midnight and remained with him until dawn, asking many questions about matters of faith, . . . (CARTAS)

The Chinese nobility, likewise, were evidently great night-people. It makes sense when you consider the fact that the nobility had to wear more clothing than other people and could not have gone out in the day-light for much of the year without roasting. Cruz described birthday parties which lasted "through the entire night, because all of these peoples live in obscurity without the knowledge of God (Deus), and, likewise, all their parties for all parts of India [the East Indies] and China are held at night." (C:TCC in my translation, ch-45.) One wonders if Cruz really believed his reason for Far Eastern people partying *at night,* or if he was just exercising his Christian wit against the *bad* night when people engaged in sex and, worse, the moon reflected the merciful Light of the Buddhist Law. Here is a haiku by Teitoku (age 16 in 1585) on what happens during the time of year when staying up late was, indeed, *de rigor* for any cultured gentlemen (the title is mine):

> *harvest dreams*
>
> sowing the seeds
> of everyman's noon nap
> the fall moon

Had the moon and moon-viewing not had the Buddhist connection, Frois might have written:

> *In Europe, only farmers astronomers and calendar-makers pay much attention to the moon.*
> *In Japan, the gentry* vaza vaza *[wazawaza: on purpose] stay up late to watch and fete it.*

Surely that must be the world's most innocent night-time entertainment. Meanwhile, all-night religious vigils at the ermitas (shrines) in Spain were infamous for disintegrating "into feasting, dancing, singing of secular songs, adultery, and fornication." (See: Sara T. Nalle *God in La Mancha: Religious Reform and the People of Cuenca,* 1500-1650), and the large number of writings *against* sleeping-in found in Europe suggest that "our" noblemen, even Iberians, did have a tendency to stay up too late. The Augustinian Fray Luis de Leon wrote in 1583 that if nature sends us light it must be good for us to wake up "and this is not negated by the habit of those people whom the world now calls gentlemen, whose principle preoccupation is to live in order to rest and regale their bodies, sleeping in until midday." (LA PERFECTA CASADA) Perhaps the biggest contrast with Japan would be in the vehemence of our opposition to this practice thought by some to be "part of a gentleman's status," as opposed to the tolerance of the Japanese (with respect to nobles, not peasants!). De Leon makes it clear that the problem was not only what one did at night, but the damage done to body and mind by sleeping in –

for the discord in life arises and has its origin in an even greater discord which is to be found in the soul and which itself is also the cause and origin of many base and ugly discords. For the blood and humours of the body, excessively kindled and harmed by the heat of day and sleep, not only damage one's health but they also hideously affect and infect the heart. And it is something worthy of admiration [i.e. of great surprise] that being in everything else great followers, or better still, great slaves of pleasure, these men forget their pleasure only in this matter and through the vice of sleeping miss out on what is most pleasurable in life, which is the morning. (L(J&L):LPC)

This passage is followed by a page on the pleasure of waking early. *It is no mere first worm, but what may well be the best description of the magical multi-sensed beauty of dawn ever written!*

13-26 In Europe, we do not eat and drink during soirees, plays and tragedies;
Em Europa em serões, autos e tragedias não se uza de comer e beber;

In Japan, these are never put on without wine and *sakana* [appetizers].
Em Japão nenhuma couza destas se faz sem vinho e sacana.

True, M & J admit, no eating and drinking took place in the chapels and monasteries used for these events in the West, but light acts called *entre-mezes* (intermezzos) and *momos* (mummery/miming) sandwiched into banquettes, so drama and food were not complete strangers.

13-27 Among us, the leaps of the *fulia* [joyful dancing] and tambourines [thrown] into the air are customary; *Antré nós os saltos nas fulias e pandeiros pera o ar hé custume;*

They are very astounded by it, and think it mad and barbaric.
Elles o estranhão muito e o tem em nós por doudice e barbaria.

The grammar for "our" side is confusing. Basques *did* throw tambourines, so I went that way, but the Japanese translators have people leaping into the air to the little belled drums (tambourines) of the *fulia,* a dance nominally one with "folly." As Miguel=Valignano pointed out in *De Missione*, Japanese dancers only jumped and whirled to depict a deranged soul. Contented people stay still. Apparently, the very idea of *jumping for joy* was foreign to the Japanese.

13-28 Among us, it would be ridiculous for a very noble man to ride bareback without a barrette.
Antré nós yr hum fidalgo muito nobre a cavalo descalso e sem barrete seria doudice;

In Japan, it is an ordinary custom to go about in this manner.
Em Japão hé custume ordinario andarem desta maneira.

Bareback and hatless! Oh, the scandal of it! In Europe, the higher the class of the man, the better his equestrian outfit. Did Japanese nobles appreciate the primal experience? Is bareback+barehead something like those unpainted wooden cups discussed in 6-30? This contrast, which ought to have been in the *Horse* chapter was apparently concocted to balance those leaps that made us look ridiculous to the Japanese. *Look,* says Frois, *you do things that look ridiculous to us, too!*

13-29 In Europe, plowing is done by one man with a pair of oxen;
Em Europa anda lavrando hum homem com hum par de bois;

In Japan, one ox with two men do the plowing.
Em Japão pera lavrar vai hum só boy com dous houmens.

No drama or dance here, either. Evidently, after proceeding from *foolish in dance* to *foolish with horse,* Frois recalled the oxen in the *Horse* chapter. In the Japanese case, one of the men might lead the ox (for the nose ring worked and they had no goad), but I doubt it was done that way all of the time.

endnote XIII
P*lays*

Not all entertainment in a society is formal, i.e. performing expected things in the proper places and times. Take the following happening (?) recorded by Edward Morse:

> An illustration of the tolerance of the people and the good manners of the children is shown in the fact that no matter how grotesque or odd some of the people appear in dress, no one shouts at them, laughs at them, or disturbs them in any way. I saw a man wearing for a hat the carapace of the gigantic Japanese crab. This is an enormous crab found in the seas of Japan, whose body measures a foot or more in length and whose claws stretch on each side four or five feet. Many looked at this man as he passed and smiled. It was certainly an odd thing to wear . . . (M:JDD)

After seeing the illustrations of the street vendors of Edo with chili-pepper salesmen sporting red chili-pepper dress and a four foot chili-pepper sack, bear-fat unguent salesmen looking out of the mouth of a bear mask, a Chinese-style candy seller riding a fake horse, a Japanese-style candy vender who is dressed like a fox and dances if you purchase anything, a dumpling seller wearing a boat with a boat-nun doll in it (who sold dumplings), a beggar dressed as a ghost with a fake knife through his throat, etc., after seeing all that (as Mitani Kazuma draws them, based on old prints and paintings in 江戸商売図絵), we realize that Japan was once a truly dramatic place to live. Unlike Europe – or the USA of my youth (1950's, early 60's) – eccentric behavior did not give others the excuse to throw things at you or beat you up (Paradoxical as it may seem, the USA did not grow up and learn to tolerate difference until the late 1960's, a time wrongly remembered as juvenile.)
..

That was, however, post-Seclusion Edo. I doubt such diversity, creativity, and the civilized forbearance that made it possible existed in Frois's time. But I cannot help suspecting Frois short-changed us a bit in the low-culture department. While he was good at observing *little* things, such as the respective sides on which we sniff melons, he missed many *low* things, perhaps because he had little interest in the low life or, if he did, felt it best not to reveal it. He mentions the chants and chanties of the watermen, but that is about it. Popular entertainment receives short thrift. This is unfortunate because Frois might have helped shed light on the beginning of *kabuki* and the institution called *geisha*. In respect to contrast 13-4, respecting the presence/lack of innovation, Cooper opines:

> As regards the traditional Japanese theatre, Frois' observation remains true to this day, for *Nô* and *Kabuki* dramas are still staged without any variation. Cocks makes several references to the latter, spelling the term indifferently *Cabicke, Caboki, Caboqui, Caboque* and *Cabuqui*; in one place he describes the *caboques* as "women plears, who danced and songe." (C:TCJ *my italics*)

And, I would add, *cabuks, cabokes* and, strangest of all *dansing beares!* (OED was no help there!) It is touching to read of Cocks' cordial relationship with the performers:

> The *cabokes* came out to sea after vs in a boate brought a banket. So I gaue them a bar of *coban* to make a banket [banquette] at their retorne to Edo . . .

> The China Capt. envited both vs & the Hollanders to dyner this day, where we had greate cheare w'th dansing beares.

> I sent ij [?] *taies* to the dansing beares, in small plate, they coming to our garden w'th a banket when we planted our trees.

> Skidayen Dono & his consortes had the feast of Baccus for their junk this day, dansing thorow the streetes w'th *caboques,* or women players, & entred into our Eng'sh howse in that order, most of their heades being hevier than their heeles, that they could not find way hom w'thout leading.
> (examples chosen at random from Cocks 1616/7 and 1620/1)

The problem is the relationship, if any, between these entertainers, geisha, and Kabuki which, together with Noh, has come to represent Japanese drama. The first recognized Kabuki *performance* took place, *according to the OJD,* in 1603, when a certain *miko,* or shrine maiden from an Izumo (Shinto) temple danced a sutra in Kyoto. Her dancing – imitators? – became very popular and the authorities, fearing a deleterious effect on public morals, forbade it and the *wakashû-kabuki,* performed by *bishonen,* or "beautiful youth" quickly replaced the women. In twenty or thirty years, that, too, was forbidden and kabuki actors were restricted to grown men. By the end of the 17c, it rivaled Noh as major theatre. Here is a take on female kabuki by Edo expert Tanaka Yûko.

> In performances called *onna* (female) *kabuki,* 50 or 60 girls around 16 years of age would dance about the stage waving the sleeves and hems of magnificent kimono (usually made from Chinese silk) perfumed with aloes (generally imported from Vietnam). Each time they waved their sleeves the exotic scent wafted down from the stage. The *yûjo* [lit. "play-women," later the name for women of the pleasure quarters] would sit on stools plucking their shamisen, whose sound commingled with that of drums and flutes, while the dancers sang, "We are but visitors to this dream of a floating world." It was said that people in the audience were so transported that they would declare that the world is an illusion and profess their indifference to wealth, property, and life itself.
>
> The impact of these performers on the large crowds that congregated in populous urban centers doubtless dwarfed anything produced by earlier itinerant entertainers. Indeed, it seems that these performances turned Kyoto's Rokujô-Misujimachi and Edo's early pleasure district into crucibles crackling with the combined energy of dance, music, and sensuality, and the shogunate regarded this as a threat to the social order. In 1612, the government arrested and executed 300 *kabukimono.* (TANAKA Yûko Vol. 30, No. 6, December 2003 *Japan Echo* "Development of the Geisha Tradition.")

There is no way that Cocks was talking about kabuki drama as we now know it; and I find it impossible to believe his delightful *kabokes* derived from the one performer in fifteen years – or did the crackdown mentioned in Tanaka's article do to the performers what the crack-down in New Orleans did to jazz: *spread it around the country?* Tanaka does make one thing clear. The word connected with entertainment that "we" all think we know today, *geisha,* is a very recent invention:

> During the Edo period [1603-1867] . . scholars of Confucianism, Shintô, poetry, and astronomy, as well as doctors (including surgeons and dentists), were all known at times as *geisha* [art/skill-person]. Masters of such martial skills as sword fighting, archery, equestrianism, . . . were called *bugeisha, bu* meaning "military." And in the Meiji era (1868–1912), *geisha* was occasionally used in reference to teachers of foreign languages. . . . In the world of *kabuki, geisha* referred to the dancers, likewise distinguished from the *yakusha* [actors]. In time, the word *geisha* came to be used to refer to people who entertain others . . . in private quarters, and it is this meaning that fits . . . with the geisha with whom we are familiar today. (Ibid – *my brackets and italics*)

Yet, the *kabuks* of Cocks seem remarkably like our (?) geisha. I feel we are talking about a country with plentiful *popular* entertainment with multiple roots that may be summed up in anything smaller than a large book. Pierre François Souyri mentions puppeteers (*kugutsu*), jugglers and other

> itinerant artists who went from inn to inn. The performers' wives (*kugutsume*) sang *imayô* – improvised songs, appreciated both at court and by the lower classes – and danced wearing colorful, shimmering costumes . . . The *kugutsume* were also prostitutes. Ôe no Masafusa, a great scholar of the late eleventh century, describes these characters . . . as people "who ignored the state, did not fear the provincial administrators, did not pay rents, and lived for pleasure." (S(R):WTU).
>
> There is a gypsy, or "traveler" feeling here. The *kugutsume* are mentioned again in a

description of "dancers and courtesans" a couple centuries later, together with *asobime,* who performed on water," enticing travelers entering port by boat with "songs and colorful clothes . . . comparable it was said to that of young women of the aristocracy," and courtesans called *shirabyôshi* (often encountered in poetry) who "went to nobles' manors to sing and dance" or could be sent for. (Ibid) Judging from the before and after, all of these, and more, were around *in one form or another* in 1585.

The lack of attention to popular music was not due to Frois's individual bias. His was the collective bias of the *Haughty Culture* (pardon my pun) East and West that still takes for granted that *Music* is classical in much the same way that *Religion* is identified with Christianity alone. I do not know how much of the following is Mrs. Busk and how much the Dutchman Meylan, but it is very revealing:

> The Japanese are passionately fond of music; and their traditions assign it a divine origin. According to this tradition, the goddess of the sun, upon a certain time, in resentment at the violence of an ill-disposed brother, retired into a cave, leaving the universe in utter confusion and darkness, and music was invented by the gods to lure her forth from her retreat. But though the presence of daylight is indubitable evidence that the device succeeded, Japanese music seems but poorly to correspond with the high purpose of its birth. It has indeed produced a variety of instruments . . . but the Japanese have no idea of harmony . . . (B:MCJ:1845)

To the Western mind, music means – or, rather *meant*, for we have seen a bit of change in the latter half of the 20c – *beautiful harmony which evokes divinity.* The matter of harmony aside, it bears pointing out that the very idea of an original "high purpose" juxtaposed *against* the reality of a low-brow music would amuse Japanese, for the common understanding is that the Goddess Amenouzumenomikoto, commonly known as Amenouzume coated her face white (the popular etymology for the word "interesting" – *omoshiroi,* or face-white – in Japanese) and did *a striptease* to that music which caused such a commotion among the delighted gods that the Sun-Goddess opened the boulder to see what was happening, at which time the "Strong-arm-god" stuck his hand in and kept the cave entrance open. I leave the matter of whether such a beginning is of *high* or *low* purpose to the reader. Suffice it to say that "we" (highly literate Occidentals) have long had a weird, restrictive idea about the nature of music that shared more with Confucian/Greek idealism than with human reality.

It is important not to judge a culture on its high art alone. Despite those repeated performances of the same Noh dramas (13-4), and the same tendency to canonize seen in *Kabuki,* lower art kept changing. Look what Kaempfer writes about the "processions and shews" in a Nagasaki festival slightly over a 100 years post-TRATADO, *i.e.*, in the Tokugawa era that was, until the research, or rather rethinking, of Tanaka Yuko and others in the 1970's and 80's, generally supposed to be lacking in originality:

> The spectacles, machines, songs and dances must be new every year, and it would be thought beneath the dignity and majesty of that great God [?], if repeating, upon occasion, the same story over again, they did not at least dress it up after a new fashion. (K(S):HOJ)

The Japanese have two sides. The traditional, unchanging side is easier to spot. It is found in the more formal arts, the arts foreigners, even Jesuits in the 16c, usually go to see *because they are what the upper-class appreciates*, and because they are *officially* "Japanese Culture." But, the Japanese *also* have a tradition of change, of improvisation. That, *too*, is their culture. It holds true for their skits (the Wooden Hands: 6-1), for their dance, and for their music. Mrs. Busk's 1845 book includes this summation of Meylan:

> . . . the girl must be lowborn and lowbred indeed who cannot accompany her own singing upon the *syamsie* [shamisen]. And this music is often *extempore*, as there is scarcely ever a party of young ladies together in which there is not some one of them capable of *improvising* a song. (B:MCJ)

Actually, the presence of a limited number of patterns which the performer knows inside and out is what *permits* such artistic freedom. It is what makes the blues so much fun. So long as you come back now and then and touch base on those blues notes, there is nothing you cannot weave into them. With a more diverse form (such as rock, which is closer to classical music because it has many quite different melodies), such *free play* is impossible. *That* is the paradox of music and, for that matter, all art. Be that as it may, look how a couple *geisha* and their *maiko* (*geisha* in training) – after putting on the usual "fan dance" and "cherry-blossom dance" and "autumn dance" have been dutifully performed – improvised in order to express their surprise at the topsy-turvy West in 1881 (Note: That is four years before Gilbert and Sullivan create their mankind that "seems to be walking on its head"). I love the story so much, that the print for the quote will be *enlarged* rather than reduced:

> The closing dance – a veritable jig, with whirls and jumps, rapid hand-clapping, and chanting by the *maiko* [young apprentice geisha] – ended in the dancers suddenly throwing themselves forward on their hands and standing on their heads, their feet against the screens.
>
> "That is what we call the foreign dance: it is in foreign style, you know. You like it?" asked the interpreter on behalf of our guests; and our *danna-san* [host] had the temerity to answer that it was very well done, but that it was now going out of fashion in America." (Eliza Scidmore: (S:JDJ))

The *danna-san* [host] has diplomatically *pretended* not to have appreciated the Japanese trying to dance Western style. (I cannot tell if Skidmore is being tongue-in-cheek on this or didn't really get it – if you recall (13-27), such jumping did not exist in Japanese music). He knew a spoof when he saw one and provided the perfect witty response (I wish I knew who he or she was!). One which, if it were properly translated, doubtless made the performers howl with laughter (once they've had a bit to drink, Japanese howl with the rest of us)!   Good Japanese parties, especially ones attended by geisha, are more than anything else, occasions for the exchange of wit.   And, unlike "our" cocktail parties, you need not be on your feet.

~~~~~~

What, then, would be the ultimate expression of instrumental topsy-turvy? Chamberlain gives it, with the possibly facetious qualification that "this is but one among many instances of the strange vagaries of the Japanese musical art."

> The perfection of Japanese classical music may be heard at Tôkyô from the Band of Court Musicians attached to the Bureau of Rites. Having said that it may be heard, we hasten to add that it cannot be heard often by ordinary mortals. The easiest way to get a hearing of it is to attend one of the concerts given by the Musical Society of Japan . . . at which the Court Musicians occasionally perform. A more curious ceremony still is the performance by these same musicians, at certain Shintô festivals, of a *silent* concert. Both stringed and wind instruments are used in this concert; but it is held that the sanctity of the occasion would be profaned, were any sound to fall on unworthy ears. Therefore, though all the motions of playing are gone through, no strains are actually emitted! (C:TJ)

> <u>A footnote to the 1905 edition of *Things Japanese*:</u>
>
> The existence of these "silent concerts" was set in doubt by a critic of the first edition of this work. Never heard, or rather seen, by ourselves, we describe them on the authority of Mr. Isawa, who, in a private communication on the subject, reminds us that such esoteric mysteries would not be willingly alluded to by their old-fashioned possessors, least of all in reply to the scientific enquiries of a foreigner, and that the very explanations given – supposing any to be given – would probably be couched in ambiguous language . . .

XIV

OF DIVERSE AND EXTRAORDINARY THINGS THAT WOULD
de algumas couzas diversas e extraordinarias que se não podem bem reduzir aos capitolos praecedentes
NOT FIT WELL IN THE PREVIOUS CHAPTERS

14-1   We strike the fire with our right hand and hold the flint in the left;
Nós ferimos o fogo com a mão dereita tendo a pederneira na esqerda;

> They strike with the left hand and hold the flint with the right.
> *Elles o ferem com a esqerda tendo a pederneira na dereita.*

"Our" way seems only natural and theirs unnatural; it is easier for right-handed people to strike with that hand; but, as it turns out, Frois is *half*-wrong. Japanese did indeed usually hold the flint with their right hand. But, they also *struck* with it. The other hand held a blackboard eraser-shaped piece of wood with a runner of metal (a piece of a *sickle blade* was common) embedded in it. Since this "striker" was larger and heavier than the flint, it was held still and the flint, or firestone, did the moving/striking. *Frois pulls a fast one by defining the striking hand as the one that does not hold the flint!* The device with the metal blade was held vertically over a nest of inflammable material (wood shavings or whatever) and *the flint held in the right hand* struck downwards to shoot the sparks along the metal blade and down into the nest. This same method of spark-throwing, called *kiribi* (cutting/separate/start-fire/s), was also used for healing, exorcism and, in Edo at least, for charming departures, in which case the device with the metal blade was held up *horizontally* by the left hand and the stone struck out along the blade to throw the sparks out in front like a subtle flame-thrower. The sparks were supposed to shoot over the right shoulder of the departing party. (See TT-long for more).

14-2   We show much emotion on losing our fortune or when our houses burn down;
Antre nós se mostra muito sentimento da perda da fazenda e qeima das cazas;

> The Japanese appear to take all of this very lightly.
> *Os Jappões no exterior passão por tudo isto muito levemente.*

While the stoicism we call Spartan and the fatalism we call Medieval were, and still are to a lesser degree, embodied by the Japanese, *they* consider *themselves* emotional or "wet" compared to "dry" and rational Western people. By specifying *no exterior* ("on the outside"), Frois did not confuse the calm appearance of the Japanese with whatever feeling lay within. That was wise, for psycho-philosophically speaking, an argument could be made (and I have read it made for Swedes) that strong emotions are, by definition, repressed; they require a pressure-cooker to build up steam, so that "we" (excitable South Europeans) have the weaker emotions. Be that as it may, the same thing Frois observed has been observed over and over. Heuskin shortly after arriving to Japan in 1856 was astonished that immediately after a typhoon destroyed a third of the town of Shimoda, "Not a cry was heard. Despair? What! Not even sorrow was visible on their faces." The same thing was said more recently about Japanese in the aftermath of the Kobe earthquake. The question that arises is *who is acting more naturally, us or them?* Is it right to marvel over how they control their emotions – or, in

Montanus' opinion, are born with a more "magnanimous [meaning large enough not to worry about things] Soul?" Or, is it not possible that *they* are behaving in a more logical and, biologically speaking, *fit* fashion than we are and that our lack of self-control is, rather, the odd thing? *What good does it do to cry over spilt milk?* What makes our histrionics *seem* so natural to us that we never point it out?

It might be instructive to see where Japanese *do* get visibly emotional. And that is, as Morse noted, for "pathetic recitals." Morse found it paradoxical. After a fire burned down an entire block, he stopped to sketch and noticed –

> The quiet way in which the sufferers of these calamities take their misfortunes is interesting; not a face that is not amiable and smiling. It is curious to see women cry at theatres and yet be so stoical . . . (M:JDD)

I cannot resist a *Faux Frois:*

We are quick to lament for ourselves, our families and our friends;
They don't lament for themselves or their own, but cry readily for fictional characters.

Perhaps the most charming comments on Japanese stoicism ever made are in Alfred Fowler's THE CURIOUSITIES OF KISSING (1905). After declaring the "wonderful control of all emotions" by the Japanese, acknowledging the fact that "deep volcanic fires glow beneath these stolid faces," and mentioning "suppression" over time (Lamarckian-Darwinism) to explain why "these genuine gentle folk, wonderful to relate, neither swear nor storm, neither curse nor kiss!" he offers a magnificent, and considering the subject of his book, magnanimous thought: "Imagine, the saving in serenity in a society that scorns both cursing and kissing." Another Western writer, not sharing Victorian Civilization's reverence for bashfulness and repression, wrote the antipodal philosophy to everything Japan stood for, without mentioning or even thinking about Japan: "With wife or husband, you should never swallow your bile. It makes you go all wrong inside. Always let fly, tooth and nail, and never repent, no matter what sort of figure you make." (D.H. Lawrence: *Fantasia of the Unconscious* 1922)

He, too, is partly right. He is right for most of "us," in most situations. But, he is wrong from a societal viewpoint, not because of social good gained by holding back, but because practice at taking things calmly over the years can actually make you calm so there is not that much bile to have to swallow. For this reason, I believe that the difference Frois mentioned was *not* only exterior.

~~~~~~

14-3 With our houses, when there is a fire, people rush in with water and dismantle neighboring houses; *As nossas cazas quando se qeimão acoden-lhe com agoa e com desfazer as cazas dos vizinhos;*

> Japanese climb up on other roofs and fanning with winnows, shout to the wind to go away. *Os Japões poem-se nos outros telhados a abanar com supis e gritão ao vento que se vá.*

Okada wonders if Frois may have been misled by paintings of large fan-like devices used to *block* flying sparks. I would add that we were not the only ones dismantling houses. A century later, Kaempfer wrote "they [the Japanese] know no better remedy at present, but to pull down some of the neighboring houses." (K:HOJ) Indeed, removing fuel was *the main method* of fire-fighting in Japan from time immemorial. Morse, who first found the weak Japanese water-pumps ridiculous and thought Western methods of fire-fighting better, changed his mind when he became more familiar with the realities of fire spreading between crowded tinder boxes. He even wrote that one reason Japanese houses came apart so easily was to enable them to be rapidly demolished in the path of a conflagration(M:JH&S). And he suggested a better contrast I will only introduce as a Frois:

In Europe, we fight fires by splashing water on the flames coming from the buildings;
In Japan, they save the water for spraying down the firemen as they tear down the buildings.

Kaempfer also mentioned something Morse, for all his interest in architecture, missed. "Almost every house hath a place under the roof, or upon it, where they constantly keep a tub full of water, with a couple maps [blueprints to help with deconstruction?], which may be easily come at, even without the house, by the help of ladders." (K(S):HOJ) But, despite all this, fires on dry, windy winter days were often unstoppable. The worst, in 1657, destroyed half of Edo and killed over 100,000 people. Not surprisingly, Japanese had fire on the mind. According to Chamberlain,

> so completely did this destructive agency establish itself as a national institution that a whole vocabulary grew up to express every shade of meaning in matters fiery. The Japanese language has special terms for an *incendiary fire*, an *accidental fire*, *fire starting from one's own house*, a *fire caught from next door*, a *fire which one shares with others*, a *fire which is burning to an end*, the *flame of a fire*, anything – for instance, a brazier – *from which a fire may arise*, the *side from which to attack a fire* in order to extinguish it, a *visit of condolence after a fire*, and so on. We have not given half. (*italics* mine C:TJ – and more in *TT-long*)

14-4 With us, to call someone a liar to his face would be a great libel;
Antre nós hé suma injuria dizer a hum homem no rosto que mente;

> The Japanese laugh it [lying] off as gallantry.
> *Os Japãos rin-se disso e o tem por galantaria.*

Japanese valued *face* as much as the Latin culture Frois knew best, but had a more sophisticated attitude toward *lying*. Tact, they knew, often requires it, and they greatly admired a good bluffer. It is possible Frois's contrast has a simpler explanation. Even today, Japanese lightly say "*uso-tsuki!*" or "liar!" when someone tells them something interesting. We are talking about an idiom meaning only *You don't say!* But the issue is probably deeper than idiom. Judeo-Christians with their tendency to make oaths on their holy book or on the name of their God have an *exceptionally* black and white *attitude* toward lying. Over a 100 years after TRATADO, in a little town called Salem, dozens of innocent people would be executed because they could not lie and admit they were witches (in which case they would have been spared!). Once, *the truth was more important to us than life* – now people will lie to avoid a traffic ticket. "Our" attitude was magnificent, but, when compared to the vast majority of human cultures, extremely rare, *i.e. abnormal.* On the other hand, Japanese lived in a society, which placed so high a premium on being secretive as to be an anomaly. Here is Valignano. After explaining how wonderfully self-controlled the Japanese were,

> On the other hand, they are the most false and treacherous people of any known in the world; for from childhood they are taught never to reveal their hearts, and they regard this as prudence and the contrary as folly, to such a degree that those who lightly reveal their mind are looked upon as nitwits, and are contemptuously termed single-hearted men. (1583 in C:TCJ)

Rodrigues was later to develop this line of thought further, writing that the Japanese had "three hearts: a false one in their mouths for all the world to see, another within their breasts only for their friends, and the third in the depths of their hearts, reserved for themselves alone and never manifested to anybody." (C:TCJ) Whether this secrecy derives from the negative influence of insecurity deriving from the long Warring Era, or the positive value given to hiding emotion as a sign of maturity, Japanese preferred to remain silent about many things. In this situation, not the liar but the person who insists upon asking the question that forces one to lie is resented. In other words, foreigners hear more lies from Japanese than Japanese do because they unwittingly force them to lie.

14-5 We can not kill [someone] unless we have the authority and jurisdiction to do so;
Antre nós não mata senão quem tem alsada e juridisão pera isso;

> In Japan, anyone can kill [someone] in their own house.
> *Em Japão cada hum pode matar em sua caza.*

This right for any man, "whether a gentleman or a common fellow" to kill any member of his household "on the smallest pretext any time he likes" was one of the first things Xavier observed about the Japanese in the same paragraph where he praised them as "white, courteous and highly civilized!" Frois puts it like this in a letter of 1565 Englished by Willis: "No public prisons, no common gaols, no ordinary justices: privately each householder hath the hearing of matters at home in his own house, and the punishing of greater crimes that deserve death without delay. Thus usually the people is kept in awe and fear." Valignano more precisely specifies that "each man is so absolutely master of his house and those under his rule that he can cut or kill them *justly or unjustly* without having to answer to anyone."(my *italics* and trans from V(A):S). Alvarez-Taladriz, in a footnote to the *Sumario* says Valignano protested that power, and that "among Christian gentry/lords (*senores*) the custom was greatly humanized. D. Augustin Konishi established three special judges in order to investigate the causes of deaths." *Marvelous*. But, we should grant one thing to the other Japanese. They, too, were killing with authority and jurisdiction, for their lords gave it to them. Moreover, as Schütte, S.J., the man who rescued Frois's TRATADO from oblivion, noted "On the other hand, in accordance with Japanese legal usage, he [a Lord] had no jurisdiction over the vassals of his feoffees[?]; these were subject to the orders of their immediate masters alone." (S:VMP)

14-6   We are terrified to kill a man, but think nothing of killing cows, chickens and dogs;
Antre nós hé espanto matar a hum homem, e nenhum matar vacas, galinhas ou cãis;

> The Japanese are afraid to kill animals, but kill men as a matter of course.
> *Os Japõis se espantão de ver matar animais e matar homens hé couza corrente.*

Valignano wrote the same (*sans* cows and chickens) about the Japanese in 1583:

> The fourth bad quality is that they are very cruel and easily kill, for they kill their subjects for slight things and think no more of cutting off a man's head or cutting a man in half from one end to another than they would a dog [in another rendition he writes *a pig*], so much so that many, if they can do it without danger to themselves, encountering a poor man may cut him through the middle just to see how his *katana* (sword) cuts. (my trans. from V(A):S&A)

Since Valignano did a magnificent job of explaining the *good* qualities of the Japanese, he had to do equally well with the *bad* qualities, too, if he didn't want to shame "us" and upset the censors in Rome. But after Maffei translated his observations into Latin and they became a hit among the intellectuals throughout Europe, Valignano either felt bad about slighting the Japanese or worried that he had created such a bad image that it would hurt support for the church in Japan, for in his LIBRO PRIMERO of 1601 (& in V(A):S&A note) he desperately tried to explain that Japanese were *not*, I repeat, *not* cruel killers as might be inferred "from what Maffei wrote."

> even if it cannot be denied that the Japanese with the profession that makes all soldiers [meaning the samurai or *buke* that formed Japan's gentry] can kill with ease . . . they cannot be called cruel and barbaric for their killing is in battle or at the order and command of their lords, as executers of justice . . . And because they will not let themselves be killed without taking vengeance [first?] when they can, it naturally follows that many times they must use dissimilitude when killing. . . But, excepting killing done in time of war or at the command of their lord, they live very peacefully with very few killings and duels, thus, they are not naturally cruel. And, while there are cases where someone kills a poor man to test a sword, this is very rare, because there is great [i.e. capital] punishment [*grandísima pena*] for homocide, or even for fighting with others, and [they] only test their swords on those who are dead by justice. (V:Libro in note (A):VS&A)

Now that is *much* more fair than his 1583 words! While there were aberrations, such as the second Tokugawa Shogun Iyemitsu's nocturnal sword-testing expeditions (years later), the rules against dueling strengthened as Japan unified, a process already underway in Frois and Valignano's time, so that within decades, *just drawing a sword* in town was what we now would call a felony, and might get the *bushi* executed! (Many students of history in Japan are rightly incensed by the ridiculous amount of swordplay at the drop of a hat shown on television Easterns). Not that any of this mattered in Europe, where Montanus in 1670, borrowing from Valignano's earlier work, wrote of how "sometimes, having no Quarrel, in a meer Frolick, they [Japanese] will try whether the Edges of their Blades be so tender, as to be bated, or turn upon one anothers Heads."

If one didn't mess in politics and were lucky enough not to be in a war, Japan was a safe place (safer than most of Europe) even then, on the tail of the Warring Era. Valignano continued to qualify himself, or rather, disavow his own *hard view* of Japan. *Harakiri* was to save the lives of their family, and not out of an outlandish cruelty so fantastic as to extend even to themselves (if the word had existed, it would have been *masochism*), as he had written earlier. Similarly, infanticide was not "even crueler" but only done by the poorest people because they thought it less cruel than letting them live in misery (Ricci, in China, facing the same was later to add that the idea was that the infants might be luckier in their next reincarnation: i.e. "Pythagorean"=Buddhist belief played a role in it (S:MPMR), and this was, after all, done by *our* gentile Romans. And speaking of Romans, Valignano added, the supposedly cruel Japanese did not make mass games out of gladiatorial and marine combat where people were proud of killing each other in front of others, nor did Japanese rulers take pleasure in having men fight lions and tigers for the joy of seeing how many men they could kill. All in all, Valignano concluded, the Japanese did have a barbarian government, as must be for a nation that is not Christian, but they were not *as* barbarian as "our" Romans and "there cannot be found a people more moderate and modest in their actions and less bad and less cruel than the Japanese." (Libro 1601)

Nihonjinron (pop Japanology) written by Japanese intellectuals in the 1970's and 80's usually attributed the Japanese reluctance to kill animals (including reluctance to put their dogs to sleep) to their lack of experience with livestock, not being part of a Christian culture where man had the right to play God with other animals, Buddhist spare-all-life faith, Shinto fear of pollution, or being a particularly peaceful farming people who simply cannot stomach the sight of blood. This also was, conversely, used to explain away massacres in World War II. Namely, Japanese soldiers went berserk because killing was so far from their nature, unlike those calloused Westerners who could easily enslave and kill people in cold blood *because* of their long experience with livestock and its extension, slavery. These intellectuals ignore the relative cheapness of human life for hundreds of years preceding and following Frois's stay and preferred to point out a 300 year period earlier in Japanese history (the Heian era (794-1185)) where there was no capital punishment and running people out of town and exiling them was considered bad enough). Incredibly, they forget the reality of hundreds of years of publicly displayed bodies and heads including the graphic scenes of killing and suicide in Japanese drama which astounded 19c European visitors:

> the wonderful endurance of the hacked victims, and the streams of red paint and red silk ravellings that ooze forth delight the audiences, who shout and shriek their "*Ya! Ya!*" and "*Yeh! Yeh!*" (S:JDIJ)

> The play itself was a little too gory to suit our present taste, as there were two suicides and three murders performed upon the stage, with every ghastly detail of blood, muscular contortion, death rattle, and final rigidity given in the most carefully worked out and realistic manner. (B:AJI)

With respect to killing or not killing animals, although Buddhism, as noted elsewhere, does not ultimately determine precisely what can and cannot be killed, its emphasis on preserving *all* life as opposed to the anthropocentrism of the Judeo-Christian morality, doubtless played a role in creating this contrast, which was first noted by Frois in a charming 1565 letter about Nara (the old capitol when Kyoto (now the old capitol) was the capitol), where he described 1) "A pond as broad as a musket-shot filled with innumerable fish dedicated to the Pagoda [temple]." Anyone who ate one was said "to turn into a leper." 2) A "great multitude of chickens on the grounds of the same Pagoda, which no one would kill, for it was taken to be the gravest sin, and when killing a man was not taken for a sin." And, 3) "The Pagoda deer who roamed the streets of the town like dogs in Spain." To bother them would be to incur a great fine, to kill one was a capital crime, and "if one were found dead on the street unless it could be proven beyond doubt to have been sick, the entire block was razed and the stores lost."

But if religion can help explain the Japanese tendency to refrain from killing most animals, our religion cannot even begin to explain why "we" were *so cruel* to them (the incredibly gory games played with live cats in much of Europe in Frois's time are sickening, worse than the behavior we often find in the boyhood of a serial murderer today). Yet, in the last half of the 20c, "we" were more eager to protect animals than the Japanese, who killed off even their little bears (hardly grizzlies) and cemented up their rivers (the last Japanese otter went extinct decades ago) in the interest of total public safety, and almost always kept their big dogs on a small chain around the clock. On the other hand, "we" (at least Usanians), are so extremely callous about *human* life that we have allowed our murder rates to climb sky-high and have priced medicine beyond the reach of many (like me).

~~~~~~

14-7 With us, one is not killed for stealing, unless it be above a certain sum;
Antre nós se não mata por furto senão até huma certa cantidade;

In Japan, one is killed no matter how trifling the sum.
Em Japão por qualquer couza ainda que seja muito peqena.

All accounts of Japan from Xavier, before Frois, to those of the newly-opened Japan of the 19c mention the draconian laws against stealing. Frois, in a 1565 letter Englished by Willis: "They detest all kind of theft, whosoever is taken in that fault may be slain freely of anybody" (W:HOT). Carletti: "And in my time many suffered crucifixion on the slightest pretext, such as theft of a radish or some similar trifle . . . But they pay no more heed to the death of those who suffer in this way than we should to the killing of a fly" (C:TCJ). Cocks: "This day a Japon was roasted to death, runing rownd about a post, fyre being made about hym. The occation was for staling a small bark [boat] of littell or no vallue."(C:TCJ) The logic of this severity was two-fold. *First*, theft is theft. A Japanese proverb says something like "he who would steal a penny would steal a pound." And, *second*, the law had to be fair to all. That ruled out fines, for as Kaempfer wrote "if punishments could be bought off with money, it would be in the power of the rich to commit what crimes they please, a thing in their opinion, and in its very nature, absurd and inconsistent with reason and justice." Finally, Japanese found corporal punishment and jails repulsive.

Here, fairness requires us to mention the children hung for stealing a bit of food (the proverbial *crumb of bread*) in our own history. As Cooper notes "It would be well to recall, however, that 'in England, until early in the 19th century, punishments for crime were ferocious' and we can agree with Gladstone's 18c observation: "It is a melancholy truth, that among the variety of actions which men are daily liable to commit, no less than one hundred and sixty have been declared by Act of Parliament to be felonius without benefit of clergy; or, in other words, to be worthy of instant death. So dreadful a list, instead of diminishing, increases the number of offenders.' (C:TCJ)

What is fascinating here is that *in Japan*, at least, the draconian laws (and large rewards posted for murderers) evidently worked! Captain Will Adams, who spent the last half of his life involuntarily in Japan, put it like this: "And their citties you may go all ower in ye night with out any trobell or perrill." It was even more true in the orderly nation Kaempfer observed a century later, and two centuries later when Golownin observed that a little peaceful city (Japan) was better than one (Europe) where the "inhabitants were rich, and had abundance of necessaries and luxuries, but they unhappily lived in constant quarrels, and there were so many rogues among them, that people durst not venture in the streets of a night for fear of being murdered." (G:MCJ) This disparity was still noticed at the end of the 19c. Morse compared the number of murders in Michigan and Tokyo with their similar-sized populations and found 87 murders that year in the former (despite its lower density) and none in the later (12 in ten years). But to return to the topic, *theft*, here is Morse:

> It is delightful to be in a country where the people are honest. I never think of keeping my hand on my wallet or watch. On my table, with door unlocked [there were no locks], I leave my small change, and the Japanese boy or man coming in fifty times a day leaves untouched everything he should not touch. (M:JDD)

> Realizing the honesty of the people in the fact I had never seen a lock, key or bolt on any sliding screen in Japan, I resolved to risk the experiment, so left eighty dollars in an open tray in a room which was probably occupied a dozen times during my absence and to which access could be had by every domestic and guest in the house. We were off for a week's trip, yet on my return every bit of change to the last cent, and the watch, of course, were in the open tray as I had left them. When one recalls the warnings and admonitions in printed notices on the doors of American and English inns . . . , one is compelled to admit the innate honesty of these people, and this is only one of the many examples I could cite. It must amuse a Japanese when he visits our country to see dippers chained to the fountain, thermometers screwed to the wall, doormats fastened to the steps, and inside every hotel various devices to prevent the stealing of soap and towels. (Ibid)

I should add that Morse did not purposely tempt the Japanese. He had asked if he could leave his valuables while he went out on a junk and had been astounded to find they did not put them in a safe-box. One example he gives elsewhere, of a produce stand left untended with a box of change, I have seen and used in Tokyo on many occasions. In this case, even if someone was secretly watching – which wasn't likely – no one could possibly notice if one pretended to pay or actually stole some of the change. So one cannot simply say that fear of the law ingrained by centuries of capital punishment, or exceedingly strong shame at being found out, i.e. external sanctions are responsible for the good behavior. A person who can put himself into another's shoes, that is to say an honest-to-god *conscience*, i.e. the moral gyroscope that is the mark of an inner-directed person must be responsible. So, honesty with respect to *things* and lying *words* (14-4) would seem to have comfortably coexisted.

During the Seclusion, the law itself, if anything, grew crueler with time, until German law codes were adopted in the late-19c. So we have the apparent contradiction of an incredibly good people with law and order that makes even the Old Testament's eye-for-an-eye a model of clemency. This may be coincidence, but one can not help but wonder whether a millennium of killing people for petty thievery increased the fitness of the most timid, affecting the very genes of these people! I joke, but Morse wondered the same in a speech given on Founder's day at Vassar college, 1894

> we find with the Japanese so many acts of the most unselfish nature blended with their good manners that one might be inclined to believe that the courtesy of the Japanese is a part of their nature and that such conditions had come about by a process of selection. With the sharp definition of classes in feudal times coupled with the dominance of the proud Samurai class over those below, it is possible that those who would not manifest good manners and a kindliness of demeanor have been exterminated and thus by a process of selection the well behaved have survived. Frankness compels me to confess that when confronted by the overbearing impertinence of public officials, the flippant serving girl and many similar kinds of people, and the pernicious influence this behavior exerts upon our children, I have sometimes wished for the power of some selective action to weed out the rude and impertinent from our midst and do it at once. (M:IGM)

One qualification must be made. The samurai and law do not deserve all the credit. Documents from the 15c to the 19c show that the most ferocious treatment of thieves (and often their families) was meted out by villagers themselves. (See *TT-long* for more)

14-8 With us, if we kill another with just cause or for our own defense, we are spared;
Antre nós, se hum mata a outro e teve justiça, ou foi por sua defensón, salva-se;

> In Japan, if someone is killed, someone must die, and if he fails to appear, another is killed instead. *Em Japão, se hum mata, á-de morrer aquelle, e se não aparese, matão outro por elle.*

The apparent discrepancy between getting away with murder as noted in 14-5, above, and automatic death for killing here is explained thus: The former concerns the rights of someone who kills someone under his or her authority, while this concerns those who kill a superior, an equal (excluding war) or an inferior who is the charge of another without the other's permission. Here, the contrast is about the absence on our part and presence in Japan of a type of *collective responsibility*. As Cocks notes about a theft in which he had been the victim: "Soe they made a comvne serche throwe the towne for the theefe Man, &, not finding hym, comitted his father, mother, & brother to pr'son, w'th an other, his m.r w'ch sould hym [indentured him as a servant], whoe the ten of the streete are bound to answer for his forth coming, &, in fallt of fynding out the theefe, must answer w'th their lives or geue vs content for what is stolne. (1620 currant [1621] 03. (22.)) If only parents were held responsible for their children, this would not necessarily be a bad idea, but, as Miguel=Valignano noted in 1589, the execution of a wife for her husband's crimes that she knew nothing about was simply "not right."

This was not an academic question for the Jesuits in their capacity as advisors to Christian rulers in Japan, for the rulers had to chose what innocent person to deliver up to the other country to avoid a more informal revenge murder that could cause further complications. This practice was the twentieth of forty-five "thorny problems of conscience" Valignano submitted to Rome for guidance. The reply, of the legal scholar Gil Vázquez (in P(B):EPJ) was that the ruler could not hand over an innocent even if it endangered the life of the ruler himself, but that he could if it threatened the well-being of his country. Be that as it may, collective responsibility was a fixture of Japanese law and it grew stronger after 1585. Consider the implications of this paragraph by Kaempfer, who, in 1692, gave by far the most detailed explanations of what some have called Japan's "police-state" of any visitor.

If quarrels, or disputes, arise in the street, whether it be between the inhabitants or strangers, the next neighbours are oblig'd forthwith to part the fray, for if one should happen to be kill'd, tho' it be the aggressor, the other must inevitably suffer death, not withstanding his *moderamen inculpatae tutelae*, pleadings of *se defendendo*, or the like. All he can do, to prevent the shame of public execution, is to make away with himself, ripping open his belly. Nor is the death of such an unhappy person thought satisfactory, in their laws, to attone for the deceased's blood. Three of those families, who live next to the place wherre the accident happen'd, are lock'd up in their houses for three, four or more months, and rough wooden boards nail'd a-cross their doors and windows, after they have duly prepar'd themselves for this imprisonment, by getting the necessary provisions. The rest of the inhabitants of the same street, have also their share in the punishment, being sentenc'd to some days, or months, hard labour at publick works . . . The like penalty, and in a higher degree, is inflicted on the *Kumi Gasijra* [*gashira*], or heads of the Corporations of that street . . . It highly aggravates their guilt, and the punishment is increas'd in proportion, if they knew beforehand, that the delinquints had been in a quarreling humour . . . The landlords also and masters of the delinquents partake in the punishment for the misdemeanors of their lodgers, or servants. This rigorous proceeding . . . seems to be grounded upon the same principle with the *Canon Facientis dist.86. Facientis culpam* . . . He is doubtless guilty of the same Crime with the delinquint, who neglected to prevent it, when he could have done it. (K(S)HOJ:1692)

With such a system of collective responsibility, the rowdy behavior tolerated as inevitable in the Occident would be nipped in the bud by people worried about their own interests. Blaming the bullied as well as the bully would not be right, but, there would be few bullies if such a system were applied to parents in the West because they would not allow juvenile behavior to grow into a habit. If a bully picks on another student, have the bully's parents' flogged. If a kid extorts money from another kid have the parents repay it a hundred times, etc. Crime would have nowhere to start. As with so much else, the Japan's system was modeled after China's, where houses were "numbered and divided into groups of 'ten and ten' households" (L:AME), but it seems to me that the Japanese emphasized the responsibility of the group to work out their troubles by themselves so they would not escalate into a criminal act, while the Chinese emphasized the responsibility to report on one's neighbors. Still, the Shogunate eventually developed an internal spy system which horrified "Commodore Perry's historian," whom Alcock quoted: "Everybody is watched. No man knows who are the secret spies around him . . . This wretched system is even extended to the humblest of the citizens." (A:COT) This may be exaggerated. Alcock also quoted another American to the effect that "the system of espionage, an abomination to foreigners, loses much of its repulsion when viewed from a Japan stand-point. . . . It exercises a wholesome restraint upon delegated powers, sitting light upon intelligent and upright officers, who regard these spies with no more disfavor than our treasurers their auditors. . . . Japan, it must be confessed, furnishes the best apology for despotism that the world affords." (A:COT) The historian should, however, have noted this did not harm family relations because relations were not expected to report each other. (The 1871 revision even made informing on relatives a felony with a 2 ½ year sentence if true and life-sentence if false!)

~~~~~~

14-9   With us, there is no crucifixion; *Antre nós se não crucifica;*
           In Japan, it is something very common. *Em Japão hé couza muito uzada.*

Being *crossed,* as Will Adams put it, was a common form of capital punishment that went back hundreds of years before the Jesuits arrived. It served as "hanging is in our land." The crosses are not identical. The Japanese cross is a "丁" rather than a "十." It is called *haritsuke*, "stretch-fix" and once could even lie on the ground. The victim was tied (not nailed) to a standing piece or pieces of wood. But imperfect or not, the equivalence was unsettling to Europeans. In *De Missione*, when Miguel=Valignano describes justice in Europe, explaining how the crime and not the soul of the criminal are punished, so they can have a last confession, beg the mercy of God and go to death with a quiet heart, he claims ingeniously that they are executed in relatively kind ways, and are never "burned [boiled?] to death in a kettle or crucified." Miguel does not elaborate on why *crossing* was crueler than other European methods of punishment. Maybe it was psychological, for the association of *crossing* with the execution of common criminals (as it was in Rome, right?) in Japan was sometimes turned against the Christians. Frois mentions Buddhist polemicists gleefully saying things like:

> the fathers say outright that the one they claim to be the creator of heaven and earth and the savior of mankind was a man who was crucified with two thieves! In Japan, only bad people are crucified, so you can imagine what sort of man this so-called savior was! (J/F:H)

Even in China, where crucifixion was *not* common, the image of the cross with the bloody body of Jesus on it was a problem. Ricci's cross almost got him a beating when the Eunuch who looked after the Emperor's interests thought it "a wicked thing you have made, to kill our king." That is to say, they saw it as we might see a figure pounded full of nails, as a device used for black magic. "As one Chinese friend said to Ricci, it was really "not good one to have someone looking like that"; another suggested that the Jesuits "crush into powder any other crucifixes they had with them, so there would be no memory of them." So the Jesuits in China pretty much had to stick with the prettier image of Virgin Mary. The result of this was that many Chinese believed that the Christian God was a woman with child! (S:MPMR) While the Japanese had stronger stomachs than the Chinese, they, too, preferred the Virgin. The Iwakura Embassy to the West in the early 1870's was amazed to find "us" enthralled by our tall-tale-like (荒唐) religion with "voices coming from the sky and executed prisoners reviving."(J/I:IR) The Japanese visitors found it hard to understand what gave rise to the tears shed by the religious kneeling down wailing at the feet of the executed Jesus.

> In every municipality in Europe and America, we find pictures of the dead prisoner, blood-stains all over him, being lowered off the cross. These are hung on hall-walls and house-niches and gives people the sensation of passing a graveyard or lodging at an execution ground. If this isn't *kikai* [eerie, monstrous, outrageous, spooky, weird] what in the world *is*! And the Occidentals find it *kikai* that the East does *not* have them . . . (J/I:IR)

As Carletti described it 300 years earlier, the Japanese, unlike the Romans, provided some support between the legs and under the feet, and tied people to crosses "with iron straps hammered into the wood" or, "bound the entire body" to the cross with ropes *before* lifting up the cross and sliding the base into a prepared hole. Then, at a judge's order – this is where the last-minute reprieve comes in the TV Easterns – lances were simultaneously stabbed up and through the bodies from the right and left, with the intention of piercing vital organs and hastening death. It was not always so merciful. Carletti saw people left alive on crosses and "they similarly crucify women with babies still nursing at their breasts, so that both the one and the other die of privation."

Okada made one comment about crucifixion in Japan that was new to me: before Frois's time, the body was often crucified head down. Now *that* is a contrast!

~~~~~~

14-10 With us, domestic servants are reprehended and other help punished by whipping;
Antre nós se reprendem os criados e se castigão os servos com asoutes;

> In Japan they are reprehended and castigated by being beheaded.
> *Em Japão a reprensão e castigo hé cortar a cabeça.*

There is a paradox here. Judging from what Valignano wrote, the Japanese dared not beat their servants, for even servants had high self esteem and might revenge the insult by killing their master and committing suicide. So, this excessive punishment may have been the result of what we might call equality of honor in Japan! Although there were notable exceptions – the famously sadistic Shogun Nobunaga, who met and liked the Jesuits, reputably decapitated a servant girl for leaving the stem of a fruit on the tatami – the Japanese were, on the whole, kind and closer to their servants (see observations in 11-27) than we were.

~~~~~~

14-11 We have prisons, wardens, bailiffs and constables;
Antre nós há troncos, alcaides, meirinhos e biliguins;

> Japanese have none of these, nor caning, de-earing, or hanging.
> *Antre os Japões não há nada disto, nem asoutar, desorelhar, nem em[for]car.*

It is clear that as far as *prisons* go, the West was far more developed (?), unless we include the clever devices – little cages in the street and whatnot – soon to be used in the large Japanese Pleasure Quarters to publicly hold Johns who wouldn't pay for their play. However, Alvarez-Taladriz notes that Japan once *had* prisons, until "they lost the feeling for" them during the long period of civil wars with decentralization and military justice. He adds that Valignano, who observed Japanese had no prisons in his SUMARIO (1583), wrote in his ADICIONES (1592) that the institution was reestablished. In *De Missione*, written in-between the aforementioned, Miguel+Leo=Valignano discuss the contrary attitudes and how they might be related to the differing situations:

> Miguel – . . . . [in Europe] no one rashly hands out death sentences; it is only done when the facts have been considered over a long period of time. Because Europeans know that their punishment is [*or*, will be] based on just laws, they do not feel great distress at being led to prison. . . . Europeans have actually seen people often leave the jail as free men without punishment according to the judges just understanding of each and every man's deeds.

> Leo – Hearing that, we Japanese can only wonder at the patience of the Europeans! From what you say, Europeans don't find imprisonment that great of a pain. But if you take the people in our country, they are of such a spirit that they would spend their blood and give up their lives to avenge a single day of imprisonment [*or*, rather than spend a single day in prison].

After this, Miguel explains that Japanese fight to the death rather than go to prison because they know that prison means they are bound to be executed, probably at the whim of the lord, rather than justice. (I wonder if the Japanese translation or the Latin rendition is a bit off, hence the bracketed suggestions). A hundred years later Kaempfer noted that prison was only a place to be held until tried, so the entire concept may have been different. In the mid 19c, Consul Harris gives us yet another explanation. It reminds us of what Frois wrote about walking (1-27):

> The Japanese cannot understand our imprisonment for punishment. They say for a man to be in a good house and have enough food and clothing cannot be a punishment to a large portion of men, who only care for their animal wants and have no self-respect; and, as they never walk for pleasure, they cannot think it hard to be deprived of wandering about. (56-10-25)

Cruel Punishment, however, is a different matter. Frois makes us the winners. Not to be beaten, Okada lists 10 methods extant in Frois's time, including crucifixion right-side-up and upside-down, skewering, ox-splitting [quartering by ox-power?], cart-splitting, roasting, pot-boiling, mat-wrapping and the only one as bad as "our" flaying: the "saw-pull," where – if the TV Easterns I've seen are accurate (which, on the whole, they are *not!*) – those who passed by were actually required to take a pull at a saw slowly cutting through a man buried by the side of the road (!), and even the above-mentioned ear-removal. As to why Japanese did not hang people, I can only guess that it was because hanging was pretty much thought a way for women to kill themselves, and that may have ruled out its use as a proper method of punishment.

Caning. We have already seen that Japanese do not cane/whip their children. Now Frois claims the same thing holds true for adults. In this, too, Japan is contrary to traditional China, the adult caning capital of the world.

14-12 With us, stolen goods are returned to the owner by the court;
Antre nós, o furto que se acha se torna por justiça a seu dono;

> In Japan, when stolen goods are found, they are confiscated by the court as if they were lost. *Em Japão o tal furto achado toma-o a justiça pera si por perdido.*

Okada cites a document showing that *by law* stolen goods were supposed to be returned to their owners in Japan and stipulating that in the meantime they were to be held by the bailiff or placed in a specified place, but adds, perhaps it was the custom for the bailiff to confiscate stolen goods. I.e., the law and practice may have differed. In *De Missione*, after Valignano=Leno points out that any tiny misdemeanor can be used as a pretext to confiscate property, Valignano=Mancio replies that

> Such things are not surprising. Japanese, being heathens, don't think about the legality or illegality of things like Christians do. Even though the law says that another's things should be returned to the original owner, the Japanese, not thinking of things in the context of an eternal future, don't obey; and think that governing people is not for the public interest but their own private interest.

As politically turbulent Japan rapidly unified, there was evidently a lot of confiscation going on under one pretext or another. It was also, however going on in Europe. Some inquisitors were infamous for teaming up with local authorities to rob others legally through carefully manipulated witch trials. And, more important yet, Mancio's reasoning is faulty because it ignores the fact that those who were not governing, by all accounts, stole *less* than their Christian counterparts in Europe.

14-13 With us, man, woman and child are afraid of the dark;
Antre nós, homens, molheres e meninos tem medo de noyte;

> In Japan, to the contrary, neither the old nor the young have any fear.
> *Em Japão polo contrario grandes nem peqenos nenhum medo tem.*

While "our" moon spawned werewolves, the Japanese moon made even savage boars take a break from ravaging farms and fall sweetly asleep. The Milky Way is identified with the home of souls and there is a Star Festival for the *loving stars* (the Herder and the Weaver) every year on 7/7. As the seventh was a half-moon night, it was relatively bright in the evening. I assume Frois's "dark" includes such nights, bright enough to find one's way around. Did many Europeans, or at least Iberians, fear the demonic night so much that they even called moon-lit nights "dark" and shuddered at the thought of going out? Or, were "we" just too unruly and prone to violence when not placed under the giant crime-light in the sky, the Sun? In Lodovico Augustini's *The Imaginary Republic*, written between 1575-1580, the citizens are forbidden to wander the streets or gather in the piazza after nightfall "in the interest of law and order." (H:CER). As far as pitch-black nights go, I wonder. Japanese have always had a greater variety of ghosts than we do, many were denizens of the night and I cannot believe parents never used them to get children to go to sleep. During the Tokugawa era, when these ghosts evidently had their heyday, it would seem that fear got the upper edge. In the *senryu* collections dating back to less than a hundred years post-TRATADO, there are poems reminding us of one of Goya's best known *caprichos*: "After the lamp dies, horrific wisdom comes out" (*cho-ga kiete-kara osoroshii chie-ga deru*: MUTAMAGAWA). By the end of the ghost-ridden Seclusion, we might even speak of a reversal between *them* and *us*. To wit, Bird in 1877 and Scidmore shortly later:

> The Japanese are terribly afraid of darkness; the poorest people keep a lamp burning all night. In these regions they will not walk along the roads after dark unless in companies. I have been compelled to make an early halt several times because the *mago* [horseboy=muleteer] would not for double pay encounter the supernatural risks to be met with in returning at night. At Shingoji I was awoke by a great disturbance because a bald-pated monster with goggle eyes and a tongue hanging out of his mouth had looked over the folding screens, a trick he often plays. (B:UTJ)

> The outer veranda is closed at night and in bad weather by *amados*, solid wooden screens or shutters that rumble and bang their way back and forth in their grooves. These *amados* are without windows or air-holes, and the servants will not willingly leave a gap for ventilation. "But thieves may get in, or the *kappa!* they cry, the kappa being a mythical animal always ready to fly away with them. In every room is placed an *andon* or night lamp. (S:JDJ)

The Japanese today usually close the *amado*, not to keep out the *kappa* but because of a fear of catching night-chills or something by drafts while sleeping. Since the room is pitch-black with the *amado* closed, one can understand why, as Bird wrote, "No Japanese would think of sleeping without having an *andon* [a type of dim lantern she calls "wretched 'darkness visible'"!] burning all night in his room."

Okada believes Frois is not describing Japanese as a whole but the character of the children of the samurai who were raised to be brave. The passage he cites from the samurai classic *Hagakure* reminds parents that cowardice even in childhood may turn into a lifelong blemish and that it would be *negligence* (*fukaku*) for them to put their young children (幼少) into a funk over thunder, allow them to fear the dark or tell them scary stories. Since most Japanese deliberately spook their little children to encourage them to cling to them or make it easier to prevent wandering, this advice is very apt indeed. Then, when the child gets a bit older, they were positively challenged, made to visit cemeteries alone at night and so forth until they learned to become fearless.

14-14 We are generally afraid of snakes and dislike holding them;
Antre nós geralmente tem medo aas cobras e asco de lhe pôr a mão;

> The Japanese pick them up easily, without fear, and some eat them.
> *Os Japões as tomão com a mão muito facilmente sem temor, e alguns as comem.*

It may be accidental that the generic term for "snake" in Portuguese is "cobra," but it seems indicative of "our" jaundiced view of snakes, that held all *poisonous*, if not in body, *in spirit*. With the snake a major presence in the pagan religions of Eurasia, it was turned into the symbolic fall-guy, or scapegoat for those who resisted "our" brazen monopolization of the sacred and banishment of all gods but our own. As the symbol of evil, the snake was also the first victim of our war against the natural world. As primates, we may well share an instinctive fear of snakes, but Judeo-Christo-Islamity magnified this to an absurd degree. Or, is this fear, in part derived from unconscious guilt at what we have done? This was, of course, a death warrant for the snakes of the Occident and, as mentioned elsewhere, a command to the rats whose fleas carried the plague to multiply and fill the earth.

Most Japanese are and were, of course, afraid of *poisonous* snakes. They never got as close to deadly snakes (were not so fatalistic?) as Indians with their cobra cults. In Okinawa, there are hours when people will not go out into the fields for fear of the *habu,* a rattlesnake-like heat-seeking viper. Snakes were indeed eaten in Japan, as they are eaten in most of the world, and there were indeed women who made a living by combining strip-teases with snakes (see *TT-long* for more details), but Japanese, on the whole, were shy about touching wild animals and did not care to become as close to snakes as Frois suggests. I think the following passage by Isabella Bird, who was riding on a packhorse led by a woman in the late 19c could have happened in Frois's day –

> We traveled less than a *ri* (about a kilometer) an hour, as it was a mere flounder among rocks or in deep mud, the woman in her girt up dress and straw sandals trudging bravely along, till she suddenly flung away the rope cried out and ran backwards, perfectly scared by a big grey snake, with red spots, much embarrassed by a large frog which he could not let go, though, like most of his kind, he was alarmed by human approach and made desperate efforts to swallow his victim and wriggle into the bushes. (B:UBJ)

There was one way the Japanese attitude toward snakes was indeed different than "ours." Shinto held them to be sacrosanct messengers from the Earth and albino snakes, in particular, were revered and considered taboo.

14-15 To sneeze is, with us, a natural thing and we think nothing of it;
O espirrar antre nós hé couza natural e de que se não faz cazo;

On the isles of Gotô, it is thought to be an omen, and anyone who sneezes that day can not speak to the *tono* [feudal lord]. *Nas ilhas do Goto se tem por agouro e não pode falar ao tono quem aquelle dia espirrou.*

Such expressions as "Gesundheit!" and "God bless you!" suggest that some in the West, too, have traditionally ascribed *supernatural* significance to sneezing. But, sneezes may have gotten a bit more attention in Japan than in Europe, for there is ample literature on masking sneezes with words and vice versa. According to the OJD, the literary word for "sneeze," *kusame* (as opposed to the modern word *kushami*), may have originally meant either "That I don't rot!" (neg. subj. of *kusaru*) or derived from "Eat shit!" (*kuso kurae*), both charms against bad spirits. Proof *kusame* was used as a charm is found in the 14c Buddhist priest Kenkô's *Tsurezuregusa*. Here is essay #47, as translated by Donald Keene:

> A certain man on his way to Kiyomizu was joined on the road by an aged nun. As they trudged along, she kept murmuring, "*Kusame, kusame,*" until finally he asked her, "Sister, why do you say that?" Without even deigning to answer, she kept up an unending stream of repetitions of the word. He persisted, and when she had been asked several times she at last became angry and said, "What a nuisance of a man! Don't you know that unless you say the magic word when somebody sneezes he'll die? The young master I brought up is an acolyte now on Mount Hiei.[1] He may be sneezing at this very moment, for all I know. That's why I said "*kusame.*" This was certainly a case of unusual devotion. (*Essays in Idleness*: Columbia University Press 1967/Tuttle 1987)

But Frois, here, does not say "Japan," but *the Gotô islands*, which are about 40 kilometers closer to China than Hirado, Japan (Frois's directions). As a contrast, it is ridiculous. Imagine substituting, say, "the Isle of Mann" for "Europe"! As is often the case for out-of-the-way places, East or West, it was indeed an incredible hotbed of superstition. Frois discusses the superstitions on the "three tiny islands" of Gotô (the name transliterates as "Five-isles," either Frois overlooked two or they sank) in three delightful pages of his *Historia*. First, Frois mentions how much the people of the Goto islands hated smallpox. Then he described the strict quarantines they observed when someone was stricken which he compared to Japanese funeral practices where the family of the deceased could not make contact with other people for months. He must have felt both of those practices were superstitions because he leapt from them directly to the sneezes!

> Another weird superstition found among the residents of the Goto islands is that they find a sneeze to be extremely ominous. For that reason, when someone has to go see the Lord or for some reason is invited to visit him, he may reply [by messenger or letter?] "I am dreadfully sorry, but as I sneezed this morning, I cannot come" and escape from the duty of visiting that day. Or, if he was actually on his way to see the lord and happened to sneeze on the way, he would have to return home and not speak to his lord on that day. (J/F:Historia ch13)

Apparently, the islanders also closely abided by the calendar of auspicious and inauspicious days – Frois neglects to write that the calendar was common to all Japan, it was only the degree to which they heeded it that was noteworthy – and, being poor, lived in great anxiety. As Frois describes it, they were "ridden with Devilish superstitions." His main example of such "superstitious customs" is far more fascinating to us than the sneezing, for it seems to be tailor-made for what we now think of as responsible stewardship of the earth. Since Frois's long *Historia* is not likely to ever be translated into English, let me give this part in full, for it deserves to be known. In the last sentence, Frois, indirectly and incredibly, recognizes the benefit of "superstition" for what we would now call *ecology*.

> Wherever they are, whatever type of place it is, when they cut the wood to fuel their salt-pots [apparently, salt (a symbol of the boondocks and exile in Japan) was one of their export items], in order that their pot not be cursed by the gods, they leave untouched an especially verdant and pleasant place, be it an entire hill or a part of the mountain=forest that is covered with particularly tall and valuable trees, for the gods. No pagans take so much of a twig from these trees though it only be for medicinal purposes. If some one were to cut even a little from those trees, it would end up costing him a lot. This is not only because of some sort of disaster or curse of the gods, but because that person must make amends in the form of ceremonies and money to fulfill his duty for the sin of cutting off tree limbs [on such a mountain] by planting a fixed number of trees. Because of that, and because when times are hard the people pledge to the gods [not to cut certain areas], the many places they dedicated to the gods are covered with green and there is beautiful scenery for the people. (Ibid)

Today, it is the *number* of sneezes that matters in Japan. *One* may mean someone is saying something bad about you, *two* that someone is saying something good about you (or vice-versa, I always forget) and *three* – well, you're getting a cold! Or maybe there are *four*. Whatever it is, repeated sneezes in an office always get attention. Omen or natural thing, Japanese are still particularly attentive to and averse to sneezing. Many Japanese men and almost all Japanese women stiffle or completely kill them. If they want to pop their eardrums, it is their business, but the perpetual sniffling (they rarely *blow* their noses) drives this foreign honker bananas!

1. Mount Hiei. I believe Kenkô made the mountain the one he did for his story because its name may be punned with *hie,* or "a chill." Since acolytes practicing austerities on such mountains had a high death rate, fear he might catch a cold and die was not unreasonable even if the old nun's manner of coping with it was!

~~~~~~

14-16 We use gold and silver coins;
Antre nós [se u]sa de moedas d'ouro e prata;

> In Japan, they circulate in pieces and [are valued] by weight.
> *Em Japão correm em pedaços sempre a pezo.*

Okada says that sometimes standardized coins were made by territorial lords, but usually not. Apparently, Japan was not sufficiently unified to agree on regional standards, much less "national" ones. European countries, on the other hand, generally used coins stamped with the sign of the king or republic. While this contrast makes Europe seem modern, we should not forget the use of paper money by the Chinese described with astonishment by Marco Polo hundreds of years earlier!

14-17   We in Europe always use a balance;   *Nós em Europa sempre uzamos de balansas;*

And, the Japanese [use] a *dachem* [(Chinese) scale].   *E os Japões de dachen.*

A balance is the type of weighing device that uses two plates or dishes called scales. A *dachem* or *dachen* was derived from the the Malaysian (*daching*) for a Chinese scale adopted by the Portuguese. It was a small lever-scale (close to a *beam-scale*, where a small weight is moved closer or further from the fulcrum to change the leverage but not quite the same). The Chinese carried them "aboutt them to wey their monies," while larger ones were used to weigh commodities and sometimes even two "stillyards" (scales?) were used at once to weigh a heavy thing, according to Peter Mundy in 1637. His editor explained that a balance was "a beam made to move freely on a central pivot with a scale pan at each end" while a dotchin (*d'achem*) "consisted of a lever with unequal arms which moves on a fulcrum." This definition was found in Boxer's notes to Gaspar Da Cruz's *Things of China*, where he writes that "everyone hath scales of his own . . . for each laboureth by all means to deceive the other, so none do trust the scales and weights of the other." Not that one's own scales will help much when hens are filled with water and have sand in their crops, etc.! (B:SCSC)

[14-17/18]   Our copper coins are whole;   *Antre nós a moeda de cobre hé inteira;*

In Japan, they have holes in the middle.   *Em Japão furada polo meo.*

Another of Frois's unnumbered contrasts. To me, what is more interesting than the hole itself is the fact that it is square rather than round as one might expect for money that might be strung up. In the Warring States period an enormous quantity of these round copper coins with square holes were imported from China and continued to circulate in Japan until Frois's time and then some. They were the most popular currency in Japan because of their crisp design and the words printed on them: 永楽通宝 (*eirakutsûhô*) = eternal-ease/pleasure-commute[pass-through]-treasure, or 開元通宝 = open-origin-commute-treasure, or 乾降通宝 = dry[drought]-[or] wet[downpour]-commute-treasure. One character was on each side of the square hole. They were *auspicious*. To wit:

   With us, good luck may bring us money.
   With them, money may bring good luck.

14-18   In Europe, copper coins are accepted as a matter-of-course;
   Em Europa se toma correntemente a moeda de cobre;

In Japan, they must be chosen, and must be old, of such and such color and markings.   *Em Japão á-de ser escolhida, e á-de ser velha e de tal cor e tais cunhos.*

With hundreds of years of domestic and foreign-made coins of diverse purity – in particular many poor copies (a good fake wouldn't be a problem, right?) of the lucky Chinese *eiraku* coins just mentioned – in circulation, in Japan, every man had to behave like a coin collector! *This is bad.* People should not have to waste time on little things. (But not so bad as the situation in the USA today, where we are constantly forced to waste our time – which is irreplaceable – choosing which of a zillion services to use, thereby losing far more than any possible gain, which in the long run usually turns out to be bogus to boot!)

14-19 In Europe, it is uncommon to use copper coins as a gift;
Em Europa comummente se não faz prezente com moeda de cobre;

> In Japan, they are very commonly sent in boxes as a *rei* [formal thank-you gift] to lords. *Em Japão hé muito corrente ir fazer* rei *aos senhores com caxas.*

According to something quoted by Okada, in the Tokugawa era, it was common to give a single gold coin and a dozen or so silver ones and other coins of various dimensions and put a closed piece of paper with that information on an accompanying stand (*tsukedai*), but "in the old days" there was no stand and "it was normal to give small change (銭)." The *old days* were those of Frois. My guess is that because the coins were considered lucky, they were probably divided up and used for the monetary New Year's gift (*toshidama*) the lord gives his underlings. With fortunes constantly gained and lost in the upheavals of that time, I also imagine that *luck* would have meant far more than money! On reflection, it is more likely that with the country settled down, lords became strong enough to demand *real* rather than *token* "gifts."

These copper coins were also strung up like beads on a necklace. Today, in their reincarnation as freshly minted 5-yen coins, they are commonly given to children for the New Year. They lack the above-mentioned lucky words, but their denomination has an intrinsically auspicious value: In Japanese, *go-en* (five yen) happens to be a homophone for "good fortune!"

14-20 We express honor through our nouns/names; *Nós pomos a honra nos nomes;*

> The Japanese express it all through their verbs. *Os Japões a põe toda no uzo dos verbos.*

With far more conjugations for etiquette (levels of politeness) than for tense, it is true that Japanese can do much more with their verbs than we can. They even have different verbs with identical meanings to use depending upon whom they speak to or about. But Japanese do not *only* rely on the verb. For some words, they *also* have different levels of nouns. And they have honorific prefixes and suffixes to be pegged on to nouns or (even on adjectives) fore and aft. Moreover, it would have been more accurate to write "honor and humility" for one can both talk *up* another and talk *down* oneself with equal ease in Japanese. Frois had to know he was vastly oversimplifying, for even Valignano, probably basing his understanding largely on what he learned from others, had written as follows about Japanese some years earlier and got the nouns, too: "As well as possessing a great variety of synonyms, it also has a kind of natural elegance and dignity; and so you may not use the same nouns and verbs when talking with different people . . ." (1583 C:TCJ *italics* mine) Only the prefixes and suffixes were missed. In 1601, Valignano qualified his remarks on Latin (he claimed Japanese was "more abundant" and "expresses concepts better") and elaborated on those honorifics:

> It is also true that the tongue of Japan is very copious and elegant. While preferring it to Latin would be odious, it could be said that it is the more courteous and dignified [*cortes y honrosa*], because it has certain particles of honor for verbs as well as nouns that greatly assists in making it courteous and . . . *it also has another manner of courtesy: that no one, though he be great and powerful, can when speaking of himself can use any of the particles or verbs of honor [i.e. honorifics], but must use verbs and words that are common and humble when speaking in the first-person* [Alvarez-Taladriz's citation suggests this was first observed by Gago in 1562] and can only use them [the honorifics] when speaking of others; and conforming to the persons and things they speak of which they speak, they must use words and particles of honor, respecting, when they speak, not only the persons with whom they speak, but of the people and things about which they speak, and, in conformance with this, must use verbs that are common or of honor. (*My italics*: Libro in V(A): S&A n)

This is impressive. Even the practice of honoring or disparaging *things* is not overlooked. I would have loved it had Frois at least picked up on the aspect of Japanese mentioned by Valignano that I italicized and written, say:

In Europe, the great men of our society speak as befit great men;
In Japan, even the greatest men must speak humbly of themselves.

There is one aspect of learning to speak Japanese that differs from the situation with European tongues. As Mexia wrote in 1584: "there is another thing which I do not think is to be found in any other language – that a person learns rhetoric and good breeding along with his language, for nobody can learn Japanese without knowing how he must address the great and the lowly, the nobles and the commoners, and the decorum to be observed with them all, for they have particular verbs and nouns and ways of speaking for one class and the other," (C:TCJ) or, as Rodrigues put more succinctly a couple decades years later, "it is impossible to learn the language without at the same time learning to speak with dignity and courtesy." (C:TCJ) Actually, it is also true for other languages where different levels of language are clear to all. *Eg. Malay.* But, all of this is hard to follow in a Western language lacking the equivalent grammar. It is hard for us to *imagine* that the verb "to be" may have various forms depending on levels of formality, politeness and whatnot (the term *honorifics* does not really cover the half of it). Percival Lowell *tries* to imagine and comes up with this unsympathetic picture:

> . . . but what excuse can be made for a phrase like the following, "It respectfully does that the august seat exists," all of which means "is," and may be applied to anything, being the common word – in Japanese it is all one word now – for that apparently simple idea. It would seem a sad waste of valuable material. (L:SOFE:1888)

His ludicrous "phrase" is a single complex word, *gozaimasu*, still in common use today! But who cares about the "waste" of a few syllabets? *It sounds nice.* Remember. Japanese sentences *end* with the verb. If you do *not* use varying speech levels, play with those conjugations, it can get awfully monotonous. *Da* is also *is* in Japanese. But who wants to hear *da, da , da* all the time? Translated, even the simplest element of Japanese *honorifics*, the wee and subtle particles – *prefixes* such as "*o*," "*mi*," or "*go*"), primarily signifying that something is someone else's rather than one's own, but *also* courteous and respectful – when Englished, turn into heavy, ie. *obvious,* artificial and fawning adjectives. *O-cha*, becomes "honorable tea," *o-kao,* "exalted visage" and *o-kuruma* "august sedan" etc.. Bird, who gave examples like this from letters, as conveyed to her by Chamberlain, writes to her reader, "they will interest you from the extreme orientalism of their expressions."

No! No! No! They are Orientalized *by default.* They do not convey the essence of the Japanese, but are *an unconscious act of revenge by the English language against forms of speech it is unfortunately incapable of matching."* The translator, who has the choice of ignoring the politeness/respect or making Japanese sound inane is a traitor *no matter what he or she does* (See my book *Orientalism & Occidentalism* for a deeper discussion of why exotic tongues cannot help but create misunderstanding). To her credit, Bird surmised that "possibly they do not go very far beyond "your obedient humble servant." *That is right.* In fact, they do not sound half so fulsome. But at the same time, Japanese does have more obvious politeness in it:

We must always chose our words carefully in order to be polite and respectful.
They learn polite and respectful ways of speaking that can be applied at the appropriate time..

Rodrigues *liked* the way "respect and courtesy" for rank – before democracy, rank was not looked down on – were pegged on to the very grammar of Japanese. So did *everybody* back then. Today, when equality is idealized, even in Japan, some people have mixed feelings about this. Moreover, the complexity of such language – strictly speaking, the redundant ways of "saying the same thing" takes time to learn – is thought of as a barrier to global understanding.

14-21 We wash our hands to touch something precious;
Nós lavamos as mãos pera tocar alguma couza preciosa;

> The Japanese wash theirs to view *dogu* [implement/s] of *chanoyu* [the tea ceremony].
> *Os Japões as lavão pera verem os dongus de chanoyu.*

Contrast 11-9 says that *dogu* were as precious to the Japanese as gems are to "us." By contrasting *dogu* with *something precious* here, we are indirectly told that *dogu* are not precious by "our" way of thinking. Rodrigues describes the context:

> As they walk along the path through the wood up to the *cha* house [hut?], they quietly contemplate everything there – the wood itself, individual trees in their natural state and setting, the paving stones and the rough stone trough for washing the hands. There is crystal clear water there which they take with a vessel and pour onto their hands . . . (R(C):TIJ)

Note that the prelude to the tea ceremony bears much resemblance to visiting a Shinto shrine – one takes a nature walk and cleans one's hands in water ladled from a trough bored into a boulder (or, better yet, a natural convexity in the boulder). The only difference is that the tea people are conscious of the masterfully arranged, generally small, if not miniature, natural elements and savor them, whereas the shrine-goers are just enjoying their walk to the shrine and may or may not pay attention to the cedar, boulder, mountain peaks and, perhaps, sea. Note, there is nothing of *soap* here; the intent is like that of the shrine-goer: *spiritual purification*. Perhaps, in both sacred grounds and the tea hut, there is a spirit of equality not present in the extremely rank-conscious outside world, so washing may also symbolize (though not obviously) *a temporary removal of the trappings of difference*. It is possible, however, that Frois here is only thinking of a situation where someone asks to view – which means pick up and feel in the case of tea cups – a valuable *dogu* in someone's possession.

14-22 Europeans kill boar mounted, with pikes, greyhounds and arquebuses;
Em Europa se matão os porcos montezes com chuças, galgos e espingardas;

> The Japanese often chase them with *catanadas* [blows of *katana*=swords].[1]
> *Os Japões muitas vezes a coço às catanadas.*

Even if the Portuguese calls them *porcos,* which sounds *piggy* and cute, we are talking about what some believe to be *the* most dangerous game on earth. Facing a boar with a sword is more dangerous than facing a lion with a spear, for a sword is shorter and the former beast is less likely to flee if wounded. The tusks are perfectly designed to cut a femoral artery and kill a man. Okada's only comment is: "this is a scene drawn from a scroll painting." I think he means that Frois has gotten this (wrong) idea from a picture! The only such scene I have on-hand shows mounted Japanese with spears, with only one exception, a man seated backwards on top of a huge boar that threatens to break through the lines, raising a knife as if to stab the boar in its rump!

1. Catanada. Amazingly, this is *bona fide* Portuguese and I need not have included it in italics. The Japanese *katana,* sword or saber, spelled *catana* became Portuguese and in *Aurelio* has no less than six meanings! *Catanada* has a separate listing and means "a blow or stroke of a sword" or, "a severe reprimand."

14-23 With us, killing flies with the hand is [considered] filthy;
Antre nós matar moscas com a mão hé sujidade;

> In Japan, princes and lords do it, pulling off their wings and throwing them out.
> *Em Japão o fazem principes e senhores e tirando-lhe as azas as deitão fora.*

Apparently, we thought flies vermin *before* we had a germ theory. I guess it wasn't hard to see what they sometimes sat on.

I cannot imagine anyone snatching flies from the air by their wings, so the Japanese side has me stymied. A Japanese friend thinks this shows how spoiled and mentally deranged young nobles were. But, surely, these men were not cruel enough to *torture* Winter flies sitting on window paper. Or, was this a clever way for pious Buddhists to avoid killing? You whack them just hard enough to knock them out but not kill them. You pull their wings off quickly while they are still unconscious. Then you toss them outside and lacking wings they cannot get back inside. And if the ants finish them off, then the bad karma is on the ants. Or were the wings pulled off for a more practical reason, to reduce friction so the body could be thrown or snapped further away? Or – my final guess – did this come from the practice of raising baby sparrows? Perhaps, Frois maligns men who were kindly assisting little birds he did not notice (For more, see my book *Fly-ku!*)

14-24 European monkeys, for the most part, have tails;
Os bojios d'Europa pola mayor parte tem rabos;

In Japan, there are many monkeys but no tails and seeing them [tails] is a novelty.
Em Japão com aver muitos não há nehum que o tenha e pera elles hé couza nova.

Had Frois been alive in the early Eocene, he might have found lemuriform primates in Europe, but the only non-human primates of "our" own to make it into human history are the Barbary apes of Gibraltar and, *guess what!* – they are tail-less macaque, like those of Japan! But, all sorts of monkeys, mostly with tails, did make it to Europe, where they were greatly enjoyed as pets and performers. I have seen a picture of what I took to be a capuchin monkey on the shoulder of a "Southern Barbarian" visitor to Japan and Frois doubtless saw or witnessed Japanese astonishment to find the monkey had what Europeans took for granted, *a tail.* That is to say, Frois's "European monkeys" are not really European monkeys but the monkeys most commonly known to Europeans or the European *image* of a monkey, as transmitted from ancient times (the classical world imported many animals from Africa).

So long as the monkey is on my back, let me add that primatology was enlisted in *nihonjinron* in the 1970's and 80's (see Donna Harraway: *Primate Visions*, and the appropriate chapter of Peter Dale: *The Myth of Uniqueness*), and I have personally overheard young Japanese at the zoo relating the character of Japanese and Western primates to our respective characters (The Japanese *Macaca fuscata* a far tenser hierarchical animal than the easy-going "Western" chimp). Two *Faux Frois* monkeys:

With us dogs and cats are considered natural enemies;
The Japanese say the same about dogs and monkeys.

To us, a monkey is a symbol of ugly and uncouth behavior.
To Chinese and Japanese monkey's stand for self-control

We can imagine how these animals would get on each other's nerves, what with the latter making a monkey of the former and the former dogging the latter. But "self-control?" It comes from Chinese philosophy. *The horse* stands for the hard-to-tame *id*, and *the monkey* as *super-ego* restrains it.

14-25 We count by quill [writing numbers down] and tallies; *Antre nós fas-se a conta por pena ou tentos;*
Japanese use *jina* [abacus]. *Os Japões a fazem com* jina.

François Caron wrote: "They reckon with little pellets, stuck upon little sticks upon a board . . wherewith they will add, multiply, and divide, with more facility and certainty then we with Counters." (C:TCJ) More precisely, metal or bamboo rods set in two rows, or decks, on a wooden frame. The oldest known counting board (abacus) is the Babylonian Salamis tablet dated ≑ 300 B.C. Basically, there are groves inscribed in marble for stones to be lined up in. The first real abacus (suan-pan) is said to have evolved about 1200 A.D. in China. For details of Chinese, Korean and Japanese abacuses, see TT-long. Whatever model the abacus, it beats the pen. Its users can calculate as fast if not faster than a computer, for entering a number *ipso facto* tabulates it. So, when your long-hand calculator begins to work out the answer, the *soroban,* as Japanese call it, is already done! Not surprisingly, people *still* use it in the small stores and, sometimes, even in the post offices and railroad ticket offices in Japan. The only thing hard to understand is why *we* have not used it.

Recently – I quote an undated *Newscientist.com* article by Jim Thomas entitled "Atomic Abacus" – James Gimzewski, head of a group of researchers at the IBM Zurich Research Laboratory, came across a ticket vender using a *soroban* in Japan and, *eureka!* his team soon had a nano-sized abacus using football-shaped Buckminsterfullerene molecules, or *buckyballs,* as the beads with copper guide rails a millions times thinner than human hair as the rods [Can copper be that thin?!]. Meanwhile, Makoto Komiyama of the dep. of chemistry and biotechnology at Tokyo University "built a molecular abacus of his own" promising "to increase computer memory capacities to undreamed-of levels and even lead to molecular computers." (LR)

14-26 We give many presents to show our love;
Antre nós dar de prezente diverzas couzas se tem por mais sinal de amor;

In Japan, few gifts show more class.
Em Japão quanto são menos hé mayor primor.[1]

Rodrigues, writing about the tea-masters: "their ideal is to promise little but accomplish much, to praise sparingly but achieve a great deal . . . finally, to desire to err by default rather than excess" (R(C):TIJ?). But, giving little may not just be a case of Japanese moderation, good taste and philosophy. In Japan, gift-giving was – and, to a degree, still is – as formalized as that of many primitive peoples. Every little gift must be matched in a given amount of time. Today, there are even specialized gift-brokers to recycle gifts received by wealthy professionals who are showered with gifts by clients. Giving a lot would set off a vicious cycle of exchange every bit as hard on the pocketbook as a potlatch. Indeed, like a potlatch, it could and was used with belligerent intentions. So, Japan is not the ideal place to live for someone who likes to give when he or she can and take when they need to take and doesn't like to keep tabs on this sort of thing.

But, I could be wrong on my reading of Frois. It might be just that so strong a connection was made between high-quality and small number in Japan (there is even a proverb to that effect!) that this was reflected in the gifts. Actually my reading of *primor*[1] favors this second interpretation.

1. Primor, again! Okada translated *mayor primor* as "more polite" (better etiquette = *reigi tadashii*). That suggests he thought along the lines of my first interpretation. Matsuda and Jorissen translate "the quality is heightened," (*hinkaku ga takamaru*) which supports my second. The French translation is "the homage is grand." (*plus l'hommage est grand.*) For some reason, French pulls this off best.

14-27 We have no custom of giving presents of medicine;
Antre nós não se uza dar mezinhas de prezentes;

In Japan, it is a common thing to give medicine in clam shells.
Em Japão hé cousa muito corrente dar mezinhas em cascas d'amejias.

Young Japanese and Korean clams are among the most beautifully marked shells in the world. They completely live up to their scientific name: *Meretrix,* or painted woman! But the clams used for gift containers were artificially painted, i.e. standardized. The idea of putting presents into shells for packaging is so unfamiliar to us that a copy-editor (?) for the French translation inadvertently turned the clam = *pruaire* into prune = *prunier*. There was another use for these and other shells:

> *We throw away the shells we eat.*
> *The Japanese paint poetry on them.*

These were painted gold and adorned with a tiny portrait of a poet together with his or her poem. Sets of these shells were then used for parlor games, so the contrast might have been made with *cards*, instead. But there are more basic contrasts involving gifts:

> *In Japan, a present of money is more honorable than pay;*
> *whereas in America pay is more honorable than a present.* (B:JG&W)

I Frois'd Bacon (19c), here. This may not have been true in the 16c, for European working classes, too, have long paid in kind. However, in Japan, even the rich gave Doctors and teachers and others they respected a gift, or rather, a token of gratitude (*o-rei*) rather than payment *per se*. Contracts and exact charges for professional services were considered disgustingly crass by both sides.

> *We give clothing and toys and other carefully chosen things to people;*
> *They give cash for everything from children's New Year's presents to weddings and funerals.*

"We" are taught that giving money was vulgar. Japanese were and are not. But, note:

> *When we pay or repay someone a sum of money, we simply hand it over as is.*
> *When Japanese do so they must wrap it up neatly or the other party will be insulted.*

Traditionally decorated, formal money-giving envelope are now sold in any convenience store. But the best example of contrary presents *today* involves neither seashells nor money:

> *Among us, men give women flowers or chocolate on St. Valentines Day;*
> *In Japan, the women always give chocolate to the men*

There is also something called *giri-choko*, "dutiful-chocolate," which female employees give to all the male employees in a firm to be certain everyone has chocolate on his desk. This can then be repaid on *huaito-dei*, White-Day, a week or two later, because, if I am not mistaken, an ad campaign by a major dairy producer convinced men to give back "dutiful white-chocolate" to the women.

14-28 With us, a visitor ordinarily brings nothing;
Antre nós ordinariamente se costumão as visitasões sem levar nada;

> In Japan, visitors for the most part always must bring something.
> *Em Japão [quem] vai visitar pola mayor parte sempre á-de levar alguma couza.*

This is still true today. Remember to bring a full load of trinkets if you visit Japan. Audubon birdcalls, if you can find them, are my first recommendation. Or, buy the usual pastry, fruit or alcohol on the way to someone's house.

14-29 With us, things brought as presents can not be enjoyed by the same person who brings them; *Antre nós das cousas que hum tras de prezente, não se pode ao mesmo convidar com ellas.*

> In Japan, it is a sign of affection between the one who gives them and the one who receives them to try them on the spot. *Em Japão em sinal de amor o que as dá e o que as recebe as hão logo de provar ali.*

As the gift is usually food, you must be sure to bring something you like, so you can enjoy giving your cake and eating it too!

14-30   We embrace on parting and arriving from elsewhere;
    Antre nós se uza de abraços ao despedir ou vir de fora;

>   The Japanese do not embrace at all, and laugh to see it done.
>   *Os Japões totalmente o não uzão, antes se rim quando o vem fazer.*

The Japanese are, as Frois's words suggest, one of the least touching people of the world. Any embracing they did, was done by adults in private. Neither men nor women went about with their arms over each others shoulders or holding hands (This is the opposite of the so-called Middle East where men and women hold hands). Even children were not generally hugged. Passing through a crowd, they made a strong effort not to touch anyone. Rather than physically squeezing through as is common in many cultures, if someone was in the way, they always said something or, if the other person were looking, might use a slight karate-chop-like gesture that a way needed to be opened. Knowing this, my only surprise was not finding *kissing* in the contrast. In 1585, even the stiff English still kissed like Hungarians (both cheeks). Did the Spanish and Portuguese *not* do so? Or was it taken for granted to be part of the above-mentioned embrace and thus not mentioned? The Japanese, at any rate, noticed *kissing*, for Kaempfer wrote in his account of an audience with the Emperor [or was it the Shôgun?] in 1692 that "Then they made us kiss one another, like man and wife, which the ladies particularly shew'd by their laughter to be well pleas'd with." (K:HOJ) The delegation was completely male. It seems that visiting the antipodes can be a trying experience. Crossing the equator for the first time, I, *too* had to kiss a male. To be precise, it was the painted toes of the ugliest sailor (Neptune's wife, Juno) on *La Traviata* (a Russian-built Swedish bulk freighter) I worked away on.

The Chinese, who also did not embrace or kiss in public, found our *skinship* (a fine 20c Japanese term) as odd as the Japanese did. A picture from a Chinese magazine article c.1890 shown in *Land Without Ghosts*, a book on how Chinese viewed the West, depicts families and relations in France saying good bye before a trip. The caption includes the following:

>   Prostrating oneself, kneeling, and bowing – each expresses civility through regulation of limbs. This is called civility of manners. Shaking hands, brushing cheeks, and kissing are also exchanges of civility by making bodies come together. This may be called civility of sentiments. Westerners esteem sentiment the way Chinese esteem etiquette. Civilities are different but the desire to be polite is the same. (A&L:LWG)

The nuanced relativism is fascinating. The caption continuing mentions a young daughter-in-law who was scolded by the elder brother's wife for sleeping in and missing the chance to kiss her father-in-law goodbye, as etiquette demanded.   Perhaps I over-associate, but I cannot help but recall a common figure in Chinese popular poetry (nursery rhymes etc.): the lecherous father-in-law chasing around the daughter-in-law who defends herself by squirting him with milk from her breasts, etc.. And, *here,* the Chinese reader chuckles to himself, she is *supposed* to kiss him! The caption writer could not resist a few more words on kissing itself. Neither can I:

>   We have also heard the way to kiss requires making a chirping sound. In the Western language/s it is called '*quasi.'* Those who do not know how to translate say the sound is like a fish drinking water, but this is wrong. (Ibid)

Hygienic types have suggested that even a handshake is too much contact and that we should copy the Japanese here. People who feel that humans need more touching, however, may find the Japanese physical standoffishness pathological. While not overly hygienic, Thoreau would have liked the Japanese way and found it refreshing. When he was visited by some preachers from somewhere out West (California, if I recall correctly) who not only hugged him familiarly but presumed in words to know him better than he knew himself, he spat back that when they dived into his belly they ought to take care not to break their necks upon the shallow bottom. Call me *cold*, but I would second Thoreau. But this coldness can be overdone.   If we confine ourselves to the physical, all humans are cold fish compared to our closest primate relation, the bonobo, who turn every greeting into a round of mutual masturbation and sex. But we forget something important: *words*. Japanese enjoy more crisp stock phrases for greeting and coming and going, entering and leaving situations than English. To a person sensitive to language, such words can be just as satisfying as "our" physical methods of greeting and send-off. For the cultured, these words were not only spoken. Reading the haiku saint Bashô (1644-1694), we find almost half of his poems composed for greeting and parting situations –using natural allusion or allegory to express gratitude, joy, respect, remorse, sorrow, etc. *Faux Frois:*

We exchange standard pleasantries and talk about people when we meet and part;
A Japanese of parts must make up an appropriate poem about nature to express his feelings.

In respect to another parting about which Frois might well have written but did not:

Before we die, we give the priest our last confession;
Japanese compose and leave the world a poem.

14-31 We use our hands to play ball; *Antre nós se joga a pela com a mão;*

The Japanese play with their feet. *Os Japões a jogão c[om o p]ee.*

Speaking of feet and hands, I must add that whereas the chimpanzee grabs and pulls one toward itself to bite, the bonobo is said to use its feet to kick one away, defensively. More to the point, the Japanese game *kemari,* literally, "kickball," was played "from time immemorial." Native Americans (who share blue-spots on their rear-end with the Japanese) were also mostly into kicking sports. The world might be divided into *kicking* and *throwing* sports cultures.

14-32 We do our play with the ball against a wall from above;
Antre nós se fazem os piqes da pella em parede pera riba;

In Japan it is done on the ground, striking it always with the ball from below.
Em Japão se fazem no chão, dando sempre com a pela pera baxo.

Europeans had long bounced balls off castle walls and churches (Okada). This, combined with the throwing devices of the central Amerindians, evolved into *jai-lai.* It is hard to say exactly how the European game was played in Frois's day. Marques writes there is no description of the ball games, that "it probably was one of throwing the ball, perhaps with intent of knocking down some obstacle or simply hitting a distant point;" but he also writes that (King) Joao I considered it very useful in training for arms "because this game makes the members of the body supple," something which suggests the game must have been far more active than his own guesses indicate!

The Japanese game *kemari* is no longer played (unless it turns out to be the root of soccer). On TV Easterns, at least, we see a prettily decorated small ball repeatedly kicked up by young nobles wearing silk formal clothing. Rodrigues explains the game as follows:

The balls are inflated and are the size of a man's head. This is played a great deal by the nobles and *kuge* [peers: imperial line, as opposed to shogunate or fief-related nobility], and many of them gather in a circle wearing on the right foot a certain shoe with a blunt point; it is a fine sight to see them kick forward the point of the foot and hit the ball upwards, and then do various tricks and clever feats with it without letting it touch the ground. Among the *kuge* there is a noble family which is head of this art for it belongs to the royal household and palace. The same applies to archery, riding and various other liberal arts. (Cooper trans. R(C):TIJ)

I continued quoting beyond the proper subject of this contrast because Rodrigues pointed out something deserving a *Faux Frois:*

We have heads of various public institutions, religious orders and learned societies;
The Japanese have heads for everything from poetry to tea-making to sword-identification.

Rodrigues explains all of this as an aside in his long essay "On Entertaining With Cha," because the "teacher or head of this religion or art" [the tea ceremony, including the construction of the tea hut and *dogu*, etc.] was called a *suki-no-oshô*, where *suki*, means fine-discrimination and *oshô*, is a term generally used for the head of a Zen temple. He explains that some heads are "promoted and chosen by the king, . . . others are recognized as such by their superiority over everybody else in an art." For the former type, he mentions "the head of the poets in every kind of Japanese verse." And, for the latter, Japanese chess and *go*. Sometimes it was a hereditary office, and sometimes elected and the top people in their fields were "wont to place a notice or inscription above the door of their house, for example, *Fude Tenka-ichi*, that is, "the best manufacturer of writing brushes in the kingdom," etc." Rodrigues explained how patents were issued by the heads of these offices. To me this is significant because he wrote it at the very start of the Tokugawa, the closed period of Japan's history which is usually *blamed* for spawning this system where every art has its master-families (*iemoto*) who dictate over it. Some today think this suffocating. I find a society striving for and admitting excellence like this laudable; but, to return to the football, the game described by Rodrigues resembles the play which Latin Americans do for hours with soccer balls. In Cooper's footnote to Rodrigues, we find this gem:

> In 905 a record was set up in the presence of the emperor by a group of courtiers kicking the stuffed ball 260 times without letting it touch the ground. (R:TIJ)

There is surely a China-connection here, because Dyer Ball gives an entire page to a form of foot-ball he calls shuttle-cock. The shuttle-cock comprises 8 to 20 layers of skin, the outer two being snake and inner ones "said to be shark's skin" with three duck-feathers (!). The kicking styles can get very elaborate, but

> the most usual form of this stroke is . . . the left leg is doubled round so that the foot is in front of the body and about ten or twelve inches from the ground: this is done while the shuttle-cock is descending: and, when it is almost near enough to hit, a spring is taken off the ground with the right foot last, and the shuttle-cock is immediately hit by the inner side of the sole of the right foot from under the left calf. . . . Another stroke is made with the sole of the right foot from behind the body . . .

I will refrain from quoting him on the more complex kicks! "The object of the play is, of course, to keep the shuttle-cock up as long as possible." Just like in Japan with that *mari*.

14-33 We have mills, water-wheels and horse-powered grinders;
Antre nós há moinhos, asenhas e atafonas;

> In Japan, all flour is ground with a hand mill using arm-power.
> *Em Japão tudo o que se moe hé com roda de mão à força de braço.*

To me, the fact that little dogs in England spent their entire days and lives working turnspits for "us" tells it all. In 1585, there was already a disparity in horsepower – "we" were using more energy per capita than the Japanese who generally ground flour or beans with a *te-usu* (hand-mill), as opposed to the Chinese style *fumi-usu* (tread-mill). But in the Tokugawa era that would soon follow, Japanese developed many types of mechanical power and complex automata enjoyed great popularity, so they were ready to reproduce steamboats, railroads and whatnot when Perry pushed open that door.

14-34 In Europe, people socialize and recreate with others in plazas and streets;
Em Europa se comonicão e recreão os homens polas praças e ruas;

> In Japan, [they do it] only in their houses, and just walk along when they are on the streets. *Em Japão somente em suas cazas, e polas ruas sempre vão de caminho.*

In Europe, squares and parks where people could socialize had a long history going back at least as far as 5c Greece, and buildings in Europe surrounded an open public square. Searching the history of public spaces on the internet brought 1 nice story (*the Corpus Christi parades where dawn-to-dusk plays were performed on stages with wheels that went from one public square to another, performing one act at each!*) for 100 horrible ones (*hanged in the public square; burned alive in the public square; publicly beheaded in the public square; slow-roasted upon an open fire in a public square; hung by the heels in a public square,* etc.). Either executions were "our" favorite recreation or people with websites tend to have historical axes to grind.

Frois was right, Japan had no such public places to socialize, unless it was the temples and shrines described in 3-15. This was to change, but not much. In the 18c, Issa complained of having to buy green – pay for tea – to escape the hot treeless streets of Edo where walled-off daimyo residences took up miles of street-front. In most of Japan, it was only a short walk to a temple ground or recreational establishment of one sort or another. But, these places were not for socializing with others in the sense Frois's word *se comunicão* suggests. This does not mean that Japanese did little socializing. They just did *more between colleagues* (such as the networks of poets) who would arrange to meet somewhere, maybe a hall at a temple, or someone's house, and *less with complete strangers*. Japanese are still like this. They tend to socialize entirely within their own cliques and, aside from the mama-sans at the bars who are almost always witty, there is relatively little of the easy-going *exchange of jokes and insults between strangers* that makes going out so much fun in most countries. But there is one difference. Japanese do almost all their socialization with their colleagues outside (not in squares but in bars and coffee shops) and *almost never at home*. I thought it a post WWII phenomenon owing to cramped housing, but Townsend Harris's mid 19c journal suggests otherwise:

> I told them they had a queer way of showing friendship and hospitality; that I had been in the country four months and a half, and had never been invited to enter the house of a Japanese, and that they had even refused to dine with me on my country's New Year's Day . . . and closed by saying that in America such conduct would be called inhospitable. (H:CJTH)

Harris's loneliness may in part derive from his high position, which warranted isolation to the Japanese way of thinking, and the official policy of keeping foreigners at arm's length. But, I feel that it is mostly that Japanese guarded their privacy. Note how the report of the Iwakura Embassy, a Japanese diplomatic mission that toured the West in the 1870's, relates to this contrast.

> East/West cultural traits or dispositions categorically differ with each other, as if they come out opposite: the Occidental enjoys outside contact [*gaiko*]; the Oriental shrinks from it. It is not only a remnant of our Seclusion. It is because we pay little attention to making fortunes and feel little urgency to trade. Occidentals enjoy going out and taking trips . . . Orientals enjoy remaining idle inside . . . *Occidentals study the science of the material and Orientals the science of the immaterial*. . . . That every Occidental city has botanical and zoological gardens and we have our *uegiya* [nursery/nurseryman] and beast-shows, excepting the difference in scale, superficially seems a point of resemblance; but the facilities' purposes are radically opposed . . . (J/I:IR 1876)

We can see here that Orientals=Japanese are pegged as stay-at-homes and Occidentals as literally outgoing – just as Frois put it almost 300 years earlier. Iwakura's point was that when Westerners went out, they gained valuable material knowledge as they enjoyed themselves. The Japanese "zoo" was a mere freak show, while Western parks served the common interest of material science, instructing children about the natural world, and this promotion of material science and progress was what lay behind the wealth and poverty gap separating West and East.

14-35 With us, a feigned smile/laugh is considered frivolous;
Antre nós ho rizo finjido se tem por liviandade;

> In Japan, refined and [a mark of] good comportment.
> *Em Japão por primor e boa condisão.*

In Portuguese, *riso,* and in Japanese, *warai* means both "smile" *and* "laugh." In English we must specify one or the other. I suspect that "smiling" is what Frois is thinking of, but considering the fact *risinho* is used for smile in 48, below, can not completely rule out "laugh" either.

> When a servant is rebuked or scolded he must smile like a Chinese cat. This etiquette in smiles is very misleading at first. I often used to think that Také, my *riksha*-boy, meant to be impertinent when he insisted on smiling while I was angry with him; but when he told me of the death of his little child with a burst of laughter, I knew that this was only one of the tidbits of etiquette in this topsy-turvy land. (S:MQTJ)

I will not bother quoting any more observations by Westerners about the "strange way" Japanese and other Far Eastern people smile or laugh when they have done something wrong, are tense, or sad because someone has died in their family, etc.. These observations are a dime a dozen. Let me just ask: *If one is going to maintain a stiff upper lip about things, it is more graceful to do so in the form of a slight smile than in a scowl or a frown, is it not?* Moreover, such a smile is actually a close relative of the grimace – as reflected, I think, by "grin and bear it" – so it has a valid physio-psychological pedigree and is not really *artificial* as "we" claim.

Moreover, essays on "the enigma of the Japanese smile" – I recall coming across a few – strangely overlook the Koreans and Chinese who do the same. The Sinosphere appreciates self-control and equanimity, which is to say, not looking troubled. Note: *Buddha shares that smile.* Christ, as we have recounted above, is generally depicted looking pretty damn wretched. In that sense, Christ was clearly an Occidental. Perhaps, there is greater difference between the way Japanese and other Far Eastern people express themselves in private (when their faces show what Ekman calls "universal emotion" (intro. to C. Darwin: *The Expression of the Emotions in Men and Animals*)) and in public – as compared to Europeans – but there is nothing strange about it; and, I think it bears noting that Japanese are no more aware of their slight smile than are most Occidentals of their tendency to stare into the eyes of other people.

It is interesting that Frois concentrates on the contrast in *facial expressions*, both in not revealing grief in calamity (14-2) and now in this matter of smiling. He never writes, "We always complain; They never do." Valignano *almost* does when he writes: "they [the Japanese] never come to discuss their troubles . . ." (*nunca vienen a contar sus trabajos ni agravios . . .*). (V(A):S&A). Confession was doubtless exceedingly difficult for Japanese, and a relief for them!

~~~~~~

14-36 In Europe, clarity of language is sought and ambiguity avoided;
Em Europa proqurão clareza nas palavras e jojem da eqivocasão

> In Japan, ambiguous words are good language and held in high estimate.
> *Em Japão as equivocas hé a milhor lingoa e são as mais estimadas.*

In the timeless classic ENGLISHMEN, FRENCHMEN, SPANIARDS, the ambiguity of our native tongue is held to be the mainstay of British diplomacy and well suited for the "allogical" (not *illogical*) national temperament. But, in England, aside from antagonism toward the cold unbending logic of the French, some of whom did indeed claim that "what is not clear is not French" – a prescriptive claim under the guise of a fact that only proved other Frenchmen used ambiguous language! – one does not find the clear-cut, conscious and unabashed *defense of ambiguity* found not only in Frois's Japan but in modern Japan.

Okada opines Frois refers to "the honorifics that reached their most complex state of development at the time" which "took a form that avoided clear ways of saying things and favored expressions that were indirect and inconclusive." I would add that avoidance is but half of it. Spelling things out insults the intelligence of a friend or an enemy. Moreover, I would not link Frois's observation to honorifics alone. Ambiguity was also couched in unfinished sentences and double and triple negatives. Finally, Frois may have regarded things like "Excuse me" (*shitsurei desuga*) meaning "And could you please tell me to whom I am talking" or "I'll think it over" (*kangaete-okimasu*), meaning "You might as well give up asking because there is almost no chance it is possible" – to use a couple expressions common today – as "ambiguous" *when actually they are not* for those completely fluent in Japanese. We must be careful about overdoing this *ambiguity* stuff for Japanese do, after all, have to communicate. Be that as it may, Frois is the first person to mention Japanese ambiguity, which is most commonly explained today as the result of years of warring and fear for losing one's head by being clear by people who do not appreciate it and as proof that Japanese are close-knit and do need not explain themselves *ad-nauseam* and have the good sense to allow for some play on the part of the other party by people who like it (see *Orientalism & Occidentalism* for more).

14-37 With us, a respected man would be thought deranged to hang the pelt of a fox or jackal from his belt; *Antre nós trazer hum homem honrado huma pele de rapoza ou adibe pindurada detras na cinta, te-lo hião por doudo;*

> In Japan, noblemen bring them with them when they have work to do, or their lackeys bring them, for them to sit upon. *Em Japão os fidalgos quando fazem obras as trazem, e os pajens, pera se asentarem nellas.*

Used to tatami, Japanese prefer sitting *down* to sitting up on chairs. *Ergo*, fur on the ground would beat a hard log for a stool. But, this custom may have a less natural, i.e. historical, explanation which harkens back to China (where there was no tatami and people often sat on stools). The Orestes' PICTORAL CHINESE-JAPANESE CHARACTERS account of the origin of the character for *tail* 尾:

> In ancient times in China, people of the common class used to carry, when working outside, traveling on foot or going places, a kind of fur cushion hung behind at the waist like an animal's tail to sit upon when in need of rest.

Vaccari also notes that Japanese miners still carried "a similar thing made of straw." (V&V:PCC) The *nobleman* aspect of the contrast would appear to be the uniquely Japanese part. Frois's description of Japan's first country-unifying shogun Nobunaga would seem to shed some light on the proliferation of pelt fashion in Japan:

> He decreed that while the work [building Nijo castle] was in progress none of the monasteries either inside or outside the city should toll its bells. [i.e. no telling of time!] He set up a bell in the castle to summon and dismiss the men, and as soon as it was rung all the chief nobles and their retainers would begin working with spades and hoes in their hands. He always strode around girded about with a tiger skin on which to sit and wearing rough and coarse clothing; following his example everyone wore skins and no one dared to appear before him in court dress while the building was still in progress. (in C:TCJ)

Needless to say, the castle was built in record time.

14-38 In Europe, an open crown for mass is only worn by a bishop; *Em Europa coroa aberta de missa não a tras senão os sacerdotes;*

> In the Gokinai [Kyoto, etc] area, *komono* [petty servant/s] who carry a lord's shoes wear one. *Nas partes de Goquinay as trazem os comonos que levão os sapatos a seus senhores.*

The profile of this open crown, or hat with an almost flat front and a back, called a *miter*, resembles the top of a bishop in chess. The barnacle-shaped *eboshi* cap worn by petty servants was not as highly decorated, but too similar for Frois to resist this otherwise meaningless contrast! I suppose it was funny to consider underlings with tall hats which were generally symbols of high position and Frois's envisioned audience being fellow clergy . . .

14-39 In Europe, we go forward with our stones/pieces when playing [a board game];
Em Europa as tabolas que se jogão se vão lançando pera diante;

> In Japan, they always pull them back toward themselves.
> *Em Japão se vai sempre tirando por ellas pera tras.*

Other translations assume "our" side concerns chess or checkers, but I wonder if it may not be backgammon IF, that is, we played it differently than their *sugoroku*. Had Frois known and cared more about board games, he would have made many more contrasts, such as:

Our chess pieces are always ours;
Their shôgi [Chinese-style chess] pieces are turned over when taken and join the other side.

Our chess pieces are discriminated by shape;
Theirs are identified by Chinese characters meaning "castle," "elephant," etc. written on them.

In the heyday of *Nihonjinron* (1970-1990), the way *shôgi* pieces do not die but are recycled was sometimes tied into stereotypes of *gentle relativistic Orientals* vs. *cruelly absolutist Occidentals*. The use of characters to indicate pieces used in the popular *shôgi* shows how deeply the written word permeated Sino-Japanese culture. If *shôgi* is the equivalent of *chess*, *go* is a cut above both:

Our chess pieces are diverse of type and movement;
Their more complex board game, go, uses only identical black and white stones;

Our chess game starts with all the pieces on the board and has no handicap;
Their go game begins with no pieces on the board, unless one player is given a handicap.

Our chess pieces move about, so that each piece might be said to have a history, or a trail.
Their go pieces are called ishi, and true to their name, remain in place like stones.

In chess, we try to checkmate the king;
In go, they compete to capture the most territory.

With chess, the winner is perfectly obvious;
With go, it is sometimes necessary to tabulate the respective territories to know the winner.

Our pieces always set within square spaces on the board;
Theirs always set on the interstices of the lines rather than on the space between.

We keep our pieces in rectangular boxes or leave them lined up on the board;
They keep them in round bowls and never leave them on the board.

Perhaps because all board games in Japan were used for gambling (*go* has a good handicap system which allows amateurs to play pros), the Jesuits, despite their love for learning, failed to appreciate the superiority of *go* to chess – *Try it and see if you still want to play chess!* – and didn't bring it back to us (Perhaps a Ricci scholar can explain why someone as bright as he obviously was failed to export it from China either!!!) And, *amazingly,* even today *go* is virtually unknown in the West. *Why? What is wrong with us?*

14-40 In Europe, hawks and falcons almost always have hoods over their eyes;
Em Europa os asores e falcões estão quasi sempre com caparões nos olhos;

> In Japan, the eyes are always uncovered.
> *Em Japão sempre tem os olhos descubertos.*

Frois must have seen a lot more hawks staring back at him in Japan than in Europe – and a glance at old prints bears this out – but the difference may not have been absolute (Okada finds a citation of a hood on a Japanese hawk, but it is almost three decades after Frois and might have been learned from the West.) Hawks probably deserve a whole chapter, like horses, for the attention the nobility gave to them in both Europe where an Emperor (Frederick II) wrote a fine book on them, and in Japan where there are dozens of terms for their feathers alone. The most touching animal-related poem in the overwhelmingly human – love-affair – centered *Manyoshu* (Japan's oldest anthology of poetry) is an eulogy for a hunting hawk that the poet raised in his living room parts of which remind me of one of "our" most touching animal eulogies, Skelton's incredible *"Phillip Sparrowe."*

14-41 We wash turnips with our hands; *Antre n[ós] lavão-se os nabos com as mãos;*

> Japanese women wash them with their feet. *As molheres japoas os lavão com os pees.*

We saw this sort of contrast twice already. Once with Herodotus in the *Foreword* and once with clothing (1-49). Hands *vs* feet are popular in topsy-turvyism. The difference between "us" and "them" is sometimes paralleled with gender. In Meiji 27 (1894), the poet Shiki was to write a pair of haiku about washing rape leaves, where men used a pole and women their feet. I do not know if this is because men's feet are dirty and they are more likely to have thin shanks with poor circulation which makes immersion in cold water for extended periods impossible, or because women have weak arms.

14-42 Our sacks of wheat and barley are made of cloth; *Os sacos de trigo e sevada antre nós são de pano;*

> The Japanese ones of straw. *Em Japão de palha.*

No one is growing hay for sacks in Japan. Rice straw, wheat straw, etc. – all are "hay" and all are kindly helping to carry themselves to market. I would guess that in Europe such hay would be eaten by the more abundant livestock.

14-43 When we warm our hands, the palm faces the fire;
Nós quando aqentamos as mãos pomos as palmas pera o fogo;

> When the Japanese warm them, the back of the hand faces the fire.
> *Os Japões quando se aqentão virão pera a parte do fogo as costas das mãos.*

The palms and finger-tips are full of nerves, while the back of the hand has big blood vessels and bones. Who can say which is better to heat up? This agrees with the Japanese tendency to "face" danger with their backs rather than fronts as we do, and their tendency to walk with their toes in rather than out, as we are taught to do, thereby exposing the outside rather than the instep of the foot.

> *We beckon others with our palm up motioning upwards and back with one or more finger tips;*
> *They beckon others with their palm downward, moving their fingers down and back.*

Perhaps they do this because we tend to make inferiors rise and they to make them get down as noted in 2-60. But I would not be surprised if a correlation between these last three mentioned mannerisms and the one in this contrast could be found. If you would like to do *pure research* in cultural anthropology, this would be the right type of question for a worldwide survey.

14-44 With us, a long message is given while standing or kneeling;
Antre nós, dando-se hum recado comprido, estaa hum im pé ou de jiolhos dando seu recado;

> In Japan, it is with both knees on the ground, and almost prone, with one hand on the *tatami* [mat] and the other turning up its sleeve and gently rubbing it. *Em Japão está com ambos os jiolhos em [te]rra e quasi de bruços com huma mão estribida nos tatamis e com a outra mão á-de arregaçar aquelle braço e estar-se levemente coçando nelle.*

I usually associate fly-like hand-rubbing with the Chinese rather than the Japanese. As Cruz wrote "the common courtesy is, the left hand closed, they enclose it within the right hand, and they move both hands repeatedly up and down towards the breast, showing that they have one another enclosed in their heart." (TCC in B:SCSC) In Japan, only the merchant – considered the most Chinese trade – seems to have done a lot of rubbing. And in Japan, it is not an etiquette with an explanation such as that given to Cruz in China. Like the disconcerting practice of hissing between the teeth still found among old Japanese men, it would, rather, seem to be *a way of showing one is as tense as one should be* in a formal situation, facing one's superior. The Japanese seem to have had an unconscious agreement that *underlings should look tense at all times*. While most young Japanese no longer do these things, one still feels that Japanese feel, however unconsciously, that being tense is the most important part of being respectful.

14-45   With us, men stand up straight with one foot in front of the other while talking;
Antre nós, quando se fala em pee, estão os homens direitos e com hum pé diante do outro;

> In Japan, when two men talk, the inferior must line up his feet side by side, cross his arms at his belt, bend his body forward and respond to what the other says by making bows like the women of Europe. *Em Japão, se [estão] dous, o que hé inferior á-de ter os pés juntos, a[s mã]os cruzados na sinta, o corpo inclinado pera diante e, segundo que o outro fala, á-de estar fazendo mizurinhas como as molheres d'Europa.*

There are actually *three* contrasts here. The *first* and least significant one is the matter of the position of the feet. Unless, that is, we can find an explanation for "ours." Did the vaunted beauty of the classic statues *contrapposto* stance come to be copied by Renaissance schools while side-by-side legs were considered stiff and lacking grace? Or, was it something about putting our best (right) foot forward? Or, was it in case the talk turned into a fight, so we could not be easily pushed over and could quickly move forward or backward? I can only move on to the *second* unstated contrast and note the comparatively greater equality of body language in Europe compared to Japan. You will note in the Japanese case, as described above, only the inferior "must" do this or that. The implication would seem to be that the superior stands (or rides) however he wants as he talks.

The *third* contrast, the bows, deserve a whole paragraph (though the concept may already have been introduced in the chapter on *Writing*, it is worth *more* notice). The fact is that "we" tend to speak in sequential monologues requiring no response, while Japanese converse in bite-sized chunks of sentence, punctuated with the listener's "yeahs" and grunts (*hai!, ha!, he!, ho!, un!* etc.) each accompanied by a bob of the head and a slight body-bow – more emphatic on the part of the inferior (but the superior also nods a bit) – so Japanese speaking to Japanese can be discriminated from non-Japanese from a hundred yards away: they are the ones who look like chickens pecking grain. If the listening party forgets to, or doesn't know enough to grunt, the Japanese speaker may even stop talking. Japanese is not unique in this. It is found in many language-cultures.

14-46   With us, the towel that serves the face is different from the one that cleans the feet;
Antre nós hé diferente a toalha que serve do rosto e a com que se alimpão os pés;

> The Japanese, when washing their bodies use the same towel for everything.
> *Os Japões, quando lavão o corpo, huma mesma toalha serve pera tudo.*

..

Before reaching the last line in Chamberlain's "Topsy-turvydom" entry, I thought of adding a Faux Frois: *We use a washcloth to wash; the Japanese also use it to dry themselves.* But, he beat me:

Strangest of all, after a bath, the Japanese dry themselves with a damp towel. (C:TJ)

"Strangest of all"? Not at all! Depending upon your lifestyle, *it makes perfect sense*. Theoretically, a huge dry towel is best; but the Japanese washcloth-towel-in-one is better for a poor bachelor in a country with high humidity. You see, when you wash yourself, you also wash your towel, so you never have to launder it and need not wait for it to get completely dry before using it again. I can imagine, though, that those of "us" who would *never* think to use the same towel for a face and feet, would be totally disgusted at "their" side (which, I guess includes *me*, for I have done it).

14-47 We clean our nostrils with the thumb or index finger;
Nós alimpamos as ventas do naris com o dedo polegar ou index;

> They have small nostrils and use their little finger.
> *Elles, polas terem peqenas, o fazem com o dedo meiminho.*

Finally, our favorite! Frois really had a thing with nostrils! He already mentioned small Japanese nostrils in 1-4! Here he adds fingers. It is hard to say for sure what he means by "clean." Are we talking about diligent ablutions? Or, that behavior that always feels fine when you do it yourself but looks gross when others do it, namely *nose-picking?* (This is how it is usually translated, for the best of reasons: because it is funniest). Or, are the fingers in question used to cover one nostril to spray out the contents of the other? Personally, I would guess that Japanese used the baby-finger because it was thought to look cooler, but I leave further discussion of this to the anthropologist. One thing is certain. Favorite or not, Frois's is not the best possible contrast for a body orifice. *This* is:

> *We clean out our own ear wax and have nothing special to do it with;*
> *Japanese men have their mother or wife do it with a specially designed wooden scoop.*

Japanese have wooden wax scoops (*mimikaki* or *mimikujiri*), that look like a cross between a crochet needle and a spoon – the Chinese character 了 is differentiated from other characters pronounced *ryô* by calling it the *mimikaki-ryô*, or "ear-scoop-*ryô*. Mothers use them on their children, and wives on their husbands. Since the scoops are wooden, thin and hard, it goes without saying that they would be dangerous in the hands of a rough person or in the ear of a child who couldn't keep still. As such, they would, like paper partitions, be impossible in "our" rambunctious world. If that is not strange enough, these tiny devices generally have some downy white feathers on the other end that LD suggests come in handy because "Asians tend to have flaky white *mimi kuso* [ear-crap] . . . while Caucasians have brown waxy (hence the name) earwax," which down-feathers would not budge.

14-48 We exchange courtesies with a serene and grave demeanor;
Antre nós as cortezias se fazem com rosto sereno e grave;

> The Japanese always, infallibly, with artificial smiles.
> *Os Japões sempre infalivelmente com rizinhos finjidos.*

14-35, narrowed down. But here, the Portuguese *risinho* is definitely a smile rather than a laugh. If it is as easy or easier to hold a grin than to maintain a grave demeanor (that, for some of us is always in danger of changing into a laugh), who says the smile is the more "artificial." Today, I believe that Occidentals usually smile when exchanging greetings, right?

14-49 Our kegs of wine are placed on boards on the ground and well sealed;
As nossas pipas de vinho estão estão sobre paos em riba do chão muito bem tapadas;

> The Japanese keep their wine in large open-mouthed vessels and keep them buried in the earth up to the mouth. *Os Japões tem o seu vinho em jarras com grandes bocas destapadas emterradas até boca na terra.*

Heat from the atmosphere cannot work its way through ground as well as through air. Since Japanese had little temperature control within their dwellings . . . Obviously, the dirt did not come quite up to the lips of the vessel, for they had to be high enough to prevent dirt from getting in!

14-50 Our pelts are colored with dye;
As nossas peles tomão sua cor com tintas;

> The Japanese color theirs very well with the smoke of straw.
> *Os Japões as pintão muito bem com fumo de palhas somente.*

..

Okada writes that one of the main "straws" in use was pine needles and that thick paper was glued on white pelts so that smoking created a clear print of the family crest. This contrast made me think: *Do we* – in the Occident or Japan – *today have any idea how our clothing is colored?* Now, *that* is a contrast with our mutually foreign country, *The Past*.

14-51 Our bamboo in Europe serves for little but spindles;
As nossas canas, tirando rocas pera fiar, servem em Europa de mui pouqas couzas;

> That [bamboo] of Japan is eaten as a morsel in *shiru* [soup] and serves for bows, arrow shafts, flooring, roof-tiles, ladders, vials for oil, wine flasks, blinds, tea whisks and many other things. *As de Japão servem de iguaria pera se comer no* xiro, *servem de arcos, frechas, solhado da caza e telhas do telhado, escadas, almotolias d'azeite, [va]zilha pera o vinho, esteiras, escovas pera o chá, e de outras muitas couzas.*

I *worship* bamboo and wonder if there is anything it can *not* serve for! Rather than list more conventional uses, which you know, let me mention just a few of my own:, for, among other things, I have pole-vaulted with it, made a fiddle bow, a fiddle (as do the Chinese) and kayak paddles, floored an anteroom floor that only required cleaning a few times a year (split the bamboo in half and put the convex side up and the dirt and lint gathers below while the top remains clean), fit a length to each arm so I could walk like an ape (good for the lower-back), invented and made a pick-stick (using the arrow-making variety) which could pick real staccato because the teeth passed perpendicular through a slit extended to the upper edge of the bamboo so they had room to bend, and made beautiful ball-point pens from the tip – imagine using a pen that was blown back and forth against the sky (though, it cannot match a quill that has flown across the ocean) because only the tip of the main stem is narrow enough yet hollow.

14-52 Our presents are sent in little boxes without any decoration/ribbons;
Os prezentes que antre nós se mandão em bocetas vão sem nenhum atilho;

> In Japan, they are tied with string or covered with paper, and in *Ximo* [Shimo] they are sent in bottles wrapped in women's belts. *Em Japão se atão com fio ou grudão com papel, e no Ximo vão as vazilhas atadas com sinjidouros das molheres.*

As far as I can tell, "we" were very slow to learn how to wrap presents. Lacking cheap and attractive paper, we were more likely to put gifts into a trunk or a cloth bag to carry them and leave them bare. In the 1830's, a wrapping paper was made from straw in Tuscany, by the mid-19c, the idea of wrapping things in paper had become commonplace – when Claude Monet visited Zaandam, he purchased from a Dutch grocer a stack of Japanese color prints he was using to wrap-up butter and cheese which he took to Paris, where they became the rage – and, by the end of the century, colored Christmas tissue and printed gift wrapping paper was sold commercially, or else, this is wrong and Hallmark invented it in 1917.

The Nagasaki (Shimo) area custom of wrapping up gifts with women's belts (beautiful *obi*?) was a singular practice. I doubt not that a strange manner of wrapping gifts can be uncovered *somewhere* in Europe as well. But, one thing is certain, the Japanese of *origami* fame, are indeed the most avid wrappers on earth. Every culture has one or two areas where creativity runs wild. In Italy, I am told it is the variety of flush devices on toilets. In Mexico, *I know* it is the dashboard of buses. (Other entries are welcome!) To shop in Japan is to be *amazed* at the variety and beauty of the packaging. From Frois, we know that this has a long history, and it began with gifts.

14-53 We refresh our faces with rose-water; *Nós resfriamos a testa com agoa rozada;*

The Japanese do it with a handful of wine. *As Japões com o vinho que tomão na mão.*

Sake on the face must not have been as common a practice in Japan as rose-water in Europe for Okada, after explaining that rose-water had some alcohol in it, opined that the *sake* was *probably* refreshing/bracing for the skin, as it, too, had alcohol.

14-54 We require a spoonful of sweetmeat or a succade to drink a dipper of water; *Antre nós pera huma pessoa beber hum pucaro d'agoa se lhe dá huma qulher de confeitos, ou huma talhada de conserva;*

In Japan, it is enough to have one sweetmeat, or something of its size per *sakazuki* [*sake* cup]. *Em Japão pera tomar o sacanzuqi basta dar-lhe hum só confeito ou couza do seu tamanho.*

Water was usually not drunken alone in Europe (6-33). Usually, *sake* is accompanied by salty tidbits, not sweet ones, which is why, I think, Frois writes "or something of its size." Okada, noting Europeans *also* had appetizers with their drinks wonders about the worth of this contrast. If I am not mistaken, the reference to "size" suggests what Frois' intended contrast might be, namely, a *sake* cup is much tinier than a *púcaro,* or ladle/dipper/mug/glass ("a small vase with a handle"). We drink a lot per morsel while they have only a sip with each. If this is the case, the "enough" (*basta*) is something rare in Frois, facetious irony.

14-55 We in Europe offer a bouquet of roses to show our affection to our friends; *Nós por a[miz]ade oferecemos em Europa a hum amigo hum molho de rozas;*

The Japanese only a single rose or pink. *Os Japões huma roza ou hum cravo somente.*

Ah, give me a culture whose people give One Rose and believe in ten-thousand gods before one whose people give ten-thousand roses and believe in One God! It is hard to say if this difference arises from different aesthetics, the flower version of paucity vs. abundance of figures in a picture (11-30) and the *tokonoma*-style of introducing a single work at a time (ch.11 endnote), from the fashion of giving *less* gifts (14-26), or simply from the lack of a tradition of cut flowers – other than those used for truly artistic creations, i.e. *ikebana.* Not a few Occidentals found Japanese taste agreeable:

> The vases which hang so gracefully on the polished posts contain each a single peony, a single iris, a single azalea, stalk, leaves and corolla, all displayed in their full beauty. Can anything be more grotesque than our "florist's bouquets," a series of concentric rings of flowers of divers colours, bordered by maidenhair and a piece of stiff lace paper in which stems, leaves, and even petals are brutally crushed, and the grace and individuality of each flower systematically destroyed. (B:UTJ)

Reading Isabella Bird's statement made me think, could the gift of one flower have suggested the person receiving it is likewise the only one in the giver's mind? In modern times, the Japanese came to adopt the Occidental bouquet. Were Frois with us, he would surely have written this:

> *We carry bouquets with the flowers right-side up, as they grow;*
> *In Japan, they are carried with their heads dangling down.*

The Japanese claim they do this not to damage the flower heads in movement, but I wonder if it was originally not a matter of modesty (hiding the sight and scent until the present is delivered).

14-56 We toss a lot of gum benjamin[1] directly upon the fire;
Nos deitamo[s] muito beijoim immediatamente sobre o fogo;

> The Japanese place an extremely thin plate of silver on hot coals and put a few pieces of aloes the size of kernels of wheat on it. *Os Japões poem sobre a sinza qente huma laminazinha de prata muito delgada e sobre ella huma pouca d'aguila tamanha como dous ou 3 grãos de trigo.*

I do not know if the abundance of European per-fume was due to its use to consecrate space and fumigate disease-causing bad airs or simply because of "our" tendency toward *lots of* this or that, as already mentioned in several contrasts. In Japan, on the other hand, Okada notes that benzoin (benjamin) was only used in combination with other aromatics and, more interestingly, that the idea was to *hear* the tiny kernel of scent, which was sometimes even smaller than a grain of rice, indeed one variety was said to be "as thin as [a hair from a] horse-tail[hair]" or "mosquito-leg," and the tray, a Chinese invention, was called a "silver-leaf" but could also be glass, crystal or gold. Needless to say, such miniscule kernels would not fill a room with smoke. Indeed, with the exception of the place where people pray for things at temples and funerals, where all who attend light-up a stick of joss for the departed, the Japanese only encountered such *fumes* as mosquito smudge. 20c Occidentals, who tend to think of incense as Oriental, have found Japanese reticence or even displeasure (*"Uh! It's like somebody died!"*) with respect to burning incense sticks in their rooms hard to understand.

While the incense burned was tiny in size, the interest was large. Aristocrats of Frois's day enjoyed incense parties called *kikikô* or *bunkô,* or "hear-scent" the likes of which the West has never known. Chamberlain, who never missed an odd thing Japanese, describes them:

> The gist of it is this: – The host produces from among a score of different kinds of incense, five kinds, to each of which he affixes at pleasure a new name founded on some literary allusion, and each name receives a number. The various kinds are then burnt in irregular order, sometimes in combinations of two or three kinds, and the guests have to write down the corresponding numbers on slips of paper by means of certain signs symbolical of the chapters in a celebrated classical romance called *Genji Mono-gatari.* He who guesses best wins a prize. When the nose gets jaded by much smelling, it is restored to normal discrimination by means of vinegar. (C:TJ)

1. Benjamin? The Chinese characters for benzoin read "ease-breath-scent" and its nicknames in English are "gum benjamin" and "friar's balsam." OED describes "a dry and brittle resinous substance, with a fragrant odour and slightly aromatic taste, obtained from the *Styrax Benzoin*, a tree of Sumatra, Java, etc." called "frankincense of Jawa" by Ibn Batuta c 1350. "Benjamin" is a corruption: *Benzoin→ Benjoin→ Benjamin.*

14-57 We are passionate with anger running free and impatience hardly tamed at all;
Nós temos a paxão da yra muy solta e a impacientia mui pouqo domada;

> They, in some strange manner, control themselves and thus are moderate and prudent. *Elles em estranha maneira a tem moderada e são nisso muito moderados e advertidos.*

While there are parts of Japan where people fly off the handle quickly, and splendidly uptight parts of the West, the contrast, on the whole, still holds. And it is the main reason why General

MacArthur's "nation of twelve year olds" has always felt, with far more justification, that *we* are about half that age! In *The Christian Century in Japan*, Boxer writes –

> he [Valignano] notes that "the Japanese are slow and deliberate in their dealings, and . . . never display outward resentment or impatience, even when they are inwardly upset. They do not lightly murmur or complain, nor do they speak evil of one another. They are very secretive in their hearts. They are greatly addicted to formal manners and empty compliments, but know how to bid their time in silence very patiently. Whereas we on the contrary are usually quite the reverse. For we are hasty, choleric, free and easy in our speech, and straightway disclose our thoughts and minds, . . ." It is amusing to find a Jesuit – traditionally the embodiment of reticence and guile – writing thus, but the celebrated French Jesuit, Jean de Fontaney, wrote the same strain about the Chinese and Europeans more than a century later. (B:CCJ)

Yes, even these Jesuit missionaries were children compared to Orientals who judged maturity on the basis of one's self-control, and most other Occidentals came across as *raging maniacs*. The Jesuits were not the only ones to notice this, either, it was the central theme of Mendez Pinto's *Peregrinations* (written 1560-80). He *constantly* bemoaned the poor character of the Portuguese, who the Chinese avoided for that reason, as if we "had a contagious disease." (details in *TT-long*) Pinto was generous to find the fault in his own countrymen, but the Portuguese were hardly the only louts in Europe. They drank less and were probably on the whole better mannered than the English and Dutch. Cocks' dairy mentions various European nationalities in Japan about a half-century after Pinto who behaved simply atrociously. Mostly, it was between themselves (as was true in Pinto's tale), as when "broyle Jno. Portus broke a Hollanders pate with his dagger" or when "There were rymes cast abrode and song up and downe towne against Matinga [Cock's concubine] and other English mens women," but sometimes Japanese were attacked: "Mr.Nealson in his fustion fumes did beate Co Jno., our *jurebasso* [interpreter], about the head with his shews in the streete, because he came not to hym at his first calle, and yet had a *jurebasso* of his owne as good a linguist as he." There were also drunken murders and major plots such as the Portuguese trying to blow up their gun-powder, etc., but it is in these smaller items that we see "our" character best: We have met the *yahoos* and, by God, they were us! To be fair, the Japanese were not always angels either. It would seem that a border city was a border city even in Japan, for toward the end of Cocks' letter [forgot to copy the date, sorry!] to the Governor of the East India Company, he wrote:

> And as som of our men goe along the streetyes, the Japons kindly call them in and geve them wine and whores till they be drunk, and then stripp them of all they have (some of them stark naked) and soe turne them out of dores.

But, even here, the Japanese are not rowdies. They are not out of control. They are in control, but happen to be criminals. This fundamental difference Pinto stressed and Frois contrasted was put into modern racial terms by the Iwakura Embassy to the West in the 1870's:

> The peoples of Europe are generally categorized as "the white race" or Caucasian race, Asian peoples "the yellow race" or "Mongolian race." Roughly considering the temperaments of these two races, whites, being afire with desires, are wild for religion and have little power to control themselves, or, to put it in a word, are a *yokubukaki* [avaricious/rapacious] race; yellows have weak desires and are strong [good] at controlling their temperament, in a word, they have little avarice [rapaciousness]. Accordingly, the purport of government also must be opposite: in the West, there is a politics of protection [(?) *hogo*], and in the East one of morality. (I:TZT)

In the early-20c, this was further confirmed by a most unlikely source. The Report of the Missions Investigating Committee "appointed to tour the world and supply an unvarnished report of the true condition of affairs in Oriental lands amongst the peoples usually termed 'heathens'" by the INTERNATIONAL BIBLE STUDENTS ASSOCIATION at its convention held September 1-10, 1911, with respect to the Japanese. They found the Japanese more "industrious, peace-loving, polite and kind" and less plagued with the "fretfulness, unhappiness, quarrelsomeness and rudeness and boisterousness frequently in evidence in Europe and America" and even noticed that the Japanese do not curse (This is generally true). They came up with a splendid rationalization for this: God sent Christianity to us because we were "the more rude or combative race" and hence needed its message of meekness and gentleness more! (see *TT-long* for more details or www.agsconsulting.com/htdbnon/r5007.htm)

14-58   In Europe, if for some reason a married or single woman happens to find shelter in a lord's house, she is helped and kept safe; *Em Europa se huma molher cazada ou solteira por algum cazo fortuito se acolhe a caza de algum senhor, ali hé favorecida e ajudada e posta a salvo;*

> In Japan, if a woman goes to the house of any *tono* [lord], she loses her liberty and becomes his captive. *Em Japão como se acolhem a casa de qualquer* tono *perdem a liberdade e ficão suas cativas.*

I do not get it. Was Europe, despite woman's relative lack of liberty we have seen in chapter II, this much kinder to women? I could understand if Frois had written "some *tono*," but *qualquer* = any = all!? It so happens that what Frois describes is common on TV Easterns in Japan, today: a woman begs the *tono* to right things for her wronged husband, or for a loan to pay for a sick child's medicine, only to be sexually assaulted (after which – or, during which – she commits suicide and is revenged by the hero, a martial artist do-gooder who usually is not the husband but feels guilty for not doing something to help the lady earlier, etc). The coincidence makes one wonder, but surely all the *tonos* of Japan were not *that* monstrous. I believe Frois must have been upset about some specific incident/s that occurred in the recent past and took out his helpless anger with this contrast.

14-59   With us, people who have made up beg apologies from one another and embrace;
Antre nós os que se fazem amigos se pedem perdão ou abraçam;

> In Japan, the one to blame rubs his hands before the other and drinks from his *sakazuki* [*sake* cup]. *Em Japão o culpado esfrega as mãos diante do outro e bebe o seu* sacanzuqi.

Hand rubbing, as mentioned in 14-44, is a sign of being contrite, and the other offers him *sake* to say, "I forgive you" and reaffirm vows of friendship. I would bet there were parts of Europe and classes of people who *also* drank rather than embraced to make up.

..

14-60   With us, the iron [blade] of a hoe is broad and shallow;
Antre nós as emxadas são largas e curtas no ferro;

> Those of Japan are very thin, long and curve.
> *O ferro das emxadas de Japão he muito estreito, comprido e concavo.*

I prefer the Japanese hoe blade. The slight curve – I say "curve" rather than *concave* because it is only concave on the up-down axis – improves the bite and driving in much deeper, it can pull out long-rooted weeds more easily. The slight curve in the hoe blade makes as much sense as the slight curve in the Usanian ax handle, which made it superior to the old world axes. Unfortunately, the handles on *all* hoes in Japan *and* in the West are too damn short. It is as if someone had the idea that the men of the soil should always be short men who should bend low, and I – a tall man who finds hoeing a great satisfaction, so long as I can stand straight – resent it!

14-61 European flutes are made of wood and have a hole to play/blow into;
As frautas d'Europa são de pao e tem buxa por onde se tanjem;

    Those of Japan are of bamboo, open on both ends.
    As de Japão são de cana e são abertas todas por baxo e por cima.

The Japanese flute works like the South American *cana,* one blows across the end of it, rather than through a hole that guarantees your breathe strikes it at the perfect angle. Because the bamboo is thicker on the large Japanese flute, it is hard for most people to even get a noise out of it! Once mastered, however, the greater freedom of attack that causes so much initial suffering permits nuances the Western flute performer cannot even dream of. (Another advantage of open ends is no place for spit to build up.) I am assuming that by "flute," here, Frois does not mean the fife mentioned in chapter 13, but the *shakuhachi,* the richest timbered of all wind instruments, which creates complex notes and texture reminding one of the brush-stroke leaving strips of white within the black (*hakke*) in sumi-e (ink-painting) or of harmonics incorporated into the overall sound, ... All classic Western musicians with guts should listen carefully to a *shakuhachi* and consider whether "our" instruments are really the only possibility for Music.

14-62 With us, the hair of domestic servants is kept short and the manes of horses allowed to grow; *Antre nós trosqião-se os moços de serviço e deixão-se crecer os topetes dos cavalos;*

    In Japan, the horse's is cropped and the *komono's* [=underling's] is allowed to grow. *Em Japão, trosqião-se os topetes dos cavalos e deixão-nos crecer aos comonos.*

One thing seems certain from this and other contrasts we have seen; the imposition of short hair on persons of inferior position in Europe (noted in 3-1) was so broad-spread a practice that the presence of hirsute help in Japan must have shocked Frois. To think that almost 400 years after Frois, growing up in the New World, the establishment still tried to keep our (speaking from the position of someone lacking power) hair short! Women in the Occident have pretty much broken free in terms of clothing (bifurcated or not) and hair (long or short), but, superficially at least, most men still live in what amounts to servitude if not slavery.

..

14-63 Portuguese grapes and figs are for us pleasing and very delicious;
As uvas e figos de Portugal são pera nós fructas aceytas e muito gostozas;

    Japanese abhor figs, and do not particularly enjoy grapes.
    Os Japões avorrecem os figos, e não gostão muito das uvas.

According to Okada, "*figos*" (written with the characters meaning "no-flower-fruit" in Chinese) were also used by the Portuguese to indicate Japanese persimmon (*kaki*), but since Japanese liked them and because Japanese figs are tiny and not very good by any measure, Frois is probably talking about *dried or sugared figs* brought in by the traders.

14-64 With us, there is no custom of a domestic servants inviting their master and mistress to their house; *Antre nós não hé costume convidarem os criados em suas cazas a seus senhores e senhoras;*

    In Japan it is often done, sometimes from obligation and sometimes otherwise.
    Em Japão o fazem muitas vezes, humas por obrigasão e outras sem ella.

It is one thing to feed the carpenter working at your house (11-27) and quite another to visit the house of your help. Perhaps this was on the servant's holiday or the day when servants were changed or their service extended (generally, they had one-year contracts). But I do not know, for this is the only mention of bosses visiting their servants' houses that I have ever come across!

As we have already pointed out (14-34), in the 19-20c, visiting homes was itself rare in Japan. I worked with a dozen or so people for almost twenty years and another dozen or so more for ten years and only saw one of their apartments, and that when a company party (at a restaurant) kept a number of us from making the last train. That, makes this practice Frois describes doubly notable. The only question, and it is a big one, is whether it was egalitarian, which is to say a social visit pleasant to both parties or authoritarian, i.e. an inspection of the quarters by the employer/master.

14-65 In Europe, household servants do not accompany their master wearing his clothing;
Em Europa os criados não vão com os vestidos de seus senhores acompanhando-os;

> The *tono* [sire/s] of Japan lend their servants their clothing and gilt *katana* [sword/s] for the sake of their own *isei* [pomp/prestige/splendor]. *Os tonos em Japão emprestão seus vestidos e catanas douradas aos criados pera seu yxei.*

..
Contradicting Frois's claim that European servants don't wear their master's clothing, M & J cite Nola's *Libro de Guisados* (1529): "forgetting the humility of old Portugal, maid-servants have adopted the new style of wearing the same good clothing as their Mistresses" and de Melo's *Carta de Guia de Casados*(1650) which "criticized this, saying that it would make it hard to tell apart a mistress from her servants, make the latter haughty and that it is sufficient for a good master to see that his or her help is dressed in clean clothing." (J/F(M&J):T). I am not sure we are talking about the same thing here. When Frois writes "the clothing of their masters'" (*os vestidos de seus senhores*), he does not necessarily mean that the clothing is identical and the servants are acting uppity trying to ape their superiors. His point is that in Japan, the master or employer makes a real effort to outfit the servants as he or she feels that their looking good reflects the fortunes of the house, and that some even go so far as to give men gilt-handled swords (since Japanese do not ordinarily wear such swords, I would guess he means for ceremonies or parade-like moves from one place to another). The De Melo quote suggests that, in the splendorific Baroque era, some Europeans began to think more like Japanese and cooperated in making their servants look good, but Frois could hardly be expected to predict that!

endnote XIV
Diverse 雑

On the whole, I think the Japanese – at least, as I explain them in this book – come across better than *us*. I am happy with that, partly because it is true, and partly because "our" national (I speak as a Usanian, but the same could be said not only for most Europeans but a surprisingly large number of Latin Americans who tend to call all Far Eastern people *"Chino."*) conceit can always use some deflating. In my books, published in Japan/ese, on the other hand, I made more of an effort to defend *us*, because in the heady 1970's and 1980's, Japanese intellectuals avoided hard thought about their *own* future by Occidentalizing (engaging in what might be called intellectual bashing of the West) and this, I felt, was bad for the world they would be playing a larger and larger role in. In other words, writing in Japanese, I tend to be hard on the Japanese, and writing in English I tend to be hard on English-speakers (and people of cognate Indo-European culture). Which is why, I guess, I am not your most popular author.

But, as I wrote the notes to the three items in this chapter touching upon and *praising the greater self-control the Japanese have over their emotions than Westerners do*, I felt there was one bad thing about Japan – something I don't care for, at any rate – that needed to be expressed if this book would be fair. *What is it?* First, let me say what it is *not*. It is *not* the usual putdown of Japanese conformity. Since Japanese have more self-control and are on the whole more literate than "we" are, their world-view and opinions tend to be more individual than "ours" (This especially goes for my fellow Usanians most of whom *seriously believe* they are giving you an *original* opinion when they are only spouting off one of a number of old saws. They have no idea how *difficult* it is to come up with anything original.) Where it counts most, *inside*, "we" are generally the more conformist than Japanese. Our greater freedom is illusory. Nor, is it Japanese lack of creativity. Who *says* we have more? (I will debate this another time, if/when I publish my *One-String Experiment*. Suffice it to say that our housing, clothing, food, music, literature, etc. demonstrates very little of what I would call creativity.)

No, the problem with Japanese is that their stoicism toward their own lot can give rise to what seems like, or *is,* callousness toward the lot of others. Here is something Kaempfer saw in 1691.
..
> In the middle of a field we found a Monk dying. The poor man lay on his face, thoroughly soak'd with water, it having rain'd pretty hard, but gave as yet some signs of life, and doubtless might have been reliev'd. Such a miserable object, one would think, should have mov'd the hardest stones to pity, but it had no effect on the merciless Japanese. (K(S):HOJ)

Remember, Kaempfer saw and liked Japan and even argued that the people seemed so happy that it might be a good idea for the country to remain closed even if some of the benefits of international discourse are lost (Perhaps the fact this was found and translated back into Japanese, helps explain why the arguments the Japanese give Golownin on the matter sound so familiar!). Yet, he cannot help marveling at "the merciless Japanese." *And this was not peculiar to the Tokugawa era.* I have saved one, possibly two lives, myself, when no one had the decency or guts to act (In one case, a yakuza was repeatedly kicking an unconscious man in the head on a train platform and in the other a drunk fell clunk onto the track when a train was coming). Less spectacularly, I have watched lost children wailing and wailing with no one helping them. The *I-don't-want-to-be-troubled* side of the Japanese has attracted the attention of many foreign visitors. I once read an article by one particularly gutsy, or rude, Occidental who *pretended* more than once to have a heart-attack on a train platform, just to see if anyone would help!

So *why are they like that?* I can think of any number of reasons. *First*, they themselves expect no help (Here, *The Golden Rule* works the wrong way!). *Second*, Japanese are terribly timid. If they are too timid to hurt a stranger, they are also too timid to help one. To put it another way, it takes courage to be bad, or to be good. *Third*, many if not most Japanese are like rich people in the West. As a number of psychological surveys (where someone has been sent out begging door to door) have shown, the wealthy tend to be smug and less likely to assist people than the poor. Perhaps, the same self-control that allows them to defer gratification and control their rowdy side, also reins in their natural sympathy, or conscience, before it can act. And, *fourth*, they have an all-or-nothing sense of responsibility, whereas we have a greyer form of incremental responsibility.

This last item requires an example to explain. One day, I had just left work – at an avant-garde publisher – on the way to give a short talk and participate in a panel discussion before hundreds of veterinarians (all because I mentioned life with a cat in one of my books and wrote a few articles!) when I found a large, apparently well-fed and badly injured dog on the sidewalk by the six-lane street. I rushed across the street to the vet training school that just happened to be there and explained the situation. After leading a veterinarian and his students to the dog, I ran to the train station and arrived just in time to talk and luckily, my first soy-bean shot from the lectern to the small fry-pan I hung on one side of the auditorium hit its target (It was one of my tools for teaching cats to behave). *The next day, my superior at work lectured me on my bad behavior.* The gist of it was that I had acted *irresponsibly* because the vet-school called the publisher – being right across the street, they knew my face – and asked: "Who is going to take responsibility for this dog, which your *gaijin* (foreigner) picked up?" *What was I to do!?* I had an appointment I couldn't be late for, the dog lay bleeding with glazed eyes on the sidewalk and the vet-school was right across the street. I compromised and did the best I could under the circumstances, and I think most of "us" would agree that *I acted as responsibly as I could*. But my superior (someone interested in moral philosophy, Leibniz, no less!) strongly criticized me for *not thinking of the responsibility incurred and bringing about a troublesome situation.* "If you get involved in something, you have to take full responsibility for it, do you understand?" I *do* understand, but I beg to disagree with her.

After experiencing this type of thing a few times, most Japanese in my shoes would have walked right by that dog, pretending one thing or another to themselves to assuage their consciences. It left a sour taste in my mouth, which, years later, still has not completely vanished.

The question is whether people can be less all-or-nothing about responsibility than the Japanese, yet still exercise splendid self-control. Or, whether these good and bad things inevitably come together.

~~~~~~

Given the title of this chapter, I had first thought to use this Note to add diverse Faux Frois's missed by Frois. But, I hope you will forgive me for, finally, *pooping out*. What readers send will be pegged on, in subsequent editions.

"We" _____.

"They" _____.

P*ost*W*ord*

"the jappyknee oppositioner"

While we wos a waitin' I spyd wun ov Mr. Harper's artists a skethcin' away like phun, makin' a pictur ov the yard, and ov the peeple, and ov the white-washed plank-walk for the Jappyknees to cum ashoar on, and the sogers, and the stemeboat we wos on, Jappyknees and awl, includin' me. But awl at wunst he seed sumthin' on the bote, and stop'd drawin', and begun to larf like phun. I looked tew see what on airth he was a larfin' at, and thair was a Jappyknee oppositioner a sketchin' away like phun teew. I deon't wundur Mr. Harper's artist was kinder knocked aback tew see this feller, and I would like tew see the tew picturs, side by side, jist tew see which feller was best.
(Benjamin Downing, 3rd. *Harper's Weekly, May 26, 1860*)

Pardon the folksy spelling. It was popular at the time. "Our" ripoorter observed the coming of the first Japanese Embassy to the United States. What he said about the painters was true for the whole affair, with the only difference being that "we" were concerned with the bad behavior of our own citizens as well as the manners and deportment of the Japanese. *Harper's Weekly* writers mention "the gentleman who smashed his hat over their eyes in Baltimore; the lady who filled up the window in Philadelphia, the shouting, staring, insulting crowd which has dogged them everywhere" and laments that, unlike the always dignified visitors, we exhibited such "barbarian and savage behavior" that the "princes" might regret their allowing the country to be opened. But, he need not have worried, the Japanese were far more impressed by the tremendous amount of flowers the women showered on them – "How lucky we are!" – after they learned it was "the highest expression of kindness on the part of the fair sex." The Japanese understood perfectly well why they were mobbed.

> None of the Ambassadors from Europe excite any curiosity here, as they are almost the same in manners and customs as the Americans. Moreover, the latter themselves were once Europeans, whereas we belong to an entirely different civilization, the Government, manners and customs of which widely differ from those of America. We can quite understand how great the interest and curiosity aroused by our party must be.

> The day appointed for our presentation to the President of the United States of America has at last come. . . . What immense crowds there were! The streets were like seas of human beings; the windows and balconies were thronged with people eager to get a glimpse of the procession. I could not help smiling at the wonder in their eyes, which reached a culminating point when they caught sight of our party wearing costumes that they had never seen before or even dreamt of. I might say that the whole procession seemed to the people of Washington to be a scene out of fairyland, as, indeed, their city appeared to us. It was however, not without a feeling of pride and satisfaction that we drove, in such grand style, through the streets of the American metropolis as the first Ambassadors that Japan had ever sent abroad . . . (A:FJE)

How *refreshing* to read of a culture, a nation of people equal to the West for as long as they've known us! From that first Embassy, we know that what was true when Frois lived in Japan remained true after Perry jammed his foot in the door. Perhaps the West enjoyed a momentary superiority in military hardware, but, as Golownin had predicted a century earlier, that was nothing a bright and well educated people couldn't fix in a generation or two. Indeed, less than fifty years later, Japan whipped Russia and turned world history on its head. The defeat of Japan in World War II put world history back on its Occidental feet; but, this time, it took Japan only one generation to knock it back on its butt. True, "Japan as Number One" proved to be short-lived, but other nations of the Sinosphere sharing much of the same topsy-turvy culture with its tradition of study and the deferment of satisfaction, which is to say self-discipline, are filling in the slack and the Occident, lead by the irresponsible (or is it criminally wasteful?) Usanian culture falls deeper into their debt every year.

Meanwhile, the East – the "them" in Frois's distiches – I am afraid, is evaporating. The world becomes more uniform by the day. As women in the Occident have tended to adopt male values rather than bring female ones to management, the people of the Orient are Occidentalizing themselves as they move into positions of world leadership. Even culturally conceited East Asian leaders who call human values "Asian values" (in the same manner that fundamentalists in the USA call them Christian values) all too often do so *while wearing a Western suit* and living the American Dream. The only exceptions are Islamic leaders, whose ability to stand up to the West (a *good* thing) comes from a common tradition of absolute religion (a *bad* thing: it is still fast at work destroying cultural diversity in Africa and Asia today), and the occasional sartorial maverick – I think of the Japanese finance minister, who gained notoriety (?) by wearing his nation's traditional dress to America in the 1980's or 90's (He also brought along his daughter on what was official government business (Good for him!)). In other words, Far Eastern culturalists talk the talk, but rarely walk the walk. And their *suits* are the least of it. The young Asian, who could be forging his or her own tradition, literally *redressing the world*, has a knack for picking up the ugliest street fashions from the West. . . .

Shades of Lafcadio Hearn and other Occidentals who bemoaned the loss of traditional Japanese culture in the late-19c? *No.* There is a big difference. Until the 1970's, when Japan came to own as much of the West as vice-versa, they *had to* mimic us to survive. For this reason, hoping for them to do otherwise was, indeed, elitism. *Today, this is no longer true.* The East has enough economic clout and toleration of diversity has grown strong enough in the West that there is no longer a need to pass. It is my opinion that had the Japanese only been bold enough to do their own thing in the 1980's (see my thoughts on male coiffure and dress at the end of chapter I) – that is *come out* culturally speaking, I think they might have found the creativity needed to translate the economic bubble into lasting global influence. Now, it may be true that genius does not care what it wears, and that clothing is only a convention. But Carlyle was no fool. *Sartor Resartus* is right: on a broader level, dress *is* everything. Unless the philosophers of *mu* (nothingness) – or whatever – in the Far East can convince others to *wear* rather than spout their metaphysics, the East will not revive as a creative entity even if it comes to completely own the West. (To paraphrase Wilde, if you think appearances are shallow, think again!)

..
Difference is a dangerous game to play, whether you emphasize your own or that of others. You must love your uniqueness enough to keep it alive yet not become so self-infatuated that you force it on the world. You must notice the difference of others but take care lest your awareness becomes another's prejudice. Valignano did everything a man could do to convince his superiors that Japanese were as different as different can be from us, *and* our cultural match. He did it in order to show why the Japanese mission needed more money and time than the people back in Rome might otherwise imagine. He did it to justify a policy of Accommodation, of doing things *their* way, and training *them* to run the Japanese church. Yet, after being published in Maffei's Latin translation, his different-but-equal cultural antipodes quickly mutated into the all-too-familiar exotic wonderland, the worst of which – I think of the fulsome illustrations in Montanus – bring to mind the *freak show*.

But *we need not be too shy*. We need not avoid mention of difference for fear of creating prejudice. Even though Valignano's qualifications in 1601 of his earlier generalizations about Japan's bad traits did not find their way into the public forum and did not prevent malicious exoticizing, his clearly expressed *respect* for the Japanese and their culture (all but *religion* and *sex*) was never completely lost. One finds scattered words of praise for the Japanese character and polity in almost every book written in the Occident over the following four centuries. And I would suggest – a new argument, if I am not mistaken – that *the depiction of the Japanese and their culture as a paragon of contrariety did not make them our inferiors; but if anything, by removing them from our scale of culture, saved them from being treated as unfairly as culturally closer traditions have been.* Perhaps there is something in culture akin to beauty, so that a truly exotic culture is attractive to us in the way a bird or a horse can be attractive, unlike the cognate ape, who looks too much like us to be measured by a separate ideal or scale of beauty. What is generally thought of as *Orientalism,* an unfavorable stereotype, *implies a single cultural yard-stick,* does it not? While topsy-turvy may be thought of as extreme *Orientalism,* it might be the case that *removing Japan (and China) from the scale altogether kept both from being fully Orientalized in the disparaging sense of the term.* (As I write that, however, I must grant that much Japanese Occidentalizing is also *beyond their scale*, and as such less prejudicial than it might seem to us.)

While I *tried* to keep things balanced as I went, sometimes by qualifying the extent of the difference and sometimes by offsetting with examples from "our" side, which might be overlooked by most readers, I could not resist playing with and expanding the numbers of contrasts. Let me be honest. I really have no idea what impression of the Japanese this book will leave on my readers. *This is spooky.* I hope I educate as I entertain. But, for all I know, I could be creating *more* prejudice instead of less. Since most of my previous books attempt to deconstruct stereotypes of difference and involved no risk whatsoever of being taken the wrong way, this has been a new and trying experience for me. My pride (?) as a well-known destroyer-of-stereotype in Japan in the 1980's (One reviewer, a translator of Gregory Bateson, even compared my logical force to that of a certain Hawaiian sumo champion!) told me to destroy the contrasts, while my instinct as a translator was to defend Frois's claims with all my heart.

It is funny, but despite the unforgivable way Frois treated Buddhist "idols," *I really came to like the guy.* An acquaintance, the famous novelist and playwright Inoue Hisashi, wrote a 100 page novelette called *Waga Tomo Furoisu,* or, "My Friend Frois" (If anyone would like to translate it, I will append the whole damn thing – with Inoue's permission – in lieu of the biographical information I should have prepared but did not because I hate writing biography, to the long version of this book TT-long.). Indeed, for all but the chapters on religion, I ended up pretty much on Frois's side. Moreover, as hinted at in the Foreword, once differences become a collectable item, *it really is hard not to join the game!* You might say I joined Frois and had my fun! My intent was to make amends for this difference-mongering by pegging on a 5-page appendix describing 16 *Ways to Make a Difference* – to make it seem like "we" and "they" are far more different, far more contrary than we really are – on to the tail of this book. As the sexy female voice on the Coca Cola commercial on Miami Cuban radio puts it, *Es mejor pedir perdón, que pedir permiso.* (Have your fun, *then* apologize.) As it turns out, however, it is not here. I published *Orientalism & Occidentalism* first, and pegged it on *it,* instead. So buy and read it, if you wish to know the tricks of the trade and bring critical judgment to bear upon the differences found in this book.

If I quoted more old books than properly called for, it is because my heart was not in my century. I lived half of the 20c longing for the fairy-land that used to exist in both the East *and* West. When I look into the mirror, I want to see that "Jappyknee oppositioner," in a *kimono* or some other *wafuku* staring back at me. The only problem is that, if he is looking for difference, he might not like what *he* sees, for I might be wearing the same! (Like Alan Watts, I am partial to non-bifurcated clothing.) ✎

p.s. All of Valignano's European-Japanese contrast-mongering may be summed up as *an apology for the Jesuit policy of adaptation,* or *cultural accommodation,* if you prefer. Could we not, then, call Frois's TRATADO *an apology of an apology and my work an apology for that?* Call it a *triple apologia!*

Be that as it may, *obrigado,* Brother Frois, *obrigado!*

Biblio*graphy*
SKETCHY

The long version of this book has a 19-page tight-lined small-font annotated bibliography which, starts with a good sob over circumstances (being outside of academia, too poor to be reunited with my own library, much less buy books, etc) preventing your author from finding every book in the world, a rationalization of why it is generally *not* good to cite page numbers and short summary/reviews of scores of books. Besides attending to the important books, I give special attention to the rarely encountered ones (mostly dug up at the British Library), such as Cornwallis's 1859 work which claims, among other things that he shot a Japanese wolf and sent it to the Smithsonian. Here, in the short version, with a few exceptions, I only give the bare bones. If you are a bibliophile and interested in things Japanese, please convince your library to buy a copy of the long (740 pg) version also (Or find it on-line).

Books in Western Languages (J/ books are separately listed below)

A:HCJ = Abbe (trans. N.N.): THE HISTORY OF THE CHURCH OF JAPAN written originally in French by L' Abbe de T. London 1705 (vol 1) and 1707 (vol 2). *A couple pages of topsy-turvy contrasts, all very favorable to Japan.* It comes from *Histoire de l'Eglise du Japon, par M. l'Abbe de T. Paris 1689*. Originally by F. Solier, rewritten(?) by F. Crasset, S.J..
A:NMH = Acosta, Ioseph (trans. by E.G.): THE NATURAL AND MORAL HISTORIE OF THE EAST AND WEST INDIES. London 1604 (vol 12?) (UMI microfilm and part is in C:TCJ) *Writing systems part is good, but short!*
A(S):AI = Al-Bîrûnî (Edward C. Sachau trans.) ALBERUNI'S INDIA (orig. London 1888; New Delhi 1964). *Al-Bîrûnî's study of the religion, science, math,, literature and all-round mindscape of Hindu civilization in the early 11c.*
A:COT = Alcock, Sir Rutherford: **THE CAPITAL OF THE TYCOON**: a narrative of three years residence in Japan. (2v) The Bradley co (NY) (Original is 1863) *by England's first Ambassador to Japan. Outstanding.   Revives topsy-turvyism!.*
Alvarez   I only read selections from Captain Jorge Alvarez's 1547 report found in C:LLFX, below.
Alvarez-Taladriz → See V(A):S&A
A:FJE = the America-Japan Society: THE FIRST JAPANESE EMBASSY TO THE UNITED STATES OF AMERICA 1920 / 1977. *The embassy went in 1860.* THE MURAGAKI DAIRY *(transl. Miyoshi Shigehiko) and US news reports, etc.*
A(M):LLT = Anonymous (W.S. Merwin trans.: THE LIFE OF LAZARILLO DE TORMES (c.1554) Anchor 1962. *Established the literary genre of the picaresque or roguery novel. Perhaps inspired Pinto?*
A&L:LWG = Arkush, R. David and Lee, Leo O. trans./ed.: LAND WITHOUT GHOSTS: CHINESE IMPRESSIONS OF AMERICA FROM THE MID-NINETEENTH CENTURY TO THE PRESENT. Univ. of California Press, 1989. *Good.*
A:HOG = Armstrong, Karen. A HISTORY OF GOD – The 4,000 Year Quest of Judaism, Christianity and Islam. *Lucid.*
A(D):AL = Aubrey, John (Oliver Lawson Dick, ed): AUBREY'S BRIEF LIVES (late 17c). *A classic. If you are even part English and haven't read Aubrey, you probably have no right to be reading me. First things first.*
Aurelio = Novo Dictionário AURÉLIO, or, NOVO DICIONÁRIO DA LÍNGUA PORTUGUESA by Aurélio Buarque de Holanda Ferreira et al Editora Nova Frontera 1st ed 15th Imp. 1985? Rio de Janeiro. *Many spellings & connotations.*
 A: TJ = Aveling, J.C.H.: THE JESUITS. Dorset Press (Stein & Day) 1981/7. *A bad book, very unfair to Valignano.*

B:AJI = Bacon, Alice Mabel: A JAPANESE INTERIOR. Houghton, Mifflin and co. 1893. *Good but much is redundant with her earlier JGW and Morse's later book on Japanese homes, unless you choose to read this first.*
B:JGW = Bacon, Alice Mabel: JAPANESE GIRLS AND WOMEN (1890?). Gordon Press (NY) reprint of Houghton Mifflin 1925 ed. *One of the finest pieces of cultural anthropology ever written, it deserves to be famous.*
B:TC = Ball, J. Dyer: **THINGS CHINESE** (orig.1890). Kelly &Walsh, ltd (Shanghai, HK and Singapore: 1925.) *On the whole, Ball is not up to Chamberlain and his* Things Japanese *– but does* very *well with* some *items.*
B:D = Barr, Andrew: DRINK – *a social history of America*. Carroll & Graf Publ. inc. (NY) 1999. *Excellent (if you like me)*
B(H):EOS = Barthes, Roland (Richard Howard trans.). EMPIRE OF SIGNS (1970) Hill and Wang 1982. *There is nothing more entertaining than an essay that boldly turns appearances into ideas. A worthy classic.*
B:FDD = Barzun, Jacques: FROM DAWN TO DECADENCE *– 500 Years of Western Cultural Life 1500 to the Present* (2000) HarperCollins. *Idea-centered and opinionated. Includes* The View From Madrid Around 1540.
B:UTJ = Bird, Isabella L.: UNBEATEN TRACKS IN JAPAN (2v), John Murray (London) 2ed 1880 (1st same year). *Her classic. Observant, opinionated, witty and brave – what more does one need in a good travel writer?*
B:KAHN = Bishop, Isabella Bird (She married so diff. name): KOREA AND HER NEIGHBORS (1897). Fleming H. Revell co (NY) mdcccxcviii??? *Worth a read for her long description of Korean ponies and Korean superstitions alone.*
 B:YVAB =   Bishop, Mrs. J.F. (Isabella Bird): THE YANGTZE VALLEY AND BEYOND. Same publisher, 1899. (reprinted by Ch'eng-wen Publishing Co., Taipei, 1972) *Married or not, still indefatigable.*
B:MM = Blyth Reginald. MUMONKAN. *Anything by Blyth is erudite and enjoyable (because he is an opinionated aesthete).*

B:CCJ = Boxer, C. R..: **THE CHRISTIAN CENTURY IN JAPAN** 1549-1650. U. of California Press, 1967. *Incredible tour de force! Boxer is as interested in warfare and piracy as he is in the interesting Jesuits.*
B:SCSC = Boxer, C.R. ed. **SOUTH CHINA IN THE SIXTEENTH CENTURY**: Being the narratives of GALEOTE PEREIRA, FR. GASPAR DA CRUZ, O.P., FR. MARTÍN DE RADA, O.E.S.A. (1550-1575), printed for Hakluyt Society (London) 1953.
Bulletin of Portuguese-Japanese Studies. *Well-edited and right up my alley. Hope to see more of them!*
B:A = Bulwer: ANTHROPOMETAMORPHOSIS. Also "The Artificial Changeling." (1652) (first is 1650). *This classic with an original name running a full page, comes under many abbreviated names. The one I have quote is dated* 1654).
B:MCJ = Busk, Mrs. W. (or M.M.) ed.: **MANNERS AND CUSTOMS OF THE JAPANESE** (*in the 19th century from the accounts of recent Dutch residents in Japan, and from the German work . . .*). Harper & Bros, 1841. *I found the editor's name in the English printing by John Murray. I think Harper & Bros stole the book, for she is not mentioned.*

~~~~~~

C(W):MVAW = Carletti, Francisco (trans. Herbert Weinstock): MY VOYAGE AROUND THE WORLD (early 17c). Pantheon, 1964. *This Florentine merchant's work is a delightful complement to the Jesuits' more high-brow observations.*
C:MKJS = Caron, Francois and Schouton (ed. C.R.Boxer): A TRUE DESCRIPTION OF THE MIGHTY KINGDOMS OF JAPAN AND SIAM (1663 English edition. Schouton describes Siam. The Argonaut Press (London), 1935.
CARTAS = (Au = The Society of Jesus?) CARTAS QUE LOS PADRES Y HERMANOS DE LA COMPANIA DE IESUS, QUE ANDAN EN LOS REYNOS DE IAPON . . . (microfiche   1547-1571) casa de Iuan Iniguez (Castilla and Aragon) 1575. *What a wealth of writing! I wish I had found more time to read!*
C(T):HML = Casanova, Giacomo (trans. Willard R. Trask). HISTORY OF MY LIFE. The John Hopkins UP. 1971.
C:TJ = Chamberlain, Basil Hall: **THINGS JAPANESE   (first ed. 1890).** *A fine, witty and tasteful book which is sometimes titled* Japanese Things *by idiot publishers. the most prolific Topsy-turvyman since Frois.*
C:CBD Chambers, Robert: CHAMBER'S BOOK OF DAYS (1869) *Next to* Aubrey's Lives, *the best window on our past* Mike Hillman is to be commended for putting it on-line, so we who cannot afford to buy the book can read it.
C:JIL = Cockburn, S.: JAPANESE IDEAS OF LONDON. London 1873. *This book written in far-from-heroic couplets is supposed to be a letter from "a Japanese scout" to his wife in Yokohama, but is utter nonsense. Not worth a read.*
C:DORC1 = Cocks, Richard: THE DIARY OF RICHARD COCKS (1615-1622) Hakluyt Society reprint.   The E.Thompson ed. *version (Burt Franklin, NY_), is expurgated. Forget it unless you are a prude.*
C:DORC2 = Diary of Richard Cocks, 1615-1622 : diary kept by the head of the English factory in Japan / [edited by The Historiographical Institute, The University of Tokyo]. Tokyo : The Institute, 1978-1980. *This is the good version.*
C:LLFX = Coleridge, Henry J. THE LIFE AND LETTERS OF ST. FRANCIS XAVIER. London. new ed 1881 *The Japanese convert Paul's description of Japan and abbreviation of Alvarez's account sent to Xavier.*
C:JA = Collins, Robert J. JAPAN-THINK AMERICA-THINK. Penguin 1992. *This "Irreverent Guide to Understanding the Cultural Differences Between Us" contains hundreds of opposites, some well-treated; but not for the discriminating reader.* (I dare say Penguin would do far better with a hyper-short version of my book. Why are books on Japan so damn juvenile?)
C:RTI = Cooper, Michael, S.J. RODRIGUES THE INTERPRETER – an Early Jesuit in Japan and China. Weatherhill 1974. *A biography of a barely educated Portuguese boy who arrived in Japan at age 15 or 16 and eventually came to play a central role in Jesuit affairs in Japan, Cooper is* always *thorough* and *entertaining to read.*
"**Cooper**" by himself means the classic book mentioned below.
C:TCJ = **Cooper, Michael (compiled and annotated): THEY CAME TO JAPAN – An Anthology of European Reports on Japan, 1543-1640**. Univ. of California Press (1965/81). *One of the best collections of readings* ever *published..   One reason I had to use so much post-1640 material is that Cooper managed to find the lion's share of the best of the older material! He also annotates it well.*
Cooper trans. This Island of Japon by Rodrigues→R(C):TIJ).
C:TJJ = Cornwallis, Kinahan: TWO JOURNEYS TO JAPAN.   1859. *I first found this book mentioned in Alcock. I like the author's humanist stance. He has a poem advising Japanese not to let Christian invaders desecrate their land.*
C:TAJ = Crosland, T.W.H.. THE TRUTH ABOUT JAPAN. London 1904. *This author had already written* THE UNSPEAKABLE SCOT *and* LOVELY WOMAN, *both savage attacks of wit upon types he considered grossly over-rated.*
C:TCC = Cruz, Frei Gaspar da (Rui Manuel Loureiro ed.): TRATADO DAS COISAS DA CHINA (Evora 1569-70). Cotavia (Lisboa), 1997. *After struggling through this in Portuguese, I was half-disappointed to find it in Boxer:SCSC! The first book on China published in Europe. Cruz was overwhelmed by the industry of the Chinese..*

~~~~~~

DR = Daniel Reff, correspondence. Please see Acknowledgments. For his books, see R.
D:A-J = Dalby, Liza et al: ALL-JAPAN: THE CATALOGUE OF EVERYTHING JAPANESE. William Morrow & co., 1984. *A more selective introduction of things Japanese than that of Chamberlain, and with many illustrations.*
D:EBJ = Dalton, William. AN ENGLISH BOY IN JAPAN. London, 1858. *Impressive. Dalton obviously read Busk's collection of Dutch writings, Kaempfer, Willis's Frois letter (the spelling of the romanized Japanese gives it away).*
D(B):DLS = Defourneaux, Marcelin (Newton Branch tr). DAILY LIFE IN SPAIN IN THE GOLDEN AGE. George Allen and Unwin, 1970. *A bold and creative* wet *style of history, faction about Spain by a very opinionated Frenchman.*
De Missione → see Japanese book J/S:DM.
De Sande→ see Japanese book J/S:DM.
D:GGS = Diamond, Jared. GUNS, GERMS, AND STEEL. W.W.Norton & co, 1997. *A good attempt to explain developmental differences by geo-ecological conditions, but asides on Chinese characters are regrettably ethnocentric.*
Dicionário Escolar Inglês-Português, Português-Inglês = Oswaldo Serpa (Ministerio da Educaçao e cultura FENAME Rio de Janeiro 7th ed 1973? *I used this mostly to read* AURELIO. *It is limited but well edited.*
D:WWM = Dower, John W. WAR WITHOUT MERCY. Pantheon, 1986. *Great book on bad stereotypes. The prejudice*

leading up to and used during WWII by Americans and Japanese includes a strong topsy-turvy element.
D:RCN = Du Pleis, Scipio. THE RESOLUER, OR CURIOUSITIES OF NATURE written in French by ~. (orig. date anyone?) London, 1635. (You must spell "resolve" with a "u" to find it in the catalog). *As much fun as Plutarch's Morals..*

~~~~~~~~~~~~~~~~~~~~

E:MP = Eire, Carlos M. N.. FROM MADRID TO PURGATORY: the art and craft of dying in sixteenth-century Spain. Cambridge University Press, 1995. *There was a saying "De Madrid al cielo," (see Venice and die) A fine book.*
E:DD = Elison, George. DEUS DESTROYED: THE IMAGE OF CHRISTIANITY IN EARLY MODERN JAPAN. Harvard UP, 1973. *Some history on the attitude of the Jesuits in Japan and more on the way the Japanese viewed the Jesuits and Christianity, with ample translation and analysis of arguments written against Christianity by two Japanese and Portuguese apostates. Elison's treatment of Valignano is excellent – and it is so rare to find a book like this giving the other side of the argument at length that I hate to quibble – but I feel his short summary of Frois' TRATADO is more flippant than fair (though, so well-done, that, ingrate that I am, I borrowed it for my book explanation.).*

~~~~~~~~~~~~~~~~~~~~

F: DWJ = Frazer, Mrs. Hugh: A DIPLOMATIST'S WIFE IN JAPAN. (v1) Hutchinson & Co; London, 1899. *The wonderfully poetic first letter I quoted from is, unfortunately, the beginning of a far less inspired book.*
F(S):T(K) = Frois, Luis (Josef Franz Schütte S.J. trans/ed.) TRATADO. The actual name of this book, the first to put Frois's original in print is **KULTURGEGENSÄTZE EUROPA-JAPAN** (1585). Jochi (Sophia) University Press (Tokyo), 1955. *Schütte S.J. deserves all our gratitude for discovering and saving the TRATADO of Luis Frois from oblivion! Printed in Japan, it has no Japanese. It has the Portuguese original [Frois's misspelling and silverfish lacuna left as is], a German translation, ample background and a fair number of notes about problematic vocabulary.*
F(C):T(EJ) Fróis, Luís = (TRATADO) = EUROPA-JAPAO UM DIÁLOGO CIVILIZACIONAL NO SÉCULO XVI. (Comissão Nacional para as Comemorações dos Descobrimentos Portugueses / Lisboa: 1993). apresentação de José Manuel Garcia ; fixação de texto e notas por Raffaella D'Intino.] *A tastefully designed book – tall, slim, on artsy paper, as I would like to publish were it not for budget problems – with a short, proper introduction, a pithy historical essay and definitions of the Japanese vocabulary used by Frois, but no other notes to speak of. My all-caps hide the clever EuropaJapao of the original. The modern Portuguese was very helpful, for Frois's old and sometimes misspelled words were not easy to look up (eventually I learned which letters to substitute, etc., but at first I had no idea!).*
F(CSG):T(T) = Frois, Luis. (Xavier de Castro & Robert Schrimpf trans., presented by (?) José Manuel Garcia: **(TRATADO) TRAITÉ DE LUIS FRÓIS, S.J. (1585)** sur les contradictions de moeurs entre Européens & Japonais (Editions Chandeigne, Paris: 1993). *It is interesting to see the word* contradiction*, which does not work in English, preserved in the title! A very smoothly reading, indeed lively translation (So I occasionally quote it) and gets a few things right that others missed. Whoever was responsible for searching out the Far Eastern Portuguese (Malay, etc.) words deserves particular commendation. Unfortunately, there are far too few notes in this beautiful book.*
Frois's TRATADO in Japanese → Please see English explanations for J/F:T entries in Japanese book section, below.
F(F&T): TJ = Fulop-Miller, (F.S. Flint and D.F. Tait trans) THE JESUITS (The Power and the Secret of the Jesuits 1930), Capricorn Books (NY), 1963. *Mistaken with respect to the roots of crucifixion in Japan, but a good book.*

~~~~~~~~~~~~~~~~~~~~

G:PPI = Gaitonide, P.D.: PORTUGUESE PIONEERS IN INDIA: spotlight on medicine. Sangam Books (Manchester) 1983. *The history of the Portuguese in India and essays of the respective systems of medicine are gems.*
G:HOM = Garrison, Fielding H. An Introduction to the HISTORY OF MEDICINE W.B. Saunders Company 1913/1966 *The progress of Western medicine traced with evident delight one doctor/pioneer at a time. A personable tour d'force.*
G:OAO = **Gill, Robin D. ORIENTALISM & OCCIDENTALISM** – is the mistranslation of culture inevitable? Paraverse Press 2004. *The very identity of Japanese is built upon contraries, that is to say identifying themselves as the opposite of "us." That is a tendency found in much of the non-West (see Basso's Portraits of "The Whiteman"). This book shows how (mutually) exotic tongues exacerbate this.*
G:RCM = Glassman, Hank THE RELIGIOUS CONSTRUCTION OF MOTHERHOOD IN MEDIEVAL JAPAN. 2001 Princeton U library has the dissertation (There is also a Religious Studies program Stanford University connection.) *Found on the internet. Good research, splendid reading. I'm surprised it hasn't become a bona fide book already!*
G:MCIJ = **Golownin,** Captain (Vasilii Mikhailovich), R. N. (3v): MEMOIRS OF A CAPTIVITY IN JAPAN 1811-1813 (Henry Colburn & co. London 1824). Oxford University Press, 1967. *To read the words of Captain Golownin and Captain P. Rickford of the Imperial Russian Navy (whose account of the affair is included in v.3) is to love them.*
G:WDW: = Goreau, A. THE WHOLE DUTY OF WOMEN. *The most incredible war of words the world has ever known. Horrible but witty put-downsof and comebacks by women mostly in verse and 17th century. An excellent selection!*
G:EOJ = Gulick, Sydney L. THE EVOLUTION OF THE JAPANESE. New York, 1903. *This seems a remarkably deep work, but I only saw it for ten minutes and it was closing time at the library in a city I was leaving.*

~~~~~~~~~~~~~~~~~~~~

Historia → For Frois's Historia, see J/F:HISTORIA in the Japanese section.
H:CER = Hale, John. THE CIVILIZATION OF EUROPE IN THE RENAISSANCE. Antheneum 1994. *Like Barzun (B:FDD), impressive for being more interested in ideas than dates. The "Discovery of Europe" and the chapter on "civility" has instructed me more than could be included in Topsy-turvy. Better had I read it earlier in my research!*
H:CJTH = Harris, Townsend (ed. Mario Emilio Cosenza), THE COMPLETE JOURNAL OF TOWNSEND HARRIS – first American consul general and minister to Japan. Doubleday & Co. (published for Japan Society, New York), MCMXXX. *This fine literate consul is so much the better man than the wealthy politicos chosen for ambassadors today! He knew something of Valignano, for when the Japanese tried to prevent his meeting with the head of the nation on the basis of there being no precedent for it, he replied: "What about Valignani?" who indeed had visited Nobunaga*

and later Hideyoshi and Tokugawa as the representative for Rome, and India, respectively!
H:JAI = Hearn, Lafcadio: JAPAN – AN ATTEMPT AT INTERPRETATION (190_). Charles E. Tuttle Company, 1955/69. *Besides the attention given to the topsy-turvy, Hearn considers Japan's future in a world of aggressive Western powers and, among other things, clearly predicts Nazism and facism and anti-semiticism.*
H:S = Hearn, Lafcadio = SHADOWINGS. Little, Brown and co..1900. *The cicada and Japanese female names are two of the more interesting topics in this book, which like all of Hearne's books is interesting.*
H:ETP = Hanley, Susan B. EVERYDAY THINGS IN PREMODERN JAPAN. Univ. of California Press, 1997. *This book, which I read too late to take much advantage of, shows that in some ways pre-modern was modern indeed.*
H(G):HH= Herodotus (trans. David Grene): HERODOTUS'S HISTORY Univ. of Chicago Press. *Herodotus is worth reading. Topsy-turvy is not all of it by any means.*
H(V&W): JJ = Heusken, Henry (Jeannette C. van der Corput & Robert A. Wilson trans/ed.) JAPAN JOURNAL 1855-1861. Rutgers U. P. 1964. *The translator/secretary for the first US consul in Japan is astoundingly astute for a man in his twenties. Were he not assassinated, there is no telling what this literate man may have eventually accomplished.*
H:HJD = Hooykaas, R.: HUMANISM AND THE VOYAGES OF DISCOVERY IN 16TH CENTURY PORTUGUESE SCIENCE AND LETTERS. North-Holland Publ. co 1965/79. *Linking the discoveries and the new science. Many great quotes.*
H:CCTT = Huc, M. L'Abbé: CHRISTIANITY IN CHINA, TARTARY AND THIBET (v2) D&J Sadlier &co (Montreal), 1884
~~~~~~
K(S):HOJ = Kaempfer, Engelbert, MD (J.G. Scheuchzer trans.): THE HISTORY OF JAPAN (Together with a Description of the Kingdom of Siam)(1690-2). James MacLehose and Sons (Glasgow), Macmillan co (NY) MCMVI. *With neither the (still missing) first volume of Frois's HISTORIA, nor Rodrigues's history of the church* (first volume: TIOJ) *yet published, Kaempfer's work provided the most complete picture of Japan available outside of the Jesuit's archives until the mid 19 c! Unlike Montanus (M:EEJ), Kaempfer observed and recorded things not in the earlier Jesuit writing. Perhaps because of Montanus' dwelling on Japanese contrariness, Kaempfer writes no topsy-turvy generalizations, but sticks to the facts, which, however, includes hearsay from Japanese). The English language translator is a very impressive son of a fine Zurich professor (More in TT-long!)* (I have not seen the recent translation)
K:AJC = Keene, Donald. APPRECIATIONS OF JAPANESE CULTURE. Kodansha International (1971) 81. *Fine selection.*
K(K):EI = Kenko (Donald Keene trans.): ESSAYS IN IDLENESS – THE TSUREZUREGUSA OF KENKO (orig1330-32) Tuttle, 1987(1967 Columbia UP). *Together with Sei Shônagon's Pillow Book, one of two top must-read books by jpse.*
K:KJ = Kipling, Rudyard (Hugh Cortazzi and George Webb ed.): KIPLING'S JAPAN. Athlone, 1988. *One editor an expert on Japan and one on Kipling. Fine notes. Too bad they are exiled to the back of the book!*
K:FMJ = Knapp, Arthur May: FEUDAL AND MODERN JAPAN (v2). L.C. Page and co (Boston) 1897 (1896). *A delightful book, content and design-wise. The electrotyping by Geo. C. Scott & Sons for Colonial Press was superb.*
K:HWJ Kurihara, Toshie: HISTORY OF WOMAN IN JAPANESE BUDDHISM / NICHIREN'S PERSPECTIVES ON THE ENLIGHTENMENT OF WOMAN (on line) the Institute of Oriental Philosophy. *Splendid! Scholarly, yet not academic.*
~~~~~~
L:AME = Lach, Donald F.. ASIA IN THE MAKING OF EUROPE. vol 1. The University of Chicago Press. *Together with B:TCC, the best overall picture of the meeting of the continents, yet incredible detail! Lach stands alone (and is absolutely correct) in* **his assessment of Frois' writing as not being given to verbosity. One may write at great length, but provided the writing is full of "concrete data and detail" (1-pg.683), it cannot rightly be criticized as verbose.**
L:JIA = Lanham, Charles: THE JAPANESE IN AMERICA. NW University Publishing Co (1872). *Lanham, Secretary for the Japanese Legation in Washington, did a fine job editing what is largely pr for Japan. A speech by Marquis Ito includes a fascinating paragraph of what might be called allegorical revisionism:* "The red disc in the centre of our national flag shall no longer appear like a wafer over a sealed empire, but henceforth be in fact what it is designed to be, the visible symbol of the rising sun, moving onward and upward amid the enlightened nations of the world." *This is the earliest instance I know of Japan* as *the rising sun, rather than the* birthplace of *the sun! Meanwhile, a student, Yashida Hisomaro noted that* "the terms oriental and occidental have not been used with strictly scientific accuracy; for the United States of America are east of Japan, and yet Japan is called an oriental nation, though in fact it is occidental in relation to them."
LR = (Lost Reference, or Forgotten Source.) *Read sometime, somewhere; the title or website either forgotten or the book not found in time to confirm whether it was indeed the source of the information. (Sorry!)*
L:TSC = Las Casas, Bartholomew de (trans M.M.S.): THE SPANISH COLONIE OR BRIEFE CHRONICLE OF THE ACTS AND GESTES OF THE SPANIARDES . . . (1641?49?) William Brome (London) 1583. *Polemic is far bolder, more powerful than I had imagined. Never has cruelty been described in so many metaphors!*
L:AJN = LaViolette, Forest E.: AMERICANS OF JAPANESE ANCESTRY (1945/ Canada Institute of International Affairs). Arno Press (NY) 1978. *A good "study of assimilation in the American community."*
Lazarillo→ Anonymous
L:IOJ = Lehmann, Jean-Pierre: THE IMAGE OF JAPAN – from feudal isolation to world power, 1850-1905. George Allen & Unwin (London),1978. *Ambivalent Western feelings about Japan's modernization. Exceptionally well-balanced.*
L(J&L):LPC = León, Fray Luis de (tr. ed. John A. Jones and Javier San José Lera): LA PERFECTA CASADA – A Bilingual Edition of ~ (the role of married women in 16th century Spain) (1583). The Edwin Mellen Press. 1999. *This Augustinian and "leading humanist of Spain's Golden Age" also did the first Spanish translation of Solomon's* Song of Songs. *Includes a 100pg sustained argument against cosmetics and essay of personal beauty..*
L:WCRS = Levathes, Louise E.: WHEN CHINA RULED THE SEAS: the treasure fleet of the dragon throne 1405-1433. Oxford UP, 1994. *Ships the length of two football fields! The spectacular rise and fall of Chinese sea-power.*

L:VJHVL = Linschoten, John Huyghen Van: THE VOYAGE OF JOHN HUYGHEN VAN LINSCHOTEN ((1596) from the old english translation of 1598, first vol. by Arthur Coke Burnell, Haklyut Society reprint 1885?) reprint Lenox Hill (Burt Franklin) 1970. *It is hard for me to tell who to credit for what with this book, but it is a fine olde read!*
L:IOJ = Littlewood, Ian: THE IDEA OF JAPAN. Secker & Warburg, London, 1996. *Much fine 19 & 20 c writing is cited; the unfavorable or patronizing element of the Western images and myths of Japan is somewhat over-emphasized – despite the well-balanced and witty introduction..*
L:SOFE = Lowell, Percival: THE SOUL OF THE FAR EAST. Houghton, Mifflin and co. 1888. *This is an outrageous attempt to use Japanese as proof that the essence of the West is individual-enhancing and the East individual-effacing. Lowell mysteriously dedicates his book "to the rose" – a very Occidental flower – in Japanese only* (Bara-no hana ni)!

~~~~~~

M:JAL = Markino Yoshio: A JAPANESE ARTIST IN LONDON. George W. Jacobs (Philadelphia) 1910. (and Chatto & Windus) *Awkward English, left unpolished to show it was the genuine work of one who is not a native speaker!*
M:DLP = Marques, A. H. de Oliveira (tr. S. S. Wyatt): DAILY LIFE IN PORTUGAL IN THE LATE MIDDLE AGES. (U of Wisconsin Press: 1971) *Particular care taken with clothing; ample illustrations depict what print alone cannot show.*
M(B):HIC = Martins, J.P. Oliveira (tr. Aubrey F.G. Bell): A HISTORY OF IBERIAN CIVILIZATION (1879). Oxford UP 1930. *As the translator writes: "history seen through a temperament." Like Cash's THE MIND OF THE SOUTH.*
M:AWE = Massarella, Derek: A WORLD ELSEWHERE – Europe's encounter with Japan in the Sixteenth and Seventeenth Centuries. Yale U P, 1990. *Massarella's attempt to balance Boxer's CHRISTIAN CENTURY . . . by giving more space to English contacts (as opposed to Iberian) and ten full pages of their intimate relations with the Japanese is fine, but Boxer is still the book to read. Massarella gives little more space (one paragraph) to the Bungo Consensus than do writers on China, who at least have the excuse of saying they are, after all, dealing with China.*
M & J, alone, or
Matsuda & Jorissen (their trans. of TRATADO and analysis) → J/F(M&J):T
M:RPJ = Matsuda, Kiichi: THE RELATIONS BETWEEN PORTUGAL AND JAPAN (Lisbon) 1965. *Half of this book by the translator/annotator of one of the Japanese translations of TRATADO is a pithy but masterful summary of the history of the earliest Portuguese and Japanese relations, and what happened to Christianity there.*
M:MFAJ = Mears, Helen: MIRROR FOR AMERICANS – JAPAN. Houghton Mifflin co., 1948. *Takes Americans to task for demonizing the Japanese, pointing out they are no more militaristic than we are, and argues for a kind Occupation.*
M:JRC = Menpes, Mortimer (and Dorothy): JAPAN, A RECORD IN COLOUR. London 1901. *Dorothy Menpes claims to simply present her father's impressions, but I wonder if it is simply a transcription. Intensely aesthetic adulation. Wow.*
M:MSB = Michel, Wolfgang: THE MEDICINE OF THE SOUTHERN BARBARIANS IN JAPAN (http://www.rc.kyushu-u.ac.jp/~michel/publ/books/) *A thorough and very readable survey of the history of Western Medicine in Japan. (first published in Japanese as part of Michel, Wolfgang: Kômôryû geka no tanjô ni tsuite. . . Kyôto, March 1997.)*
M:LRY = Mikes, George: LAND OF THE RISING YEN. Andre Deutsch 1970 (Penguin 1973) *Lines like "I am for untidiness and a modicum of dirt" make Mikes' irreverent, but never mean criticism a delight to read.*
M:BGE = Moges, Marquis de. BARON GROS'S EMBASSY TO CHINA AND JAPAN IN 1857-58. London (Richard Griffin & Co) 1860. *Baron Gros and Lord Elgin's Embassy and War-party might more accurately describe the Chinese part of the book! the China part of the book is enriched with a plunder of observations, if I may coin a new term of venery!*
M(F):CEM = Montaigne, Michel de (Donald M. Frame trans): THE COMPLETE ESSAYS OF MONTAIGNE (c1570~88).. Stanford U P, 1943 /85 *If you have not read Montaigne's Essays, do. Find out how far we have not come in 500 years!*
M:EEJ = Montanus, Arnoldus: AN EMBASSY TO THE EMPEROR OF JAPAN [also, *Atlas Japannensis*]. (Engl. transl: 1670). *This book of wonders is allegedly about the Dutch Embassy, but actually a hodge-podge of Japan-lure, the best part of which repeats Valignano's contrasts, adding commentary that makes them seem even stranger, and serving up the whole with magnificent illustrations by an artist who obviously never went to Japan. Early Orientalism.*
M:JM = Moore, Charles E, ed. THE JAPANESE MIND. University of Hawaii Press: 1967 *Very readable papers by academics (including a world-class physicist) about what Japanese logic has to offer (something different?) in the greater (Western?) world of philosophy. I would recommend reading T:SJT before and my O&O after reading it.*
M:JJ = Moran, J.F.: THE JAPANESE AND THE JESUITS – Alessandro Valignano in sixteenth century Japan. Routledge, 1993. *Valignano is given due credit for the great work he did, while his overworked amanuensis Frois is sympathetically described. If a reader wishes to understand Frois' circumstances better, see this book.*
M:IGM = Morse, Edward S. ON THE IMPORTANCE OF GOOD MANNERS. 1894. *This speech to the graduates of Vassar might be the first attempt at* Learn-from-Japanism. *Harvard charged me an arm-and-a-leg for the microfiche*
M:JDD = Morse, Edward S.: JAPAN DAY BY DAY 1877, 1878-9, 1882-3 (2v). Houghton Mifflin Company, 1917. *Even if the book, which was taken from thirty-five hundred pages of journal by the author himself, were not blessed by 777 illustrations, this scientist/observer's ample and absolutely unaffected observations would be fine reading.*
M:JHTS = Morse, Edward S.: JAPANESE HOMES AND THEIR SURROUNDINGS. Harper & Brothers, 1904. *A fine book, well illustrated by the author and worth reprinting.*
M:CL = Mungello, D.E.: CURIOUS LAND: JESUIT ACCOMODATION AND THE ORIGINS OF SINOLOGY. U of Hawaii Press, 1989. *The role of Valignano and Japan in the development of a policy of Accommodation is overlooked.*

~~~~~~

N:GIL Nalle, Sara T. GOD IN LA MANCHA: Religious Reform and the People of Cuenca, 1500-1650 THE LIBRARY OF IBERIAN RESOURCES ONLINE *Full of both statistics and local color, entertaining quotes from the mouths of the people as recorded by the notaries. You feel like they are standing right before you.*
NIPO = Nihon-Portuguese, i.e. Japanese-Portuguese dictionary of 1604. *I wish I had a copy but I don't.*
N:MAR = Nelson, Randy F. ed. THE OVERLOOK MARTIAL ARTS READER. The Overlook Press (NY) 1989. *A fine*

"anthology of historical and philosophical writings." *Lafcadio Hearn on judo was a new discovery for me.*
N(O):EC = Nieuhoff, John (John Ogilby): AN EMBASSY FOR THE EAST-INDIA CO. TO . . . . THE GRAND TARTAR CHAM EMPEROR OF CHINA. 1673 *The folklore explanations of the magical natural world of the Orient (obviously gathered from local sources with relish) equals the best – i.e .most fabulous – passages of Pliny. Indeed, Pliny is often quoted. The Gods of the Formosan's and the Chinese are listed and described in great detail without any moralizing..*

OED = **The OXFORD ENGLISH DICTIONARY.** *Why mention it? Because I only realized just how much help it was for* TRANSLATING *a few months before finishing the first edition* (TT-long) *for that reason, it helps the last half of the book more than the first). It has not a few, but many old Portuguese words not even found in AURELIO!*
OJD → **J/OJD,** in the Japanese section.
Okada = i.e., his annotated trans. of TRATADO → **J/F(O):T** My debt to him is the largest of all.
O:IOE = Okakura, Kakasu: THE IDEALS OF THE EAST WITH SPECIAL REFERENCE TO THE ART OF JAPAN. John Murray, 1903. *OK but not so interesting as his writing on The Way of the Tea!*
O:EEM= Oliphant, Laurence: Earl of Elgin's Mission to China and Japan, v2 1860, New York, Harper & Brothers, (first US edition).. *Unlike his French counterpart Moge, Oliphant has almost nothing to say about the Chinese. Vol 2, on Japan, is 90% culture and history. Oliphant cites nearly every major writer on Japan that precedes him.*

P:AOE = Palliser, D.M.: THE AGE OF ELIZABETH under the late Tudors 1547-1603. Longman (London) 1983/92.
P(P):SMS = Peréz-Mallaína, Pablo E. (Carla Rahn Phillips trans.). SPAIN'S MEN OF THE SEA: DAILY LIFE ON THE INDIES FLEETS IN THE SIXTEENTH CENTURY. John Hopkins, 1998. *Excellent writing/wit and, beautifully translated.*
 P:GUG = Perrin, Noel: GIVING UP THE GUN: JAPAN'S REVERSION TO THE SWORD 1543-1879. G.K. Hall & co (Boston) 1979. *An masterful essay proving that good sense counts more than language skills, because the author* (who did not know Japanese) *slowly gathered material with the help of translators and . . . read it and see for yourself!*
P:EAE : Picaza, Jorge, MD.: "The European-Amerindian Encounter: An immunodeficiency lesson" in *Mercy medicine*, vol.2 #4 1984. *The citation is from* Oviedo FG. HISTORIA GENERAL Y NATURAL DE LOS INDIOS. Mexico City: Fondo de cultura economica, 1950. *Picaza describes diseases to which the Europeans were the more vulnerable as well as the usual destruction caused by "our" diseases to "them."*
 P(C):TMP = Pinto, Fernao Mendez (Rebecca D. Catz trans./ed.) THE TRAVELS OF MENDES PINTO. (written1560-80, publ. 1614) U. Chicago, 1989. *The full edition, with ample notes. Everyone should read Pinto at least once.*
P(L):TMP = Pinto, again. (Michael Lowery trans/abridge) THE PEREGRINATION OF FERNAO MENDES PINTO . . . Carcanet Press (Manchester) 1992. *The abbreviated parts are summed up and the book is long enough for most readers. Pinto's honest-to-goodness (and badness) history reads like Don Quixote crossed with Candide and The Arabian Nights.*
P:LJ = Ponting, Herbert J. THE LOTUS-LAND JAPAN. London & NY, 1922. *Not bad, but nothing much.*
PRINCIPIO = See **V(W):HPP.**
P(B):ETPJ = Proust Jacques. (Elizabeth Bell trans.) EUROPE THROUGH THE PRISM OF JAPAN – Sixteenth to Eighteenth Centuries. U of Notre Dame Press, 2001. *Like Perrin's* Giving Up the Gun, *it proves that (not having)reading knowledge of Japanese is less important than brains and taste. Includes the relationship between the Jesuit Almeida being a New-Christian (Jewish roots) and his practice of medicine in Japan, the reaction of "one of the most famous casuists of the time" to Valignano's list of predicaments faced by the Jesuits in Japan.*

R:DPC = Reff, Daniel T. DISEASE, DEPOPULATION, AND CULTURE CHANGE IN NORTHWESTERN NEW SPAIN 1518-1764. *This classic book documenting the demographic and cultural consequences of the spread of Old World disease.*
R(R&A&D):HOT = de Ribas, Andrés Pérez (Trans. of 1645 Spanish orig. by Daniel T. Reff, Maureen Ahern and Richard Danford): HISTORY OF THE TRIUMPHS OF OUR HOLY FAITH Amongst the Most Barbarous And Fierce Peoples of the New World. 1999. U. of Arizona Press. *In Book 7 ch.1 of this huge work, the author wrote "My motivation for writing this Treatise was augmented by the fact that I learned that a modern-day heretic had published a treatise against the Company, saying that its missionary sons seek out and choose ministries only among the richest, noblest and most powerful peoples and republics such as China, Japan, and other similar nations."*
 R(C):TIJ = **RODRIGUEZ, JOAO (Michael Cooper trans./ed): THIS ISLAND OF JAPON** (book 1 of *Historia da Igregja do Japao:*1620-33). Kodansha Int'l ltd (Tokyo and New York). *The first part of Rodrigues's History of the Church in Japan, perhaps the best single introduction to Japan ever written. I wonder if it may not have utilized Frois's missing summary to his HISTORIA, which includes some* Tratado *related material.*
R:MD = Rodrigues João (Michael Cooper trans. intro) "THE MUSE DESCRIBED: Joao Rodrigues' Account of Japanese Poetry" Monumenta Nipponica, Vol.26, No.1/2 (1971), 55-75). (A selection from Rodrigues' huge *Arte da lingoa de Iapam* (dated 1604, prob. not printed until 1608)) *If you are interested in the history of the translation of Japanese poetry, this is where it started. Most of the examples of poetry are the first poem in Japanese collections of poetry.*
R(L):TOES = Rodriguez, João (Jeroen Pieter Lamers trans+intro): TREATISE ON EPISTOLARY STYLE – João Rodriguez on the Noble Art of Writing Japanese Letters. (selection from *Arte da lingoa de Iapam* (1604-8)) Center for Japanese Studies, U. of Mich. 2002 *Good translation, good introduction and good notes, but too expensive!*
Ross, A.C. = A VISION BETRAYED 1994 Edinburgh. ***Unfortunately, I missed this!*** *At last minute, I read a book review suggesting Ross made overly large claims for the depth of Valignano's challenge to Eurocentric understanding of culture. I suspect I will agree with Ross and hope to see a copy before the second edition!*
R:TKM = Rudofsky Bernard. THE KIMONO MIND. Van Nostrand Reinhold Company 1965. *Rudofsky likes ideas, so intelligent readers will enjoy him, but the tasteful illustrations fail to offset his often tasteless swipes at the Japanese.*

de **Sande** → **See the Japanese books J/S:DM**
S:HOJ = Sansom, George: A HISTORY OF JAPAN, 1334-1615. Stanford UP:1961. *A standard.*
S:JDJ = Scidmore, Eliza Ruhamah: JINRICKSHA DAYS IN JAPAN. Harper & Bros, 1891. *If Skidmore is not an adventurer of Bird's class, she is an even better writer. She is the one who called the Japanese "a nation of poseurs – . . ." long before modern cultural anthropologists came up with the concept of a theatre-state.*
S(C):VMP = Schütte, Josef Franz S.J. (John J. Coyne, S.J. trans): **VALIGNANO'S MISSION PRINCIPLES FOR JAPAN** (v.1). The Institute of Jesuit Sources (St. Louis), 1980. *Schütte not only found and presented Frois's TRATADO to the world, but, with this book, gives Valignano the full treatment he deserves. Any scholar pretending to understand the Jesuit's policy of Accommodation in Japan and China, and the Bungo Consultation [that became the Consensus?] that hammered out the modus operandi and vivendi to make East-West cultural equality a reality for the first time since the Renaissance (my claims, not Schütte's), must start from this in-depth but easy-reading study. This book may sound very specialized, but it is a far better read than most books published by academic presses and deserves a pb reprint!*
S(M)PBSS = Sei Shonagon (Ivan Morris trans/ed): THE PILLOW BOOK OF SEI SHONAGON (c 1000 AD) Columbia U P 1967/Penguin 71. *Read Shônagon and die. I think Sei Shônagon would appreciate my putting it that way!*
S:QTJ = Sladen, Douglas. QUEER THINGS ABOUT JAPAN. Anthony Treherne & Co., Ltd., 1903.
S:MQT = Sladen, Douglas (and Norma Lorimer): **MORE QUEER THINGS ABOUT JAPAN,** Anthony Treherne & co. (London), 1905. *I read and enjoyed Sladen's first book twenty years ago, but was unable to obtain it by library loan. The book includes "the famous letters of Will Adams" and a retranslation of a Japanese "Life of Napoleon"!*
S:JPMC = So Kwan-wai: JAPANESE PIRACY IN MING CHINA DURING THE 16TH CENTURY. Michigan State U, 1975. *Chinese documents show much if not most Japanese piracy was actually done with Chinese cooperation and leadership.*
S(R):WTU Souyri, Pierre François (trans. Käthe Roth) THE WORLD TURNED UPSIDE DOWN – Medieval Japanese Society. (Columbia University Press 2001. Orig is 1998). *Detail of rock warfare and riots, and the survey of the religious communes that took over much of the country and degree of autonomy won (and later lost) by many peasants, etc. was fascinating and more than made up for what began as an overly complex history – one warlord after another (to a generalist like me). While the author could not resist quoting Valignano on contrary Japan, the title refers to inversion of the social hierarchy, with the warriors that served in the Heian Era turning into the rulers.*
S:MPMR = Spence, Jonathan D.: THE MEMORY PALACE OF MATTEO RICCI. Viking, 1984. *Something for every good reader but Valignano and things Japanese are bent a bit to fit the author's evident affection for Ricci and China.*
S:MOA = Steadman, John. **THE MYTH OF ASIA** (A Refutation of Western Stereotypes of Asian Religion, Philosophy, Art and Politics) Simon and Schuster. 1969. *I cannot for the life of me understand why this book should be so unknown. The first book to grasp the complexity of Orientalism – it described the diverse stereotypes (some good and some bad) and analyzed the ways by which differences become generalized and exaggerate – Steadman deserves more attention than a certain man about whom more than enough has been said.*
S:SCP = Sutton, Richard L.: SIXTEENTH CENTURY PHYSICIAN AND HIS METHODS – a Mercuralis on diseases of the skin (1986) The Lowell Press, Kansas City, Missouri. *A translation of Hieronymus Mercuralis' 1572 book.*
S:GT = Swift, Jonathon. (ed Greenberg) GULLIVER'S TRAVELS. (1726) W.W. Norton & co. 1970. *Japan is clearly the model for one scene and provided ideas for others. (Note: Norton critical edition anthologies should be given the best place in every bookstore, because the additional matter beats that of their English rival.* Norton fails to promote itself.)
SUMARIO → **See V(A):S&A**. But note that there is also Frois's lost **Summary** mentioned in J/F:Historia.

~~~

T:SIH = Taylor, Gordon Rattray SEX IN HISTORY (1954). *A great way to get students to start reading history!*
T:RAD = Thomas, Keith RELIGION AND THE DECLINE OF MAGIC (1971). *Plentiful and interesting primary material. Enjoy it, then peek at Valerie Flint's RISE OF MAGIC in Europe, which argues that the church was more attentive to and incorporated more pagan 'magic' than Thomas suggests. For earlier hist., see Daniel T. Reff's Plagues, Priests, Demons – Sacred Narratives and the Rise of Christianity in the Old World and the New* (Cambridge 2005).
T:MNW = Thomas, Keith. MAN AND THE NATURAL WORLD Changing Attitudes in England, 1500-1800 (1983). *Thank you Sir Thomas, (he was since knighted) for letting us share with you the words of the past in the words of the past!*
T:TEAA = Thunberg, Charles Peter, M.D.: TRAVELS IN EUROPE, AFRICA AND ASIA (between 1770 and 1779). Engl. trans. printed for F. and C. Rivington and sold by W. Richardson, London 1795/96. vol.3 is all Japan. *Little is added to Kaempfer's more substantial work. Thunber's main contribution was Botony, but I have not examined that work.*
T:COA = Todorov Tzvetan (Richard Howard trans.): THE CONQUEST OF AMERICA HarperPerennial: 1984. (1981 Editions du Seuil). *This book stressing mis/communication is the best modern book on what happened when the Iberians met the "Indians." The book is dedicated to the memory of a Mayan woman devoured by dogs (after she kills herself rather than submit to sex with captain Alonso Lopez de Avila).*
T:SJT = Tsunoda, de Bary, Keene compiled: SOURCES OF JAPANESE TRADITION v2. Columbia University Press, 1964. *Part of Theodore de Bary's "Introduction to Oriental Civilizations" series. Gives the reader a far better feel for the intellectual traditions in non-Western civilization than any analytical one-topic book. A must-read classic.*

~~~

V&V:PCC = Vaccari, Oreste and Enko: PICTORAL CHINESE-JAPANESE CHARACTERS. Vaccari's Language Institute (Tokyo), 1950/70.
Valignano = for *De Missione* → J/S:DM in the Japanese books (below).
Valignano=Miguel/Leon, etc., as above, → J/S:DM
Valignano (1601) , or (1602) or 1603 → V:LIBRO, below (but also sometimes cited in V(A):S&A).
Valignano (1579)(1582?)(1583) → V(W)HPP or some quotes from C:TCJ or from V(A)S&A.
Valignano (1583) (1592)(1602) → V(A)S&A

V:LIBRO = Valignano, Padre Alexandro, LIBRO PRIMERO DEL PRINCIPIO y progresso de la religion christiana en jappon . . . Compuesto por el Padre Alexandro Valignano, 1601. (Ms. British Museum Add. Mss.9857) *Comments in this work which soften and explain earlier criticism of the bad qualities of the Japanese, show that despite all the hardship encountered by the Church in Japan, Valignano had not hardened but rather came to understand and appreciate Japan over the years (This is contrary to the impression left by Spence (S:MPMR.)). Partly read in Alvarez-Taladriz. Regardless, all trans. are mine from the Spanish.*

V(A):S&A = **Valignano, Alejandro S.I. (ed. José Luis Alvarez-Taladriz): SUMARIO DE LAS COSAS DE JAPÓN (1583), ADICIONES DEL SUMARIO DE JAPON (1592).** Sophia U. (Tokyo), 1954. *Much of it is a summary of the good and bad character and customs of the Japanese, with some of this given in what might be called prosaic distiches, i.e. simple contrast. The editor supplies ample and excellent notes citing other Jesuit letters and other writing by Valignano. Splendid scholarship. If you read Spanish, this book is the book on Valignano's contrary Japan.*

V(W):HPP = **Valignano, Alessandro (ed. Joseph Wicki S.I.): HISTORIA DEL PRINCIPIO Y PROGRESSO DE LA COMPANIA DE JESUS EN LAS INDIAS ORIENTALES 1542-64** Institutum Historicum S.I. (Rome) 1944. (1579~1603?). *Includes the earliest summary written by Valignano in 1579, largely about India + the topsy-turvy China vs Japan, the next rendition which gave Japan more space and compared it to Europe, instead, and the next, which refined that in 1583. I did not spend enough time with this book, but remember enough to recommend it.*

V:RCJ = Vivero, G. San Antonio y R. de: RELACIONES DE LA CAMBOYA Y EL JAPON. (Cronicas de la America, Historia 16?). *Vivero enjoyed bad company, for he is the only early observer to find Japanese vicious in drink.!*

~~~~~~

W:HOT = **Willes, Richard.(also Willis) HISTORY OF TRAVAYLE (1577) in ENGLAND AND JAPAN** (pref. M. Paske-Smith). J.L. Thompson & Co. (Kobe), 1928. *The History can also be found on microfilm and its full name is The (Pleasant) History of Travayle in the East and West Indies. Wiles writes only a few words on Japan prefacing his translation of "my old acquainted friend" Maffei's Latined version of a 1565 Frois letter. According to P-S' preface, since Marco Polo was not Englished until 1579 (There is a wee mention of a fabled land called Zipangu), this book was "the first notice in English of Japan." So, our "Father Froes" was the father of Japanology in English.*

~~~~~~

XAVIER → C:LLFX, above.

~~~~~~

Books in *Japanese*

..
J/A:NGK = Aramata Hiroshi. NIHON GYÔTEN KIGEN (Japan-shocking-origins) Shûeisha: 1994
J?De Sande → See J/S
J/E:NBJ = Ebisawa Arimichi transl. *Nambanjikyôkaiki* (c.1700); *Jakyô Daii* (1648); *Myôtei mondo* (1605); *Ha-deusu* (1620) Tôyô Bunko = Heibonsha 1964/1989. *I was just looking for a copy of Ha-deusu* (Destruction/Destroying Deus), *the famous attack on Christianity and the Jesuits by the apostate Fukan Fabian, but his Myotei-Mondo a lively attack on Buddhism, Taoism/Confucianism and Shinto was actually much more fun to read and revealing (If you read Japanese, read this rather than Elison, for the bunko is cheap and, wow! 3 works in 1.)*

J/F:HISTORIA = Frois, Luis. (trans. by Matsuda Kiichi and Kawasaki Momota) kanyaku FUROISU-NO NIHON-SHI (complete translation Frois's Japan-History) 12v. Chuokoronsha, 1977-80. *This is a full translation of Frois's Historia de Japam, which is actually a history of the Church in Japan, but probably includes more first-hand information on the Japanese rulers (who the Jesuits knew personally) than any other single source. The important Prologue to the lost Summary vol. of the Historia , placed in the back of the first volume, is extremely significant for reading between the lines of TRATADO, for it proves Frois was not naïve about the implications – i.e., misunderstanding – arising from translation. The Japanese translators provide a plethora of excellent notes.*

J/F(O):T = Frois, Luis (Okada Akio trans./ed.: TRATADO:1585) YOROPPA-BUNKA TO NIHON-BUNKA (European culture and Japanese culture). Iwanami Shoten (Tokyo), 1996 (1965). *My copy is the thirteenth printing of the pocketbook. About half of the 611 items are annotated, with annotations averaging several lines. They tend provide a bit more information on Japan than Europe, perhaps because many Japanese today know little about their own history, or because Okada had more of an opinion about his side. I find many useful and cite or quote them in my notes. I even considered translating Okada's book, but, since the Western reader needs different information than the Japanese reader and Okada failed to address many items I felt had to be solved, thought it better to write my own.*

J/F(M&E):T = Frois, Luis (Matsuda Kiichi and Engelbert Jorissen trans./ed: TRATADO:1585): FUROISU-NO NIHON-OBOEGAKI – *nihon to yoroppa no fûshû no chigai* (Frois' notes on japan – the difference in the customs of Japan and Europe). Chuô-shinshô, 1983. *(The ss's in Jorissen are actually a big B-like letter and the J pronounced Y.) This book, unlike the case with Okada, has Matsuda and Jorissen down as co-authors rather than translator-annotators. Most of their translation is virtually identical with Okada's (even the mistaken 2-29 and trickier 2-59). There are no notes and TRATADO is squeezed into one 77 pg chapter, but the route by which the manuscript arrived at the Museum, its relationship to Francesco Carletti's* Voyage Around the World *(which borrowed much from it) and its authenticity are carefully analyzed for the first 60 pages of the book and the veracity of Frois's observations (especially on Europe) with respect to some chapters are essayed for 30 pgs in the back. Like Okada's book, published as a pocket book.*

J/F = Fukan Fabian. → F/E:NBJ and E:DD.

J/G:NRT = Gill, Robin: NIHONJIN-RON TANKEN. TBS Britannica, 1985. *An attempt to cure what I called "The Uniqueness Syndrome," the Japanese fixation on themselves and the West as antithetical. It is also good medicine against the difference-mongering I enjoyed here (See* Ori & Occi *in Engl.). Mea culpa, mea maxima . . . (This & 4 other of my bks are mentioned in* TT-long. *If you read Japanese, check on them in my bio at www.paraverse.org.)*

J/I:FPM = I, Oryon (= Lee O-young)= FUROSHIKI-NO-POSUTO-MODAN. Chuokoronsha, 1989. *My riposte to this Japanese-Korean-Occidental book of contrasts was published in the same publisher's monthly magazine* Chuokoron. *People sometimes get the wrong idea of my criticism. I usually do not bother with someone unless I like their work.*

J/I:WTF = Inoue Hisashi: WAGA TOMO FUROISU (my friend Frois). Nesco (Bungeishunju) 1999. *A delightful novelette of Frois' life almost entirely comprising letters, based upon fact but crafted with artistic license. A letter from Frois to Vilela written over 10 years before Valignano's SUMARIO and 15 years before TRATADO has almost a dozen topsy-turvy contradictions.* [If real, I better find it by the second edition]. *Inoue apparently judges the idea came from Frois rather than Valignano. Among the deceased Frois' scanty personal effects, Inoue writes, there was one sheet of Japanese Sugiwara paper with the words* par in parem imperium non habet: *"equal has no right to rule equal."*

J/I:IR= Iwakura Tomoi: tokumei zenken taishi bei-ō kairan jiki ("special rights plenipotentiary ambassador america-europe tour report," or, commonly: THE IWAKURA REPORT) 1872. *The reporting is, on the whole, heavy-going, for the mission was to learn about the West's industry & economy. But social topics are occasionally interesting.*

J/Lee O-young → See J/I

J/M:KZJ = Minegishi Sumio ed. (& 8 other contibutors) KAZOKU TO JOSEI. Furukawa Kobunkan: 1992. *Solid & good.*

J/N&T:SCK : Nakano Miyoko and Takeda Masaya: SEKIMATSU CHUGOKU-NO KAWARABAN. Fukutake shoten 1989. *Selected feature stories from a late 19c Chinese tabloid of interesting and often significant Chinese subjects.*

J/OJD = NIHON-KOKUGO-DAI-JITEN. **Shogakukan**. *This 20 vol (10v small print) dictionary is more interesting than Johnson's English one, because the literary examples are entire, thanks to the brevity of Japanese poems! Many are senryû and very risqué. Useful 90% of the times I look up an obsolete or archaic word, I call it THE ONLY JAPANESE DICTIONARY, OJD for short and because it is the Japanese OED. Okada also relied heavily on it.*

J/O:KGB = Ôhara Rieko: KUROGAMI NO BUNKA-SHI (cultural history of black-hair) 1988. *Hundreds of illustrations of Japanese hairdos (90% women), all of which have names and a short description.*

J/R:ALJ = Rodrigues, Joao (Doi Tadao trans.): NIHON DAI-BUNTEN (ARTE DA LINGOA DE JAPAM). Sanseido, 1955 (Nangasaqui-no Collegio de Japao da Compania de JESV, 1604). *Or, to give the English title provided:* A GREAT JAPANESE GRAMMAR. *I seriously doubt that anyone wrote so substantial a book on English grammar! And, not only is there grammar, but more information on poetry than I have ever seen in a modern grammar book!*

J/S:DM (DE MISSIONE) = de Sande, Duarte [Eduardo] de trans., (au=Valignano) DE MISSIONE LEGATORUM IAPONEN (Macao 1589) *More precisely, the Japanese trans. of the same from Latin by Izui Hisanosuke: Tensho nenkan ken'o shisetsu kenbun taiwaroku; Sande, Duarte de, Tokyo : Toyo Bunko, 1942. Also with Nagazawa Nobuhisa, Mitani Shouji and Sunami Ichiro trans./notes published by Yushodo Shoten (Tokyo), 1969. This is an introduction to Europe in dialogue form, created by Valignano with the help of abundant reports he received from his brainchild, the Japanese Embassy to Europe (1582-1588) We cannot know exactly what information and opinions came from the four young Japanese envoys Mancio Ito, Miguel Chijiwa, Martin Hara and Julian Nakaura (Michael=Miguel, Martinus=Martino, Iulianus=Julian and Mancius=Mancio) and what from the apparent editor/author Valignano. So I credit "Miguel=Valignano," "Mancio =Valignano"etc.. I quote heavily because DE MISSIONE is not available in English and is the only Japanese opinion on the subject of some of Frois's contrasts, even if it is biased by passing through and dialogued by Valignano, and further changed into poor Latin by De Sande (whose humble apologies = he was immersed in Chinese = are touching), rather than coming directly from the pens of the Japanese youths. The Japanese trans. team did a prodigious amount of research for their notes which I appreciate much more than their stiff translation. A team comprising a native English speaker who is a Latin+Renaissance expert and a Japanese capable of helping with the notes for the Japanese side should English this book!*

J/U:BNS = Umesao Tadao: BUNMEI NO SEITAISHI-KAN (a historo-ecological view of civilization). 1974. *Some of what Diamond did in D:GGS was already done by Umesao.*

J/U:KNS = Umesao Tadao: KYOTO-NO SEISHIN (Kyoto's Espirit). Kadokawa-sensho: 1987. *Umesao thinks Kyoto is no mere tourist city, but a center, if not the center for Eastern civilization. Europeans talk about Americanization as a* culture *problem, but Umesao argues Kyoto has bigger fish to fry: it would defend a* civilization.

J/W:F = Watsuji Tetsuro: FÛDO (1935/44). Iwanami Bunko, 1983. *A classic book about the effect of climate on culture with a focus on explaining Japanese and Western differences. Cogent. If there is a translation, read it & debate it.*

ACKNOWLEDGMENTS

When I mentioned Frois's *Tratado* to Professor of Comparative Studies Daniel Reff (DR) in 1998, he suggested we do a book. At that time the *Tratado* was only one of several Japanese books (for I had Okada's translation of *Tratado*) I was thinking about translating. But, thanks to Dan's interest, I switched into high gear for Frois. He was working on Jesuit activities in the New World (see R(R,A&D):HOT, above) introduced me to Schütte: *Valignano's Mission Principles*, which was a real eye-opener, and taught me the word *distich*, which I must confess to not knowing. We planned to do *Tratado* together, but I ended up going overboard (researching the Japanese side *and* the European, and finally invading Dan's Jesuit territory), as you can imagine from reading this book, while he was slowed down by other obligations and found my idea for three versions (*short, medium*, and *long*: This is the *medium* though I wanted to make it really *short*) hard to take. Economic circumstances also made it impossible for me to properly complete an academic style work, while making premature publication necessary. Thank you, Dan, for getting me started, the letter that enabled me to read Valignano's 1601 work at the BL, the incisive and probing questions about some of the chapters, of which I only wish there could have been more (and likewise for your brilliant student KT – I wish she could have read and commented on the whole thing rather than only a chapter!) and your work (together with H) on the translation which helped get me back into thinking critically in English (in 1998, my vocabulary was not quite *there* after 20 years of writing in Japanese!). And thank you, Prudence (my sister in Columbus), for introducing me to Dan.

My debts to other researchers is acknowledged directly and indirectly in the Bibliography. Without Father Schütte's discovery and transcription into readable print of the *Tratado* (F(S):T), this book would not exist, but my largest debt *in terms of understanding the content* is to Okada's heavily annotated translation of *Tratado* (J/F(O):T), followed by Cooper's *They Came to Japan* (C:TCJ), and quite a bit further down the line, Matsuda and Jorissen's (M&J) translation of Tratado (J/F(M&J):T), the *De Missione* translation (J/S:DM), Matsuda + Kawasaki's translation of Frois's *Historia* (J/F:HISTORIA), and *Valignano's* writing (especially: V(A):S&A).

Reference-wise, Mary McCarthy at the Santa-Fe + St Leo library made my stay with my other sister in Gainesville (actually, Newberry, Watermelon Capital of the World) *extremely productive*. I am very grateful to her and the kind, mostly Southern and none-to-wealthy universities who were especially cooperative. Thank you, Susan, for putting me up so long and allowing me a big chunk of bookcase. More recently, Kristina Troost at Duke's Perkins Library helped me obtain the *Monumenta Nipponica* (Rodrigues's introduction of Japanese poetry) and Catarina Marot Mendez of the Biblioteca National de Portugal was kind enough to respond to a few language-related questions, giving me confidence.

On the local side, thanks to Jacques of France on Key Biscayne for buying me the French translation of *Tratado* and answering my questions re. the French (and his son Alexis, too!); Alexandra for answering questions about Schütte's German and lending me her dictionary, though I must say, I find German dictionaries a *horror*; Camila and her daughter Gabriela for living without *Aurelio* and their other Portuguese-English dictionary for 10 months as of this writing; my mother for likewise doing without her OED;, and, I almost forgot, ER, whose uncanny ability to find the word on the tip of my tongue when I phone him for one is much appreciated!

On the Japan side, I thank Hiroko-san, the owner of a small used-book store, for helping me round up a number of books; "Tenki-san," host of the charming haiku website Ukimido, for setting up a Frois Questions and Answer's Site (フロイス問答場) and all those who visited it to answer questions (or answered them elsewhere). The overall champion is Furiko-san. I hope that after this is published, it gets enough attention to draw some professional historians and specialists in some of the fields Frois covers to the website, for there are still all-too-many unsolved questions! I also thank Midorikawa Machiko for letting me try the PMJS bbs, though , I got no response (T_T).

I am grateful to web-sites *that offer information easily accessible to all*, such as Iberian Resources On-line and the University of Washington's Nagasaki-magazine (old copies, any way – but it is better than nothing). For anyone who is too poor (in time=money) to travel, or has ecological qualms about wasting resources, the ability to find information (not just information about information) *on the net* cannot be overstated. LD, who read the first chapter, wrote that she had one stylistic bone to pick with me and that was my constant use of the verb "google, because it will eventually date me." I appreciate her faith in the longevity of this book, but will continue using it because it feels natural. Rather than snorkeling around, you goggle+oogle, or *google*. And, besides, I have derived great benefit from Google's intelligently designed search-engine, so using the verb is a deliberate show of gratitude.

At the end of the introduction to his *Epochs of Chinese and Japanese Art*, one of many books read but not cited here, Fenollosa acknowledges the help of eight of his Japanese colleagues and pegs the following onto the tail: *"Other scholars to whom I owe tribute might be enumerated by the dozens. Marco Polo is surely worth something."* (Some way or another, *my* Marco Polo slipped the bibliography: *Oops!*)   — r.d.g. (April Fool's Day, on Key Biscayne)

Appeal (to be read only *after* you have read this book, if you like it)

1) This book is found in few bookstores because it is "No Return" (it must be to keep the price low) so the only way most people will learn about it is if their friends inform them of it. **Please pass the word and write reviews.**
2) If you are a scholar and want to add a gloss supplementing or debating anything I write or do not write, please read *TT-long* (to be sure I have not already noted the same) and write me. The entire 740 pg content of *Topsy-turvy 1585* is, as of this writing, up at Google and searchable. **You will be free to put in a line or two about your own book or research or whatever else you wish to advertise to make the time spent writing the gloss worthwhile.**
3) If you have any media connections, please contact me, for author-publishers are generally ignored, and this author/publisher has little time for publicity. (Even fine reviews of *Rise, Ye Sea Slugs!* in the most prestigious haiku magazine in English, *Modern Haiku* (↓) and, more recently (Spring 2005) in *Metamorphoses: a journal of the five college faculty seminar on literary translation,* have failed, so far, to bring a single response from a book review editor of a major magazine or newspaper. Whatever I send them might as well be shot into a black hole.)

Reviews of Previous Work by the Author

re: *Rise, Ye Sea Slugs!* 1000 holothurian haiku (2003)

"Gill **appeals to readers who revel in ideas and expansive footnotes.** ... Some of the most engaging commentary on haiku (and senryu and the occasional tanka or kyôka) ever to see print. ... may be our best English-language window yet into the labyrinth of Japanese haikai culture. ... As a translator, I find Gill's approach stimulating and challenging. **He has raised the bar very high in terms of a translator's responsibility** (. . .) to the text. ... **If you have read Yasuda, Blyth, Henderson, Ueda, and Shirane, then read Gill**. He will expand your mind. If you have not read those guys yet, then read Gill first. He's more fun.** – William J. Higginson, dean of haiku editors in the USA and author of the international classic *Haiku World,* in *Modern Haiku* (a 5-page review in vol. 35.1 winter-spring 2004)

". . . If you ever thought haiku were not erotic, this book alone could change your mind forever. **If you read it, I can guarantee you will not be the same when you finish it!** ... Incredible work." – Jane Reichhold (host of the Aha! poetry web-ring) in *Lynx* (Feb., 2004)

"Gill's tone is relaxed and informal and he doesn't take himself too seriously or struggle for academic respectability, but he is still **precise in his own way, and insanely erudite**. ... All told, it's **an original undertaking carried out with style**. ... [An example haiku in the review]: *a few drinks / and i am a sea slug / out of water* Gijô (1741) – Danny Yee in Danny reviews.com (solid reviews of eclectic books Down-under)

"This book gets my vote for **the most original literary theme of the decade.**" – Jim Nollman, author of *Dolphin Dreamtime,* in "Interspecies" (Spring 2004).

"**Already a classic . . .** like the work of Blyth." "The *ante y después* of critical studies of haiku" – Vincente Haya, author of *Corazon de Haiku* from 2 postings at El Rincon de Haiku (an online haiku forum in Spanish).

re: Anti-stereotype books published in Japanese only.

"**I bow my head to the author's linguistic prowess.**" – Inoue Hisashi (on a reader's card) – a top Japanese novelist and playwright. [re. *Eigo wa konna ni nippongo = English is This Japanese!* (Chikuma bunko)]

"What felt good about reading it [*Han=nihonjinron* = anti-Japanology, (Kousakusha: 1984) was that the book **doesn't get bogged down in Japan, but develops into a theory of culture** [bunkaron] . . . it is **remarkable for not being prejudiced either for or against the past**." – Itasaka Gen (in *"Honyaku no Sekai"*), a Japanese literature scholar who formerly taught at Harvard and later became the president of Tenri University.

"**The author's Thoreauvian naturalism is splendid . .** and the book [*Han=nihonjinron*] leaves you feeling better than reading ten of those popular Japan-as-Number-One type books." – Matsuoka Seigow (in an NTT book) – a legendary editor and avant-garde thinker.

"**A splendid deconstruction** [on Ibid] **of longstanding stereotypes of Japanese national/ cultural character** (nihonjinron) that, wearing the academic guise of cultural anthropology and topographic/climatic reductionism, (fudoron), have titillated our pride." – Kyodo News Service (a review carried nationally).

"Re: [*Nihonjinron Tanken* TBS-Britannica (1984)] **the author's point is that we must not allow our obsession with "Japaneseness" to stop us from facing up to the human agenda in this Age where we are capable of spoiling the earth.**" – TSUMURA Takashi (also Kyodo News Service), a well known practitioner and advocate of Eastern medicine and meditation.

More Books & Reviews at
http://www.paraverse.org

1 Men, 2 Women   ITEM BY ITEM CONTENTS   455

In Lieu of an

INDEX   i hope a future edition can have a full index but, for now, this incomplete outline will have to do.

Introduction: The Appeal of Topsy-turvydom

i The Origin of Topsy-turvy Herodotus, Al-Bîrûnî Valignano & Frois (champions of black & white contrast)
ii The Nature of Topsy-turvy How Frois's Contrasts relate to the Respect Jesuits had for Japanese and the admirable policy of Accommodation. The *Tratado* as cultural shock therapy, etc.
iii Some Types of Topsy-turvy Contrasts in *Tratado* that contradict stereotypes or confirm them, concern important things, or small. Frois and the discovery of culture with a small c.
iv Tokugawa Topsy-turvy Carletti, Montanus, L'Abbe de T, Kaempfer, Golownin, Thunberg, etc.
v Modern Topsy-turvy: Alcock, *Alice* and Kipling
vi Modern Topsy-turvy: Chamberlain (An attempt to patent Topsy-turvy?)
vii Modern Topsy-turvy: Lowell (A grandiose metaphysical venture in Topsy-turvy socio-psychology)
viii Modern Topsy-turvy: Knapp (the Principle of Inversion and appreciation for what is objectively good.)
ix Twentieth Century Topsy-turvy Sladen, Ripley, Singer, Pop Japanology and the publication of *Tratado*.
x Topsy-turvy in Broader Perspective From simple dichotomy to complex contrast. The fixed Indian knife.
xi Envoi *De Missione,* or 16c Japanese in Europe.

1 Men

1-1 Body
1-2 Eyes, size
1-3 Eyes, whites.
1-4 Noses
1-5 Beard
1-6 Beard vs. topknot
1-7 Hair-cut vs. shaving pate
1-8 Freckles
1-9 Pockmarks
1-10 Fingernails
1-11 Sword scars

1-1+ Dress, seasonal
1-2+ Clothes, colorful
1-3+ Dress, fashion *vs.* tradition
1-4+ Vests
1-5+ Sleeves
1-6+ Breeches, design
1-7+ Breeches, material
1-8+ Dress with/without gender
1-9+ Dress, tight *vs.* loose fit
1-10+ Dress, access of hands
1-11+ Dress, best side out *vs.* inside
1-12+ Lining
1-13+ Fur, on inside or outside

1-14+ Shaving head for relief
1-15+ Shaving beard *vs.* top-knot
1-16+ Robe, wrap direction
1-17+ Mantle vs. open lapel collar
1-18+ Folding clothing
1-19+ Handkerchiefs, material
1-20+ Removing hat *vs.* shoes
1-21+ Swords, double/single-edged
1-22+ Scabbards
1-23+ Sword handles
1-24+ Sword-testing
1-25+ Worn sword: which side up
1-26+ Raincoats
1-27+ Walking just to walk
1-28+ Valuable sword adorned
1-29+ Standing vs. sitting to greet
1-30+ Black, white and psyche
1-31+ Nudity front *vs.* back
1-32+ Nudity on the road
1-33+ Spitting vs. swallowing
1-34+ Swords 1 and 2-handed
1-35+ Shoes, leather/straw
1-36+ Shoes: removal shows respect
1-37+ Shoes: remove at entrance
1-38+ Washing faces

1-39+ Kneeling-obeisance
1-40+ Hat shape
1-41+ Patches on clothes
1-42+ Scissors and knife
1-43+ Fans and Men
1-44+ Torches
1-45+ Nudity before fire
1-46+ Looking in mirrors
1-47+ Paper Clothing
1-48+ House-robes
1-49+ Laundry by hand *vs.* foot
1-50+ Handkerchief carrying
1-51+ Pockets *vs.* Purses
1-52+ Things in Purses
1-53+ Bathing in private/public
1-54+ Shoes and *geta* in rain
1-55+ Shoe and *tabi* leathers
1-56+ Glove length
1-57+ Unfinished clothing
1-58+ Shoe soles
1-59+ Shoe length
1-60+ Walking style
1-61+ See-through clothing
1-62+ Skirt and robe length
1-63+ Black cloth, white stitches

2 Women

2-1 Chastity
2-2 Desirable Hair-color
2-3 Hair-parts
2-4 Hair perfume *vs.* oil
2-5 Wigs
2-6 Hair ornaments
2-7 Hair ties
2-8 Bonnets

2-9 Shampoo location
2-10 Trains *vs.* Wig-trains
2-11 Eyebrow treatment
2-12 Forehead cosmetics
2-13 White hair
2-14 Pierced Ears
2-15 Heavy make-up
2-16 Tooth color

2-17 Bracelets
2-18 Necklaces
2-19 Sleeve-length, nudity
2-20 Bare feet
2-21 Belts, tight *vs.* loose
2-22 Rings and other jewelry
2-23 Purses and belts
2-24 Dress-front Open/Closed

2-25 Gloves
2-26 Mantle length
2-27 Mantle design
2-28 Uniforms
2-29 M and F Walking Order
2-30 M and F Property
2-31 Divorce frequency
2-32 M and F Divorcing party
2-33 Abduction
2-34 Seclusion *vs.* Freedom
2-35 Husband's Permission
2-36 Relatives
2-37 Umbrella bearers
2-38 Abortions
2-39 Infanticide
2-40 Pregnancy belts
2-41 Post-partum rest
2-42 Post-partum ventilation
2-43 Nuns, strict *vs.* profligate
2-44 Nuns stay in *vs.* go out
2-45 Writing
2-46 Letters signed or not
2-47 First Names
2-48 Shoe material
2-49 Horse-riding style
2-50 Saddle pads/cloths
2-51 M & F Which is cook?
2-52 M&F Which is tailor?
2-53 M&F Height of tables
2-54 Drinking
2-55 Eating Meat
2-56 Talking and Mantles
2-57 Talking and partitions
2-58 Out-of-bounds for women
2-59 Carrying Things
2-60 Greeting guests stand/sit
2-61 Masks, collars *vs* towels
2-62 Hair cut-off
2-63 Sitting
2-64 Drinking method
2-65 Hair braiding and tying
2-66 Make-up powder quantity
2-67 Thimbles
2-68 Taking apart garments

3 *Children*

3-1 Hair, trim *vs.* long
3-2 Swaddling *vs.* freedom
3-3 Cradles *vs.* nature
3-4 Age of baby-carriers
3-5 Securing baby clothing
3-6 Eating by hand *vs.* chopstick
3-7 Whipping
3-8 Schooling
3-9 Write first *vs.* read first
3-10 Catechism *vs.* pederasty
3-11 Giving messages
3-12 Carrying swords, age of.
3-13 Respect for custom
3-14 Ability to perform in public
3-15 Gifts and affection
3-16 Parents & children
3-17 Godparents
3-18 Mothers & children outside
3-19 Name-changes
3-20 Relatives & children
3-21 Inheritance, age of.
3-22 Health, bleeding *vs.* burning
3-23 Cosmetics on children
3-24 Sleeves, restricted *vs.* free

4 *Monks & Bonzes*

4-1 Reasons to join an Order
4-2 Chaste monks, sinful bonzes
4-3 Fleeing riches, seeking riches
4-4 Obedience to Superior
4-5 Property, collective/indivual
4-6 Patronage, collective/indiv.
4-7 Condemning sins & situation
4-8 Humble *vs.* fine clothing
4-9 Titles, seeking/avoiding
4-10 Peace-loving, War-loving
4-11 Promises to God
4-12 Working as Envoys
4-13 Marriage
4-14 Succession methods
4-15 Reasons to join an Order
4-16 Clean inside *vs.* outside
4-17 Hating lies, Living off them
4-18 Beards and Hair
4-19 Hats
4-20 Decency *vs.* Indecency
4-21 Drinking
4-22 Singing and Playing
4-23 Immortality: belief *vs.* disbelief
4-24 One Church *vs.* 13 sects
4-25 Devil-hating *vs.* liking
4-26 Temple ownership
4-27 Stole worn inside *vs.* outside
4-28 Stole vertical vs. diagonal
4-29 Medical activity
4-30 Fans for preaching
4-31 Preaching posture
4-32 Preaching dress
4-33 Pulpits *vs.* chairs
4-34 Give rosaries *vs.* Sell charms
4-35 Burial gowns given/sold
4-36 Funeral in church *vs.* house
4-37 Yellow
4-38 Hating other sects
4-39 Sorcerers
4-40 Sock color
4-41 Funeral suicide
4-42 How we beg God's mercy

5 *Temples & Images*

5-1 Deep church, shallow temple
5-2 Pews *vs.* tatami mats
5-3 Books in-common *vs.* individual
5-4 Books folded *vs.* rolled up
5-5 Images *retabulo* vs. sculpture
5-6 Polychrome *vs.* gilt images
5-7 Life-size *vs.* gigantic images
5-8 Beautiful *vs.* horrid images
5-9 Bells, hung high *vs.* low
5-10 Clapper within; struck without
5-11 Bells, tolling *vs.* not tolling
5-12 Clocks, iron *vs.* water
5-13 Hours, number in a day
5-14 Hours, method of counting
5-15 Vegetation in the church
5-16 Candles, shape
5-17 Candles, wicks
5-18 Prayer-bead moving direction
5-19 Deceased, the hair of.
5-20 Coffin shape
5-21 Deceased, position of.
5-22 Burial *vs.* incineration
5-23 Prayers posted in- *vs.* outside
5-24 Funeral, aftermath
5-25 Changing faith
5-26 Initiation
5-27 1 *vs.* 2 religions for 2 worlds
5-28 Images, painted on what.
5-29 Oil-color vs. black-ink value
5-30 Transporting prelates

ITEM BY ITEM   Midword *China*   6 *Food*   7 *War*   457

Midword: *China* vs. *Japan*

i. Battle of the antipodes Is Japan too idiosyncratic to be a *bona fide* opposite culture or "antidote" for us? Embree vs. Moore, Pollack.
ii. Japan over China? European view of Japanese superiority to Chinese. Pinto on the wonders of China. But Frois corrects mistaken idea that Chinese can't fight!
iii. The Chineseness of Japan How contrary Japan comes from China shown by contrary China in Moge, Ball and Ripley's.
iv The Un-Chineseness of Japan Japan born in opposition to China – Valignano and Van Linschoten.
v Japanese-Chinese Topsy-turvy How Japan can be seen as contrary to China, rather than following China (Valignano's pre Europe-Japan contrast).
vi Japan more Chinese than China? On the Chinese roots of things Japanese, and the Japanese way of preserving culture intact.
vii The True Orient Get a shovel and start digging?
Envoi: What about Marco Polo? Diversity, yes; the contrary, no.

6 *Food & Drink*

6-1 Fingers *vs.* chopsticks
6-2 Bread *vs.* Rice
6-3 Tables, stationary *vs.* carried
6-4 Tables, high *vs.* low
6-5 Chairs *vs.* tatami mat
6-6 Dishes sequential or all at once
6-7 Soup
6-8 Service, silver *vs.* lacquer
6-9 Pots, earthenware *vs.* iron
6-10 Tripods, legs up or down.
6-11 M & F eat together *vs.* apart
6-12 Fish, cooked *vs.* raw
6-13 Fruit, eating ripe *vs.* green
6-14 Melons, direction of cut.
6-15 Melons, sniffing top or bottom
6-16 Melons, pared or not pared
6-17 Green grapes
6-18 Covering food
6-19 Sweet-lovers *vs.* Salt-lovers
6-20 Cleaning up after meals
6-21 Washing hands after meals
6-22 Vermicelli, eaten hot *vs.* cold
6-23 Vermi., with sugar, with chili
6-24 Our foods, their *strange* foods
6-25 Trout
6-26 Wine, cooled or heated
6-27 Wine, grape *vs.* rice
6-28 Drinking, one *vs.* two hands
6-29 Drinking posture
6-30 Drinking cups, fine *vs.* crude
6-31 Drinking, forced.
6-32 Drinking from a dirty dish
6-33 Water, drunken cool *vs.* hot
6-34 Water, drunk with burnt rice
6-35 Drinking, time it starts
6-36 Water drunk from dirty dish
6-37 Toothpicks
6-38 Drunkenness, attitude toward.
6-39 Dairy products
6-40 Spices *vs. miso*
6-41 Beef-eating *vs.* dog-eating
6-42 Fish-gut
6-43 Noise while eating
6-44 Drinking, expression while.
6-45 Conversing/dancing at table
6-46 Guest/Host – who thanks whom
6-47 Fried fish *vs.* fried seaweed
6-48 Fishing
6-49 Cleaning teeth, time of.
6-50 Root-eating poor
6-51 Rotten fish
6-52 Wine-selling citizens
6-53 Pets
6-54 Pastry material
6-55 Boar, boiled *vs.* raw
6-56 Salt
6-57 Saltiness
6-58 Rice with or without salt
6-59 Mullet
6-60 Belching

7 *War & Weapons*

7-1 Swords, straight *vs.* curved
7-2 Hilt length
7-3 Baldrics *vs.* sashes
7-4 One sword per side *vs.* two
7-5 Daggers, short *vs.* long
7-6 Swords, things hanging from.
7-7 Swordplay, stabbing
7-8 Presented swords
7-9 Scabbards, extra things in.
7-10 Swords, New *vs.* Old as better
7-11 Number of blades worn
7-12 Knife handles
7-13 Knife Cutting direction
7-14 Beads cut by knife *vs.* lathe
7-15 Nails cut by knife *vs.* scissors
7-16 Carving decoration
7-17 Spearhead shape
7-18 Spear shaft finish
7-19 Halberds vs. *Naginata*
7-20 Mortars and Guns
7-21 Powder horns
7-22 Bows
7-23 Arrows
7-24 Bows, Shooting and Clothing.
7-25 Shouting while shooting
7-26 Shields, curved *vs.* flat & long
7-27 Armor, weight
7-28 Armor, material
7-29 Helmet plumes
7-30 Helmet visors
7-31 Helmet, shape
7-32 Armor, what is underneath
7-33 Armor, on horses
7-34 Music in battle
7-35 Battle standards
7-36 Ranks
7-37 Fighting on horseback
7-38 Salary of soldiers
7-39 Rewards of battle
7-40 Carriers, animal vs. human
7-41 Suicide
7-42 Treason
7-43 Executioner's status
7-44 Helmet wigs
7-45 Razor shape
7-46 Whetstones, oil *vs.* water
7-47 Shaving, by barbers, by oneself
7-48 Shaving beards and heads
7-49 Match (for matchlock) hand
7-50 Match material
7-51 Yell with each blow, fencing
7-52 Placement of gun butt

8 Horses

8-1 Horse's appearance
8-2 Horse's handling
8-3 Riding on rumps
8-4 Riding abreast
8-5 Tail, full vs. tied in knot
8-6 Manes, full vs. clipped
8-7 Horse shoes material
8-8 Straw shoe carrier
8-9 Bits
8-10 Mounting side
8-11 Reins, material
8-12 Stirrup length
8-13 Stirrup shape
8-14 Spurs
8-15 Saddle bows
8-16 Trappings
8-17 Saddle material
8-18 Stable location
8-19 Reception in the Stable!
8-20 Curry comb vs. Rope
8-21 Mangers vs. Buckets
8-22 Sleeping
8-23 Stable ground vs. floor
8-24 Ladle for stale (urine)!
8-25 Mules, zebras, etc.
8-26 Saddle cloths
8-27 Rider holding halter!
8-28 Reins, 1 or 2 in hand
8-29 Medical treatment
8-30 Reins, tight and loose
8-31 Tilling, Horse & Ox
8-32 Pack-saddle material
8-33 Crupper for loads
8-34 Bells and Jingles
8-35 Bulls, character
8-36 Carriers help horses!
8-37 Loading by eye vs. scale
8-38 Leading, with 2 men per horse!
8-39 Girth tie location

9 Disease & Medicine

9-1 Scrofula, stones, gout, pest
9-2 Bleeding vs. Moxibustion
9-3 Bleeding, location
9-4 Clysters and Syringes
9-5 Prescriptions
9-6 Pulse-taking
9-7 Urine
9-8 Healing speed
9-9 Wound Sewing vs. Paper
9-10 Medical Cloth vs. Paper
9-11 Burning Abscesses
9-12 Force-feeding
9-13 Beds, soft and hard
9-14 Food for the sick
9-15 Dentistry tools
9-16 Mortars
9-17 Pearls for medicine
9-18 Licensing of practitioner
9-19 The Pox

10 Writing

10-1 Letters vs. infinite characters
10-2 Study books vs. characters
10-3 L-to-R vs. R-to-L & vertical
10-4 Where Books Begin
10-5 Printing
10-6 Pens vs. Brushes
10-7 Ink
10-8 Inkwells vs. slabs of stone
10-9 Inkwell paraphernalia
10-10 Paper variety
10-11 Notary public vs. indiv. chop
10-12 Constant mark, changing chop
10-13 Paper, rag vs. bark
10-14 Length of Letters
10-15 Writing between lines
10-16 Letters, folded vs. rolled
10-16a Dating letters
10-17 Christian vs. Japanese eras
10-18 Sealing Letters
10-19 Mailing Letters
10-20 Making Paper
10-21 Ink, wiping vs. sucking!
10-22 Writing, on desk vs. on hand
10-23 Unsealing?
10-24 Blotting
10-25 Size of Lettering
10-26 Poems
10-27 Reading speed
10-28 Desks
10-29 Book binding

11 Home & Garden

11-1 Houses, tall vs. low
11-2 Stone & lime vs. mud & straw
11-3 Foundations
11-4 Doors
11-5 Partitions
11-6 Roofs
11-7 Interior wood
11-8 Windows
11-9 Valuables: gems vs. old pots
11-10 Tapestry vs. byôbû
11-11 Carpets vs. Straw mats
11-12 Chests and baskets
11-13 Sleeping high vs. low
11-14 Beds Out vs. hidden
11-15 Pillows
11-16 Pavilions vs. mosquito net
11-17 Sweeping noblemen!
11-18 Linen for faces
11-19 Lavatory placement
11-20 Defecating posture
11-21 Night-soil value
11-22 Horse dung
11-23 Locks
11-24 Compartments vs. drawers
11-25 Carpenters' work posture
11-26 Gimlets
11-27 Carpenters fed or not fed
11-28 Adze
11-29 Prefab. lumber!
11-30 Figures in paintings, # of.
11-31 Fruit vs. flowering-trees
11-32 Fireplaces vs. kotatsu
11-33 Hiring sawyers or saws?
11-34 Lawns
11-35 Street Drain location
11-36 Entrance ramp
11-37 Entrance, patent vs. hidden
11-38 Pools
11-39 Trees, straight vs. bent
11-40 Basins (for washing)
11-41 Water to wash hands
11-42 Roofs with things on them!
11-43 Pines and pine-nuts
11-44 Cherry Tree's product
11-45 Rose and its scent
11-46 Japanese blossoms lack scent
11-47 Rose water, like vs. dislike
11-48 Strong scents?

ITEM BY ITEM   12 *Ships*   13 *Plays & Music*   14 *Sundry*   459

12 *Ships*

12-1   Types of Ships only "we" have
12-2   Ribs and Decks
12-3   Sailing without oars
12-4   Pitch
12-5   Bow and Stern height
12-6   Sail material
12-7   Rope material
12-8   Anchors
12-9   Bows, armored *vs.* open.
12-10 Rowing, sit/stand, silent/sing
12-11 Oars, one *vs.* two-piece
12-12 Oar blade
12-13 Rowing *vs.* Sculling
12-14 Fire aboard
12-15 Honor in Bow *vs.* Poop
12-16 Mast shape
12-17 De-masting
12-18 Sails only "we" have
12-19 Night travel
12-20 Rain
12-21 Hiring Boat or boatmen?
12-22 Capacity measurement unit
12-23 Ship Carpenters
12-24 Freight bills
12-25 Flag shape
12-26 Taboo goods
12-27 Superstitions of sailors
12-28 Water on board
12-29 Torn sails ignored?!
12-30 Disembarking, which end?

13 *Plays & Music*

13-1   Play performance time
13-2   Actors' stage appearance
13-3   Plays, in verse *vs.* prose
13-4   Various & *ad hoc vs.* fixed
13-5   Acts
13-6   Dressing rooms
13-7   Plays, Spoken *vs.* Sung
13-8   Noise during play
13-9   Mask size
13-10 Music with drama
13-11 Dances with/out song
13-12 Dancers
13-13 Dancing by day *vs.* night
13-14 Foot *vs.* hand movement
13-15 Singing poly *vs.* monotone
13-16 Singing with full throat?
13-17 Instruments sweet/harsh
13-18 Organ music
13-19 Music of nobility & folk
13-20 Octave of voice
13-21 Guitar *vs. biwa*
13-22 Noble *vs.* Blind guitar play
13-23 Clavichord *vs. koto*
13-24 Blind-men, gallant lovers!
13-25 Noblemen up all night!
13-26 Food during performances
13-27 Jumping while dancing
13-28 Bareback and hatless
13-29 Plowing 1-man 2-ox & opp.

14 *Sundry*

14-1   Flintstone striking hand
14-2   Emotion *vs.* no emotion
14-3   Fire fighting
14-4   Lying
14-5   Killing people at home
14-6   Killing men *vs.* animals
14-7   Execution for stealing
14-8   Killing substitutes for killing
14-9   Crucifixion
14-10   Punishment of servants
14-11   Prisons and punishment
14-12   Stolen goods
14-13   Fear of the dark
14-14   Fear of snakes
14-15   Sneezing
14-16   Coins *vs.* scrap by weight
14-17   Balances *vs.* Scales
14-17/18 Coins with holes
14-18   Coins, face-value *vs.* choice
14-19   Coins as gift
14-20   Honorifics by noun *vs.* verb
14-21   Washing hands for *dogu*
14-22   Boar-hunting
14-23   Fly-killing!
14-24   Monkeys
14-25   Counting by hand *vs.* abacus
14-26   Present-giving, number of.
14-27   Present, giving medicine?
14-28   Present, brought by guest
14-29   Present enjoyed by guest
14-30   Embracing
14-31   Ball play, hand *vs.* foot
14-32   On wall or just ground?
14-33   Mills and horse-power
14-34   Socializing, town *vs.* house
14-35   Smiles
14-36   Clear *vs.* ambiguous Lang.
14-37   Wearing pelts
14-38   Crowns
14-39   Board games
14-40   Hawk and falcon hoods
14-41   Turnip washing, hands/feet
14-42   Sack material
14-43   Warming hands in fire
14-44   Message giving posture
14-45   Posture while speaking
14-46   Towels for head & feet!
14-47   Nostril-cleaning fingers!
14-48   Courtesy-exchanging face
14-49   Wine keg storage
14-50   Pelt coloring
14-51   Bamboo usages
14-52   Present package adornment
14-53   Rose-water *vs.* wine on face
14-54   Sweetmeat and drinks
14-55   Bouquet *vs.* single flowers
14-56   Incense quantity
14-57   Passionate *vs.* restrained
14-58   Treatment of woman in refuge
14-59   Apologies
14-60   Hoe blades
14-61   Flutes
14-62   Hair of Servants and Horses
14-63   Grapes and Figs
14-64   Visiting Servant's Houses
14-65   Servants in Master's clothing

If any reader would like to contribute time or money toward making a real index for this or future books, please write me at Paraverse Press / PMB #399 / 260 Crandon Blvd. Suite #32 / Key Biscayne, FL. 33149-1540, or E-mail me at info@paraverse.org. – rdg (author-publisher/publicist/editor & whatnot). Or, if a major publisher would like to do up this book big (give me an advance, a good editor and help gathering illustrations, etc.) please let me know. I am also looking for a bilingual agent (Japanese-English) if any such person exists, in the event that those big publishers fail to find me on their own.

www.ingramcontent.com/pod-product-compliance
Lightning Source LLC
Chambersburg PA
CBHW081213170426
43198CB00017B/2604